LAWRENCE OF ARABIA'S WAR

LAWRENCE OF ARABIA'S WAR

THE ARABS, THE BRITISH AND THE REMAKING OF THE MIDDLE EAST IN WWI

NEIL FAULKNER

YALE UNIVERSITY PRESS

NEW HAVEN AND LONDON

For information about this and other Yale University Press publications, please contact:
U.S. Office: sales.press@yale.edu   yalebooks.com
Europe Office: sales@yaleup.co.uk   yalebooks.co.uk

Typeset in Minion Pro by IDSUK (DataConnection) Ltd
Printed in Great Britain by Gomer Press, Llandysul, Ceredigion, Wales

Library of Congress Cataloging-in-Publication Data

Names: Faulkner, Neil, author.
Title: Lawrence of Arabia's war : the Arabs, the British, and the remaking of the Middle East in WWI / Neil Faulkner.
Description: New Haven : Yale University Press, 2016. | Includes bibliographical references and index.
Identifiers: LCCN 2015048301 | ISBN 9780300196832 (cloth : alk. paper)
Subjects: LCSH: World War, 1914–1918—Campaigns—Middle East. | Lawrence, T. E. (Thomas Edward), 1888–1935. | Middle East—History—1914–1923.
Classification: LCC D568.4.L45 F38 2016 | DDC 940.4/15—dc23
LC record available at http://lccn.loc.gov/2015048301

A catalogue record for this book is available from the British Library.

10 9 8 7 6 5 4 3 2 1

CONTENTS

MAPS AND ILLUSTRATIONS

Maps

Illustration credits

Plate 1 is photographed by Harry Chase, 1917, © 2005 TopFoto. From T.E. Lawrence's *Seven Pillars of Wisdom*, subscribers' edition, 1926, the following images (artists' names follow in parentheses): plate 5 left (W. Nicholson), right (Augustus John) and bottom (William Roberts); plate 6 bottom right (Eric Kennington); and all three images on plate 7 (Eric Kennington). Plate 6 top of the Emir Feisal is by Augustus John, 1919 © Ashmolean Museum, University of Oxford (WA1936.30). Plate 8 right of Sir Henry McMahon is by Walter Stoneman, 1920 © National Portrait Gallery, London. Plate 11 top and plate 17 top are courtesy of the Imperial War Museum (Q58863 and Q59193). Plate 13 top is courtesy of the Huntingdon Library, San Marino, California. Plate 13 bottom is a photograph from Lt George Pascoe's album, courtesy of John B. Winterburn. Plate 20 bottom left is by Eric Kennington at Clouds Hill, Dorset © National Trust/R. Goldsmith.

NOTE ON THE TEXT

THE TRANSCRIPTION OF foreign-language names is always problematic. I have avoided the somewhat pedantic academic practice of using a standardised system of transcription, since this is of little use to a general reader unfamiliar with the language in question. The matter, anyway, is hopelessly complicated by changing conventions, to the extent that arbitrary use of a modern standard can render some places referred to in the primary sources unidentifiable to the uninitiated.

Instead, in each case, I have adopted whatever form seemed most natural, both as it appears on the page and as a rough guide to pronunciation. I have, however, been wholly consistent in always using the same transcription for any particular name. Djemal Pasha is always Djemal, never Cemal or Jemal, and I have done this partly because this spelling was widely used in contemporary sources, partly because it more closely resembles the Turkish pronunciation.

Another problem arises in relation to place-names. Different names for the same place were sometimes used in the past, and these are often different from those in use today. I have generally opted for the names most commonly used in contemporary British military sources.

Military terminology is another source of difficulty. It is useful to know that an Ottoman regiment was the equivalent of a British brigade, and that both typically comprised three battalions. A battalion at full strength numbered about 1,000 men, but on campaign actual strengths tended to be far lower, in the case of the Ottomans very much so. Regiments/brigades were, of course, incorporated into divisions, corps and armies. In numbering these, I have followed the convention of using words for armies, Roman numerals for corps and Arabic numerals for divisions, brigades and battalions, as in Seventh Army, VIII Corps, 43rd Division, 130th Brigade and 3rd Manchesters.

In relation to occasional references to money, it is worth knowing that in 1914 a British pound was worth about US $3, a Turkish pound 50 cents and a German mark about 25 cents. I have rounded any figures used because values varied considerably in the course of the First World War.

I have modernised, standardised and corrected the punctuation in the quotes, and also standardised spellings, so that they are easier to read and do not jar.

ACKNOWLEDGEMENTS

THANKS ARE DUE to a great number of people. Many Jordanians supported the Great Arab Revolt Project's nine annual seasons between 2006 and 2014. They include: King Abdullah, Prince Hassan, Prince Mired and the staff of the Royal Court; Dr Fawwaz al-Khraisha, Dr Ziad al-Saad, Dr Monther Jamhawi, Jihad Haroun, Hani Falahat, Khalil Hamdan, Aktham Oweidi, and Saata Massadeh of the Department of Antiquities; Jihad Kafafi of the Jordan Museum; Engineer Hussein Krishan of the Aqaba Railway; Dr Fawzi Abudanah, Dr Mansour Shqiarat, Dr Zeyad al-Salameen, Dr Saad Twaissi and colleagues at the University of Al Hussein bin Talal in Maan; Muhammad Twaissi and the staff of the Edom Hotel in Wadi Musa; and, not least, Salah Hassanat and all our local drivers. Mention must also be made of the valuable assistance given by Professor Bill Finlayson, Nadja Qaisi and the staff of the Council for British Research in the Levant, and by Bob Bewley and David Kennedy for use of their air reconnaissance photographs of southern Jordan.

An especially deep debt of gratitude is owed to the personnel of Bristol University's Great Arab Revolt Project (GARP). The core included the following: David Thorpe and Ali Baldry, with whom I conceived and planned the project on a recce to Jordan in 2005, the former then serving as site director, the latter as site photographer; Susan Daniels, our long-serving, ultra-efficient and exceptionally hard-working project administrator; John Winterburn, GARP's (official) landscape archaeologist and (unofficial) archive researcher; Cat Edwards and Anna Gow, responsible respectively for overall site supervision and overall finds processing; Roger Ward, the project's indispensable 'techie' and metal-detectorist; and also Fizz Altinoluk (site supervisor), Angie and Dave Hibbitt (geophysicists), Odette Nelson (finds assistant), David Spencer (site supervisor) and Duncan Ward (site supervisor).

In addition, all of the following participated in one or more of GARP's field seasons: Linah Ababneh, Suzanne Auckerman, John Austin, Fabrice de Backer, Ali Baldry, Mohammad Bataineh, Peter Besler, Len Blasiol, Esther Breithoff, David Brown, Martin Burgess, Susannah Chapman, Richard Clayton, Lisa Corti, Nick Dawson, Neil Dearberg, Karen Deighton, Chrissie Eaves-Walton, Charles Eilers, Jo Gilbert, Michael Gill, Andrew Green, Fred Hay, Ian Heritage, Owen Humphrys, Caroline Jennings, Guy Jillings, Tim Johnson, Nick Kelly, Alice Kilroy, Erica Kratz, David Long, Bill Loughner, Alistair MacLellan, Ian McKenzie, Heinrich Natho, Phillip Naylor, Yvonne Neville-Rolfe, Simone Paturel, Kelly Pool, Brian Powell, John Raiswell, Mike Relph, Jerry Revell, Rob Riddett, Vicky Roads, Hilary Sanseverino, John Scott, David Shepherd, Paul Smith, James Stejskal, Bill Sutherland, Guy Taylor, Véronique Thévoz, Dennis Thompson, Barbara Wagner, Steve Walker, Roger Ward, Benjamin Wimmer, Jan Woolf and Zheng Xu.

It must be stressed that in practice the distinction between team and volunteers dissolved, everyone working together in a warm, enthusiastic, mutually supportive group. Some volunteers participated in all nine seasons, and many contributed much valuable time and expertise. The lobby of the Edom Hotel in Wadi Musa was often buzzing with late-evening activity as notes were written up, plans finished, finds cleaned, identifications made and breaking news sent out on the daily blog.

This book could not have been written without the involvement and support of all the people listed above. A few, however, deserve special mention in relation to the information and ideas presented here. John Winterburn, GARP's landscape archaeologist, was responsible for much detailed archive and landscape research, and for numerous powerful insights derived from this, many of which are reflected in this text. Jeremy Wilson, whom I regard as the world's leading authority on the biography of T E Lawrence, proved an exceptionally thorough and critical reader of the draft text, purging it of much error – though he is responsible for nothing that remains, since in places, where our interpretations diverged a little, I have sometimes proved stubborn. Jan Woolf may be partly responsible for this, since we shared many psychoanalytical thoughts about Lawrence, and those who both read my book and see her new play, *The Man with the Gold*, may notice the concurrence. The staff of both the Imperial War Museum and the British Library are to be thanked for their assistance in accessing primary sources. Rachael Lonsdale of Yale University Press has also been a most conscientious, sensible and supportive critical reader. In an age when relationships between authors and publishers have often become highly attenuated, Rachael and her colleagues at Yale are notable exceptions. I am most fortunate in my publisher. I might add that relationships between authors and copy-editors can also sometimes be awkward; but not in the case of Sophie Richmond, with whom it was a delight to work on this book.

Finally, and above all, there is Nick Saunders of Bristol University. Strong, enduring, fruitful academic partnerships are rare; when they occur, they can be immensely enriching, both for the partners and, I hope, for the discipline to which they contribute. Nick and I have complementary experience, knowledge and thinking, but our respective intellectual orientations are in close alignment. Many of the more significant ideas in this book owe much, and virtually all something, to discussions with Nick – as often as not conducted in the back of a Toyota pickup on long drives through the Jordanian desert. His book – due for publication in a year or so – will be the essential complement to mine.

Neil Faulkner
November 2015

INTRODUCTION

WHEN LAWRENCE CHOSE *Seven Pillars of Wisdom* as the title of his military memoir, it was mere whimsy. The title had no meaningful relationship with the content. The subtitle was hardly more helpful: *a triumph* was not only vague, but also deliberately – and bitterly – ironic.

My own choice of title is less opaque. Nonetheless, it may be misleading, for the book is not a military biography of T.E. Lawrence, nor even a military history of the Arab Revolt – though it involves large elements of both. Rather, it is an attempt to understand the war that played out in the Middle East between 1914 and 1918 in all its dimensions – the war that has given the region its essential form throughout the century since. Lawrence provides a unique lens through which to observe and interpret the conflict, since, having a pivotal role in it and being an especially intelligent, thoughtful and sensitive participant, he experienced its multiple contradictions as inner torment. His angst-ridden psyche thus becomes a metaphor for the tragedy of the war.

Lawrence, then, is the central character. But he takes his place among many others, both major and minor, some who fought alongside Lawrence in the desert, others who fought in parallel campaigns in Sinai and Palestine. For this was a war of two fronts, a hybrid conflict in which the Ottoman Empire was defeated west of the Jordan by a conventional mechanised army dependent on industrialised supply, and east of it by a tribal insurgency of camel-mounted guerrillas.

These two campaigns are usually studied and written about separately. This impedes understanding of both, for they were interdependent and profoundly symbiotic. Britain's wartime alliance with the sherif of Mecca undercut the appeal of a German-backed Ottoman call for global *jihad* designed to destabilise the British, French and Russian empires. The loyalty of Ottoman-Arab soldiers became conflicted and uncertain, feeding an epidemic of desertion, while the drain on Ottoman manpower and materiel of an unwinnable counter-insurgency war in the desert was a crucial ingredient in the success of British operations in Palestine. Allenby's soldiers, by contrast, as allies of the sherif, enjoyed a clear run in their advance across Arab lands.

So this is an attempt to tell the story of the campaigns in Sinai, Arabia, Palestine and Syria as an integrated whole. It involves much conventional military history, but is not restricted to this. A number of good accounts exist, and there are, of course, Lawrence's own writings, both *Seven Pillars of Wisdom* (1922/1926/1935) and, for those wanting a pared-down military narrative, his radical abridgement *Revolt in the Desert* (1927). To add significantly to the modest corpus we have would almost certainly depend upon access to Arabic and Turkish primary sources. The former are, in fact, few: most Arab participants in the war were not literate, and those who were usually made plans and gave orders without writing anything down. The latter are no doubt extensive, but the Turkish military archives are closed to independent scholars. Attempts to access them, working with Turkish colleagues, were fruitless. I cannot be certain of the reason, but I can guess. Genocide denial is the policy of the Turkish state, and it is safe to assume that abundant evidence for the wartime destruction of the Armenian people lies buried in the official archives.

So even had I wished to write a new military history, perhaps in part from 'the other side of the hill', it would have been impossible. But that was never the intention. Rather, *Lawrence of Arabia's War* is an attempt at an inter-disciplinary study of the conflict that unfolded in Egypt, Arabia, Palestine and Syria during the First World War; a conflict which, multi-dimensional and multi-layered, created the modern Middle East; a conflict whose violent consequences have ricocheted across the region for a century; a conflict from whose coils we have not yet escaped.

* * *

The interdisciplinary approach is fundamental to modern conflict archaeology and was the academic basis of the Great Arab Revolt Project (2006–14). We put a team of about 30 archaeologists and volunteers into the field for two weeks each autumn, working mainly in the desert regions of southern Jordan along the line of the former Hijaz Railway between Maan and Mudawwara. The archaeology comprised fortified railway stations, hilltop redoubts, blockhouses, campsites and scatters of expended munitions, discarded military equipment and the detritus of everyday army life: evidence of the Ottoman counter-insurgency effort between 1916 and 1918. Occasionally, too, we caught a glimpse of the shadowy enemy, the Bedouin guerrillas and the British demolition experts, weapon specialists and liaison officers who supported them. Using archive sources, satellite imagery and ground reconnaissance, we plotted the sites spread across the desert wilderness. Some we then investigated in detail, clearing wind-blown sand from breastworks and tent-rings, digging out trenches and machine-gun posts, drawing and photographing loop-holed blockhouses. And so, bit by bit, we built a picture of 'Lawrence of Arabia's war'.

The archaeology transformed our understanding of the conflict. It also provided the anchor for an attempt to comprehend the totality of the First World War in the Middle East in all its complexity and contradiction. Such, indeed, is the richness of the insights afforded that two books are necessary, this one, which is essentially a military history, and another currently in preparation by my colleague Nick Saunders, which will be a synthetic analysis of the archaeology and anthropology.

Our most basic discovery was that the Turks had a military post watching every yard of the railway, implying that they were engaged against a chronic and pervasive menace. And wherever it could be tested, we found Lawrence's account confirmed, implying that detractors who have portrayed him as a liar, a charlatan and a self-promoter are wrong, and that *Seven Pillars* should be regarded as one of history's great war memoirs.

But our scope was wider. Modern conflict archaeology begins with the material remains of the past, viewed in their landscape setting. Understanding of these is informed by written and visual sources, and draws on the insights of many disciplines. Because the social world is an integrated whole, full understanding of the past requires a holistic approach. Take the Hijaz Railway, the spine of the war, our project's centre of gravity. Here was a projection of industrial and military power into a traditional landscape; here, too, an expression of traditional Islamic piety; not one or the other, but both, for the railway conveyed soldiers and pilgrims alike into distant Arabia. It soon became something more: a frontier of sorts, what the Romans would have called a *limes* (in their day a road, but here a railway), a fortified line separating 'civilisation' from 'barbarism' – the civilisation of Ottoman-controlled Syria and the western Arabian littoral as against the barbarism of the desert.

Unsurprisingly, therefore, the railway was contested throughout its (short) history, at first by camel tribes ruined by 'the iron donkey', later by a desert potentate set upon raising rebellion and making himself 'king of the Arabs'. The railway forthwith took on a new role, becoming a military artery supplying the garrison of Medina, the holy city whose possession allowed the Ottoman sultan in Constantinople to sustain his claim to the caliphate and his call to Holy War. But in the war that followed – between the train and the camel – between, if you will, modernity and tradition – it was the camel that triumphed. For it was the camel that enabled the Arabs to become, in Lawrence's evocative phrase, 'the silent threat of a vast, unknown desert'.

This book, then, is an archaeologically and anthropologically informed politico-military history. It attempts to weave together the theoretical insights of diverse disciplines in an effort to create a holistic history of the First World War in the Levantine heart of the Middle East. If the biography of T.E. Lawrence is a central thread – and it is – this is because his peculiar role and deeply introspective nature meant that he experienced the cross-currents and contradictions of the evolving conflict as an inner personal crisis that culminated in psychic implosion. The war can be seen in sharp outline through the prism of Lawrence's mind; and, equally, Lawrence's breakdown becomes fully explicable only by reference to the war's tragic character. Individual psychology and military history are entwined. More simply, Lawrence becomes the metaphor for the imperialism, violence and betrayals that tore the region apart a century ago and has left it divided into warring fragments ever since.

* * *

In other respects, my approach will be familiar to readers of modern – as opposed to traditional – military history. I attempt to understand the experience of campaigning and combat at the level of the individual soldier, making plentiful use of first-hand testimony, not simply to 'add colour', but because I believe that the course of military events cannot otherwise be understood. We still need military history 'from above' – the strategic overview, the logistical challenges, the plans of the high command, the massing of guns, the movements of divisions and brigades. But the outcome depends equally on nuances of terrain, vagaries of weather, the reactions of the enemy and the behaviour of ordinary men amid the chaos, roar and terror of combat. Much can be anticipated and prepared for, but 'no plan survives first contact with the enemy', and battle is always a journey into the unknown, to a place where the actions of small groups of soldiers may matter as much as the orders of their generals.

This observation is nothing new. But I have attempted to place it in a wider anthropological context. Men at war are shaped by the social order to which they belong. How they think and act on the battlefield is affected not only by formal military training, but also by cultural conditioning. The extraordinary stoicism and resilience of the Anatolian Turkish soldier during the Great War was a phenomenon. Why did he – ragged, hungry, outnumbered, outgunned – defend trenches with such gritty resolution? Perhaps in part because he was recruited from a peasant village, where attachment to the land was innate. The Bedouin was quite the opposite: reluctant to defend fixed positions, but superb as a mobile guerrilla fighting a war of hit and run. Of course: for his people were the camel-nomads of the desert. Part of the brilliance of Lawrence was his instinctive grasp of the anthropology of war, and his willingness to adapt strategy and tactics to men, not to recast men in a conventional mould.

But if it was a war of peasants and nomads, it was a war fought with modern weapons and ideas. A Rhineland rifle and a Prussian officer turned the Turkish peasant-conscript into a modern soldier. A wadge of gun-cotton turned the Arab tribesman into a modern insurgent. So it was also a war of empires, firepower and mass production. As many modern scholars have been at pains to explain – notably Hew Strachan, Eugene Rogan and Kristian Ulrichsen – the war in the Middle East was no mere 'sideshow'. Not if you lived there. For the people of the region were encompassed by a global industrialised war in which one in ten lost their lives – some in battle, many more in epidemics, famines and massacres – and millions of others were crippled, displaced or impoverished. And as the old order crumbled, and the societies that formed it were torn apart, the region came to constitute what imperial statesmen call a 'vacuum' – as if the people had somehow vanished into a black hole – and set about imposing a new order, one controlled by themselves, serving their inter- ests, imposed by diktat and force, using clubs, machine-guns and poison gas. They called it 'a peace settlement', but it was not: for the imperial powers created a Middle East of petty states, petty rivalries and petty hates that has now been at war with itself for a century. They imposed what David Fromkin has called 'a peace to end all peace'.

This book is an attempt to explain how and why this Middle East was created. It is an attempt to explain 'Lawrence of Arabia's war'.

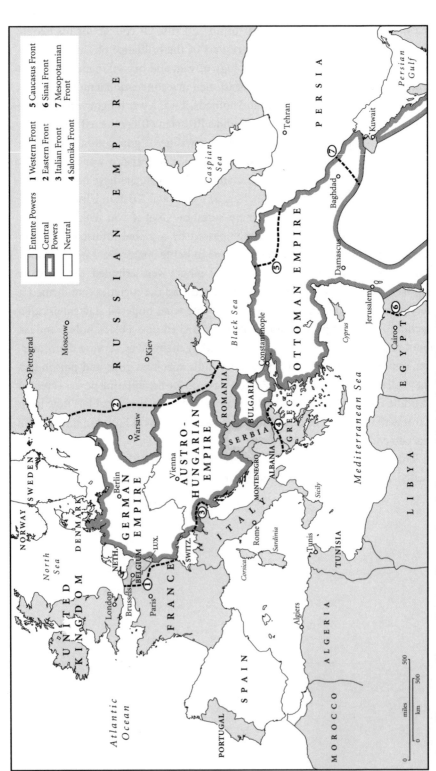

1. The world war in early 1916, showing alliances, the main fronts and the 'siege' of the Central Powers.

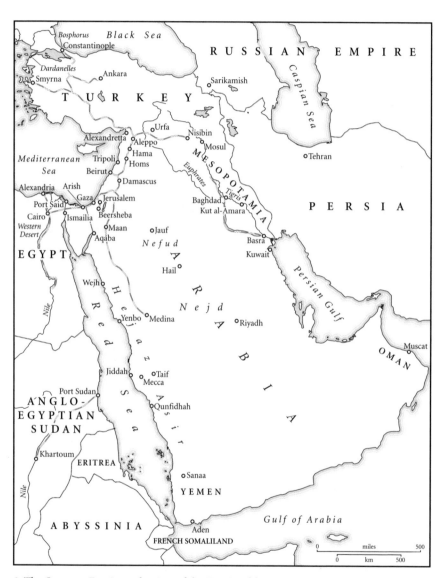

2. The Ottoman Empire at the time of the First World War.

3. Sinai, Palestine and Syria, showing major towns, communication lines and the principal battle sites.

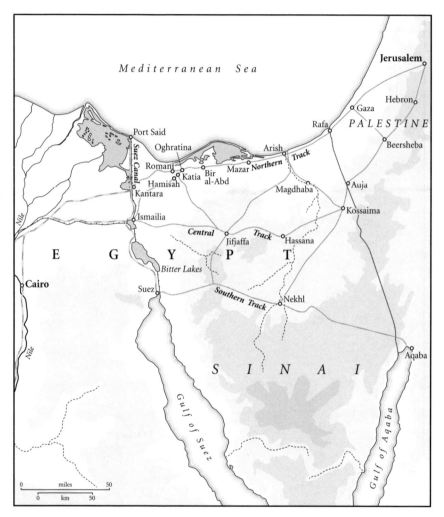

Mediterranean Sea

Jerusalem

Hebron

Gaza

Rafa

PALESTINE

Beersheba

Port Said

Oghratina

Arish

Romani

Mazar

Northern

Track

Suez Canal

Katia

Bir al-Abd

Hamisah

Magdhaba

Auja

Kantara

Kossaima

Ismailia

Central

Track

Nile

E G Y P T

Jifjaffa

Hassana

Bitter Lakes

Cairo

Suez

Southern Track

Nekhl

Nile

Aqaba

S I N A I

Gulf of Suez

Gulf of Aqaba

| 0 | miles | 50 |
| 0 | km | 50 |

4. The Sinai Desert, showing the Suez Canal, the larger oasis settlements and the main route-ways. The British railway, water-pipe and wire road followed the line of the Northern Track.

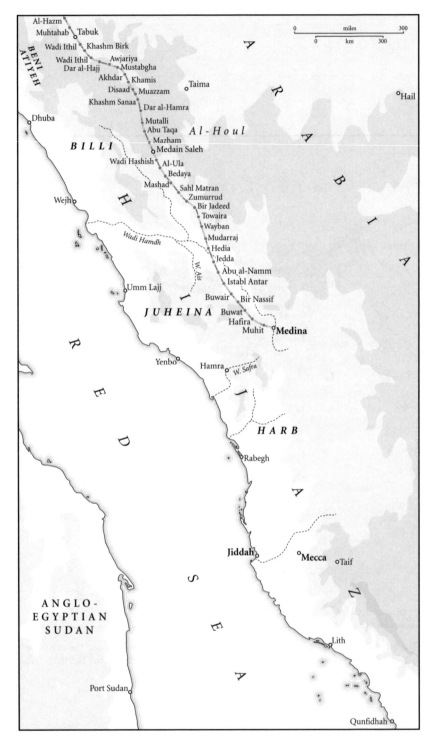

Al-Hazm
Muhtahab · Tabuk
BENI ATIYEH
Wadi Ithil · Khashm Birk
Wadi Ithil · Awjariya
Dar al-Hajj · Mustabgha
Akhdar · Khamis
Disaad · Muazzam · Taima
Khashm Sanaa · Dar al-Hamra
Dhuba
BILLI · Mutalli
Abu Taqa · Al-Houl
Mazham
Medain Saleh
Wadi Hashish · Al-Ula
Bedaya
Mashad · Sahl Matran
Zumurrud
Wejh · Bir Jadeed
Towaira
HIJ · Wayban
Mudarraj
Wadi Hamdh · Hedia
Jedda
W. Ais · Abu al-Namm
Istabl Antar
Umm Lajj · Buwair · Bir Nassif
JUHEINA · Buwat
Hafira
Muhit · Medina
ARABIA
Hail
RED · Yenbo · Hamra · W. Safra
I
HARB
Z
Rabegh
A
ANGLO-EGYPTIAN SUDAN
SEA
Jiddah · Mecca · Taif
Lith
Port Sudan
Qunfidhah

miles
0   300
0   km   300

5. The Hijaz in 1916.

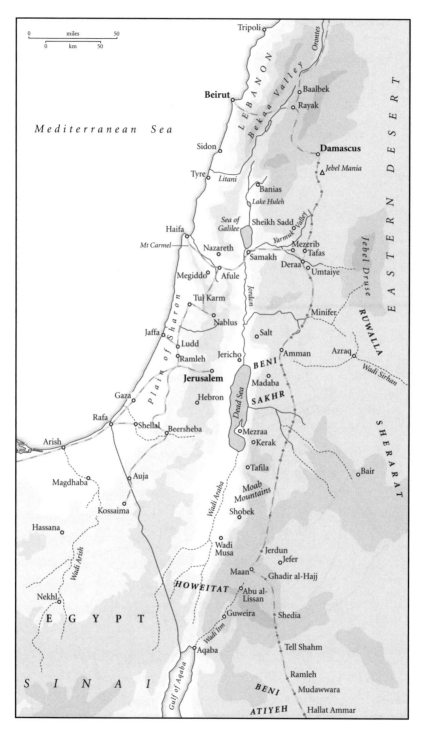

Scale bar:
```
0        miles        50
0         km          50
```

Mediterranean   Sea

Tripoli

L E B A N O N

Bekaa Valley

Orontes

Baalbek

Beirut

Rayak

Sidon

Damascus

Jebel Mania △

Tyre

Litani

Banias

Lake Huleh

Sea of Galilee

Sheikh Sadd

Haifa

Mt Carmel

Nazareth

Samakh

Yarmuk Valley

Mezerib

Tafas

Deraa

Umtaiye

Megiddo

Afule

E A S T E R N   D E S E R T

Jebel Druse

Tul Karm

Nablus

Jordan

Minifer

RUWALLA

Jaffa

Ludd

Salt

Amman

Azraq

Ramleh

Jericho

BENI

Wadi Sirhan

Jerusalem

Dead Sea

Madaba

SAKHR

Hebron

Gaza

Rafa

Shellal

Beersheba

Mezraa

Kerak

SHERARAT

Arish

Auja

Tafila

Bair

Magdhaba

Wadi Araba

Moab Mountains

Shobek

Kossaima

Hassana

Plain of Sharon

Wadi Arish

Wadi Musa

Jerdun

Jefer

Maan

Ghadir al-Hajj

Nekhl

HOWEITAT

Abu al-Lissan

E G Y P T

Guweira

Shedia

Wadi Itm

Aqaba

Gulf of Aqaba

Tell Shahm

Ramleh

S I N A I

BENI

Mudawwara

ATIYEH

Hallat Ammar

6. The zone of operations on the Arab front between May 1917 and August 1918.

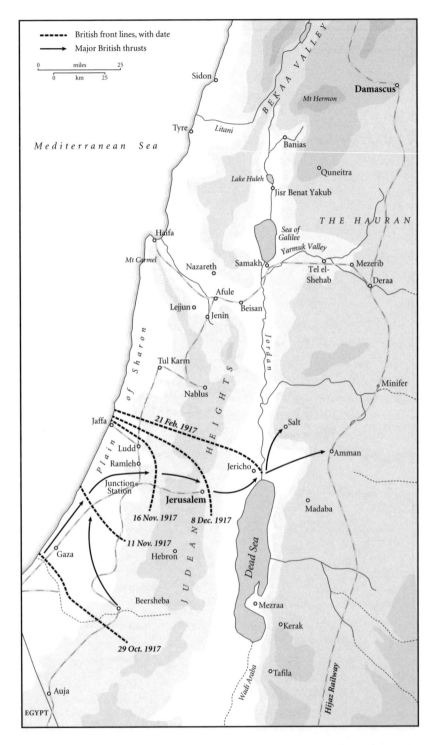

7. Palestine, showing major British military advances, November 1917–September 1918.

CHAPTER 1

Holy War?

O N ABOUT 10 December 1913, a letter arrived for the two British archaeologists working on the Carchemish excavations in northern Syria.
Would they be willing to join a survey expedition in eastern Sinai over the
winter? As a subsequent letter from the chairman of the Executive Committee
of the Palestine Exploration Fund explained:

> The country, of which the survey is now to be taken in hand, is that south of
> the previous survey, up to the line of the Egyptian frontier, which extends
> from Rafa, on the Mediterranean coast about 20 miles south-west of Gaza,
> in a south-south-east direction, to the head of the Gulf of Aqaba ... This
> country, notwithstanding its proximity to Palestine and Egypt, is but little
> known, and, though it has been crossed by travellers in certain parts, is to a
> great extent unexplored.

It was, in fact, a disconcerting cartographic lacuna, a triangle of uncharted land
situated between that shown on the Palestine Exploration Fund's maps of
western Palestine and that on the Egyptian Survey Department's maps of Sinai.
The former had been surveyed in the 1870s, the latter more recently, following
the British seizure of Sinai – a classic imperial land-grab – in 1906.[1] War with
Germany looked increasingly likely. The stance of the Ottoman Empire was
uncertain. The security of Egypt and the Suez Canal was a vital British interest.
The military needed comprehensive map coverage of what might soon become
a theatre of operations. The problem was that the unmapped territory was on
the Ottoman side of the frontier. Thus the invitation to the two British archaeologists, who were to be the academic cover for an essentially military survey.
The real leader of the expedition would be Captain Stewart 'Skinface' Newcombe
of the Royal Engineers.

Newcombe had anticipated a couple of elderly professorial types. When the pair turned up, he decided they looked about 24 and 18, and that his arrangements for their reception had been too polite: 'undue deference ceased forthwith'.[2] Whatever their ages (they were actually 33 and 25), they worked with professional efficiency, and an academic monograph – *The Wilderness of Zin* – later appeared. The authors suspected they were stooges, but remained hazy about details. 'We are obviously only meant as red herrings, to give an archaeological colour to a political job,' wrote one of them. The work had been gruelling – long days on camel-back, nights sleeping rough and a diet mainly, it seems, of bread and Turkish Delight. The older of the two, Leonard Woolley, found the going particularly hard. 'Woolley is the more uncomfortable, since he is a flesh-potter,' his companion explained in a letter to a mutual friend at the Ashmolean Museum. 'I can travel on a thistle, and sleep in a cloak on the ground.' The younger man seems to have relished the adventure. The work had also set him thinking: 'It shows how easy it is in an absolutely deserted country to defy a government.' So mused a young Oxford archaeologist called Thomas Edward Lawrence.[3]

* * *

The maps would be needed. A year after the British survey, in January 1915, eastern Sinai had become a routeway to battle: 25,000 Ottoman soldiers of the Canal Expeditionary Force were marching to the Suez Canal, intent on severing the British Empire's jugular, rousing its Egyptian subjects to Holy War and restoring the sultan's authority over one of his richest provinces. 'I want to start an offensive against the Suez Canal to keep the English tied up in Egypt,' the Ottoman War Minister Ismail Enver Pasha had explained to the man appointed to the command.[4]

The British had studied their maps and guessed that 5,000 men and 2,000 camels constituted the largest force that might be projected across the 150 miles of desert between Beersheba and the Suez Canal.[5] Though it turned out to have been a gross underestimate, it reflected well enough the immense logistical challenge of desert warfare for large conventional armies.

The civilisations of the Nile had been divided from those of the Levant throughout most of human history by the desiccated liminal space of the Sinai Desert. On the map it is a wedge-shaped peninsula extending roughly 240 miles north–south and 120 miles along its base. It is bounded to the west by the Gulf of Suez, to the east by the Gulf of Aqaba and to the north by the Mediterranean. The northern zone comprises a narrow coastal plain, varying from 5 to 25 miles wide, formed largely of sand dunes, but with extensive tracts of salty mud-flat, especially near the coast, and numerous 'hods' (stands) of date-palms in the depressions between the dunes, where supplies of brackish water are available in pools, wells and cisterns. The central zone is a wider band of barren, stony, undulating plateau, much of it scrub-covered, rising in places to almost 1,000 metres. The southern zone is a great mass of high, rocky, precipitous, granite mountains, the highest of them, the Mount Sinai group, in excess of 2,500 metres.[6]

The essentials of desert warfare are water, supplies and mobility – in that order. Sinai in 1915 supported little more than occasional clusters of mud-walled houses around an ancient cistern and scattered encampments of nomadic Bedouin. So few were the native inhabitants of Sinai that the presence of the soldiers of the Canal Expeditionary Force probably doubled the population of the peninsula. The British assumption was that the emptiness of the desert, the hard going on its trackways and the ramshackle logistics of the Ottoman Army would preclude anything more ambitious than a large-scale raid. In fact, by the morning of 2 February, the Ottomans had got the 13,000 men of their advanced strike-force across the wilderness and into position for a direct assault on the canal. Then, mid-afternoon, the wind got up, a violent sandstorm blotted out the sun and, for the time being, military operations ceased.

* * *

Squinting into the dirty brown swirl of the sandstorm from trenches along the west bank of the canal near Tussum were the men of the 62nd and 92nd Punjabis, the 2nd Rajputs and the 10th Gurkhas – regiments of Indian Army sepoys belonging to an expeditionary force recently arrived to guard the link connecting the Raj to the British Isles. Faces were shrouded in flaps of turban and rifle breeches clothed in rags against the blizzard of sand. The defenders knew the enemy were close, but the sentries strained for sound of them in the howling wind.[7]

Along the 100-mile extent of the canal between Port Said and Suez there were about 30,000 men in total – 24 battalions of infantry, a cavalry brigade, a camel corps and four batteries of artillery. Except for some Egyptian gunners, virtually all were soldiers of the Indian Army. These had recently replaced European troops redeployed from Egypt to the Western Front. The newly arrived 42nd (East Lancashire) Division remained around Cairo, along with various other British, Australian and New Zealand units. Acclimatisation, re-equipment and training were still in progress; in any case, white soldiers were needed near the capital as an internal security force.[8]

Lacking the strength to defend any part of Sinai, the British had withdrawn behind the canal and were treating it as a defensive moat. It was a formidable obstacle, being 34 feet deep, between 65 and 100 yards wide, and with banks up to 30 feet above the water-level in places. Along some two-thirds of its length, moreover, effective assault was precluded by the presence of lakes.

The 25-mile northern sector between Port Said and Kantara (designated Section 3) ran along the eastern edge of Lake Menzaleh, a shallow but extensive sheet of salt water that would have hemmed in any attackers who succeeded in crossing the canal at this point. The previous November, moreover, the British had closed off this possibility, at least for the winter months, by flooding the low-lying Plain of Tineh on the eastern side of the canal. The southern sector (Section 1) was also difficult for an attacker. The Great Bitter and Little Bitter lakes extended for more than 20 miles, and the final 15-mile stretch of canal down to the sea at Suez passed through a relatively remote region. The logistics and risks involved in trying to bring a large force to bear against Section 1 were prohibitive.

It was the central sector, between Kantara and the Great Bitter Lake (Section 2), that was critical. Lake Timsah accounted for 7 miles of this 30-mile extent, and elsewhere the banks tended to be high and readily defensible. On the other hand, it was here that Ismailia was located, the strategically vital transport and water-supply hub of the entire defence system, and the line of approach from the east was direct, firm-footed and well watered.[9] It was opposite Ismailia, then, that some 13,000 Ottoman soldiers of the strike-force massed on the night of 2/3 February, waiting for the sandstorm to pass over.

The coming battle – the first major clash of the war between the Ottoman and British Empires – was to be fought by the subject-peoples of the rival powers. The attackers were mainly Arab peasants conscripted from the villages of Syria, the defenders Punjabi, Rajput and Gurkha regulars from northern India. The Indians were volunteers, but they were fighting a white man's war far from home. How would they fare amid the cross-currents of conflicting loyalties unleashed by the Great War? How, in particular, would Muslim soldiers of the British Raj view a war against fellow Muslims on behalf of their Christian rulers?

* * *

Suez was the narrowest stretch on the great maritime highway that linked the twin pivots of Britain's global power: India and the homeland. But when the Government of India declared war on the enemies of the British Empire, it had elicited a less than enthusiastic response from many of its 300 million

Indian subjects. For sure, pledges of allegiance and support flowed in from numerous official bodies set up by the British colonial regime, and John Buchan, the writer and wartime propagandist, was able to proclaim that the imperial mission was affirmed as India 'took the world by surprise and thrilled every British heart'.[10]

The reality was more complex. Unqualified enthusiasm was restricted to a layer of privileged collaborators, men like the Maharaja of Rewa, who offered his troops, his territory, his private jewels, and ended an official letter with the words 'What order has my King for me?'[11] The majority of Indians in the villages and smaller towns probably knew little of the war and cared less. Their British overlords – jingoes like Buchan notwithstanding – were no doubt content that it was so: since the trauma of the 1857 Mutiny, the Government of India's policy had been a combination of light touch and deliberate underdevelopment.[12] Anything potentially destabilising was to be avoided. Indifference was the ideal.

But the Indian nationalists were now a sizeable minority, and among them the war evoked a more forthright response. Moderate nationalists – like Gandhi – urged support, but largely on the basis that military service would demonstrate good faith and qualify Indians for national independence. Radical nationalists, on the other hand, opposed it outright and saw Britain's crisis as India's opportunity.

The Congress Party, a middle-class nationalist organisation founded in 1885, had by now swelled into a mass movement against British rule, fuelled by anger over lack of support for native industry and racial discrimination in government employment. In 1907, a combination of state interference in the freedom of the universities and a decision to partition the ancient province of Bengal gave rise to a wave of nationalist agitation, causing Congress to split into moderate and radical wings, the former still seeking to negotiate change, the latter calling for immediate action.[13]

Rash Behari Bose emerged as a leading advocate of 'propaganda of the deed', arguing that 'the commission of outrages' would trigger 'a strong desire . . . among the masses for open revolution'.[14] A series of terrorist attacks culminated in an attempt on the life of the British Viceroy, Lord Hardinge, in December 1912. Hardinge and his wife were riding on a ceremonial elephant in a procession through the streets to mark the transfer of the imperial capital from Calcutta to New Delhi. A homemade bomb was hurled at their howdah and exploded behind them. Hardinge was injured across much of his back by fragments of metal. The gang of three assassins were later hunted down and executed.[15]

The main centres of radical nationalism were Bengal and the Punjab, and by the outbreak of war its primary expression was the Ghadar Party, a network of revolutionary groups organised around an illegal newspaper published abroad and smuggled into the country. Hardinge detected a sinister conspiracy to overthrow the Raj. Ghadar, in his view, was an 'anarchist' organisation whose 'predominant plan is to reduce the province to chaos by the murder of police and officials'; it was, he claimed, 'encouraged by a few crazy people in the United States and western Canada, and probably subventioned by Germany'.[16] That German agents were active in India during the war is certain. At the end of 1915, Hardinge's police exposed a conspiracy to launch a full-scale revolt, claiming 'ample evidence that German assistance, financial and otherwise, has been given to agitators'.[17]

* * *

The British took the risk of Indian nationalist revolution very seriously. After the Mutiny – the central event of nineteenth-century Indian history – they had remodelled their entire administration to minimise the risk of a repetition, proclaiming Queen Victoria 'Empress of India', creating a new Government of India headed by a viceroy and staffed by a professional Indian Civil Service, and fostering a network of relationships which extended from native princes and other notables, through an administrative middle class, to village notables enlisted as collectors of rents and taxes.[18] They also remodelled their army of native sepoys.

The Indian Army was not in any sense a 'national' army; rather, it was an 'anti-national' army, contrived in the shadow of 1857. The proportion of British troops serving in India had been increased from one in six to one in three. The standard pattern was to brigade one British battalion with three Indian. The establishment of British officers in a typical Indian battalion had been raised to twelve, and Indian officers rarely served above the level of platoon command. All field artillery was kept in British hands; only mountain-guns were served by Indian crews.[19] Thus were the guardians guarded, for the loyalty of the Indian sepoy, a mercenary in foreign colonial service, could never be taken for granted.

Recruitment was restricted to the one-tenth of the population considered to comprise 'martial races'. This meant that virtually all the 150,000 men of the Indian Army in 1914, and virtually all the 1.3 million Indians who served overseas during the war, were recruited from a pool of about 3 million young men from traditional villages in northern India.[20] Regiments formed of these carefully selected volunteers were bound together by a mix of religion, caste solidarity and feudal fealty. The individual sepoy was motivated by a strong sense of personal 'honour' and by bonds of comradeship with men who were often relatives and neighbours.[21] 'You will be the first Indian soldiers of the King-Emperor who will have the honour of showing . . . that the sons of India have lost none of their ancient martial instincts', George V told the first batch of Indian soldiers to reach the front. 'In battle you will remember that your religions enjoin on you that to give your life doing your duty is your highest reward . . . You will fight for your King-Emperor and your faith, so that history will record the doings of India's sons, and your children will proudly tell of the deeds of their fathers . . .'[22]

Thus were the pomp and mysticism of medieval India reconfigured to serve a modern capitalist empire. The Indian Army sepoy was a traditional warrior dressed in khaki and armed with a magazine rifle. Behind the façade, the Raj was about profit and power. Early twentieth-century India was a primary market for British industry. It absorbed 10 per cent of Britain's overseas investments and almost half the output of its cotton mills.[23] And as the original 'workshop of the world' lost its lead to newly rising industrial powers, India loomed ever larger in the calculations of British statesmen. 'As long as we rule India, we are the greatest power in the world,' claimed Lord Curzon, the Indian Viceroy, in 1901. 'If we lose it, we shall drop straightaway to a third-rate power.'[24]

* * *

The Indian Army had two primary roles: frontier defence and internal security. The former involved regular deployment and frequent combat experience on the North-West Frontier. What made this frontier – *the* frontier – along with Afghanistan beyond so sensitive was the advance of the tsarist empire across Central Asia during the mid to late nineteenth century. This had pitted the British and the Russians against each other in a 'Great Game' played out between the Black Sea and the Pacific Ocean. The primary pressure-point had always been the approaches to India through the Hindu Kush. Anxiety in this region was heightened by the fact that the loyalty of both Afghan emirs and Pathan hill-tribesmen was for sale.

A succession of events in the first decade of the twentieth century had, however, brought the Great Game to a sudden and unexpected end. In 1902 the British formed an alliance with Japan and, in 1904–5, the new ally inflicted a crushing defeat on the old rival in the Russo-Japanese War. This triggered a proletarian revolution that almost toppled the tsar, and, before the situation stabilised, rising tensions inside Europe had compelled Britain and Russia to forget former differences over Afghanistan and forge a defensive alliance against Germany and Austria-Hungary.[25]

What now should the role of the Indian Army be? Internal security and the defence of the frontier remained paramount, but the Government of India did concede in 1912 that its army should be 'so organised and equipped as to be capable of affording ready overseas co-operation, when the situation allows of it, in such direction as His Majesty's Government may determine'.[26]

In fact, the Indian sepoy had always been something of a transferable asset in the struggle for global supremacy, contributing to British campaigns as far apart as China, Sudan, Uganda and even the Mediterranean in the later nineteenth century. In any case, the Government of India took a broad view of security, taking a keen interest in events across a great arc of territory from East Africa, through the Arabian Peninsula, to South-East Asia.[27] On the brink of war, it firmed up its commitments by offering a cavalry brigade and two infantry divisions for overseas service.[28] In the event, even before the end of 1914, the Indian Army had dispatched four separate expeditionary forces – to the Western Front, Mesopotamia, Egypt and East Africa – and by the end of the war it would have more than a million men in the field, twenty times the number originally envisaged. British India in the First World War was not only 'the jewel in the crown'. It was also a pillar of empire: a vast reserve of military manpower, much of it composed of professional long-service volunteers seasoned by combat experience.

* * *

India's mighty contribution to the British Empire's war had been made possible by a modernisation programme overseen in the preceding decade by Lord Herbert Kitchener of Khartoum. By the time he became war minister in August 1914, Kitchener was Britain's greatest living soldier. A monument to Victorian militarism and a *Boy's Own* hero of the jingo press, his portrait on a million recruitment posters, all steely-eyed stare and walrus moustache, had quickly made his the most familiar face of the war in Britain. He had made his reputation as the architect of, first, the industrialised destruction of the Sudanese Dervishes at Omdurman in 1898, and then the counter-insurgency war that had brought the South African Boers to the negotiating table in 1902. But from 1903 to 1909 he had served as the commander-in-chief of the Indian Army, and his achievement in this less glamorous assignment had been no less significant. At the time, he had still envisaged a reform of the army to make it better suited to war on the frontier. But the effect was to turn it, for the first time, into an effective instrument of world power. Kitchener's aim was to reduce dispersal across the country in local policing roles and instead to concentrate the army close to the frontier in new war-fighting divisions –

all-arms miniature armies in which the stolid qualities of British regulars, the mobility and panache of Indian sepoys, and a full complement of cavalry, artillery, sappers and transport services would be combined.[29]

This was the reformed army to which the Indian soldiers manning the trenches along the Suez Canal early in 1915 belonged. It was limited in many ways. General conscription was impossible in India and even general enlistment would have risked placing guns in the hands of men who might one day turn them against the Raj. So recruitment remained restricted – to the more trustworthy 'martial races' – and the shortage of officers in particular, both commissioned and non-commissioned, remained acute. Nonetheless, the 1.3 million men of the Indian Army who eventually fought in the Great War amounted to 15 per cent of the British Empire's mobilised manpower.[30]

Jewel in the crown and pillar of empire: profit and power: such was India. Now, in early February 1915, an Ottoman Army stood poised on the banks of the Suez Canal intent on choking off the flow of men and materiel from India to the Motherland at the outset. This was the importance of Egypt: it guarded Britain's routeway to India; it was the western bastion of an imperial domain centred on the subcontinent that extended across the Indian Ocean from the Red Sea and East Africa on one side to the South China Sea and Australasia on the other. This was the reason Britain had invaded Egypt in 1882; this the reason she had reconquered the Sudan in 1898; this the reason she had 40,000 men guarding Cairo even as the Ottomans prepared to launch an attack on the canal.

* * *

Among the guardians of Cairo that winter were the men of 10th Battalion, the Manchester Regiment, 126th Brigade, part of the newly arrived 42nd East Lancashire Division. The battalion was a product of the late Victorian craze for part-time soldiering. First raised in 1859 as the 31st Lancashire Volunteers, it had been reincorporated as a territorial battalion of the Manchester Regiment in 1908. The men of the Territorial Force (later the Territorial Army) were, in effect, part-time militia dedicated to the defence of the homeland in the event of war. During the Boer War, however, many volunteer units had served overseas, and the assumption was that the territorials would do the same on a future occasion; thus they were regarded as Britain's first-line reserves. In the event, 95 per cent of the men of 10th Battalion had volunteered for overseas in August 1914, and fresh recruitment had quickly made the numbers up to a full battalion complement of 1,008 men.[31]

The 10th Manchesters had sailed for Alexandria in September, along with the rest of the East Lancashire Division – the first complete territorial division, 16,000 officers and men, to leave for overseas service. They were replacements for the pre-war garrison of 5,000 regulars, whose services were urgently required on the Western Front that autumn. The 10th was moved by train to Cairo and then marched to an encampment on Heliopolis racecourse – a featureless expanse of sand that disappointed expectations – four miles from the city. Here they commenced a three-month programme of acclimatisation and intensive training designed to turn these 'Saturday after-noon' amateurs into combat-ready soldiers.[32] At the same time, they acted as a colonial police force.

'The withdrawal of the whole of the regular troops from Lower Egypt,' recalled Captain Wynne, 'and their replacement by what was considered "raw material", encouraged the rebellious element in the country to try conclusions.' On 20 October, therefore, the entire 126th Brigade was marched through Cairo, where there was 'a great feeling of unrest' and 'the natives of all classes were inclined to be both sullen and insolent'. This was followed a week later by another show of force, now involving the entire 42nd Division, 'which presented a magnificent and impressive spectacle'; the effect, in Captain Wynne's view, 'upon the many thousands of natives who lined the streets and occupied every point of vantage was obvious'.[33]

The mood remained tense in the Egyptian capital throughout the following winter. Among those who sensed it was a newly arrived wartime intelligence officer. He had originally taken up a civilian post in the map department of the War Office in London, but had soon donned military uniform as Temporary 2nd Lieutenant-Interpreter T.E. Lawrence.[34] He had then been sent to Cairo as one of a small group of officer-intellectuals with Middle Eastern experience who were to form a new intelligence service.

None of the 'five musketeers' – as they came to be called – was a professional soldier. One of the others was Woolley, now a lieutenant, and then there was Captain George Lloyd, a businessman and Tory MP, Captain Aubrey Herbert, a linguist, traveller, diplomat and another Tory MP, and one Lieutenant Hay, about whom little is known. The officer in charge was Captain Stewart Newcombe, and he in turn reported to Captain Gilbert Clayton, the Director of Intelligence. The new department was built from scratch. 'There wasn't an intelligence department, it seemed, and they thought all was well without it,' Lawrence wrote shortly after his arrival, 'till it dawned on them that nobody in Egypt knew about Syria.' Lawrence, the youngest by far and most junior in rank, was 'map officer'. Woolley wrote reports and press releases. Lloyd looked after Mesopotamian affairs, Herbert did the same for Turkish politics, and 'between them in their spare time they locate the Turkish army'. Newcombe ran 'a gang of most offensive spies' and liaised with high command.

Alongside his other responsibilities, Herbert was much preoccupied with internal security, unearthing 'futile conspiracies', and rounding up opponents of British rule. Though Lawrence implied that nationalist activity was a comic-opera affair, he was in no doubt about the widespread popular hostility it represented: 'the Egyptian townsmen do hate us so. I thought it was only a coldness ... but it is a most burning dislike. They are also very much afraid.'[35]

* * *

Hatred and fear: the Egyptians had good reason for both. The British had invaded and occupied their country in 1882, in order to overthrow a nationalist government, secure control of the Suez Canal and ensure a continuing flow of revenues to foreign creditors. Previously, the British had preferred to keep Egypt at arm's length. They had intervened to clear out the French after Napoleon's invasion in 1798, but had then withdrawn. Prime Minister Palmerston had summed up the British attitude in the first half of the nineteenth century in wry patrician style:

> We do not want Egypt, any more than a rational man with an estate in the north of England and a residence in the south would wish to possess the inns on the road. All he could want would be that the inns should be always accessible to him and furnish him, when he came, with mutton-chops and post-horses.[36]

But if Egypt seemed to imperial statesmen little more than an 'inn' on the route to India, it appeared otherwise to its own leaders. The country had an unfortunate tendency to produce ambitious nation-building modernisers. The British felt obliged to send the Royal Navy in 1841 to break the power of Muhammad Ali and restore the authority of the Ottoman sultan. They later opposed the Khedive Ismail's canal scheme – Prime Minister Benjamin Disraeli professed to believe it 'a most futile attempt and totally impossible to be carried out'. Then, after the Suez Canal was opened in 1869 – a triumph of Egyptian nationalism and French engineering – the very same Disraeli seized the opportunity to buy a controlling interest at a rock-bottom price from the heavily indebted Egyptian government. 'The entire interest of the khedive is now yours,' he gleefully informed Queen Victoria.[37]

There was much more to be had. Ismail's modernisation programme had left his government hopelessly mired in debt. In 1877 the Egyptian revenue was £9.5 million, but of this, £7.5 million went in interest to foreign bondholders. The khedivial regime thus became, in essence, a mechanism for extracting taxes from the desperately poor Egyptian peasantry, the *fellahin*, for the benefit of investors in London and Paris. To sustain the flow, the British and French governments imposed 'Dual Control' in 1876 – effectively a joint financial dictatorship – to consolidate Egypt's debts and impose a strict repayment schedule. When Ismail, responding to rising popular anger, became obstructive, the Ottoman sultan, still the nominal suzerain, was persuaded to depose him and appoint his more compliant son Tewfik as khedive.[38]

The imposition of a colonial client regime controlled by Anglo-French finance-capital coincided with crop failure and famine in Upper Egypt. Thousands starved to death. Flogging and imprisonment became routine. The radical journalist William Scawen Blunt wrote that the *fellahin* 'were in terrible straits of poverty ... the European bondholders were clamouring for their "coupons" and famine was at the door'.[39] The canal and the debt: for the British Empire, Egypt had become a trade route, a revenue stream and a strategic asset – for the protection of which it would be prepared to conduct a succession of military interventions and crackdowns from 1882 onwards.

Egypt under Tewfik quickly acquired the appearance of a colony. The 90,000 European residents were exempt from taxation and, effectively, from Egyptian law. While Egyptian civil servants were sacked or had their pay cut, foreign officials were hired on gargantuan salaries, such that the pay of 1,300 Europeans was soon absorbing 5 per cent of government expenditure.[40] The growing resistance of all classes coalesced around the leadership of Colonel Ahmed Arabi Pasha and a group of nationalist army officers. By 1882 a tide of popular revolution was threatening the survival of the client regime. But the Royal Navy bombarded the port of Alexandria in July, smashing Arabi's batteries, and a British expeditionary force of 30,000 men then invaded Egypt and won a decisive victory over Arabi's outnumbered army at Tel el-Kebir in September, killing up to 10,000 Egyptians.[41]

Arabi was exiled, the Egyptian Army disbanded and the khedive transformed into a puppet. The real ruler of Egypt henceforward was the 'British agent and consul-general'. The country became what one senior British statesman dubbed a 'Veiled Protectorate'. The first consul-general was Evelyn Baring (nicknamed 'Over-Baring'). Later ennobled as Lord Cromer, he served from 1883 to 1907. The Egypt being defended by the 10th Manchesters and their comrades in the winter of 1914/15 was essentially Cromer's Egypt.

* * *

British colonialism at the turn of the century combined self-righteous paternalism and racial and social arrogance with a commitment to top-down reform and corruption-free administration designed to maximise profit and put a favourable spin on empire. Less use of the *corvée* (press-gang) and the *kourbash* (rhinoceros-hide whip) could be expected to raise the productivity of agricultural labour – and therefore the tax revenue – while improving the image of British rule in the eyes of an increasingly well-informed and critical public. And, Cromer mused, a more prosperous small peasantry might evolve into a bulwark of the colonial regime, a conservative rural bloc with which to flatten the nationalism of the more politically advanced towns. But there was no substantive land reform, so the condition of the *fellahin* actually improved very little. At the end of Cromer's quarter-century as ruler of Egypt, the poorest 80 per cent of landholders owned less than 25 per cent of the land, while the richest 1 per cent owned 40 per cent, and almost a million *fellahin* were farming less than 5.5 acres.[42]

An incident in the delta village of Denshawai in 1906 tore away the mask of British benevolence. A group of Britons had gone pigeon-shooting. The pigeons they shot belonged to the villagers. There was an altercation and a scuffle. A British officer went for help but died of concussion and heat-stroke. A peasant tried to assist him, but a party of British soldiers mistook him for an assailant and beat him to death. Cromer, backed by the newspapers, then demanded exemplary punishment of the villagers. A special tribunal was set up under an English judge who knew little Arabic. Four men were sentenced to hang and nine to fifty lashes. The sentences were carried out on site and the villagers were forced to watch.[43]

* * *

The British had also taken control of the Sudan. A Turco-Egyptian army had conquered and occupied the country in the 1820s, and paramilitary tax-collection squads had then battened onto such of its impoverished people as they could reach. The Sudanese had endured their oppression for sixty years, and then a holy man had arisen among them claiming to be the *Mahdi*, the 'Expected One', a new Islamic prophet sent by Allah to guide his people in a war to extirpate infidels and restore justice to the world. The Dervishes – as they came to be known – crushed their enemies in pitched battle in late 1883, and then captured Khartoum in early 1885, killing the British general sent to defend it before a desert relief column could reach him.[44]

The British accepted the outcome for a decade: Sudan was not worth the military investment necessary for reconquest. What reconfigured the calculation was the 'Scramble for Africa'. As the European empires rushed to gobble up 'vacant' territory before their rivals, Britain's rulers became obsessively preoccupied with the security of Egypt, the Suez Canal and the Red Sea route to India and the Dominions. The Sudan, of course, was the back-gate to Egypt, and therefore to Suez. The more ambitious British colonialists, moreover, dreamed of a Cape-to-Cairo strip of unbroken red the length of the continent. The French, on the other hand, dominant across the vast western bulge of Africa, imagined a band of blue stretching crossways from the Atlantic to the Indian Ocean. These two visions collided in southern Sudan. Khartoum became the key to locking the French out of East Africa.[45]

Between 1896 and 1898, Major-General Herbert Kitchener, at that time sirdar of the Egyptian Army, waged what was, in effect, an industrialised war to bring down a medieval theocracy. Building a railway line parallel with the Nile as he went, he edged his army slowly southwards, until, in September 1898, he was able to bring 22,000 men to Omdurman, on the opposite bank of the Nile from Khartoum, and compel the main forces of the Dervish Empire to give battle. Kitchener's men were armed with modern rifles, machine-guns and artillery. Most of the Sudanese were armed with spears and swords. The Battle of Omdurman was a massacre. Kitchener's army suffered fewer than 500 casualties. The Sudanese lost 10,000 killed, 13,000 wounded and 5,000 taken prisoner. The British murdered the wounded or left them to die where they lay. Meanwhile, a small French military expedition had arrived at Fashoda on the upper reaches of the Nile in southern Sudan. Kitchener moved upriver to confront them and Britain threatened war if they did not withdraw. The French backed down.[46] The back-gate to Suez had been locked.

* * *

In late 1914, Lieutenant-General Sir John Maxwell, the newly arrived British commander in Egypt, had good reason to be anxious about security, irrespective of anything the Ottomans might do. He had spent much of his military career in the country, serving with the Black Watch at Tel el-Kebir in 1882, commanding the 2nd Egyptian Brigade at Omdurman in 1898 and acting as sirdar of the Egyptian Army between 1908 and 1912.[47] He was, in fact, a blood-stained colonialist. The young Winston Churchill – who was there – considered Maxwell's men mainly responsible for the bayoneting and shooting of the Sudanese wounded after Omdurman. Maxwell himself, put in charge of the occupation of Omdurman after the battle, privately admitted that he 'quietly made away with a bunch of emirs'.[48]

Maxwell can have been in no doubt about the dangers he faced in 1914. The outbreak of war had plunged Egypt into an economic crisis which saw the value of exports – mainly cotton – fall by more than 75 per cent. 'The present crisis,' opined *The Times*, in characteristically pompous and stilted prose, 'affected all classes, and caused a very general *malaise*, more especially among the very poor. The risk that sedition-mongers would attempt to stir up trouble among the ignorant and needy had to be taken into account.' Four classes of 'sedition-mongers' were identified: 'the khedive and his supporters, the extremist nationalists, German agents and Turkish agitators'.[49] The danger was partly that 'the numerically small but vocal extremist party' – whose ranks seem to have included students, lower professionals and some urban workers – might have succeeded in mobilising wider forces on the basis of economic grievances. But there was also worry about jihadism: 'Religion was the side on which this town population was most easily approached by intriguers, and it is noteworthy that the connexion between Egypt and Turkey was popular among them, and among some of the *fellahin* for religious reasons.'[50]

A particular concern was the Egyptian Army. The native soldiers of a newly constituted army created by the British after 1882 had done the bulk of the fighting during Kitchener's campaigns in the Sudan. In 1914 this army comprised about 20,000 men. There were: seventeen infantry battalions (eight Egyptian, seven Muslim Sudanese, one Christian Sudanese and one Bedouin Sudanese); three mounted-infantry companies, two cavalry squadrons and a camel corps; six batteries of field or mountain artillery and three companies of garrison artillery; sappers, medics and other support services; and sundry militia, gendarmerie and coast guards (not all technically part of the army). The soldiers were commanded by British volunteer officers and were relatively well-equipped; most men began the war with single-shot Martini-Henrys, but these were replaced by magazine Lee-Enfields during the war, and there were also some machine-guns.

The victors of Omdurman might have been regarded as a valuable military asset in the war that had just broken out across the Middle East. They were not. Maxwell did not trust them and they played almost no role in either the defence of the canal or the garrisoning of Cairo. A few were posted to southern Sinai, some saw action against the Senussi in the Western Desert, but most were deployed to the Sudan.[51]

There is no question that the Sudan required a garrison. It was huge, disaffected, hard to police and vulnerable along its extensive borders; the rebellion of Ali Dinar of Darfur in 1916 would, in due course, confirm the dangers.[52] But the decision to rely solely on Egyptian Army troops in Sudan – and deploy virtually none to Egypt itself – reflected Maxwell's deep distrust. What, he wondered, would be the effect of the Ottoman *jihad* on these Muslim soldiers? How might they respond to an outbreak of nationalist agitation on the streets of Cairo and Alexandria? He was right to be anxious: the fragility of the

Egyptian Army's allegiance was exposed when a number of soldiers defected to the Senussi in 1915.[53]

The British position in Egypt was made more awkward by the attitude of the country's nominal ruler. The Khedive Abbas Hilmi was known to be pro-Ottoman and anti-British. This created an exceptionally delicate dilemma, for Egypt remained constitutionally part of the Ottoman Empire and legally subject to the Ottoman sultan – a paper authority which British officials had sustained with urbane hypocrisy for more than a generation. Since the Ottoman sultan might be expected to object to one of his provinces being used as a base for military operations against his own armies, the outbreak of war had rendered the 'Veiled Protectorate' untenable. The veil would have to be removed.

On 2 November, General Maxwell imposed martial law on Egypt, declaring that he had been directed 'to assume military control of Egypt in order to secure its protection'. The Egyptian government and civil administration were to carry on as before, and private citizens were informed that 'they will best serve the common end by abstaining from all action of a nature to disturb the public peace, to stir up disaffection, or to aid the enemies of His Britannic Majesty and His Allies, and by conforming promptly and cheerfully to all orders ...'

Five days later came a second proclamation, announcing that a state of war existed between Britain and the Ottoman Empire, and that 'Great Britain was fighting both to protect the rights and liberties of Egypt ... and to secure to her the continuance of the peace and prosperity which she has enjoyed during the 30 years of the British Occupation.' Perhaps anticipating a certain lack of enthusiasm for the cause, Sir John stressed that there would no interference by the military authorities in citizens' lives, and that any requisitions 'necessitated by military exigencies' would be paid for.[54] Though Egypt was at war, apparently in its own interest, the Egyptians were not expected to play any part in it.

The declaration of martial law compounded Egypt's anomalous constitutional status. From a technical point of view, the country was now at war with its sovereign ruler, the Ottoman sultan.[55] This was resolved on 18 December with a British announcement that Egypt had become a 'Protectorate'. The Khedive Abbas Hilmi – who, conveniently enough, was on a visit to Constantinople – was deemed to have abdicated, and the Ottoman sultan's suzerainty to have been terminated. Abbas Hilmi was replaced by his uncle, Hussein Kamel. This more compliant puppet now enjoyed enhanced status as 'sultan'; while the title of the puppet-master was changed from 'consul-general' to 'high commissioner'.

The British imperial class had long experience of managing such things. On 20 December the Sultan Hussein Kamel was to make his ceremonial entry into the Abdin Palace. A 21-gun salute boomed out over Cairo at 9.30 in the morning, the soldiers lining the route presented arms and the grand procession set out. British Yeomanry on grey horses, Egyptian Lancers in red fezzes, and the Cavalry of the Bodyguard in black and dark blue preceded the sultan's state carriage, which was drawn by four white horses and driven by coachmen liveried in scarlet and gold. The sultan's ministers followed behind, then another squadron of Yeomanry and, finally, clip-clopping tactfully along at the rear of the procession, the carriages of the country's actual rulers, the British High Commissioner and Lieutenant-General Sir John Maxwell. A six-hour grand reception followed inside the Palace. The day passed off without a hitch. The populace, according to *The Times* – with the apparent implication that it might have been otherwise – had showed 'good humour and obedience'. The long lines of British soldiers on the streets may have helped.[56]

* * *

Sir Reginald Wingate, who was both governor-general of the Sudan and sirdar of the Egyptian Army, was, like General Maxwell, somewhat anxious about allegiances. He announced the state of war to assembled British and Egyptian officers in Khartoum on 7 November, and summoned the leading sheikhs and imams to a meeting the following day. For the occasion, Wingate enlisted the support of the Grand Mufti, who informed the audience that the conflict had been forced on Britain by a 'syndicate of Jews, financiers, and low-born intriguers . . . in deference to the demands of Germany . . . who had gone to war with the one power who by her actions and the sentiments of her people has ever been a true and sympathetic friend to the Muslims and to Islam.' In view of Sudan's recent history, some listeners may have considered this a surprising claim; if so, they passed no comment. The Grand Mufti continued:

> Great Britain has no quarrel with Islam or its spiritual leaders. She will ever maintain and enforce on others the sanctity and inviolability of the Holy Places. They need not fear that the war would affect the situation of Islam in the world. Their fears are groundless, for the British Empire will not change the position of a single Muslim subject for the worse, or repudiate a single privilege granted to its Muslims.[57]

The British coup was accomplished without resistance. Both Egypt and the Sudan remained quiet. But when the official war historians inform us that 'the populace acquiesced' and 'the sultan and his ministers cordially supported the high commissioner and Sir J. Maxwell in utilising the resources of Egypt as they required', they paint an incomplete picture.[58] Fear of mass resistance impelled the British government to give a solemn pledge that the whole burden of the defence of Egypt would fall on Britain alone, and that no call would be made on the Egyptian people.[59] In time, this would prove far short of the truth; but at no stage did the British contemplate any form of general conscription or war tax. Egypt was a base for the protection of the British Empire's maritime communications, and it would become a platform for the projection of imperial power into the wider Middle East; but it was never engaged as an active partner in the prosecution of the war. The Egyptians may have remained indifferent to the Ottoman claim on their allegiance as long as the war lasted, but they did so as neutrals, never belligerents; many showed their true feelings by cheering German victories in the Cairo cinemas; and in 1919 they would demonstrate clearly enough whom they regarded as the real enemy.[60]

* * *

The Canal Expeditionary Force had marched at night by the light of the moon, seeking concealment from enemy planes active in the day, treading ancient desert tracks that had been used for thousands of years by traders, pilgrims and soldiers. The Pharaohs and the Persians, Alexander and the Caesars, the Crusaders, the Ottomans, even Napoleon had come this way. For Sinai was the land-bridge joining Asia to Africa and, throughout history, great tides of commerce, religion and war had flowed across its barren wastes. The opening of the Suez Canal in 1867 had now given it new significance as the principal chokepoint on the maritime route between Europe and the East. At the head of the latest military expedition was Ahmed Djemal Pasha, a leading 'Young Turk', the Ottoman government's minister of marine and now also commander of the newly formed Fourth Army in Syria and Palestine.

The Young Turk regime, in power since 1908, was brash and bombastic – a style that perhaps reflected the Ottoman Empire's uncertain geopolitical status in an age of steelworks and dreadnoughts. The ruling party – the Committee of Union and Progress (CUP) – and the Ottoman Cabinet were dominated by ambitious men in their thirties or forties from modest backgrounds. Members of the inner clique often held multiple posts. Djemal Pasha, a former staff officer from a military family, was one of these. Short, stocky and somewhat stoop-shouldered, with dark eyes and black hair and beard, he belonged to a triumvirate of top figures alongside Enver Pasha, minister of war and *de facto* army commander-in-chief, and Talaat Pasha, minister of the interior and *de facto* CUP party manager in the capital.

Henry Morgenthau, the US ambassador to Constantinople, detected cunning, ferocity and ruthlessness in Djemal Pasha; to this scion of America's East Coast elite, the minister of marine seemed to lack the urbane charm of some of his CUP colleagues. The ambassador had observed his departure for the east from Haidar Pasha Station on the Asian shore of the Bosphorus in early November 1914. It had been the occasion of a great demonstration. An Ottoman imperial satrap was setting out on a new campaign of conquest. The crowd hailed him 'Saviour of Egypt'. The would-be hero replied: 'I shall not return to Constantinople until I have conquered Egypt.'[61]

Imperial revanchism was an understandable response by an ambitious new leadership to the ongoing dismemberment of the Ottoman Empire – a century-old process that had recently accelerated to an alarming degree. But the dynastic claims of a medieval despot – Egypt had been conquered by Sultan Selim I in 1517 – did not provide the most compelling of arguments in the early twentieth century. The Young Turks were therefore tapping two other ideological springs: pan-Turkism and Islamism. Djemal, in his heart of hearts, was a pan-Turk nationalist. Morgenthau had the impression 'he despised the subject-peoples of the Ottoman country – Arabs, Greeks, Armenians, Circassians, Jews; it was his determination to Turkify the whole empire'.[62]

The difficulty for the Young Turks was that Ottomanism, pan-Turkism and Islamism did not readily blend. The Ottoman Empire was not a modern nation-state with a common language and culture, but a polyglot collection of territories taken in war between the early fifteenth and the late seventeenth centuries. Though much territory had since been lost, it still sprawled from Thrace to Mesopotamia, from the Caucasus to the Yemen. Ethnic Turkish Muslims, concentrated in the core Anatolian landmass, made up only 12 million of the empire's 22 million people. The Arab Muslims of Syria, Iraq, Palestine and Arabia numbered perhaps 6 million. The Armenian Christians and Kurdish Muslims of Transcaucasia each formed sizeable minorities well in excess of a million, as did the Greek Christians of Constantinople, the eastern Aegean and the Levant. Albanians, Bulgarians, Circassians and Jews were among the smaller groups. The empire was a palimpsest of ethno-religious sects formed by thousands of years of demographic and cultural churn.[63]

The subject-peoples of the Ottomans were, in varying degrees, loyal or disaffected. Some of the smaller minorities were arch-loyalists out of self-interest. The regime had its Cossacks in the Kurds, who lived uneasily in their mountain villages with their Armenian neighbours, and in the Circassians, Muslim refugees from persecution in tsarist Russia during the late nineteenth century. But most of the subject-peoples were indifferent or hostile, and how to manage them had for long been a central question of Ottoman statesmanship. Were they to be seduced or coerced? Was Ottomanism or pan-Turkism to be the programme? Was the aim a culturally inclusive *imperium* or a modern nation-state? Were the subject-peoples to be integrated into a greater whole, or were they to be precisely that – *subjects* of their Turkish masters – harnessed to a programme of Central Asian imperialism designed to create a Turkic super-state? The CUP leaders could never quite decide. And, compounding the uncertainty was what Imperial Germany, the CUP's all-important ally, considered the great genie in the Ottoman bottle: Islamic Holy War.

The matter had been explained to Henry Morgenthau by his German counterpart in Constantinople a few months before. Baron Hans Freiherr von Wangenheim, a huge, upright, domineering product of the Prussian diplomatic corps, had sat puffing on a big black cigar as he calmly described how the Turks would conjure the nemesis of Germany's enemies in the world war. 'Turkey herself is not really the important matter,' Wangenheim explained. 'Her army is a small one, and we do not expect it to do very much. For the most part it will act on the defensive. But the big thing is the Muslim world. If we can stir the Muhammadans up against the English and the Russians, we can force them to make peace.'[64]

Here was a question. The Europeans, masters of most of Asia and Africa, had fallen out over the global distribution of empire and profit. In consequence, having invested heavily for a generation in the creation of mass industrialised armies, they were now engaged in full-scale war. But the war had failed to conform to expectations, and it now looked to become more protracted and costly than any previously known. The Germans had hoped to capture Paris and knock France out of the war in the first six weeks; instead, they had been defeated at the Marne, hurled back onto defensive lines and then found the Western Front going into lockdown all the way from Switzerland to the sea. Meanwhile, despite their own success in repelling a Russian invasion of East Prussia with a surprise victory at Tannenberg, their Austro-Hungarian ally had crashed to catastrophic defeat, both at the hands of the Russians in Galicia and at those of the Serbians in the Balkans. In short, on the Western Front the Kaiser's army was bogged down in attritional trench warfare, while on the Eastern it found itself 'shackled to a corpse'.[65] The Germans were left searching for additional allies to help them break the deadlock. Who better than the world's 300 million Muslims?

The possibilities were enough to make otherwise sober diplomats like Baron Wangenheim dizzy. Germany was a European power with only a handful of overseas colonies and almost no Muslim subjects. The three Entente powers, on the other hand, all ruled over large Muslim populations. There were 20 million under the Russians in Central Asia, 20 million under the French in North and West Africa, and as many as 100 million under the British, predominantly in India (55 million) and in Egypt and the Sudan (15 million).[66] Were these great masses to be set in motion against their imperial masters, the war would be transformed into a truly global conflagration, with Russian, French and British troops perforce diverted from European battlefields to defend their colonies; the balance might then tip decisively in favour of the Central Powers. The Russian revolutionary Leon Trotsky had described Imperial Germany as 'a feudal turret on a capitalist base' – a compound, that is, of traditional Prussian militarism and the railways and arms factories of the Industrial Revolution. In the Middle East, a further ingredient was added to the mix, for here the feudal turret flew the star-and-crescent banner of Ottoman Islam.[67]

The Ottoman Empire was nothing if not Islamic. Of late, indeed, the Ottoman sultan's claim to be the caliph – the supreme religious leader of all Muslims in succession to the Prophet – had grown more strident, holy authority perhaps providing a substitute for waning imperial power. The main trajectory of political Islam was already that of traditionalist reaction to Western imperialism and, in this respect (if not in others), Ottomanism and Islamism were in harmony. This was the relationship that Imperial Germany now sought to exploit. Wangenheim and his colleagues saw the Ottoman caliphate as the main cog in a mechanism of Central Asian, Middle Eastern and North African *jihad* that might destroy their enemies' colonial empires. The Ottoman alliance had not only harnessed 12 million Anatolian peasants to the German war-machine; it might yet unleash the revolutionary potential of the 140 million Muslims living under British, French and Russian rule.

* * *

The Turks had been Muslims for a millennium, but they had their origins among the pastoral nomads of the Central Asian steppes. Hordes of them had swept across much of Iran, Mesopotamia and Anatolia during the eleventh century, imposing themselves on those they conquered – Persians, Arabs, Kurds, Armenians – as a new ruling elite. Their domain later splintered into a mosaic of petty states ruled by rival Turkic warlords. One of these, called Osman, emerged in the years around 1300 as a rising hegemon among the Turks of north-eastern Anatolia. Because he and his successors – the 'Ottomans' – had to fight for their place in the world, the empire they created was based on war and conquest. It eventually extended, after some 250 years of almost unbroken fighting, from Algeria to the borders of Persia, from southern Ukraine to the tip of the Arabian Peninsula. But this Turkic empire was also an Islamic empire.

Islam had been central to the identity of the Turks since their first eruption from the steppes. The Ottomans claimed that Allah had appeared in a dream to the founder of their dynasty and tasked him with a holy mission.[68] This seemed confirmed when the armies of his early sixteenth-century successors, Selim the Grim and Suleiman the Magnificent, captured the greatest Arab cities – Damascus, Jerusalem, Cairo, Medina, Mecca and Baghdad – and thereby shifted the empire's centre of gravity towards the Orient and Islam. Holy relics – the Prophet's banner, cloak, sword, seal and even some of his teeth, hairs from his beard and the sun-baked impression of his footprint – were removed from the East and installed in a new shrine in Constantinople's Topkapi Palace. The sultan henceforth gloried in the title 'Servant of the Two Holy Places'.[69] The connection between the Ottoman capital and the cities of Mecca and Medina was reaffirmed each year when a Sacred Caravan set out from Uskudar, on the Asian shore of the Bosphorus, on the 1,500-mile pilgrimage to the Hijaz. Along the most dangerous part of the route, from Damascus southwards, the sultans built a string of Hajj forts to guard the routeway and its watering-places – an exercise in imperial largesse in which piety, public service and military security could be conveniently combined.[70]

Later Ottoman tradition maintained that when Selim the Grim returned from his eastern conquests in the early sixteenth century, he did so vested with the authority of caliph. If so, he made little use of it. Only with the decline of Ottoman authority during the eighteenth and nineteenth centuries – with loss of territory to the Austrians in Central Europe and to the Russians around the Black Sea; with the growing assertiveness of independent-minded vassals in North Africa; with the mounting rebelliousness of reluctant subjects, especially in Rumelia, the Ottoman-ruled Balkans, where most people were neither Turkish nor Muslim – only then did the Ottoman caliphate take wing. By the reign of Abdulhamid II (1876–1909) it was in full flight. At his succession, Abdulhamid chose to be girded with the swords of both Osman, the first sultan, and Omar, the second caliph: a dual claim to both dynastic and religious authority. When, a short while later, he promulgated a modern liberal constitution, it made reference, somewhat incongruously, to the Ottoman Empire's claim to the 'supreme Islamic caliphate'. And when the tsar went to war against the Ottoman Empire in the name of 'Orthodoxy and Slavdom' in 1877, the sultan proclaimed a Holy War and had the banner of the Prophet paraded outside the Topkapi Palace.[71]

The greatest monument to Abdulhamid's latter-day 'Islamic empire' was the 800-mile-long Hijaz Railway linking Damascus and Medina (with the unfulfilled intention that it should eventually extend to Mecca). Built between 1900 and 1908, and partly funded by (more or less) voluntary pious donations, it cut the journey time for Hajj pilgrims from a month to three days.[72] Like its predecessor, the line of Hajj forts and cisterns along the caravan route, the railway served multiple purposes and revealed the many public faces of the

Late Ottoman sultanate. On its long passage through the desert wilderness, it was a symbol of modernity and industrialism, of imperial power and the mailed fist, and, not least, of Islamic piety, marking Abdulhamid as a true caliph who honoured the Hajj and the holy cities.

Abdulhamid was gone when the war broke out, replaced by a cipher sultan-caliph (Mehmed V) and, of course, by the Young Turks of the CUP. But the empire's pan-Islamist pretensions remained, and Enver, Talaat and Djemal, whose self-appointed task it was to create a modern great-power, found themselves the unlikely impresarios of a bottled genie of unknown potency which their German allies were keen to test. The CUP regime, in the minds of German strategists, was to become the transmitter of Islamic insurgency across Central Asia, the Middle East and North Africa.

* * *

For Kaiser Wilhelm II, Turkey was 'a bridge to world dominion'. His accession in 1888 had triggered a shift in Imperial German policy from the cautious nation-building *Realpolitik* of veteran Chancellor Otto von Bismarck ('world dominion is a term that finds no place in my political dictionary') to the vaunting *Weltpolitik* of a new generation of Prussian warlords. Germany was Europe's rising industrial colossus. 'World Policy' expressed the imperatives of German capital accumulation. The bombastic militarism of the Kaiser, the figurehead of the Prussian military caste that dominated Germany, was not mere eccentricity: it reflected the aggressive energy being generated by the country's fast-expanding economy.

The year after his accession, the Kaiser made a state visit to Constantinople, opening a new channel for Germanic endeavour – from bank loans to archaeological digs – in the course of the next decade.[73] When the Kaiser returned for a second visit in 1898, steaming up the Bosphorus in a gleaming white luxury yacht and mooring off the sultan's Dolmabahche Palace, it was something of a triumphal procession.[74] He was entertained in lavish *belle époque* style, the Dolmabahche being a fashionable, neo-rococo, French-built replacement for the Topkapi (which was too much associated with such oriental exotica as harems, tulip gardens and bowstring executions to provide an appropriate setting for the rituals of nineteenth-century diplomacy). From there, he headed off on a state visit to the Holy Land, becoming the first ruler of a Christian state to enter Jerusalem in more than six centuries. Yet – he was at pains to explain to his hosts – he came not as would-be Crusader but as ally of Islam. He reserved his most dramatic gesture for Damascus, the ancient Arab capital, where he laid a wreath on the tomb of Saladin and proclaimed that 'His Majesty, the Sultan Abdulhamid, and the 300 million Muslims who reverence him as caliph, may rest assured that the German emperor will ever be their friend.'[75] The rumour on the Arab street was that the Kaiser had visited Mecca and converted to Islam; he was dubbed 'Hajji Wilhelm'.[76]

The German emperor was playing with a fire that could not harm him. The imperial masters of numerous Muslim subjects – British, French and Russian – winced at the news from Damascus. The Hohenzollern 'friendship' with Ottoman Islam – dubbed *Islampolitik* – strengthened in subsequent years, becoming a factor of growing weight in European diplomacy as the likelihood increased that, in the event of war, Constantinople would intervene as an ally of the Central Powers. Thus, in the fevered atmosphere of the July Crisis of 1914, the Kaiser responded to British threats by invoking the spectre of *jihad*: 'Our consuls in Turkey and India, our agents, etc., must rouse the whole Muslim world into wild rebellion against this hateful, mendacious, unprincipled nation of shopkeepers; if we are going to shed our blood, England must at least lose India.' The aspiration – to conjure an Islamic Holy War – was shared by other, more sober members of the German elite: Field-Marshal Helmuth von Moltke, Chief of the General Staff, wrote to his Foreign Office colleagues demanding action to foment *jihad* in India and Egypt.[77]

The very man for such work was already at hand. In the event of a great European war involving the Ottoman Empire as a German ally, he had informed Reich Chancellor Bülow as far back as 1908, 'one may certainly expect an overall revolt of the Muslims in the British colonies'; so serious would this be, he continued, that 'England would need a large part of its navy and almost its entire army in order to keep its colonies.' So averred Max von Oppenheimer, a scion of the famous banking family, a Christian convert from Judaism, and a Middle Eastern explorer and archaeologist considered to be a leading expert on Arab and Islamic affairs. By early 1915, Oppenheimer had an office in Constantinople, a small staff of German academics and 100 million marks of German government money with which to create a network of propaganda stations and a flood of jihadist literature. Oppenheimer's bureau eventually had twenty-five regional offices across the East, and was responsible for a total of more than 1,000 publications in 9 European and 15 Asian languages, totalling some 3 million copies, in the course of the war.[78]

Constantinople was catapulted into war on 2 November 1914. Less than two weeks later, the Grand Mufti proclaimed Holy War against Germany's enemies. 'O Muslims,' he intoned, 'know that our empire is at war with the mortal enemies of Islam: the governments of Muscovy, Britain and France. The Commander of the Faithful summons you to the *jihad*.' The faithful were assured that the reward of those who answered the call would be 'felicity' if they survived, 'martyrdom' and 'paradise' if they fell.[79]

By January 1915, the Holy War was in motion. Djemal Pasha's men were advancing through the desert night towards the Suez Canal. According to their commander, they sang 'The Red Flag Flies over Cairo', and 'everyone was absolutely convinced that the canal would certainly be crossed, that we should dig ourselves in securely on the further bank, and that the Egyptian patriots would then rise and attack the English in the rear.'[80] Some of the column were indeed *dervish* volunteers (the German ambassador complained that their high conical hats would make them conspicuous targets).[81] But the regulars, too, seem to have been infected by the jihadist mood. Stories circulated that the British were massacring Muslims, the regimental imams promised victory and paradise, and 'the Sacred Banner' was given out as a watchword. Among some, at least, expectations of success against the odds seemed to acquire a messianic tone. One Turkish officer wrote on the eve of the assault: 'It would be false to say that our march was not difficult and full of hardship, but every difficulty has … been conquered thanks to our perfect organisation, and tomorrow we shall be across the canal and on our way to Cairo.' (He was to be killed in the battle, and the letter containing these words was never sent.)[82]

* * *

Once the force had been concentrated at Beersheba, its commanders faced a choice of three main routes: the old coast road that ran from Gaza through Rafa, Arish and Katia to Kantara on the northern sector of the canal; the central track through Auja, Kossaima, Hassana, Jifjaffa and then down the Wadi Muksheib towards Ismailia in the central sector; or, moving from either Auja in the north or Aqaba to the east, the mountain path via Nekhl to the town of Suez at the southern end of the canal. The coastal option would have involved an arduous march through sand dunes and the risk of attack from the sea. The Nekhl route was longer, harder and debouched too far south; it was, in any case, impassable for wheels. The central track, on the other hand, offered firm ground and headed directly towards Ismailia, the linchpin of the canal defences; if the Ottomans could force a passage here, they might not only block the canal (which they could do anywhere), but also cut both the railway line and the fresh-water channel that supplied the garrisons all down the line. To keep the British guessing, however, and to prevent them concentrating near Ismailia, the plan was for small forces to follow the northern and southern tracks, while the main assault force took the central one.[83]

The latter was divided into two echelons. The first, whose mission was to force a crossing of the canal and secure a bridgehead on the western side, was about 13,000 strong and formed mainly of the Arab 25th Infantry Division.

The second, mainly the Turkish 10th Infantry Division, was to follow behind in a reserve capacity. The decision to spearhead the assault with Arab soldiers – generally less reliable than Turks – may have been prompted by exaggerated hopes of an Egyptian uprising and the greater likelihood of fellow Arabs being welcomed as liberators. Supporting the infantry were nine batteries of field artillery (pulled by horses) and one of 150mm howitzers (pulled by oxen).[84]

Three things made the movement of this force possible: heavy winter rains, 12,000 camels and Colonel Baron Freiherr Kress von Kressenstein. The rains had filled the pools and cisterns along the desert tracks, a fact well known to the local Bedouin guides in Ottoman service; in particular, just two days' march short of Ismailia the invaders could expect to find several million gallons of water in the pools and cisterns of the Wadi Muksheib.[85] As for camels, a sufficient number had been commandeered in southern Palestine to carry the water, food, fodder and munitions required by an expedition of 25,000 men, 1,000 horses and 300 oxen. And Kress, a Bavarian aristocrat, an experienced German staff officer and, in the view of one of his enemies, 'a gallant, resolute, and able soldier', managed the entire operation with exceptional efficiency.[86] Despite the 'great difficulties' of the route – Kress listed them as 'lack of water, absence of roads and cultivation, [and the] irregularity and impassable nature of the sandy soil, intersected as it was by deep, steep-sided torrent beds' – he was later able to report that the guides were good, not a man or beast had been lost, and the march was completed in ten days.[87]

Bavarian staff-work had not, however, been able to ensure any real measure of surprise. Despite the diversionary columns on the northern and southern tracks, and the precaution of marching at night and lying low during the day, the British had observed the movement and divined the plan. Kress recalls a few aerial bombs as 'the only inconvenience' on the march across Sinai. But at this stage in the war, dropping the occasional small bomb was not the main role of aircraft: it was reconnaissance. Here was one of the many ingredients of the military revolution wrought between 1914 and 1918. Cavalry had traditionally been the eyes of armies, but the exigencies of modern industrialised warfare had tapered their usefulness. In a war of movement they tended to exhaust themselves tracking mass armies over vast spaces, while in a war of trenches they were perilously vulnerable to modern firepower. So intelligence-gathering became increasingly reliant on aircraft.

Though dependent on good weather – both to be able to fly at all and to see anything when they did – the airmen achieved startling results in the early months of the First World War. Flimsy biplanes and monoplanes – each essentially a superstructure of wood, wire and canvas, a steel engine in an aluminium casing and an open cockpit – would fly across the battlefield looking for the enemy. The defenders of the canal in early 1915 were well served by a French squadron of seven Nieuport two-seater seaplanes commanded by Lieutenant de Vaisseau de l'Escaille. The squadron was based on a captured cargo steamer converted into a carrier and moored at Port Said. The energy of the commander and his men, and their willingness to push their machines to the limit, ensured that, as early as 11 January, the British were certain that an attack on the canal was coming and, soon after, that the main thrust would be directed at the central sector.[88]

The first clashes occurred at Kantara on the 26th and at Kubri on the 27th, but these were skirmishes involving the small northern and southern columns: artillery fire and air strikes served to keep the Ottomans at a distance, both now and over succeeding days.[89] By 31 January, however, the 25th Division had reached its planned forward assembly-zone a few miles east of Ismailia. After a day's rest and preparation, it moved forward during the night of 1/2 February to its jumping-off positions on the east bank of the canal, the men ensconcing themselves amid sandhills and brushwood, as guns were hauled into position to support the attack, and sapper detachments brought forward the craft in which the canal was to be crossed – 20-man galvanised iron pontoons manu-factured in Germany that looked like elongated bath-tubs, and improvised rafts built of kerosene tins in rectangular wooden frames measuring 15 by 12 feet. The actual assault was then delayed by the sandstorm, which began mid-afternoon on 2 February and continued until the early hours. The stillness as the wind died away became the signal to attack.[90]

* * *

The Ottoman sappers hurried the pontoons and rafts to the gaps in the canal bank, and the first wave of assault troops massed for embarkation. Some of the Indian sentries on the western bank became aware of the activity. Then the quiet of the night was broken by howling exhortations to Allah – in defiance of strict orders – from the *mujahedin* volunteers accompanying the 25th Division on the approaches to Tussum. Guard dogs – chained at points along the eastern bank to give early warning of attack – started barking.

A machine-gun fired into the darkness, spraying towards the noise. Then mountain-guns and more machine-guns opened up, along with the riflemen lining the trenches. The Ottomans fired back, and a frantic firefight – men on both sides shooting towards flashes in the darkness – erupted along the canal as the assault troops struggled to get waterborne.

The cloud cleared and the moon revealed the dark shapes of men and craft moving about near the water's edge. The defenders now had proper targets.

They began shooting the figures on the eastern bank, while such pontoons as entered the water were quickly holed and sunk. 'It was', recalled one Ottoman soldier, 'as if the Gates of Hell were opened and its fires turned loose upon us'. Along a frontage of a mile and a half, wherever gaps in the bank gave ready access to the water, the Ottoman assault parties were either gunned down or dropped their pontoons and rafts under the hail of fire and abandoned the attempt. 'The boats were hit and started sinking, and most of our men could not shoot back', reported a Syrian veteran of the Balkan Wars. 'Those who could swim saved themselves, but those who could not drowned and went down with the boats.'

Only three pontoon-loads made it across. One was immediately charged with the bayonet by a detachment of 62nd Punjabis and all were killed or wounded. The other two parties found each other in the gloom and formed a group, but they too were attacked by the Punjabis: six were killed, four wounded and about twenty others who fled and hid were later rounded up. These were to be the only enemy soldiers to cross the canal in the course of the war.[91]

As the sky brightened in the east, the sepoys bore witness to their work: the far bank of the canal was littered with the wreckage of a failed amphibious assault – contorted humps of men, some still moving, iron canoes, wooden rafts, a scatter of abandoned kit. But the battle was not yet over.

In addition to the trenches on the western bank, the defences of the canal comprised a series of fortified posts on the eastern bank, each formed of trenches revetted with sandbags and protected by barbed wire. These covered the ferry-crossings, enfiladed the approaches to the canal, and provided launch-pads for counter-attacks.[92] Three of these posts, at Tussum, Serapeum and Ismailia Ferry, came under attack on the morning of 3 February from Ottoman infantry supported by artillery.

None of the assaults could make much headway in the face of superior enemy firepower, and an artillery duel raged from first light to early afternoon as the Ottoman gunners struggled to neutralise the threat to their infantry. They might have succeeded had they faced only the field and mountain batteries on the western bank, but the defenders were also supported by the fire of several naval warships stationed along the canal as floating batteries.

At one point the Ottoman heavy guns – the 150mm howitzers hauled across the desert by oxen – engaged the unarmoured Indian warship *Hardinge* and forced her to withdraw lest she be sunk in the canal and block it. The gun battle continued when the howitzers re-directed their attention to the French coast-guard vessel *Requin*, berthed in Lake Timsah, firing at an extreme range of more than 9,000 yards. Though the Ottoman gunners forced the crews of the *Requin's* unprotected 100mm deck guns to take cover, the warship's single

270mm turret gun remained in action and homed in on the battery in the desert. Three giant shells were enough to silence the Ottoman howitzers. Victory in the artillery duel enabled the *Requin*, now supported by the French cruiser *D'Entrecasteaux*, to shift target onto the Ottoman infantry still threatening the posts at Tussum and Serapeum.[93]

The morale of 25th Division's Arab infantry was sinking. Parties of the 73rd Regiment had gained some of the outer trenches around Tussum Post, but one group had been destroyed early on by enfilade fire from machine-guns, and another, 350 strong, was driven back in two separate counter-attacks during the morning, and then completely overwhelmed mid-afternoon. Seven Ottoman officers and 280 other ranks were killed or captured.[94]

The thrust at Serapeum by the 74th Regiment fared no better. Companies of the 2nd Rajputs, the 92nd Punjabis and the 10th Gurkhas were by now mounting an active defence, manoeuvring for position across the open ground beyond the east bank of the canal, attempting to take the Ottomans in flank. The 74th Regiment was soon pinned down by a determined Anglo-Indian firing line, backed by naval guns, and never got closer than 1,200 yards to the enemy trenches.[95]

The fighting at Tussum and Serapeum fizzled out in the middle of the afternoon. The attack on Ismailia Ferry Post was never seriously pressed, and secondary attacks on Kantara and Ferdan in the north, and Kubri in the south, were mere feints. The following morning, 4 February, the Ottomans were gone, retreating back across the desert the way they had come. They had lost about 1,500 men, their opponents barely a tenth as many.[96] They had failed to cross the canal or to damage it in any way, and their efforts, such as they were, had not evoked any discernible activity on the part of their Egyptian co-religionists.

* * *

The Sinai campaign of January–February 1915 appeared to some to have been a comprehensive failure. But this was so only when measured against the vaulting ambition of some of the Young Turks. Kress von Kressenstein, the Bavarian colonel who had managed the whole operation with such proficiency, offered a more sober assessment based on the military principle of economy of force. He conceded that the setback was real: 'A sandstorm delayed the movement of the troops, who were insufficiently trained and disciplined for their difficult work; the Arab units chosen to make the attempt went over in large numbers to the enemy . . .' (The latter view is mistaken – there is no corroboration in the British sources – but it reflects the reality that Arab soldiers in the Ottoman service were under-motivated, reluctant to press attacks and willing to surrender under pressure: here was a critical weakness.) On the other hand, Kress reported, 'The effect of this offensive, though it failed to secure material results, was to increase the British anxiety for the security of Egypt, and hold fast in that country a large number of their troops.'

Kress himself continued to feed that anxiety, remaining in Sinai until the middle of the year, with three battalions, two mountain batteries and a camel squadron, in order to carry out 'a number of raids and minor operations which considerably disturbed traffic through the canal'.[97]

As long as Ottoman soldiers were within reach of the canal, the British high command could not sleep easy. In November 1915, the General Staff at the War Office estimated the force required for the defence of Egypt at six infantry divisions and five mounted brigades on the canal, two infantry brigades and two mounted brigades in the Western Desert, and fifteen garrison battalions and one mounted brigade in the delta.[98]

A spectre haunted the Middle East during the Great War: the spectre of Islamic *jihad*. It may have existed more in imaginations coloured by Orientalist prejudice than in real possibilities. The contemporary Western mind – both German and British – readily accepted the colonial-racist stereotype of the Muslim 'fanatic'. But it was no less a factor in strategic thinking for that. How might the spectre be roused, asked men on one side. How might it be laid to rest, asked men on the other. One such, much given to imaginative flights of fancy, was the young archaeologist-turned-intelligence officer currently engaged in drawing military maps in a Cairo office. He took a rather dim view of the plodding efforts of the Government of India to control Arabia by 'the old game of balancing the little powers there'. A grander scheme was needed. 'I want to pull them all together,' he wrote to David Hogarth on 22 March 1915, 'and roll up Syria by way of the Hijaz in the name of the sherif . . . we can rush right up to Damascus, and biff the French out of all hope of Syria. It's a big game, and at last one worth playing.' But, he added, 'Don't talk of it yet.'[99]

CHAPTER 2

Young Turks

A SPECIAL TRAIN pulled into Constantinople's main station on the evening of 16 October 1914. Having left Berlin four days before, it had completed its thousand-mile journey across Central Europe in near record time. It was carrying valuable cargo: a Prussian prince, a Rumanian ambassador and a million Turkish pounds in gold coins. Emboldened by the success of this first transit – there had been concerns about Russian pressure on the Rumanians to block it – the Germans sent another shipment less than a week later. The Russians, already at war with Germany, believed that an Ottoman attack on them was likely at any moment.[1] They were right. The German gold was to buy the services of Turkish soldiers in the Great War.

The Ottoman Empire's financial capacity to wage a modern industrialised war was close to zero. The state treasury was almost empty. The government was heavily in debt and its financial affairs were in the hands of foreign banks. Paper currency was almost non-existent.[2] The tax-base comprised mainly impoverished peasant villagers. It was partly for this reason that the Sublime Porte (as the Ottoman government was known in foreign diplomatic circles) had delayed a declaration of war.

Once the German and Ottoman governments had signed their secret military pact on 2 August, the Porte had ordered full mobilisation. But at the same time it had issued a public declaration of neutrality, and Ottoman ministers spent much of the next three months in negotiation with powers on both sides of the conflict. By implication, the German alliance remained fragile, and the cost of securing it rose in consequence, the Ottomans playing the diplomatic market for the best deal. The October gold shipments were advance payments on a T£5 million contract eventually signed on 10 November – and already the German ambassador was promising further loans should they be needed.[3]

A pattern was set, for the flow of German gold to the Ottoman Empire would continue throughout the war. Post-war German estimates were that combined credits and loans to their erstwhile ally amounted T£235 million, representing about 80 per cent of Ottoman war expenditure (and 3 per cent of German war expenditure).[4] Two-thirds was advanced in the form of German treasury notes, the remainder as German marks, Turkish pound bills, and gold and silver coins. The financial arrangements included German underwriting of Ottoman issues of paper money, direct payment for procurement and delivery of war materiel to Ottoman forces, cash and credits to pay for non-military supplies like grain, coal and machinery, debt repayments to German private creditors and, not least, subsidies to German firms working on unfinished sections of the Baghdad Railway. A particular bone of contention was the Ottoman government's intractable prejudice against paper money. The German authorities were required to provide full coverage for virtually all wartime issues.[5] Despite their modernising aspirations, when it came to money, the Turks, like the Arabs, were men of the East: only gold counted.

* * *

Imperial Germany was a late participant in the succession of diplomatic intrigues which nineteenth-century statesmen called 'the Eastern Question'. Four great powers had been competing for influence around the decaying Ottoman Empire since the Napoleonic Wars – Austria-Hungary in the Balkans, Russia in the Straits and the Caucasus, and Britain and France in North Africa and the Middle East. All four had interests essentially antagonistic to those of the Ottoman Empire; all had, at different times, whenever mutual rivalry had not prevented it, hacked off chunks of Ottoman territory. Only Germany among the great powers had played no part. This was partly for historical reasons: Germany had become a unified state only in 1871, and prior to that the whole of its political life had revolved around its unresolved 'national question'. But it was also a matter of geography. Even as the German industrial economy began to grow exponentially in the last quarter of the nineteenth century, the country's position in the centre of Europe precluded any direct conflict with an empire located on the continent's south-eastern edge. Paul Rohrbach – a German nationalist writer, proponent of colonisation and author of the influential polemic *The German Idea in the World* (1912) – sensed the geopolitical opportunity: 'In the very nature of things, Turkey, surrounded on all sides by envious neighbours, must seek the support of a power that has practically no territorial interests in the Orient. That power is Germany.'[6]

Not that Imperial Germany was a disinterested suitor in a play for Ottoman favour. German economic growth was breaking records. Coal production rose from less than 40 million tons in 1871 to 280 million in 1914. Steel production expanded more than eight-fold between 1880 and 1910. On the eve of the First World War, Germany was the main producer of both heavy and light chemicals, and accounted for nearly half the world's trade in electrical goods. An industrial colossus had emerged in the heart of Europe in little more than a generation. One measure of its growing appetite for raw materials, markets and investment opportunities was a three-fold increase in the value of German exports, two-thirds of which were finished industrial goods.[7] The economy of Germany was fast overhauling that of Britain, the original 'workshop of the world', and was in consequence bursting its national shell. *Weltpolitik* – 'World Policy' – was not the aberration of a neurotic Prussian warlord; it was an expression of breakneck capital accumulation.

For sure, German penetration of the Ottoman economy on the eve of the First World War still lagged behind that of Britain, France, and even Austria-Hungary; but it was catching up.[8] Between 1888 and 1905, the value of German exports to the Ottoman Empire had increased six-fold, that of German imports from the Ottoman Empire no less than 22-fold.[9] The value of German investments in the Ottoman Empire totalled about T£20 million by 1914. The giant Deutsche Bank, which controlled a quarter of German banking, was heavily involved, along with two specialist finance-houses, the German Orient Bank and the German Palestine Bank. The arms manufacturers Krupp (supplying artillery) and Mauser (supplying small-arms) were important investors, as was the electrical giant Siemens (building telegraph lines). The most important enterprises, however, were railways, which accounted for about two-thirds of all German investment, the great bulk of it in the famous 'Berlin-to-Baghdad Railway' – widely viewed, by friends and enemies alike, as the supreme symbol of the Kaiser's *Drang nach Osten* ('Drive to the East') policy.[10]

* * *

Railways were the beating heart of turn-of-the-century imperialism. The biggest infrastructure projects of their age, they returned gargantuan profits for the consortia of banks, industrial suppliers and construction firms involved. Competition for contracts was intense, above all in the Ottoman Empire, with its vast extent and urgent need for modern communications. Though British and French companies secured major concessions (mainly in Syria), the most lucrative eventually went to the Germans, who were first contracted to build the Anatolian Railway, linking Constantinople to Ankara, in 1888, then granted the right to build a line across Anatolia, Syria and Iraq, all the way to Baghdad, in 1903.[11]

The terms of the contracts reflected the Ottoman Empire's semi-colonial status. Unable either to raise the loans necessary to pay the contractors for their work, or to ensure sufficient traffic to make the railways a going concern when they opened, the government offered a guaranteed return on each kilometre of track laid, while giving the Deutsche Bank, the main lender, the right to collect taxes from a number of its provinces. Thus German finance-capital battened vampire-like onto the Anatolian peasantry. It operated through local intermediaries, each tier of corrupt administration taking its cut, such that, in the words of German socialist Rosa Luxemburg, 'the tithe grows like a landslide as it approaches the farmer'.[12]

Railways were strategic as well as economic assets – arteries in a global struggle for power. 'The Baghdad Railway', explained Paul Rohrbach, 'was destined from the start to bring Constantinople and the military strongholds of the Turkish Empire in Asia Minor into direct contact with Syria and the provinces on the Euphrates and on the Tigris.' The primary target of this railway-building offensive was Britain:

> England can be attacked and mortally wounded on land in Egypt … A Muhammadan power like Turkey, moreover, could exercise a dangerous influence over the 60 millions of Muhammadan subjects of England in India, Afghanistan, and Persia … But Turkey can subjugate Egypt only if it possesses an extended system of railways in Asia Minor and Syria …

The Baghdad Railway, a potential transmitter of Ottoman power and Islamic insurgency across the Middle East, was nothing less than 'a political life insurance policy for Germany'.[13]

The British had many reasons to be alarmed by the Berlin-to-Baghdad Railway. Railways had been considered vital strategic assets ever since their capacity to move armies and deliver victories had been demonstrated in the American Civil War (1861–5) and in Bismarck's wars against Austria (1866) and France (1870–1). The construction and control of railways became as important to war as dreadnoughts and artillery. The Deutsche Bank's concession to build the Baghdad Railway was not just a matter of profitable contracts for German heavy industry in the supply of track and rolling stock. What was in prospect was a 2,000-mile-long spine of geopolitical power linking Germany, Austria-Hungary, the Balkans, Anatolia, Syria and Iraq – effectively a single line from the Baltic to the Persian Gulf.[14] Here was an implicit threat to Russian interests in the Straits, the Caucasus and Persia; to French interests in Syria and the Levant; and, above all, to British interests across the Near East all the way to India.

'It is unpleasant to contemplate', wrote Sir Nicholas Roderick O'Conor, the British ambassador to the Porte, in a letter to the foreign secretary in 1901, 'the construction of a railway traversing the whole of Asia Minor and terminating in the Persian Gulf, in which Great Britain takes no part or share.'[15] O'Conor's main concern at the time was the prospective railway's capacity to project military power and Islamist ideology in the direction of Egypt and India. Soon, however, a new concern was added: the black gold of the Persian Gulf.

* * *

A revolution in naval technology had begun. The mobility of the coal-fired warships of the Victorian era had been constrained by the need to access coaling-stations at frequent intervals; at the turn of the century, the existence of numerous such stations on friendly coasts remained a precondition of global maritime power. The routine of coaling a ship also took time and exhausted the crew. Even at sea, the shovelling of coal from one steel chamber to another was the eternal task of a hundred men on all large battleships. Oil, on the other hand, could be moved in pipes. This made resupply by tankers possible, and also cut to a fraction the labour involved. To these obvious advantages of oil, the second generation of warships spawned by the Anglo-German naval arms race – the so-called 'super-dreadnoughts' – gave rise to another. The require-ment to carry heavier armour and guns reduced speed – all three equally vital in naval warfare – unless engine power could be increased. But with the advent of the 15-inch-gun battleship, the design problem became intractable on the basis of coal-fired technology.

The solution was oil fuel. It burned more fiercely than coal and gave off more heat. The greater steam-pressure increased the speed of shafts and propellers. It might be the difference between 21 knots and 25. 'Speed! Speed!' exclaimed Admiral 'Jackie' Fisher, Britain's famed first sea lord. 'Do you remember the recipe for jugged hare in *Mrs Glasse's Cookery*? First, catch your hare ... The first of all necessities is speed so as to be able to fight When you like, Where you like, and How you like ...'

Britain, however, produced abundant coal, but no oil. To retain the all-important lead in naval power on which maritime supremacy and imperial security depended, the British Empire needed control over foreign oil supplies. 'This liquid fuel problem', wrote Winston Churchill, the first lord of the Admiralty, 'has got to be solved.'[16]

In 1901 a middle-aged former adventurer and entrepreneur called Knox D'Arcy, who had made a fortune in the Australian gold-rush, bought a conces-sion to prospect for oil across half a million square miles of Persia. Five years later, having found nothing after spending £200,000 and exhausting his resources, he went in with Burmah Oil, which put up fresh capital and shifted drilling to a new area. Two years after that, on 26 May 1908, the prospectors struck oil. A column of black gold suddenly spurted 50 feet out of the ground.

A year on and D'Arcy and Burmah Oil had formed a new company, Anglo-Persian Oil (later British Petroleum). The company enjoyed the protection of the British authorities from the outset. The Indian government sent a detachment of troops to guard the drillers, and British Resident Sir Percy Cox negotiated an arrangement with the local sheikh for the oil to be transported in a 130-mile pipeline to the island of Abadan for refining and onward shipping by tanker. Churchill, installed at the Admiralty in 1911, was soon taking a keen interest in the company. Having told the House of Commons in July 1913 that 'we must become the owners, or at any rate the controllers, at the source of at least a proportion of the supply of natural oil which we require', he finally obtained authorisation a year later to acquire a 51 per cent interest in Anglo-Persian on behalf of the British government.[17] The Navy had its oil. And the Gulf had begun its long primacy as one of the pivots of global power.

* * *

The Kaiser, meanwhile, was sponsoring a railway headed in the general direction of the British oilfields. Around the time of the British government's part-nationalisation of Anglo-Persian, the German engineers had got as far as the upper Euphrates, where they were busy building a bridge. As chance would have it, this had brought them abreast of the British Museum's excavations at the Hittite site of Carchemish, causing tensions between the rival teams over the route of the railway, the quarrying of stone and the hiring of local labour.[18] When the German engineers were threatened by a revolt of their own workmen in March 1914, however, the two English archaeologists – Leonard Woolley and Edward Lawrence – turned out to rescue them, having been alerted by the sound of gunfire. The Germans had an unfortunate reputation for defrauding their mainly Kurdish labourers. An incident occurred in which a labourer protesting against being paid less than his due was attacked by one of the armed Circassian guards employed as site security. By the time Woolley and Lawrence arrived – their excavation house was only 200 yards away and they gained a clear view of events from the top of the ancient town walls – the incident had escalated from stone-throwing into a full-scale gun battle with rifles and revolvers, about 30 Germans and Circassians ranged around the offices on one side, up to 300 Arab and Kurdish workers along the railway embankment and on the slopes of the ancient tell on the other. The defenders were few, and a massacre threatened. Only by 'superhuman efforts and good humour' did the two Englishmen, assisted by two native headmen and two others of their work-force, succeed, at great personal risk amid the flying bullets, in calming the situation.[19]

Labour relations were usually bad on the Baghdad Railway. Work records were often inaccurate, the paymaster had a reputation for corruption, wages were docked for inadequate subsistence, and fines were frequently imposed.[20] Most labourers preferred a job on the excavations if they could get one. This seems to have been partly due to the popularity of the young Arabic-speaking deputy director who managed the native workforce.[21] Shy, awkward and rather introverted, he seems to have been more at ease in the alien culture of the East than in his own. Increasingly, he had chosen to stay in Syria between excavation seasons, improving his language skills and exploring more of the region; in one eighteen-month period he spent only three weeks at home. 'I don't think that I will ever travel in the West again,' he wrote to his family in April 1914; 'one cannot tell, of course, but this part out here is worth a million of the rest. The Arabs are so different from ourselves.'[22]

This year, though, there was post-excavation work to be done back home, so Lawrence and Woolley travelled back together in June 1914. They used the completed part of the Baghdad Railway on the first leg of their journey, having been enlisted in another of 'Skinface' Newcombe's spying missions (he of the Sinai survey earlier that year). They accomplished their task with aplomb, meeting a disgruntled Italian engineer who had been sacked by the Germans and was happy to tell them everything Newcombe wanted to know about plans for the Taurus Mountains stretch of the line. Both men took boyish delight in another minor triumph over their German rivals.[23]

Lawrence would never return to Carchemish, nor Woolley for many years – and the Baghdad Railway was not the least of the reasons. Looking back in 1917, it seemed to the American-Polish orientalist Morris Jastrow that:

the Baghdad Railway will be found to be the largest single contributing factor in bringing on the war, because through it more than any other cause, the mutual distrust among the European Powers has been nurtured, until the entire atmosphere of international diplomacy became vitiated.[24]

* * *

The German Military Mission was surely a 'contributing factor' only margin-ally less alarming to British, French and Russian statesmen in the years before the war. In 1884, Colonel Colmar Freiherr von der Goltz, a Prussian staff officer and veteran of the Austro-Prussian and Franco-Prussian wars, had arrived in Constantinople to head a newly established German Military Mission to the Ottoman Empire. The sultan, fretting over the defeat of his armies in the Russo-Turkish War (1877–8), had turned for help to what was, undoubtedly, the most professional army in the world at the time. The Germans were only too willing to oblige. Though only a handful of German officers were involved – and though their work was much impeded by suspicion, corruption and vested interests – progress was real. The Ottoman military was reorganised to speed up mobilisation and improve command and control. Promising young Turkish officers, up to twenty each year, were sent to Potsdam for staff training. Ship-loads of Krupp cannon and Mauser rifles were dispatched from Hamburg to Constantinople. Unsurprisingly, foreign ambassadors began sending alarmist reports to their governments about the apparent evolution of the Ottoman Army from *ancien régime* anachronism to what looked increasingly like an extension of Prussian militarism.[25]

But others were modernising too, notably the Balkan states, and the reforms of the German Military Mission were barely sufficient to enable their Turkish *protégés* to keep pace with developments elsewhere. The relative decline of Ottoman power continued. Further wars exposed the gap between ambition and capacity. In 1908, Austria-Hungary annexed Bosnia-Herzegovina, Bulgaria announced its independence and Crete declared union with Greece: the Ottoman government had been unable to prevent any of these coups.[26] In September 1911, the Italians invaded Libya. Ottoman soldiers fought alongside jihadist insurgents under Young Turk officers, and the Italians found themselves pinned down in the coastal towns and unable to pacify the hinterland. But an alliance of Balkan states – actively encouraged by the embattled Italians – chose this moment to strike a body-blow at Turkey-in-Europe. Hopelessly overextended, the Ottomans crashed to defeat. By January 1913, they had lost Libya to the Italians, and Albania and Macedonia to a hostile coalition of Bulgars, Greeks, Serbs and Montenegrins.[27]

Defeat in the First Balkan War sent a new shock-wave through an already unstable political system. 'The defeat has proved', ran an Ottoman newspaper editorial in April 1913:

that the road we have been following was not the right one. It has also proved that we still have much to achieve if we really mean to exist and develop. We must free ourselves from our old mistakes and weaknesses, and give up the old incapacity, the old ignorance, and the old vanity. We can no longer halt at half measures, at half education, at half knowledge.[28]

In fact, the defeat had already triggered a coup by Young Turk hardliners against a government largely of the party's own making. The coup installed a new leadership that was younger, more nationalist, less tolerant of time-servers, less willing to accommodate vested interests. High priority was given to a renewal of the German Military Mission. The new grand vizier duly dispatched a request to the Kaiser and, on 14 December 1913, General Otto Liman von Sanders stepped off the Berlin train at Sirkedji Station in Constantinople, to be met, amid a crash of military music, by the Ottoman minister of war and a guard of honour formed of the city Fire Brigade (a regular army regiment). He came with a team of thirty officers and forty men. His mission was to take command of the Ottoman Army – Liman was to hold the rank of inspector-general – and, in the words of Ambassador Wangenheim, oversee 'the uniform and purposeful reformation of the Turkish Army . . . to serve as the basis for the work of mobilisation and for the operations of some future war'.[29]

Liman was highly strung and irascible. He glares out of wartime photos with an air of petulant irritation. He quarrelled easily with colleagues, and his reactions to the inevitable frustrations and slights of the Ottoman service were volatile. But though he dispatched a string of missives to Berlin requesting recall, he was always turned down and ended up serving in the East throughout the war, presiding over both Ottoman victory at Gallipoli in 1915 and Ottoman defeat in Palestine in 1918.[30]

Neurotic disposition was not unusual among Prussian officers at the time. The Kaiser was a textbook case. (Post-war psychoanalysts would blame the loveless patriarchal-authoritarian families in which they were reared.) The consequences often included stress, ill-temper, risk avoidance, paralysis of will, and even psychological breakdown during a crisis. But the obsessive-compulsive personality also tended towards professional dedication and punctiliousness in the performance of duty. Liman was an archetype: a methodical, thorough, expert manager of industrialised war. Henry Morgenthau, the cynical, worldly wise, sharply anti-German US ambassador to the Porte, observed the startling effects of the new German commander's work at a grand military review in July 1914:

> What in January had been an undisciplined, ragged rabble was now parading with the goose-step; the men were clad in German field-grey, and they even wore a casque-shaped head covering, which slightly suggested the German *Pickelhaube*. The German officers were immensely proud of the exhibition, and the transformation of the wretched Turkish soldiers of January into these neatly dressed, smartly stepping, splendidly manoeuvring troops was really a creditable military achievement.[31]

Appearances did not deceive: though the reform programme was incomplete when war broke out, the Ottoman Army was much improved since its Balkan War defeats. Not the least reason for a string of Entente setbacks in the first three years of the war was the misguided assumption that the Ottoman resistance would readily crumble.[32]

Another German visitor turned up in Constantinople later that year: Richard von Kühlmann. Nerves were frayed in Berlin by the Porte's continued shilly-shallying and the apparent inability of the German ambassador – the mountainous, cigar-smoking Baron von Wangenheim – to engineer an Ottoman declaration of war. Kühlmann had been sent to chivvy things along. Kühlmann embodied the nexus of finance, industry and state that was the essence of early twentieth-century imperialism. Born in Constantinople, where his father had worked on railway projects funded by the German banks, he had served as a diplomat in London before the war, engaged in awkward negotiations with the British aimed at easing the passage to completion of the Baghdad line. Returning to Turkey in October 1914, Kühlmann came empowered to offer a large subsidy to induce the Ottoman leaders to enter the war.[33] Kühlmann was Imperial Germany's man with the gold.

By the end of October, Anglophile and neutralist sentiment in the Ottoman Cabinet was ebbing away, and the Young Turks were preparing to embark on their greatest adventure.

* * *

What had brought the Ottoman Empire to the brink of war as an ally of the Central Powers was the military coup of 23 January 1913. Until this moment, the nationalist officers behind the Young Turk Revolution of 1908 had been content to operate as string-pullers in a political theatre of superannuated *ancien régime* politicians. But when the Ottoman armies crashed to defeat in the First Balkan War (1912–13), when the Bulgarian guns could be heard pounding the Chatalja Lines, the capital's last line of defence, when it appeared that Grand Vizier Kamil Pasha was about to surrender Edirne and extinguish virtually all that remained of Turkey-in-Europe, they could restrain themselves no longer. 'I would not like to act as a revolutionary,' wrote the 32-year-old Ismail Enver Pasha to a German friend on 14 January 1913, 'but I do not know where it will all end ... To save the Fatherland or to die with honour I will try to overturn everything.'[34]

A small, handsome, dapper figure who sported a waxed Kaiser moustache, perhaps to signal the Germanophile enthusiasm acquired during his time as military attaché in Berlin, Colonel Enver was a strange mix of idealism and ambition. A junior officer of modest origin who had joined the underground opposition while serving in the Ottoman Army in the Balkans many years before, he now emerged from the shadows. For it was he, along with Talaat, the burly ex-postman, and Djemal, the middle-aged career officer destined shortly to carry the banner of Islam to the banks of the Suez Canal, who led fifty or so party activists into the Sublime Porte at three o'clock on the afternoon of 23 January. The telephone line had been cut and a battalion loyal to the Committee of Union and Progress (CUP) assigned to guard duty (the soldiers saluted as the rebel officers swept past them). Enver's party rushed up the stairs, waving flags and brandishing revolvers, and made for the grand vizier's office. Bursting in, someone shot dead General Nazim Pasha, the minister of war. The officers then demanded the resignation of Kamil Pasha. New army commanders were appointed, Djemal was made commandant of the capital, and Enver commandeered the Grand Mufti's car and sped off to the palace to secure the sultan's signature on the installation of a more agreeable grand vizier. Meantime, a smiling officer appeared before a crowd of about 500 people gathered outside the Porte and told them, 'We have made a little revolution.'[35]

Henceforward Enver would be the dominant figure in the Ottoman state. From early 1914 through to autumn 1918, he effectively combined the roles of war minister, chief of the general staff and commander-in-chief of the army. It was Enver, more than any other Young Turk, who promoted the German connection and pushed for war against the Entente. This – the launching of a great war to rebuild the empire, the declaration of an Islamic *jihad*, the attempt to rouse the Turkic tribes of Central Asia, the catapulting of the Anatolian and Arab peasantry into the maelstrom of modern industrialised war – this was to be the culmination of a mission begun six years before in the city of Salonika.

* * *

Now known as Thessaloniki in Greece, Salonika under Sultan Abdulhamid II was a cosmopolitan port city of 100,000 inhabitants. Slum tenements lay a minute's walk from grand waterfront villas. Jewish dockers and Greek shop-keepers lived cheek-by-jowl near the port, while Turkish dignitaries sat at ease in private gardens or pavement coffee-houses farther inland. Synagogues, mosques and the churches of Orthodox, Catholic and Protestant Christians testified to the city's diversity. Yet, as Lucy Garnett, an English resident in the 1880s, discovered, a charity fête at a Jewish school might be attended by the Ottoman governor and the Greek archbishop as well as the chief rabbi. Such was Salonika in its golden age before twentieth-century wars of nationalism and hate tore apart its social fabric.[36] It was here, amid the cultural cross-currents, in urban backstreets where young Turkish officers might come across Greek nationalists, Jewish socialists and European ladies of advanced ideas, that the CUP was formed.

Salonika gave concentrated expression to a wider Balkan ferment. Many troops were stationed here, yet the Ottoman Empire seemed weak, its power slipping away as hostile nationalisms cast a growing shadow over Rumelia – 'the land of the Romans', the Ottoman-ruled Balkans, the 500-year-old historic lodgement that was 'Turkey-in-Europe'. Experiencing the crisis to an acute degree were the army officers, civil servants, and educated professionals who represented the Ottoman state in Rumelia. They perceived at once the manifold faults of the Abdulhamid regime. The government was autocratic, corrupt and a perpetrator of medieval-style pogroms (an estimated 100,000 Armenian Christians had been murdered by the *Hamidiye*, units of Kurdish Muslim tribal irregulars fiercely loyal to the regime, in a rolling wave of massacres in the mid-1890s).[37] The administrative structure was not that of a unitary state but a mosaic of separate ethnic-religious *millets*, each dominated by traditional notables, mere time-serving appointees preoccupied with defending local fiefdoms and touting for favour. The economy was semi-colonial: more than 80 per cent of industrial enterprises and 70 per cent of railway track were foreign-owned.[38] The state was in hock to foreign bankers, spending 60 per cent of its budget on army and administration, 30 per cent on debt servicing, and virtually nothing on infrastructure. Symbolic of the empire's economic and financial dependency were the much-resented 'Capitulations' – grants of commercial and diplomatic privilege to various foreign powers, including exemption from Ottoman taxation and jurisdiction for their nationals. The Capitulations provided the main pretext for outside interference in Ottoman affairs. The great powers routinely proclaimed themselves 'protectors' of both their own nationals and adopted minority communities like the Maronite Christians (in the case of the French) or the Orthodox Christians (in the case of the Russians).[39] The Crimean War had begun with a row between two orders of monks over the keys to the Christian holy places in Jerusalem; the French had backed the Latin monks, the Russians the Greek.[40]

Incremental losses of territory were the milestones of decline. During the eighteenth century, Hungary and the north-western Balkans had been lost to Austria, the Crimea and northern Black Sea region to Russia. The Serbs won their autonomy in 1817, the Greeks full independence in 1830. At the Congress of Berlin in 1878, following Ottoman defeat in the Russo-Turkish War, Bosnia-Herzegovina became a protectorate (of Austria), Bulgaria autonomous and Rumania fully independent. This had been a turning-point. The great majority of the departures from Ottoman authority were Balkan Christians (while significant numbers of Muslims entered the empire as refugees, both in the Balkans and in the Caucasus). Though the sultan's North African territories – Algeria, Tunisia, Libya and Egypt – had become effectively autonomous under local potentates in the early nineteenth century, and were later gobbled up the imperial powers – Algeria (1830) and Tunisia (1881) by the French, Egypt by the British (1882), Libya by the Italians (1911–12) – it was losses in Rumelia, the Ottoman Balkans, that mattered most. Here were the empire's richest and most populous territories; here was a large part of its multi-ethnic tapestry; here was its modernist pole. With Rumelia reduced to a rump, the Ottoman centre of gravity shifted eastwards; thenceforward, three-quarters of the sultan's subjects would be Muslims.[41]

The tilt to the East hardened the conservatism of the *ancien régime*. The young nationalist officers debating matters in Salonika coffee-houses knew that change had for long been sought, and had for long remained elusive. Ever since the *Tanzimat* reforms were first proclaimed in 1839, it had been an endless cycle of grandiose promise, followed by obstruction and delay, then a relapse into the usual stagnation and drift. The most recent false dawn had been Abdulhamid's inauguration of a new liberal constitution shortly after his accession in 1876. It had lasted three months. Then the reform ministry had been dismissed, parliament dissolved and the constitution suspended indefinitely. Shortly afterwards, with mainly Christian Rumelia reduced to little more than Macedonia and Thrace, Abdulhamid had made his 'Islamic turn'.[42] One symbol of this was the Hijaz pilgrim railway. Another was the Armenian pogrom.

The underground opposition was not tightly organised, but it was extensive and influential – more so, in fact, than its activists realised. Public mood is hard to gauge under autocratic rule. The degree to which Abdulhamid's regime had been hollowed out was unclear. So the CUP dithered, uncertain if, when and how to act; and then it was bounced into revolution when one of its cells was uncovered by regime spies and a maverick army major took unilateral action in an effort to save himself. On 3 July 1908, the major, at the head of 200 soldiers and some civilian supporters, issued a revolutionary manifesto demanding restoration of the December 1876 constitution. The rebels expected a glorious death. Instead they found themselves leading a mass movement. Fearing a retaliatory crackdown, the CUP leadership in Salonika moved into action: on 23 July, it proclaimed the constitution restored. With the firing of this signal gun, the revolt immediately became general across the Ottoman armies in the Balkans and, the day after the CUP proclamation, Sultan Abdulhamid announced parliamentary elections. With its army in revolt, the dictatorship had capitulated with hardly a shot fired.

The CUP's principal spokesman in Salonika during the 'July Days' was Major Enver Bey. The young officer, intoxicated by the revolutionary atmosphere of flags, meetings, processions and crowds, addressed a gathering outside the cafés in the hastily renamed Place de la Liberté: 'Citizens! Today the arbitrary ruler is gone. Bad government no longer exists. We are all brothers. There are no longer Bulgarians, Greeks, Serbs, Romanians, Jews, Muslims. Under the same blue sky we are all equal. We are all proud to be Ottomans!'[43]

* * *

The CUP was a party of middle-class nationalists angered by the authoritarianism, corruption and weakness of Sultan Abdulhamid II's regime; in particular, by its inability to enact the reforms necessary to halt the empire's accelerating disintegration. The party's self-appointed mission was to rescue the country from oblivion. Its aim was not social revolution, but a liberal constitution and a programme of modernisation to restore great-power status. For this reason – and perhaps because they were young men of limited experience – the CUP leaders proceeded with exceptional caution.[44] For almost a year, Abdulhamid continued to reign and, between July 1908 and April 1909, the Ottoman Empire was subject to an unstable dual power, with palace and barracks involved in an extended tussle over political authority. Then Islamist conservatives, with the tacit support of the sultan, staged mass demonstrations against the new reform government in Constantinople. In response, on 22 April, troops from the Balkans loyal to the CUP entered the capital to forestall attempted counter-revolution. Within a week they had occupied the Yildiz Palace, forced Abdulhamid to abdicate and replaced him with his more pliant brother, who became Mehmed V.[45] This second revolution put state power in the hands of the CUP leadership (though the most powerful party figures still remained in the background). But the accumulated contradictions of the decaying Ottoman Empire proved insoluble.

Banners inscribed 'Liberty, Equality, Fraternity, and Justice' had been raised in Salonika's main square on 23 July 1908.[46] This was the mood which had captivated Enver and other young officers. Revolutions usually begin this way – in a carnival of solidarity and optimism. But as new political forms crystallise, the clash of social forces resumes. The workers were soon on strike for higher wages, the peasants in revolt against taxation and conscription, and the subject-peoples, especially the Armenians, agitating for autonomy. Yet none of these forces had either the social weight or political organisation to provide effective national leadership. Industry was underdeveloped, so the working class was very small. Outside the large towns, Ottoman society was geographically dispersed, socially fragmented and culturally diverse. Only the state-service middle class, above all the army officers, constituted a sufficiently centralised and powerful social force to take the reins from the *ancien régime*. This, of course, was the class represented by the CUP, with its programme of modernisation and nation-building. But such aspirations could not easily be squared with strikes, social reform and grants of regional autonomy. For the Ottoman Empire was poor, and its scarce resources were needed to pay for telegraph lines, railways, artillery and battleships. So strikes were banned, conscription enforced and agitation among the national minorities suppressed. The possibility of a deeper, more democratic, more socially progressive revolution ebbed away after the heady days of late 1908 – leaving a residue of bitterness on one side, an instinct for authoritarian government on the other.[47]

Other contradictions proved more intractable. The CUP aspired to national independence, but modernisation was impossible without foreign loans and investment. The party was dominated by Turkish officers for whom the European nation-state was the model, but almost half the population of the empire was non-Turkish. It was a secular nationalist movement eager to retain the support of large non-Muslim minorities – Armenians, Greeks, Jews – yet some form of Islamism might be the ideological glue to cement together the majority Turks and Arabs. And what exactly were the priorities? Was the aim to restore the Ottoman Empire to its former greatness, build a new Turkic empire in Central Asia or trigger an anti-colonial Holy War? What balance, in short, should be struck between the conflicting demands of Ottomanism, pan-Turkism and Islamism?

Such questions threatened to tear the empire apart. To allow them free play in a liberal parliamentary system was to risk paralysis as a plethora of traditional interests and new forces battled for influence. What was needed was a strong centralised state that could impose a unified programme of national regeneration. The idealism of 1908 therefore gave way to the *Realpolitik* of state-building. Finding themselves at the head of an antiquated dynastic empire threatened by forces of modernity, determined as Ottoman patriots to make their country great again, the CUP leaders evolved into military dictators. The Young Turks became a state power *over* society, instead of the political expression *of* society. They attempted to marshal the empire's slender resources, human and material, by diktat from above. When they encountered obstacles, they tried to bludgeon their way through. When the means failed – when poverty and backwardness frustrated modernising ambition – they resorted to bombast. They would rekindle the warrior spirit of the Turcoman. They would rouse the Muslim world. They would set the East ablaze.

Enver seemed to embody the contradictory essence of the Young Turk Revolution. He had been the main voice of its idealism during Salonika's exuberant July Days. He had since commanded an army in Libya against the Italians in 1912, led a military coup to prevent the surrender of Edirne in January 1913, and then ridden at the head of his troops to retake the city during the Second Balkan War. By the eve of war he had emerged as one of a triumvirate of dictators – the 'Three Pashas' – who now held in their hands the fate of some 22 million people.

US Ambassador Henry Morgenthau recalled sitting in Enver's house one evening and noticing that 'on one side hung a picture of Napoleon, on the other one of Frederick the Great, and between them sat Enver himself!' The ambassador put it down to vanity, to Enver's estimation of himself as 'hero of the revolution' and 'man of destiny'; and to his friends' flattery when they dubbed him *Napoleonlik* – 'little Napoleon'.[48] Perhaps; but it also reflected the complex character of the revolutionary-nationalist regime.

The 1908 revolution had been a curious blend of French idealism and Prussian militarism. But the relative proportions had changed through the six years of war and revolution since. The brief revolt of workers, peasants and subject-peoples had been suppressed. The faltering experiment in liberal constitutionalism had ended. The pretence that a sultan-caliph still ruled in Constantinople had faded. And Enver Pasha had completed his metamorphosis from revolutionary demagogue to military autocrat. All that remained was for him to lead the country into war alongside Imperial Germany, the greatest power in Europe, and so secure its place among the victors in the distribution of spoils. Thus, as the oriental auxiliaries of Prussian militarism, might the Ottomans leap the barrier of their own backwardness and restore their former grandeur.

* * *

Enver was certain about the policy the Ottoman Empire should adopt in the war, but as yet, in August 1914, he was in a small minority among Turkish statesmen. Of the thirty or so men who formed the CUP leadership – party bosses and Cabinet ministers – only a handful favoured intervention alongside the Central Powers. Most wanted to stay neutral, either strictly so, or with a stance of armed neutrality directed against Russia. Some even preferred an alliance with the Entente, usually on the basis that their superior resources made them the more likely victors in the conflict.[49]

The secret military pact agreed with Germany on 2 August reflected these divisions and at the same time exemplified the curious character of the Young Turk regime, where formal authority – that of sultan, grand vizier and Cabinet – masked a machinery of power controlled by Enver, Talaat and Djemal. The pact had been crafted by Enver in his capacity as war minister, with the support of Talaat, now minister of the interior, and signed by the German ambassador and the grand vizier (who doubled as foreign minister). It seems, however, to have been kept secret even from the majority of the Ottoman Cabinet. Articles 1 and 2 provided for Ottoman intervention on the side of Germany in the event of war with Russia arising from the Austro-Serbian conflict (already a fact by the time the pact was signed). Article 3 left the German Military Mission at the disposal of the Porte but required the Ottomans to allow it 'effective influence'. Germany also undertook to help protect Ottoman territorial integrity. The signatories pledged themselves to secrecy and to a commitment lasting until the end of 1918.[50]

Any expectation the Germans might have had of an immediate Ottoman declaration of war were confounded, however. Said Halim, the grand vizier, seems to have been an opportunist trimmer equally susceptible to pressure from pro-German and pro-Entente ministers. Vanity and ambition were, in the opinion of Ambassador Morgenthau, at the root of this. Said Halim had attached himself to the CUP as the rising force in Ottoman politics, becoming their main funder from the earliest days, and 'in exchange they had given him the highest office in the empire, with the tacit understanding that he should not attempt to exercise the real powers of his office, but content himself with enjoying its dignities'.[51]

This worked well enough when the Three Pashas were in agreement. It was hard to manage when they were not. And the opposition to the pact with Germany at first included no less a figure than Djemal Pasha, who, as minister of marine, had developed a close relationship with Admiral Arthur Limpus, head of the British Naval Mission.[52] Just as the Ottoman authorities had sought German advice on the modernisation of their army, they had turned to the British for the upgrading of their navy and coastal defences (and, as it happened, to the French with regard to reform of the *Jandarma*, the paramilitary police and border guards). Limpus, who had arrived in 1912, was the third British flag officer to serve in the role, and he and his staff of about seventy officers and men were an obvious counterweight to Liman von Sanders' contingent of German army officers.

If the Kaiser regarded the German Military Mission as an opportunity to work for 'the Germanisation of the Turkish Army', the British harboured comparable – if more tactfully expressed – aspirations for their Naval Mission. Limpus had in fact chalked up two notable successes in this respect: an order for a second dreadnought battleship in addition to one already under construction in British yards; and a contract for British arms manufacturers Armstrong-Whitworth and Vickers to build new naval dockyards. If Enver, the Ottoman

Army, and the German Military Mission formed one nexus of power inside the CUP regime, Djemal, the Ottoman Navy, and the British Military Mission formed another. Unsurprisingly – given the turf war between rival Young Turk politicians – the minister of marine was, for a while, markedly unenthusiastic about war with the Entente.[53] But this domestic spat was soon consumed by a far weightier matter: the naval arms race in the eastern Mediterranean.

* * *

Armaments are a form of waste expenditure. They satisfy no human need and therefore, in the final analysis, can have no rational purpose. An arms race, moreover, involves a rising curve of waste expenditure as rival teams of scientists and engineers compete to gain the lead in weapons technology. There are few more dramatic instances than the launch in 1906 of the Royal Navy's HMS *Dreadnought*. Mounting ten 12-inch guns in her five rotating turrets, each protected by 11-inch thick armour, and speeding through the water at 21 knots, *Dreadnought* rendered every other warship afloat obsolescent; these at once became 'pre-dreadnoughts'.[54] Dreadnought battleships were henceforward the must-haves of all aspiring world-class navies. This was especially the case for maritime empires, and the Ottoman Empire was girded by salt water – by the Black Sea, the Aegean, the eastern Mediterranean, the Red Sea, the Arabian Sea, the Persian Gulf and the Caspian. In particular, it was imperilled by the Black Sea Fleet of tsarist Russia, its most unrelenting historic foe. So the Ottomans wanted their own dreadnoughts. The problem was how to pay for them.

The Young Turks thought it could be done by public subscription – in the same way as for Abdulhamid's pilgrim railway – and the CUP party machine set about raising money in towns and villages for the great patriotic (or was it holy?) cause. When the ships were completed ahead of schedule, a complement of 400 Ottoman naval officers and seamen was dispatched to Tyneside to take possession of the vessels, and plans were advanced for a celebratory 'Navy Week' on the Golden Horn (the wide waterway on the northern side of the old city of Constantinople), when the new battleships were to be escorted to their anchorages by the assembled ships of the Ottoman Fleet.[55] Then, a hammer-blow.

On 28 July, First Lord of the Admiralty Winston Churchill requisitioned both Ottoman dreadnoughts – *Reshadieh* and *Sultan Osman I* – for the Royal Navy. 'I took this action solely for British naval purposes,' he later claimed. 'The addition of the two Turkish dreadnoughts to the British Fleet seemed vital to national safety.'[56] This is nonsense. Britain enjoyed overwhelming naval superiority with twenty-nine dreadnoughts to Germany's seventeen.[57] The concern was the balance of naval power in the eastern Mediterranean and the Black Sea, where delivery of the two dreadnoughts would have constituted a direct threat to British, Russian and Greek interests. Churchill did not act unilaterally: he had the full backing of the British Cabinet. With the British Empire on the brink of war, with Germany and the Ottoman Empire closely aligned, with sensitivities about the security of Egypt and the route to India heightened, with Russia an actual ally and Greece a potential one, it is inconceivable that the British would have allowed the two dreadnoughts to have sailed to join the Ottoman service.

The Ottoman Empire in 1914 was a revanchist power. It wanted to retrieve lost territory: in Egypt, annexed by the British in 1882; in the Balkans, where Salonika and Macedonia had been overrun by Greeks, Serbs and Bulgars in the First Balkan War; in the Aegean, where the Greeks had also seized Chios, Mytilene and Lemnos; above all in the Caucasus, where lay the 'lost provinces' of Kars, Ardahan and Batum, won by the Russians in 1878.[58] Before all this, Ottoman statesmen perceived in Russia a mortal threat to the empire's continued existence in any form. The Turks had lost each of their seven wars against Russia since 1711. Of late, they had been saved only by foreign inter-vention – by an Anglo-French army sent to the Crimea in 1854; by an Anglo-German diplomatic démarche in 1878. Throughout, the Ottomans knew that the tsars wanted Constantinople. And now Britain and France were allies of the Russians, whereas the Germans and Austrians were at war with them.[59] The two British dreadnoughts, delivered to the Ottoman Empire, would have tipped the naval balance in the eastern Mediterranean decisively against the Entente. They could not, for this reason, have been sent.

The British assured the Turks that the seizure of the warships was not a hostile move. Churchill sent a 'sympathetic and friendly message to the minister of marine', and another to Enver offering to pay £1,000 a day in compensation for the use of the commandeered battleships as long as Turkey remained neutral. It made little difference. Enver declined the bribe, the Turks were indignant and the pro-Entente faction inside the CUP leadership was discredited.[60]

This tale of two battleships had exposed underlying fault-lines and thrown the Ottoman Empire's relationship with the Entente into crisis. It was soon compounded by a second tale concerning another two battleships. With an uncanny symmetry common in fiction but rare in fact, no sooner had the British taken possession of their prizes than two replacements appeared on the Turkish horizon.

* * *

The captain of HMS *Gloucester*, a light cruiser deployed to watch the southern exits from the Straits of Messina, first caught sight of them on the evening of 6 August. The outbreak of war had found two German cruisers, the *Goeben* and the *Breslau*, commanded by Admiral Wilhelm Souchon, at large in the Mediterranean and being tracked by far more numerous British and French warships under orders to prevent a breakout into the Atlantic and to eliminate the enemy presence. Souchon was driving his engines to the limit in the effort to evade his pursuers. Stokers fell unconscious trying to raise steam in the summer heat on the *Goeben* – which had boiler problems – and four were scalded to death.

The *Gloucester* was a scout for Admiral Ernest Troubridge's squadron of four armoured cruisers. Troubridge was a direct descendant of one of Nelson's captains at Trafalgar. But under orders not to attack a 'superior force' – and *Goeben*'s 11-inch guns were certainly superior to his – Troubridge preferred discretion over valour, declining battle and turning away early on 7 August. Souchon steamed on and disappeared for three days. Where had he gone? Where was he headed? Had he doubled back? The British naval commanders were unsure.

Then, at five o'clock in the afternoon on 10 August, having re-coaled at sea among the Greek Islands, Souchon dropped anchor at the entrance to the Dardanelles. Admiral Sir Berkeley Milne, commanding the Mediterranean Fleet, knew nothing of the political situation in the Ottoman Empire, but believed the Straits were mined and closed to shipping. What now transpired does not seem to have entered his calculations. The German vessels were guided into Constantinople, and then, on 12 August, were announced as having been 'sold' to the Ottoman government and their German crews transferred to the Ottoman service.[61] The ships were renamed *Yavuz Sultan Selim* and *Midilli*, the German crews donned Turkish fezzes, and Admiral Souchon became Commander-in-Chief of the Ottoman Fleet. By 15 August, Admiral Limpus's British Military Mission had ceased to function; he and his men were shortly afterwards ordered to Malta.[62]

Ambassador Morgenthau was suitably impressed by the extraordinary coup engineered by his German counterpart at the Porte. For it was Baron Wangenheim who had proposed the wheeze, having prepared public opinion over the preceding fortnight by arranging for the Ottoman press to be filled with stories about British perfidy and illegality in seizing the two dreadnoughts on Tyneside. At a stroke, he had found refuge for the two hunted battleships, positioned them in the strategically vital Dardanelles Straits, altered the whole balance of naval power in the region, seen off the British Naval Mission and, not least, greatly strengthened the pro-German faction inside the CUP regime.

No-one believed the fiction that the *Yavuz Sultan Selim* and *Midilli* were now Turkish ships. The German crews certainly made light of their new status as honorary Turks. One night the *Goeben* sailed down the Bosphorus and dropped anchor opposite the Russian embassy. The men removed their fezzes, put on German caps, and sang 'Deutschland über Alles' and other patriotic songs to the accompaniment of the ship's band. After an hour serenading the national enemy, they restored their fezzes and sailed back to their station.

In Morgenthau's judgement, the arrival of the two German warships was the decisive event in the countdown to war. The *Goeben*'s 11-inch guns were more powerful than any in the Russian Black Sea Fleet; their mere presence therefore secured Constantinople against a Russian naval assault. These same guns, moreover, might be used to 'terrorise the Turks'; specifically, if required, to intervene in the fractious internal politics of the CUP regime in support of the pro-German elements. 'I am convinced that ... the passage of the Strait by these German ships made it inevitable that Turkey should join Germany the moment that Germany desired her assistance, and that it likewise sealed the doom of the Turkish Empire.'[63]

The Ottoman leadership was far from oblivious to the dangers. Morgenthau spoke of 'the doom of the Turkish Empire' with the benefit of hindsight, but the peril was apparent in August 1914, and, like statesmen elsewhere that tumultuous summer, the Ottoman leaders hesitated at the brink. The logic of history may have pointed in a single direction, but the human agents through whom it worked felt their way in a fog of conflicting impressions and myriad fears. But logic there was. The British, the French and the Russians all had designs on Ottoman territory; all were predatory wolves wearing masks of friendship and fidelity only while bidding for the sultan's favour. The British had grabbed Egypt. The French wanted Syria. The Russians craved Constantinople itself. What tangible gains could be expected from these powers in return for an Ottoman alliance? What long-term security would there be in the event of Entente victory? What benefit for the Turk in a world reshaped by Anglo-French finance and the tsar's armies?

Djemal, the most pro-Entente of the triumvirs, eventually grasped the logic.

Germany ... was the *only* power which desired to see Turkey strong. Germany's interests could be secured by the strengthening of Turkey, and that alone. Germany could not lay hands on Turkey as if she were a colony, for neither geographical position nor her resources made that possible. The result was that Germany regarded Turkey as a link in the commercial and trading chain, and thus became her stoutest champion against the Entente governments, which wanted to dismember her, particularly as the elimination of Turkey would mean the final 'encirclement' of Germany. The only way in which she could escape the pressure of the iron ring was to prevent the dismemberment of Turkey.[64]

* * *

But if geopolitical imperatives drove the Ottoman Empire into the arms of Germany, it was the internal contradictions of the Young Turk Revolution that turned it into an active belligerent. The CUP regime rested on a narrow social base of middle-class officers. It had crushed an embryonic popular movement to its left. It faced opposition from traditional interests to its right. It was hamstrung by the backwardness and indifference of a largely peasant country. Presiding over a stagnant economy, a lethargic society and a corrupt administration, it had turned itself into a dictatorship and was attempting to drive through modernisation with the *kourbash* and the gun. Lacking firm roots in society, moreover, the government was unstable and fractious. Lacking the resources to realise its ambitions, it was prone to fantasy and bombast. Military adventurism thus became an alternative to political implosion. War was the only way to strap together the CUP leadership and dragoon the Ottoman masses in the service of the state.

The militarists in the government had been strengthened by a purge of potentially disloyal army officers in January 1914, and by an influx of Muslim refugees from the Macedonian territories lost in the First Balkan War. Both officers and refugees were strongly 'irredentist', favouring war to restore Ottoman territory and power.[65] The press, too, was increasingly belligerent and pro-German, reacting with jingoistic fury to the British seizure of the two dreadnoughts and harbouring a deep suspicion that the Entente powers were planning the dismemberment of the Ottoman Empire.[66] This suspicion was justified: the only substantive issue was whether it would be done through an intensification of the existing semi-colonial dependency or though outright annexation and partition. Germany had, in fact, been involved in negotiations with all three Entente powers between 1910 and 1914 in an effort to agree 'spheres of influence', while the Ottomans had also been negotiating in the hope of modifying the terms of the notorious Capitulations. Underlying all these discussions was an assumption of the subordinate status of the Ottoman Empire. Prince Lichnowsky, the German ambassador to London, was unequivocal:

The real purpose of these treaties was to divide Asia Minor into spheres of interest, although this expression was avoided out of regard for the rights of the sultan. Russia's share consisted in the eastern provinces; France had

Syria and the adjoining provinces; Great Britain, Mesopotamia and the territory crossed by the Smyrna–Aïdin railway; Germany, Asia Minor proper.[67]

The difference, of course, was that Germany had no capacity to impose a military solution at the expense of the Ottoman Empire; on the contrary, it was seeking a military alliance.

Still, the Ottoman government continued to dither through the summer and into the autumn. Even after Djemal aligned himself with Enver and Talaat, the triumvirs could not win a majority among their CUP and Cabinet colleagues. One effect of the further delay was the higher price Germany was prepared to offer – those trainloads of gold dispatched from Berlin in late October. Another was the delivery of secret orders from the Ottoman war minister to Admiral Souchon to 'gain command of the Black Sea'. The real purpose was almost certainly to contrive a military clash with the Russians. Once at sea, Souchon, an Ottoman officer only in name, went much further: on 29 October he launched an attack on Sevastopol, Odessa and other coastal towns. Port facilities were shelled, several vessels destroyed and mines dropped in shipping lanes. Casualties and damage were slight, but it was an open act of war. Souchon radioed to Constantinople the disingenuous message that hostilities had begun in response to Russian interference with Ottoman naval manoeuvres.

The news opened the final phase of the long drawn-out political crisis in the capital. Talaat convened a meeting of the CUP Central Committee on 30 October. More bellicose than the Cabinet – though membership overlapped – the Committee voted 17 to 10 for war at this meeting. To maintain government unity, however, the triumvirs then agreed to the dispatch of a conciliatory note to St Petersburg. The Russians, hard-pressed on the Eastern Front and desperate to avoid a new war in the south, responded favourably, but, reasonably enough given Souchon's unprovoked attack, demanded the expulsion of all German military personnel from the Ottoman Empire. Whatever the intention, this amounted to an ultimatum which the CUP leaders were bound to reject. Souchon's raid had triggered a Russian response which left the Young Turks with a stark choice between war and a clear break with their German allies.

Britain and France had broken off diplomatic relations with the Porte on 30 October. Russia declared war on 2 November. Britain's gung-ho first lord of the Admiralty was jubilant. Churchill, with ships on stand-by near the mouth of the Dardanelles, had sent out a general order on 31 October to 'commence hostilities at once against Turkey'. The day after the Russian declaration of war, Admiral Carden's ships opened fire on the outer fortifications of the Dardanelles

Straits. French warships followed suit. The British and French governments were thus bounced into war by Churchill and Carden, much as the Ottoman government had been bounced by Enver and Souchon. Formal declarations followed on 5 November.[68]

* * *

The Ottoman Empire entered the First World War for its own reasons. The bargaining position of the CUP regime was strong and it was able to extract a high price from its German ally. It had its own objectives and to a large degree would pursue these throughout the war. Nonetheless, viewed in global context, the Ottoman Empire had become an outpost of German imperialism, its primary role in the wider war being to tie down men and materiel that might otherwise have been deployed on more decisive battlefields; its fate was henceforward inextricably linked to that of Imperial Germany and Habsburg Austria.

The Anatolian peasant-conscript – armed with a Rhineland gun, commanded by a Prussian officer, financed by a Berlin bank – was now the hired auxiliary of the German Kaiser. How would he fare in the maelstrom of modern industrialised war into which his leaders were sending him?

CHAPTER 3

Little Mehmet

FARTHEST FORWARD WERE sixty men of Captain E.W. Tulloch's company of 11th Battalion, 3rd Brigade, Australian and New Zealand Army Corps (Anzac). Tulloch was a Melbourne brewer in private life, and his men, like all of 11th Battalion, were from Western Australia. Now they were scrambling up steep, scrub-covered slopes above a small cove on a remote Mediterranean shoreline. They were the forward elements of an ambitious plan to strike at the very heart of the Ottoman Empire and knock it out of the war. The objective was Constantinople itself.

An earlier attempt to force the Dardanelles Straits by naval power alone had been defeated by coastal guns and minefields. Tulloch's company was part of the first wave of a 75,000-strong army that was going to seize the Gallipoli Peninsula on the western side of the Straits and facilitate the passage of the fleet. The main objective was the Khilid Bahr plateau, the high ground over-looking the narrowest stretch of the Straits. But the Anzacs had missed their intended landing-place and, instead of moving rapidly inland over relatively low-lying ground, they found themselves climbing a series of precipitous ridges, with the commanding height of Chunuk Bair above them.

The Aussies had piled off their boats at 4.30am, just before dawn, and immediately headed up the slopes, heavily laden, each with rifle, 200 rounds, entrenching tool and two days' extra rations of bully beef, biscuits and tea. Shortly after 9am, having crossed a succession of rises and dips, they had advanced just over a mile, climbed more than 500 metres, and could see the looming mass of Chunuk Bair ahead. Deployed in a widely extended line, carefully conserving their water, they were pushing forward in a succession of rushes, displaying the discipline and field-craft of veterans (which they were not). The heavily outnumbered enemy was falling back ahead of them. A decisive victory appeared imminent.[1]

Tulloch caught sight of a Turkish officer standing by a lone tree. Messengers came and went. The Australian captain fired at him, but he did not move. It seems likely – though far from certain – that the officer in question was Lieutenant-Colonel Mustapha Kemal Bey, commander of the Ottoman 19th Division, which had been stationed in reserve on the eastern side of the peninsula. Kemal, alerted by the sound of gunfire, had set out for Chunuk Bair at the head of his 57th (Turkish) Regiment, which had been parading that morning, leaving orders for the rest of the division, the 72nd and 77th (Arab) Regiments, to follow as soon as possible. The panoramic view from the heights confirmed that a full-scale invasion was under way. The Anzacs were landing some 12,000 men that morning, and the Ottoman defenders were outnumbered about ten to one.

'Why are you running away?' Kemal demanded of a group of soldiers fleeing towards Chunuk Bair. It turned out they had run out of ammunition and a line of enemy skirmishers was moving fast on their position. Kemal ordered them to fix bayonets and lie down. The bluff worked: the advancing Aussies, suspecting they were about to come under fire, followed suit and went to ground. Vital time was gained, and the first elements of 57th Regiment, along with a mountain artillery battery, arrived to reinforce Kemal's improvised line. By 10am the 57th Regiment was strong enough to take the offensive.[2]

Tulloch's men were among the first to feel the pressure as Ottoman resistance hardened. Brought to a halt by enemy strongly posted in the Chunuk Bair foothills, they soon found themselves being flanked, first on the right, then on the left, their whole position under increasingly heavy fire. With a third of his men down and in imminent danger of envelopment, Tulloch staged a fighting withdrawal, his four sections alternately firing and retiring.[3]

Around 11.30am the battle reached its crisis. The Anzacs in forward positions were strung out in widely dispersed company-size packets. Kemal's 57th Regiment, on the other hand, had become a concentrated force of three battalions on the Anzacs' left flank, while the neighbouring 27th Regiment was maintaining pressure in the centre. 'But this was no ordinary attack,' Kemal later recalled. 'The deciding factor in our favour was our troops' determination to kill or be killed. My order to the commanders was: "I don't order you to attack. I order you to die. When we die, other troops and commanders can take our places."'[4]

In the fighting that followed, on this and subsequent days, the 57th Regiment was virtually destroyed. Outnumbered never less than three to one, its counterattack threw the Anzacs back down the slopes and secured the high ground. So grim, in fact, had the tactical situation become at the end of the first day that the Anzac commander proposed immediate evacuation. This was refused, so his men dug in.

The resulting Anzac beachhead comprised a triangle of ground about two miles long and barely half a mile deep. The trenches were cut along the western edge of a narrow ridge. The Ottomans held the eastern edge. In many places the opposing lines were less than 50 yards apart. What followed was eight months of attritional trench warfare and 'mission creep', as each side poured in more men and materiel. The same was true of the fighting at Cape Helles, where the British and French had landed on the same day as the Anzacs, and later at Suvla Bay, where a further landing was made in August: all three Gallipoli fronts went into lockdown. By the end, a third of a million men were contesting control of a tongue of land barely 20 miles long by 5 miles wide.

* * *

For the British, Gallipoli had turned out little different from the Western Front: murderous trench warfare against a courageous, resourceful, immovable opponent. No-one had expected it. Even the Ottoman Empire's allies had discounted its military potential. 'Turkey is militarily a nonentity', wrote the German Chief-of-Staff Helmuth von Moltke to his Austrian counterpart in March 1914. 'If Turkey was described before as a sick man, it must now be described as a dying man ... Our military mission is like a medical board that stands by the deathbed of a hopeless invalid.'[5] To outsiders it seemed that forty years of defeat – at the hands of Russians, Italians, Serbs, Bulgarians and Greeks – had demonstrated the hopeless decadence of the Ottoman military tradition. It was a view informed by the racism and Social Darwinist pseudo-science fashionable among imperial elites at the time. The European upper classes had become accustomed to looking down on native people in the colonies (as well as their own working classes) as inferior species.

'Taking the Turkish Army as a whole', wrote one British staff officer in November 1914, 'I should say it was [a] militia only moderately trained, and composed as a rule of tough but slow-witted peasants as liable to panic before the unexpected as most uneducated men.'[6] Another, writing in anticipation of the Gallipoli landings, expressed the view that 'It will be grim work to begin with, but we have good fighters ready to tackle it, and an enemy who has never shown himself as good a fighter as the white man.'[7]

General Sir Ian Hamilton, the British commander-in-chief at Gallipoli, seems to have found the prospect of fighting men as lowly as Turks with extreme distaste:

Here are the best the Old Country can produce; the hope of the progress of the British ideal in the world; and half of them are going to swap their lives with Turks whose relative value to the well-being of humanity is to theirs as is a locust to a honey-bee ... Let me bring my lads face-to-face with the Turks in the open field, we must beat them every time, because British volunteer soldiers are superior individuals to Anatolians, Syrians or Arabs, and are animated with a superior ideal and an equal joy in battle ... To attempt to solve the problem by letting a single dirty Turk at the Maxim [machine-gun] kill ten – twenty – fifty – of our fellows on the barbed wire, each of whom is worth several dozen Turks, is a sin of the Holy Ghost category.[8]

Lawrence, the bookish Cairo intelligence officer, did not share the crude, broadbrush racism of men like Hamilton. His view of the East was coloured by a romanticised form of Orientalism and, perhaps, by more than a touch of neurotic obsession with the 'clean' and the 'pure'. The Bedouin – the man of the desert – stood tall in this vision.[9] But this was no less a race myth than Hamilton's undifferentiated disdain for the people of the East; and its dramatic counterpoint was Lawrence's generic antipathy towards the Turks. He would later write of 'the meanness of our enemy'. In self-deprecation, he would proclaim, 'The Turks were too-poor creatures for me to fight. Admiration of a beaten enemy had always in it something of the infect; admiration of the Turks would have been blatant self-praise ...'[10]

The Anatolian peasant-conscript confounded the bigotry of his enemies. On Gallipoli, enemy soldiers came to know him, in a mix of admiration and awe, as 'Johnny Turk'. Official estimates of his military calibre were radically revised. To Colonel Archibald Wavell, a staff officer in Palestine in 1918, he was 'a fine soldier of the rough-and-ready type, with extraordinary powers of endurance, great patience under hardships and privations, a certain inherited aptitude for warfare, and stolid courage in battle'.[11] To his own people he was *Mehmetchik* – 'Little Mehmet' – an affectionate term that was the Turkish equivalent of the British 'Tommy' or the Australian 'Digger'.

The 21-year-old Lieutenant Mehmed Fasih commanded a company of the 47th (Turkish) Regiment in the trenches at Lone Pine on Gallipoli. Though a dapper, educated, professional soldier with a fashionable Kaiser moustache in peacetime, service in the trenches had left him so haggard that no-one believed his age, while his ragged appearance caused him to be mistaken for an enlisted man.[12] He formed a deep emotional bond with the men alongside whom he shared the privations and dangers. 'And what about my soldiers?' he wrote in his diary on 22 November 1915: 'My beloved children! In what shape are they? Take the sentry at my door. Due to the cold, his shoulders are hunched and his head buried between them. His legs are huddled, his lips are blue, his nose is running. Yet his grip on his rifle is firm.' This despite seven months of murderous attrition: 'Where are our old soldiers? While we originally had 200 soldiers in each of our companies, we are now down to 50 or fewer apiece. The rest have been martyred, are missing, or have been wounded. Others have had to be evacuated on medical grounds. Which means all the veterans are gone.'[13]

Yet the line held. Thanks to the resolve of men like Fasih, the Ottomans retained Chunuk Bair to the end. The other Gallipoli fronts – Cape Helles and Suvla Bay – proved equally intractable, and when the last Entente forces were finally evacuated in January 1916, they had suffered a quarter of a million casualties. The Ottomans had suffered equally grievously; but they were the victors.[14]

Gallipoli was the supreme triumph, but there were others. For *Mehmetchik* was now engaged in the greatest war in Ottoman history, and his dogged resistance, on widely dispersed fronts, against vastly superior forces, through four years of industrialised warfare, was nothing less than a modern military epic.

* * *

The triple declaration of war upon the Ottoman Empire by the Entente powers, soon followed by attacks on Ottoman territory in the Gulf, the Caucasus and the Straits, seems to have kindled the nationalism inherent in the Young Turk Revolution, especially among senior officers – many of them recently promoted Committee of Union and Progress (CUP) party loyalists like Mustapha Kemal – and among the more modern-minded junior officers from Constantinople and the towns of Rumelia and north-western Anatolia. A somewhat histrionic patriotism infected a letter Kemal wrote to a friend while serving against the Italians in Libya in 1912. Detecting a 'desire to die for the fatherland' among fellow officers, he reported that 'a feeling of great joy and pride welled up in my heart, and I told my comrades: the fatherland will surely be safe, the nation will surely find happiness, because the fatherland has many children willing to sacrifice their safety and happiness for those of the country and the nation'.[15] Even after his company had spent more than six months in the trenches at Gallipoli, and notwithstanding his bitterness about the war, the government and the military staff, Mehmed Fasih was sustained by his patriotism, writing in his diary, 'There is no fate worse than having to watch the tearing down of one's flag and the trampling of one's country under enemy boots. This is the most dreadful poison one can imagine.'[16]

Among ordinary soldiers, nationalism was less important than religion. A young American oil prospector who happened to be in Jerusalem in early November 1914 watched in awe as streams of young Muslim men poured into the Old City on their way to the Al-Aqsa mosque, beating their breasts and declaring their willingness to die for Islam. It looked like a scene from the Crusades, he thought, and it 'sent shivers up and down our spines'.[17] Though many detected a cynical ruse by irreligious politicians and their German mentors, the Grand Mufti's call to *jihad* a few days later was not without echoes in the streets of the East. Members of Sufi or *dervish* military orders like the Mevlevi fought as jihadist volunteers; some joined the Canal Expeditionary Force in January 1915, and a battalion of them formed part of Djemal Pasha's guard in Damascus for much of the war.[18] Other Islamic enthusiasts, known as *fedais* ('self-sacrificers'), were recruited during the war, mainly from among Muslim men displaced during the Balkan Wars; the *fedais*, who numbered several thousands, combined religious passion with a yearning for vengeance.[19]

Though the committed jihadists were a minority, most Ottoman soldiers – Anatolian and Arab peasant-conscripts serving in the regular army – shared a simple Islamic piety. Religious leaders blessed military standards, regimental imams preached in the trenches and the most common battle-cry of Ottoman soldiers was 'God is Great!' (*Allah al-Akbar*).[20] Ambassador Morgenthau, witness to a practice firing on Gallipoli, was struck by the symbiotic relationship between German professionalism and Turkish passion:

> Everything was quickness and alertness. Evidently the Germans had been excellent instructors, but there was more to it than German military precision, for the men's faces lighted up with all the fanaticism which supplies the morale of Turkish soldiers ... Above the shouts of all I could hear the sing-song chant of the leader, intoning the prayer with which the Muslim has rushed to battle for thirteen centuries. 'Allah is great, there is but one God, and Muhammad is his Prophet!'[21]

Islamic sentiment was linked with defence of territory. Turkish nationalism may have had no traction in Beirut, Damascus and Baghdad, but even in the Arabic-speaking parts of the Ottoman Empire appeals on behalf of an Islamic state under attack by infidels resonated. Djemal Pasha claimed that 'brotherly affection prevailed' among the Turks and Arabs campaigning together in Sinai in January 1915, providing 'a brilliant revelation of the fact that the majority of the Arabs stood by the Caliphate with heart and soul'.[22]

In all armies it is a minority of front-line soldiers who do most of the fighting. Often they are junior officers or NCOs, though they may be private soldiers, and either way they provide the personal leadership necessary amid the chaos and terror of combat.[23] They are usually motivated by some cocktail of nationalism, religion and professional pride, combined perhaps with an instinct to defend territory, assert dominance and exact vengeance.

Sometimes, no doubt, they are touched with madness – a suppressed psychotic rage that may erupt into aggression and frenzied killing on the battlefield.[24] Often there are words for such men. Lieutenant Fasih used the Turkish word *delikanli* (literally 'one with crazy blood') to describe one such soldier on Gallipoli. Sergeant Kamil had been lobbing grenades across no-man's-land in November 1915 when one exploded prematurely and blew off his hand and wounded another soldier. 'I was here to seek revenge,' lamented the injured man as his wrist was bound. 'Not to hurt myself or a comrade. Now I've done both.' Tears flowed and he turned to his officer: 'Be the one to avenge me! I have failed to do it. I had come here for that purpose … Avenge me!'[25]

Men like Kamil form an essential part of the micro-structure and moral economy of successful armies. They embody the obligations of duty, honour, professionalism and comradeship which bind soldiers together on the battle-field. They achieve a partial dissolution of self – with its memories of home and family, its everyday discomforts and fears, its hopes for the future – into the collective. They become lightning rods of *esprit de corps* and a brotherhood of trench-fighters.

Among the more forward-looking officers this often fused with both personal ambition and patriotic aspiration. Mustapha Kemal epitomised the new type of educated, professional, modernising Turkish officer, at once resentful of German influence, contemptuous of Ottoman failings and deter-mined to leap the barriers of backwardness. 'After spending so many years acquiring higher education, enquiring into civilised social life, and getting a taste for freedom, why should I descend to the level of the common people? Rather, I should raise them to my level.'[26]

But there was a shortage of such officers: they were the exception rather than the rule. The Balkan Wars had done terrible damage to the old officer class. The empire had lost 20 per cent of its population in total, and an even greater proportion of the educated middle class from which its best officers were recruited. It had suffered a quarter of a million casualties, destroying a large part of its trained and experienced military cadre at junior officer and NCO level.[27] It is impossible to understand Turkey's war – and to evaluate properly the country's astonishing achievement in sustaining resistance for four years – without comprehending the entire sequence of events between 1908 and 1923. Throughout this period, all the active forces of Ottoman social life were consumed in an uninterrupted series of revolutions, wars and human cataclysms. There was no pause of any duration; no time for rest and recupera-tion. From Salonika's July Days insurrection in 1908 to the Proclamation of the Turkish Republic in October 1923, the train of history ran unchecked.

The losses sustained in 1912 and 1913 were irreplaceable. They were compounded by a political purge in January 1914, when Enver Pasha, the new war minister, dismissed more than 1,000 older officers. Ostensibly done to weed out superannuated or incompetent men, in fact, given the desperate shortage of experienced officers at the time, the primary motive must have been political. The fact that a number of the sacked officers were immediately imprisoned confirms this.[28] The greater political reliability of the purged officer corps may have enhanced its coherence, but it cannot have improved its professionalism. In most armies, corps are commanded by lieutenant-generals and divisions by major-generals; in the Ottoman Army of the First World War, corps were commonly led by colonels, divisions by majors.[29]

As the war escalated, there was no alternative to the employment of poorly educated Anatolian and Arab officers promoted from the ranks. Colonel Hans Kannengiesser, the German commander of the Ottoman 9th Division on Gallipoli, was scathing about such *alayli* ('from the ranks') officers:

> There were many who had been raised from the troops without having attended any training schools, and there were actually company commanders who could neither read nor write and were therefore not really effendis . . . Noticeably small was the number of officers who could read a map correctly.[30]

An obvious consequence was lack of confidence and initiative on the battle-field. But, he continued, 'I don't mean to say that all the officers were like this. There were quite a large number who were independent and acted independently, and who were full of initiative and ideas.'[31]

Other officers were recalled to the colours from retirement, and many of these proved corrupt as well as incompetent and negligent. Army logistics were often dependent on the services of ageing officers from Abdulhamid's day, typically from lowly rural backgrounds; in many cases they had achieved their rank in preference to more able middle-class men liable to have revolutionary sympathies. Known as *takauts*, these officers were, according to the Venezuelan mercenary Rafael de Nogales, who served four years with the Ottoman Army and travelled extensively across the empire:

> the greatest plague that devastated that unhappy country [Syria] during the war . . . those inveterate human parasites sold the medicines and rations of man and beast, and, had they found a buyer, would certainly have sold the very locomotives of the Baghdad Railway.[32]

Many senior officers were of high quality, especially those who had been trained in Germany. The rank-and-file would prove resilient and hard-fighting. What the Ottoman Army lacked was the 'professional depth' provided by a strong cadre of junior officers and NCOs.[33] Liman von Sanders, the German commander-in-chief on Gallipoli, noted the contrast between officers and men. Many of his officers lost their nerve and urged retreat; Kemal was exceptional. Liman attributed victory – in the face of daunting odds – 'to the stoic calmness of the Anatolian soldier and to his freedom from wants'.[34] At this level, the camaraderie of the trenches was surely decisive. Closely bonded with a small group of other men with whom he shared the brutal ordeal of modern industrialised war – the monotony and toil, the discomfort and sickness, the terrors and horrors of combat – *Mehmetchik* ended up fighting not for sultan and caliph, nor even for nation and religion, but for his 'brothers'.[35] The deep-rooted psychic need to belong, to be cared about, to feel affection and security – something not peculiar to soldiers but inherent in the species-being of humanity – is heightened *in extremis*. This is the real root of endurance and courage among men at war. Soldiers sacrifice themselves for one another, not for gods, rulers or causes. The Ottoman soldier of the First World War was no exception.

Lieutenant Fasih may have been typical. He resented both politicians and staff officers. He considered the soldiers and their families victims of ambition and greed. 'My heart bleeds,' he wrote in his diary, 'for the mothers, wives, and children of our martyrs.' But when his friend and comrade Sergeant Nuri was torn apart by high explosive, he was consumed with grief.

> As I gaze at his face, my sorrow overwhelms me, so that when I throw into the grave the first handful of earth, I break down . . . After the last shovelful of earth, I conduct our religious rites. As I recite the opening verse of the *Koran*, with all the compassion, conviction, and eloquence I can muster, I again find it difficult to control myself. Warm tears stream down my cheeks. As everything must, this also ends. Turn my back to the grave and walk away. However, everything I see seems to be telling me, 'Nuri has been martyred. You have again lost one of those for whom you cared.'[36]

* * *

It was the bonds between men like Lieutenant Fasih and Sergeant Nuri that enabled the Ottoman Empire to fight the Great War. It was these that enabled ordinary soldiers to endure the hardships and privations imposed by the empire's economic backwardness. For whatever the measure, the empire was weaker than its enemies. Its total population of 22 million was only 56 per cent that of France, 49 per cent that of Britain, and just 13 per cent that of Russia.[37] Yet this is to understate the disparity, for it includes the Ottoman subject-peoples (10 million) but excludes the colonial and dominion forces available to the French and the British. A more telling contrast appears in the estimates for total wartime manpower mobilisation: compared with an Ottoman total of 2.9 million men, the French raised 8.3 million, the British 8.9 million, the Russians 12 million.[38]

The imbalance in industrial capacity was even more acute. The First World War was the first fully industrialised 'total war'. It involved a process of protracted attrition of men and materiel, such that sustaining (and increasing) the flow of food, fodder, equipment and munitions to the fighting fronts became decisive. It was a war of logistics – of transport and supply – dependent upon a strong industrial base. This the Ottoman Empire did not possess. Total coal production was just 0.3 per cent that of Britain's, iron and steel production was insignificant, and there was no chemical production of any kind. Arms industries were limited to a single cannon and small-arms factory, a single shell and bullet factory, and a single gunpowder factory. Even the processing of agricultural products – wool, cotton, leather, wood – to manufacture uniforms, boots and personal equipment, proved unequal to the demands of war. For virtually everything – including the finance to pay for it – the Ottoman Empire was dependent on its allies.[39]

During the first year of the war, however, the main supply-route from Germany and Austria passed through enemy (Serbian) and neutral (Bulgarian) territory. This was the great railway line that ran from Berlin, through Vienna and Budapest, then across the Balkans via Belgrade and Sofia to Constantinople – the European half of the planned Berlin-to-Baghdad Railway. 'The valleys of the Morava and Maritza, in which this railroad is laid', explained Henry Morgenthau:

> constituted for Turkey a kind of waterless Dardanelles. In her possession, it
> gave her access to her allies; in the possession of her enemies, the Ottoman
> Empire would go to pieces. Only the accession of Bulgaria to the Teutonic
> cause could give the Turks and Germans this advantage. As soon as the
> Bulgarians entered, that section of the railroad extending to the Serbian
> frontier would at once become available. If Bulgaria joined the Central
> Powers as an active participant, the conquest of Serbia would inevitably
> follow, and this would give the link extending from Nish to Belgrade to the
> Teutonic powers. Thus the Bulgarian alliance would make Constantinople a
> suburb of Berlin, place all the resources of the Krupps at the disposal of the

Turkish army, make inevitable the failure of the Allied attack on Gallipoli, and lay the foundation of that oriental empire which had been for thirty years the mainspring of German policy.[40]

Even after the opening of the Berlin–Constantinople line with the entry of Bulgaria into the war (October 1915) and the over-running of Serbia (November 1915), the problem remained of the dire condition of the internal transport-network. The Ottoman Empire was vast, with 8,000km of land frontier and 12,000km of coastline, and found itself fighting on a war on four widely dispersed fronts – Rumelia (Turkey-in-Europe), the Caucasus, Mesopotamia and Syria/Palestine/Arabia. Its sea transport was quickly paralysed by superior Entente naval power. By the end of the war, the steam tonnage of the Ottoman merchant marine had been halved. And despite more than half a century of railway building, the empire in 1914 still had less than 6,000km of track – compared with 64,000km in Germany, a country with barely one-fifth the land-mass.[41]

The First World War was a railway war. Its mass armies were moved and supplied by train. Beyond the railheads, without large-scale use of motor trans-port, armies moved at the speed of marching men, and supplies were limited to what could be carried by carts and pack-animals. The Ottoman Empire was exceptionally ill-served. The only line to the three eastern fronts was the Baghdad Railway, which at that time extended from Konya, where it connected with the Anatolian Railway, to Jerablus in Syria, where the bridge over the Euphrates was unfinished and the line beyond was still under construction; about 825km of track was yet to be laid as of August 1914.[42] Both the Caucasus and the Mesopotamia fronts were, in consequence, several hundred kilometres from the nearest railhead. A second line extended southwards from Aleppo to Damascus, and from there, as the Hijaz Railway, all the way to Medina. A subsidiary line ran westwards from the Hijaz through Lebanon to Beirut, and another through northern Palestine to connect with a network of local lines serving Haifa, Jaffa, Gaza, Jerusalem, Beersheba and other towns. But the distances were huge and the impediments numerous. It was around 2,000km from Haidar Pasha on the Asian shore of the Bosphorus to Gaza at the southern edge of Palestine, and the journey was liable to take more than a month.

Compounding the basic lack of rail capacity was the fact that different gauges were in use, and in two places there were breaks in the line where tunnels had yet to be cut, one of 37km at the Taurus Mountains, another of 97km at the Amanus Mountains. The successive transhipments that this made necessary tied up resources, wasted time and created bottlenecks. There were soon more than 100,000 conscripts in labour battalions working as porters at the Taurus and Amanus gaps, along with thousands of camels, buffaloes, horses and mules. Corruption thrived: requisitioned carts and animals were sold to local tribesmen by transport officers, and dozens of animals died each day for lack of basic veterinary care.[43]

Fuel was another problem. What little coal the Ottoman Empire produced was used in the Constantinople munitions factories and on the northern section of the Anatolian Railway. Wood was the main alternative source of fuel, but its calorific value is well below that of coal, and its use is especially inefficient in fireboxes designed for coal-burning. This meant huge quantities were required, but wood was scarce across most of the Middle East. Fuel was scavenged from anywhere. All abandoned houses in Medina are reported to have been stripped of their woodwork by February 1918. Such was the level of consumption that only industrial-scale wood-cutting and transportation could keep the railways running. A special army bureau was established to deal with the problem, and more than 30,000 men assigned to it. The Syrian woodlands were plundered; entire forests were destroyed in the Yarmuk Valley. Orders were issued that one in ten fruit trees were to be felled, and it is estimated that over 22,000 acres of olive trees were cut down. A 40km-long railway line was built from Shobek to Unayza in 1915 for the sole purpose of transporting wood from the Jordan Valley Escarpment to the Hijaz Railway.[44]

Roads were few and usually in poor repair. According to Liman von Sanders: 'Most of the roads on Turkish territory which appear on the map receive no official attention. Their breadth changed constantly depending on whether they went through open country or dwindled to narrow trails between walls of rock and steep precipices.'[45] This slowed railway transhipments and all movement beyond the railheads. Carts and animals were routinely overloaded and often brutally treated, and the military veterinary staff numbered just 250; in consequence, the attrition was appalling, and the relentless demands of requisition squads eventually so denuded the countryside of draft animals that famine threatened.[46]

Djemal Pasha, *en route* to take command of the Fourth Army in Syria in November 1914, had first-hand experience of the state of the Ottoman roads. Two years of negligence by the company responsible for repairs had left the main road from Alexandretta to Aleppo impassable for motor traffic following winter rains. 'All the stones had been taken from the crown of the highway, and they were piled in two long heaps on each side. The holes between these heaps had filled with rainwater, and the result was a perfect canal.' Djemal was forced to continue his journey on horseback, aware that the road in question was the only one 'which keeps my army in touch with the home country'.[47]

* * *

The weakness of the Ottoman infrastructure was soon exposed by the demands of war. Though the soldiers at Gallipoli, fighting in the vicinity of the richest parts of the empire, were relatively well-fed, men serving in the Caucasus, Mesopotamia, and Syria were badly supplied from the outset. The diet varied according to local availability. The staples were bread, bulgar, rice and/or beans. Meat and other vegetables, when supplied, were commonly incorporated in a stew. Fruit usually came in dried form, typically raisins. Sometimes, however, men were forced to subsist for months on a thin gruel of flour and water. The laconic comment in the British Army's 1916 *Handbook of the Turkish Army* is indicative: 'In war the soldier has little to eat: his rations are 1½ lbs per day of bread with vegetables or rice. Meat is seldom given, and pay is seldom forthcoming.'[48] The iron rations carried in backpacks during an advance might comprise biscuits and dates. Tea and coffee, preferably sugared, were the main beverages. Smoking was universal, with tobacco consumed in the form of packet cigarettes, roll-ups, long-stemmed pipes and water-pipes (*hookahs* or *nargiles*).[49] Commanders would distribute cigarettes as morale-boosters; the German officer Kannengiesser would make a point of distributing two cigarettes to each man in the front-line when inspecting the Gallipoli trenches.[50]

Large ovens were constructed for the mass production of pitta bread, and meals were prepared in large copper cauldrons. Ottoman soldiers seem to have maintained a quiet collective dignity in the sharing and consumption of meagre food. Sometimes each would receive his portion in his own dish, other times half a dozen men might squat or sit cross-legged on the ground around a communal plate. 'Each threw a piece of bread into the soup,' Kannengiesser reported, 'and calm and dignified, each without haste, recovered it with his spoon. I have never seen a battle for food, no matter how great the hunger.'[51]

Officers, of course, were better provided for: all First World War armies were, in this respect, mirrors of the class societies of their time. Officers were addressed deferentially, had personal servants to do their chores ('batmen' in the British Army), and enjoyed generous baggage-allowances. Lieutenant Fasih reports eating such savouries as cheese, sausage, meat-balls, ravioli, pilaf, stuffed aubergines, rice soup and tinned soup, along with traditional eastern sweetmeats like halva and baklava, as well as occasional fresh fruit, plentiful dried fruit and sometimes chestnuts, hazelnuts and walnuts. Relaxing in his dugout, he might drink from glass or china cups and take puffs at his water-pipe while reading a newspaper, magazine, or novel by the light of a kerosene lamp.[52]

But conditions were grim enough even for officers. Fasih's dugout was tiny – barely two metres across and a metre high – and infested with lice, fleas and rats. It required a log roof and wire-netting as protection against the enemy grenades regularly tossed over. The young lieutenant was almost always leaden with lack of sleep, and he day-dreamed of a wife, children and home life he feared he might never know.[53] Conditions were far worse for the rank-and-file. Most were, of course, from poor rural backgrounds and were used to sleeping on a mattress, carpet, or mat on the floor, perhaps the entire family in a single room.[54] This cannot have been much different from living in an army tent in Mesopotamia, Syria or Arabia. Each 12-man section occupied a canvas bell-tent with a footprint only 4 metres across. The floor might be dug out to increase head-room and the sides revetted in stone if a long stay was antici-pated. The bottom of the canvas was usually weighted down with rocks as a precaution against high wind. There might be a stone hearth cut into the floor, and a kerosene lamp fixed to the central pole. Mats were often laid across the floor. Here, in a fug of intimacy, a small group of comrades-in-arms ate, drank, smoked, talked, sang folk songs, played cards, shared troubles, helped each other cope and created the bonds that held the Ottoman Army together through four years of war.[55]

* * *

The supply of replacement uniforms, boots, equipment and weaponry was as erratic as the supply of food and fodder. Even before the outbreak of war, some units were in a shocking state of neglect. When the newly arrived head of the German Military Mission, Liman von Sanders, inspected the 8th Division, he found the following:

> The officers had not received pay in six or eight months, and they and their families were forced to get their subsistence from the troop messes. The men had not seen pay for years, were undernourished, and dressed in ragged uniforms. Of the company sent to the railway station ... as guard of honour, a considerable part wore torn boots or shoes, others were bare-footed. The division commander explained that he could not hold large exercises because the men were too weak and could not march with such defective footwear.

Liman goes on to state that when he reported this to the war minister, the divisional commander was sacked for telling the truth.[56]

Matters could only get worse as the creaking infrastructure took the burden of modern industrialised war. New recruits sometimes arrived at the front still wearing their civilian clothes.[57] Elsewhere, especially on more distant fronts, and increasingly so as the war dragged on, uniforms fell apart and could not be replaced, so soldiers ended up wearing a ragged assortment of whatever they could get; footwear, for example, often comprised rags or animal skins tied with string.[58] The basic kit of the Ottoman soldier was simple enough. He wore khaki tunic, trousers and puttees, and either a distinctive khaki *kabalak* in the shape of a flattened pith-helmet but formed of strips of cloth, or a khaki *keffiya*; Turks typically wore the former, Arabs the latter. A waterproof canvas backpack carried all personal equipment, and each man was also equipped with brown leather waist-belt, two ammo pouches or a bandolier, a haversack, an aluminium water-bottle and a greatcoat. In addition, each man carried part of a communal tent, one in three a shovel, one in ten a cooking pot, and one in twelve a pick. Two days' iron rations were carried in the haversack, occasionally three, though it was five on the march across Sinai in January 1915.[59]

The Ottoman Army began the war with about 500,000 antiquated Martini-Henrys and Martini-Peabodys of 1870s vintage; these were single-shot weapons that required the soldier to load another bullet after each firing. But they also had 700,000 Mausers – modern rifles of German design that took a clip of five cartridges and allowed rapid individual fire. More Mausers were imported during the war, but demand always exceeded supply, and the Ottomans were forced to improvise. One measure was to convert Martinis to take Mauser ammunition – which the Ottomans were manufacturing themselves in a modern factory outside Constantinople – to simplify the problem of ammunition supply. But many men had no modern rifle of any kind and were forced to make do with antique firearms or revolvers. Liman inspected a depot regiment of 8,000 men in March 1916 which had barely 1,000 rifles between them.[60]

Each soldier, in addition to his rifle, was supposed to carry 120 rounds on his belt and a reserve of 30 in his backpack.[61] Many also carried grenades, whether old-fashioned ball grenades, local versions of the German 'potato masher' stick-grenade or crude imitations of the British Mills grenade, formed like a miniature pineapple to increase the number of flying fragments; at Gallipoli the Anzacs found their enemies well-supplied with grenades and were forced to improvise their own 'jam-tin' bombs in response.[62] All Ottoman soldiers were also equipped with a standard-issue bayonet, though many appropriated a variety of supplementary close-quarters weapons – knives, daggers, wooden clubs, even modified agricultural implements like bill-hooks.[63]

The supply of infantry-support weapons, above all machine-guns, was a yet greater problem. The Ottomans had suffered massive losses during the Balkan Wars and retained only modest numbers of German Maxim and French Hotchkiss machine-guns in 1914. Each infantry regiment (of three battalions) was supposed to have four machine-guns, but even this inadequate allocation was not achieved: the Ottoman Army began the war needing about 200 machine-guns to bring it up to strength. Ideally, however, there should have been machine-guns at battalion and even company level – several thousand more than the Ottomans possessed. The Germans supplied quantities of new Maxims during the war, both the MG Model 1908 heavy machine-gun that was the German Army's standard weapon, and the MG Model 1909 light machine-gun, which fired the same ammunition as the Mauser rifle and became the most widely used machine-gun in the Ottoman service; but there were never enough.[64]

The artillery establishment was also below par. The Ottoman Army's medium field-guns – usually German Krupp 75mm quick-firers, occasionally Austrian Skodas or French Schneiders of equivalent calibre – were too few to provide each of its thirty-six divisions with its full complement of twenty-four pieces. The same applied to the corps artillery. Each of the army's thirteen corps should have had eighteen howitzers and twenty-four mountain-guns, but it seems that none at all were so equipped. The shortage of heavy artillery was especially acute, with just three batteries of 105mm howitzers (12 guns in total) available as field artillery at the start of the war (though an additional 900 guns were in fixed or semi-fixed positions in fortresses and coastal defence-works). Overall, having lost up to half its field artillery during the Balkan Wars, the army needed almost 300 field-guns, and perhaps a similar number of mountain-guns, to bring it back up to establishment.

To make up the shortfall, some guns were removed from fixed positions to create additional mobile batteries, and fresh deliveries began to arrive in quantity from German and Austrian factories once direct communications were opened with the entry of Bulgaria into the war. Lieutenant Fasih reports that several new batteries of heavy guns reached the Gallipoli front between October and December. The Ottoman artillery henceforward included an impressive range of heavy calibres, albeit in limited numbers: 107mm and 120mm field-guns; 105mm, 150mm and 305mm howitzers; and 240mm, 280mm and 315mm mortars.[65] (In trench warfare, high-trajectory howitzers and mortars, and heavy calibres of shell with high explosive power, were necessary to destroy enemy defences.) But against this was the steady attrition of industrialised warfare, such that the supply of guns, especially heavy ordnance, never matched need.[66]

Equally worrying was the army's limited stockpile of ammunition. At the beginning of the war this amounted to fewer than 600 shells per gun, and productive capacity seems to have been limited to the 200-rounds-per-day output of a single factory.[67] Fasih reports that a mortar battery in the trenches behind Lone Pine fired just three or four rounds during an artillery duel and then fell silent. Why? 'No shells,' he was told. 'Today we received just ten rounds. Only three fit the guns. The others don't. If we try to force them into the barrels, they explode.'[68]

The supply of small-arms ammunition was also problematic. In addition to the 150 rounds issued immediately to each soldier and the 190 rounds per man held in unit depots, the entire army reserve amounted to just 200 million rounds. Though the Ottoman powder mills could turn out enough powder to fill 100,000 cartridges a day, the arms factories needed to burn 300 tons of coal a day (13 per cent of Ottoman output), and this, due to Russian naval activity in the Black Sea, had be transported the 150 miles from Zonguldak to Constantinople on small sailing vessels or on pack-animals over mountain tracks.[69] Nothing in the way of military logistics was ever straightforward in the Ottoman Empire. In the supply of munitions, as in so many other respects, the Ottomans were largely reliant on their European allies to be able to fight at all.

* * *

If the flow of rations and munitions to the front was often inadequate, the quality of the military support services was far worse. Each corps was supposed to have four field hospitals, each division a field medical unit. These were never up to strength: the Ottoman Empire's lack of education and training infrastructure ensured there were never enough doctors, medics or nurses. Though the hospitals had a total of 37,000 beds, more than a third of these were in Constantinople, and arrangements for the evacuation of the wounded from battlefield to hospital ranged from poor to non-existent. This, combined with undernourishment, contaminated water and general lack of hygiene, ensured massive levels of sickness and disease. The Ottoman Army recorded 462,000 cases of malaria, 147,000 cases of dysentery, 103,000 cases of intermittent fever, 93,000 cases of typhus and 27,000 cases of syphilis during the war. In this respect, it remained a medieval institution. Among Europeans, the First World War was the first in which the numbers killed in combat outnumbered those who died of disease. Not among the Ottomans: while an estimated 244,000 died in battle or from wounds, no less than 467,000 died from disease. While the British Army listed one man dead for every two men wounded, the Ottoman record was one dead for one wounded.[70] It is little wonder that many European observers had occasion to comment on the docility and stoicism of wounded Turkish soldiers: men who fell in the service of the Ottoman Empire had so little expectation of proper care that they succumbed instinctively to a feeling of hopeless resignation.[71]

* * *

The First World War in the Middle East – the most terrible war in Turkish history – began slowly. One reason was the three-month delay imposed by the squabbling indecision of the CUP regime. Another was the absence of a coherent war plan and enduring uncertainty about where troops should be deployed. Even when decisions were made, the empire's rudimentary infrastructure precluded haste. It took soldiers a month to reach Syria from Constantinople, two months to reach Mesopotamia. The Caucasus front was thirty-five days' march from the nearest railhead. Not before early November was the Ottoman mobilisation, a process begun a full three months before, completed.[72]

The empire had an estimated military-manpower reserve well in excess of 2 million, but the logistical infrastructure enabled only about half this number to be mobilised at any one time. Of these, around half were required for fortress garrisons, coastal defence, and the servicing of lines of communication and transportation. Thus, in mid-November 1914, the Ottoman Empire might have had half a million men deployed to front-line combat units.[73] More likely, the actual number was lower. Official military records probably exaggerate unit strengths because officers had an interest in inflating numbers so as to maximise supply allocations – the conscientious in the interests of their men, the corrupt in order to market the goods. Many units certainly began the war well below strength. Liman reports finding 'infantry companies with no more than twenty men for duty' in the summer of 1914 (instead of 250).[74]

Military service was universal in the Ottoman Empire. Men usually enlisted at the age of 20 and served for three years in the active army (*Nizamiye*). Thereafter they returned to civilian life, but remained members of the reserve army (*Ihtiyat*) for the next sixteen years, and then of the territorial force (*Müstahfiz*) for another seven. The wartime army therefore comprised active regulars aged 20–3, trained reservists aged 23–39 and territorials/home guard aged 39–45. In addition, there were the 42,000 gendarmes of the French-trained paramilitary *Jandarma*, who acted primarily as border guards and internal security police, but were often heavily armed and, in theory at least, properly trained. Since the 1908 revolution, moreover, the obligation to perform military service had been extended from Muslims to non-Muslims – that is, to Armenians, Greeks and Jews – but these, being less trustworthy, were usually enrolled in labour battalions.[75] Alongside these formal state forces were various militia and volunteer units, including Kurdish, Circassian, Laz and Arab irregulars serving under their own tribal leaders, several thousand *fedais* (jihadists), and small contingents of *dervishes*. A further curiosity of the Ottoman Army was the elite paramilitary character of the Istanbul Fire Brigade: it comprised several battalions of 700 men, armed and trained as infantry as well as being firefighters.[76]

Given its multiple inadequacies, given that it was small, dispersed, lacking in firepower and operating at the end of long and tenuous supply-lines, the

Ottoman Army might have chosen to remain on the defensive. Several factors militated against this. One was the relative weakness of the empire's enemies at the beginning of the war: an opportunity beckoned that might later be lost. Another was the potential leverage of offensive action: the fact that it might trigger anti-colonial revolt. No less important, however, were the CUP regime's inherent adventurism and the German high command's wider strategic needs.

Politics does not tolerate a vacuum. The contradiction between the great-power ambitions of the CUP dictatorship and the underdevelopment of the Ottoman Empire had created a political space. This had been filled with fantasies of Turkic and Islamist revolt. This, in turn, suited Germany's military leaders well enough. Deadlocked on the Western Front, 'shackled to a corpse' on the Eastern, the German high command was keen to see British, French and Russian military strength diverted from what it regarded as the principal battlefronts in Europe. Neither the CUP leaders nor the German generals, therefore, favoured a defensive war in Asia. What was wanted was a spectacle of advancing Turkic-Muslim armies such as might set the East alight. This was the global context for the Ottoman offensives of the winter of 1914/15 – a major one in the Caucasus, a minor one in Sinai.

* * *

The Russians knew the Caucasus as the 'Turkish Siberia'.[77] In the blizzards of mid-winter, temperatures might plunge to –20°C in the mountains around the town of the Sarikamish. Small, remote, surrounded by peaks, sometimes inaccessible for weeks at a time, the Russians had seized the place in 1877. Now the Ottomans wanted it back. Here would begin the great drive to create a new Central Asian empire of Turkic peoples. Enver Pasha – the Ottoman 'Napoleon' – would lead the national crusade in person. The omens were good: the news had reached Constantinople that General Hasan Izzet's Third Army had been victorious at the Battle of Köprüköy in early November, throwing back an impetuous Russian thrust across the frontier and inflicting heavy casualties. Enver conceived an ambitious plan to exploit this success by launching an immediate offensive. One corps would hold the Russians in front while two others marched across the mountains to turn the enemy's right flank. The Third Army's 95,000 men would then storm into Sarikamish. The reservations of Liman von Sanders were brushed aside. The German general considered Enver's plan to march 'through Afghanistan to India' to be 'fantasy'.[78]

The mountains rose to heights of 3,000 metres or more. The valleys and passes were narrow funnels, the roads through them mere tracks, blocked in winter under metres of snow. The landscape was barren, the population sparse and impoverished: everything the army needed in order to live and fight had to be carried hundreds of miles from the railhead and through the mountains by ox-wagon, camel and mule. No winter kit was issued. No forward supply-depots were established. Many units began their arduous advance on 22 December with only dry bread and olives in their haversacks.

As they climbed, the snow deepened and temperatures plummeted. Soon, the whiteness along the line of march became speckled with the black humps of exhausted, starving, frostbitten men who had fallen never to rise again. The 17th Division was trapped in a blizzard and lost 40 per cent of its men frozen to death. The 29th Division bivouacked in the open at a temperature of −20ºC and lost 50 per cent dead or deserted. At the end of a week, IX and X Corps, the two-thirds of the army forming the flanking force, had been reduced to about 12,000 men, less than a quarter of the original strength. Many of the shrunken divisions, advancing on widely separate tracks, had lost contact with each other. The survivors were at the limit of endurance.[79]

Even so, on 29 December, when the fighting reached its climax, matters seemed to hover for a moment in the balance. The Russian high command was nervous and divided. The defenders had been weakened and demoralised by their November defeat. But the lingering hope was momentary. The Russians had had time to regroup, bring up reinforcements and dig strong defences. Their railway supply-line ran all the way to the front. Some 65,000 of them were now ensconced on the high ground with clear fields of fire across the slopes. At the end of a day of savage attacks, IX and X Corps were reduced to 6,000 men. Even Enver conceded that further efforts were pointless.

But the forward elements were now deep inside the Russian lines. The remnants of IX Corps – 2,500 men and 14 guns and machine-guns – were cut off in woodland outside Sarikamish. On 2 January the Russians counter-attacked, attempting a giant encirclement of their own to trap and destroy Enver's army. In this they largely succeeded. When the retreat from Sarikamish ended, and those who were left had been counted in the Ottoman forward-base at Erzerum, the Third Army's losses were found to total 75,000 men and all its artillery.[80]

The Ottomans would never recover from the catastrophe of Sarikamish. A year later, they would lose Erzurum, the third most powerful fortress in the empire, and the anchor of the entire defence of eastern Anatolia. Straining to halt the Russian advance, between November 1915 and February 1917 the Ottomans would suffer three-quarters of their casualties on the Caucasus front.[81] Viewed in wider perspective, the campaign undoubtedly contributed to victories over the tsar's armies elsewhere. In particular, by playing on Russian anxieties about *jihad* in Central Asia, Ottoman operations in the Caucasus tied down enemy soldiers, reducing the numbers available for service against the Germans and Austrians on the Eastern Front, and contributed to the attrition that would eventually bring them to mutiny and revolution. This, though, did nothing to diminish the crisis engendered inside the Ottoman Empire.

Enver was strong-willed, visionary and charismatic, but he was profoundly lacking in political and military talent; less the Napoleon of the Young Turk regime than its Mephistopheles – a mischievous sprite who had sold the Ottoman Empire to Germany for a pot of gold and a dream of glory. The pot could be refilled, but Enver's dream of pan-Turkic conquest perished in the winter snow of Sarikamish, and he never sought field command again. A month later, Djemal's Islamic *jihad* ended equally ignominiously on the sands of Sinai. Defeated and deflated, thrown onto the defensive both militarily and politically, the triumvirs cast about for an enemy within, upon whom to place the blame and vent their rage.

* * *

Rafael de Nogales, the Venezuelan mercenary who had taken a commission in the Ottoman Army, was passing through remote Transcaucasia in June 1915. He had stopped at Sak, a small town south of Lake Van, and was having lunch at the government office. Looking out of the window he saw the market-place had filled with several hundred exhausted women and children.

> Their sunken cheeks and cavernous eyes bore the stamp of death. Among the women, almost all of whom were young, were some mothers with children, or, rather, childish skeletons, in their arms. One of them was mad. She knelt beside the half-putrefied cadaver of a new-born babe. Another woman had fallen to the ground, rigid and lifeless. Her two little girls, believing her asleep, sobbed convulsively as they tried in vain to awaken her. By her side, dying in a scarlet pool, was yet another, beautiful and very young, the victim of a soldier of the escort. The velvety eyes of the dying girl, who bore every evidence of refinement, mirrored an immense and indescribable agony.

When the order to move was given, 'one after another of those filthy, ragged skeletons struggled to its feet and, taking its place in that mass of misery that shrieked silently to heaven, tottered off, guarded by a group of bearded gendarmes'. Their oppressors also stirred themselves into motion: undeterred by the half-hearted efforts of the gendarmes to fend them off, 'a mob of Kurds and ruffians … kept fluttering about their future victims like carrion buzzards, hurling curses and brandishing weapons in the faces of the unhappy creatures'.[82]

What Nogales had witnessed was one of hundreds of similar processions that wound their way along the highways of eastern Anatolia and Transcaucasia between April and October 1915. When the reports of American consuls and missionaries reaching Ambassador Morgenthau in Constantinople became a flood, he realised that a vast movement of ethnic-cleansing and genocide was in progress.

> From thousands of Armenian cities and villages these despairing caravans now set forth; they filled all the roads leading southward; everywhere, as they moved on, they raised a huge dust, and abandoned debris, chairs, blankets, bedclothes, household utensils, and other impedimenta, marked the course of the processions.

At the outset the travellers 'bore some resemblance to human beings', but this did not last, and 'what had started a few hours before as an orderly procession soon became a dishevelled and scrambling mob'.[83]

These columns of people were not so much deportations as death marches. In the stream of horrified reports from the field, Morgenthau could discern a pattern. Armenian soldiers serving in the Ottoman Army were disarmed and redeployed in labour battalions. Armenian civilians were ordered to hand over their arms (virtually all men carried guns in Transcaucasia), and there were ruthless searches of Armenian homes and sometimes shootings of those who resisted or were found to have concealed weapons. Deportation orders were then issued, and the death marches began. Able-bodied men were soon taken aside and murdered, leaving women, children and old folk defenceless as the column moved on. They were then prey to the greed and lust of the gendarmes, tribal paramilitaries and random thugs on the road. Some young women were raped and discarded, while others were carried off as sex-slaves. Most deportees were plundered of their property, some even of the clothes they wore, reducing the victims to nakedness as they stumbled along under the broiling sun. Jesse Jackson, the American Consul in Aleppo, saw one such column. About 1,000 women and children had set out from Harput in temperatures of more than 40°C. Only 300 or so made it to Aleppo, arriving 'entirely naked, their hair flowing in the air like wild beasts'; they were, Jackson reported, 'burned to the colour of a green olive, the skin peeling off in great blotches, and many of them carrying gashes on the head and wounds of the body as a result of the terrible beatings'.[84]

The survivors were dumped in desolate deportation camps, where they died in their tens of thousands, deprived of food, water and medical care. At Ras al-ain camp in Syria, miles of large black tents filled with dead and dying people stretched across the desert. Flies, insects and birds fed on the corpses.[85] The German nurse Armin Wegner inspected this camp in November 1915. He found it a place of hunger, disease and death, smelling of shit and decay. Most pitiful were the growing numbers of orphans. 'At the sides of the camp,' he reported:

> a row of holes in the ground covered in rags, had been prepared for them. Girls and boys of all ages were sitting in these holes, heads together, abandoned and reduced to animals, starved, without food or bread, deprived of the most basic human aid, packed tightly one against the other and trembling from the night cold, holding pieces of still smouldering wood to try to get warm.[86]

For six months, across the north-eastern regions of the Ottoman Empire, scenes of apocalyptic horror were enacted. Nogales spent much of the summer of 1915 on the road. Again and again he witnessed the stumbling columns of the walking dead.

> It was terrible to see some of the stragglers in the rear. After crawling for a long time like wounded animals, shrieking to their families, they finally fell at the roadside, to die and become carrion. Among them I saw many a very old man, many an aged woman, carrying a great-grandchild in withered arms, perhaps the last survivor of a once numerous family. I saw children covered with hideous sores, with suppurating eyes black with flies, bearing a little brother, dead or new-born, whose mother had died along the way.[87]

The camps were even worse, for here the great dying mass of the Armenian people became a concentrate.

> As the epidemics increased, camps and roads became clogged with carrion, which attracted the hyenas from the desert; and jackals grew so numerous that even by day they could be seen feeding on the corpses. Sometimes, I was told, they even ate the dying. I remember one case when the animals tore a child to pieces even while it slept at its mother's side. When she awoke, she went mad, and stood screaming . . . with the fragments of her baby in her arms.[88]

No-one is sure how many died: the murderers kept no records. Journalists at the time estimated that between 600,000 and 1 million Armenians were killed in 1915, but that more died later, perhaps another 200,000, in the summer of 1916, when many survivors of the death marches were murdered in the camps, and yet more in fresh pogroms in 1920 and 1922. It is possible that the final death toll in the Armenian Genocide of 1915 to 1922 was 1.5 million.[89]

* * *

By late summer, something of what was happening in the eastern provinces of the Ottoman Empire had become widely known. 'The women and children of Armenian villages have all been expelled from Cilicia to Mesopotamia and Syria,' Lawrence wrote to fellow intelligence officer George Lloyd in September, 'but the men of fit age all sent to labour battalions.' Lawrence detected a military opportunity: 'So north Syria is full of unarmed battalions of Armenians and Christians, fit men, with no relations or home ties. In addition, there are many outlaws, Muhammadan and Christian, in the hills: all of it good material for a rising backed by us ...'[90] This was optimistic. The genocide and ethnic-cleansing was already far advanced.

A history of oppression under Ottoman rule had for long encouraged the Armenians to organise for self-defence and self-determination, and, as a beleaguered minority, to look to tsarist Russia for support. This had, of course, increased suspicion and repression, and tensions tended, for obvious reasons, to peak in moments of national crisis. None was ever graver than the outbreak of war in November 1914 and the catastrophe of Sarikamish two months later. Many Armenians – including an estimated 50,000 army deserters – made the journey into Russian-controlled territory to take service with the tsar's army. Others formed guerrilla bands, supplied with Russian arms and ammunition, and commenced local attacks on Ottoman police. Some Armenian civilians made no attempt to conceal their joy at news of Entente military successes.

The Ottoman authorities responded by arresting leading Armenians, deporting Armenian residents from front-line areas and attempting to confiscate all arms in Armenian possession. The conflict exploded into full-scale war with an uprising of the Armenian population in the eastern Anatolian city of Van in late April 1915. The fighting lasted a month and was merciless. Nogales, who took part, had rarely experienced anything like it. 'Nobody gave any quarter, nor asked it.' The Ottomans eventually withdrew as a Russian army approached. The Muslims fled with them.[91] But anything that had happened up to this point was dwarfed by what followed.

That all-out genocide was ordered by the CUP in Constantinople is not in doubt. A thin paper trail exists. On 15 September 1915, for example, Talaat, the party boss and interior minister, cabled this instruction to the Ottoman prefect in Aleppo:

It has been previously communicated to you that the government ... has decided to destroy completely all the indicated persons living in Turkey ... An end must be put to their existence, however tragic the measures taken may be, and no regard must be paid to either age or sex, or to any scruples of conscience.[92]

Indeed, by this time, the regime was so steeped in blood and guilt, that its leaders were convinced there was no turning back. 'We have already disposed of three-quarters of the Armenians,' Talaat told the American ambassador. 'The hatred between the Turks and the Armenians is now so intense that we have got to finish with them. If we don't, they will plan their revenge.' More simply, on another occasion, he told Morgenthau that 'no Armenian can be our friend after what we have done to them.'[93]

Morgenthau tried again and again to intercede on behalf of the Armenians, but the CUP leaders were immovable. They had made a cold-blooded decision to liquidate the Armenians living inside the Ottoman Empire. 'Our Armenian policy is absolutely fixed and nothing can change it,' Talaat declared. 'We will not have the Armenians anywhere in Anatolia. They can live in the desert but nowhere else.'[94] Enver was equally adamant. If Talaat's persona was that of the murderous tribal chieftain, Enver retained an air of urbane refinement. As if discussing the latest French novel, he calmly explained to Morgenthau the need for mass murder. The Armenians had been warned not to make trouble. They had not heeded the warning. They were supporting the Russians. They had organised an insurrection in Van. They were separatists working for an Ottoman defeat. In a military emergency it was not possible to make fine distinctions between the innocent and the guilty. All Armenians were a threat, a fifth column, an enemy within. All that mattered was the war. 'The only important thing is to win,' Enver explained. 'That's the only thing we have on our mind. If we win, everything will be alright; if we lose, everything will be all wrong anyhow. Our situation is desperate ... and we are fighting as desperate men fight. We are not going to let the Armenians attack us in the rear.'[95]

When Morgenthau implied that the worst excesses may not have been the government's intention, Enver stiffened. You are greatly mistaken,' he said:

We have this country absolutely under our control ... The Cabinet itself has ordered the deportations. I am convinced that we are completely justified in doing this owing to the hostile attitude of the Armenians towards the Ottoman government, but we are the real rulers of Turkey, and no underling would dare proceed in a matter of this kind without our orders.[96]

Enver and Talaat were the leaders of a bourgeois-nationalist dictatorship in an underdeveloped country threatened with defeat and dismemberment. Their heady hopes of pan-Turkic or pan-Islamic revolution had been crushed at Sarikamish and Sinai. They were now engaged in a desperate struggle for existence on the Gallipoli Peninsula. They viewed the liquidation of the Armenians as a necessary wartime measure. Many of their German allies were equally clinical. Baron Wangenheim, the German ambassador, steadfastly refused to lobby the Ottoman government on behalf of the Armenians, telling Morgenthau, 'The Armenians have shown themselves in this war to be enemies of the Turks. It is quite apparent that the two peoples can never live together in the same country.'[97] The German naval attaché was blunter still. A fluent Turkish speaker and personal friend of Enver, Captain Humann was a Social Darwinist: 'Armenians and Turks cannot live together in this country. One of these races has to go. And I don't blame the Turks for what they are doing. I think that they are entirely justified. The weaker nation must succumb.'[98]

Humann clearly saw the Armenian Question as something transcending the immediate exigencies of war. Talaat, too, seems to have regarded the war as an opportunity to implement some sort of 'final solution'. He told Morgenthau that he considered the destruction of the Armenian people 'inevitable'. He was quoted in the German press saying, 'We have been reproached for making no distinction between the innocent Armenians and the guilty; but that was utterly impossible, in view of the fact that those who were innocent today might be guilty tomorrow.'[99] He boasted to his friends that he had 'accomplished more towards solving the Armenian problem in three months than Abdulhamid accomplished in 30 years'.[100]

* * *

Total war was the context which made genocide possible. It turned the whole of Ottoman society into an armed camp, creating a pervading sense of crisis and insecurity. Fear, suspicion and xenophobia were normalised, and virtually any sort of 'emergency' procedure could be validated. This provided opportunities for those with otherwise marginal political agendas to become leading protagonists in the development and implementation of policy. It also unleashed dammed-up forces of psychotic rage from the social depths.

Zia Gökalp, the founding father of Turkish nationalism, was one of these agents of genocide. Born in Diyarbekir in eastern Anatolia, his reaction to the intricate mosaic of ethnicities, religions, tongues and customs around him – the cultural residues of movements of people ongoing since the dawn of time – was a virulent 'blood and soil' myth. In Gökalp's vision, Turkish Muslims were the master-race, and the revitalisation of the Ottoman Empire depended upon their cultural dominance over lesser peoples like Armenians, Greeks and Jews. To be strong again, Turkey had to become 'a society consisting of people who speak the same language, have had the same education, and are united in their religious and aesthetic ideals'; a nation, he proclaimed, required 'a common culture and religion'. The Turks, moreover, should seek to recover their lost national virtues and emulate the great military achievements of their ancestors. Accordingly, Gökalp welcomed the war and admired the aggression of the CUP politico-military leaders; they in turn regarded him as an ideological guru. Like other reactionary nationalists of his era, Gökalp saw war as redemptive: it would inspire the people, rouse them from apathy, unite them in a great struggle to remake the nation. He and his followers – his 'Turkish Hearth' movement had more than 2,500 members in Constantinople – were hypnotised by the vision of a Central Asian super-state: they seemed to see in the more than 20 million Turks who lived outside the borders of the Ottoman Empire, the great majority in Russia, most of the rest in Persia, China and Afghanistan, the ghosts of the Turkmen of the medieval steppes. 'The country of the Turk is not Turkey,' Gökalp announced. 'It is not Turkestan. It is a great and eternal land: Turan.'[101] From this mystical mish-mash, the Young Turk militarists selected what they needed; Talaat, in particular, discovered an ideology of extermination in the muddled outpourings of the nationalist propaganda circles.

The main apparatus of the genocide was supplied by a new department of security police – the Special Organisation (SO) – which seems to have been set up by Talaat's Ministry of the Interior, but to have received funding from Enver's Ministry of War. It soon took on a life of its own, growing into an organisation of 700 officers and 30,000 operatives subject only to the authority of the two triumvirs. The SO's former head later described it as 'a secret body designed to achieve the internal and external security of the Ottoman state' – one more powerful than the 'official government'. The SO's main focus was 'non-Turkish and non-Muslim races and nationalities', since their loyalty to the empire was 'suspect'.

In the winter of 1914/15, the SO was given full autonomy in the eastern provinces, and it was the SO which organised the death-squads and planned the massacres and deportations.[102] Heading the operation was Dr Behaeddin Shakir, a medical doctor and leading CUP member who regarded the Armenians as 'tubercular microbes' infecting the Ottoman state.[103] The work of the SO was given retrospective legitimacy by a 'Temporary Law of Deportation' enacted in May and a 'Temporary Law of Expropriation and Confiscation' enacted in September.[104] But the real decisions had been taken at a secret party meeting in December 1914 or January 1915. They were summarised in a document later dubbed – after it fell into British hands in 1919 – 'The Ten Commandments'. The document amounts to a full and explicit programme of deportation, ethnic-cleansing and genocide in the eastern provinces of the Ottoman Empire.[105]

Two decades before, the regime of Abdulhamid had massacred 100,000 Armenians by unleashing upon them the *Hamidiye* – local units of mainly Kurdish irregulars in the Ottoman service. Now, under a modernising bourgeois-nationalist regime, genocide was bureaucratised, becoming the business of a specialised government department, and expanded into a state-wide programme of ethnic-cleansing. Thus, the most senior murderers might receive a foreign ambassador in their palatial government offices and discuss the matter as dispassionately as they might any other matter of state.

On the ground, however, the genocide assumed a medieval form, for the Ottomans lacked the resources to transform mass murder into an industrial process. The actual killing had to be done personally, at close quarters, often with primeval brutality. Armenians were shot and hanged, bayoneted and bludgeoned, drowned and burned alive. Many died on the road, usually from hunger, thirst and beatings, but sometimes because they were deliberately killed. Many more died later, in the camps, either because they were deprived of every necessity of life, or because they were rounded up for extermination. In one bizarre precursor of what was to come, 5,000 people were herded into a cave complex and asphyxiated by a bonfire at the mouth: a primitive gas-chamber, a mini Auschwitz.[106]

To carry out the deportations and the killings, it was necessary to construct an infrastructure of genocide across the eastern provinces. But in doing so, the CUP leadership stirred into motion the muck of ages, the accumulated cultural sediment of tribalism and hatred that festered in the poverty at the base of the social order. A chaotic, churning mass movement of improvised extermination, of murder, rape, torture and plunder, quickly swelled and spread across hundreds of miles of Transcaucasia, eastern Anatolia and northern Syria.

The SO created death-squads known as *chetes* that employed tens of thousands of convicted criminals. But the killing was also done by the gendarmes of the paramilitary provincial police – ostensibly 'guards' of the deportees – by gangs of Muslim jihadists and refugees, and by bands of irregulars, tribesmen and brigands, usually Kurdish, often enrolled in auxiliary cavalry units.[107] The killers' motives were a mix of greed, lust, sadism, bigotry and religious fanaticism. They operated in a context of increasing political fragmentation, where the formal state was in retreat and real power was exercised by local potentates, often tribal leaders who were little more than licensed brigands, and where traditional ethnic and religious divisions could be used to legitimise the use of violence. Local Ottoman officials, police and paramilitaries were, to a large degree, embedded in this social substrate. The killers operated in a world of feuds, vendettas and vigilantism; a world of armed men among whom tribal violence was habitual; a world of damaged psyches filled with pathological rage.[108]

The Armenian Genocide elevated men of unsurpassed bestiality to positions of absolute power over the lives of thousands of helpless people. These included Fakhri Pasha, the commander destined to defend Medina against the Arabs, a man whom Lawrence would later describe as 'the courageous old butcher who had "purified" Zeitun and Urfa of Armenians'.[109] Also Khalil Pasha, whom Lawrence was destined to meet outside Kut in April 1916, and whose bloody work at Sairt was witnessed by Nogales, where he saw a hill 'crowned by thousands of half-nude and still bleeding corpses, lying in heaps, or interlaced in death's final embrace'.[110] And then there was Djevdet Bey, brother-in-law of Enver Pasha, appointed to the governorship of Van in place of a more conciliatory predecessor. A psychotic racist and sadist, described by Henry Morgenthau as a 'connoisseur in torture', Djevdet became known as 'the Horseshoe Master of Bashkale' for his practice of nailing horseshoes to the feet of his Armenian victims.[111] And what, finally, is one to make of the nameless men – their identities lost to history – who had been at work at Malatia shortly before Aurora Mardiganian, a holocaust survivor, arrived there? Not only were the wells along the approaches stuffed with the corpses of dead women, but at the entrance to the town hung the crucified remains of sixteen Armenian girls. 'Each girl had been nailed alive upon her cross, spikes through her feet and hands,' wrote Mardiganian; 'only their hair, blown by the wind, covered their bodies'. Vultures were eating the corpses.[112]

* * *

In six short years, the Young Turk Revolution had degenerated from carnival of liberation into genocidal dictatorship. The workers, peasants and national minorities had appeared briefly on history's stage in its opening act, but their protests had been crushed, their voices silenced, and power assumed by a narrow caste of army officers without a social base. Transformed into a triumvirate of military despots, their authority underpinned by German gold and guns, Enver, Talaat and Djemal had floated for a while on a cloud of pan-Turkic and pan-Islamist fantasy. Then, defeated and disillusioned, they had been forced to confront the intractable fact of the Ottoman Empire's poverty and weakness. But by this time they had committed it to a military struggle for national existence of unprecedented ferocity; one from which they could not withdraw without themselves losing power. So it was, trapped by the contradictions of imperial decline and their own ambition, victims of their own delusion and bombast, in fear and frustration, they turned in murderous rage on the Armenian people in that terrible summer of 1915.

CHAPTER 4

For Sultan and Caliph

A T THE BEGINNING of 1916, it may have appeared that the Ottoman Empire had chosen the winning side in the Great War. The prospects for the Central Powers were perhaps better than at any time since August 1914. For one thing, the Ottoman victory at Gallipoli, signalled by the Entente evacuation between 7 December 1915 and 8 January 1916, was one of the war's most decisive. It not only put paid to Anglo-French hopes of knocking the Ottoman Empire out of the war with the capture of Constantinople; it also kept the Straits closed to Russia, denying it access to world markets for its Ukrainian wheat, and preventing any inward flow of military materiel from its allies. Russia's manpower reserve was greater than that of all the Central Powers combined; but without guns and munitions, it could only ever mobilise a fraction of it. At the Battle of Gorlice-Tarnow in May 1915, the tsar's armies had collapsed. The line was stretched too thin and many men did not even have a rifle. The Russians lost 2 million men and were forced to retreat 300 miles, abandoning Galicia and most of Poland.[1] The German Military Mission's Colonel Hans Kannengiesser saw Gallipoli as the final shattering blow to Russian morale at the end of a disastrous year, cutting them off from their allies and, in the long run, sealing the fate of the tsarist regime: 'Without Gallipoli they would probably have had no revolution,' he wrote.

Meanwhile, on the Western Front, if the success had been less spectacular than on the Eastern, it was solid enough. The Germans had seized most of Belgium and a large part of north-eastern France in August 1914. The French had thereby lost most of their coalfields, all their iron mines and much of their heavy industry, while the nearest enemy soldiers were entrenched only 60 miles from Paris.[2] Knowing that the Entente powers were bound to take the offensive in an effort to liberate their territory, the Germans, secure in control of higher ground along most of the front, opted to remain mainly on the defensive.

Despite British War Minister Lord Kitchener's judgement in January 1915 that 'the German lines in France may be looked on as a fortress that cannot be carried by assault', a series of increasingly violent assaults had nonetheless been launched. These had culminated in a coordinated offensive in Artois and Champagne involving almost a million men and 5,000 guns. It had begun on 25 September, lasted a month, achieved nothing and cost about 250,000 casualties.[3]

Matters were yet more cataclysmic in the Balkans. Italy entered the war against the Central Powers in May 1915, and its soldiers were immediately committed to a campaign of conquest aimed at the seizure of the northern Adriatic port of Trieste. Though heavily outnumbered, the Austro-Hungarians improvised a strong defensive line in the mountains along the frontier, and by the end of the year the Italians had lost a quarter of a million men in four failed offensives on the Isonzo line (to be followed by another seven, all equally futile, over the next two years).[4]

Worse happened in the southern Balkans. Germany had been able to secure the allegiance of Bulgaria by offering her Macedonia – which the Entente powers could not, in deference to the interests of their existing Serbian and prospective Greek allies. A combined German, Austro-Hungarian and Bulgarian offensive then overran Serbia in a lightning campaign in October and November. The remnants of the Serbian Army were evacuated by sea and redeployed to the Salonika Front – a new line running across the southern Balkans from the Adriatic to the Aegean, formed in the wake of an abortive Anglo-French effort to bring succour to the Serbs. The Allied 'Army of the Orient' stationed here – eventually including British, French, Serbian, Italian, Russian and Greek troops – would swell to a peak strength of 600,000 men in the summer of 1917. Sardonic German commentators would describe it as 'the greatest internment camp in the world'; the French press dubbed its well-entrenched defenders 'the Gardeners of Salonika'.[5] The Army of the Orient's passivity reflected the defensive resilience of Bulgaria's huge, tough, experienced army: the small Balkan state appears to have mobilised a higher proportion of its national manpower than any other belligerent, eventually having perhaps 900,000 men under arms out of a population of barely 6 million.[6] The Bulgarian intervention transformed the war in the Balkans, not least for the Ottoman Empire, whose western flank was now protected, and whose rail communications with Central Europe were secured.

The situation in the Caucasus was more worrying for the Central Powers, but there had been no general collapse after the Sarikamish disaster. The factors which had wrecked the Ottoman winter offensive thereafter played in reverse. The force of an attack reduces as it advances, since it involves attackers moving ahead of their supporting arms and sources of supply, while defenders fall back on theirs. This was especially so in the Caucasus campaign, where two over-stretched and under-resourced armies faced each other across hundreds of miles of remote, inaccessible, mountainous terrain. When the Russians advanced from their railhead at Sarikamish, they quickly lost momentum. The Ottomans, meantime, rushed reinforcements to Erzerum. A reinvigorated Third Army under Mahmud Kamil Pasha was able to sustain a war of movement around Lake Van throughout 1915.[7]

Even a major breakthrough by the Russian Caucasus Army, following a surprise attack along the whole front in January 1916, could not be transformed into a war-winning victory. By late spring, the Russians had captured Erzerum, Trebizond and a band of territory some 200 miles deep. But the basic strategic problem remained: they lacked the manpower and resources to sustain an offensive that pushed deep into the vast Ottoman hinterland and, from June onwards, they faced powerful counter-attacks from a reinforced Third Army and a newly deployed Second Army. Though the Ottomans continued to suffer heavy defeats – their casualty toll for the Caucasus campaign in 1916 would eventually reach more than 100,000 – by late August a rough balance of force and mutual exhaustion had combined to bring the campaign to an end. With nearly half the Ottoman Army deployed there, the Caucasus Front stabilised along existing lines. In the event, the Russians would come no farther. The tsar's army had reached breaking-point, and the peasant-conscripts manning the trenches in Transcaucasia would soon be joining the revolution.[8]

* * *

The Ottoman Empire's military resilience had serious political implications for its imperial rivals. British and French prestige had been badly damaged, especially in the East, by defeat at the hands of the 'lowly Turk'. Kannengiesser was clear that Gallipoli had been a victory against the odds for the Anatolian peasant-soldier: 'Firm will, stubborn devotion, unshakeable loyalty to their sultan and caliph, on the part of the Turks, gained them the victory against the superior might and crushing material of the Entente. Psychological powers triumphed over physical, the spirit over the material.' The war in the Middle East now looked set to be long and hard: 'England did not give up her aim on Constantinople, but was forced to take up the weary and difficult operations through Mesopotamia and Palestine. This, in addition to work, would cost money and blood – for years, instead of months by the short route over Gallipoli.'[9]

Not only had hopes of a quick-fix end to the war in the Middle East been dashed; the fear was that the European colonial regimes might themselves succumb. The Ottoman veterans of Gallipoli had become a military elite that would henceforward stiffen the resistance on other fronts. The Muslim masses had borne witness to the fragility of British power.[10] Prestige mattered; it was inseparable from empire. Because the colonial subject-peoples were many and their rulers few, the continued domination of one by the other depended to a large degree on the mere semblance of power. Stripped to its essentials, colonialism was based on fear of the bully. In the end, native people paid taxes, did coolie work and soaked up abuse because they were frightened of the policeman. The victory of the Turk at Gallipoli in 1915 – like the victory of the Japanese over the Russians in 1905 – posed questions about the inevitability of European colonial rule. This could only further complicate the cross-currents of rival nationalisms that the war was fanning into flame across the Middle East. And it was in the very heart of that region – on the River Tigris a hundred miles or so south of Baghdad – that another dramatic demonstration of the fragility of British imperial power was to be acted out in the early months of 1916.

* * *

It had all seemed so easy. The Government of India had landed two brigades of troops at the head of the Persian Gulf in November 1914. Their mission had been to secure the oilfield at Ahwaz, the oil port at Abadan, and the 100-mile pipeline connecting the two. Because of the proximity of the border, this had necessitated the seizure of Basra from the Ottomans and the occupation of southern Mesopotamia. All of this had been accomplished by the end of the month; the Ottoman – and Arab – resistance had been easily routed.[11]

There matters might have rested. But the senior ranks of the Government of India and the Indian Army contained ambitious men with empire-building vision. Sir Percy Cox had, for this very reason, resigned as foreign secretary to the viceroy in order to take up the post of political officer with the expeditionary force, and Lieutenant-General Sir John Nixon, appointed commander-in-chief in April 1915, was cheerfully optimistic about the prospects for an advance up the Tigris. For sure, there was a solid practical reason for pushing forward: the Land of the Two Rivers was one of the world's great bread-baskets, the annexation of which might lift the shadow of famine from India.[12] Another consideration was the impact of Gallipoli on Muslim opinion, once Hamilton's last major offensive, in early August, had failed. According to the *Official History*, Britain's political leaders saw in Iraq an opportunity 'for a great success such as we had not yet achieved in any quarter, and the political (and even military) advantages which would follow from it throughout the East could not easily be overrated'.[13] For the men on the ground, there was also personal ambition. A dazzling prize lay before them: Baghdad, the fabled medieval City of the Caliphs. History beckoned. Cox and Nixon aspired to a place in the annals.[14]

It is 500 miles from Basra to Baghdad. As the Mesopotamia Expeditionary Force fought its way upriver in the summer of 1915, the temperature in the shade sometimes hit 49°C. Because the Indian Army had no experience of large-scale military operations – it was accustomed to sending small punitive columns into the mountains – the logistics were a shambles. Basra became a bottleneck, and there were never enough river craft. The inadequate medical services were overwhelmed by sunstroke and dysentery sufferers even before large numbers of combat casualties began to arrive. But the Ottoman resistance seemed weak, the British and Indian troops won a succession of quick victories, and Major-General Charles Townshend, spearheading the advance with a rein-forced 6th Division, was urged to press on.[15]

The euphoria ended at the Battle of Ctesiphon, fought 20 miles south of Baghdad over the four days of 22–5 November. The entrenched Ottomans, recently reinforced by a crack Anatolian division, were 20,000 strong. Townshend's ambitious plan was to fix the main enemy line while hooking around his open left, but he had only 12,000 men with which to do this: far too few. Deluged with Ottoman artillery and machine-gun fire as they advanced over flat ground almost devoid of cover, the British and Indian soldiers of 6th Division lost 4,500 men on the first day of the battle. Though subsequent counter-attacks were repulsed, and the Ottoman commander felt obliged to pull back, Townshend's force was broken-backed: with 40 per cent casualties at the end of the battle, he retreated to his forward base at Kut al-Amara.[16]

Reaching Kut on 3 December, Townshend decided to hold fast. Three days later, the Ottoman Army closed around the town, a collection of mud-houses in a sinuous loop of the Tigris about a mile wide, and put it under siege. Townshend seems to have lost his grip. He retained within his perimeter a population of 6,000 Arabs – extra mouths to feed – in addition to the garrison of 13,000 British and Indian troops. He failed to organise a systematic search for food, and he did not reduce rations until two months had elapsed. He sent a succession of messages to his superiors that were often inaccurate, sometimes contradictory, occasionally hysterical. He made no attempt to support relief operations by mounting sorties even when the sound of heavy gunfire indi-cated a major battle in progress.[17]

The relief effort was hamstrung by the same logistical failures that had viti-ated the entire campaign. Witness to this was none other than T.E. Lawrence, the Cairo-based intelligence officer, who arrived in Mesopotamia at the begin-ning of April. Though still a very junior officer (he was now a captain), he had been dispatched to assist in a mission of exceptional importance – one with which, owing to its morally unsavoury character, more senior officers had disdained to be associated. Being Lawrence, he took the opportunity to carry out an unofficial military inspection. According to one of his superiors, the report he submitted when he returned to Egypt was so scathing that it had to be bowdlerised before it could be set before Sir Archibald Murray, the new commander-in-chief in Egypt.

> He criticised the quality of the stones used for lithographing, the system of berthing barges alongside quays, the inefficiency of the cranes for handling stores, the lack of system in shunting and entraining on the railways, the want of adequate medical stores, the blindness of the medical authorities and their want of imagination as to their probable requirements. And, horror of horrors, he criticised the higher command and the conduct of the campaign in general![18]

In due course, however, a parliamentary enquiry would come to substantially the same conclusion as the obscure captain. The fatal weakness was lack of river transport:

> Large reinforcements could not be moved to the front in time to take part in critical battles … Looking at the facts, which from the first must have been apparent to any administrator, military or civilian, who gave a few minutes' consideration to the map and to the conditions in Mesopotamia, the want of foresight and provision for the most fundamental needs of the expedition reflects discredit upon the organising aptitude of all the authorities concerned.[19]

The shambles was of Crimean proportions. Without adequate river transport, arrangements for the evacuation of the wounded degenerated into chaos and filth. Men with untreated wounds lay in their own shit on the open decks of slow-moving riverboats as they chugged southwards. 'When the *Mejidieh* was about 300 yards off,' recalled one observer describing its arrival at the base hospital at Basra, 'it looked as if she were festooned with ropes. The stench when she was close was quite definite, and I found that what I mistook for ropes were dried stalactites of human faeces. The patients were so crowded and huddled together on the ship that they could not perform the offices of nature clear of the ship's edge.'[20]

Inside the besieged town, meanwhile, conditions had deteriorated rapidly in the early months of 1916. With temperatures below freezing each night through January and February, men were afflicted with frostbite and trench rheumatism. The annual Tigris floods reached Kut the following month, collapsing trenches and creating lakes of mud. The landscape became a sweltering marsh; the air filled with disease-bearing insects; a foul stench assailed the soldiers sweating and wilting in the trenches. By this time, rations had been cut back heavily and men were so weakened by hunger that they fainted on sentry-duty and were incapable of fatigues. The Indian soldiers – many of whom steadfastly refused to eat horsemeat for religious reasons – appeared to be in a state of semi-starvation. The disease rate soared, and by late April there were fifteen men dying from dysentery alone every day. By then, too, food was running out. Surrender negotiations commenced on 26 April.[21]

* * *

Three days later, three British officers advanced under a white flag a couple of hundred yards into the no-man's-land between the opposing trench-lines at Kut. The senior was Colonel Edward Beach, and he was accompanied by Captains Aubrey Herbert and Edward Lawrence, both of Cairo Military Intelligence. Since they were seeking a meeting with the Ottoman commander, General Khalil Pasha, they were kept waiting in the sun several hours while the necessary enquiries were made. Standing on an open plain with the river to the north, they became aware of 'an unpleasant battlefield smell round us'. They then noticed that 'the place [was] crawling with huge black beetles and singing flies that had both been feeding on the dead'.[22]

The prospect of surrender at Kut – within six months of the defeat on Gallipoli – had been concentrating British minds since the failure of a second attempt to relieve the town on 8 March. There were gloomy predictions of pan-Islamic insurgency all the way from India to Egypt.[23] Townshend had become preoccupied with securing 'reasonable and honourable terms' while still able to negotiate from a position of relative strength. His superiors were horrified. The new GOC (general officer commanding) in Mesopotamia, General Sir Percy Lake – a steady pair of hands sent out to replace the swashbuckling Nixon as the latter's plans unravelled – could see no advantage in negotiations 'at this stage'. 'Moreover,' he continued, 'the mere fact of your asking for terms would at once be published abroad, and would produce evil effects as regards loss of prestige scarcely less than those involved by the enforced surrender of Kut ...' London and Simla (as the Government of India was commonly known) concurred. The British were subsequently to find reassurance in the fact that it was Khalil who first sought negotiations: his overtures could surely be taken as confirmation that 'the difficulties of the Turks are serious'.[24]

But on 22 April the relief force suffered a third major defeat. Despite three weeks of fighting and almost 10,000 casualties, it was still 12 miles from Kut, with no chance of launching another attack any time soon. Three days later, moreover, a paddle-steamer – armour-plated, sandbagged and loaded with 270 tons of supplies – failed in its attempt to run the blockade; it was stopped by a steel hawser stretched across the river and all of the crew killed, wounded, or taken prisoner.[25] The fall of Kut became inevitable. The only question remaining was the terms.

The three British officers waiting in no-man's-land were hoping to nego-tiate something more 'honourable' than unconditional surrender. A prior attempt to instigate an anti-Ottoman revolt of the Iraqi tribes had crashed. Lawrence, acting on intelligence reports of an underground network of Iraqi-Arab nationalists, had held a secret meeting with one its presumed leaders in Basra, just prior to his journey downriver to Kut. The Iraqi notable in question had been aghast at the proposal.[26] Now, in company with Beach and Herbert, he was engaged in a final – and distinctly shady – attempt at damage limitation. At stake was the prestige of the British Empire.

The three men were in the unusual position for king's officers of being empowered to offer a bribe of up to £1 million. The idea seems to have origi-nated with Kitchener, whose experience of the endemic corruption inside the Ottoman Empire gave him hope that a well-placed payment might loosen the enemy's grip on Kut. Many were sceptical. Some were affronted and refused to have anything to do with the matter. Others feared that the damage to British prestige when the news got out – as surely it would if the bribe were rejected – would be every bit as serious as actual capitulation. Such, indeed, was the dubious nature of the project that responsibility for it had descended to a rela-tively junior officer. Lawrence would later become 'the man with the gold' – the bearer of British treasure with which to buy Arab service. His arrival at Basra on 3 April was an early anticipation of this role – only it was a Turk, not an Arab, he had come to buy. 'Most secret and for you personally,' cabled London to General Lake in Mesopotamia. 'Captain Lawrence is due at Basra ... to consult with you and if possible purchase one of the Turkish leaders of the Mesopotamian Army ... You are authorised to expend for this purpose any sum not exceeding one million pounds.'[27]

By the time the three officers had been led blindfold through the Ottoman lines to Khalil Pasha's tent 4 miles behind the front, it was mid-afternoon. Colonel Khalil Pasha was an exemplar of the Young Turk. An officer in his mid-thirties, he was trim, good-looking and moustachioed, much like his close kinsman, the War Minister Enver Pasha. His association with Enver, combined with party loyalty, had ensured rapid ascent in just three years from captain to colonel. He would shortly be promoted to general in recognition of his newly acquired status as 'Hero of Kut' – a status now assured by the fact that General Townshend had given his surrender in the early hours of that very morning.[28] This, though, had not been known to the three British officers when they had stepped out into no-man's-land. Nor, it seems, were they aware that the bribe had already been rejected. Townshend had made the offer to Khalil two days before, Khalil had forwarded the information to Enver, and Enver had returned a categorical refusal to accept payment for improved surrender terms.[29] The Ottomans craved the glory of another unequivocal triumph over the British Empire.

Beach, Herbert and Lawrence were soon made aware that Townshend had surrendered and destroyed his guns. Khalil had already agreed to another British request: that the British sick and wounded be evacuated in exchange for healthy Ottomans in British prisoner-of-war camps. Might the exchange be extended to cover all men, Beach enquired, through Herbert, who spoke in French? The matter would be referred to higher authority, replied Khalil. But he was not optimistic; and he would insist on exchanging Britons for Turks, Indians for Arabs. The matter lapsed. Then the money question was raised, suitably disguised: might 'financial support for the civilians of Kut' be acceptable? This was brushed aside with contempt.

Then it was Khalil's turn. Were the British able to lend riverboats for transporting the prisoners up the Tigris to Baghdad, these to be returned afterwards? Beach knew this was impossible – the British did not have enough river transport for their own use, even had they believed the Ottomans could be trusted. Then Khalil referred to the Arab population of Kut: he could give no guarantees regarding their fate. The meeting fizzled out. The Ottoman commander yawned, gave his apologies, and explained that he had much work to do. The hour was late, so the three officers were fed and accommodated.[30] Thus did the man who would become Lawrence of Arabia spend the night of 29/30 April 1916 sleeping in an Ottoman Army camp of 20,000 men.

Khalil Pasha's middle-class manners belied his true nature. He may have observed the courtesies when receiving Beach, Herbert and Lawrence, and he subsequently ensured that General Townshend travelled in comfort by road and rail to a pleasant confinement for the rest of the war in the former British Consul's summer residence on the Bosphorus. But Khalil was a mass murderer, one of the leading architects of the Armenian genocide, and the fate of the British and Indian soldiers taken prisoner at Kut was very different from that of their general. Already weakened by hunger, many died as they were marched through the desert with inadequate provision for water, food and medical care. The officers were then interned in tolerable camps, but the common soldiers were confined in conditions which made survival barely possible. The Indians suffered most: both soldiers and non-combatants – amounting to three-quarters of the prisoners from Kut – were employed as slave labour on the Baghdad Railway. More than two-thirds of the 12,000 men who surrendered at Kut never returned home.[31]

It was the worst mass surrender in the long history of the British Army. It ratcheted official worries about *jihad* up to a new level. The official report, published in June 1917, was damning. 'I regret to have to say', intoned Lord Curzon, the former Viceroy of India and current War Cabinet member, 'that a more shocking exposure of official blundering and incompetence has not in my opinion been made, at any rate since the Crimean War.'[32] Imperial *hubris* had been partly to blame. Cox and Nixon had shared the racial arrogance of Hamilton, proceeding without due planning and preparation in the conviction that their enemy was contemptible. But the Ottoman soldier had again confounded expectations. General Lake was in no doubt that success had eluded the British 'owing to the undoubtedly fine fighting qualities of the troops who are now opposed to us'.[33]

* * *

Mesopotamia – with its oil and overland access to the Raj – was too important to be left to the amateurs of the Government of India. The British War Office assumed responsibility and appointed Lieutenant-General Sir Stanley Maude to command. Maude, a veteran of South Africa, the Western Front and Gallipoli, was a competent manager of an industrialised war.[34] Basra was transformed into an efficient supply-port. The river transport and medical services were reorganised and massively expanded. The Mesopotamia Expeditionary Force swelled to 150,000 men, giving Maude a three-to-one numerical advantage over the Ottomans, and in December 1916 he began a methodical campaign to fight his way up the Tigris to Baghdad. Khalil Pasha's Sixth Army suffered decisive defeat at the Second Battle of Kut in late February, and the City of the Caliphs fell to the British on 11 March 1917.[35]

But this was not the knock-out blow it might have been. Baghdad was separated from Damascus by almost 500 miles of desert. For modern armies, with their huge logistical tails, the only manageable routeways ran north–south. Beckoning from the north, moreover, lay the oil-wells of Mosul, a valuable imperial prize in themselves, some 250 miles distant. These became the new objective once the summer heat had waned. But Ottoman resistance in northern Mesopotamia, well directed by German officers, proved intractable. By the end of 1917, though the Anglo-Indian Army had grown to more than

400,000, it was unable to finish a war against an enemy with barely a tenth of its strength.[36]

The Russian Revolution added a new layer of complexity. The vacuum left by the collapse of the tsarist state saw rival British and German-Ottoman forces racing for the Baku oil-wells in early 1918. The conflict soon spilled over the border into the oil-producing regions of north-western Persia. The whole Caspian Basin was convulsed by a chaotic multi-sided struggle involving the Ottomans, the British, local irregulars, tsarist Cossacks and the Bolsheviks. Oil was the prize: the Mesopotamian war had been transformed into a naked imperialist land-grab. The British seized Baku in August 1918, but were ejected the following month. They then took both Mosul and Baku during separate operations in November.[37]

Logistics, the lure of black gold and the dogged resilience of the Turkish soldier: all three factors helped keep the huge Mesopotamian Expeditionary Force tied up east of the Euphrates for the rest of the war. By the end, Lieutenant-General Sir William Marshall – who replaced Maude when he died of cholera – had 500,000 men and the largest river-fleet in the world under his command. The Ottoman forces in theatre may have shrunk to as few as 20,000.[38]

* * *

There was something else about Anglo-Indian operations in Iraq: another factor that Captain Lawrence had noticed during his visit to the front in April 1916 – though it had not found its way into his official report. He had been shocked by the attitude of Indian Army officers both to their own native troops and to the local Arabs. He had judged it a fatal weakness that the Anglo-Indian Army made no attempt to win hearts and minds: cooperation with the Arabs 'was not the way of the directing parties there . . . and till the end of the war the British in Mesopotamia remained substantially an alien force invading enemy territory, with the local people passively neutral or sullenly against them.'[39]

Lower Mesopotamia's intricate maze of waterways, with its mud-houses, irrigated gardens, date palms and green expanses of reed-bed, was densely populated by Shia 'Marsh Arabs'. The arid plains beyond, to east and west, were the haunt of nomadic Bedouin. A few of the tribes were pro-British, more were pro-Ottoman, and a majority were neutral. Raiding was widespread, however, and being neutral simply meant that targeting was indiscriminate. The Anglo-Indian forces found themselves fighting organised tribal contingents on the battlefield, and an epidemic of sniping and pilfering in the rear. Attacks on military bases became so frequent that they took on a ritualistic character, with drumming, dancing and war-cries followed by sporadic fire from a variety of modern rifles, single-shot breech-loaders and antiquated muskets. British soldiers called these attacks 'Salvation Army Meetings' and dubbed one notable individual equipped with a large-bore musket 'Blunderbuss Bill'; they referred to hostile Arab irregulars in general as 'Budhoos'.[40]

More serious were two full-scale attacks by combined forces of Ottoman regulars and Arab or Kurdish irregulars, the first about 10,000 strong against the Persian oil installations at Ahwaz in January 1915, the second, almost 20,000 strong, against Basra itself the following April. Later, on the night of 13/14 July, during an operation to dislodge strongly entrenched Ottoman regulars at Nasiriyeh, the British were attacked in the rear by hostile Marsh Arabs. At the Battle of Ctesiphon in late November, it was partly the action of Arab horsemen on his desert flank that compelled Townshend to retreat to Kut.[41] 'Many of them had joined what they now believed to be the winning side,' reported *The Times*, 'and it was evident that the British might soon find their retreat intercepted. Enemy horsemen were reported even below Kut.'[42] Enthusiastic crowds celebrated Ottoman victories that year in both Baghdad and the Shia holy city of Najaf.[43]

The problem eased with the British capture of Baghdad and growing efforts by some of the more enlightened Anglo-Indian officers to win local support. Many tribesmen abandoned the Ottoman service as the tide of war turned, while units of Arab police, Bedouin scouts, and Kurdish cavalry were raised by the British.[44] But the shift of allegiance was but a veneer; most Iraqis were loyal to their own interests, not to any imperial power. Anglo-Indian policy did nothing to change that. After the war, Lawrence, then a retired colonel, wrote a scathing letter to *The Times* about the occupation of Iraq:

> The government we have set up is English in fashion, and is conducted in the English language. So it has 450 British executive officers running it, and not a single responsible Mesopotamian. In Turkish days, 70 per cent of the executive civil service was local. Our 80,000 troops there are occupied in police duties, not in guarding the frontiers. They are holding down the people. In Turkish days, the two army corps in Mesopotamia were 60 per cent Arab in officers, 95 per cent in other ranks.[45]

The Anglo-Indian intervention in Mesopotamia was, then, an imperialist occupation based on racial exclusion and military repression. This was not the least of the reasons that the Mesopotamian Expeditionary Force became bogged down north of Baghdad in a war it seemed incapable of ending even as its strength in theatre soared towards half a million men. The problem was not simply the deeply ingrained assumptions of racial superiority imported from

India along with the baggage and batmen of the white officer caste. Memory of the Mutiny weighed on the minds of the Anglo-Indian elite as a nightmare. They feared nationalist and jihadist revolt above all else, and in consequence viewed with deep suspicion even the most minimal proposals for the advancement of native people to a role in government.

Lord Hardinge, the viceroy, put it thus in a cable to London in October 1915:

> We have always regarded . . . the creation of a strong Arab state lying astride our interests in the East and in the Gulf as a not unlikely source of ultimate trouble . . . We have always contemplated as a minimum the eventual annexation of Basra *vilayet* and some form of native administration in Baghdad *vilayet* under our close political control.

This view was shared by General Nixon, at the time still GOC Mesopotamia:

> The formation of an autonomous state in Iraq appears to be impossible and unnecessary. Here in Iraq there is no sign of the slightest ambition of the kind among the people, who expect and seem to be quite ready to accept our administration . . . we are of the opinion that . . . it is highly inexpedient and unnecessary to put into the heads of the backward people of the country . . . visionary and premature notions of the creation of an Arab state – notions which will tend to make endless difficulties for Great Britain here and serve no present purpose but to stimulate a small section of ambitious men to turn their activities to a direction from which it is highly desirable to keep them for many years to come.[46]

Cairo took a different view. Indeed, an influential group of diplomats and officers – including the Intelligence Department's most hyperactive officer – was hatching an elaborate scheme liable to do precisely what men like Hardinge and Nixon feared most: encourage 'visionary and premature notions of the creation of an Arab state'. It was not that the Anglo-Egyptian elite feared popular revolt any less than their Anglo-Indian cousins; but they had rather more creative ideas about dealing with the danger. While 'Indian' officials thought in terms of repression, 'Egyptian' officials envisaged incorporation. Their ambitious proposal was to attempt to transform both the embryonic Arab national movement and the Bedouin tradition of desert raiding into proxy forces in the service of the British Empire. Kut had heightened the sense of urgency. In the view of Sir Henry McMahon, the British high commissioner in Egypt, 'The serious situation . . . now facing us in Egypt and Mesopotamia renders the alienation of Arab assistance from the Turks a matter of great importance, and we must make every effort to enlist the sympathy and assistance, even though passive, of the Arab people.' Whitehall agreed; so alarmed were some Foreign Office officials that they warned of possible wholesale British withdrawal from the Western Front 'to face Muhammadan risings in all our possessions'.[47]

Iraq was not the only source of anxiety; another had emerged on the opposite flank of Britain's growing Middle Eastern empire. In November 1915, just as the British generals were facing up to the reality of defeat on Gallipoli, Egypt had been invaded from the Western Desert – by a formidable alliance of Ottoman officers, Senussi jihadists and Berber tribesmen.

* * *

The invasion had been a long time coming. Nine months before, a small boat loaded with cheap arms and ammunition had been run to shore on the Libyan coast at Dafnah, just west of the Egyptian border. It was operated by a Beirut gun-runner, but he was working to hire for two enterprising Ottoman officers, Nuri Pasha, a half-brother of Enver, and Jafar Pasha al-Askari, an Iraqi Arab.

Jafar was 30 and already somewhat wide of girth – not ideal for active service, especially in the heat of the desert. (An escape attempt subsequent to his capture by the British would be frustrated when a rope of army blankets gave way under the strain, causing him to fall and break his ankle.) He was, nonetheless, a thoroughly professional officer. He had sailed down the Tigris from his home-town of Mosul on a *kalak* – a crude river-raft buoyed by inflated animal-skins – to enter the Military School at Baghdad. From there he had transferred to the Military College at Constantinople, before graduating as a lieutenant in the Ottoman Army at the age of 19. Like many young career officers, both Turkish and Arab, he had been radicalised by the corruption, misgovernment and backwardness of the decaying empire. After the 1908 Revolution, he had enjoyed the privilege of being selected for further military training in Berlin – where he had been impressed by 'German efficiency, earnestness and industry' – before returning home to take part in the Balkan Wars. Now, in February 1915, this exemplary officer found himself landing on an alien shore to undertake a mission of supreme importance; one that would require political finesse, organisational skill and strategic vision, all in the highest degree.[48]

Two days after landing, Nuri and Jafar had their first meeting with Sayyid Ahmad al-Senussi, the politico-religious leader of the Senussi, an Islamist revival movement founded in the middle of the nineteenth century. The movement had spread its influence across much of the Sahara, establishing *zawiyas*

or 'lodges' in most of the major oases of the Western Desert. Though fundamentalist in advocating a return to the true Islamic *tariqa* or 'way', the Senussi
were not persecutors, and their influence among the nomadic Berber tribes of
the desert – who wore their religion lightly – was strong.

The success of traditional Islamist movements often depended upon cooperation between 'desert and sown'. So it was with the Senussi. The oases, with
their pools, wells and cisterns, were the crossing-points and way-stations of the
desert trade-routes; but they also sustained a modest settled life based on cultivation, and Senussi settlements typically comprised a warren of mud-brick
houses, courtyards, gardens and narrow lanes, along with mosque, schoolroom, barracks and storerooms. An outer defensive wall often enclosed the
whole. The resident *ikhwan* or 'brothers' were organised as both a religious
community and a military force. Thus, with its 'capital' at Kufra, deep in the
Sahara, and a web of local *zawiyas* extending across 1,500 miles, the Senussi
power was a loosely structured theocratic confederacy that filled the desert
spaces between Italian-dominated coastal Libya, French-dominated Central
Africa, and British-dominated Egypt and Sudan.[49]

Though the Senussi had declined to make common cause with the Sudanese
Dervishes, they had demonstrated their military potential in recent wars
against both French and Italian colonial forces – especially the latter. Ottoman
resistance to the Italian invasion of Libya in 1911 had been defeated quickly in
the coastal areas, but Senussi guerrilla warfare in the hinterland, especially in
Cyrenaica, had been a different matter, continuing long after the Turks themselves had given up the struggle; indeed, the Italians would not succeed in fully
'pacifying' Libya for twenty years. On 26 August 1914 – the very day the British
Expeditionary Force was making its gallant little stand at Le Cateau on the
Western Front – an Italian supply-column was attacked and virtually destroyed
by Senussi guerrillas. Despite the use of mobile columns, local proxies, aerial
bombing and telegraph lines, the Italians found themselves bogged down in an
intractable counter-insurgency campaign; widespread atrocities seem merely
to have fuelled the resistance.[50]

The success of Nuri and Jafar's mission depended upon persuading Sayyid
Ahmad to open a third front against the British. All the great powers had, for a
variety of reasons, been willing to grant Italy a free hand in Libya in 1911; all,
equally, had been content that Italy should then have become tied down there.
The outbreak of the European war had, however, reconfigured the Libyan
crisis. The Kaiser and his Ottoman allies now hoped to redirect Senussi ener-
gies against the British. A message was dispatched from Berlin – written in
Arabic and carried in an embossed casket – in which 'Emperor William, son of
Charlemagne, Allah's Envoy, Islam's Protector' expressed a desire to see Senussi

warriors 'expel infidels from territory that belongs to true believers and their commander'. To assist, the Kaiser offered 'arms, money and tried chiefs'. Thus, he suggested, 'our common enemies, whom Allah annihilate to the last man, shall fly before thee'.[51]

Meantime, the Entente powers were as eager to quench the Senussi insurgency as the Kaiser was to inflame it. When Nuri and Jafar arrived in Libya, the British had only just repelled Djemal Pasha's assault on the Suez Canal. They feared a war on two fronts that would trigger insurrections across Egypt and the Sudan. This was precisely what the two Ottoman officers were aiming at. 'We lived in hope that some of the Egyptian tribes would join our forces,' Jafar later recalled, 'stage internal revolts in Egyptian cities and start guerrilla operations, thus distracting and tying down enemy troops as much as possible.'[52] His British enemies would later acknowledge the Iraqi officer's worth, rating him 'an excellent trainer of men' who ensured that 'the troops of the Senussi would be formidable opponents'.[53]

Time – alongside space, force and morale – is one of war's primary dimensions. It favoured the British as events unfolded around Egypt between February 1915 and August 1916: at no point over these eighteen months were the Ottomans able to coordinate the variegated strategic threats to British rule in Egypt. Sayyid Ahmad had enjoyed good relations with the British and was loath to jeopardise these by hurling his followers into a war against them on behalf of the Ottoman Empire and its German allies. Nuri and Jafar's efforts to persuade him otherwise were for long unavailing. Among other things, they found themselves hamstrung by the predictions of an Algerian astrologer, 'who was forever fiddling with an astrolabe and reciting our names one by one,' recalled Jafar. 'All the divinations and auguries he conjured from this instrument pointed to the same conclusion: that all our operations would end in complete failure.'[54] Thus did a medieval mystic delay the work of modern warlords.

But a steady trickle of guns and gold was destabilising the desert. Sayyid Ahmad had only loose control over his tribal confederates, and Nuri and Jafar were colluding with the wilder elements to engineer cross-border raids. At the same time, they told the Senussi chief that, since Italy had joined the Entente, 'there was no way of getting rid of them and saving his country unless he salvaged what he could from the situation by joining the Ottoman side wholeheartedly'. Now was the time, they argued, for him to make common cause with the Ottoman Empire and the Muslim masses living under infidel rule; 'much better to take advantage of such circumstances and not let the opportunity slip by'.[55]

It was events, though, rather than entreaty, that finally bounced Sayyid Ahmad into action. The fighting on the border escalated, engulfing the Awlad

Ali tribe, which was loyal to the Senussi but lived on the Egyptian side. A reli-gious leader and some tribesmen were killed in a skirmish. The British retreated and their abandoned camp was pillaged. Arab confidence rose and calls for vengeance became strident. With the Senussi chief's prestige at stake, he was left no scope for further procrastination: the invasion of British-ruled Egypt was on.[56]

* * *

The Ottoman-Senussi war plan was to raise an insurgency along the entire western border of Egypt and the Sudan. This would involve operations in three distinct zones: along the coastal strip; between the western oases and the lower Nile in Egypt; and between Darfur and the upper Nile in Sudan.

A string of scruffy settlements and areas of cultivation extended along the coastal strip. They were linked by a railway line that ran for about 100 miles west from Alexandria to Daaba, and then by a cleared track – grandly titled the 'Khedivial Motor Road' – that ran another 150 miles beyond that, passing through Mersa Matruh, Sidi Barrani and Sollum before reaching the Libyan border. Relatively large forces could operate in this zone – though movement might occasionally be paralysed by sticky mud during the short rainy season between December and March. A short distance inland, a high rocky escarp-ment rose above the plain, marking the edge of a hard desert plateau which extended about 150 miles southwards before dropping down to the Siwah oasis. This was the most northerly of a series of oases – the others were Baharia, Farafra, Dakhla and Kharga – that ran roughly north-west to south-east across almost 500 miles of desert. Between the oases and the Nile lay approximately 100 miles of soft, shifting sand dunes. Kharga was the effective limit of Senussi authority: the desert to the south was an impenetrable waste for hundreds of miles. But on the far side of this, at the western edge of the Sudan, some 1,200 miles from the coast, lay the semi-arid scrubland of Darfur, the territory of the Sultan Ali Dinar, a distant ally of the Senussi, the commander of an army of about 5,000 tribesmen, and the only major Sudanese leader who had failed to send a message of support to the Anglo-Egyptian authorities at the outbreak of war.[57]

The Senussi army that headed down the coast road into Egypt in November 1915 was the finest in the movement's history. Khaki-clad regulars of the *Muhafizia* battalions marched alongside hordes of tribal irregulars in white and yellow robes, many on horses or camels, the poorer men on foot. Also in the column were two mountain-guns and four machine-guns with their Ottoman crews. In total it was probably well above 2,000 strong – though the tribesmen tended to come and go – and its quality was a testimony to the organisational skill and political tact of Jafar, an Arab officer unusual in his ability to lead both regulars and irregulars with equal facility, and to weld them into an effective combined-arms force.[58] The defection of three Egyptian Camel Corps officers along with their men gave the invaders a welcome fillip.[59]

The outnumbered British fell back, pending the arrival of an improvised desert column – the Western Frontier Force – formed of a composite mounted brigade (cavalry, yeomanry, Australian Light Horse and Royal Horse Artillery) and a composite infantry brigade (three British territorial battalions and one of Indian Army Sikhs). This was supported by a Royal Naval warship offshore and a detachment of four Royal Naval armoured cars. The British were used to this sort of colonial 'small war', and they struck back suddenly at the Battle of Wadi Majid just west of Mersa Matruh on 25 December. Taking Jafar's men by surprise and panicking his tribesmen, they forced his regulars to abandon their position by raking them with naval gunfire, fixing them with a frontal attack, and sending a mounted column round their desert flank. The invasion was then rolled back along the coast.

When the Senussi attempted a major stand two months later, they fared no better. Jafar had handled his men well, keeping them to rough tracks and broken ground to still their fear of armoured cars. (There was less he could do, however, about aerial 'bombing' by reconnaissance pilots in the habit of lobbing grenades over the side of their planes as they passed by.)[60] Now, at Agagir on 26 February 1916, he deployed them in an area of sand dunes, 4 miles long by 3 wide, overlooking the coast road. But the British repeated their earlier tactics, pinning the Senussi riflemen with a frontal attack of infantry – this time involving two battalions of South Africans – while Dorset Yeomanry circled around the left flank and mounted a headlong charge across a thousand yards of open ground under machine-gun and rifle-fire from the 150-strong Senussi rearguard. Jafar was in the thick of it:

> In an instant enemy cavalry were charging down upon us regardless of life and limb. Soon they were in among us with their swords drawn, while we fought back with our rifles in savage close-quarters combat. I was slashed by a sword on my right arm and my pistol fell to the ground, and glancing behind I saw the officer who had wounded me a few paces away, having fallen from his horse, hit by a bullet from one of our men.

The Dorsets lost 58 of their 184 men, but the charge decided the battle: Jafar and two other Ottoman officers were captured, and the Senussi army was put to flight. There was little further fighting on the coast, and the British reoccupied Sollum on 14 March.[61]

The battle of the oases was more protracted. Sayyid Ahmad himself led the Senussi force that occupied the Baharia, Farafra, Dakhla and Kharga oases in February. The British were forced to deploy an infantry division and several brigades of yeomanry to defend Upper Egypt during the summer of 1916. Only in the autumn did a force of camel corps and armoured cars succeed in retaking the oases. Sayyid Ahmad was eventually pursued to Siwah, where the armoured cars inflicted a final defeat upon him in February 1917.[62] Long before this, his ally in Darfur had also been defeated – in May 1916 – by an Egyptian Army column supported by a detachment of BE2 aircraft of the Royal Flying Corps. The Battle of Beringia was a 40-minute miniature Omdurman, in which a small African army equipped with swords, spears and antiquated firearms was blasted off the battlefield by modern soldiers.[63]

The Senussi threat was liquidated and the war in the Western Desert ended. But the cost had been prodigious. The Ottomans had sent no more than 300 men to North Africa, and they had supplied only modest quantities of gold and munitions. The Senussi had never been able to field more than a few thousand warriors at any one time, and latterly they had defended the oases with probably no more than 2,000. Yet they had tied down more than 100,000 British, French and Italian troops.[64] The British, moreover, with 35,000 men committed, had been compelled to build a 350km narrow-gauge railway across the desert from the Nile to Bahariya oasis, defended by a string of fortified blockhouses.[65]

Such marked disproportion in the relative efforts of the protagonists made the Senussi War a spectacular lesson in the principle of 'economy of force'. As such, it both confirmed a danger and hinted at a possibility: the clear and present danger of an Ottoman-Islamic *jihad* directed at the European colonial regimes; and the intriguing possibility of an Arab revolt inside the Ottoman Empire that might cripple its military capacity.

Among those taking an interest was T.E. Lawrence. 'Perfect peace here,' he wrote home on 28 December 1915, 'except on the west, where there is a little war going on.'[66] Though his personal role in the anti-Senussi campaign was slight, the Cairo intelligence bureau to which he belonged was heavily involved, and its small size and informal *modus operandi* ensured that responsibilities were shared and all major developments intensively discussed. Lawrence in particular, because of his exceptional talents, seems to have had a hand in most aspects of the bureau's work. 'T.E. Lawrence,' wrote his Oxford mentor and wartime colleague David Hogarth, 'whose power of initiative, reasoned audacity, compelling personality, and singular persuasiveness I had often had reason to confess in past years, was still a second lieutenant in the Cairo Military

Intelligence, but, with a purpose more clearly foreseen than perhaps that of anyone else, he was already pulling the wires.'[67]

One specific task assigned to Lawrence was the invention of a new code for use by the Western Frontier Force in November 1915. The British high command was concerned that the Ottomans, with German technical assistance and/or information supplied by nationalist sympathisers in the Egyptian State Telegraph, might have broken the old cipher. After a morning devising the new code, Lawrence travelled down the coast to Sollum, near the Libyan border, to deliver it in person to the British commanding officer; a mission which earned him official listing for 'exemplary service' in the Western Desert campaign.[68] It would be surprising if this most perspicacious of officers had not drawn lessons from the Senussi War.

* * *

British Intelligence in Cairo acquired a new member on 26 November 1915: the renowned Middle Eastern traveller, explorer, and archaeologist Gertrude Bell. She was met by Hogarth and Lawrence upon arrival – after a 'horrible journey' from Marseilles due to 'almost continuous storm'. Hogarth, an old friend of Bell's, and the former director of the Carchemish dig, had arrived in Cairo in July in the hope of finding useful wartime employment for his talents. It was he who had invited Bell, thinking her recently acquired knowledge of the north Arabian tribes might come in useful. She was also acquainted with Lawrence, having spent a day in his company during a visit to Carchemish in May 1911. The two men escorted Bell to their hotel – the Continental – and the three later dined together. There was purpose in this solicitude.

Hogarth and Lawrence wished to enlist Bell's support for the intelligence bureau's favourite scheme. The assumption was that their guest's prestige as a Middle East expert, and her connections at the highest levels of British society, would prove advantageous to the advancement of a year-long obsession the arguments for which seemed inescapably compelling. They were not disappointed: three days later, Bell wrote a long letter to Lord Cromer, the former consul-general of Egypt, setting out forcefully the Cairo case she had heard over the dinner table. Her obligations to her hosts fulfilled, she then seems to have settled down to routine duties: 'I am helping Mr Hogarth to fill in the intelligence files with information as to the tribes and sheikhs,' she wrote. 'It's great fun and delightful to be working with him.'[69]

The Cairo scheme involved using British naval power to land a small army somewhere on the Syrian coast, so as to cut Ottoman communications with their armies in Mesopotamia and Palestine, and perhaps trigger an Arab nationalist rising in Syria. The obvious place at which to strike was Alexandretta, the point at which the Ottoman railway passed closest to the coast, before bifurcating into separate lines running east and south. A British lodgement astride the railway would, the argument ran, paralyse Ottoman offensive capability in the wider Middle Eastern theatre. The Suez Canal and the Persian oilfields were be secured by a bold application of what would later be called 'the indirect approach'. So obvious did it seem, in fact, that the scheme pre-dated the formation of the Cairo intelligence unit. General Maxwell, the British commander in Egypt, had proposed it to Kitchener as early as December 1914: 'If any diversion is contemplated, I think the easiest, safest, and most fruitful in results would be one at Alexandretta. There . . . we strike a vital blow at the railways and also hit German interests very hard . . . Alexandretta would not want a very large force. All other places . . . are too far from the Turkish lines of communications.'[70]

Lawrence and his colleagues may have been unaware of the origins of the scheme. They seem to have believed the conception theirs. Lawrence in particular later claimed that 'the Alexandretta scheme . . . was, from beginning to end, my invention, put forward necessarily through my chiefs'. What is true is that the Cairo Intelligence Department developed and promoted the idea during 1915. A memorandum issued in January stressed the strategic importance of Alexandretta itself: it had the only natural harbour on the Syrian coast and, because the Amanus railway tunnel had not yet been completed, the road that ran through the town was the main supply-line for the Ottoman armies to the east and the south. A second January memorandum focused on the Arab question. The Ottomans:

[feared] nothing so much as a landing by us in the north of Syria – they say themselves that this would be followed by a general defection of their Arab troops. There is no doubt that this fear is well founded, and that a general Arab revolt . . . would be the immediate result of our occupation of Alexandretta following on a defeat of the Turkish forces in the south . . .

And there was an interesting caveat: 'Within the last few years the Arab national feeling has developed to an astonishing degree, and while European [assistance] is a general demand, the partition of the Arab country between different European powers would be deeply resented.'[71]

This was an oblique reference to Britain's French allies, for whom 'partition of the Arab country' was precisely the intention; and herein lay an insuperable obstacle to fulfilment of the Alexandretta scheme. Each of the great powers had designs on the Ottoman Empire. Each had leverage. The Germans, with the

Austro-Hungarians in tow, currently held prime position, for they had an alliance with Young Turks and supported their ambitions with gold, armaments and military specialists. The Russians traditionally posed as defenders of the Armenians and the Orthodox Church. The French had for long proclaimed similar patronage of the Lebanese Maronites and other Catholics. These 'humanitarian' concerns overlapped with more substantive considerations – the territorial claims of the Russians on the Bosphorus and in the Caucasus, and the business interests of French capitalists in the Levant.

French banks had invested heavily in Ottoman debt and railway construction, and they had formed especially close links with the Maronite-Christian bourgeoisie. Lebanon had become France's Trojan Horse inside the Ottoman Empire, and the more outspoken French colonialists made no secret of their designs on Syria as a whole. For this reason, the French were regarded with grave suspicion by Arab nationalists in Beirut and Damascus; so much so that any successful Arab revolt in the region could be guaranteed to result in a strongly anti-French regime. This was well understood by the French. The Alexandretta scheme – described explicitly by one of its instigators as designed to trigger 'a war for liberty and small peoples, not for French financiers' – therefore hit a wall of hostility from Britain's principal wartime ally.[72] Sir Edward Grey, the British foreign secretary, cabled Sir Henry McMahon, the British high commissioner in Egypt, with the bad news: 'You must be careful ... not to arouse the susceptibilities of France about Syria; if this were done, our relations with France would be impaired in a way that would be most unfortunate while we are prosecuting a war in common.'[73]

Neither a British army on the Syrian coast nor an Arab rising in the Syrian hinterland were to be contemplated. The Middle East had been contracted out to the British, but they were there as guardians of the interests of their allies. That was the basis on which the French carried most of the burden of the fighting on the Western Front. The Cairo intelligence wonks were despondent. 'Everything has been left undone, that we ought to have done,' wrote Lawrence to a friend at home, 'and we have done nothing at all. So I'm as sick as might be, and yet not so sick as the rest of us ... do curse and spit at and abominate the F.O. [Foreign Office] and all its desolations. It has cogged all our dice against us.'

Lawrence's bitterness against the French was extreme – 'so far as Syria is concerned, it is France and not Turkey that is the enemy' – and this would henceforward shape his view of the war as a whole.[74] At stake was not simply a much canvassed strategic plan. There was something else: a quite different conception of empire. The French treated their colonies as outposts of France, appointing French officials to run local administration, encouraging the adoption of French language and culture, and regarding their subject-peoples as, in effect, trainee French citizens. The imperialists of the Third Republic took their responsibilities seriously: theirs was a 'civilising' mission, and, naturally, to be 'civilised' meant to be 'gallic'.[75]

The British were much more hands-off. They preferred to rule through local clients and let native custom prevail. Both approaches were equally arrogant, since both assumed that the native populations of the colonies were in some sense 'uncivilised'. The difference arose over whether the imperial mission involved teaching 'civilisation' (the French view) or 'respecting native traditions' (the British view). The latter position could be interpreted in one of two ways. The implication might be that the natives were beyond hope: mere racial inferiors who could never aspire to European standards. Alternatively, they might be seen as following their own pathway to independent nationhood, the imperial power acting as guardian and facilitator of this journey. This allowed a romantic Orientalist like Lawrence to regard the British imperial mission far more positively than he did the French: it could be squared with his ideal of a form of local autonomy and self-government little short of full independence. What was offensive was French determination to 'gallicise' the Arabs; whereas Lawrence, both during the war and after, was aiming for Arab self-rule under British hegemony. He would later claim, when something approximating this emerged in Iraq and Transjordan in 1921, that this was 'the big achievement of my life: of which the war was a preparation'.[76]

The failure of Gallipoli saw a brief revival of the Alexandretta scheme. Maxwell, fearing a flood of Ottoman soldiers to the Palestine front, again cabled London to urge an immediate occupation. Hogarth and Lawrence's assignation with Gertrude Bell was therefore part of a wider flurry of activity. Kitchener was persuaded at an emergency war council held aboard a warship in the Aegean; such was the sense of crisis in the Middle Eastern theatre that he had attended in person. But Kitchener's star was waning, and other senior officers harboured serious doubts about the strategic feasibility of the plan.[77] All agreed that it would require at least 100,000 men, perhaps 150,000, and 'the results of Gallipoli did not encourage further experiments in landing operations on a large scale'.[78] But it was the French who killed the idea. A note from the French Embassy to the British Foreign Office was unequivocal:

> French public opinion could not be indifferent to anything that would be attempted in a country they consider already as being intended to become a part of the future Syria; and they would require of the French government that not only could no military operation be undertaken in this particular country before it has been concerted between the Allies, but even that,

should such an action be taken, the greater part of the task should be entrusted to the French troops and the generals commanding them.[79]

Since no such troops were available, this ended the matter. Though Cairo continued its agitation for a month or so, it was now a forlorn effort. There would be no more 'indirect approaches': the Ottoman Empire was to be fought to its destruction from the bottom up.

The Intelligence Department plotters were, in any case, already hard at work on another scheme. They were assisted by a letter received in August 1915 from the Sherif Hussein, the Arab ruler of the Hijaz region of western Arabia. A direct descendant of the Prophet, Hussein was the guardian of the Muslim holy cities of Mecca and Medina. As such, he occupied prime position in the complex politics of Islamic *jihad* and Arab allegiance. Courted by the Turks, he had maintained a certain distance; most significantly, he had failed to endorse the Grand Mufti's declaration of Holy War in November 1914. In fact, he was already in secret correspondence with both the Arab nationalist underground and the British authorities in Egypt. Nonetheless, as Lawrence later recalled, Hussein's August letter came as something of a 'bombshell'. In it, he offered the British a military alliance in the war against the Ottoman Empire. His condition, however, was their agreement to a new Arab caliphate embracing the whole of Arabia, Syria and Mesopotamia.[80] The war in the Middle East was about to change shape.

CHAPTER 5

Sinai Bridgehead

'THE ENEMY SEEM to be contemplating pushing out a force into the Katia region at no very distant date . . . We are going to push out as soon as we can to Katia and deal with such of the enemy as may be there. I should not wonder if we had quite a scrap in that region before very long.'[1] Thus wrote Major-General Sir Arthur Lynden-Bell, chief-of-staff of the Mediterranean Expeditionary Force (MEF), to Brigadier-General Sir Frederick Maurice, director of military operations at the War Office, on 8 February 1916. He was right. The dissolution of the Gallipoli front had permitted a rapid build-up of Ottoman military strength on the far side of Sinai.

Djemal Pasha's Syrian command had been run down to just twelve Arab battalions without machine-guns or artillery during 1915. But he had used the time to levy fresh conscripts, build new railways and roads, and strengthen his defences. In particular, he had overseen the construction of 120 miles of railway line from Tulkeram in central Palestine, through Beersheba, the main Ottoman base in the south, to Auja and Kossaima at the eastern edge of Sinai.[2] The year 1915 was, he said, 'the year of preparation and consolidation'.[3] Then, as troops became available in early 1916, plans were advanced for a renewed assault on the canal – though Djemal remained cautious about what might be achieved: the declared aim was no longer to conquer Egypt, but to seize and fortify a position near Kantara and attempt to block the canal, or at least to bombard the ships using it.[4]

The ever-enterprising Bavarian Colonel Kress von Kressenstein – whose strategy of occasional pinprick desert raids had kept the British on edge over the preceding year – assembled a new Canal Expeditionary Force.[5] It comprised the 3rd (Turkish) Division, an Ottoman camel regiment and the German 'Pasha I Expedition' – 12,000 rifles, 38 machine-guns and 30 cannon, some 16,000 men in all. Pasha I was an elite composite formation, one of two making up the

German 'Asia Corps' that had been dispatched to bolster the Ottoman war-effort. It comprised a flight detachment of new Fokker fighters, eight machine-gun companies, four 150mm howitzers, two 100mm field-guns, two 210mm mortars, four anti-aircraft sections, two trench-mortar companies, a signal detachment, some motor-transport guns and two field hospitals. Kress's force also included two Austro-Hungarian mountain batteries.[6] In all, it amounted to a formidable battle-group: a solid mass of Turkish peasant-infantry framed by German staff officers, weapon specialists and modern kit. Smaller than the First Canal Expeditionary Force, the Second packed a harder punch.

Nonetheless, Kress's actual military potential was modest in comparison to the panic assessments circulating in Cairo. Lieutenant-General Sir Archibald Murray, the newly appointed MEF commander, had written to Sir William Robertson, Chief of the Imperial General Staff, on 15 February suggesting that the Ottomans might push a force of 250,000 across the desert come the spring. Robertson had replied on 27 February revising the estimate down to 100,000. But even this was wildly alarmist.[7] It grossly exaggerated the numbers of soldiers available to Ottoman commanders (a basic intelligence failing that recurred throughout the war), and failed to take proper account of the insuperable logistical constraints bearing down on all Ottoman military enterprise.[8] Even had the soldiers been available, only a fraction of the numbers in the British estimates could have been supplied in any advance across Sinai. This, according to Kress, was always the dominant factor: 'from the first day of the war to the last, the lines of communication worked badly, and to this must largely be attributed the series of disasters which befell the Turks.'[9] None was in a better position to know. The Second Canal Expeditionary Force must therefore be regarded as another startling exercise in 'economy of force': because it triggered acute anxieties about the security of Egypt and the canal, and because its size was magnified many times over in the minds of British generals, Kress's little army was responsible for tying down men and materiel out of all proportion to the actual threat posed.

What made sober assessment harder was the British high command's growing worry about social discontent and nationalist agitation as the war entered its third year. Lynden-Bell and Maurice were friends – they addressed one another as 'Belinda' and 'Freddie' even in official letters – and they used their correspondence to share a range of fears and frustrations. At home there were strikes on the Clyde in the spring of 1916. As Maurice explained on 30 March: 'They [the government] are ... having considerable difficulty with the Clyde strike, which is really a syndicalist "Stop the War" movement and is not in connection with any labour organisation.'[10] A little later, news of the

Easter Rising in Dublin seems to have reinforced Lynden-Bell's worries about security in Cairo: on 22 May he wrote:

> I don't like to take too many of these garrison battalions away from the delta, because ... the Boches are doing their very best to make trouble, and above all we want to avoid any chance of having a show such as they had in Dublin. I feel quite certain that the Boches are doing everything they can to cause trouble among the native population, and we must be prepared for outbreaks ...[11]

Early the following month, with an Ottoman attack on the canal looking ever more imminent, Lynden-Bell was reporting a security crackdown in Cairo. Twenty foreign nationals – 'nearly all Austrians and Germans protected by Swiss nationality' – had been arrested, suspected of trying to foment a nationalist rising; though there was no direct proof, 'the situation ... is such out here that we cannot afford to take any risks'. The enemy within proved a many-headed hydra. Further round-ups were soon cutting a swathe through the ranks of known and suspected Egyptian nationalists: 'The arrest and deportation of undesirables has had a most excellent effect here ... We are preparing another scoop and are gradually getting rid of Egyptian undesirables to St Helena.' The estimated 80,000 Turks in Egypt were also cause for concern, Lynden-Bell reporting that he hoped 'to make a big hole in this lot before long'.[12]

The British were also taking measures to improve the military security of the canal itself. Pre-war planning had assumed the canal to be the obvious main line of defence on Egypt's eastern frontier. There were three main reasons for this. First, it forced the Ottomans to bear the heavy logistical burden inherent in attempting to project military force across the Sinai Desert. Second, it allowed the British to fight close to their main base of supply, with ready access to existing railheads and ample fresh water. Third, it permitted the use of naval warships as mobile artillery along the whole of the front-line. These factors had proved decisive in the defeat of the First Canal Expeditionary Force in January–February 1915. But there was an obvious disadvantage. To forego control of the east bank was to expose the canal to a crippling attack should the enemy establish himself within artillery range. It was to treat the canal as a defensive moat, turning a global strategic asset into a local tactical feature; it meant, in the words of the British *Official History*, 'the employment of the Empire's main line of communication as an obstacle in front of a fire trench'.[13] This was acceptable only as a last resort: that is, in the absence of the forces necessary to contest control of the desert beyond. Such forces became available with the arrival of Gallipoli evacuees from November 1915 onwards, and

Kitchener, visiting at this time, is reported to have asked the British high command the acid question: 'Is the garrison of Egypt defending the canal, or is the canal defending the garrison of Egypt?'[14]

The truth was that the British in Egypt had succumbed to a siege mentality. Lynden-Bell, viewing matters with the critical eye of a newly arrived Anglo-Irish professional, suspected that 'oriental' lethargy had got a grip. 'The great difficulty in Egypt has been to produce an atmosphere of war,' he wrote to Maurice on 16 January. 'Up to the time of our arrival, the whole idea in Egypt appeared to be amusement and having a good time, and the state of Cairo and Alexandria was a positive scandal, thousands of officers hanging about the hotels, and an enormous number of women, mostly Australians and Americans.'[15]

The root of the problem, according to Lynden-Bell, was Lieutenant-General Sir John Maxwell, the British commander in Egypt. References to Maxwell were frequent and acerbic in Lynden-Bell's letters to the War Office. Maxwell, it seems, was 'quite incapable of running a big show' and forever 'making rather an ass of himself'.[16] London appears to have concurred. The Gallipoli evacuation had created an anomalous divided command in Egypt, with Maxwell in charge of the existing garrison, and Murray, Lynden-Bell's GOC (general officer commanding), in charge of the Mediterranean Expeditionary Force, which was now guarding the canal. On 10 March a telegram duly arrived informing Murray that the two forces in Egypt were to be united under his sole command and renamed the Egyptian Expeditionary Force (EEF). Maxwell was to return home. Lynden-Bell thought the news 'came as an absolute bomb to him'.[17]

* * *

The war had already entered a new phase. The British had begun work on a forward line in December, located on average about 11,000 yards east of the canal, beyond the limit of long-range artillery fire. A second line of works was planned midway between the first and the canal, while a third was to comprise fortified bridgeheads on the bank itself. Construction required a heavy expenditure in labour and materials over many weeks. Mile upon mile of trenches had to be dug, wired and revetted. More than a hundred miles of light railway, metalled road and pipeline were laid down.[18]

This was not the limit of Murray's endeavours. He was in fact implementing an 'offensive-defensive' strategy, not only pushing his principal line around 6 miles forward of the canal, but also attempting to block the main avenues of advance across the desert beyond by securing the oases. He had no orders to take the offensive *per se*; on the contrary, he was explicitly reminded that the force under his command was 'a general strategic reserve for the empire', that 'France is the main theatre of war' and that no more troops were to be maintained in Egypt than were 'absolutely necessary'.[19] For the time being, Egypt was to be thought of as a staging-post (on the route from the East), a training camp (for troops in transit) and a strategic reserve (for the war-effort as a whole) – but not as the base for an attack on the Ottoman Empire.[20] On the other hand, 'no formed body of the enemy should come within artillery range of the canal', and, furthermore, he was 'to endeavour by all means to interfere with the enemy's advanced base and lines of communication'.[21] Given that the enemy's forward base lay more than a hundred miles from the canal on the opposite side of Sinai, it is a moot point whether Murray's orders were internally consistent. They certainly appeared to give scope to an enterprising commander and his more gung-ho subordinates.

Murray concluded that passive defence of the canal – on whatever line – was wasteful of men and materiel. The key to its defence was control of the northern routeway from Arish via Katia to Kantara. Arish, indeed, could be considered the key to Sinai as a whole, since its possession would block the northern route, threaten the flank of any attempt to use the central or southern routes instead, and provide a launch-pad for operations against the enemy's main bases in southern Palestine. To secure Arish, however, it would be necessary to build a railway, this being the only way to supply a large garrison at such a distance. This in turn would necessitate a series of jumps forward as the railhead advanced across the desert. The first jump would necessarily be to Katia, some 25 miles east of the canal, the westernmost of a series of major oases which extended for 15 miles to Bir al-Abd. In this zone – but not beyond – the water supply was plentiful and drinkable, though somewhat brackish. Murray duly received War Office authorisation to make the initial move to Katia. The question of a subsequent advance to Arish was left open for the time being: the working assumption remained that the British would meet an offensive threat on their own side of the desert.[22]

In the early spring of 1916, therefore, both the Ottomans and the British were pushing forward in Sinai. Since sustained large-scale operations were possible only in the north, where water was relatively abundant, both sides were edging towards each other from either end of the coastal route. The focus on the northern edge of the desert suited the British well, since they enjoyed naval supremacy and the ships of the Mediterranean Fleet could secure the left flank, bring in supplies, and provide fire support for land operations.[23] The 40-mile zone between Kantara and Bir al-Abd was thus about to become the war's new centre of gravity. It would remain so throughout the hot summer months to follow.

On 22 April, the British 5th (Yeomanry) Mounted Brigade was in the Katia district, covering the construction of the railway, which had now reached

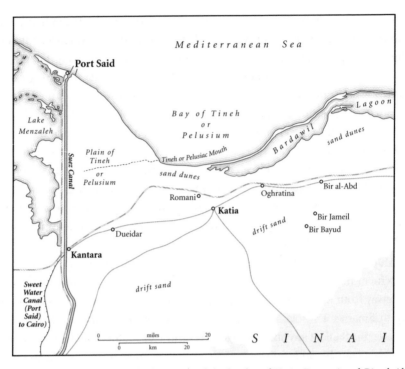

8. North-west Sinai, showing the locations of the battles of Katia, Romani and Bir al-Abd in 1916.

Romani, a few miles to the west. Two squadrons of Worcestershire Yeomanry were at Oghratina, 6 miles north-east of Katia, guarding a group of engineers working on some wells. One squadron of Gloucestershire Hussars was at Katia itself, and two others further back at Romani. Three squadrons, two of Warwickshire Yeomanry, one of Worcesters, were concentrated at a place called Hamisah, around 3 miles south-west of Katia, preparatory to an attack on an enemy force out in the desert sighted the previous day.

Approaching from the east along the coast road was Kress von Kressenstein with an advanced detachment of the Canal Expeditionary Force – two battalions and one company of the 32nd (Turkish) Regiment, a squadron of regular cavalry, four machine-guns, six mountain-guns and a detachment of camel-mounted Arab irregulars: 3,500 men in all.[24] Sinai's fourteen months of phony war was about to end.

* * *

The 5th Mounted's commander, Brigadier-General E.A. Wiggin, had assumed personal command of the three squadrons of yeomanry assembled at Hamisah.

An enemy formation about 200 strong had been reported at Mageibra, about 7 miles to the south-east, and he was keen to lead his men in their first attack, even though it would take him out of contact for a time with his other squadrons. It may not have been very professional – a general's job is to remain at the head of his command, not lead a night-time raid – but it was certainly in the spirit of the yeomanry. These were the mounted equivalents of territorial infantry battalions – part-time militia in peacetime, volunteer soldiers in wartime.

Traditionally recruited from the English shires, they had first been raised during the Napoleonic Wars, mainly for home defence in the event of invasion, but, being of conservative social character, they had also been employed in the suppression of popular demonstrations. They had not seen service overseas until the Boer War, when many new units had been raised, the need being for large numbers of mounted infantry to take part in counter-insurgency operations on the South African *veldt*. Even in the early twentieth century, the yeomanry retained something of their semi-feudal character. Officers were often landed gentry, and they rode to war as if to hounds, well attended by batmen, well supplied with the genteel comforts of home. The troopers – typically recruited from deferential village communities – regarded military service as a great adventure.[25] 'What a lark!' exclaimed Trooper S.F. Hatton of the Middlesex Imperial Yeomanry shortly after joining up; 'real scouting, real trekking, real bullets, and real charging. Crumbs! I was a schoolmaster. No more going back to that stuffy classroom and those kids ... Real war: see a bit of the world, have a man's life. This was going to be great fun, one big adventure.'[26]

Brigadier-General Wiggin set out with his three squadrons of Warwicks and Worcesters on the afternoon of 22 April and reached Mageibra at dawn the following day. But the enemy camp was deserted: the yeomen found themselves punching the air. Wiggin doubled back to Hamisah, arriving around 9 o'clock. He was greeted by alarming news.

The Ottomans sighted at Mageibra the day before had long since passed by. They were in fact approaching Dueidar, 20 miles farther west, around the time that Wiggin's detachment reached their former campsite.[27] (A recurring feature of the Sinai campaign was the extraordinary speed of Turkish and Arab infantry moving across heavy sand, often outpacing enemy horsemen.)[28] A second Ottoman force – which had not been sighted at all – had meantime been approaching Oghratina.

The two squadrons of Worcesters under Major Williams-Thomas guarding the Royal Engineers detachment working at Oghratina stood to arms before daylight on the morning of the 23 April. They were defending an oasis 'hod' – a stand of date palms – surrounded by dunes of soft sand that had the effect of muffling sound. By chance, a heavy mist had drifted in from the sea that morning, drastically reducing visibility around the camp. Despite this, the night patrols were withdrawn. The Turkish infantry were, in fact, perilously close. They now crept forward undetected through the fog.[29]

The 5th Mounted Brigade was dispersed across some 15 miles of desert in four separate packets, each too small to defend itself, each too distant from the others to provide mutual support, especially when operating over heavy sand. Yet the British did not know where the enemy was. The German Fokkers had air supremacy and were reconnoitring and bombing British positions on a daily basis. Bedouin in the Ottoman service were moving freely about the desert. In contrast, Wiggin's yeomanry – who should have been the eyes of the British advanced force as a whole – were operating blind. In the early hours of 23 April, Kress seems to have known the precise position of British posts at Oghratina, Katia, Dueidar and Romani; Wiggin, on the other hand, was unaware of the location of either of the two enemy detachments.[30]

As the fog lifted at Oghratina around 5.30am, the Ottomans opened fire at close range with rifles, machine-guns and light artillery from the north and east. The British were taken completely by surprise. They had not had time to dig proper trenches around the camp, and the best they could do was to improvise firing-lines as a confused shoot-out developed around them. Williams-Thomas discounted the option of mounting up and breaking away, for it would have meant abandoning the men on foot it was his duty to protect. But he was hopelessly outgunned. His first line was driven in, then his second, allowing the Turkish infantry to surround the camp with a tight ring of riflemen. British casualties mounted rapidly. Half the rifles became clogged with sand. Ammunition began to run out. As the defenders' fire fizzled down, the Turks rushed the position from all sides and the survivors surrendered. All 200 men of the British force were killed, wounded or taken prisoner. The Ottomans, some on captured horses, then pressed on towards Katia, a few miles distant across the dunes to the south-west.[31]

* * *

Captain Lloyd-Baker's squadron of Gloucester Hussars, 95 strong, had heard the firing at Oghratina. They had also received two telephone reports, one at 6 o'clock informing them that the enemy had been beaten off, another an hour later reporting a heavy attack on all sides. Then the wire was cut. Half an hour later, the firing stopped, and the desert was ominously silent for a while.

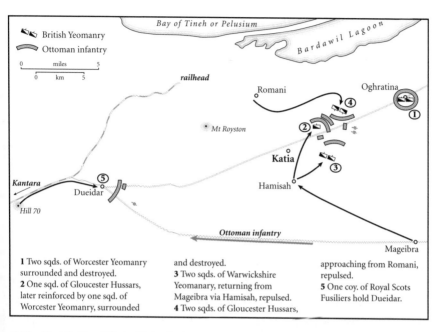

9. The First Battle of Katia, 23 April 1916.

The Gloucesters were ensconced in a low-lying hod surrounded by dunes. The sea mist reduced visibility around their position to 100 yards or so until about 8am. Around 8.45, a messenger came in from a patrol to report that two long lines of infantry, each about 300 strong, supported by cavalry, were advancing across the desert towards Katia; they were roughly a mile and a half away. Lloyd-Baker was heavily outnumbered and he could have chosen to fall back on Romani. But, like Williams-Thomas at Oghratina, he had men on foot to protect, so he decided to stand and fight. He was strengthened in this decision by telephone messages to the effect that support would shortly arrive, both from Romani itself, where the brigade reserve was stationed, and from Hamisah, to which Wiggin had by now returned following his abortive night-time raid.[32]

But the British were again underestimating their opponents. Several light guns opened fire on the Gloucesters' camp from some rising ground to the east around 9 o'clock, quickly ranging in on the horse-lines: within ten minutes most of the animals were dead. A German reconnaissance plane then flew over and redirected the artillery fire onto the yeomanry's hastily assembled line. Around the same time, Turkish riflemen opened fire on the camp at a range of about 1,000 yards. Over the next few hours, these infantry were to demonstrate superb field-craft, moulding themselves to the landscape as they crept forward in small parties under covering fire.

To understand how this might be done is to understand the micro-topography of the desert. Lieutenant-Colonel R.R. Thompson of the 52nd (Lowland) Division described it thus:

> As the scrub and camel-weed, the latter a diminutive cactus, grow in the dew-moistened desert, they collect the wind-driven sand about them, and with them there rise up hummocks of sand, usually about three feet in height, but sometimes as much as six and over. These hummocks occur every dozen yards or so in all parts of the desert where the sand is firm enough for the roots of the scrub to fasten. They form ready-made breast-works for the sniper, and usually have a fringe formed by the leaves and branches of their bushes.[33]

Employing modern 'fire and movement' tactics across such ground, the Turkish riflemen slowly closed in around the yeomanry, reducing the range of their firing-line, yet taking minimal casualties themselves. By early afternoon, many of the Turks were only 300 yards from the British camp. The mountain-guns were moved up behind them and machine-guns were also brought into action.

One squadron of Worcesters, approaching from Hamisah, had dismounted close to the little battlefield and advanced on foot to the Gloucesters' camp before the Ottoman cordon closed around it. The other two squadrons, following behind, managed an attack on the southern flank of the Ottoman position, but were unable to break through and relieve the garrison. The two squadrons dispatched from Romani clashed with the enemy to the north, but were also driven off.

Meantime, the Turkish infantry had tightened the squeeze around the British camp. By mid-afternoon, many of them were within 50 yards of the slowly disintegrating line of Gloucester and Worcester yeomanry. When mounting casualties and lack of ammunition had reduced the defenders' fire to an occasional splutter, the Turks rushed the camp with the bayonet. Some men escaped across the desert, but most not already dead were taken prisoner.[34] Another two squadrons of yeomanry had thus been destroyed: virtually half the strength of 5th Mounted Brigade.

The other Ottoman attack that day – by a camel-mounted column of about 300 that had marched overnight from Mageibra to Dueidar – was altogether less successful. The post was held by about 120 men of the Royal Scots Fusiliers and another 30 or so yeomanry and cameliers. The Ottomans struck shortly after dawn, around the same time as the attack on Oghratina 20 miles to the north-east. They emerged from the mist, hoping to rush the defences with bomb and bayonet before the garrison could respond, but the Scottish sentries were alert and their approach was swept with rifle and light machine-gun fire. Surprise lost, the battle continued as a firefight for several hours, until British reinforcements came up around noon and the Ottomans made off into the desert. British casualties numbered 55, those of the attackers 75, with another 30 or so taken prisoner by pursuing horsemen.[35]

* * *

The relative success of the Royal Scots Fusiliers at Dueidar underlined the mishandling of the 5th Mounted Brigade that had led to disaster at Oghratina and Katia. Their dispersal, and the partial breakdown of command and control, had exacerbated the essential weakness of mounted infantry: lack of firepower. The smaller size of mounted units, and the need for at least one man in four to act as a horse-holder, meant that the firing-line of an entire mounted brigade was no more numerous than that of a single infantry battalion.[36] Dismounted yeomanry could not, therefore, be expected to hold fixed positions against strong enemy attack without support from their own infantry and artillery. To attempt to use them in this way, moreover, was to negate their primary advantage: mobility. The defence of an advancing railhead through the desert was a combined-arms mission, requiring cooperation between strong infantry posts well provided with artillery, aggressive cavalry patrols and effective air reconnaissance.

Time and space are intimately related in war: the application of force depends upon the time taken to move across space. The landscape of Sinai could not have been more different from English shires where Wiggin's yeomanry were recruited. And while time is a universal, space is always geographically specific. An hour of time is always an hour of time; but a mile of Gloucestershire plough-land is quite different from a mile of Sinai sand. The First Battle of Katia had shown that much of the British Army, for all its colonial 'small war' experience, including that in the Western Desert the previous year, had not yet adjusted to the demands of desert fighting. Murray had given Wiggin inappropriate orders: he was to 'dispose his brigade in such a way as to protect all railway, topographical and water survey parties', and to 'observe the route eastwards towards Bir al-Abd'; this notwithstanding the fact that it would take two days to reinforce him with infantry in the event of a strong enemy attack.[37] Too few men had been given too much to do, and the result had been dispersion and over-extension.

Kress von Kressenstein, on the other hand, had emerged as a minor master of desert strategy, the soldiers under his command as canny desert warriors. The Prussian military system encouraged flexibility and creativity; field commanders,

junior officers and NCOs were expected to exercise initiative in the fluid conditions of the battlefield: this was evident in Sinai in April 1916. Equally apparent
were the qualities of the Anatolian peasant-soldier, who, inured to hardship and
a tough outdoor life, seems to have adapted easily to the demands of movement
and combat in the desert. The Ottoman Army was working with the grain of the
landscape. It was reading the wide spaces of the wilderness from the reports of
airmen and local nomads. It was moving swiftly along desert trackways, usually
by night to avoid both the enervating heat of the day and observation by enemy
patrols. Its soldiers were dissolving into the ripples and humps of the dunes as
they moved upon their enemies, caring nothing for drill and the dressing of
lines, displaying an instinctive feel for the latest ideas in small-unit infantry
tactics imparted to them by their officers. Those officers, moreover, were proving
themselves adept at combining the efforts of Turkish riflemen, Arab camel-men,
German machine-gunners and Austrian light artillerymen, creating compact,
multi-skilled, mission-oriented 'battle groups'.

As the broken remnants of 5th Mounted Brigade drifted back across the
desert, Murray rushed forward reinforcements. Orders were to make all speed
to Hill 70, 7 miles east of Kantara, to cover the withdrawal of the yeomanry. A
fresh mounted brigade duly clattered across the pontoon-bridge over the canal
in the bright moonlight of Easter Sunday and rode eastwards into the desert.
They were big, tough, hard-living men from the outback, mounted on superb
horses in peak condition. They viewed the scattered detachments of yeomanry
they passed going in the opposite direction with cynical disdain. Eager and
confident, sometimes brash and swaggering, the pride of a young nation
fighting its first war, they were the Australian Light Horse (ALH).[38]

* * *

Their baptism of fire had been rough and bloody. Horsemen from ranches
measured in tens of thousands of acres had found themselves shipped as
infantry to the narrow, jagged Gallipoli Peninsula, where they lived and died in
the cramped ridge-top trenches of a tiny battlefield barely two miles long by
half a mile wide. The nadir came on 7 August 1915. The dismounted Light
Horse were required to launch a series of frontal attacks uphill, over bare
ground, in broad daylight, against well-defended Ottoman trenches. The 1st
ALH lost 150 of its 200 men at Pope's Hill, and had to be withdrawn from the
line. The 2nd ALH lost 50 of its 55 men within seconds of leaving its trenches
at Quinn's Post.

The fate of the 8th and 10th Regiments at The Nek was yet more soul-
destroying. Four separate waves were sent over the top. Each was scythed

within yards of the trenches. Of the 400 men involved, 362 were killed or wounded. Charles Bean, the Australian war correspondent and official historian, saw the aftermath: 'During the long hours of that day, the summit of The Nek could be seen crowded with their bodies. At first, here and there, a man raised his arm to the sky, or tried to drink from his water-bottle. But as the sun that burning day climbed higher, such movement ceased. Over the whole summit, the figures lay still in the quivering heat.' Most of a brigade had been destroyed in less than an hour.[39]

Eight months later, riding into Sinai, the Australian Light Horse had been transformed. Half the men were now replacements, fresh drafts of enthusiastic young recruits untainted by the torments of Gallipoli. These had been fastened onto a solid framework of rejuvenated combat-veterans, men whose morale had soared when reunited with their mounts and sent out on desert patrols or refresher training. Observers noted how 'the Gallipoli stoop of the men [due to long service in shallow trenches under fire] changed into the old swing of the cavalryman'. Given that many senior officers had served in the Boer War, and virtually all junior officers and NCOs had been on Gallipoli, the Australian Light Horse had become that perfect military mix of an experienced, professional cadre with keen, idealistic volunteers.[40]

The men from whom the Light Horse was recruited were of the highest calibre. Cultivators and lumberjacks, stockmen and sheep-shearers, pioneers, prospectors and squatters, they came from the small farms of the coastal plain, the forested slopes of the mountain ranges, and the sprawling sheep and cattle ranches of the interior. Some were from outback stations hundreds of miles from a railway line, where the mail and newspapers arrived at intervals of weeks. Most could ride a horse, and many could handle a gun. Much of Australia was a frontier society of people both on the move and on the make; an open, fluid society of self-reliant men who were physically tough and independent-minded. Rugged individualism was mixed with boisterous male brotherhood – what Australians called 'mateship'. When the call to war was heard, men, more often than not, joined up with one or more of their mates – and the macho culture of the outback sheep-station became the culture of the Light Horse.[41]

The 'spirit of Anzac' – epitomised by the Light Horse – has become an Australian national legend. Australia had existed as an independent nation-state for only thirteen years when the First World War broke out, and its army had been little more than a volunteer militia until as late as 1911. Universal military training had then been introduced, but the army still comprised barely 2,000 regulars and 20,000 trained militiamen three years later – a tiny force in a population of 7 million. Yet, when the Australian prime minister announced that 'when the empire is at war, so also is Australia', there was surge of volunteers to join the Australian Imperial Force formed for overseas service on 15 August 1914. More than 52,000 had been enrolled by December, and some 330,000 Australians would join up before the war's end. Of these, two-thirds would become casualties, and one in five would be killed.[42] All would be volunteers, for Australians twice voted down government attempts to impose conscription.[43]

Why did so many young Australians volunteer to fight a war for the British Empire on the other side of the world? The Australian elite of big ranchers and city capitalists were tied by a thousand threads to the British imperial trading system.[44] Many had come to regard the French, Germans, Russians and Japanese as competitors for empire in the Western Pacific.[45] Many saw the Royal Navy and British maritime supremacy as a vital national interest.[46] So they supported the war and favoured conscription. But what of ordinary Australians?

The Australian *Official History* later defined the national cause in the language of blood-and-soil mysticism. The Anzac soldier, it maintained, was inspired by an 'unconscious loyalty of blood', by 'racial patriotism', by 'the honour of the old land of his fathers'.[47] The term 'racial patriotism' seems apposite, given the country's origin as a colonial settler-state, its recent history of genocidal warfare against the Aborigines and its 'White Australia' policy of racial exclusion, designed, in the words of Charles Bean – who perhaps did more than anyone else to foster the Anzac spirit – 'to maintain a high Western standard of economy, society, and culture' through 'the rigid exclusion of Oriental peoples'.[48] The latent racism in the Australian ranks contributed to occasional violence on the streets of Cairo during the war. The most notorious incident – the so-called 'Battle of the Wozzer' on Good Friday 1915 – involved hundreds of Anzacs rioting in the city's red-light district in protest at rising prices, poor-quality drink and the incidence of venereal disease.[49]

Embryonic nationalism, laced with racism, was strongest in the small, conservative, rural communities where light-horsemen were usually recruited. But even in the big cities, the labour unions had pushed the 'White Australia' policy as a form of job reservation, and the very fact that workers were well organised and militant gave them a sense that they too had a stake in the nation. The absence of titled aristocracy, inherited wealth, and traditional privilege added to the feeling that Australia was a society of opportunity and freedom where everyone could expect 'a fair go'.[50]

Most, however, probably had more prosaic motives than a desire to fight for Australia, let alone the British Empire – the lure of adventure, the challenge to manhood, the pull of mateship. War seemed the ultimate test of both individual worth and male bonds. 'I was dead scared when I went to join up,' one veteran recalled years later. 'Scared it would be all over before I got there!' Charles Bean tells the story of a man arriving in the front trench before the Australian attack at Lone Pine on Gallipoli in August 1915. 'Do you chaps mind shiftin' up a piece,' he said once he had located the man he was looking for. 'Him and me are mates, an' we're goin' over together.'[51]

Australian egalitarianism and mateship clashed with the class-based traditions of the British Army. No end of stories circulated in British officers' messes concerning Australian indiscipline: the man who put two fingers in his mouth and whistled to summon his lieutenant when asked a question he could not answer; the man who did not bother saluting because he considered himself 'a fighter' rather than a soldier; the man who walked off saying 'tie your horse to these bloody railings' when asked to hold an officer's reins; and many more.[52] Especially at odds with military discipline were the imperatives of mateship. Its central precept – that 'a man should at all times and at any cost stand by his mate' – might not always be compatible with obedience to authority. Army orders to leave the wounded to the stretcher-bearers were routinely ignored by Australian soldiers; the unwritten code that you did not leave 'mates' to the enemy was overriding. In two and a half years of constant fighting, only 73 light-horsemen were taken prisoner, most of them wounded, and not a single officer; whereas they succeeded in capturing between 40,000 and 50,000 enemy soldiers.[53]

The Anzac Corps was a strange mix of racial patriotism, labour solidarity and mateship – a mix that would turn them into the military elite of the Egyptian Expeditionary Force.

* * *

A Light Horse regiment was divided into three squadrons, each of six troops, and at full strength numbered about 500 men.[54] Three regiments formed a brigade, and in March 1916 all were consolidated into a single Anzac Mounted Division comprising the 1st, 2nd and 3rd Australian Light Horse Brigades and the New Zealand Mounted Rifles Brigade.[55] As the Anzacs had no guns, four British Territorial Force batteries of Royal Horse Artillery were attached to the division.[56]

Most men were mounted on Australian 'walers' – not a breed, but a class of strong stock-horses used on the land and of variable size and form. They were expected to carry up to 280lbs and to require 6 gallons of water a day; in practice, they sometimes carried 500lbs, went without water for two days or more, and easily outpaced transport camels across the desert sand. 'Bill the Bastard' – an exceptional horse named for his unruly behaviour – on one occasion carried five wounded troopers to safety. Though few walers could match Bill's stamina – and some fell short of any acceptable standard and had to be culled – the majority proved superior in toughness and endurance to all but the best of British officers' hunters and chargers.[57] This, though, depended upon good horse maintenance. Most light-horsemen were skilled riders, but they had to be trained to look after their mounts. At home, horses had ample time for rest and recuperation when not in use; on campaign, they would sometimes be driven to the limits, with hard riding day after day in the heat of the desert. This placed a premium on 'the value of ceaseless grooming, of extreme care in the balanced packing of saddles, and of the greatest possible regularity in feeding and watering'.[58] The waler, well looked after, was to be essential to the success of the Australian Light Horse in Sinai, Palestine and Syria.

The troopers wore khaki tunics and breeches, usually of wool, occasionally lighter cotton drill designed for hot weather, leather ankle boots and spiral-strapped leggings, and, most characteristically, an emu-feather plumed slouch hat, designed to provide all-round sun protection. They were armed with a standard Lee-Enfield rifle – a .303-calibre, bolt-action, magazine-loaded repeater used throughout the British armed forces in the first half of the twentieth century – and wore a leather bandolier carrying 90 rounds. They were equipped with a bayonet, but, at this stage in the war, no sword, for the Light Horse were mounted infantry, not cavalry.[59] Both arms had similar roles – scouting, patrolling, surprise attacks on isolated detachments, the advanced seizure of key positions, screening ahead of the main force, worrying at the enemy's flanks, the rapid exploitation of breakthroughs – but they sometimes performed them in different ways, mounted infantry dismounting to form a firing-line, cavalry occasionally resorting to the shock action of a charge.[60]

* * *

The commander of the Anzac Mounted Division, the 50-year-old Major-General Harry Chauvel, was a rare example of a long-service Australian professional. Born into a New South Wales family that owned 100,000 acres, 12,000 head of cattle and over 300 horses, he had spent the first part of his life as a rancher. He doubled, however, as a volunteer militia-officer, and, getting a taste for the military, in 1896 he had swapped grazing for soldiering and signed on as a regular officer. A year on active service in the South African war had led to promotion to lieutenant-colonel and left him one of the most experienced and accomplished officers in the country.[61] Even so, in the bitter rows that later erupted over compulsory military service, Chauvel took a relatively moderate position, remaining a keen supporter of the militia system, the citizen-soldier and the mounted-infantry tradition.[62] In this apparent contradiction – between regular soldier and people's cavalier – perhaps lies the secret of his greatness as a commander of horsemen.

Chauvel valued the boisterous martial qualities of his command. 'They are a fine lot of men and horses,' he wrote to his wife on 15 December 1914.[63] But he knew, too, that without order and method, the potential would be wasted. He was little interested in petty matters like saluting and sartorial elegance. His real concern was with such essentials as horse maintenance, care of weapons, good march discipline and high standards of marksmanship. What was needed to harness the fighting power of Australian horsemen was a discipline that was moderate and self-willed: 'I do not mean that we can expect to establish a hard and fast discipline such as obtains in the regular army [of Britain], but by a proper organisation ... and above all by the establishment of an *esprit de corps*, a higher and even better form of discipline can be obtained.'[64] Chauvel ideal-ised the free citizen-soldier, but sought to place him in a framework of modern military organisation. He was less 'Jeb' Stuart – the Confederate cavalry commander he especially admired – than Oliver Cromwell.[65]

The day after the Katia disaster, 24 April 1916, Chauvel was ordered to assume command of all British forces in the Romani sector. A month before he had criticised the folly of establishing mounted infantry in a series of small, widely dispersed posts. Since then, his Light Horse had demonstrated their prowess in two successful long-range raids.[66] The Australian mounties – big men from the sun-baked outback on the toughest of horses – were clearly at home in the desert. Murray was impressed enough to put Chauvel in overall charge. The new commander in Sinai was soon planning a decisive battle. It would take time to prepare, but when it came it would turn the tide of war in the Middle East and begin the long march of the British Army from Suez to Damascus.

* * *

The desert in summer is a furnace inimical to life. Men who try to live in it are consumed by it – burnt-up, dried out, crushed by heat and thirst. Temperatures in Sinai hit 45°C in the shade in mid-May. 'Our daily water ration was increased from half a bottle to a full bottle per day, issued at 6pm,' recalled Private Loudon of the 52nd (Lowland) Division. 'We were forbidden to drink any till noon next day. The flies were very troublesome. For two days, 16th and 17th, the heat became unbearable, reaching 125°F [52°C].' Loudon, a farmer's son turned junior civil-servant, had failed the eye-sight test at an Edinburgh recruiting centre, so he had learned the test-card by heart and got himself accepted into the 4th Royal Scots, a territorial unit, the previous summer. Having served briefly on Gallipoli, he and his mates had hoped for evacuation home, but they had been shipped to Alexandria, dressed in new desert kit – 'khaki cotton-drill uniform and pith helmet' (though Loudon had cut his trousers into shorts) – and sent into the line defending the Suez Canal.

As the summer heat approached its peak, the desert sun struck down legions of soldiers. Exposed flesh reddened, swelled and burst open. Heads were frazzled with sunstroke, leaving men debilitated by splitting headaches and constant vomiting. Nearly everyone suffered from septic sores, huge numbers from diarrhoea and heart trouble, and many were hospitalised by one form of sun-induced sickness or another.[67] The cold grey drizzle of the Scottish Lowlands seemed like paradise to men tossing inside roasting tents. It was no better in the offices of the high command. Lynden-Bell complained to Maurice on 22 May 1916: 'We have had five days of the most appalling heat that has ever been experienced here . . . 123 in the shade was a bit tall, especially when it was accompanied by a fiery wind from the south and myriads of flies.'[68]

Only the flies thrived. The common house-fly has conquered the world by feeding on the garbage and shit of human settlement. Originating in the steppes of Central Asia, it now occurs on every continent and in all climatic zones, coexisting with humans wherever they are active. The fly's life-cycle can be completed in as little as a week, and a female can lay up to 500 eggs in a few days. Warmth increases reproduction, with temperatures above 25°C optimal. It has been estimated that a single pair of flies beginning reproduction in April could, under perfect conditions and assuming all offspring survived, give rise to 190 quintillion flies by August. Ideal feeding and breeding habitats are, in descending order, horse manure, human excrement, cow manure, fermenting vegetable matter, and kitchen waste.[69] Filthy human encampments do not 'attract' flies: they breed them in their millions in a matter of days. The men and beasts of the Egyptian Expeditionary Force were the royal banquet of the flies of Sinai.

The flies, like the heat, penetrated everywhere, turning routine tasks into a flailing struggle against a black swarm. The torment was relentless, but the spread of sickness – food poisoning, diarrhoea, dysentery – was the greater problem. Flies are primary carriers of disease because they pick up pathogenic organisms from the filth on which they feed and transport them to human and animal food on their mouthparts, other body-parts, and in their vomit and faeces.[70] Large-scale warfare has the effect of turning this micro-biological process into a pandemic. One medical officer, commenting on the movement of bulk supplies from base-depots to forward posts, reported that 'it was a common sight to see camels coming in loaded with quarters of beef which had the light cloth covering torn off, covered with myriads of flies, and a dirty camel-driver seated on top of the load'.[71]

Contact with the Ottomans was minimal that summer. Flies were the main enemy: a plague of flies meant disease, misery and degradation enough to crush the will of the hardiest of warriors. 'It was a pitiful sight,' recalled the Middlesex Yeomanry's recently promoted Lance-Corporal Hatton, 'to see men who had evacuated some twenty times a day lying almost beside the latrine pails, as they had insufficient strength to trust themselves further afield.' He had a bad turn himself and discovered that 'nothing . . . will sap away vitality so quickly and cause such excruciating stomach pains as dysentery'.[72]

Various 'de-flying' measures were attempted. When the Light Horse rode into the abandoned yeomanry camp at Romani in April, their senior medical officer had been appalled by what he saw: 'The camp was found in a filthy condition; heaps of manure were lying everywhere; horse-lines were feet deep in manure . . . The whole camp was a huge fly-breeding area.' It took time, resources and ingenuity to make a difference. Eventually, camp incinerators were constructed from thousands of recycled bully-beef tins; well-designed to ensure plenty of draught, they were fed only with refuse sieved of sand, so as to maximise efficiency. Medical staff also manufactured sticky streamers to serve as fly-traps. Units were encouraged to compete to have the most fly-free camp; some went to the extreme of 'de-flying' personnel and stores entering their site.[73] The officers of the Worcestershire Yeomanry discovered that a chameleon 'proved most useful in eating all the flies in the mess'; they consequently adopted a number of these little animals, among whom the champion was one called Cuthbert, who 'held the record for eating 50 flies before breakfast'.[74]

* * *

Sand was also an enemy. Unless baked hard by the sun, it sucked at the feet of marching men and slowed their movement to a wearisome trudge. Private Albert Surry of 7th Battalion, the Essex Regiment, thought the misery of a desert march almost beyond words: 'The agony of mind, the agony of body, the ceaseless plodding, the ceaseless longing for the end of the journey, the torment of thirst, the horrible vermin, the stench of half-decomposed camels, the stretches of deep soft sand . . .'[75]

Equally exhausting was digging in sand, for it slipped down the walls of trenches and doubled the labour of constructing them. Surry again:

Digging in the sand is a wearisome business . . . we were perpetually digging and re-digging trenches . . . One can dig and dig and dig for hours on end, only to find that the quick-drying action of the sun causes the sides of your trench to fall in ... These digging operations took place on six days of the week and sometimes on the seventh by way of a change.[76]

Then there was the grit that got sprayed into everything with each gust of wind. Captain Ernest Hinde of the Royal Army Medical Corps found that a sand-storm left him with 'sand in my hair, sand in my ears, sand in my eyes, sand in my nose and in my mouth, sand in my clothes – in fact, sand everywhere. The food is gritty with sand.'[77] Sometimes, in a sandstorm, men might be besieged inside howling tents for days at a time. Hatton recalled a three-day *khamsin* – 'insufferably hot' in the lulls, 'like a blast from a ship's furnace' when the wind blew – in which his camp was cut off and the consequent water shortage became 'very serious indeed'.[78] Trooper Ion Idriess's squadron of 5th Light Horse was hit by a *khamsin* while out on patrol in May 1916:

> The sun rose, a ball of quivering fire, hurrying from the east, a wind straight from the furnace. The horses bent their heads and gasped ... I think this is the most hellish wind I've experienced. It sears through the oasis, through our blanket shelter, and scorches our naked bodies ... I walked out in the sun ... and the burning wind seemed actually to strike me. The leather of our boots is shrinking from the blazing sand ...[79]

The sand also harboured legions of predators. Camps would be infested with biting ants, spiders or centipedes.[80] Sandflies would suddenly arrive in myriads – small, biting, sometimes disease-bearing – perhaps in the wake of a sand-storm.[81] Yet more loathsome were the ticks which infested the sand in and around settlements, awaiting their chance to attach themselves to a passing body and bore under the skin, where they would inflate by gorging on blood, lay their eggs, and contaminate the unwilling host with sickness.[82] Meantime, lurking under rocks, were scorpions and snakes.[83] Just occasionally, one species of vermin would make war on another, and offer the desert's human residents a little solace: 'An interesting and useful discovery was made by some of the men,' reported one yeomanry medical officer, 'namely, that the numerous ants in our camp were rapidly clearing the regiment of lice! These little insects, when allowed to run over a man's clothing, appeared to be much more effica-cious than any insect powder.'[84]

Heat, sand and vermin: little wonder that many veterans recalled the joy of swimming. It was, of course, a physical escape from the torments of the desert and the toil of fatigues. But it was something more: the sensual luxury of immersion in warm water, the subliminal experience of its womb-like embrace, meant a momentary withdrawal from the harsh realities of war and a cathartic regression to foetus-like security; especially so if one bathed naked, at night, under the moon. Hatton described it thus:

> To take a towel, and a companion, and stroll off through the silent date palms, down to where Lake Timsah lay gleaming 'neath a golden moon; to slip silently into the water, and swim side-by-side to a sand-bank half a mile from the shore, to feel the cooling salt water along the flanks so lately tried by heat of sun; there to stretch one's length in the shallows, prone in the lazy ripples on the sand, and look back at the palm-shadowed shore: this was bathing fit for Grecian gods.[85]

* * *

The struggle to tame the desert – to make it a place in which men could live and fight – was a matter of materiel. 'The new defensive line east of the canal . . . is getting on,' explained Lynden-Bell to Maurice on 16 January 1916, 'though an enormous amount of revetting material is required to keep the sand from falling in.'[86] 'Revetting material' meant wood, wire and canvas or matting. Early attempts to revet trenches using sandbags alone had failed: the bags dried out so completely in the sun that the sand slowly trickled away and the walls collapsed; double-bagging was more successful, but too expensive in bags. The problem was solved using wooden hurdles, to which matting or canvas was attached on the inside. The trenches were dug to the necessary width at the bottom, with the front and rear walls sloping at about 45°. The hurdles were then placed at their correct slope and wired to anchorages of either wooden pickets or sandbags. Sand was then used to backfill the space between hurdle and cutting, and mounded up front and back to form parapet and parados, which were finished off with two or three layers of sandbags.[87] To make a trench a metre wide in this way involved opening almost 5 metres of ground. A line of such trenches and redoubts ran for 80 miles down the eastern side of the canal. Periodically, moreover, they had to be repaired or dug out afresh, for a *khamsin* could fill a trench with sand in a single night.[88] Only thus, with stupendous expenditure of labour and material, could the desert be engineered to provide the protected spaces on which modern war depended.

Sand also clogged up military movement. Lynden-Bell reported to Maurice on 4 September that the EEF was experimenting with:

> a new kind of sand-shoe, which is in the nature of a snow-shoe, and we have great hopes that if it turns out successfully we may be able to increase the

pace of infantry across this desert to three miles an hour. The Turk has a distinct score off us in this respect, as the way he moves across the desert on his flat feet is nothing short of amazing.[89]

A number of prototypes were tested, but it was four months before a wholly successful pattern was devised.[90] By then, however, the wire sand-shoe was being superseded by a monumental application of the same principle: a wire road. Australians knew of the technique back home, for wire would be laid across the sandy beds of inland rivers to give firm footing in the dry summer season. In Sinai, a few widths of wire-netting, securely pegged down, were sufficient to provide a roadway that could accommodate marching infantry four abreast.[91] By February 1917, 86 miles of wire or brushwood road would run across northern Sinai from the canal to the border of Palestine.[92] 'By palm-grove, sand-dune, bir, and hod,' Rex Scott would later write in *Palestine News*, the Egyptian Expeditionary Force paper, 'there's a long, snaky ribbon, far-winding – the toil-saving, thrice-bless'd Wire Road.'[93]

The road was one of three parallel strips of industrialised infrastructure constructed during 1916 to allow the British to project their military power across the desert. Alongside the road ran also a railway and a water-pipe. 'Who can the desert's strength subdue?' wrote Crawsley Williams, another EEF soldier-poet. 'Pipe, Rail, and Road. Pipe to carry your drink to you; Rail to speed your rations through; Road to march on firm and true . . .'[94]

Work had begun on the railway at the end of February 1916, and it progressed thereafter at a rate of about 15 miles a month for the next year. It eventually ran for 140 miles from Kantara on the canal, where it was connected to the Egyptian railway system, through Romani, then along the northern fringe of the desert to Arish and Rafa, ending at the Wadi Ghuzze opposite Gaza (with an additional branch and spur built later). A standard gauge railway with an average capacity of thirteen trains a day, it was to become, in the estimate of war correspondent W.T. Massey, 'the keystone of our strategic structure in Eastern Egypt . . . the backbone, the arteries, the very life-blood of the army.'[95]

The railway would enable the British to supply a military force on the opposite side of Sinai far larger than could be supported by the available water supplies. The water in the desert was of essentially three kinds: winter rain-water stored in various pools and cisterns; 'fossil water' tapped by wells that reached down to the water table; and water carried into the desert by camels from either Egypt or Palestine. Supplies were always limited, especially so during the summer, and not all the water in the oases was drinkable. The Royal Engineers devoted much effort to renovating old wells and digging new ones. Regimental medical officers were responsible for sterilising the facilities in their areas. A particular problem was a 60-mile-wide waterless tract on the northern routeway between Bir al-Abd in the west and Arish in the east.[96]

Digging new wells in sand is immensely arduous, but army engineers successfully employed an alternative device, 'the spear-point pump', to access buried water. 'A 2½ inch pipe was pointed, perforated, and covered with a sheet of fine perforated brass,' explained Lieutenant-Colonel Guy Powles of the New Zealand Mounted Rifles. 'This was driven down into the water area by means of a small pulley bar and monkey, or by a sledgehammer; and additional lengths of pipe were added if necessary. The ordinary General Service "lift and force pump" was then attached.' Water could be produced in minutes. It worked so well that spear-points were issued to every squadron in the Anzac Mounted Division.[97] But such measures were mere stopgaps.

The priorities in the desert war were water, water and again water – water for men, water for horses, and water for camels and mules. It simply could not be supplied in the quantities required without an industrial-scale pipeline. In September and October, therefore, two consignments of American piping were landed, and the construction of a 12 inch water-pipe running parallel to the railway began. Pipeline construction was faster than railway construction and had caught up with the latter by December, around the time both projects reached Arish. The pipeline was connected to the Sweet Water Canal at Kantara West, where there was a filtration plant designed to handle 600,000 gallons a day. This additional plant was made necessary by the water's contamination with bilharzia (a parasitic worm whose short-term effects included stomach cramps, diarrhoea, and blood in the urine and faeces, with long-term effects far worse). As well as the filtration plant, there were pumping-stations and reservoirs at Kantara East, Romani, Bir al-Abd and Mazar, these to keep the water moving along the pipeline, since the most powerful pump available could push only about 100 tons of water an hour a distance of no more than 30 miles.[98]

An old Arab prophecy predicted that when the waters of the Nile came to Palestine, Jerusalem would be retaken from the Turks. This would come to pass the following year: the pipeline would arrive a short distance from Gaza and Beersheba on the edge of Palestine in October 1917, just prior to the offensive that would carry the British forward to the capture of Jerusalem by Christmas. That which the prophecy had assumed impossible was achieved by the industrialisation of the desert. Colonel Archibald Wavell, a classically educated EEF staff officer, was reminded of Tacitus' famous epigram about the Romans in Scotland in AD 84 – 'they make a desert and call it peace' – and inverted it to describe the British advance across Sinai in 1916: 'They turn the desert into a workshop and call it war.'[99]

Kantara, indeed, had become a vast improvised desert city of dockyards, transport depots, storehouses, workshops and tents. At peak, there would be thousands of tons of supplies and hundreds of thousands of gallons of water passing through it every 24 hours. 'Probably no town built during a gold-rush grew so rapidly,' thought Massey; 'certainly none was extended so methodically. I passed through the place on an average once a fortnight for many months, and I never saw it twice the same. Something had always been added, but no-one ever saw congestion or confusion . . .'[100]

* * *

The conquest of the desert by industrialised logistics involved prodigious expenditure of resources and labour. By early 1917, the EEF's passage of Sinai had consumed 30 million sandbags, 2 million square feet of timber, 50,000 rolls of wire-netting, and 7,000 tons of barbed wire. The Royal Engineers had constructed a total of 220 miles of tarmac road, 359 miles of railway and 300 miles of pipeline.[101]

Soldiers performed much of the heavy labour, but their efforts were supported by those of the Egyptian Labour Corps (ELC) and the Egyptian Camel Transport Corps (CTC). The ELC expanded from 3,000 men at the beginning of 1916 to 56,000 by the middle of 1917. They were drawn from a pool of 186,000 general labourers, who worked three-month contracts, and were dressed in uniforms comprising khaki shorts and smocks with 'ELC' in red letters across the chest.[102] Similar numbers were mobilised by the CTC, which employed an average of about 25,000 camel-drivers at any one time, with some 170,000 in all serving during the war.[103]

These, however, were far from happy arrangements. Many were volunteers in name only. According to Colonel Wavell, 'to produce these numbers, very active recruiting was necessary'.[104] This was a euphemism for widespread abuse. Men were press-ganged and compelled to work at gunpoint. Pay was low and fines were imposed for infringements. Working conditions were appalling: men were sometimes marched long distances across the desert without water, to the point where a good number died of sunstroke and thirst. Lieutenant Joe McPherson, a transport officer, recalls one particular death-march: 'The heat was most intense and the sand burnt and cracked the natives' feet. Half of them were unprovided with water-bottles . . . It was a pitiful sight, the poor devils fainting with thirst, heat and weariness, falling out or plodding on blindly . . . Lieutenant Hill, one of our officers, went mad and tried to kill himself.'[105]

The flogging of 'Gyppos' seems to have been routine. Sent down the Nile to Aswan on a camel-buying expedition, McPherson found it relatively easy to recruit the labourers he needed in the impoverished villages of the district. But the men then found themselves unexpectedly subject to military law. 'I held my little courts martial when necessary,' he explained. 'Cases were tried and, if necessary, the accused punished summarily by a small fine or a mild flogging.' Not always mild: one man suspected of 'disaffection and tampering with others' was sentenced by McPherson to 25 lashes with a rhinoceros-hide whip. The fourth stroke drew blood, by the twentieth the victim 'looked like a piece of raw beef', and the remaining five had to be applied to the feet.[106] Socialists and paci- fists among EEF soldiers were sometimes shocked. 'The treatment of these Egyptians is a scandal,' observed a conscientious objector serving in a field ambulance. 'They talk about modern civilisation and abolishing slavery, yet these men have task-masters paid by the British government to whip them like dogs with long leather whips. Even the British and Australians kick and bully them unmercifully. Let us take the beam from our eyes before talking about Germany and her allies.'[107]

British soldiers were forbidden to strike natives – so formal floggings were usually administered by Egyptian overseers – but the injunction was widely flouted. The violence was typically justified in racist terms. Bernard Blaser's unit of the London Scottish witnessed an attack 'with a thick stick by a short, thick-set British soldier on police duty'. The reaction was mixed: 'Many men who witnessed this incident ejaculated murmurs of protest, while others, more callous and hardened, laughed, thinking it great sport.' But, Blaser continued, 'We learned very soon afterwards . . . that this summary treatment is the only logic these natives understand . . .'[108]

Approval came from the highest levels. 'Everyone who knows the country considers the power of flogging to be necessary,' explained a cable from EEF headquarters to the War Office in December 1917. 'The general behaviour of the Egyptian Labour Corps is very good; but there are now and then cases for the lash. Do you think that could be specially legalised . . .?'[109]

Mutiny was an ever-present danger. On 1 February 1916, 400 men of the 4th and 7th Royal Scots were marched to the barracks of Egyptian reservists protesting against being called up to perform menial tasks for miserable pay.[110] Egyptians had not been consulted about the war when it began, but they had been reassured that 'there would be no interference by the military authorities in citizens' lives'.[111] This turned out to have been a lie. They found themselves conscripted into a white man's war, only to be underpaid, overworked, racially abused and brutally treated. The ground was being laid for an explosion of anger that would, in 1919, shake British rule in Egypt to its foundations.

* * *

To fight their war, the British needed native labour. They also needed camels. The industrialisation of the desert by railway, pipeline and road had strict geographical limits; beyond these was the domain of the camel. Before widespread use of motor transport, camels were essential in desert warfare. Railways and pipelines were expensive to lay and ran in straight lines to fixed points. They were useful in transporting bulk supplies – whether of artillery shells, bully-beef or drinking water – but, in and of themselves, could not sustain mobile operations any distance from their terminuses. Bulk had to be broken down into small packets and transported across the desert to widely scattered operational units.

'Our scheme is to try and make a mobile force of two divisions and two mounted brigades,' Lynden-Bell had written to Maurice in January 1916, 'for which ... some 60,000 camels will be required.'[112] Easier said than done: Lynden-Bell remained preoccupied throughout the first half of 1916 with a crippling shortage of both baggage and riding camels fit for desert service. The war had created a massive surge in demand for animals that were central to the local economy. A further complication was the many different types of camel – around a dozen were recognised by the British military authorities. A delta camel, for example, needed to drink every day, whereas a desert camel could go six days without water.[113] A 'heavy-burden' camel could carry up to 350lbs, a 'light-burden' camel only between 200 and 250lbs. A typical 'heavy' load might be: six cases of preserved meat, four cases of cheese, two cases of bacon, four bags of rice, two sacks of grain, six cases of biscuit, four cases of jam, four chests of tea, six cases of milk, four bags of sugar, four cases of tobacco or cigarettes, four cases of candles, two bales of compressed forage, and two fantasses (10-gallon zinc tanks) of water. These loads were substantial, but the pace was slow: 15 miles a day was considered a good distance for a camel, 25 miles possible but liable to put strain on the animal. The military supply of a division therefore required the services of about 2,000 transport camels.[114] The Camel Transport Corps was divided into companies of approximately this size – eventually there would be 17 of them – each with 7 British officers, 11 British NCOs, 45 native NCOs and about 1,000 camel-drivers.[115]

A camel column approaching over the desert sand was something out of time in this war of machines. 'While sitting in Green's shelter after dinner,' recalled the yeomanry medical officer Captain Hinde:

> our attention was called by an unusual sound and ... we saw a long line of camels with empty fantasses, and it was the rattling of these which had attracted our attention ... the length of line that was visible to us was a good quarter of a mile long, and it seemed to go on a long time. We went down to

the well area later and saw these camels arrive and file right round the fence dumping their fantasses down. It was a wonderful sight in the bright moonlight.[116]

* * *

In Sinai, train and camel worked in combination. Both were sinews – one of iron and steam, the other of flesh and blood – of a single war-effort. Tradition and modernity were melded into one, such that the military power of the British Empire could be deployed to achieve the conquest of Sinai and an invasion of Palestine.

Long before railway, pipeline and wire road were finished, however, Harry Chauvel and the Light Horse had fought their decisive battle. Brilliantly conceived and carefully prepared, the Anzacs had lured the Ottoman enemy into an elaborate trap, and there, at the Battle of Romani, had crushed them with thirst and firepower under a burning August sun.

CHAPTER 6

The Battle of Romani

BRIGADIER-GENERAL EDWARD Chaytor may have been the most senior officer to fly a 'Tac R' – tactical reconnaissance mission – during the First World War. It was certainly not 'standard', especially given the hazards of early aviation. Chaytor was commander of the New Zealand Mounted Rifles Brigade, part of Harry Chauvel's Anzac Mounted Division, and his decision to make a personal reconnaissance of Sinai's eastern oasis area may have been motivated by growing anxiety about the enemy's whereabouts. What he saw astonished him.

Repeatedly had British airmen and Anzac patrols reported the area east of Romani clear of large enemy forces. But, flying along the eastern edge of the oases on 19 July, Chaytor saw between 3,000 and 3,500 men massed at Bir al-Abd in the north, and two groups in the desert several miles to the south, one of about 2,000 men at Bir Jameil, another of 3,000 men at Bir Bayud. Returning to base, Chaytor dropped a message over to 2nd Light Horse Brigade camp. The news caused consternation: the Ottomans had moved several thousand men across the 60-mile-wide waterless waste between Arish and Bir al-Abd without being detected. They had done this at the height of summer, when many thought the debilitating heat precluded major operations. And this, unlike the Katia expedition in April, which had involved only 3,500 men, was obviously no raid: the entire Canal Expeditionary Force, 16,000 strong, appeared to be on the move.[1]

Much was due to the efficiency of the German personnel attached to the Ottoman forces. A flight of Austrian and German fighters – Aviatiks, Albatrosses and Fokkers – was supplementing the work of pro-Ottoman Sinai Bedouin to help build a detailed intelligence picture of British positions.[2] Artillery and machine-guns were largely German-operated.[3] Most of the planning was done by Kress von Kressenstein's small staff of German officers. But success also depended on the quality of the infantry, and, advancing in force across Sinai at the height of summer, the Turkish soldier had demonstrated remarkable speed, stealth and endurance. Lynden-Bell, Murray's chief-of-staff, reckoned the enemy infantry had three times the speed of their British counterparts over the desert. The yeomanry medical officer Captain Teichman thought them 'wonderful at disappearing and appearing again' – a result, it seems, of their habit of going to ground under camouflage during daylight hours and marching only at night.[4] The First Canal Expedition in early 1915 had been formed of untested Arab conscripts. The Second, in the summer of 1916, involved men of the 3rd Infantry Division, a crack Turkish formation of Gallipoli veterans.[5] The combination of German method and Anatolian toughness made the Second Expedition, despite smaller numbers, a more formidable challenge than the First.

Measured against the titanic battles raging at Verdun and the Somme, the struggle that unfolded in Sinai in the first two weeks of August 1916 seems small scale. But the appearance is deceptive. Both armies were fighting at the end of long, slow and sometimes contested supply-lines; both were attempting to project military force across a hostile desert environment; both were waging war at the furthest limit of logistical possibility. The men at the sharp end – the combat soldiers – were an exceptionally small proportion of the total numbers involved. Behind each few thousand in the line were tens of thousands employed on steamships and railways, in ports, supply-depots, and workshops, and supervising the camel-trains passing endlessly back and forth. What made such effort worthwhile was the Suez Canal. 'The two empires were fighting at the ends of very long lines of communication,' explained Lieutenant-Colonel Thompson, the official historian of the 52nd (Lowland) Division, 'so that only comparatively small forces could be kept in the field. That, however, does not alter the magnitude of the decisions arrived at . . .'[6]

Chastened by the Katia debacle in April, General Murray had decided that Sinai must be cleared of Ottomans. Such was the strategic importance of the canal that the presence of even a small enemy force within striking distance was sufficient to tie down 100,000 men in static garrison duties. 'The canal is still holding out,' Lawrence had written to Hogarth just before Katia:

and we are forgetting all about it. Turkey, if she is wise, will raid it from time to time, and annoy the garrison there, which is huge, and lumbersome, and creaks so loudly in the joints that you hear them eight hours before they move. So it's quite easy to run down and chuck a bomb at it, and run away without being caught.[7]

As so often with Lawrence, flippancy packaged insight. The greater the value of a strategic asset, the smaller the force necessary to generate anxiety: this was the essential asymmetry of Kress von Kressenstein's little war in the desert. Murray understood this and, in the summer of 1916, he was planning a decisive battle to extinguish the threat for good.

*　*　*

The British plan was based on the assumption that the Ottomans were preparing a new advance on the canal, and that it would be advantageous to lure them forward and fight the battle as close to Egypt as possible. The military axiom that an attack loses momentum as it advances is writ large in the desert. The summer heat reduced British infantry mobility to a maximum of about 6 miles per day. The cavalry could range much farther, but Katia had demonstrated the vulnerability of isolated mounted units to attack by strong combined-arms forces. Every leap forward, moreover, increased the logistical strain and reduced the size of the spearhead. The ideal was to shift the burden of heat, sand, distance and a lengthening supply-line onto the enemy. Murray planned to draw the Ottomans onto prepared positions in north-western Sinai, where their desert-weary force could be 'fixed' by entrenched infantry and attacked in flank and rear by a mobile *masse de manoeuvre*; in this way, they might even be surrounded and destroyed altogether.[8]

From the middle of May, the 52nd (Lowland) Division had occupied a fishhook-shaped line of eighteen redoubts covering the railhead and the main British forward-base at Romani. It extended from Mahemdiya on the coast to a complex of sand dunes about 6 miles inland. The northern flank rested on the great Bardawil Lagoon, the southern on a giant 70m-high dune called Katib Gannit, around which, perched on secondary dunes, curved the line of redoubts. Running west from Katib Gannit was Wellington Ridge, which bounded the southern edge of the sandy plain across which the railway ran from Kantara, via stations at Gilban and Pelusium, to Romani. Beyond Wellington Ridge – and outside the British position – lay a series of isolated dunes, the largest being Mount Meredith, a mile or so to the south, and Mount Royston, a similar distance to the south-west (the two heights were named after the commanders of the 1st and 2nd Light Horse Brigades respectively). Various gullies cut through Wellington Ridge and the dunes to its south. A gap extended from this vicinity across an expanse of heavy sand to the fortified post at Dueidar, about 10 miles to the south-west in the direction of Kantara, the main British base on the canal. The gap was deliberate: it was the mouth of the trap.[9]

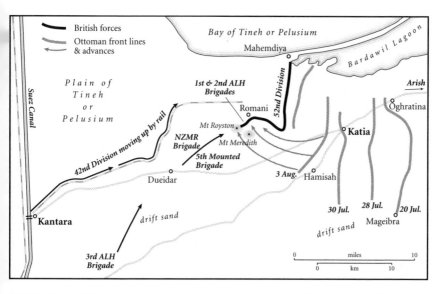

10. The Battle of Romani, 4 August 1916, showing the stages in the Ottoman advance, the farthest point reached and the British/Anzac response.

The position was held by about 11,000 infantry, 3,000 cavalry and 36 guns (mainly 18-pounder field-guns, but also two batteries of 4.5-inch howitzers and one of 60-pounder heavies). A similar number again were deployed within easy marching distance, in the vicinity of Kantara. Combat strength tended to fall well below this in the summer months, however, by as much as 50 per cent in some units, as men were incapacitated by the heat, which could soar above 50°C.[10] Each redoubt – essentially a circular trench fronted by barbed-wire – was defended by about 100 men, with perhaps two heavy machine-guns and some Lewis guns (portable light machine-guns). Typically, the redoubts were located on low sand-hills, roughly 900 yards apart, with good fields of fire of between 1,000 and 2,000 yards. In the south, where there was much dead ground around the redoubts, some were also supplied with Stokes trench-mortars. Deliberate efforts were made to conceal the strength of the defences: the redoubts were positioned below the sky-line, the sand-hillocks around them were not levelled, and the gaps between them were not wired until immediately before the battle. The aim was to encourage an attack, and in this the deception may have succeeded: Kress perhaps underestimated the size of the force opposing him at Romani, which, on the second day of the battle, would swell to twice the size of his entire force.[11]

British success depended on the Ottomans using the northern route across Sinai – not the central one, as they had in early 1915. To ensure this, Murray ordered the Light Horse to destroy the pools and cisterns at Wadi

Muksheib, about 35 miles south-east of Ismailia. They used hand-pumps to drain the cisterns and a combination of explosives and deep channels to drain the pools; the cisterns were then sealed to prevent them refilling. Three days of heavy labour in the summer heat destroyed stores of about 5 million gallons of water and effectively closed the central routeway across Sinai to large military forces.[12]

The whole of the Light Horse was active throughout the summer, moving across the desert on long-range patrols, men and horses often pushed to the limits of endurance. The intention, apart from keeping tabs on the enemy, was to toughen them and make them both desert-wise and desert-worthy: to prepare them for battle. After Chaytor's air reconnaissance on 19 July, patrolling intensified and clashes with small groups of the enemy became more frequent, heightening the sense that a major collision was imminent, despite the furnace-heat.[13]

* * *

Kress moved his men forward again on the night of 19/20 July, and then halted for a week on a line between Oghratina in the north and Mageibra in the south. The British suspected that he was planning to come no further, intending instead to fortify a forward line in the oasis zone and sit tight. In fact, he was delayed by logistics. Shortage of water in the oases had compelled him to move his infantry by echelons, while his heavy guns had to be manhandled across the desert in short stages by running the wheels through specially-cut gullies or over lengths of movable planking.[14] (In this respect, the British had a distinct advantage, having adopted 'pedrails' – short wooden planks fastened to the wheels of guns, carriages, and wagons, designed to distribute weight and prevent bogging in sand or mud.)[15]

Then, on the night of 27/28 July, the Ottoman forward movement was resumed. Five days later, the entire Canal Expeditionary Force, 12,000 rifles, 36 machine-guns and 30 guns, including relatively heavy 4.2-inch howitzers and 5.9-inch field-guns, was massed along a curving north-east to south-west line just beyond Katia, a mere 5 miles or so from the 52nd Infantry Division's line of redoubts.[16]

Alerted by patrols to the enemy advance, Chauvel began sending out a Light Horse brigade each night to form an outpost line between Katib Gannit and Hod al-Enna, covering the approaches to the area of sand dunes south of Wellington Ridge. On the night of 3 August, it was the turn of the 1st Light Horse. About three and a half miles long and echeloned back towards the south-west, this line, 750 strong, lay at right angles to the enemy's anticipated line of advance should he, as expected and hoped, attempt to manoeuvre around the open desert flank of the main British position.

Chauvel's instructions in the event of attack were clear: the brigade was not to break away but to conduct a fighting withdrawal, the line pivoting on Katib Gannit and falling back slowly on the right, squadron by squadron, in a series of rushes covered by fire. The aim was to lure the attackers forward – into the sand-filled mouth of the trap – but also to delay and tire them as they came on.[17] This was wholly in keeping Chauvel's strategy for mounted operations in the desert: instead of dispersal in small static posts – the worst possible way to use cavalry – he favoured concentration of force combined with aggressive patrolling.[18] This strategy now became the mechanism to achieve a tactical triumph.

* * *

The night was dark and quiet. Then, around 10pm, a light flashed in the Katia area. It showed four times for ten seconds on each occasion, then ceased: a signal. Nothing more was seen or heard for almost two hours, until, just before midnight, movement was detected in front of the outpost line. Immediately, amid panic shouts, firing erupted at different points in the darkness, rifles flashing at shadows in the sand. Then it died away. The Turks had not expected resistance so far forward; their advanced elements halted, uncertain of the strength opposing them, lacking appropriate orders, in need of reinforcement.

Around 1 o'clock the attack was renewed. The battle-cry *Allah al-Akbar* and the imprecation 'Finish Australia' could be heard above a roar of rifle-fire from the Ottoman line. The Light Horse fired back, and for the next hour a fierce gun-battle raged over the blackened sand as the Turkish infantry slowly worked their way forward, moulding themselves to the ground as they had at Katia, eventually closing the gap to 30 or 40 yards.

In places, groping through the darkness, men stumbled into each other. Two eight-man posts of the 3rd Light Horse Regiment were almost entirely destroyed in a frenzy of point-blank fire and bayonet stabbing when the Turks got among them. Command and control began to break down: it was dark and the line was widely spaced. Squadron and troop leaders assumed local control, pulling their men back when they sensed the Turks around them becoming too threatening. By 2 o'clock a disjointed fighting withdrawal was under way along the length of the Light Horse line.[19]

The firing eased for a while as the Turks regrouped and massed for the next push. Then, for half an hour, it flared up again in a tremendous battle for possession of Mount Meredith, the 70m-high sand dune that dominated the battlefield. A small Anzac contingent held the summit. The Turks discarded their boots to get better footing on the sliding wall of sand and mounted a succession of frontal assaults. Each was hurled back, the assailants bowled over by the defenders' fire and sent rolling away down the slope.

But eventually the Anzacs were flanked and forced to withdraw, and by around 3 o'clock the Turkish infantry were on the height – the decisive capture of the night, for they soon had a machine-gun in position on the top, poised to rake the wafer-thin line of light-horsemen below them as dawn broke over the desert. The Anzacs were now being driven back by up to 8,000 Turkish infantry, more then ten times their number. Often, groups of them had to cut and run. 'The bullets were making little spurts of flame all around us . . .' recalled the 2nd Regiment's Lieutenant-Colonel Bourne. 'Here we experienced for the first time the moral effects of turning our backs on the enemy, and the question arose in our minds as we rode, "Can we reform?"'[20]

They could and did; but for how long? As the sun came up, the disparity of force became apparent. As well as facing fire from the machine-gun and riflemen on Meredith, the line of Australian skirmishers lying in the desert was soon being sprayed with shrapnel as shells burst overhead. Meantime, thousands of Turkish infantry were moving forward on the left, threatening to flank the entire brigade and destroy it in enfilade.[21]

The Australians fell back on Wellington Ridge, troop covering troop as before, the khaki line still, against the odds, retaining its cohesion. Major W.R. Kermack of the 7th Royal Scots, watching with a brother officer, 'had a fine view of the Australians fighting their retiring action, galloping back over a ridge, leaping off their horses at the foot, and doubling up again to form a line on the crest. Rifle bullets fired too high for their targets came singing over in our direction . . .'[22] W.T. Massey, the official London press correspondent, also had a good view of the Australian horsemen in action and was equally impressed: 'I saw the Light Horse on Wellington Ridge when shrapnel was bursting over them with wonderful accuracy, but the Australians never showed the slightest sign of movement until the enemy attempted a rush.'[23] The German field-guns and howitzers also had some of the British infantry redoubts under fire: one fort, more exposed than the others, was to receive about 500 shells during several hours of bombardment.[24]

But relief was at hand, for at around 4.30am, the sun now well up, the 2nd Light Horse Brigade hoved into view. Chauvel had deliberately held them back, determined they should not become embroiled in the night-time struggle and leave him without a strong reserve before daylight revealed the shape of the battle. He could now see that the main threat was on the western flank, so he dispatched two regiments to extend the Light Horse line rightwards. The Turkish infantry, meantime, pushed forward along the whole line between

Mount Royston and Wellington Ridge, supported by artillery and machine-guns; and the light-horsemen continued to give ground. Chauvel's reinforcement was sufficient to sustain the line, not to reverse the tide. It was not intended to: the aim was still to draw the Turks forward, making them pay heavily for each 100 yards gained, degrading their capacity to continue the battle through the heat of the long daylight hours ahead.[25]

At 7am the Turks took Wellington Ridge, a 30m-high rise of sand that offered good shooting northwards, and shortly afterwards also seized Mount Royston, the 65m eminence dominating the western limit of the battlefield. But for an hour the Turkish infantry made no use of the ridge, keeping below the crest, and when they later appeared on the sky-line were almost immediately swept back by British fire. The balance had tipped against them. The Light Horse had been reinforced by a British infantry battalion, which had swung into line on the left, while British batteries deployed to the rear had ranged in on the enemy-controlled ridge.[26]

About Mount Royston, too, the battle stalled. The Turks had continued to extend westwards in their effort to envelop the Light Horse, but had been checked, first by the Wellington Mounted Rifles (acting under Chauvel's orders), then by a squadron of Gloucestershire Hussars (acting on the initiative of their commanding officer). This was just sufficient: the Turks, at the end of their endurance and lacking fresh reserves, went to ground. By 11 o'clock the battle had lapsed into relative passivity. The offensive was losing momentum.[27]

* * *

The reason for the pause was simple. The Turks were tired and had run out of water. The enemy line, on the other hand, had filled out and firmed up. There was a momentary balance of force. But the scales were set to tip.

The Turkish infantry had been moving and fighting in shifting sand for eight hours. They had been wilting under the rising heat of the summer sun for the last four. Most had now drunk the modest ration of water in their bottles. The Light Horse were better served. Each man carried a quart of water, and, operating close to Romani, could easily be resupplied; the 7th Regiment was in fact so close to one of the British camps that the cooks – under heavy fire – served tea in the afternoon to the men in the firing-line as they lay in their little scoops of sand.[28]

Moving up and down the line, in close contact with his officers, Chauvel sensed the change in tempo. The lull signalled that the moment to close the trap had arrived, for the exhausted Turks now lay before the British lines, their forward impetus used up, their left flank wide open to attack from the west.[29]

Ideally, Chauvel's men, having drawn the Ottomans deep into the mouth of the Romani position, should have been relieved by infantry, given time to water their horses, and then used to reinforce the mounted counter-stroke now in preparation. But Chauvel was not in overall command; both he, as commander of the Anzac Mounted Division, and General Smith, as commander of the 52nd (Lowland) Division, took their orders from General Lawrence, whose head-quarters were not at Romani at all, but at Kantara on the canal. Nor was that all: Lawrence had reserved to himself direct control over the cavalry strike-force on the western flank, the New Zealand Mounted Rifles and the 5th Mounted Yeomanry. It was a clumsy arrangement – made more so when the telephone line between Romani and Kantara was severed early on the morning of the battle. Smith refused to use his reserve to relieve Chauvel's men, since he was planning his own assault eastwards towards Abu Hamra. Lawrence, acting on delayed intelligence, did not get the New Zealanders and Yeomanry moving until the morning was well advanced.[30] Had Chauvel – 'the brain of Romani' – had full battlefield command, the counter-stroke might have been truly crushing.[31]

As it was, the speed and weight necessary to destroy the now-spent Ottoman force was lacking. Late morning, a body of troops was spotted approaching from the south-west. Major Whyte, a New Zealand officer serving with the 2nd Light Horse, flashed a heliograph message: 'Who are you?' The reply came back: 'Chaytor'. This was welcome news. After a further brief exchange, Whyte asked: 'Will you attack Mount Royston?' The reply flashed out over the desert: 'Advancing to attack Mount Royston.'[32]

The attack got under way early in the afternoon. There were about 2,000 Turks hidden in the piles of heavy sand about Mount Royston. Facing them to the north were the 3rd and 6th Light Horse Regiments, backed by some of Chauvel's horse guns and two British 18-pounder batteries (it was the fire of this artillery that had forced the Turks to go to ground). Deploying on their western flank was the whole of the Canterbury Mounted Rifles, part of the Auckland Mounted Rifles, and several squadrons of 5th Yeomanry: a firing-line of perhaps a thousand. These were supported by a Somerset territorial battery of horse guns.[33]

The offensive capability of the Turkish infantry may have been exhausted, but not their determination in defence. Chaytor's men, trudging forward in heavy sand under intense heat, rarely saw their enemy in the maze of little hills and gullies. The Turkish defenders fought stubbornly and shot well throughout the afternoon. The German artillery continued to rake the British lines. Lieutenant Joe McPherson of the Camel Transport Corps, detailed to deliver water to the Worcester Yeomanry, discovered that 'the whole region we were traversing was at present a battlefield. Shells and bullets whistling over us, the rattle of machine-guns and rifle-fire, and the roar of artillery made that obvious to me . . .'[34] A short while later, standing before a precipitous drop, he gained a grandstand view of the battle below:

Suddenly, hell opened beneath our feet. Out of the peaceful palm-grove came shot and shell . . . and our troops responded with terrible effect. A hail of shrapnel crashed into the trees and a fusillade opened upon it. Men rushed out and attempted to climb, [but fell and] remained dead, framed on the sand. Horses and camels burst out and fell spouting blood . . . I was so fascinated by the sight, and it was so theatrical and dramatic, that I felt rather like the occupant of a stage-box at the fifth act of a tragedy.[35]

Only around 6 o'clock did the Turks' morale finally break. By then, British infantry of the 42nd Division, marching up from the south-west, were entering the battle and tipping its balance. Many of the Turks were suffering from dysentery; all were hungry, tormented by thirst and shattered by their 18 hours' exertion, most of it under a broiling sun. Slowly losing ground and in increasing danger as the enemy firing-line closed and thickened around them, the defenders of Mount Royston hoisted the white flag and around 500 surrendered.[36]

The Worcesters' medical officer was soon on the scene.

The wounded Turks were most grateful for the water and food, as they only had with them a few dates and a little dirty water. They looked so grateful when they found that we were not going to leave them out in the desert, and made no sound while we dressed their wounds. One great bearded fellow, badly shot through the thigh, had the grateful look of an injured dog in his expressive eyes as we lifted him onto a horse.[37]

Teichman was later struck by the variegated appearance of the prisoners. They were a living microcosm of the globalised war of empire.

There seemed to be representatives of many races among them, from the desert Arab and negro soldier to the fair-haired and blue-eyed European Turk. Infantry wearing the enverene hats, brown fezzes or skullcaps, dressed in dark-brown khaki and corduroy breeches (most unsuitable for this climate), gunners in astrakhan caps and blue uniforms, Arab irregulars in flowing garments, transport drivers with red facings to their uniforms and yellow sashes, and German machine-gunners in khaki drill and wearing yachting caps.[38]

The victory was won; but it was not as decisive as it could have been. Sand, heat and Turkish resilience had slowed the counter-attack on the afternoon of 4 August. The 42nd Division had come up too late to deliver a knockout blow before darkness fell. The 52nd Division had done little fighting, its commander refusing to provide Chauvel with the weight needed for a punch at the Turks on Wellington Ridge.[39] The following morning, when the ridge was finally stormed and retaken, the Anzac troopers – begrimed in dust and sweat, eyes bloodshot from lack of sleep – were still in the front-line. The 7th Light Horse, the Wellington Mounted Rifles, and the 8th Scottish Rifles burst onto the ridge at dawn, covered by fire from the 7th Scottish Rifles. Another 1,500 Turks were captured.[40]

Chauvel's light-horsemen immediately swept forward over the desert, their exhaustion held in abeyance by the adrenalin-surge of victory and the chase. The ground was littered with abandoned kit, and they took the surrender of hundreds of straggling Turks. Lieutenant P.G. Sneath, a trench-mortar officer with the 52nd Division, watched the early stages of the spectacle through a periscope:

> An Australian Light Horse patrol was approaching the post with a batch of prisoners ... As they approached, Turks could be seen rising from behind the cover of scrub and sand dunes as far as the eye could see. They were throwing down their rifles and holding up their hands. Some were waving white flags in token of surrender ... The Australian Light Horse were rounding them up like sheep.[41]

Was Kress von Kressenstein's little army disintegrating? Chauvel, finally given command of all the mounted troops and ordered to conduct a vigorous pursuit, may have thought so as his four brigades approached the Katia oasis around 3.30 on the afternoon of 5 August.[42]

* * *

In fact, Kress had been granted the time and space he needed to extract the bulk of his army and orchestrate an effective fighting withdrawal; his consummate German professionalism and the discipline of his Gallipoli veterans did the rest. Chauvel assumed that the Turkish line confronting him at Katia was weak and shaky; a rapid mounted charge, especially by men brandishing cold steel, might be enough to break it. He therefore deployed his men in a long line, 5th Yeomanry on the left, 2nd and 1st Light Horse in the centre, New Zealand Rifles on the right: several thousand mounted men ranged across several thousand yards of ground. Bayonets were snapped onto rifles and the men waved their weapons aloft, more like warriors of antiquity than the soldiers of an industrial war. The moral effect might compensate for the awkwardness of managing a charging horse while gripping a Lee-Enfield rifle with fixed bayonet.[43]

'The colonel with the adjutant rode in the lead,' recalled Trooper Ion Idriess of the 5th Light Horse Regiment:

> the squadron majors leading their squadrons . . . We held the horses in so as to have their strength in the last great clash. But they were getting excited . . . we rode knee-to-knee . . . and our bodies felt the massed heat of the horses that tugged and strained as the horses broke into a swift canter. Then a horse reared high and screamed, and we were into a mad gallop, the horses' mouths open and their great eyes staring as the squadrons thundered on.[44]

The mounted brigades had formed up on the solid ground of a salt-pan about a mile and a half from the edge of the oasis. They anticipated good going across the intervening distance and only ragged fire from the far side. Both assumptions were wrong. Along most of the front, the hard salt-pan quickly gave way to salt-water swamp about 2,000 yards wide. The exhilaration of the charge was short-lived as the line of horsemen plunged into the mire and came to a standstill, bogging to their knees. Orders were given to dismount and send the horses to the rear, and the troopers began wading forward on foot. But the fire coming from the distant line of palm-trees in front proved to be a full-on storm, not a faltering patter.

Katia was a reserve position and, using the trunks and cut-down branches of the palm-trees for cover, the Turks defending the oasis had established a strong firing-line along its western edge, with concealed machine-guns along its length and heavy guns in support behind. The position, moreover, was growing stronger all the time, as men trailing in from the Romani debacle found refuge, were revived with water and food, and then sent straight into the line.[45]

The attackers' task was hopeless. Some units completed their charge – the 5th Yeomanry Brigade on the left and the 5th Light Horse and Auckland Mounted Rifles on the right – because they had charged beyond the northern and southern limits of swamp. But they then ran into heavy machine-gun and artillery fire from positions hidden in the palm-hods. The men of the 1st and 2nd Light Horse Brigades, on the other hand, never got closer than between 600 to 1,000 yards. Hauling themselves through the mire on foot, some of them now continuously in the saddle or the firing-line for 60 hours, they made feeble progress. Nor could they see the enemy ahead to deliver effective counter-fire. By dusk, the attack had come to a standstill half way across the swamp. Chauvel ordered a general withdrawal. His men were sent back to Romani to water their horses. Meantime, the victors in the battle – for whom this had been but a holding action – also pulled out, the tired Turkish infantry slogging east in the direction of Oghratina.[46]

* * *

The fate of the British infantry on 5 August confirmed the desert's crushing power. The Lowlanders of the 52nd Division, defending the line of redoubts east of Romani, had had several weeks to acclimatise. Having done little on the 4th, their advance on the 5th had started late, and they failed to make contact with the enemy that day, leaving the mounted brigades to fight alone at Katia. The East Lancashire men of the 42nd Division plumbed the depths of misery. New to the desert, they had been marched up to Romani from the canal the previous day, and then marched on to Katia during 5 August, trudging across the desert all day long under the furnace-sun in full kit. Water discipline broke down and bottles were soon empty. Before noon, many battalions were in acute distress and, by the end of the day, as the forward elements neared Katia – too late to play any part in the battle – the stragglers numbered thousands. One battalion lost 300 men along the way. Many fell unconscious. Others went mad, scraping frantically at the burning sand in search of water. Not a few died of sunstroke.[47] A New Zealand officer reported seeing men 'in a fearful state through lack of water, with blackened lips and swollen tongues'.[48]

* * *

In the fighting on 4 and 5 August, both sides in their turn had been reduced to prostration by the desert. The Ottoman left hook against Romani had been defeated by sand, heat and lack of water; it was, reported Chauvel, 'the empty Turkish water-bottle that won the battle', adding that 'Meredith and Royston [commanders respectively of his 1st and 2nd Brigades] had put six hours on to it ... Meredith, by his gallant stand in the night, was chiefly responsible for the success of the delaying action, and Royston, by his ceaseless activity and fearlessness, for the holding of the line we gradually withdrew to.'[49] The Anzac charge at Katia, on the other hand, had dissolved in a salt-swamp as men finally succumbed to utter physical exhaustion. In each case, victory had gone to men fighting defensively close to water; in each case, the desert had shrivelled up the efforts of their opponents to traverse its wide, fiery, desiccated spaces.

General Murray, the EEF (Egyptian Expeditionary Force) commander, under pressure from the War Office to press the pursuit after Romani, cabled back the ineluctable realities:

> I cannot pursue with the vigour I should like, because the horses of the Anzac Mounted Division are exhausted. After a short march on the 5th, 800 men were missing from one brigade of the 42nd Division, and the GOC (general officer commanding) the 52nd Division tells me that many of his men are undersized and quite incapable of sustained effort. The Turkish infantry is almost as fast over the desert as my cavalry. They are fine, active men, in good condition.[50]

Lynden-Bell shared his chief's assessment, seeing in the relative failure at Romani and Katia further evidence of the vital need for more camels. He had demanded 50,000 camels in January 1916, but the War Office had baulked at expense and effort 'which did not appear necessary'. But if the infantry had had full camel-transport trains to bring up water and supplies, and if some of the cavalry had been camel-mounted for wide desert sweeps, Lynden-Bell complained to Maurice, the outcome might have been radically different. 'It comes back to camels every time . . . If we had had the camels the other day at Romani, I feel certain that not a single Turk would have got away.' The central lesson of the campaign was that the camel deficit had to be made good: given sufficient numbers, it should be possible 'to smack the enemy next time he comes on' by getting 'the whole of our mounted troops in his rear'.[51]

* * *

In his slow advance towards Romani in late July, Kress had prepared a number of fall-back positions. Having pulled his men out of Katia on the night of 5 August, he had them stand again at Oghratina, where for two days more they blocked Chauvel's advance. Attacks by dismounted light-horsemen alone were hopeless against entrenched infantry supported by machine-guns and artillery, and the men of the 42nd and 52nd Divisions simply could not march fast enough in the desert heat to keep pace with the moving front. On the night of 7 August, the Turkish infantry again withdrew, falling back to a third position at Bir al-Abd, more than 20 miles east of Romani.[52]

The British decided to attempt another frontal assault. They still hoped to smash the enemy rearguard and expose his retreating army to destruction. The

Mounted Division was moved up on 8 August and readied for battle the following day. The Battle of Bir al-Abd was a rerun of Katia – but against more daunting odds. The Turkish infantry had had time to refresh themselves and recover from the shock of defeat. They had been reinforced, the rearguard now having some 6,000 men in the line. Much labour had been expended on constructing trenches and redoubts in a line of sand-hills at Bir al-Abd. Chauvel, on the other hand, had no more than 3,000 dismounted rifles with which to fight the battle and, while his horse artillery could match the enemy's mountain-guns, he had nothing to oppose to their 5.9-inch howitzers.[53]

The light-horsemen went forward on horseback until the volume of shot became too heavy, then dismounted and sent their horses to the rear. But they could make little further progress as a tremendous fire of rifles, machine-guns, and cannon raged along the line. Though some enemy posts were rushed, most of the line stalled, much of it no closer than 1,000 yards to the enemy trenches.

Around midday, the Turks began to counter-attack along the entire line. They had greatest success on Chauvel's left, where, in the late afternoon, having lapped around the northern flank of the 1st and 2nd Light Horse Brigades, they also sent between 2,000 and 3,000 men against the front. The firing-lines were soon only a few hundred yards apart, and the pressure here, and also on the right, began to unhinge Chauvel's line. With the Anzac flanks 'in the air', the 1st and 2nd Light Horse were forced back on the left, the 3rd Light Horse on the right, and this left the New Zealanders in the centre increasingly exposed to enfilading fire from either side. The position had become untenable. Chauvel ordered a general withdrawal at 5.30.

As soon as the Turks perceived the movement, they pushed forward on a front of two and a half miles. Troop by troop, squadron by squadron, the little bands of dismounted horsemen withdrew, some stumbling across the heavy dunes while others lay in the scalding sand, rifles poised, arms blistered. They had ridden all night and fought all day on two pints of water. A fighting withdrawal from close contact with a more powerful enemy tested discipline to the limit. It did not fail: casualties were heavy, but not a single troop broke and ran. Almost all the wounded – all save a handful of New Zealanders who could not be reached – were carried away: 210 men in total.[54]

Chauvel's horsemen rode back to Oghratina, leaving the field, on which lay 73 of their dead and 33 wounded, to the enemy. But the Turks did not stay. That night they abandoned the oasis zone of north-western Sinai and trudged back over the largely waterless 60-mile waste separating Bir al-Abd from Arish. They had lost more than 5,000 men, a third of the Canal Expeditionary Force, of whom nearly 4,000 were prisoners. They had lost also a mountain battery, 9 machine-guns, 2,300 rifles, and 1 million rounds of ammunition. Total British casualties over the five days of fighting were 1,100, the great majority Anzacs.[55]

* * *

The lesson of Romani was clear: without industrialised water supply and camel-based mobility, the desert itself was the real master of war. Each side had been defeated in its turn when its water ran out. Without some combination of water-pipe and camel train, the projection of decisive military force across the desert was a logistical impossibility. Once again, 60 miles of desert separated the rival armies, and this imposed a pause on the fighting while the logistics caught up.

Nonetheless, Romani was the turning-point of the war in the Middle East. The Ottoman attempt to frustrate the British advance across northern Sinai had failed. That advance, once threaded with water-pipe, railway and wire-road, would continue, carrying British arms to the gates of Palestine, thence to Jerusalem, and eventually to Damascus and Aleppo. The stand of the 1st and 2nd Light Horse on the morning of 4 August, followed by Chaytor's mounted counter-stroke that afternoon, was the moment when the Ottoman Empire lost the initative, never to regain it.[56]

This was made certain that summer by events far from north-western Sinai. A new front in the Middle Eastern war had opened in June 1916. The Hashemite Arabs of Mecca had risen in revolt and a tribal insurgency was swelling across the western Arabian Desert.

At first the two wars were widely separated. Yet the effect of the second was soon felt on the first, as Ottoman reserves were drawn down by the demands of the new Arab front. And, in due course, the two wars would converge in time and space. Before the year was out, the British army would be on the southern edge of Palestine, while the Arab insurgency would be spreading ominously northwards towards the Syrian heartland of the Ottoman East.[57]

CHAPTER 7

The Arab Revolt

ARABIA IN 1916 was as different from the cosmopolitan churn of Constantinople as the latter was from London, Paris or Berlin. It was defined by the dichotomy between 'desert and sown', the tense symbiosis of nomads and peasants. Despite mutual dependence and shared kinship, ethnicity, religion and language, they regarded each other with suspicion and unease. The true Bedouin wandered through the wilderness from one watering-place to another with their herds of camels, horses, sheep and goats, inhabiting temporary encampments of large, black, square, animal-hair tents. For thousands of years, though, they had been depositing a human sediment of settlers and cultivators into the fringes and oases of the desert. The most recent of these still lived in villages that were half mud-brick hut, half goat-hair tent.[1] Others were descendants of families sedentary for hundreds of years, and the villages and towns of the larger oases were hives of horticulture and handicrafts. The villagers cultivated dates, figs, vines and other fruits, or tended little fields of grain (for making bread) or vetch (for feeding camels), working to the timeless creaking of wooden irrigation wheels.[2] In the souk worked tailors, wood-turners, metal-smiths, stone-cutters and saddle-makers; dealers in camels, horses, drugs, spices, sugar and coffee; grocers trading onions, eggs, salt, matches, nails and bread; and veiled peasant-women squatting on the ground with chickens, milk and leather water-carriers for sale.[3]

The nomads came frequently to these little desert settlements – for rice, grain, coffee, sugar and tobacco; for cooking pans and serving dishes, coffee-pots and drinking cups; for horse harness and camel saddles; for weaponry, jewellery and trinkets. But the nomads were also warriors of the blood-feud and the raid – the *ghazzu* – and they were liable to descend upon the village, encampment or camel-caravan of a rival tribe and carry off whatever they could gather as plunder. Fear and poverty were, in the Arabian explorer Charles

Doughty's view, at the root of such cruel violence. The spirits of the Bedouin were 'made weary with incessant apprehension of their enemies, and their flesh with continual thirst and hunger'; by the necessitous life of the desert they were 'constrained to be robbers'.[4] So townsmen welcomed their trade, but dreaded their raids; from the perspective of the town, the Bedouin were 'the demons of this wild waste earth'.[5]

Doughty had travelled the wild lands of middle Arabia in the 1870s, and his travel memoir, *Travels in Arabia Deserta*, had become a classic. Thomas Edward Lawrence knew it well, and loved it, despite its inordinate length (more than 600,000 words) and its eccentric and sometimes near-impenetrable prose. As preparation for a walking tour in Syria to collect data for his undergraduate dissertation in 1909, Lawrence had written to Doughty seeking advice (it had been discouraging), and had then sat in the Bodleian reading *Arabia Deserta*. Three years later, when on his way back to Carchemish, he had called in on the great man, again with travel plans in mind. Doughty became a role model for the young archaeologist, the veteran explorer appealing to Lawrence's Romantic-Orientalist world view and his yearning for adventure. 'I am not trying to rival Doughty,' he wrote to his parents in 1911. But clearly he was, for, in reference to his own plans for travel in the East, he continued: 'You remember that passage that he who has once seen palm-trees and the goat-hair tents is never the same as he has been: that I feel very strongly, and I feel also that Doughty's two years wandering in untainted places made him the man he is, more than all his careful preparation before or since.'[6]

Its danger was, of course, part of the allure of the desert for men like Doughty and Lawrence. The policing of it was a routine responsibility of the more powerful Arabian lords. The emir of Mecca, the Hashemite Sherif Hussein ibn Ali, was one of these. As the guardian of the holy places, he had a special responsibility for the protection of pilgrims. In 1909 he ordered attacks on the Bani al-Harith – 'notorious brigands and highway robbers' – and on the Mutair – who were 'frightening the pilgrims and refusing to pay their tithes'. The order was executed by a composite posse: 'a police force on camels, a mounted force of the emir's men, together with levies from the loyal tribes'.[7]

Thus the violence of the desert made it also despotic. The one gave rise to the other: the insecurity of social life, its ruthless law of 'survival of the fittest', ensured that the desert was ruled by military strongmen, warlords who offered protection in return for submission. The Bedouin were in thrall to great tribal lords who stood at the head of a tributary system in which wealth in camels, horses, bond-men, metalwork and foodstuffs was siphoned upwards.

The Emir Ibn Rashid, for example, the lord of Jebel Shammar in northern Arabia, ruled over 5 desert towns, 25 oasis villages and the 500 miles of desert between them. Up to 20,000 settled people and perhaps 15,000 nomads owed him allegiance and tribute at the time of Doughty's visit in the 1870s. He ruled his wilderness fiefdom from Hail, a fortified town of several thousand dominated by its whitewashed, high-walled, mud-brick *Kasr*, where ancient cannon and a great coffee-hall strewn with Baghdad carpets symbolised the ruler's power and wealth. He would hold court in the morning in the public square outside, dispensing justice in a feudal-tribal *mejlis* ('council'). He would sometimes process through the streets with his retinue to pray at the Great Mosque. And if his authority were to be challenged, perhaps in some distant encampment, a 500-strong miniature army of household cavalry and camel-mounted tribesmen would muster at his summons, ready to sally forth and restore obedience.[8]

* * *

Six lords of comparable standing dominated Arabia in the years before the First World War. Their rivalries with each other were paramount, and allegiances were formed accordingly. Ibn Rashid of Hail was firmly pro-Ottoman. He sold the Turks camels. They paid him subsidies. He needed support against his desert rivals, the ancient Hashemite dynasty of Mecca, and now also the rising power of Ibn Saud, who was contesting control of the Nejd region of central Arabia. The Ottomans, eager to assist, supplied Ibn Rashid and his Shammar with 12,000 rifles and large sums of money shortly before the outbreak of war, enabling him to double the size of his army.[9]

To the north, dominating the eastern desert and in control of the 200-mile chain of oases along the Wadi Sirhan, one of the region's great highways, was Nuri al-Shaalan of the Ruwalla. He was anti-Ottoman, but discreetly so, for he was close to the main centres of Ottoman power, and his people needed access to the urban markets of Damascus and Baghdad.[10]

Ibn Saud was equally hostile to the Ottomans and for similar reasons: he had a yearning for independence from foreign overlordship. His active programme of conquest in both central Arabia and on the Gulf coast – not to mention his long-term aspiration to pan-Arabian supremacy – could hardly be squared with loyalty to his nominal sovereign.[11] But for Abdul Aziz ibn Saud, *Realpolitik* was reinforced by religion.

The Saudis were adherents of the puritanical Wahhabi sect, whose exceptionally joyless form of Islam seems to have found a natural home in the desiccated wastes of central Arabia; Doughty thought the Nejd region 'soured by the rheum of the Wahhabi religion'. Adherents abhorred smoking, drinking, dancing and womanising, and perceived the general laxity of Ottoman culture with sanctimonious disdain.[12] The Wahhabi *ikhwan* ('brotherhood'), 11,000 strong in 1912, 30,000 strong by 1919, formed the core of Ibn Saud's army; their ferocity – which extended to the routine slaughter of men and occasionally of women and children – gave it a medieval character. The *ikhwan* were supported by tens of thousands of Bedouin irregulars. Though many still fought with swords, spears and muskets, the process of modernisation had begun and, in the course of the war, Ibn Saud would acquire 8,000 modern rifles, 4 machine-guns and about a dozen 7-pounder mountain-guns.[13]

The formidable Saudi army was not, however, about to be directed against the Ottoman Empire. Ibn Saud may have told Captain Shakespear, Britain's representative in Riyadh, that he cordially hated the Turks, did not consider himself a vassal of the Ottoman sultan, and regarded the sultan's claim to the caliphate as a preposterous abomination.[14] But it hardly mattered: Ibn Saud was too far from Syria to be a real threat to the Ottomans, and he was, in any case, wholly preoccupied with the struggle for power in Arabia, first and foremost with Ibn Rashid of Hail.[15] These two potentates waged a private desert war in north-central Arabia for as long as the world war lasted. They fought in their own interests and as proxies of the great powers, for Ibn Rashid was armed by the Ottomans, Ibn Saud by the British (or, more precisely, by the Government of India). They thereby neutralised each other (though Shammar power slowly weakened). This had the coincidental effect that it freed their mutual enemy, the sherif of Mecca, to initiate a revolt against Ottoman rule – albeit with an ever-anxious eye on his eastern flank.

Two other Arab rulers were held in check by the presence of Ottoman troops. One was the Imam Yahya of Yemen, based at Sanaa, the dominant polit-ical figure in the remote and rebellious south-western corner of the peninsula. The imams had led a succession of revolts against Constantinople in the late nineteenth and early twentieth century, but the Young Turks, weary of the mili-tary drain, had cut a deal, granting extensive powers and a generous subsidy to the Yemeni ruler, so as to transform him into an Ottoman client. The existence of the Protectorate of Aden, a major coaling station run by the Government of India, and the policy of the British authorities there of cultivating the allegiance of Sunni tribes on the coastal plain, gave the Imam, a Shia whose main base of support was among the tribes of the more mountainous interior, additional reason for remaining at peace with the Turk.

The 39th and 40th Divisions of the Yemen Army Corps, comprising 14,000 mainly Ottoman Syrian soldiers, were therefore at liberty, under their enter-prising Circassian officer, Ali Said Pasha, to mount aggressive operations against the British. An Aden Field Force was hastily assembled, and by 1916 this comprised six infantry battalions (one British, the rest Indian), two cavalry squadrons, a company of sappers, and some antiquated guns. Both sides also raised local tribal forces. The British threw back a major assault on Aden in July 1915, and thereafter the situation remained more or less stable until the end of the war. The garrison was too strong to be dislodged and could be supplied indefinitely by sea; on the other hand, it had neither the inclination nor the means to challenge Ottoman/Yemeni control of the hinterland. Though cut off from their base, the Ottoman divisions were sustained by local supply and enjoyed either the active allegiance or at least the passive acquiescence of most of the Yemeni tribes.[16]

Asir – the region of southern Arabia between the Hijaz and the Yemen – was also under religious leadership, that of Sayyid Muhammad al-Idrisi. Al-Idrisi was the descendant of a family of Moroccan pilgrims who had undertaken the Hajj, founded a Sufi religious order, and settled in the mountains of Asir at the end of the eighteenth century. Having studied at a religious academy in Cairo and met with the Senussi leader in Cyrenaica, Sayyid Muhammad had no sooner succeeded his father after returning home than he launched a rebellion against Ottoman rule, calling for the restoration of the Arab *umma* ('community') and the establishment of a just and holy state ruled by *sharia* ('religious law'). By the end of 1910, Al-Idrisi had driven the Ottomans from most of Asir, and his agitation was beginning to infect the Yemeni tribes to the south and the Hijazi to the north. This gave the Ottomans the opportunity to enlist the active assistance of the Sherif Hussein, and combined Ottoman-Sherifian forces inflicted heavy defeats on Al-Idrisi in 1911 and 1912, thereby containing his *jihad* within the mountains of Asir.

Though succoured by the British from 1915 – they supplied him with rifles, ammunition, and field-guns – Al-Idrisi was held in check by the Ottoman 21st Division, which, though cut off from Constantinople like the two divisions in Yemen, remained operationally effective throughout the war.[17] In any case, whatever ambitions he might have harboured, Al-Idrisi's geopolitical position was similar to that of Ibn Saud: both were too far from Syria to aspire to lead a pan-Arab revolt against Ottoman rule; neither could hope to be anything more than desert lords.

Nor, for that matter, did their British sponsors wish otherwise. Simla – not London – ran the British imperial operation in Arabia. As well as having the port-city of Aden under its direct rule, the Government of India had treaties with many of the Arab chiefs around the southern and eastern seaboards. Kuwait was of particular strategic importance: under British influence, its huge, natural, deep-water port at the head of the Persian Gulf made it an ideal outpost of maritime power; in other hands, it might have become an equally useful terminus for the planned Baghdad Railway. But the Gulf as a whole was already, to all intents and purposes, a British protectorate, the Ottoman sultan's authority reduced to a letterhead well before the outbreak of war.[18]

Yet Simla had no inclination to turn any of its Arabian allies into active belligerents. The new wartime treaties concluded with Ibn Saud and Al-Idrisi in 1915 concerned only local issues.[19] India's colonial elite of expatriate civil servants and officers lived in perpetual fear of the social volcano beneath them. Tremors induced panic. They had no wish to stir up revolts of any kind. What unforeseeable consequences, they asked, might an Arab-Islamic revolution in the Middle East have for the security of the Raj – especially at a time when so much of the overextended Indian Army was serving abroad?[20]

* * *

Only Sherif Hussein, the emir of Mecca, was neither a client of Simla nor an Ottoman loyalist; only he, of the six great potentates of Arabia, had the capacity, the reach, the will and the freedom of action to lead a general native revolt against colonial rule.

Much of his territory, the Hijaz region of north-western Arabia, which extended about 750 miles north–south from Aqaba to Asir, and about 200 miles east–west from the Red Sea into the Nejd, was a waterless, uninhabited wilderness. But not all. Along the western and southern rim of the Arabian Peninsula the land tips upwards, creating mountain ranges which cool the hot air rising off the coastal plains and turn it into rain. The highlands run from the Levant through the Hijaz to Asir and Yemen, and wherever they run, there are patches at least of rainy upland where cultivation is possible. Hijazi mountain villages enjoyed a modest abundance of vines, almonds, peaches, pears, plums, pomegranates, sesame seeds, jujube fruit and honey.[21] Even so, the entire population was perhaps only a third of a million, a mixture of townsmen, villagers and Bedouin nomads, and the whole life of the Hijaz revolved around the city of Mecca, with about 60,000 people, and the annual Hajj pilgrimage. The control, management and safeguarding of pilgrims was a primary government responsibility, and the supply of food, accommodation, transport and guides to pilgrims was the foundation of the economy.

The sherifs – the title means 'noble' or 'honourable' – were direct lineal descendants of the Prophet through his daughter Fatima, her husband Ali, and their eldest son Hussein. As such, they enjoyed immense prestige across the Islamic world, and Ottoman sultans had traditionally been circumspect in dealings with them. The existence of more than one Sherifian clan, and the right enjoyed by the Ottoman sultan, in his role as caliph, to appoint the emir of Mecca, provided some opportunity to ensure that incumbents were compliant. But the Hijaz, because of its religious significance, had special status within the empire, and the emirs had greater, if ill-defined, authority than other vassals of the sultan. This was often a source of tension, especially during the nineteenth century, as the Ottoman regime see-sawed between reform and reaction, at times seeking to create a more centralised and modernising state, at others relapsing into stasis. The inner struggle between tradition and modernity intensified under Abdulhamid II, his reign a contradictory mix of Islamism, absolutism, military reform and railway construction; and yet more so with the advent of the Young Turk regime in 1908. This struggle found the Hashemites of the Hijaz firmly on the side of reaction.[22]

* * *

Sherif Hussein ibn Ali had been born in Constantinople in the middle of the nineteenth century, but had spent his adolescence and early manhood in Mecca, where he had acquired intimate knowledge of the desert, the tribes and the manners of the Sherifian court. He later spent long periods in Constantinople – he and his sons were effectively hostages of the sultan in the capital between 1892 and 1908 – and there became familiar with the affairs of the Ottoman court and the politics of the empire. Yet Hussein remained a traditional tribal potentate and a slave-owning aristocrat: a medieval relic in an age of steamships, railways and telegraphs. He considered women working in the Constantinople post office to be wickedness, and Ottoman soldiers who did not observe the Ramadan fast to be violators of Islam.[23] When the Committee of Union and Progress (CUP) proposed 'constitutional changes for progress and safety', his response was intractably conservative:

> I have ascended to the position of my fathers on the same conditions as those given to Sultan Selim I [in the early sixteenth century]. This is the land of God, in which no other law can prevail but the law of God ... Let, therefore, everyone ... go to his work, the civil servant to his office, the merchant to his business, the tradesman to his trade ... This country abides by the constitution of God, the law of God, and the teachings of His Prophet.[24]

The emir's vision was of a static social order, controlled by a self-perpetuating elite, bolstered by a medieval conception of Islam, that simply replicated itself forever. True to his word, after taking power in Mecca, Hussein imposed a brutal form of *sharia* law which set him at odds with liberal Arab nationalists. Cafes were shut at prayer-times, alcohol and gramophones banned, and hands and feet amputated in grotesque punishment rituals. Later, when the fighting began, Turkish prisoners were enslaved – chained and whipped to perform forced labour.[25]

Hussein had his sons educated in the same medieval code. They were first sent to be raised by nomads in the desert – to toughen them up, teach them the Bedouin life-way and endow them with the popular touch required of the Sherifian class. They were then given a traditional education: learning to recite the Koran by heart, mastery of the Arabic language, skill in calligraphy; and the cane was liberally applied. Only later, in exile in Constantinople, was the curriculum enriched with more modern subjects: Turkish, geography, arithmetic, Islamic and Ottoman history. But education still took place privately, in the home, in a manner considered appropriate to desert princes, and in such a way as to insulate them from wider social contacts and political influence. The sons of Hussein – Ali, Abdullah, Feisal and Zeid – were pickled in the aristocratic tradition of Arabia.[26]

и и и

Reaction in the Hijaz to the 1908 Young Turk Revolution had been hostile. The reigning sherif – Hussein's predecessor – had refused to proclaim the news that liberal constitutional rule had been restored, and even ordered the public flogging of men overheard discussing the new freedoms. He was promptly dismissed and the sultan appointed Hussein to replace him.[27] But Hussein was no more sympathetic to the Young Turks than his predecessor. Before leaving Constantinople to assume office, at a private audience with Abdulhamid (who remained in power for a year after the revolution), he assured the old despot of his allegiance: 'Your Majesty has in the Arab countries a group which can save the situation, and when Your Majesty calls, the first country to respond will be the Hijaz.'[28] Hussein owed his elevation not to any affinity with the revolutionaries, but to the fact that the middle-class officers of the CUP were not yet securely enough in power to challenge the traditional prerogative of the sultan-caliph to choose the emir of Mecca. The effect was to place a determined enemy of the new regime in control of the Hijaz.

Hussein had many reasons to revolt. Personally ambitious and deeply religious, he embodied the traditional Arab aspiration to reconstruct the medieval Islamic caliphate, when Arabia, Syria and Iraq had been united in a single polity. To this was added a more parochial concern with the security of the Hijaz, which was threatened by the rising power of Ibn Saud. When Napoleon was conquering Europe, the Wahhabis were conquering Arabia. They had captured Mecca and Medina, smashed the holy shrines, turned away pilgrims as 'idolaters' and united most of Arabia under their rule, the Saudi *imperium* extending at its height from the Gulf to the Red Sea, from the borders of Syria to the borders of Yemen.[29]

The first Saudi empire had not endured, but it taken a seven-year military campaign to bring it down.[30] And now, a century later, a second Saudi empire was building in the eastern deserts, and Ibn Saud made no secret of his pan-Arabian ambition: the Hijaz was in his sights. Hashemites and Saudis almost went to war in 1910 over the allegiance of the Utaiba tribe. The caravan routes from the Nejd to the Hijaz ran through their territory. Ibn Saud claimed the right to levy tribute and manpower from the tribe. The crisis passed and agreement was reached; but only because Ibn Saud was distracted by a tribal revolt at home.[31] In the long run, Hussein knew, the desert tribes would gravitate towards the stronger power, especially in troubled times. Ibn Saud already looked to some richer and better armed than the emir of Mecca. And the times were indeed troubled: drought, the railway and the war had wrecked the economy of the Hijaz.[32]

Though little could be done about the drought itself, the effect on crops and herds of several dry years became the background to a growing crisis centred on the Hajj, the main source of such modest prosperity as Hussein's desolate domain allowed. Almost 140,000 pilgrims had made the journey in 1908, the first year of Hussein's emirate, and for thousands of Hijazis the associated trade was immensely lucrative.[33] But that trade now suffered a double blow.[34] First, the construction of the Hijaz Railway, completed as far as Medina in 1908, had cut the travelling time from Damascus from a month to three days, and shifted the bulk of the overland pilgrims from camel caravans to 'the iron donkey'.

Gertrude Bell had encountered divided opinions about the railway during her travels across Syria in 1905 (construction had begun at Damascus in 1900), reporting the enthusiasm of Ottoman officials and urban traders, but scepticism in the countryside, since it facilitated troop movements and created fresh opportunities for peculation and bribes. Scepticism seems to have increased farther south, becoming outright hostility in Arabia, for the more traditional the social structure, the greater the threat to existing patterns of economic life and political power. Bell knew of 'the opposition of the sherif of Mecca and all his clan'; she attributed this to the sherif's rejection of the sultan's claim to the caliphate and his reluctance to see the Ottomans brought 'into closer touch with the religious capitals'.[35]

There were other concerns, bound up with the sherif's fragile relationship with his supporters, since, irrespective of how Hijazi tribesmen made money from the Hajj – escort duties, the hire of camels, the supply of water and victuals, 'protection' (the extortion of tolls, bribes and subsidies), or, in some cases, simply attacking the caravans – the Bedouin economy was hit hard. Hussein, in any case, had his own reasons for disliking the railway. It appeared to menace his own political pre-eminence. These two strips of steel running across 800 miles of desert from Damascus represented the advent of the Industrial Revolution and centralised imperial power in the Hijaz. They pinned Hussein's medieval domain to the modern world, allowing soldiers, cannon and wireless to penetrate the holy cities and began to dissolve their age-old social order. The railway tied the Hijaz into a worldwide geopolitical network, for the line between Damascus and Medina was connected to the Berlin-to-Baghdad Railway: a German-dominated transcontinental network of train power to rival the British-dominated maritime network of steamships.[36]

Then came the war. By 1916 the number of pilgrims travelling to the Hijaz had fallen to less than a quarter of pre-war levels, and the British had imposed a naval blockade in the Red Sea that choked off the supply of foodstuffs and fuel. The Hijazi food crisis was further compounded by the cessation of the annual tribute of grain traditionally sent from Egypt to succour the poor of the holy cities. Rice and coffee almost disappeared from local markets, the price of sugar trebled, and Meccans were reduced to using doors, windows and furniture as firewood.[37] The economic disaster helped propel Hussein and the Hijaz into war, since it comprehensively undermined Ottoman authority, both by demonstrating the empire's inability to safeguard the interests of its Arabian subjects, and by highlighting its willingness to sacrifice Arab welfare in pursuit of Central Asian conquest. The Bedouin, moreover, impoverished by the collapse of the caravan trade, viewed the railway with such bitterness that they needed little encouragement to turn it into a military target.

* * *

The tension between the Hashemites of Mecca and the Ottoman government had been palpable from the outset. The CUP had wanted to impose centralised administration and modernising reforms on the Hijaz in line with the rest of the empire, but when they made overtures to the newly installed sherif, they immediately discovered that 'Abdulhamid has sent a man who cares for nobody and acknowledges neither constitution nor reforms.'[38] The government responded by appointing a hawkish governor-general (*vali*), but when Wahib Pasha attempted to ram things through – in particular, to clear the obstacles to an extension of the Hijaz Railway to Mecca – the Harb tribe rose in revolt. Roads were cut, the towns blockaded and famine threatened. Eight battalions of Ottoman troops had to be sent down the line to restore order. The CUP backed off, ordering the *vali* to make peace with the sherif, which he did at a public ceremony by kissing the hem of Hussein's garment in token of respect for his office.[39]

The reconciliation was but a lull; Hussein's relationship with the Ottoman regime lurched from crisis to crisis. His reaction to the 1909 coup and the over-throw of Abdulhamid was predictably hostile. The Hashemite view was that the CUP had usurped power and opened a rift between Turks and Arabs; they were 'despotic' and set upon converting 'the imperial caliphate into a racial "constitutional" government' and replacing 'the Islamic and therefore ultimately Arab supervision of the state by a Western juridical control'.[40] Even military cooperation between Sherifian and Ottoman in the Asir campaign of 1911 proved problematic. The Arabs bore witness to Turkish atrocities against civilians that they were powerless to prevent, and, according to Hussein's son Abdullah, 'He [Hussein] could not forget the mutilation of the Arab dead which he had seen with his own eyes, and the atrocities committed by the Ottoman Army. It was after his return from Asir that my father began laying the foundations of the Arab Revolt.'[41]

Relations reached a new low with the 1913 coup and the passage of the Law of the Provinces. In reaction to defeat in the First Balkan War, the Young Turk leadership seized direct power, established a dictatorship and attempted to drive through reform by diktat. The new law implied administrative centralisation, general conscription, and an end to the special status of the Hijaz. When the governor-general attempted to enforce the law, he triggered demonstrations, and Government House in Mecca echoed with shouts from the streets of 'Down with the Law of the Provinces! We want our rights. No railway from Medina to Mecca! Long live the emir!' Army posts were attacked, and the police chief was taken prisoner.

Constantinople again backed down – the prime minister sent a telegram saying that the rights of the emirate would be respected, the business of the Hijaz would be left undisturbed and the railway extension would not be insisted upon.[42] But the matter did not end there. Abdullah, acting as his father's emissary, met the grand vizier and the minister of the interior (Talaat) in Constantinople, but he was sent home with a non-negotiable demand that Hussein allow railway construction to proceed. To sweeten the pill, the Ottomans offered Hussein one-third of the revenues from the line between Medina and Mecca once operational, and a guarantee that the emirate would remain in his family after his death.[43]

The war crisis terminated the tussle over the railway – there would be no construction work for the duration – but immediately gave rise to another concerning Hussein's attitude to the Ottoman cause. He maintained, in view of Ottoman weakness, that the war was a grave mistake:

the end of the Balkan War left us weak and ill-prepared for hostilities. It would be extremely dangerous to enter this war on the side of Germany. We depend upon Germany for the greater part of our arms and ammunition. The Ottoman arms factories are not sufficient to provide our armies with essential supplies, nor are they in a position to replace losses of guns or equipment.[44]

The most significant corollary was Hussein's refusal to endorse the Turco-German *jihad* of November 1914.[45] This weakened its general appeal and reduced the likelihood that it would ignite a conflagration. It also exposed it for what it was: a cynical ploy of secular politicians. The brazen lies published in Syria and Iraq – to the effect that the sherif of Mecca *had* endorsed the Holy War – is a measure of the Ottoman authorities' frustration.[46] Hussein dissembled, however, as yet unwilling to risk an outright breach with Constantinople: he supported the Holy War, he explained, and would pray for its success, but was prevented from coming out openly in its favour in view of the vulnerability of the Hijaz to retaliation by the British Red Sea Fleet; as tokens of goodwill, he added, he was sending the Prophet's banner to Damascus, and he would recruit a local force of *mujahedin* ('holy warriors').[47]

The banner was duly paraded with great ceremony from Damascus to Jerusalem in December 1914, whence it accompanied the First Canal Expedition across Sinai early in the New Year. But the Sherifians themselves were signally absent, and the whisper on the street was that it was not the Prophet's banner at all, for the emir of Mecca did not in truth support the *jihad*.[48] Nor did the Sherifian *mujahedin* show up; much to Djemal's irritation, they remained firmly at home in the Hijaz, where they were, of course, a reinforcement to the power of the emirate.[49] Relations were hardly improved when a trove of documents fell into Hussein's hands that revealed the CUP leadership and Wahib Pasha to have been discussing the assassination of the sherif and his sons. Feisal was sent to Constantinople to demand an apology and the recall of Wahib Pasha. Talaat and Enver acceded: Wahib was replaced by the more conciliatory Ghalib Pasha.[50]

* * *

Despite all, the Hashemites remained uncertain about their course. As the dismissal of Wahib demonstrated, the war had strengthened the bargaining position of the Ottoman Empire's subjects, and Hussein's sons were deeply divided on whether or not to take advantage of this. Rebellion was risky, and the Ottomans had a formidable reputation for vengeful terror. Might it not be better – safer – to offer support for the war-effort in return for guaranteed autonomy and the shelving of the Medina-to-Mecca railway? Might not the Arabs earn national advancement through loyalty and service? In any case, could a war against fellow Muslims in alliance with European infidels be expected to garner wider Arab support? Was there not the danger that it would simply open the Middle East to a European carve-up? Were the French not set upon grabbing Syria?[51]

'The Arab intellectuals were divided into two camps,' recalled Feisal:

> One party considered that the complete separation of the Arab countries from the Ottoman Empire, or a revolutionary movement against the sultan, would cause the breakup of the whole empire, including the Arab countries themselves. This party advocated a gradual and progressive solution. My eldest brother Ali and I belonged to this group. In the other camp were extremists like my brother Abdullah, who wished to start a revolution without any preparation, and without counting the heavy sacrifices it would entail.[52]

Hussein explored all options. He corresponded with both Ibn Saud and Al-Idrisi. He dispatched Feisal to Constantinople and Damascus, for talks with both the Ottomans and the Syrian nationalists. And he charged Abdullah with responsibility for negotiating with the British. From Feisal's mission arose the Damascus Protocol, which encapsulated the Arab nationalist viewpoint – common to Beirut liberals and Bedouin sheikhs as the events of 1916–18 unfolded – that the aim was a unified state encompassing Arabia, Syria and Iraq. From Abdullah's efforts arose the McMahon Correspondence, by which the British Empire came close enough to endorsing this vision to persuade the emir of Mecca to proclaim a revolt – to be funded and armed by Cairo – against the 400-year-old Ottoman Empire in the Middle East.

Feisal seems to have reached a tipping-point in the middle of 1915, when involved in his shuttle diplomacy, much of it secret, between Constantinople, Damascus and Mecca. Several factors were at work: the knowledge that the CUP leadership wanted to overthrow the Sherifians and terminate the special status of the Hijaz; their determination at some point to extend the railway from Medina to Mecca; their wider programme of centralisation, Turkish nationalism and pan-Turkish imperialism; their inability to guarantee the military security of Arab territory; and the hangings of Syrian notables charged with nationalist agitation in August 2015.[53] Feisal's conversion to anti-Ottomanism brought unanimity to the leading family. But the time for revolt had not yet come, and Hussein continued to scheme.

His principal political agent was his second son, Abdullah, the most worldly, popular and well known of the four. 'His object,' Lawrence reported in *Seven Pillars*, 'was ... the winning of Arab independence and the building up of Arab nations, but he meant to keep direction of the new states in the family.' The caveat was crucial: Abdullah was a tribal politician, not a nationalist revolutionary. He was therefore 'too balanced, too cool, too humorous to be a prophet'; he lacked 'the flame of enthusiasm that would set the desert on fire.'[54]

The Sherifian vision was, of course, a limited one. The aims were: Arab independence under Hashemite rule, not Arab independence *per se*; and regime change at the top, not social revolution from below. A Hashemite political elite was to replace an Ottoman colonial administration, but the traditional tribal and class structures of the Middle East were to remain unaltered. The sheikhs and the landlords would continue to rule; the mass of Arabs would remain subordinate.

A land war of the Syrian and Iraqi peasantry might have brought down the Ottoman regime by its own efforts. In its absence, the Arab Revolt was bound to be underpowered, making it dependent on external support. Because of the conservatism of its leadership, therefore, and because of its narrow social base, the revolt, from beginning to end, was to be an artefact of British imperialism.

* * *

Abdullah had been the go-between with the British from before the war. In the first week of February 1914, Kitchener, at that time consul-general of Egypt, had invited Abdullah, who happened to be staying in Cairo on his way back home from Constantinople, to pop in for a chat. It would have been churlish to refuse. The consul-general had been solicitous, having provided an ambassadorial yacht to convey Abdullah to the Ottoman capital on his outward journey, letting it be known at the same time that the British government was 'not anxious to see the present peace of the country of pilgrimage disturbed', and 'would not look favourably upon a disturbance of that peace by Turkey.'[55]

Kitchener, all walrus moustache and piercing eyes, listened intently as the sherif explained how much the Arabs hated the Turks and how close the Hijaz was to revolt. So did Oriental Secretary Ronald Storrs, who was also present. What, the sherif wondered, would the British attitude be in the event of revolt? Kitchener was non-committal, even discouraging: British policy was to maintain good relations with the Ottoman Empire. Nonetheless, he instructed Storrs to make a return call two days later, to explore the matter further. And when Abdullah passed through Cairo again in April, he and Storrs met for a third time. Storrs, like his master, could offer nothing on either occasion. But an idea was lodged – an idea which, in Kitchener's imaginative mind, would in due course swell into a heady vision of the dissolution of German influence in the Middle East and a map painted red from Cairo to Baghdad.[56]

Kitchener's appointment as war minister in August that year, followed by the British declaration of war against the Ottoman Empire in November, brought that heady vision to the centre of British imperial decision-making. Civilian ministers were in awe of Kitchener. His austere, repressive, glowering personality was mistaken for strength of character. His pronouncements were received as oracles from some shrine; which, in a sense, they were, for Kitchener was a national institution, a living legend, the biscuit-tin hero of the British Empire.

'He was an almost symbolic figure,' recalled the prime minister's daughter, 'and what he symbolised, I think, was strength, decision, and above all success ... Everything he touched "came off". There was a feeling that Kitchener could not fail.' In particular, Cabinet colleagues deferred to Kitchener on Middle Eastern matters. 'Does Lord Kitchener agree?' wrote Sir Edward Grey, the foreign secretary, on a telegram from Cairo. 'If so, I will approve.'[57] And the men on the ground – the Cairo staff – were, of course, Kitchener's men.

Storrs was one of these. A Cambridge-educated intellectual in his mid-thirties, he had made himself a Middle East expert through ten years' service in Cairo. Though his diplomatic rank was lowly (that of a second secretary), he was a confidant of the field-marshal and a man whose opinion counted. Another member of Kitchener's circle was Lieutenant-General Sir Francis Reginald Wingate, who had served in the Sudan Campaign of 1896–8 and then succeeded his chief as sirdar of the Egyptian Army and governor-general of the Sudan in 1899. Gilbert Clayton was also an old Sudan hand, who had then stayed on, eventually becoming the Egyptian Army's director of intelligence; he was, therefore, the obvious man to head the whole Cairo-based intelligence operation when the war broke out (making a rapid ascent from captain to general by 1918).[58] Storrs, Wingate and Clayton were soon reinforced by the little group of Arabists sent out to form the new Cairo Military Intelligence Department – Stewart Newcombe, George Lloyd, Aubrey Herbert, Leonard Woolley and, of course, Thomas Edward Lawrence.[59] These men now become the leading protagonists of Kitchener's vision of a British-sponsored Arab revolt against Ottoman rule.

Cairo's position was founded on several considerations. First, a revolt might undermine the loyalty and reliability of the one in three Ottoman soldiers who were Arabs. Second, it could be expected to tie down a proportion of the Ottoman Army in static garrison and counter-insurgency duties away from the main fronts. Third, it might remove entirely the danger of the Arabs throwing in their lot with the Turks and their German backers. Fourth, it should help liquidate the Ottoman threat to the Suez Canal and the security of Egypt. And, finally, it ought to dissolve the possibility of anti-colonial revolt in the Middle East, Central Asia and India conjured by the Ottoman call to Holy War.

This last was paramount. The British wanted to trump the Turkish *jihad* by pitching themselves as the champions of Arabism and Islam. Their greatest wartime fear – the emergence of an Islamic prophet armed with Krupp guns – was given literary expression in John Buchan's 1916 novel *Greenmantle*. Buchan was an insider, having been appointed director of information at the Foreign Office in London. 'The Syrian army is as fanatical as the hordes of the Mahdi,' Buchan has a Foreign Office mandarin tell his hero. 'The Senussi have taken a hand in the game. The Persian Muslims are threatening trouble. There is a dry wind blowing through the East, and the parched grasses wait the spark. And the wind is blowing towards the Indian border.'[60]

* * *

In the autumn of 1914, Kitchener instructed Storrs to reopen discussions with Abdullah. In the event of war between Britain and the Ottoman Empire, he wanted to know, what would be the position of the sherif of Mecca? When, soon after, war was declared, the British position became more forthright: 'Whereas the Ottoman Empire has broken her traditional ties of friendship with Great Britain by allying herself with Germany,' wrote Storrs to Abdullah, 'His Majesty's Government now feels itself free from those obligations which bound it for so long to Turkey. If you and His Highness your father still favour a movement such as would lead to the full independence of the Arabs, Great Britain is prepared to assist such a movement by all the means in her power.'[61]

This was followed by an exchange of letters between Wingate and Hussein in the first three months of 1915. No-one committed to anything definite, but it became clear that the British were angling for an alliance, or at least an 'understanding', and that Hussein was an equally eager party to the discussions. Then there was a pause. One reason for this was that the remoteness of the Hijaz and the need for secrecy meant that, in an age of written communication, diplomatic intrigue took time. In particular, Hussein, having been given to believe that the British might provide the funds and arms to sustain a revolt, needed to consult prospective allies – the nationalist underground – and agree with them what the Arab conditions should be.[62] This was Feisal's work, and the Damascus Protocol the result.

The British, too, had matters to grapple with. It had become clear that no alliance would be possible without a cast-iron commitment to Arab independence, so, after some discussion, the Cabinet was persuaded by the war minister to authorise the new high commissioner of Egypt, Sir Henry McMahon, Kitchener's successor, to make a public declaration to that effect. But there was a glitch. The British pledged recognition of the independence of the Arabian Peninsula.[63] The Damascus Protocol had stipulated Arabia, Syria and Iraq.

The seriousness of the glitch became clear when a letter from the Sherif Hussein dated 14 July 1915 arrived in Cairo. It gave as the Arab conditions for revolt those contained in the Damascus Protocol, a document drawn up by the Syrian underground a short while before, on the basis of which they had formed an alliance with the Hashemites. In essence, they would recognise Hussein as 'king of the Arabs' if he put himself at the head of a movement fighting to create an Arab super-state encompassing the whole of Arabia, Syria and Iraq. Hussein's July letter, written on behalf of the entire Arab nationalist movement, demanded British support for a unified Arab-Islamic entity on a scale unknown for a millennium.[64] This was the letter described by Lawrence as a 'bombshell'.

McMahon's reply, composed in consultation with the Foreign Office, was a curious cocktail of flummery and flannel. The strange Turco-Persian compliments and honorifics, coupled with a vague reference to 'our desire for the independence of the Arab countries and their inhabitants, and our readiness to approve an Arab caliphate upon its proclamation', could not distract from the document's obvious evasion of the substantive issue. In relation to this, McMahon's arguments were absurd. He claimed it would not be appropriate to discuss the boundaries of the future Arab state because the war was ongoing, the Turks were in occupation of the territories in question, and many of the inhabitants were serving with the Ottoman forces.[65]

Hussein's reply of 9 September betrayed his irritation: 'the conditions which are essential to our future shall be secured on a foundation of reality, and not on highly decorated phrases and titles.' His attitude to the caliphate was dismissive: 'As for the caliphate, God have mercy on its soul and comfort the Muslims for their loss!' The only thing that really mattered was 'whether you will reject or admit the proposed frontiers'.[66]

The fourth letter in the sequence, McMahon's reply of 24 October, was the most important. It represented a sea-change in the British position. In part this was a response to McMahon's realisation that Hussein was not to be fobbed off with a desert kingdom. Hussein's second letter had, of course, been unequivocal about the centrality of Syria and Iraq to the whole discussion. But the British had meantime received independent confirmation of this from an Ottoman-Arab deserter, Lieutenant Muhammad Sherif al-Faruqi, who had informed them that there was an extensive nationalist underground whose aim was the establishment of a post-war Arab super-state spanning the Middle East.

In fact, Al-Faruqi seems to have misled British intelligence about his own role and influence, and may have exaggerated the size – or more precisely, the influence – of the underground. We will never know, for the Syrian branch of the movement was about to be destroyed by Ottoman repression. What mattered at this moment, however, was that Clayton, the Cairo intelligence chief, was persuaded that an extensive fifth-column existed behind Ottoman lines – what General Maxwell, the British Army commander in Egypt, called a 'powerful organisation' in a cable to Kitchener. This, as Storrs put it, brought 'the Arab question' to 'an acute crisis'. The choice appeared straightforward: either the British aligned themselves with this 'powerful organisation' – perhaps triggering widespread mutinies and uprisings across the Middle East – by becoming the sponsors of an Arab struggle for independence; or, as Al-Faruqi warned, they ran the risk that the nationalists would cut a deal with the Turks and the Germans instead.[67]

What made the matter more pressing was the deteriorating strategic situation. A second landing on Gallipoli had failed to break the trench stalemate. Serbia had been overrun and direct communications opened between Germany, Austria-Hungary and the Ottoman Empire. The Middle Eastern rail network was developing apace. 'The Germans have not failed to see what is our most vulnerable spot and are making for it,' Clayton wrote to Wingate on 9 October. 'Please reply urgently, giving any information you may have on the progress of the Turkish railway across the desert has made towards Egypt,' Kitchener cabled Maxwell on 12 October. 'The German invasion [of Serbia],' he continued, 'will very probably lead to their being able to send troops and guns to Constantinople and from there organise an attack on Egypt.' A curious alliance of British imperialists and Bedouin tribesmen – each with very different motives – was forming for the purpose of destroying a desert railway network.

Hovering in the background, as ever, was the spectre of *jihad*. Maxwell to London: 'As all the great camel-raising tribes are pan-Arab, a satisfactory settlement of the Arab question would go far to make a serious invasion of Egypt impossible.' On the other hand, 'I feel certain that time is of the greatest importance, and that, unless we make a definite and agreeable proposal to the sherif at once, we may have a united Islam against us.' Maxwell's assessment was based on a lengthy memorandum supplied by Clayton, who had convinced himself that successful Turkish resistance was spreading 'doubt and uneasiness' among the Arabs and reducing the chances of revolt. Whereas, he continued

A favourable reply to the Arab proposals, even though it did not satisfy their aspirations entirely, would probably put the seal on their friendship . . . On the other hand, to reject the Arab proposals entirely, or even to seek to evade the issues, will be to throw the Young Arab party definitely into the arms of the enemy. Their machinery will at once be employed against us throughout the Arab countries, and the various Arab chiefs, who are almost to a man members of, or connected with, the Young Arab party, will undoubtedly be won over. Moreover, the religious element will come into play, and the *jihad*, so far a failure, may become a very grim reality, the effects of which would certainly be far-reaching and at the present crisis might well be disastrous.[68]

To avoid this 'very grim reality', the British Empire promised the Arabs the independence of virtually the whole of Arabia, Syria and Iraq. There were two major qualifications. These were made necessary by French colonial ambition in relation to Lebanon, and by existing British arrangements with local chieftains at Basra, Kuwait and elsewhere on the Gulf. As McMahon explained in his letter:

> The districts of Mersin and Alexandretta, and portions of Syria lying to the west of the districts of Damascus, Homs, Hama and Aleppo, cannot be said to be purely Arab, and must on that account be excepted from the proposed delimitation. Subject to that modification, and without prejudice to the treaties concluded between us and certain Arab chiefs, we accept that delimitation. As for the regions lying within the proposed frontiers, in which Great Britain is free to act without detriment to the interests of her ally France, I am authorised to give you the following pledges on behalf of the Government of Great Britain, and to reply as follows to your note: 'That, subject to the modification stated above, Great Britain is prepared to recognise and uphold the independence of the Arabs in all the regions lying within the frontiers proposed by the sherif of Mecca.'[69]

This was an extraordinary diplomatic coup for Hussein, and a measure of the urgency with which the British were pursuing an Anglo-Arab alliance by the autumn of 1915.[70] Though the emir opposed virtually all the territorial exclusions in a letter dated 5 November, and though he received an unsatisfactory reply on 13 December, the main issue had in fact been settled: the British had committed themselves to supporting an independent Arab state on the lines of the Damascus Protocol. In the seventh letter of the exchange, therefore, on 1 January 1916, Hussein agreed to postpone the final settlement of frontiers until after the war, and the Egyptian high commissioner was then able to close what has come to be known as 'the McMahon Correspondence' with his letter of 30 January.[71] The British had a deal.

* * *

That Hussein had settled without clear agreement on outstanding issues is to be explained by his own pressing needs. The nationalist movement in Syria had continued to disintegrate – ground down by arrests and executions, the deportation of nearly 5,000 families, the reassignment of Arab regiments to other theatres, and the beginning of a famine that would consume tens of thousands in the course of the year (and perhaps half a million before the end of the war).[72] Hussein's grand plan had been for a proclamation of independence in Mecca to trigger a tribal uprising in Arabia, insurrections in the towns and villages of Syria, and mutinies by Arab soldiers of the Ottoman Army. A simultaneous British landing at Alexandretta was to have created a forward supply-base to sustain such a revolt. Fantastic claims were made on behalf of this conception. On 18 February 1916, in a letter to McMahon, Hussein estimated at 100,000 the number of his supporters ready to rise in Syria; two weeks later, in another letter, it had become 250,000.

Eager to support the scheme, half convinced that the Middle East was set to explode, the British landed large quantities of gold, a consignment of 5,000 Japanese rifles, and 2 million rounds of ammunition on the Hijazi coast.[73] But there was no rising in Syria, and no question of a Royal Navy swoop on Alexandretta. Then, in May, the leaders of the Syrian underground were executed. The combination of British deference to French colonial ambition – which had precluded the Alexandretta landing – and Ottoman repression had destroyed whatever chance there might have been of a Syrian revolution.[74]

The ramifications are incalculable. The Syrian purge did not prevent the Arab Revolt, but it meant that, when it came, Hussein would act as an Arabian tribal potentate, not as the leader of a pan-Arab nationalist insurrection; that he would, in consequence, be excessively dependent on British gold, guns and grain; and that the 'liberation' of Syria in 1918 – if that is what it was – would be the act not of the Syrian people as whole, nor even of any substantial segment of them, but of a Bedouin army from the desert.[75] The historical 'what-ifs' multiply exponentially; what is safe to say is that the modern Middle East has its current form largely as a consequence of the success of Ottoman crackdowns in August 1915 and May 1916 in aborting revolution in Syria.

But this did not end the crisis. The Ottomans appeared to be coming for Hussein, and the survival of the Hashemite regime itself was in question. Word had reached Mecca in April that Khairi Bey's 3,500-strong Yemen Expeditionary Force was on its way, an elite force of picked and specially equipped troops. They were acting in cooperation with a small German expedition – four officers, two radio operators and some assistants – led by Baron Othmar von Stotzingen. The combined mission's objectives were to establish a base in southern Arabia, support Ottoman operations against Aden, open wireless contact with German

East Africa, broadcast propaganda to the Horn of Africa (and if possible India), and arrange arms shipments to foment revolt in Abyssinia, Eritrea, Somaliland and Sudan.[76] Southern Arabia was to be transformed into a forward base for the projection of a Turco-Ottoman *jihad* into Africa.

It seemed unlikely there would be a place in this for anyone so suspect, so obdurate in resisting reform, so unresponsive to the needs of the empire in its wartime crisis, as the emir of Mecca. The exchanges between Constantinople and Mecca had by now become acerbic. Hussein demanded a general amnesty for political prisoners, autonomy for Syria and Iraq, and recognition of his hereditary status in the Hijaz: 'on no other terms will the Arab nation co-operate in a war which was declared against my will'. The Ottoman prime minister cabled back: 'Outside your province to state terms and talk of rights. The traitors at Damascus will receive punishment. You will not see your son Feisal again unless you send the volunteers to the front as you promised.'[77]

Djemal accused Hussein and Ali of treason at a meeting with Feisal in Damascus in April. Feisal protested his family's loyalty, and was subsequently granted permission to return to Medina so that he could join his brother in leading forth the long-promised *mujahedin* for the Sinai front. Back home, a warning was whispered to him in the Mosque of the Prophet by someone in the know: it would be unsafe for him to go back to Damascus. (He would not, in fact, do so before September 1918, and then only in very different circumstances.)[78]

The tension became unbearable. Though the British logistical operation had not yet cranked up, though Feisal advised delay until the harvest was in and provisions amassed, the risk of an Ottoman coup was too great, and Hussein launched his revolution before anyone was ready.[79] The following ultimatum was delivered to the Ottomans on 9 June:

> The moderate Arab demands have been rejected by the Ottoman government. The troops who have prepared themselves for the Holy War consider that they are not bound to sacrifice themselves except in the interests of the Arab nations and Islam. If the conditions laid down by the sherif of Mecca are not immediately fulfilled, there will be no need of a formal declaration that relations between the Arab nation and Turkey have been severed. Twenty-four hours after receipt of this letter, a state of war will exist between the two nations.[80]

* * *

As the call to prayer from the minaret of the Great Mosque died away at dawn on 10 June 1916, a single shot rang out across the holy city of Mecca. It had been fired by the emir himself. It was the signal to his followers that the long-rumoured insurrection against 400 years of Ottoman rule had begun. And, as the sky brightened over Mecca that morning, its people saw the Hashemite flag fluttering defiantly over Hussein's residence.[81]

Most of the Ottoman garrison had moved to Taif – a resort 40 miles south-east of Mecca and 4,000 feet higher – for temperatures were liable to soar to 45°C in the holy city during June, the hottest month of the year. Only some 1,500 men were left, commanded by Major Derwish Bey. Supporters of the sherif, on the other hand, had been infiltrating into the city for several days, responding to a secret proclamation issued on 5 June. Around 30,000 volunteers and tribal irregulars in all had assembled at various points across the Hijaz, poised to move on the Ottoman garrisons at Mecca, Medina, Taif and the Red Sea ports of Jiddah, Rabegh and Yenbo. Several thousand of these were in Mecca, and all the Ottoman posts in the city were soon under attack.[82] As the volume of rifle-fire rose over the city, one beleaguered garrison commander is reputed to have phoned Hussein asking for assistance. The officer explained that the Arabs had declared their independence and were in revolt. Would the sherif do what he could about it? 'I have also heard that they want their independence,' replied Hussein.'I shall certainly do all I can about it.'[83]

Only one in five of the insurgents possessed a modern rifle, however; the rest were equipped with a variety of antiquated firearms. Nor did they have any artillery or machine-guns. Consequently, they found themselves pinned down by Ottoman fire and without the means to breach any walls. The Sherifians took the Bash Karakol, a small post at the south-eastern corner of the Great Mosque, on the second day of the rising, and Government House on the third; the prisoners, who included the deputy governor-general, were escorted to the Sherifian Palace. But the defenders of the two main positions on the edge of the city, the Jirwal Barracks, which guarded the roads to Jiddah and Medina, and Fort Jiyad, located on a hill dominating the whole of the city, held out. There was stalemate: the Sherifians lacked the firepower to force surrender; the Ottomans were unwilling to attempt a sortie through narrow streets infested with insurgents.[84] The main excitement occurred when Ottoman shells landed on the Great Mosque, one of them close enough to the Kaaba to set the sacred pall on fire.[85] The Arab Revolt had no sooner begun than it seemed to have stalled.

* * *

The British received their first news of the somewhat alarming developments in the Hijaz on 6 June. Ronald Storrs and David Hogarth (now head of the newly formed Arab Bureau) had just arrived at Jiddah expecting to meet Sherif

Abdullah to discuss the planned revolt, only to discover that it had already started. The emir's youngest son, Sherif Zeid, had been sent instead; his older brother, the British emissaries learned, was engaged in more active business. Zeid brought a letter from Hussein with an urgent request for gold and guns – 80,000 sovereigns, 10,000 rifles, 6 machine-guns, 6 mountain-guns (with Muslim crews) and a good supply of food and ammunition.

Most British assessments of the prospects were sombre. The principal exception seems to have been Captain Lawrence: 'It has taken a year and a half to do it,' he wrote home on 1 July 1916, 'but now is going very well. It is so good to have helped a bit in making a new nation – and I hate the Turks so much that to see their own people turning on them is very grateful ... This revolt, if it succeeds, will be the biggest thing in the Near East since 1550.'[86]

Hogarth, on the other hand, considered the revolt:

> about to be undertaken upon inadequate preparation, in ignorance of modern warfare, and with little idea of the obligations which its success would impose on the Sherifial family. In both the organisation of the tribal forces and the provision of armament, far too much has been left to the last moment and to luck. If the Arabs succeed, it will be by their overwhelming numbers and by the isolation of the Turkish garrisons.[87]

Sir Reginald Wingate in the Sudan was blunter: he thought Hussein's army was 'practically a rabble and run on Dervish lines'.[88]

Wingate nonetheless dispatched two batteries of mountain-guns and one of machine-guns, all with Egyptian crews, along with 3,000 spare rifles and many tons of barley, flour, rice, coffee and sugar. Three ships left Port Sudan on 27 June and arrived at Jiddah the following day.[89] The Egyptian mountain-guns were rushed to Mecca, 40 miles inland, where they transformed the tactical situation. The guns blasted a breach in the wall of the fort on 4 July, and the Arabs stormed in and captured it. The guns were then hauled into position opposite the barracks and opened fire; but, on 9 July, before a breach could be made, the defenders raised the white flag.

In a month's fighting, the Ottomans had suffered about 250 casualties. A total of 30 officers and 1,120 men had been taken prisoner, and the insurgents had seized 5 guns, 8,000 rifles and huge quantities of ammunition (thus beginning, in classic guerrilla manner, to equip themselves with captured enemy kit). For a loss of just eight men killed, the Arabs had retaken the holy city of Mecca.[90]

* * *

Sherif Hussein's forebears had first sworn allegiance to an Ottoman sultan in 1517. The subordination of the holy cities of Islam – Mecca, Medina, Jerusalem, Damascus and Baghdad – to Ottoman rule had transformed sultans into caliphs; they became, through the power of the sword, both temporal rulers *and* spiritual leaders. Of late, under Abdulhamid II – with encouragement from the German Kaiser – the caliphate had taken on new significance, becoming a device to conjure a global *jihad* against the British, French and Russian Empires. Now, the keystone of the Ottoman caliphate had been knocked away, and the Ottoman call to *jihad* reduced to an echo in the wilderness. Such was the mystic power of Mecca.

An ancient town on the desert caravan-route through western Arabia, it had developed around a sacred well (the Zamzam), close to a sacred mountain (Arafat), and as home to a widely venerated pagan god-block (the Black Stone of the Kaaba). Because of these things, and the stories told of them, it had become a place of local pilgrimage. Only later did it become hyper-charged with wider, universal meaning, first through an imagined association with the mythic patriarch Abraham, then by its role as the stage on which the Prophet Muhammad performed the founding rites of Islam.

Pious Muslims came to conceive of the world as a circle with Mecca at its centre. They would face towards it when they prayed, and also when they were laid in the grave at death. Any Muslim, therefore, anywhere in the world, needed to know the direction of Mecca; so important was this that a rich man's *qibla* – a scientific instrument that pointed the way – was often a prized possession. The Prophet, moreover, had ordained that all Muslims should endeavour to perform the Hajj at least once, undertaking the long, arduous, expensive, often dangerous journey to the holy city. For this was the place where the first and the last of the Prophets had communed with God; the place where a crack in the universe allowed the divine to reach down and touch frail humanity; the place where the worshipper could enter into complete oneness with his Creator. Mecca thus became the centre of a sacred geography whose routes of pilgrimage were etched across thousands of miles of mountain, steppe, desert and ocean; a network that extended across half the planet, linking West Africa, Central Asia and the East Indies to a remote Arabian hill-town.[91]

In a world of believers, control of such a place, and of the approaches to it, conferred power. The Prophet himself had led the first Hajj in 632, and the early caliphs, Abu Bakr, Umar and Uthman, had led it every year as long as they ruled. Later, as the Islamic domain expanded and its rulers took up residence elsewhere, they remained jealous of their role as leaders of the *umma*, the community of the faithful, and therefore of its most visceral expression, the annual pilgrimage; a role soon bitterly contested as the once-unitary caliphate fractured into rival polities.[92]

Umayyads, Abbasids, Fatimids, Ayyubids, Mamluks, Ottomans, even Mughals: each great Islamic dynasty in its turn laid claim to Mecca, the Hajj and the caliphate. Each monumentalised its claim by threading forts, khans and cisterns along the sacred routes.[93] The Ottoman sultans built a great caravan station at Damascus and a line of twenty-two forts between there and Medina during the sixteenth and seventeenth centuries. They paid *sürre* to the Bedouin tribes along the way to buy protection for pilgrims on the desert road. Each year, they supplied a *mahmal*, an elaborate camel-borne palanquin, to lead the procession, and a new *kiswa*, an embroidered black cloth, destined to be draped over the Kaaba. It was by these marks of piety and patronage that generations of Ottoman sultans asserted their claim to the leadership of Islam.[94]

Such was the meaning of Mecca. The eight men killed in its capture were a small price for such a prize. But could the Arabs hold it? That depended upon events elsewhere in the Hijaz during the hot summer of 1916; most urgently, upon events on the Red Sea coast, where the revolt had to succeed if it was to secure a supply-line to access British treasure and materiel.

* * *

The capture of Jiddah on 16 June had already proved decisive in tipping the balance in Mecca. A Harb tribal force of 4,000 men under Sheikh Mansur had attacked the port on the same day as the rising in Mecca, though at first with similar results: the Arabs had been stopped by artillery and machine-gun fire. 'We were horrified at the Arab method of attack,' recalled a sailor watching from a British warship anchored offshore. 'They were simply advancing in a mass, quite openly, some of them firing their rifles in the air. The Turks simply waited and then poured a withering fire into their ranks.'[95]

The garrison continued to hold out even after their water-supply had been cut off and they found themselves under naval gunfire. Two events seemed to have triggered their surrender: the arrival of the seaplane-carrier *Ben-my-Chree*, whose three aircraft commenced bombing runs over the Ottoman trenches; and the receipt of news from Mecca that no reinforcement could be expected. The white flag was raised, 2,500 men surrendered, and 15 machine-guns and 20 cannon were captured.[96]

Two other forces, again assisted by British naval power, had an easier time taking Rabegh, 100 miles north of Jiddah, and Yenbo, 100 miles farther north again, on 27 June. The land operation was managed by Major Nuri al-Said, an Iraqi officer who had defected from the Ottoman Army.[97] Described by Sir Percy Cox, the Indian viceroy's representative in Mesopotamia, as 'a delicate Arab youth of about 25 years of age' who was 'highly Europeanised' and 'a visionary socialist', he was an exceptional professional officer who would soon be training the first regular battalions of the embryonic Hashemite Army.[98]

Nuri's coup was followed by another on 15 August, when Lith and Qunfidhah, 100 and 200 miles south of Jiddah respectively, and Umm Lajj, 300 miles north of it, were all captured, giving the Sherifian forces (and the Red Sea Fleet) control of all the ports along the 500 miles of coast adjacent to Mecca and Medina. The capture of Umm Lajj was the work of Sherif Nasir bin Ali, the 27-year-old brother of the emir of Medina, a man destined to become one of the principal leaders of the revolt.[99] The political alliance of the two leading Hijazi families, those of the emirs of Mecca and Medina respectively, the former Sunni, the latter Shia, both in direct line of descent from the Prophet, gave the revolt a firm political foundation. Nasir certainly impressed Lawrence when they were introduced in early 1917: 'He was the opener of roads, the forerunner of Feisal's movement, the man who had fired the first shot in Medina, and who was to fire the last shot at Muslimiya beyond Aleppo ... and from beginning to end all that could be told of him was good.'[100]

Taif, too, was eventually taken; but the operation was protracted. The governor-general of the Hijaz, Ghalib Pasha, had retired to the highland town with at least 2,000 men to escape the summer heat of Mecca. By 10 June, Abdullah had assembled an army of 5,000 tribesmen outside Taif. Having first cut the telegraph line, they launched a series of attacks. But the Turks had dug trenches, strengthened the walls of the town, and were well supplied with machine-guns and two batteries of 75mm Krupp mountain-guns, and each attack was beaten back.[101]

Lacking the firepower to break into the defences and with ammunition running low, Abdullah commenced a war of nerves. 'As darkness fell, we lit bonfires on all the hills overlooking Taif, and we kept up a continuous shouting and beating of drums to make the enemy believe that the tribes were gathering in great numbers.'[102] Jovial and somewhat hedonistic, more politician than general, Abdullah was reluctant to risk heavy casualties through determined fighting. Lawrence would later comment on the 'pleasure-loving, laughing entourage' in his camp, and, while considering Abdullah 'head and cause of the Hijaz revolt', nonetheless criticised him as 'incapable as a military commander and unfit to be trusted alone with important commissions of an active sort'.[103] Despite the arrival of tribal reinforcements and new rifles, success in taking out one or two smaller enemy posts, and the arrival of machine-guns, mountain-guns and even howitzers from Mecca, the siege dragged on. 'We now had a far stronger armament than the enemy', Abdullah later admitted; yet, 'I did not use the guns more than was necessary, as the outcome was now a foregone conclusion, and

I was determined to save lives on both sides.'[104] The garrison, far from any possible relief, eventually surrendered on 22 September.[105]

* * *

The fall of Taif gave the Sherifians control of the whole of the Hijaz except for Medina and the railway to the north. The first shots of the revolt had, in fact, been fired not at Mecca, but when some 6,000 tribesmen under the Sherifs Ali and Feisal attacked two stations north of Medina. The aim had been to sever the town's lifeline and put the garrison under blockade. But the attacks, by ill-armed and disparate tribal contingents, were shambolic, and a strong Ottoman counter-attack drove them off.

Equally unsuccessful were the opening clashes in and around the town itself, where antique muskets proved no match for modern artillery, and the tribesmen were terrified by a weapon they had never faced before. Feisal and Ali moved about in the open amid the bursting shells to demonstrate their limited effect, but to no avail: the Arabs fell back, and the Ottomans pushed outwards from the town.

As they did so, they gave the Arabs a taste of their counter-insurgency methods: they attacked the villages of the Beni Ali tribe at Awali and massacred the inhabitants. While this opened the dykes of blood-hatred between Arab and Turk, it did nothing in the short run to steel the resolve of the tribesmen in the first shock of defeat. Ali and Feisal were forced to withdraw into the hill country west of Medina as their men deserted in droves. Running short of ammunition, rations and money, the brothers attempted to sustain morale by subterfuge. According to Lawrence, 'Feisal filled a decent chest with stones, had it locked and corded carefully, guarded on each daily march by his own slaves, and introduced meticulously into his tent each night. By such theatricals, the brothers tried to hold a melting force.'[106]

The uneven military geography of the Hijaz had dislocated the northern arm of the revolt even as it triumphed in the south and the west. On the coastal plain, the ports had fallen to a combination of local tribal uprising and British naval action. This, with the dispatch of Egyptian guns, had made possible the capture of Mecca, which nestled among hills on the edge of the plain only 40 miles or so from Jiddah, and then Taif, 40 miles farther into the uplands. The Red Sea steamship had, in a sense, been decisive, delivering the firepower to crack open the Ottoman defences (as, henceforward, it would supply the munitions, food and gold to sustain the Arab effort). Beyond the Red Sea littoral, however, lay a lava-strewn labyrinth of jagged black mountains, more than 80 miles wide. Whereas Mecca was a hill-town near the coast, Medina sat on a scorching dust-plain on the far side of this massif, more than 100 miles from Yenbo, the nearest port, at the point where the eastern slopes graded down to hillocks and merged into the great sand desert of central Arabia.[107] And while Mecca was supplied by steamship, Medina was supplied by train, for it was the southern terminus of the Hijaz Railway. With Damascus, the headquarters of Djemal Pasha's Fourth Army, only three days' journey away, Medina could support a large garrison, and it was here that the bulk of the Ottoman forces in the Hijaz were stationed in June 1916. In addition to more than 10,000 men of Fakhri Pasha's Hijaz Expeditionary Force, there were also 3,500 men of Khairi Bey's newly arrived Yemen Expeditionary Force, plus several batteries of artillery and some dozens of machine-guns. Thousands more men were strung out in numerous defended posts along the railway, keeping the line open, both to sustain the Medina garrison and to allow a build-up of force at what had now become the Ottoman forward base for the region.[108]

Elsewhere in the Hijaz that summer, outnumbered Ottoman forces had been holed up in forts or behind old-town walls. Fakhri Pasha's men, by contrast, had gone onto the offensive, driving the Arabs out of the suburbs of Medina and into the desert. Pushing forward again in early August, they tumbled the tribesmen backwards in a day-long running fight and established a perimeter up to 20 miles distant from the town.

With the urban revolt crushed and a wide security circuit set up around the town, Fakhri Pasha now awaited imminent reinforcement, both military and political. Eight battalions were on their way, along with a new sherif of Mecca, Ali Haidar, whom the Turks intended should replace the rebel Hashemite and inspire a loyalist fight-back.[109] Fakhri was planning a full-scale offensive to smash the revolt and recapture Mecca. Nothing less could be expected. A veteran of the Libyan and Balkan Wars, Fakhri was a moustachioed war-horse with a reputation for grit and ruthlessness (his defence of the holy city – during the war and beyond – would earn him the soubriquet 'Tiger of Medina'). Not only was the Arab Revolt – now represented in the north by little more than a line of snipers in the hills midway between Medina and the coast – about to face a massive military counter-attack; its adherents had every reason to fear a retributive campaign of murder, rape and dispossession.

* * *

It was a strange beginning. Arab nationalism – an advanced ideology of Syrian towns and Ottoman military academies – seemed to have found its sharpest edge among the benighted desert elites of ultra-conservative Arabia. Few had expected this; at most they had speculated on the emir of Mecca becoming the figurehead leader of a revolt centred in Beirut, Damascus and Baghdad, and among Arab officers in the Ottoman Army. Though still a fragile flower, Arab nationalism had seemed set to blossom in the wake of the Young Turk Revolution, which had both awakened and at the same time frustrated aspirations for political freedom among Syrian and Iraqi liberals.

The contradictions were encapsulated in the troubled career and *cause célèbre* of Major Aziz Ali al-Masri. A distinguished professional officer of Egyptian extraction, he had joined the CUP, played a leading role in the 1908 insurrection, and subsequently served in Yemen and Libya. He had supported the revolution, however, as a liberal Arab nationalist, and he soon found himself at odds with his Turkish colleagues. He therefore founded a secret Arab nationalist society, Al-Qahtaniya (named after a town in the Kurdish region of Syria), whose aim was to convert the Ottoman Empire into a 'dual monarchy' along the lines of Austria-Hungary. When he learned that he and other Arab officers were to be marginalised by transfer from Constantinople to distant provincial garrisons, he reached breaking-point and resigned his commission in disgust, setting up a new secret society, Al-Ahd ('the Covenant'), in late 1913, which quickly developed into a substantial underground network of Iraqi officers in the Ottoman Army.

Whether or not the Young Turks knew of the existence of Al-Ahd, they were certainly aware of Al-Masri's nationalist sympathies, and he was arrested, put on trial and condemned to death on trumped-up charges by a military court. The news prompted a wave of Arab agitation, supported by foreign diplomats and press, and the Ottoman government was forced to release the nationalist officer and allow him to pass into exile in Egypt. A backwash of suspicion and resentment among Arab-Ottoman officers remained.[110]

Al-Ahd was not the only Arab nationalist secret society. Al-Fatat ('the Youth') had been formed by Arab students studying in Paris in 1911. It moved its headquarters first to Beirut, then Damascus, at the beginning of the war, and it seems to have gathered a fair number of adherents among the educated Syrian middle class, which had a tradition of moderate nationalism, especially in Levantine literary circles, going back at least as far as 1875.[111]

Even so, neither society had the makings of a popular mass movement. In part this was a consequence of their liberal politics, which offered little or nothing to the Arab peasantry. But it was also inherent in the contradictory socio-political context of the early twentieth-century Middle East. What exactly did it mean to be an Arab nationalist? What was it that 'Young Arabs' aspired to? What would freedom look like? Would it entail greater autonomy within the Ottoman Empire, or must it involve full national independence? If the latter, who exactly would constitute the nation, and what territories would be included?

To none of these questions was the answer straightforward. Neither Arabs nor Muslims had been united under a single polity for a thousand years. In place of the relatively coherent Arab-Muslim caliphate of the tenth century there was now a complex mosaic of ethnicities, religions and tribes. The 'Arab world' – itself only part of a wider 'Islamic world' – extended from Morocco to Mesopotamia, from Aleppo to Aden and, even its inner core, the Middle East proper, was so diverse and subdivided as to make the concept of 'nationhood' little more than a literary abstraction. The dreamers of the Beirut coffee-houses found themselves grappling with an intractable social substrate of rival creeds and identities, of clans and blood-feuds, of bitter class antagonisms, and of innumerable small towns and villages where politics were irredeemably personal and parochial.

Of the 3.3 million people who lived in the Ottoman territories of Syria and Palestine, mainstream Sunni Muslims accounted for fewer than 60 per cent, for the population also included 1 million Christians (divided into twelve separate churches), 150,000 Druses, 120,000 Alawites and 90,000 Jews. These religious differences were interwoven with others, of race and culture, some very ancient, some as recent as the last century, creating an ethnographic tapestry of bewildering complexity. The main Syrian population was descended from Aramaic-speaking peasants from the time of the New Testament, but they had become admixed since with Arabs, Turks, Kurds, Armenians, Circassians and others.[112] Further complexity arose from the physical geography of the Levant, whose multiplicity of ecological niches – coastal plain, upland plateau, mountain massif, dry scrubland, desert oasis – fostered a plethora of distinct life-ways. What was it that united the wealthy Christian Arab of Salt, the owner of vineyards, orchards and corn-land, a man whose house had glazed windows, thick carpets and European furniture, with, say, the Muslim shopkeepers, metalsmiths and handloom weavers of the urban bazaars, the impoverished inhabitants of mud-built huts and animal-hair tents, eking out a living as wage-workers in the fields of northern Syria, or the Druse boy standing guard with couched musket over a herd of goats on a mountain slope?[113]

That there was much combustible material – much from which revolution might be made – could not be doubted. The Middle East was ruled by a corrupt and brutal ruling class of Ottoman officials and Arab landlords. The officials enriched themselves through corruption and extortion, and the landlords passed on the cost to the peasantry; though in fact, official and landlord were often one and the same, for Ottoman practice was to rule through local clients. The power nexus was based upon armed force: that of Ottoman military garrisons and the feudal-tribal retinues of the landlords. This guaranteed a continuing flow of surplus extracted from Syrian and Iraqi peasants, the *fellahin*, the generic beasts of burden at the base of the economic system.[114]

Few *fellahin* owned their own land; most worked for hire on the estates of rich men. The poverty was absolute. The villages were places where father and son shared a single pair of shoes, and the women and children went barefoot.[115] Draining away the pittances paid to the *fellahin* for their labour were taxes and rents, interest on debts, bribes to corrupt officials, exemption payments to escape conscription, and the ever-present threat of sudden, arbitrary, forcible seizure of property. Gertrude Bell, travelling through Syria in 1905, was convinced that the Ottoman soldiers who accompanied her as escorts fed themselves and their horses on provisions and grain taken from the peasantry by force.[116] After being entertained by an Ottoman governor, she learned that the local Alawite peasantry had been fleeced to provide the feast – the eggs, chickens and lambs had been stolen from them, and, compounding the abuse, they had been compelled to gather the necessary firewood.[117] The year before, she learned, rural transport had been paralysed because government officials had commandeered all the baggage-camels for a war in the Yemen.[118] She bore witness as a ragged peasant, pleading for debt relief, was met with rage and threats by a great lord who 'squeezes the last cent from the poor, seizes their land, and turns them out of their houses to starve'.[119] She observed, too, the fear of rape at the hands of magnates or soldiers prevalent among local peasant girls.[120]

Ottoman rule empowered a minority of imperial officials, native landowners and tribal potentates. The Syrian and Iraqi poor experienced it as a system of exploitation, oppression, and brutality. The stark contradiction in the Arab countryside between a corrupt elite and an impoverished agrarian proletariat and peasantry might have given rise to social revolution. The Mexican *campesinos* had exploded into violent resistance in 1910. The Russian *muzhiks* would do so in 1917, and the Egyptian *fellahin* in 1919. Why not the Syrian and Iraqi *fellahin* in 1916?[121] But this conception of revolution was far from the thoughts of the middle-class conspirators of Al-Ahd and Al-Fatat. Their aim was much more limited: not radical land reform to end the poverty of the peasantry, but a political reconfiguration to facilitate the advancement of educated men like themselves. This, however, had only minority appeal. Most of the self-interested Arab elite were too comfortable and secure under Ottoman rule to want to challenge it; they would shift allegiance, if at all, only when the wind of change was blowing so strongly that it became expedient to do so. Whereas the *fellahin*, browbeaten by feudal overlords, terrorised by imperial soldiery, could hardly be expected to risk revolt for anything less than possession of the land itself. The nationalists, trapped by their own timidity, were perforce compelled to seek external allies to realise their ambitions.

* * *

The war complicated Arab politics. Many nationalists were suspicious of French, British and Russian designs on the Middle East, regarding the European powers as a greater threat to Arab independence than the Ottoman Empire. Some, especially Muslims, for whom an alliance with infidels against an Islamic state was problematic, thought they might cut a deal with the Ottoman author-ities – greater autonomy in return for support for the war. On the other hand, the weakness of the Ottoman Empire – the very thing that made a deal seem possible – increased the chances that the war would end in European annexa-tion. The nationalists equivocated. Al-Fatat passed a resolution arguing that the Arab provinces of the Ottoman Empire were 'seriously imperilled' by the war, that every effort should be made 'to secure their liberation and independence', but that 'in the event of European designs appearing to materialise, the society shall be bound to work on the side of Turkey, in order to resist foreign penetra-tion of whatever kind or form'.[122]

For or against the Ottoman Empire: that was the question. Though it was never fully resolved – Arab opinion remained divided throughout the world war – the logic of the situation did tend in one direction. The space for a deal had, in fact, been narrowed rather than widened by the war, because of the CUP regime's pan-Turkish ideological trajectory and its heightened suspicion of Arab nationalism. This being so, the options were limited. Either the Ottoman Empire would prove strong enough to endure, or it would be overthrown by Entente military action. If the former, there would be no Arab nationalist revo-lution. If the latter, the Arabs would have no influence on the post-war settle-ment unless they had become active belligerents. Events therefore drove the nationalists towards an alliance with the British (and, in practice, the French, however unpalatable this may have been). The only alternative – social revolu-tion from below – was precluded by the conspirators' middle-class liberalism. Encouraged by the Hashemites – Sherif Feisal was in secret communication with members of both Al-Ahd and Al-Fatat – the nationalists issued a new statement in May 1915, in effect setting out their terms for cooperation with the British. This was the Damascus Protocol, which defined the prospective post-war independent Arab state to include virtually the whole of Syria, Iraq and Arabia. It also stipulated that the 'Capitulations' (exceptional privileges to foreigners) should be abolished, but allowed for a defensive alliance with, and economic preference for, the British.[123]

* * *

Deteriorating relations with the Ottomans gave added urgency to the plotting. Ottoman officials had raided the French consulates in Beirut and Damascus at the beginning of the war and recovered documents that incriminated a number of leading Arab nationalists. Djemal Pasha made known the discovery, but took no immediate action, merely locking the papers away in a drawer: the Ottomans still hoped to win over their Arab subjects with an appeal to imperial and religious solidarity.

The honeymoon in wartime relations between Arab and Turk was soon shattered by the double disaster at Sarikamish and Suez in early 1915. It was not simply that defeat exposed the weakness of the empire and the hollowness of its anti-imperialist and Islamist rhetoric. Iraq had been stripped of troops and Arab soldiers sent to fight in the Caucasus, allowing the British to land at Basra with minimal opposition and begin an advance down the Tigris. Arab lives were being sacrificed in pursuit of pan-Turkish empire in Central Asia, while Arab land was exposed to invasion by infidels in Mesopotamia.[124] To this grievance was added the growing burden of wartime conscription and requisitioning. Djemal was soon demanding that Arab leaders 'render the armies of the caliphate some real service'.[125] Camels, oxen and mules, along with peasant carts, were seized and driven off by military transport officers.[126] Arab peasants from 'the interior of Syria and Palestine' were conscripted into new divisions, while Jews, Greeks and Armenians were dragooned into labour battalions to work on new railways, roads and defences.[127]

Lawrence had had first-hand experience of Ottoman recruitment and requisitioning while on the Carchemish dig, as he explained in a letter home on 15 October 1912: 'They visited the Euphrates bridge works and decimated the workmen, and entirely broke up the construction of the station: they have only old men and boys left.' The archaeologists offered their dig house as a refuge, and forbade the police and soldiers to set foot on the excavation site; they also 'recovered the village donkeys which had been impressed'.[128]

All such operations were conducted with the medieval barbarism of a pre-industrial empire. Discipline was maintained by flogging; 'the whip of soft, flexible, stinging leather, which seldom leaves the Turkish officer's hand, was never idle', recalled one reluctant conscript.[129] *Bastinado* – foot whipping – was widely practised as both punishment and torture.[130] Rations were sometimes unavailable; other times they were appropriated by corrupt officers and sold on. In either case, soldiers took to plundering, and it became routine for Ottoman units to support themselves by stealing from local villagers.[131] The commissariat and transport services formed an empire-wide network of corruption, its requisition squads, which reached into every Arab village, often little more than criminal gangs operating for the profit of the officers who controlled them. Alexander Aaronsohn – an Ottoman Jew, Zionist pioneer and accomplished agronomist who had spent time in the United States – thought 'the plundering under the name of "military requisitions", the despotic rule of the army officers, and the general insecurity were even more desolating' than the plague of locusts he and his brother were charged with eradicating.[132]

Rafael de Nogales, the Argentine mercenary, was also witness to Ottoman Empire's escalating inner crisis of corruption and brutality. He encountered a scam at Aleppo where several labour battalions were being starved to death by officers who were selling off their men's rations. An original 6,000 men had been reduced to 2,000, and 'the salary and rations of the other 4,000 went into the pockets of the officers'. The process was slowly destroying the remainder: '500 of those 2,000 "unarmed soldiers" were dying, and the remaining 1,500 wasting away with famine and anaemia; all except the sergeants, who in the role of companions and confidants of the officers were swimming in wealth and living in grand style.'[133] The wider effects of the Ottoman regime's rapaciousness were to be seen everywhere in town and country. Nogales found Beirut to be in acute economic depression when he visited in 1915, its commerce paralysed, its middle class ruined, many of the common people dying of starvation.[134] 'Bread was to be had only on tickets issued by the government,' reported Aaronsohn, 'and prices in general were extremely high. The population was discontented and turbulent, and every day thousands of women came before the governor's residence to cry and protest against the scarcity of bread.'[135]

Not least worrying, from the perspective of the Arab underground, were rumours of terrible events in the far north. If true, if the Turks were indeed massacring the Armenians, what might not be the fate of other perceived enemies within? As the shadow of suspicion hanging over the nationalist conspirators of Syria and Iraq darkened into a storm-cloud, the pressure to act increased.

* * *

But Djemal struck first. It was the act of a weak, frightened, vindictive colonial administrator. Suez had badly damaged his prestige. Djemal had invested his army with a jihadist expectation that it might sweep the British aside and liberate Egypt. 'Soldiers!' he had proclaimed. 'Behind you stretch the empty deserts, before you stands the craven foe. Beyond the enemy is rich Egypt, avid to welcome you. If you falter, death only shall be your lot. Forward, for before you lies Paradise!'[136]

Aaronsohn noted that enthusiasm and excitement were at fever pitch in Jaffa before the advance on Suez.

Parades and celebrations of all kinds in anticipation of the triumphal march into Egypt were taking place, and one day a camel, a dog and a bull, decorated respectively with the flags of Russia, France and England, were driven through the streets. The poor animals were horribly maltreated by the natives, who rained blows and flung filth upon them by way of giving concrete expression to their contempt for the Allies.[137]

For a short while after the fiasco, Djemal's officials reported victory and encouraged celebrations. Then the truth trickled out as the defeated soldiery returned, and the mood became ugly. Rumours circulated that Djemal had been bribed by the British. Turkish officers turned on their German mentors. The Arab street recalled that, 'though they hated the infidel, they loved the Turk not at all, and the country was exhausted, and the blockade of the Mediterranean by the Allies prevented the import and export of articles'.[138]

The danger for Djemal was that the nationalist underground might trigger a revolution against war and empire. He found himself desperately short of reliable troops in the spring of 1915. His Anatolian Turkish regiments had been withdrawn to reinforce the defence of Gallipoli, and he was down to just twelve battalions, all of them Arab units recruited in Syria and Palestine, and without a single artillery battery or machine-gun company to support them.[139] 'If a revolt had broken out as a result of foreign intrigues,' he reported, 'there would have been no way of suppressing it, and the government would have lost all its Arab territories.'[140] In Djemal's dark mind the sense grew of having been betrayed by those whose cause he had espoused, for he was the most pro-Arab and pro-Islamist of the Young Turk triumvirate. 'Work for the elevation of the Arabs and Arabism,' he had told assembled notables in a public speech in Damascus in January 1915. 'Renew your civilisation ... Nothing will repel evil more than the continuing unity of Arabs and Turks under one caliph ...'[141] But the evidence was mounting that some of the leading men to whom he directed such appeals were plotting against him.

Al-Fatat had, in fact, extended its base beyond the Arab middle class and secured the allegiance of some powerful tribal leaders, notably Emir Nuri al-Shaalan, head of the mighty Ruwalla confederation that controlled the eastern desert. Al-Ahd's membership now included at least one general.[142] The danger was unquantifiable. It now seems that the combined membership of Al-Fatat and Al-Ahd was never more than about 100, roughly half of them army officers, amounting to just 0.5 per cent of the one-quarter of Ottoman officers who were Arab.[143] The great majority of Arab officers remained Ottoman loyalists to the end, inspired by a mix of professionalism, camaraderie, suspicion of British and French intentions, lack of confidence in the opportunistic leadership of the Arab Revolt, and antipathy towards its feudal-tribal social base and reactionary programme. But Djemal could never be sure.

How extensive was the nationalist underground? How many currently uncommitted officers might join an uprising in the event? How stable was the political ground beneath the Ottoman Fourth Army?

In April 1915 – at the very moment that the Armenian massacres began – the Ottoman police in Syria arrested a number of known Arab nationalist sympathisers. They were subsequently tried by a specially convened military court, and thirteen were found guilty of treason and condemned to death. On 21 August, eleven men were hanged in Burj Square in Beirut. Most were young. They included lawyers, journalists and scions of leading Lebanese and Syrian families.[144]

A watching Turkish officer was struck by the noble demeanour of the condemned.

> I came to Beirut on the day of the executions. It was before Government House. There was a series of gallows, and some had already been executed. There was one among them who marched among the condemned. He had been a reserve officer and wore a *kalpak* [a lambskin hat worn by Ottoman officers]. He was quiet and entirely above the fear of death. He sat on one of the benches and smoked until his turn came. He chose his own particular gallows, and he passed the knot around his neck and said, 'Born an Arab, I have served the Arabs, and I am dying for the Arabs.'[145]

A second wave of arrests followed in the autumn, and this too eventually resulted in show trials and public executions. Twenty-one nationalists were hanged in Beirut and Damascus on 6 May 1916; this time, in addition to officers, lawyers and writers, the victims included four former members of the Ottoman parliament.

The crack-down sent shock-waves across the region. Sherif Feisal, visiting Damascus at the time and staying at the farmhouse of friends a short distance from the city, received the news when a special edition of an official Arabic newspaper was brought to the breakfast table. One of the family read out the report of the executions, including the list of eminent names, along with the charge of 'treasonable participation in activities of which the aims were to separate Syria, Palestine, and Iraq from the Ottoman sultanate and to constitute them into an independent state'. A long silence followed, broken only by muttered prayers, invocations for the dead and a verse from the Koran. Then Feisal, usually restrained and dignified, jumped to his feet, hurled his *keffiya* to the ground, trampled it underfoot, and cried out, 'Death has become sweet, O Arabs!'[146]

Al-Fatat's underground organisation in Beirut and Damascus was effectively destroyed by the round-ups and executions. Al-Ahd's capacity had also been crippled by the redeployment of Arab divisions and a dispersal of nationalist officers to distant fronts. Feisal bore witness to the change:

> During these three months [of his absence from Damascus], the Turkish authorities had dispersed a great number of Syrian and Iraqi nationalists; some had been hanged; others imprisoned or expatriated far away in Anatolia. The 25th Division, composed of Arab officers and men, which was to have been the kernel of the revolutionary army, and also the officers of the reserve, all young nationalists, had been sent to Rumania and Galicia. The psychological moment for a rising had passed.[147]

A social revolution of the Arab peasantry had never been considered. The liberal revolution of the Arab middle class had been aborted. By one of history's many tragic ironies, the standard of modern Arab nationalism passed into the hands of the tribal reactionaries of the desert, where it would amount to little more than traditional Bedouin raiding inflated by foreign gold and guns. The historical consequences of this travesty are with us still.

* * *

Despite the lack of preparation and the suddenness of the outbreak, the Arab achievement by the end of September was impressive. They had taken 6,000 prisoners, tied down 14,000 enemy soldiers in a siege, cut off the three Ottoman divisions in Asir and Yemen, and brought to nought the Khairi Bey/Stotzingen mission to overwhelm Aden and detonate an African *jihad*.[148]

But these successes were largely due to surprise. Scattered Ottoman garrisons had been overwhelmed – eventually – because they had been engulfed by a sudden eruption of tribal violence, leavened by British firepower. In the period of readjustment following, the Ottomans had recovered their balance, and the bullish Medina commander, Fakhri Pasha, was determined to extinguish the revolt before the end of the year. With the arrival of further reinforcements, bringing the strength of the Hijaz Expeditionary Force up to twelve battalions of infantry, supported by artillery and aircraft, he went onto the offensive.

The direct overland route to Mecca was impossible for a large conventional force due to the mountainous terrain and lack of water, so Fakhri sent two columns towards the coast, one directed at Yenbo, the other at Rabegh. Once the coast road was open and the western flank secure, the Ottomans were to push on to Mecca. The Yenbo column clashed with Feisal's Northern Army in the hill country about Yenbo al-Nakhl and tumbled it backwards towards the coast. The Rabegh column also made good progress, Ali's Southern Army giving ground rather than face an uneven fight against a large, well-equipped modern force. Demoralised by having to retreat, traumatised by the long reach of the enemy's guns, and the bombing and strafing runs of his fighter aircraft, fearful of Ottoman reprisals in the event of defeat, the Sherifian irregulars began to melt away. Pro-Ottoman tribal chiefs about Medina and on the coast – enemies of the Hashemites – stirred into action.[149] The flame of the Arab Revolt burned low.

Early in 1916, as the McMahon negotiations with the emir of Mecca concluded, a specialist 'Arab Bureau' had been set up in Cairo, headed by David Hogarth, under the overall authority of intelligence chief Gilbert Clayton. One of its principal roles was the publication of an internal *Arab Bulletin*, giving updates on everything to do with Arab affairs as they related to the British war-effort, which was circulated among senior colonial administrators and military personnel. Captain T.E. Lawrence was a regular contributor and, in October 1916, his formal transfer to the Arab Bureau was arranged. Before it came through, however, he had made his first visit to Arabia. Alarmed by the peril facing the revolt, Clayton had dispatched Storrs and Lawrence to Jiddah for a conference with Sherif Abdullah.

The journey took four days and the two men were jettisoned into the searing heat of the Hijaz on 16 October 1916.[150] Storrs' white tunic and trousers had been stained red by his sweating into the armchairs on the deck of the small converted liner on which they had taken passage. Walking through what his companion called 'the oppressive alley of the food market' towards the British consulate, he now shone like varnish, while spreading patches on Lawrence's khaki drill went a deeper shade of brown and left him wondering whether the colour would be the same all over by the end of the walk. 'In the air, from the men to the dates and back to the meat, squadrons of flies danced up and down like particles of dust in the sun-shafts, which stabbed to the darkest places of the booths through torn places in the wood and sackcloth awning overhead. The atmosphere was like a bath.'

Captain Lawrence, the *Arabia Deserta* enthusiast, had finally arrived in the land explored by Doughty forty years before. It was the beginning of a two-year association that would eventually bring him far greater fame than his model. It would also provide a theatre of action replete with tragedy.

CHAPTER 8

A Crusader, an Unknown Desert and a New Way of War

THE LEGEND BEGAN in dream-world. It had lived in the imagination before Captain Lawrence ever set foot in Arabia, before he first disembarked at Jiddah and 'went down into the dust and noise of the eastern market-places'. 'All men dream,' he later wrote, 'but not equally.'

> Those who dream by night in the dusty recesses of their minds wake in the day to find that all was vanity: but the dreamers of the day are dangerous men, for they may act their dream with open eyes, and make it possible. This I did. I meant to make a new nation, to restore to the world a lost influence, to give 20 million of Semites the foundation on which to build an inspired dream-place of their national thoughts.

By the time he wrote those words, it had become 'a faded dream'; worse, he was 'continually and bitterly ashamed'; for his attempt to live the dream had transformed him into a 'conspirator', a 'fraud' and a 'trickster'. Into other things, too, equally hard to live with: a war hero, an early twentieth-century celebrity, a 'matinee idol' (his phrase); but one riddled with guilt and self-loathing, such that he was fascinated by his fame yet felt compelled to flee from it, causing its architect, Lowell Thomas, the American newsman and impresario who created the legend of 'Lawrence of Arabia' in 1919, to accuse his hapless *protégé* of having 'a genius for backing into the limelight'.[1]

Lawrence's tragedy was to be vulnerable, conscience-ridden and too clear-sighted. He was his own Cassandra, and his mind became a psychic prism for the accumulated contradictions of the Arab Revolt, until finally it was shattered by their intensity, and his personality imploded into a black hole of neurotic self-scrutiny and suicidal self-hate. The desert war was the hinge on which T.E. Lawrence's life turned, because, for him, it involved the dissolution of a romantic myth into a lived experience of murder, greed and betrayal. He entered Arabia in the autumn of 1916 full of ambition, enthusiasm and zest for life; he left Syria in the autumn of 1918 with his mind darkened and destabilised. The war ended in the desert, but would rage on inside Lawrence's head.

* * *

Born in the village of Tremadoc in North Wales on 15 August 1888, Thomas Edward Lawrence – 'Ned' as he was known in the family – was the second of five brothers born to Thomas Chapman and Sarah Junner. Lawrence's father was a member of the Anglo-Irish gentry, but he had left his wife and their four daughters to go off with the family governess when their illicit relationship was exposed. Because Thomas Chapman's wife refused to grant a divorce, Ned's parents were never able to marry. They assumed the name Lawrence and maintained a façade of upper-middle-class respectability, but they lived in fear that their secret would be exposed; consequently, they tended to keep themselves to themselves.

The family moved around at first, living successively in Wales, Scotland, Brittany, the Isle of Man and the New Forest, before settling down in 1896 in a large town-house in north Oxford, where Ned in due course attended the City of Oxford High School and then Jesus College. Mr Lawrence appears to have been quiet and easy-going. Born to wealth, he never worked, even after his separation, his new family living well enough on the income from his property. He enjoyed traditional gentlemanly pursuits, was a keen cyclist and photographer, and seems to have had a special interest in the architecture of medieval castles and churches. Ned embraced a number of these enthusiasms.[2]

Ned's relationship with his mother was far more problematic. Sarah Junner was working class and illegitimate. Her mother may have died of alcoholism, and she seems never to have known her father. Guilt about her origins was compounded by guilt about her elopement, illicit love and bastard children. She became repressive, opinionated and deeply religious. Family Bible readings were daily events, and the Lawrences were regular members of a fundamentalist Evangelical congregation. A strict mother, it was Sarah rather than Mr Chapman who administered corporal punishment. This took the form of severe beatings on the buttocks, and Ned, the most unruly of the Lawrence boys, was usually the victim; his youngest brother later opined that the intention was to break his will. In so far as she loved her sons, Sarah Lawrence tended to smother and devour them; when they showed defiance, she projected her own guilt onto them and punished them for the sin of their parents. Ned became the psychic mirror of his mother's neurosis, especially when he found out, seemingly at a young age, that his parents were not married. He craved his mother's approval, yet resented her deceitfulness, hypocrisy and brutality. He may have seen his father as diminished and demeaned by his mother: degraded in his manhood by a relationship with a strong-willed woman who was – as respectable Edwardian society would have viewed it – a seductress, his mistress and a social inferior.

Lawrence later accused his mother of making him 'a standing civil war'. Even she, late in life, conceded partial responsibility for his 'nervousness'. He carried the burden of his illegitimacy and his mother's guilt for the rest of his life. The role he played in the war – and his reaction to it – was the expression of a deep-rooted neurotic complex. Physically small – he was notably shorter than his brothers, only 5 feet 5 inches, and had a somewhat over-large head – he subjected himself to gruelling tests of stamina and endurance: for he needed to prove himself worthy.[3] Socially ill at ease, he kept others at a distance through mischievousness and make-believe. Frightened by his own desires, he came to regard sex and any form of physical contact with disgust. Regarded by his mother as a product of sin, tainted in his own eyes by moral pollution, burdened with a secret that called into question his 'breeding' and 'respectability', he escaped into a world of fantasy. This was easily done, for he was bright, intellectually engaged, a voracious reader, and full of drive. He experienced no real adolescence: his development was arrested at a boyhood stage of fascination with heroes and history. But this evolved into exceptional academic accomplishment.[4]

As a schoolboy, Ned used to visit construction sites in the town to recover archaeological artefacts, and he would undertake long bicycle rides into the Oxfordshire countryside to explore medieval churches and make brass-rubbings. He later cycled across France in his summer holidays, again to pursue his interest in the Middle Ages, visiting numerous castles and cathedrals. Awarded an Exhibition to read history at Jesus in 1907, he specialised in the medieval period. This culminated in a four-month walking tour of Syria in the summer of 1909 to collect primary data on Crusader castles for an undergraduate thesis. Lawrence was awarded First Class Honours in Modern History in July 1910 (Oxford, oddly, considers modernity to begin with the fall of the Roman Empire), by which time his talents had been noted by academic mentors in a position to advance his career.

David Hogarth, Keeper of the Ashmolean Museum, used his good offices to secure Lawrence a 'Senior Demyship' at Magdalen College – essentially a junior research fellowship – worth £100 a year for five years, to enable him to join the planned British Museum excavations at Carchemish, a Hittite site on the Euphrates in northern Syria. His role, effectively that of deputy director, included on-site photography and recording, cataloguing finds, work on pottery and sculptures, and supervising the native workforce.[5]

By the outbreak of war, therefore, Lawrence was exceptionally experienced and accomplished for his relatively young age: a medievalist and a field archaeologist, he was also well travelled, an excellent linguist (with command of Greek, Latin, French and Arabic), very widely read (including in French medieval literature), and physically tough, self-reliant and skilled in the management of men.

Despite all this, he was a dreamer. His fascination with the Crusades was that of a romantic in the manner of William Morris. His interwar friend, the novelist E.M. Forster, later wrote: 'The notion of a Crusade, of a body of men leaving one country to do noble deeds in another, possessed him, and I think never left him . . .'[6] He was interested in castles as monuments to an epic narrative and a code of chivalry. Heroic figures like Richard the Lionheart loomed large in his imagination. He devoured the *chansons de geste* and *romans d'aventure* of twelfth-century France because they expressed a mythic idealisation of the Crusades. Tellingly, one of only three books he would carry with him on campaign in Arabia was a copy of Sir Thomas Malory's *Le Morte d'Arthur*, the best-known version of the Arthurian legends in English.[7] That he identified himself with the heroes of medieval myth seems beyond doubt. Driven by his own insecurity and lack of self-worth, he imagined himself a latter-day Arthur or Richard. 'I had dreamed, at the City School in Oxford,' he admitted, 'of hustling into form, while I lived, the new Asia which time was inexorably bringing upon us.'[8]

Another interwar friend, the military historian and Lawrence biographer Basil Liddell Hart, confirms his hero complex:

The idea of a crusade, the idea underlying it, revolved in his mind, giving rise to a dream crusade, which implied a leader with whom, in a sense, he identified himself . . . Naturally, it would be a crusade in the modern form – the freeing of a race from bondage. Where, however, was he to find a race in need of release and at the same time of historical appeal to him? The Arabs seemed the only suitable one left, and they fitted in with the trend of his interests. Thus, early, did the dream of his mission come . . .[9]

* * *

War is the natural arena of the Crusader-hero, and Lawrence was no different from thousands of other young men of his time and class for whom the virtues of patriotism and militarism were instinctive. He had been among the first to join the Oxford University Officers' Training Corps (OTC) when it was formed in 1908, and had attended its summer camp on Farnborough Common in 1910, when, among other things, it fought a mock battle with the Cambridge OTC.[10] He was exhilarated by the outbreak of war. Just as Brooke thanked God 'who has matched us with his hour, and caught our youth, and wakened us from sleeping', Lawrence later wrote of autumn 1914 that 'it felt like morning, and the freshness of the world-to-be intoxicated us'.[11]

Like so many, his greatest fear was missing the moment. Completing *The Wilderness of Zin* survey report delayed him for a while, and he fretted in the meantime that his own special skills might not be required: 'I have a horrible fear that the Turks do not intend to go to war,' he wrote to an American friend on 18 September. 'There is nothing to do but wait, and waiting is very hard.'[12] Though he got a war job in London a month later, he still despaired of a Middle Eastern appointment, writing on 19 October: 'Turkey seems at last to have made up its mind to lie down and be at peace with all the world. I'm sorry, because I wanted to root them out of Syria, and now their blight will be more enduring than ever.'

But he did not have to wait much longer. No sooner had he been commissioned as Temporary 2nd Lieutenant-Interpreter T.E. Lawrence – exchanging civilian bags for army khaki to ease relations with senior officers – than the British and Ottoman empires found themselves at war. Sir John Maxwell, the British commander in Egypt, was shortly afterwards informed by the War Office that he was being sent 'a youngster, 2nd Lt. Lawrence, who has wandered about in the Sinai Peninsula, and who came in here to help in the map branch'. Lawrence set out on 9 December and arrived in Cairo six days later.[13]

The British authorities assigned Lawrence to the Cairo Military Intelligence Department because he spoke Arabic and had an intimate knowledge of Syria and its people. This suited him well. He had come to view the Arabs – or, more specifically, the Bedouin of the Arabian Desert – through an Orientalist lens, transforming them into stereotypical 'noble savages' and the needy objects of 'heroic' leadership; a perception coloured by the racism of empire and his private neurotic obsession with moral pollution.[14] 'The perfectly hopeless vulgarity of the half-Europeanised Arab is appalling,' he had written in a letter home from Carchemish in 1911. 'Better a thousand times the Arab untouched.'[15]

Lawrence seems to have regarded the people of the Middle East as moral categories on a social spectrum, with the depraved town-dweller at one end, the desert nomad at the other, and the Syrian *fellahin* somewhere in between. The inhabitants of Jerusalem were 'characterless as hotel servants', while 'Beirut was the door of Syria, a Levantine screen through which shop-soiled foreign influences flowed in, and represented Syria as much as Soho represented the Home Counties.'[16] Worse had been his characterisation of the labourers on an Egyptian excavation, who were 'horribly ugly, very dirty, dull, low-spirited, without any of the vigour or the self-confident independence of our men [on the Carchemish dig] ... and one could not stand or work close to them for a few minutes without catching fleas or lice ... They were frenetic, and querulous, foul-mouthed, and fawning.'[17]

Some Arabs, then, were repulsive, while others were paragons. One of the latter was Dahoum, a dark-skinned teenager employed as a donkey boy on the Carchemish excavations, who was, according to Leonard Woolley, 'beautifully built and remarkably handsome'. Lawrence spent much time with Dahoum, both on the dig and travelling between seasons, and the intimacy of their relationship scandalised local opinion, especially when Lawrence had Dahoum pose naked while he carved a stone figure of him. The relationship may never have been consummated – Lawrence's sexuality seems to have been highly repressed – but there is little doubt that it was erotically charged. It is all but certain that Dahoum – a model 'noble savage' – is the object of the famous dedication of *Seven Pillars of Wisdom*. 'I loved you,' runs the first verse of the dedicatory poem, 'so I drew these tides of men into my hands and wrote my will across the sky in stars to earn you freedom, the seven-pillared worthy house, that your eyes might be shining for me when we came.' The identity of the dedicatee seems confirmed by other clues. 'The strongest motive throughout [the Arab Revolt] had been a personal one,' he wrote in *Seven Pillars*, '... present to me, I think, every hour of these two years.' And in a private letter composed while working on the book, he explained that 'I liked a particular Arab very much, and I thought that freedom for the race would be an acceptable present.'[18]

The Crusader knights of twelfth-century romances had performed gallant deeds both to reclaim the Holy Land from the infidel and as acts of worship for their lady loves.[19] Lawrence, too, seems to have acted out a heroic role in deference to both a sacred mission, the freedom of the Arabs, and a private love, for a donkey boy from a Syrian village. But Dahoum died in a typhus epidemic in 1916, a fact of which the latter-day knight became aware before the end of the war, adding grief to the cocktail of emotions by which he was eventually overwhelmed. The dedicatory poem is an echo of a mental implosion, as romantic idealism dissolved into longing for lost love, bitterness at betrayal and a pervading sense of corruption.[20]

This, though, was yet to come. In October 1916, the ideal was still intact. But if the men of the desert were 'clean' and 'uncontaminated', they were also like children. Lawrence admired the Bedouin – or rather, his idealisation of the Bedouin – because they were pre-modern and fitted an escapist fantasy that involved 'working against the twentieth century'.[21] But for precisely this reason – and in the contradictory manner of Orientalist discourse – they required guidance. 'The Arabs are even less stable than the Turks,' he reported in February

1916. 'If properly handled, they would remain in a state of political mosaic, a tissue of small jealous principalities, incapable of cohesion ...' The Arab super-state envisioned by nationalists was impossible to realise. 'Leaving out of account the great distances, and the lack of effective communication, long years spent in the struggle of bare existence have engendered in the Arabs a distrust of their neighbours, and a passion for independence which put any permanent union, or submission to one single authority, out of the question.'[22] His famous 'Twenty-seven Articles' – briefing notes written in August 1917 for British personnel assigned to the Arab front – are couched in the terms of colonial paternalism: 'Handling Hijaz Arabs is an art ... The Bedu are easy to lead ... Better the Arabs do it tolerably than that you do it perfectly ... The beginning and ending of the secret of handling Arabs is unremitting study of them ...'[23]

Arabia offered Lawrence two things: anonymity and heroism. It enabled him to play the role of a great lord, a leader of men, a figure from legend, without the risk of exposure and shame attendant upon public prominence at home. He was able to prove his worth and create his own myth in the liminal space provided by an alien landscape and culture, his neurosis having driven him to seek a refuge out of time and place. And in this way, by this convoluted route, his peculiar psychology became an historical force.

* * *

The twelfth-century Crusaders bore almost no relation to the chivalric ideals embodied in the *chansons de geste* and *romans d'aventure*. Nor did the Bedouin tribesmen of the Arab Revolt bear much relation to their Orientalist stereo-types. Subordination and oppression pervaded desert society. A handful of emirs or princes dominated most of Arabia, competing with each other for power, levying tribute and man-service on their vassals, executing swift retri-bution on the refractory. More or less subject to the great lords were the tribal sheikhs, some with thousands of followers, some with only a few dozen, and these were ranged in loose hierarchies and confederations of kin.

The networks of power were unstable. Allegiances could shift, and if they did, the eroding power of one lord became the accumulating power of another: a process of change mediated, as often as not, by war. Because of this, fighting strength was the real measure of an emir or sheikh. Control of territory – of its towns, villages and encampments; of its wells and oases; of its routeways – meant control over manpower. The desert – the apparently empty desert – was dissected by hundreds of invisible lines, and the tribes who defended these lines were divided one from another by a folk history of raids and feuds fostered through the generations by tireless iteration around the campfire. Danger was everywhere, for, as Doughty put it, 'the open desert is full of old debts for blood' and 'a Bedouin hated all Bedouin not his tribesfolk'.[24] To leave village or encampment was to enter a contested space: 'The life of the Arabians is full of suspicion,' said Doughty of his travelling companions; 'they turned their heads with continual apprehension, gazing everywhere about them.'[25] And while abroad, there was no peace of mind, for 'every Bedouin's heart is with his household, and he has no rest in absence, because of the cattle [camels] which he has left in the open wilderness'.[26]

Because desert society was at war with itself, no man could face it alone. Access to grazing and water, and security of household and property, were dependent on blood-brotherhood: on a man's relationship with kin, tribe and sheikh. In the desert, to be shunned, to be cast out, was more than social extinction: it was physical annihilation. The social hierarchy of the desert was held together by the iron hoops of necessity. Most tribesmen were pitifully poor, whether villagers or nomads. Only sheikhs and their retainers had horses, and even the camel-men were a minority; the majority of Arabians were foot-warriors and, if they carried a gun, it was likely an ancient musket and prized family possession. But even the poorest of tribesmen was a patriarch, for Bedouin society was a cascade of oppression with women and slaves at its base.

In the desert, the role of men was to herd animals, wage war and make decisions; little else, for the Bedouin motto was 'toil not'. The whole work of household and encampment fell upon women. They collected firewood and prepared food; they spun, wove and sewed; they erected and dismantled tents; they loaded and unloaded camels; they suckled and cared for children; and they were used as sexual property. Their labour and their bodies belonged to men. They might even be passed from man to man, as when a sheikh took a younger wife and gave his old one to a poor man. Domestic violence was endemic: the beating of women was widespread in Bedouin society. Doughty, an acute observer of the condition of women in Arabia, thought that 'the woman's lot is here unequal concubinage, and in this necessitous life a weary servitude'.[27]

Labour and sexual services were also provided by slaves. They were brought across the Red Sea from Africa and sold on arrival in the Hijaz, and the better-off households might own four or five, who worked at domestic chores or in the family's garden-plots. Some were paid pocket-money, but they had no legal rights, beating was routine and slave families could be broken up at will. Between 15,000 and 25,000 slaves worked in the Wadi Safra and Wadi Yenbo, the two main agricultural districts of the middle Hijazi coastal plain, making the slave element in the population perhaps half or more of the total, in these districts at least.[28]

If most labour was performed by women and slaves (and also children), and if Arab men were a domestic elite who exercised power over persons and property yet did little work themselves, then sherifs, sheikhs and ordinary tribesmen shared a common interest in the existing social order. However browbeaten by social superiors, the poorest tribesman remained a conservative patriarch living off the labour of his own household. His interest in this arrangement cemented him into the tribal hierarchy. And outside this structure – beyond its protective (and suffocating) embrace – there was only a vast and hostile desert.

This was the anthropological substrate from which the Arab Revolt arose. The Bedouin could fight only as a member of his tribe, and only at the direction of his traditional leaders. Thus, when the Emir Hussein abolished modern administration and taxation, replacing it with the rule of sheikhs and *sharia*, most men welcomed the change.[29] Whatever else the revolt may have been, it was never a popular uprising.

This explains the role of Lawrence. The aspiring hero was a neurotic English maverick, rejected by his mother and at risk of exposure and shame in mainstream bourgeois society at home. Arrested development and infantile regression had been the psychic results as his mind reacted against this unmanageable reality. He had retreated into a mythologised past and came to imagine himself as one of its great protagonists. Fittingly, he had chosen the medieval past, for he was aware of his descent from landed gentry, and, mainly thanks to his father, was imbued with many of its habits and values. Flight from his dark secret was also escape from the materialism, snobbery and petty-mindedness of bourgeois society, as he found his refuge in the romantic myths of the feudal past.

A man afflicted like Lawrence could never have played a leading role in a modern revolution. A puppet-show character could perform only in a make-believe world. Such was the Arab Revolt. An artefact of Hashemite ambition and British imperialism, it was a fake. Neither a liberal-nationalist 'Young Arab' uprising, nor a land war of the Syrian and Iraqi *fellahin*, it was not a real revolution at all.[30] Abdul Aziz al-Masri – the former Ottoman officer who had founded Al-Ahd and was now, in late 1916, organising the embryonic Hashemite regular army – soon became disillusioned with the Sherifian family, considering them 'medievally monarchical' and 'a sort of Arabian Habsburg'. One senior British officer thought him 'so evidently disappointed at his position and so bored with the whole thing that I suspect his one idea is to get out of it'.[31] It was because the Arab Revolt had this superficial character – because it lacked social substance – that it could accommodate and make use of the fantasy that Lawrence brought to it.

* * *

Lawrence had grown increasingly restless as an intelligence officer. He was instinctively a man of action. Bike rides across France, a 1,200-mile trek through Syria, and several years excavating an archaeological site were proof enough of this. His young imagination was filled with images of legendary warriors. Now, ironically, when the drums of war had summoned millions to battle, he found himself behind a desk in a Cairo office. The death of two brothers on the Western Front in 1915, Frank in May, Will in October, left him deeply unsettled. As he wrote to a friend at the Ashmolean in Oxford, 'they were both younger than I am, and it doesn't seem right, somehow, that I should go on living peacefully in Cairo'.[32] Returning from his brief adventure in Mesopotamia in May 1916, he feared that 'I will again be nailed within that office at Cairo'.[33] The outbreak of the Arab Revolt the following month increased his keenness for an active role. Though he remained cheerful and busy, designing a set of postage-stamps for the newly independent Hijaz – with flavoured gum 'so that one may lick without unpleasantness' (an idea never implemented) – he craved service in the field.[34]

To make matters worse, circumstances had changed in Cairo. The easy-going Clayton had been relegated to take charge of the Arab Bureau alone, and a new, more conventional officer, Thomas Holdich, had been appointed head of Military Intelligence as a whole.

Thwarted in his initial request for transfer to the more donnish atmosphere of the Arab Bureau, Lawrence began making a nuisance of himself.[35] Disdainful of both bourgeois and military convention, he had always been somewhat scruffy and insolent. He would wear his peaked cap askew, his hair too long, his uniform dirty, his buttons unpolished; his Sam-Browne belt, if worn at all, would be buckled loose over his unbuttoned shoulder-strap.[36] Worse was his arrogance towards less talented but older and more senior men, and his intolerance of pretension and pomposity, especially when (as so often) it was a cover for stupidity or incompetence. He now seems to have made himself as objection-able as possible: 'I took every opportunity to rub into them their comparative ignorance and inefficiency in the department of intelligence (not difficult!) and irritated them yet further by literary airs, correcting Shavian split infinitives and tautologies in their reports'.[37]

Such behaviour came naturally, of course: his general air of superiority concealed an inner lack of self-worth. It may have been satisfying – cathartic, indeed – but it is unlikely to have been productive within a rigid military hier-archy. Clayton's efforts on his behalf were probably more efficacious. The wily spymaster remained a supreme string-puller despite his apparent demotion. Lawrence thought that 'he worked by influence rather than by direction ... He was like water, or permeating oil, soaking silently and insistently into every-thing. It was not possible to say where Clayton was and or was not ...'[38] He came through on this occasion, circumventing the Cairo staff and routing a request for Lawrence's services through London. Before the transfer came through, however, Lawrence had been sent to accompany Ronald Storrs on his October trip to the Hijaz.[39]

Lawrence was present when Storrs, accompanied by Colonel Wilson, the British Representative at Jiddah, Wingate's man in the Hijaz, met with Sherif Abdullah. He had no official role and, on the first occasion, remained quietly in the background. Attention focused on Arab requests for an Allied brigade to defend Rabegh against a possible Ottoman thrust to the coast, and for a flight of British aircraft to support operations inland. At a second meeting the following day, Lawrence became more talkative as discussion turned to the location and composition of various Ottoman forces, drawing on the encyclopaedic knowledge he had accumulated during two years in Cairo Intelligence. Abdullah was stunned: 'Is this man God, to know everything?'

Lawrence, with Storrs' backing, took the opportunity to ask permission to visit both Ali and Feisal, having determined, if possible, to meet all of Hussein's sons and assess their respective characters. An official report on conditions on the ground might increase the flow of practical support, it was pointed out. But this was not straightforward. No British officer had so far been allowed to travel inland – they were infidels, the Hijaz was the Islamic Holy Land and Hussein's supporters were tribal conservatives. Abdullah had to argue hard down the telephone to overcome his father's caution and suspicion. But permission was granted and Lawrence would soon be on his way.[40]

Between their two meetings with Abdullah, Lawrence and Storrs had dined in Jiddah with Colonel Edouard Brémond, head of the newly established French Military Mission. In conversation, they had gained a clear understanding of the radical difference between theirs and their ally's vision for the Arab Revolt. Brémond was a veteran career soldier with long experience in North Africa and a deep commitment to his nation's assumed 'civilising mission'. To help validate France's ambition to extend that mission to Syria, he had a 200-man contingent of military specialists on hand for deployment to the Hijaz.[41] But – as his two eager listeners were informed over dinner – precisely because the French wanted Syria, they did not want an Arab uprising in the north and, to prevent this, they wanted the insurgents contained in the Hijaz, where they would be useful in tying down Ottoman troops, but incapable of influencing the course of events in the wider Middle East. Brémond was remarkably candid, the views he expressed to Lawrence and Storrs being precisely those he cabled to Paris that same day: 'If the Arabs took Medina, they would immediately try to go into Syria. It is therefore in our interests that Medina does not fall into the hands of the sherif of Mecca before the end of the war.'[42]

His distrust of the French fully confirmed, Lawrence headed off to meet the other Arab leaders. He and Storrs first went up the coast by sea to consult with Ali and Zeid at Rabegh, and then, after three days, he set off alone with only Arab guides as company on a 100-mile journey inland to find Feisal.

* * *

Lawrence had been two years behind a desk and was not acclimatised. His eyes and muscles ached, and his skin blistered with 'the pestilent beating of the Arabian sun and long monotony of camel pacing'. When he arrived at Hamra, a village of about a hundred houses in the Wadi Safra, where Feisal's army was encamped, he was exhausted. Nonetheless, as he reports it, his first meeting with 'the man whom I had come to Arabia to seek' was a moment of high drama. Lawrence was led up a walled path to a mud-brick house with a double courtyard standing on a gentle mound. In the inner courtyard, motionless in the black-framed doorway of the house, he saw Feisal:

> very tall and pillar-like, very slender, dressed in long white silk robes and a brown headcloth bound with a brilliant scarlet and gold cord. His eyelids were dropped, and his close black beard and colourless face were like a mask against the strange still watchfulness of his body. His hands were loosely crossed in front of him on his dagger.[43]

Lawrence had already met Hussein's three other sons. None of them had much impressed him. Abdullah – short, round, jovial, charming, looking younger than his 35 years – he considered a politician rather than a great warrior or popular leader; one with unrealistic aspirations to be 'a far-seeing statesmen', for in fact he was working mainly to 'establish the greatness of the family' and for 'his own particular advancement'. Ali – short, slim, bent, bookish, prematurely aged at 37 – was 'without force of character, nervous, and rather tired'. Zeid was 'a shy, white, beardless lad of perhaps 19, cold and flippant, no enthusiast for the revolt'.[44] That left only the third son, the 31-year-old Feisal.

Lawrence could not afford to be disappointed, for he had journeyed to find 'the leader alone needed to make the Arab Revolt win through to a success'.[45] Nor, later, in his description of Feisal in *Seven Pillars of Wisdom*, could he do other than write of him hagiographically, for the sherif's qualities had by then become entangled in the post-war question of independence. The official report he wrote immediately after the first meeting, on the other hand, betrays reservations: Feisal was 'hot-tempered, proud, and impatient, sometimes unreasonable'; he lacked 'prudence' and was 'perhaps not over-scrupulous'; he was 'rather narrow-minded and rash'. But there were redeeming qualities, for Feisal was 'almost regal in appearance ... Far more imposing personally than any of his brothers ... A popular idol, and ambitious; full of dreams and the capacity to realise them, with keen personal insight, and a very efficient man of business'. In a revealing remark – especially in the unlikely context of a military report – Lawrence observed that Feisal 'looks like a European, and very like the monument of Richard I at Fontevraud'.[46]

Feisal was serious and hard-working in a way that Abdullah was not, yet he was also charming and hospitable, had an intimate knowledge of the leading sheikhs, their tribes and their feuds, and, above all, was infinitely patient in the detailed, day-by-day diplomacy necessary to sustain an Arabian tribal alliance. Much of his working day was spent giving audiences to a long succession of sheikhs, petitioners and disputants. Bedouin manners deprecated haste and directness. Coffee and tea were expected. To be forward with questions and matters of import would give offence. Audiences were slow-motion rituals. And since the sherif's tent was busiest of all, the greatest test of his virtue and fitness to command was social endurance.

'He was accessible to all who stood outside his tent,' said Lawrence, 'and he never cut short petitions, even when men came in chorus with their grief in a song of many verses ... His extreme patience was a ... lesson to me of what native headship in Arabia meant. His self-control seemed equally great.' Listening, knowing, mediating, Feisal acquired an invisible authority. 'I never saw an Arab leave him dissatisfied or hurt – a tribute to his tact and to his memory; for he seemed never to halt for loss of a fact; nor to stumble over a relationship.'[47] In consequence, he exercised a strange, subliminal power, such that he 'seemed to govern his men unconsciously: hardly to know how he stamped his mind on them, hardly to care whether they obeyed. It was a great art ... and it concealed itself, for Feisal was born to it.'[48]

Feisal was, indeed, the man Lawrence was seeking; but this was as much for his failings as for his strengths. The latter made him an effective leader of a tribal revolt; the former ensured that he might become a malleable instrument of Lawrence's will.

Feisal, like Abdullah, was more politician than warrior – and one of greater ambition and forcefulness than his brother – but he lacked the imagination, know-how and materiel to win the war on his own, and his dignified regal exterior concealed a certain hollowness, apparent not only to Lawrence ('Feisal was a timid man who hated running into danger'), but also to some other British officers ('he is easily frightened and lives in constant dread of a Turkish advance'). These weaknesses allowed Lawrence to insinuate himself into Feisal's confidence. Needing help, both material and psychological, Feisal would readily lend an ear to those able to provide it, especially if they were assiduous in their regard for his public dignity. 'Win and keep the confidence of your leader,' Lawrence advised others in his 'Twenty-Seven Articles'. 'Strengthen his prestige at your expense before others when you can.' The foreign advisor's job was not to give direct orders, nor even to proffer advice before a wider audience, but to work only in the shadows: 'Your ideal position is when you are present and not noticed. Do not be too intimate, too prominent, or too earnest.'[49]

Feisal's aim was to take Damascus, not as the leader of a Syrian revolution but as the chief of an Arab tribal army. His motives were both dynastic and personal: he sought the victory of the Hashemites, but also hoped for a kingdom of his own, which, as Hussein's third son, he could hardly aspire to within the confines of the Hijaz.[50] In the scales against him, in different ways and for different reasons, were the Ottoman, French and British Empires. The secret of the special relationship that shortly developed between Arab leader and British officer was contained in Lawrence's neurosis. On the one hand, it made him a romantic with a hero complex who was at odds with his own world and its crude ambitions. On the other, along with his innate brilliance, it enabled him to break the paradigm of conventional military thinking and reconfigure the strategy and tactics of the desert war in a way that would indeed carry the insurgency all the way to Damascus. Feisal's ambition, British materiel, and Lawrence's thinking would combine to frustrate Brémond's determination to keep the Arabs bottled up in the Hijaz.

Lawrence's classic account of his first audience with Feisal therefore rings true.

I greeted him and he made way for me into the room, and sat down on his carpet near the door. As my eyes grew accustomed to the shade, I saw that the little room held many silent figures, all looking at me and Feisal steadily. He remained staring down at his hands, which were twisting slowly about his dagger. At last, softly, he enquired how I had found the journey. I spoke of the heat, and he asked how long from Rabegh, commenting that I had ridden fast for the season. 'And do you like our place here in Wadi Safra?' 'Well: but it is far from Damascus.' There was a quiver, and everybody present stiffened where he sat, and held his breath for a silent minute. Some perhaps were dreaming of how far off success seemed to be; others thought my word a reflection of their late defeat. It had fallen like a sword in their midst, but Feisal at length lifted his eyes and smiled at me and said, 'Praise be to God, there are Turks nearer us than that.' We all smiled with him, and then I got up and excused myself for the moment.[51]

* * *

Lawrence was soon on his way back to the coast. He had spent a mere twenty-four hours with Feisal, and only ten days in total travelling in the Hijaz. But he came away with a far more nuanced understanding of the war than longer-serving and more senior officers who had remained corralled in the coastal ports. In particular, he had visited Feisal and his tribesmen in the field and – informed perhaps by his unconventional education in medieval warfare – discerned the hidden quality of the former and, despite recent setbacks, the high morale and fighting potential of the latter.[52] He sailed from Jiddah with Admiral Rosslyn Wemyss, the senior naval commander in the Middle East, bound for Port Sudan. He was to travel overland to Khartoum with Wemyss for a meeting with Sir Reginald Wingate – governor-general of the Sudan, sirdar of the Egyptian Army and soon to be high commissioner of Egypt. There was no particular reason for thinking that Lawrence would ever return to Arabia. The special relationship with Feisal and the new strategy for the Arab Revolt were all in the future. No doubt Lawrence dreamed, but he was still, for the time being, no more than a lowly intelligence officer with a desk job in Cairo. Events were now unfolding, however, that would transform his chances of a more active role. While Lawrence and Wemyss were *en route*, a cable had reached Wingate to the effect that the military situation in the Hijaz had worsened and the Ottomans were now only three days from Rabegh. The crisis focused attention when the three men met. What should be done? Opinions were divided.

The Arab leaders had insistently requested artillery, aircraft, machine-guns, munitions, supplies and money; and efforts were being made to provide these. The Navy was also playing a key role in transporting materiel and protecting the Hijaz ports. And it was now agreed that a British Military Mission (initially of four officers) should be formed to provide technical training and advice.[53] But what of boots on the ground?

The Emir Hussein had periodically requested the urgent dispatch of foreign troops, only subsequently to change his mind. Senior British officers argued about its advisability. General Murray, the Egyptian Expeditionary Force (EEF) commander in Cairo, was dead against: he wanted concentration of force for his operations in Sinai and had a realistic fear of 'mission creep' in Arabia.[54] Wingate, an old Sudan hand viewing matters from Khartoum, was less adamant. He was influenced by Wilson, a man he trusted who was on the spot, and by Brémond; both were convinced interventionists (though for different reasons), and both harped on about Arab military incompetence. In his concern, Wingate had recently cabled London demanding the immediate dispatch of six battalions.[55]

It transpired, however, that Lawrence and Wemyss were against intervention (though not for the same reason as Murray). Both men were enthusiasts for the Arab Revolt, but they had a keen sense of the political dangers inherent in landing infidel soldiers in the Islamic Holy Land. Some Egyptian troops had, of course, already been sent – mountain-gunners and machine-gunners – but few further could be spared without imperilling the security of the Sudan. The French Military Mission was available – and this included Muslim colonial troops from North Africa – but it was too small to be risked on its own. The concrete question was whether a British brigade should be sent to Rabegh to secure the port against any possibility of an Ottoman *coup de main* to sever the Arab supply-line and open the road to Mecca. The War Committee in London had debated sending a British brigade to Rabegh three times in the space of a month – each time deciding against – but this had not settled matters: the issue remained live as long as the military crisis in the Hijaz lasted.[56]

Back in Cairo, Lawrence was asked by Clayton to write a military assessment. He was unequivocal:

> We have appropriated too many Muslim countries for them [the Arabs] to have any real trust in our disinterestedness, and they are terribly afraid of an English occupation of Hijaz. If the British, with or without the sherif's approval, landed at Rabegh an armed force strong enough to take possession of the groves and organise a position there, they would, I am convinced, say 'We are betrayed', and scatter to their tents.[57]

That was not all: a scattering of the tribesmen was, he charged, exactly what the French wanted, for it would make the emir of Mecca more dependent on foreign support and, in the presence of a large force of foreign soldiers, more open to pressure. 'They say, "Above all things, the Arabs must not take Medina." This can be assured if an Allied force landed at Rabegh.'[58]

This was one argument: but there was another, of deeper, more long-term significance. For a paradigm-shift in strategic thinking had already begun in Lawrence's mind. What he had grasped at this early stage was that, while the Arabs could not defend Rabegh itself – indeed, could not defend fixed positions anywhere – neither had the Turks been able to capture it. Its security lay in its distance from Medina and the insurgent-infested hills between the two towns.

> All the forces fighting for the sherif are made up of tribesmen, and it is the tribal army of 3,000 to 4,000 under Sidi Feisal ... that has held up the advance on Mecca or Rabegh of Fakhri Pasha's army for five months. Rabegh is not, and never has been, defensible with Arab forces, and the Turks have not got there because these hill tribes under Feisal bar their way.[59]

These ideas were fleshed out in a more detailed report written around this time, where he explained that 'the tribal armies are aggregations of snipers only', in consequence of which 'they are not to be relied on for attack in mass', but 'are extremely mobile, and will climb or run a great distance to be in a safe place for a shot – preferably at not more than 300 yards range . . .' The tribesmen should not mount charges or fight pitched battles: their forte was defensive guerrilla warfare, whereas 'one company of Turks, properly entrenched in open country, would defeat the sherif's armies'. The mountain tribesmen were especially adept and resilient, and their home terrain, which they knew so well, was perfect for their style of warfare. Their best strategy was to preserve their elasticity and avoid decisive action against a concentrated enemy. 'A difference in character between the Turkish and Arab armies is that the more you distribute the former, the weaker they become, and the more you distribute the latter, the stronger they become.'[60] Here was the seed of a very big idea.

Lawrence's memorandum bolstered the majority position: there would be no British brigade sent to Rabegh. It also raised his profile, and the decision was soon taken that he should be sent back to Yenbo on a temporary liaison posting. The quality of his reports, the soundness of his judgements and, not least, his 'influence with Feisal' made him the obvious choice. He seems to have baulked, insisting on his 'complete unfitness for the job', but his reservations were overridden; as, no doubt, he wished them to be. By the beginning of December 1916 he was back in Arabia – just as the slow-burning military crisis there reached its climax.[61]

* * *

For the best part of two months, the opposing sides had faced each other in the hill-country between Medina and the coast, a region of ragged peaks and twisting gorges where the tracks in the valleys narrowed to 200 yards, even 20 yards, and were flanked by 'pitiless hills of granite, basalt, and porphyry: not polished slopes, but serrated and split and piled up in thousands of jagged heaps of fragments as hard as metal and nearly as sharp'. The mountain tribesmen would run from peak to peak, their tactics a fluid defence in depth, the 80-mile-wide belt of hills 'a paradise for snipers', such that 'two or three hundred determined men knowing the ranges could hold any section of them'.

Though they had sometimes gained momentary success, pushing forward into the massif, the Ottomans had never been able to break clean through to the coast. Whatever immediate tactical advantage was gained, they had always been hamstrung by their supply-line through the mountains.

The enemy would never be sure that the fickle population might not turn again, and to have such a labyrinth of defiles in the rear, across the lines of communications, would be worse than having it in front. Without the friendship of the tribes, the Turks owned only the ground on which their soldiers stood: and lines so long and so complex would soak up all their thousands of men in a night, and leave none in the battle-fronts, for it was not as though their passage of the hills ended their affair. Before them lay the length of the parched Tihama [the coastal plain], along which their regular army would require great trains of camels to provide its food and water . . .[62]

Brave words: but things were set to change. On 1 December, Fakhri Pasha marched out of Medina at the head of fresh reserves to join his army at the front and renew the push towards the coast. He followed a side-road through the hills to outflank the Harb holding the eastern entrance to the Wadi Safra, and, with the Ottoman infantry in their rear, the tribesmen melted away to protect their families. Moving fast down the wadi, the highway to the coast, the Turks took the Sherif Zeid's force at Hamra by surprise and scattered it; so sudden was their onset that Hussein's youngest son was almost captured while still asleep in his tent.

Fakhri was now astride the main Sultani Road, with the route south-west to Rabegh open; beyond lay Jiddah, then Mecca, his ultimate objective. He could not risk an advance this way with Feisal still undefeated on his north-western flank, however, so he led his main force to Wadi Yenbo.

Feisal, encamped about Kheif Hussein, almost 50 miles from the coast, was forced to fall back down the wadi to protect his supply-line, taking up a new position at Nakhl Mubarak. Here Lawrence reached him on the evening of 3 December, his 5,000 tribesmen now encamped around two large clusters of mud houses and palm gardens. 'As we got near we saw through the palm-trees flame, and the flame-lit smoke of many fires, and the hollow ground re-echoed with the roaring of thousands of camels, volleys of shots, and the shoutings of men lost in the darkness and looking through the crowd for their friends.'

A day or two later, Zeid and around 800 of his broken men rode in, spreading gloom, and the day after that, Feisal's forward positions were driven in by an Ottoman force of three battalions supported by camel-men and mule-mounted infantry. Feisal kept his nerve, re-ordered his line at Nakhl Mubarak, and sent the Juheina in a wide sweep to the left so as to threaten the Ottoman flank and rear as they came down the wadi.[63]

But the Battle of Nakhl Mubarak on 9 December seemed to confirm every British officer's anti-Arab prejudice. The battle had been going well, when suddenly, inexplicably, the word went round that the Juheina had broken, panic at the news dissolved the Arab line, and in no time all Feisal's tribesmen were streaming away down the wadi towards Yenbo. Later, at an informal enquiry into the disaster, the risible truth was learned. 'And why did you retire to the camping-ground behind us during the battle?' Feisal asked one of the Juheina sheikhs. 'Only to make ourselves a cup of coffee,' came the answer. 'We had fought from sunrise, and it was dusk, and we were very tired and thirsty.'[64]

It is defeat, not victory, that tests the mettle of a military leader. The supreme crisis of the Arab Revolt had come. Feisal's slowly crafted and delicate alliance of the tribes, an alliance glued together by promise of easy victory and ample reward, now began to unravel with alarming speed. As the Turks came on, the majority of tribesmen fled, fearing retribution and attacks on their homes. Fewer than 2,000 remained as the fugitive Sherifian army entered Yenbo. Feisal knew the gravity of the crisis, yet he concealed this from his followers. When told of the cataclysmic coffee-break, he laughed with the Juheina at their folly and chided them gently, without causing offence. Lawrence had already borne witness to this power of self-control and charismatic leadership that Feisal had. When Zeid's defeated men arrived at his camp at Nakhl Mubarak, 'he took it all in public as a joke, chaffing people on the way they had run away, jeering at them like children, but without in the least hurting their feelings, and making others feel that nothing much had happened that could not be put right. He is magnificent, for to me privately he was most horribly cut-up.'[65]

Lawrence, too, was shaken. He had set much store by the Arabs' mountain shield ('their initiative, great knowledge of the country, and mobility make them formidable in the hills'). Now he U-turned and wondered whether or not a British brigade was needed after all, for, as he reported dismally, 'The Arabs, outside their hills, are worthless.'[66]

* * *

The crisis appeared worse than it was. The Ottoman offensive was overextended. The bleeding away of men to defend its line of communications had eroded the size of the spearhead in front of Yenbo, and Feisal, who had kept his head, endeavoured to keep it so by sending the Juheina back down the Wadi Yenbo to shoot up the enemy supply-columns. The British, meantime, organised the defence of the port, Lawrence having rushed there from Feisal's camp with early warning of the emergency. Major Herbert Garland – a tall Scottish chemist who had turned himself into an explosives expert and was now in the Hijaz to teach the Arabs how to blow up trains – improvised a defensive line by strengthening and raising the ancient town-walls, stringing barbed wire in front, and emplacing machine-guns and mountain-guns at appropriate angles. Captain William 'Ginger' Boyle – a career naval officer who had earlier had a brush with Lawrence, describing him as 'a small, untidily dressed, and most unmilitary figure' – had concentrated five warships off the coast in less than twenty-four hours. These included the shallow-draught monitor *M-31* (a monitor was essentially an armoured gunboat), which had been anchored at the end of the south-eastern creek of the harbour, whence it could rake the open approaches to the walls. The larger ships were positioned to shoot either over the town or from the opposite flank. The minaret of the mosque was taken over as an observation post by naval signallers equipped with lamps and telephones. The Arabs had suffered few casualties at Nakhl Mubarak, and their morale soared under the protective mantle of naval gun-power. They scurried willingly to their positions on the ramparts on the night of 11/12 December. Then everyone waited, British naval ratings and Arab tribesmen peering into the gloom as the searchlights of HMS *Dufferin* and *M-31* performed an eerie dance across the darkened plain in front of them.

But the enemy did not come, for, as Lawrence reports, 'their hearts had failed them at the silence, and the blaze of lighted ships end to end of the harbour, and the slow beams of the searchlights revealing the openness of the glacis they would have to cross. So they turned back, and that night, I believe, the Turks lost the war.'[67]

Perhaps; but it did not seem so at the time. The Ottomans had been thwarted by the naval guns at Yenbo, and they soon found their camp under seaplane attack. They also had alarming news from the south: the Sherif Ali's Southern Army was on the move. Fakhri was undeterred. Confident that he had sufficiently degraded Feisal's Northern Army to prevent it threatening his communications with Medina, he screened it with a small force and headed south with the rest. He had an easy passage. Ali's advance had ended before Fakhri's arrival – his confidence shaken by rumours of tribal treachery – and he had scurried his tribesmen back to the coast. By early January, Fakhri, at the head of about 5,000 soldiers, had edged to within 50 miles of Rabegh.[68] Again, the very existence of the revolt seemed to hang in the balance.

Once more, however, the Ottoman offensive was undone by the peculiar asymmetry of the war. Control of the Red Sea enabled the British to move naval and air power along the coast to protect any port threatened with attack; this placed a solid backstop behind any Arab reverse. At Yenbo the Turks had been attacked by RNAS (Royal Naval Air Service) seaplanes. At Rabegh, where a landing ground had been established near the beach, they were bombed by RFC (Royal Flying Corps) fighters. Inland, meantime, no sooner had the tribesmen melted away in front of the advancing Turks than others had appeared in their rear. 'Always,' recalled Lawrence, 'the activity of the tribesmen behind their backs hampered them. Clans sometimes fell away from the Arab cause, but did not therefore become trustworthy adherents of the Turks, who found themselves operating in consistently hostile country.'

Attacks could come anywhere in the belt of hills between Medina and the coast, and in the first fortnight of January the Turks were averaging losses of forty camels and twenty men a day. 'The administrative developments of scientific war had clogged their mobility and destroyed their dash: and their troubles grew in geometrical rather than arithmetic progression each new mile they put between themselves and Medina.'[69] This was not the whole of it. The underlying principle – the stretching of the enemy's flanks – was about to be writ large; so much so, indeed, as to constitute a qualitative change in the character of the war, transforming it from a localised tribal uprising into an uncontainable guerrilla insurgency. The effect would be to paralyse the Ottoman Army in Arabia by tying down so many of its men in static garrison duties that no strike-force, no *masse de manoeuvre*, would henceforward be available.

The plan to make this happen was not new. At a conference in Rabegh on 16 November attended by Ali, Feisal, senior Arab officers, and British and French representatives, it had been decided that the three main Arab armies would surround Medina in a loose ring. Abdullah's would take position to the north-east of the city, where it would also threaten the railway line to the north, Ali's would place itself across the route south to Rabegh, Jiddah and Mecca, and Feisal's would operate to the west, with Yenbo as its main base. That was not all. Once his western front was secure, Feisal was to detach part of his force and send it 200 miles north to establish a new forward base at the port of Wejh. This, as one of the Arab officers at the conference explained, was to be:

> a fast-moving column equipped with light weapons with the task of operating behind Turkish lines in Arabia, right up to Syria. This column was intended to terrify the Turks, disrupt their communications, and paralyse their movements. The Turks would not be able to inflict heavy losses on it, because it could move at will north or south, and return to its bases for reinforcements and supplies.[70]

Fakhri's offensive two weeks later had thrown the whole scheme out of gear; but only temporarily. Now, as the tribal armies dissolved into the desert and left the Turks stranded, the Arab offensive restarted. In conformity with the original plan, Abdullah had, in fact, taken position at Hanakiyeh, about 60 miles north-east of Medina. Assembling a tribal army of many thousands, he then moved west, crossed the railway line, and ran into a sizeable Ottoman force defending a hilltop, which he surrounded and forced to surrender. The bag was impressive, including machine-guns, howitzers, an Ottoman general and subsidies for Ibn Rashid of Hail, Ibn Saud of Riyadh and the Imam of Yemen amounting to T£38,000 in total.[71]

This, from Fakhri's perspective, was bad enough, given his position near the coast and his worries about food, fodder and water at the end of a 150-mile-long communications line under guerrilla attack. But there was worse. The Wejh part of the original Arab plan was also being implemented. Not only was Wejh one of the last Ottoman-held ports on the Red Sea; its possession would give the Arabs a forward base for extending their attacks on the railway all the way north, almost as far as Syria.

There was no alternative: on 18 January 1917, Fakhri ordered his army back to Medina.[72] There it would remain for the rest of the war. The Ottoman Army would never regain the initiative against the Arabs.

* * *

Most British officers were, in varying degrees, contemptuous of Arab military capacity. The classified *Arab Bulletin* was a litany of complaints. 'Their preference is for the showy side of warfare,' announced issue number 6 (23 June 1916), 'and it will be difficult to hold them together for any length of time, unless pay and rations are attractive.'[73] 'That the Hijaz Bedouins were simply guerrillas, and not of good quality at that,' intoned issue 52 (31 May 1917), 'had been amply demonstrated, even in the early sieges; and it was never in doubt that they would not attack or withstand Turkish regulars.'[74]

Officers actually working with the Arabs in the field could be positively tetchy. Major Garland, the explosives expert, was typical of some: 'It is of course obvious to anyone knowing Arabs at all that military work of any kind is difficult for the best of them ... In military operations they continually incur unnecessary risks by their stupid conduct, such as singing and shouting within hearing of the enemy ...'[75] An RFC officer stationed at Rabegh was equally disparaging: 'If the Turk is disliked, it is only because all authority is disliked, even the most rudimentary law and order ... Serious contact with Turkish troops would mean wholesale desertion by men who are with the sherif only because of what they can get.'[76]

Lawrence's reports made a sharp contrast. He did not deny the vices, but he saw them as the flip-side of equally significant military virtues; and the trick, he implied, was to adapt military strategy to human resources, not to try and work the other way round.[77] It was far harder for a conventionally trained professional soldier, a man moulded in the traditions of an Edwardian regimental mess, to reach this conclusion than it was for a wartime officer who was both medieval scholar and romantic dreamer. The military anthropology of the Bedouin tribesman was as antipathetic to the one as it was thrilling to the other. And this, of course, is one of the marks of a great commander: to know that armies mirror societies, and, knowing it, to be able to work with the grain of social reality in leading them.

Understanding did not come in a flash. Lawrence had grasped immediately that 'the tribal armies are aggregates of snipers only'; that 'their real sphere is guerrilla warfare'; that 'the Hijaz war is one of dervishes against regular troops'. But he had considered the hill-country decisive: here the Arabs could employ mobility and cover to maximum effect, whereas on the open plain they were 'worthless'. This being so, 'the value of the tribes is defensive only'.[78]

So it had seemed in the autumn of 1916; this had then been the limit of Lawrence's vision, and it amounted to a prescription for only the most cramped and trivial kind of war. It hardly measured up to the grandeur of Arab military history, with its sweeping blitzkriegs that had brought down ancient empires in the seventh century and medieval kingdoms in the twelfth. Lightly equipped and highly mobile, the Arabs had once destroyed ponderous armies of tight-packed foot and heavy horse in dust clouds of swirling manoeuvres and long-range archery. What has been called 'the western way of war', with its emphasis on pitched battle, head-on collision and rapid decision, may have its origins in Ancient Greece and may have been characteristic of warfare west of the Eurasian steppes and south-west of the Black Sea ever since. If so, it was brought to a new level with the rise of European capitalism between the sixteenth and nineteenth centuries, when armies ceased to be agglomerations of individual warriors and became highly drilled blocs of men marching, manoeuvring and volleying with machine-like uniformity. But this had never been the Arab way. The people of desert and steppe – not just Arabs, but also Scythians, Persians, Medes, Berbers, Huns, Turks, Mongols, Cossacks and many others – had always favoured a more distant, evasive, tentative style of combat, where the aim was to minimise risk by keeping the enemy at arm's length, and to wear him down by harassment, missile-shooting and hit-and-run attacks.[79]

This suited a tribal society where the authority of leaders was personal, and where the standing of a sherif or sheikh was measured in tribesmen; no man who led his followers into a bloodbath could expect to retain his influence. Lawrence was quick to grasp this: that the Bedouin were out of synch in a world of industrialised slaughter, belonging to an older, Eastern culture which regarded every death as tragedy.

Avoidance of casualties became a guiding principle for Lawrence: 'Governments saw men only in mass: but ours being irregulars were not formations but individuals. An individual death was like a pebble dropped in water. Each might make only a brief hole, but rings of sorrow widened out from them. We could not afford casualties.'[80] Bloodless victories were the ideal. Battles were not governed by discipline, obedience, and sacrifice. Superior numbers and sudden appearance might permit a wild rush to overwhelm the enemy at the first onset. More often, men would spread out, mould themselves to the ground and engage in duels of long-range sniping. A tribal army was but an aggregate of tribal raiding parties; and a raiding party was but an aggregate of tribesmen. In a conventional army, the mass was greater than the sum of its parts, for the parts were drilled to act as one and thereby multiply their power. In a tribal army, the mass was merely the sum, no more.

At first, Lawrence failed to perceive the *offensive* potential inherent in this 'Eastern way of war'. He had not yet grasped the dialectical relationship between the defensive tactics he had observed and the offensive strategy these made possible. For if the Arabs were not committed to pitched battle, they could spread out; and if they spread out, they would stretch the Ottomans; and if they did this, the advantage would pass from those who fought best *en masse* to those who fought best as guerrillas.

Lawrence groped towards a new understanding as he reconfigured in his mind the scheme of 16 November for an Arab advance on Wejh. In the original, the move north was to have been a subsidiary operation contingent upon the Arabs being able to keep the Ottomans bottled up in Medina. Specifically, Feisal was to strengthen his lines in the hills east of Yenbo and dispatch only part of his force to capture Wejh. This was the plan that had been scuppered by the Ottoman offensive. But it was now revived in a radical new form, even though Fakhri's army had defeated Feisal, driven back Ali and was still hovering outside Rabegh. The proposal was nothing less than that Feisal, right now, should take his *entire* army to Wejh.

The risks seemed prohibitive. 'Our fear was not of what lay before us,' Lawrence later wrote, 'but of what lay behind.'

We were proposing the evacuation of Wadi Yenbo, our only defensive line against the Turkish division in Wadi Safra, only 15 miles away. We were going to strip the Juheina country of its fighting men, and to leave Yenbo, till then our indispensable base, and the second sea-port of the Hijaz, in charge of the few men unfit for the march north, and therefore unfit for anything at all dangerous. We were going to march nearly 200 miles up the coast, with no base behind and only hostile territory in front ... If the Turks cut in behind us, we would be neatly in the void.[81]

To reduce the danger, Abdullah was asked to move his Eastern Army from its present position at Hanakiyeh, 60 miles north-east of Medina, to a new position at Wadi Ais, a well-watered valley about 100 miles north of the city on the western side of the railway. Wadi Ais had many advantages: it was much closer to the coast and therefore more easily supplied; it placed a long stretch of the railway within easy reach of Abdullah's tribesmen; it virtually precluded any sudden Ottoman thrust towards the ports; and it positioned the Eastern and Northern Arab Armies close enough to provide mutual support.[82] With this, Feisal was persuaded to make his great leap into 'the void' and, once he knew that Abdullah was on his way to Wadi Ais (he would arrive there on 19 January), he put his own army in motion, setting out in early January on a march that would take three weeks.[83]

* * *

It was a spectacle from another age. When the starting signal sounded, Feisal and his Ageyl bodyguard passed through the camp, where each tribal contingent under its sheikhs was waiting to mount and fall in behind. 'Peace be upon you!' he said to each head-man as he passed, and the greeting was by each returned. Afterwards the tribesmen of each contingent would mount, sway into motion and enter the swelling surge behind the sherif. 'Then the march became rather splendid and barbaric,' recalled Lawrence.

> Feisal in front, in white; Sharraf on his right in red headcloth and henna-dyed tunic and cloak; myself on his left in white and scarlet; behind us three banners of faded crimson silk with gilt spikes; behind them the drummers playing a march; and behind them again the wild mass of 1,200 bouncing camels of the bodyguard, packed as closely as they could move, the men in every variety of coloured clothes and the camels nearly as vibrant in their trappings. Everyone suddenly burst out singing with full throat a war song in honour of Feisal and his family. We filled the valley to its banks with our river of camels, and poured down in a flashing stream.[84]

Behind the bodyguard came a contingent of Harb tribesmen and many contingents of Juheina; and as the army advanced into new territory, more Juheina joined them, and also Billi of the northern Hijaz. For this was a traditional tribal army, where most men fought only in home territory, drifting away again as the war passed on. So the Sherifian army was in permanent flux. The tribal structure was like a great sheet lying across the desert, and the Arab Revolt like a strong wind blowing beneath it, raising the sheet momentarily in each place.

The only lasting change was that the human dust of the Ottoman occupation was each time blown away; otherwise, as the sheet settled with each passing, everything was again the same.

There were, however, some exceptions among the men of the Arab Northern Army in January 1917. Eventually it would be 10,000 strong and would include a good number who had volunteered to fight far from their own camping-grounds, alongside ancient blood-enemies, having sworn to set aside their feuds for the duration of the war. Feisal became the great peacemaker of the desert, carefully assessing the balance of profit and loss in each ancient vendetta, some of them centuries old, and apportioning what was due in settlement, often paying the debit from his own reserves. 'During two years, Feisal so laboured daily, putting together and arranging in their natural order the innumerable tiny pieces which made up Arabian society [that] there was no blood feud left active in any of the districts through which he passed.' Thus his army became a confederation, a mighty host, 'splendid and barbaric': the greatest tribal army in living memory; and more than that, for, in the words of one old sheikh, 'It is not an army; it is a world that is moving on Wejh.'[85] So it was: a 'flashing stream' of men and beasts flowing northwards, carried on a new tide of history, as their forebears had been under the early caliphs thirteen centuries before.

Feisal's communications were provided by the Red Sea Patrol. An Indian troop-ship, the *Hardinge*, was assigned to the mission as mobile stores-depot and sailed up the coast parallel with Feisal's army, carrying water, food, fodder, guns, munitions and an Arab landing-party of 550 tribesmen and armed slaves. In the event, Feisal's army missed the rendezvous at Wejh, and the British command ordered an immediate attack without waiting, mainly because of the food and sanitary situation aboard the *Hardinge*. The Arab force was landed and mounted an assault under the cover of British naval gunfire on 23 January. The action was messy and protracted – the Arabs kept breaking off the attack to plunder buildings they had overrun – but the Ottoman resistance lacked determination, for the garrison, only 200 strong, was demoralised by the desertion of its commander and several weeks of tribal raiding. The soldiers surrendered before the day was out. Twenty Arab fighters had been killed. Feisal's men, hearing the firing in the distance, rushed forward to join the looting. The frenzy and relentlessness of it shocked British observers: the town, said one officer, was 'ransacked from roof to floor'. Lawrence affirmed the thoroughness of it: the looters 'broke every box and cupboard, tore down all fittings, cut open every mattress and cushion for gold . . .'[86]

Though the cost in casualties had been slight – and even this, in Lawrence's view, had been unnecessary, since the garrison, without food or transport, would have been forced to surrender after a few days anyway – the capture of Wejh was the strategic turning-point of the Arab Revolt.[87] It placed a large Arab army 200 miles north of Yenbo and 150 miles west of the railway. The immediate effect was to double the size of insurgent territory by turning the northern Hijazi tribesmen from passive sympathisers into active combatants. An indirect effect was to alert the sheikhs of the eastern desert tribes – notably the Ruwalla and the Howeitat – of the imminent possibility of the insurgency spreading yet farther north into their own territories.

The military consequences were transformative. Instead of maintaining an Arab 'front' around Medina, Abdullah's move to Wadi Ais and Feisal's to Wejh had stretched the Ottoman flank like a piece of elastic, bringing some 450 miles of desert railway line within easy reach of Arab raiding parties. The Northern Army was soon at work. In mid-February, Garland and fifty Bedouin used two mines to derail a train and bring down a bridge near Tuweira. In early March, a much larger force – a thousand camel-men, some mounted regulars, four machine-guns and two mountain-guns – engaged a full Ottoman battalion at Muazzam (though they were driven off with heavy loss). Around the same time, another raiding force, with Newcombe to supervise demolitions, launched a more successful attack on Dar al-Hamra Station, taking 15 prisoners and ripping up 2,800 yards of line. In late March, three bridges and part of the line were destroyed south of Al-Ula Station.[88] Thus, the seizure of Wejh, at a stroke, had made the security of his communications Fakhri Pasha's principal strategic preoccupation. He was forced to fall back on Medina and disperse much of his army in static penny-packet garrisons along the length of the line, depriving him of any concentrated strike-force, crippling his offensive capacity. Mecca, which had been under threat when Feisal's army was only 200 miles away, had been made safe by redeploying the army to twice the distance.

* * *

Lawrence at first played no active part in the railway war; indeed, he was almost relegated from any role in Arabia at all. He had only been filling in for the absent Stewart Newcombe, who was slated for the role of official liaison officer with Feisal's forces. When Newcombe showed up at the commencement of the march on Wejh, Lawrence's temporary posting was technically terminated. Newcombe, though, was no prima donna, liked Lawrence's company, and could see the value of the established relationship between Feisal and his junior colleague: he asked his stand-in to stay on for a while to ease the transition.

History turns on the smallest of things. Newcombe was an enterprising but conventional officer. Nothing about him suggested that he did not share the reservations of other British officers about both the political aspirations and the military capacities of the Arabs and, on the road to Wejh, Feisal was given time to assess the relative merits of Colonel Newcombe and Captain Lawrence as prospective liaison officers. On the very day of his arrival in the town, he then sent a secret cable to Colonel Wilson in Jiddah, and Wilson in turn wired Gilbert Clayton in Cairo, telling him that the sherif was 'most anxious that Lawrence should not return to Cairo, as he has given very great assistance'.

Lawrence knew nothing of this, but by the time he got back to his office, the decision that would shape the rest of his life had been made: he was to return immediately to the Hijaz on a permanent appointment as the British liaison officer serving with Feisal's Arab Northern Army. 'I do not suppose that any Englishman before ever had such a place,' he was writing to his family as early as 31 January. 'I act as a sort of advisor to Sherif Feisal, and as we are on the best of terms, the job is a wide and pleasant one. I live with him in his tent, so our food and things . . . are as good as the Hijaz can afford.'[89]

*　*　*

While Garland and Newcombe were out wrecking railway line, Lawrence was heading south-east on an urgent mission to Abdullah's camp at Wadi Ais. The five-day trek was miserable. Lawrence experienced a severe bout of dysentery that had him fainting in the saddle and, by the second day, his back was also covered in boils. Worse was to come: bickering among his fourteen-strong escort turned into a violent vendetta.

A shot rang out in the camp on the second night, bringing the exhausted Lawrence to his senses. A Moroccan had killed an Ageyl. The dead man's kinsmen immediately demanded blood-vengeance. But if an Ageyl now killed a Moroccan, a full-scale feud would be under way. Only Lawrence, the outsider without kin, could carry out an execution without further repercussion. So the Oxford archaeologist and wartime officer, who had never been in combat, let alone killed anyone, went into a narrow gully to shoot a defenceless and whimpering man in cold blood. Lawrence was shaking with fever and aimed badly. The first shot, in the chest, was not fatal and the Moroccan fell to the ground shrieking and thrashing. The second struck the wrist. Only the third stilled the victim.

The following day, Lawrence was so ill that he had to be hoisted into the saddle. When he arrived at Abdullah's camp on 15 March, he had a brief meeting with his host and then retired to his tent, racked with fever, remaining there for ten full days.[90]

His mission had to wait – despite the urgency. It arose from a British intelligence intercept that seemed to reveal an Ottoman plan to evacuate Medina and concentrate forces 500 miles to the north, just as the British were preparing to launch a full-scale assault on Gaza in an effort to break into southern Palestine. Murray, the EEF commander, wanted the retreat of the Medina garrison blocked, and Lawrence had trekked across the desert to concert a plan with Abdullah, whose forces were far closer than Feisal's to both the railway and the town.

As it happened, the intelligence was incomplete. The British knew that Djemal had ordered the evacuation, but not that he had quickly changed his mind. Medina was the second city of Islam and the location of the Tomb of the Prophet. As long as the Ottomans held it, they could substantiate their caliphate and make credible the claims of the puppet sherif they had installed there as rival to Hussein's regime in Mecca. Unknown to the British, political ideology had trumped military strategy.[91] Nonetheless, there was value in Lawrence's expedition. When he finally rose from his sick-bed, it was to find his earlier view of Abdullah's leadership qualities confirmed. Military activity was minimal. Abdullah spent his time eating, sleeping, reading, listening to poetry and playing practical jokes. His 3,000 tribesmen seemed 'very inferior as fighting men', their leaders 'ignorant, lacking in influence and character, and apparently, without any interest in the war'.[92]

Lawrence tried to stir up some activity. He found an enthusiast in Sherif Shakir – a tall, pale-skinned, well-groomed aristocrat whom Lawrence thought 'a very centaur on horseback'. Abdullah, of whom Shakir was an intimate, appointed him to lead a raid on the railway. Lawrence set off with a small advance-party to reconnoitre the target, Abu al-Naam Station, which turned out to be garrisoned by about 400 infantry. When Shakir arrived with the main force, they numbered only 300, a third of the number promised. This ruled out a direct assault. The revised plan was to shell the station with the two mountain-guns available to distract the garrison, and to blow up the line north and south of it to trap a train that had halted there.

This was a partial success. A shell hit the train and set all the carriages on fire. The engine was uncoupled and began reversing towards Medina, but was then derailed by the detonation of the southern mine. The crew got out and in about half an hour succeeded in jacking the engine back onto the rails. This should not have been possible, since the location was covered by a machine-gun; but the crew had disappeared. The engine moved off down the line again, though now 'at foot pace, clanking horribly'.

Meanwhile, Shakir's men had overrun two outposts, and the station itself had been abandoned, some Turks surrendering, others rushing for the cover of some nearby hills. Though he seemed disappointed – his comment was 'we did not wholly fail' – Lawrence's first action had been a considerable success: the engine had escaped, but the raiders had wrecked a station and a set of carriages, and had killed, wounded, or taken prisoner about 100 Turks – all for the loss of just one man wounded.[93]

A second raid followed almost immediately. It was led by Dakhil-Allah, Chief Justice of the Juheina and, according to Lawrence, the only other sheikh in Abdullah's camp who could be relied upon to take action. Short, wrinkled and weather-beaten, dressed in 'few and filthy old clothes', he had no sooner drawn his monthly T£56 subsidy from the authorities for keeping the railway intact than he was off with the rebels to blow it up. He brought with him forty of his own tribesmen, and there were also six men with a machine-gun (a heavy German sledge-maxim carried by mule) and seven Syrian regulars.

Lawrence planted a mine on the line between Hadiya and Mudarraj stations on the night of 4/5 April, but a train ran straight over it the following morning without detonating it; fortunately so, for it was packed with women and children. However, in their excitement, the Juheina had exposed themselves and alerted the local Ottoman garrisons to their presence, attracting long range fire.

The following night, Lawrence re-set the charge. After blowing up other sections of the line – 200 rails and a four-arched bridge – and pulling down sections of telegraph wire, the party made off. They heard the explosion in the distance when the main charge detonated, and they heard later that it had been set off by a troop train with 300 men on board.[94]

Nor were these the only raids. Lawrence reported nine separate attacks in the fortnight between 24 March and 6 April. Most involved the destruction of track and telegraph, but no contact with the enemy; yet these were victories, for the activation of Abdullah's sector with a series of pinprick raids imposed upon the Ottomans a growing cost in manpower, time and materiel – and with virtually zero casualties to the assailants.[95] This conformed precisely to the new conception of war that had been germinating in Lawrence's mind for months and had finally reached completion in those periods of consciousness which had punctuated his ten fever-ridden days at Wadi Ais before he had ridden out on the first of his railway raids.[96]

* * *

The paradigm of modern conventional warfare involves an industrialised version of the Western way of war. This envisages a struggle between mass high-tech armies fed through long and heavy logistical 'tails'. The aim is a concentration of firepower on defined battlefields or fronts sufficient to break the enemy's military strength in head-on collision. Most theoretically educated soldiers of the First World War, including Lawrence, considered this to be a 'Clausewitzian' conception.

But this is false. Carl von Clausewitz (1780–1831) was a Prussian officer and military theorist of the Napoleonic Wars. His great work, compiled from his notes and published shortly after his death, is a profound work of philosophy in the German tradition. Lesser men, unable to grasp its dialectical subtleties, have mined it selectively and with prejudice. Clausewitz was no more an advocate of pitched battle than of guerrilla war, for he was fully aware that the former favoured the strong and not the weak. The aim in war is always to overcome the capacity and will of the enemy to resist, and this necessarily involves 'the wastage of his forces', but this can be achieved in different ways, one of which is 'the wearing out of the enemy'. As Clausewitz explained: 'The idea of wearing out in a struggle implies a gradual exhaustion of the physical powers and the will by the long continuance of action.' The effect is to increase 'the enemy's expenditure of force' to a point where 'the price of success' becomes too high.[97]

Lawrence professed to have found 'broader principles' in the work of Marshal Maurice de Saxe (1696–1750), but this seems tendentious, for *Reveries on the Art of War* is a relatively short, shallow and undialectical work. 'I do not favour pitched battles,' avers de Saxe, 'and I am convinced that a skilful general could make war all his life without ever being forced into one. Nothing so reduces the enemy to absurdity as this method; nothing advances affairs better. Frequent small engagements will dissipate the enemy until he is forced to hide from you.'[98] This is sometimes true: it was true for the Arabs in 1916. But precisely because of this, it was not true for their enemies: a pitched battle in which they could have brought concentrated firepower to bear would have been ideal for the Ottomans. De Saxe seems opinionated and one-dimensional when set against Clausewitz.

Nor was de Saxe in any way original. Avoidance of battle is inherent in the Eastern way of war and finds its earliest surviving theoretical expression in Sun Tzu (c. 551–496 BC): 'Ultimate excellence lies not in winning every battle, but in defeating the enemy without ever fighting. The highest form of warfare is to attack strategy itself.'[99] Clausewitz towers above all other military thinkers because he thought dialectically. He was scathing of those who sought a manual of military principles that would guarantee success, insisting that such principles as existed were simple and obvious, whereas the actual conduct of war involved countless variables and possibilities, such that theory and practice were inseparable.[100] The genius of Lawrence was not to have alighted upon the right manual; it was to have evolved a conception of war appropriate to the specific circumstances in which he found himself. This was the essence of his Wadi Ais epiphany. It shows him to have been a true Clausewitzian.

The war had been an indecisive see-saw confined to the Hijaz for six months. It had then been transformed by the advance to Wejh. By marching 200 miles north – away from the main enemy concentration in and around Medina – Feisal's army had paralysed Ottoman operations and reconfigured the entire conflict. This reconfiguration, moreover, had involved minimal actual fighting. Supplied from the Red Sea by the Royal Navy, the Arabs were conducting camel-mounted raids on the Hijaz Railway about 150 miles inland. This line – a single track running through hundreds of miles of wilderness – the Ottomans had no choice but to defend. But against an insurgency that was everywhere and nowhere – against an enemy who could appear suddenly out of the desert at any point – to defend the line at all was to defend all of it. So instead of concentration of force at a single point of decision – at Medina, from which a thrust towards Mecca might have snuffed out the rebellion – the Ottomans became strung out like beads on a necklace, forced to plant a garrison of 100, 200, 400 men every 10 or 20 kilometres to watch, patrol and guard the line.

Modern guerrilla warfare involves turning conventional warfare upside down. For the guerrilla leader to offer his forces for destruction in pitched battle against more numerous and better-armed opponents would be madness. Because guerrilla warfare involves an 'asymmetrical' pitting of small groups of highly mobile and lightly equipped insurgents against logistically heavy regular forces, it is extensive rather than concentrated, involving the active contesting of entire landscapes, and protracted rather than decisive, involving a succession of fleeting, small-scale encounters at widely dispersed points.

Conventional war seeks to compress time and space. Guerrilla war does the opposite: it seeks to stretch them. Lawrence mused about this 'algebraic factor'. Control over tens of thousands of square miles was being contested. 'And how', he asked, 'would the Turks defend all that?'

> no doubt by a trench line across the bottom, if we came like an army with banners ... but suppose we were (as we might be) an influence, an idea, a thing intangible, invulnerable, without front or back, drifting about like a gas? Armies were like plants, immobile, firm-rooted, nourished through long stems to the head. We might be a vapour, blowing where we listed. Our kingdoms lay in each man's mind, and as we wanted nothing material to live on, so we might offer nothing material to the killing. It seemed a regular soldier might be helpless without a target, owning only on what he sat, and at what he could poke his rifle.

The active contesting of the entire landscape and the stretching of time and space achieved an extraordinary 'economy of force'. Because the Arabs were no longer to be found at a defined 'front-line' – because they had disappeared into the desert, their whereabouts unknown – the Ottomans could not concentrate their forces against them. Instead, because the Arabs could strike anywhere, anytime, the Ottomans were obliged to defend every threatened point all the time; whereas the Arabs, at any particular moment, were only obliged to attack one. Moreover, by dispersing and remaining mobile – rather than concentrated and static – the Arabs increased the velocity of their operations, and this was as good as an increase in manpower. The Ottomans needed more men than before, while the Arabs could manage with fewer, yet retain the initiative and act with greater effect.

To sustain and deepen the imbalance – so it seemed to Lawrence – the enemy should be offered no targets: he should be given no opportunity to inflict casualties and achieve an attrition of his own. The guerrillas should strike only where the enemy was weak; they should target his material – trains, supplies, guns, bridges, railway track, telegraph lines – rather than his manpower; they should avoid the 'effusion of blood' which the 'war-philosophers' had elevated into 'the height of a principle'.

> Most wars were wars of contact, both forces striving into touch to avoid
> tactical surprise. Ours should be a war of detachment. We were to contain
> the enemy by the silent threat of a vast, unknown desert, not disclosing
> ourselves till the moment of attack ... Many Turks on our front had no
> chance all the war to fire at us, and correspondingly we were never on the
> defensive except accidentally, and in error.

This was the opposite of what Lawrence had argued six months earlier: that the Arabs were good only for defensive fighting, as mountain snipers. Now they were the protagonists of a mobile strategic offensive. But with this critical difference from conventional 'murder war': their strategy was to create a war zone of endemic and chronic insecurity that would overwhelm the enemy's logistical infrastructure; but at a tactical level, on the battlefield itself, combat was to be only occasional, fleeting and small scale. The Ottomans were to be frustrated at every turn in their efforts to close with and kill the insurgents; they were to discover that 'to make war upon rebellion was messy and slow, like eating soup with a knife'.[101]

It is possible to identify fifteen principles of modern guerrilla warfare in Lawrence's military writings – principles reflected in the practice of Sherif Feisal's Arab Northern Army as it projected the insurgency into the northern and eastern deserts between January 1917 and October 1918. They establish Lawrence as a seminal military thinker. They are these:

- Strive above all to win hearts and minds
- Establish an unassailable base
- Remain strategically dispersed
- Make maximum use of mobility
- Operate mainly in small, local groups
- Remain largely detached from the enemy
- Do not attempt to hold ground
- Operate in depth rather than *en face* (i.e. not in lines)
- Aim for perfect intelligence about the enemy
- Concentrate only for momentary tactical superiority
- Strike only when the enemy can be taken by surprise
- Never engage in sustained combat
- Always have lines of retreat open
- Make war on materiel rather than on men
- Make a virtue of the individuality, irregularity and unpredictability of guerrillas.[102]

This radical new conception of war was about to be splashed across a wider canvas. For Lawrence was being summoned back north. Returning from the second of his two railway raids, he found a letter from Feisal awaiting him. It bore testimony to an extraordinary intimacy and dependence; and to a human relationship that had become an historical force. 'I was very sorry to hear that you were ill,' wrote the sherif. 'I hope that you are already better and that you would like to come back to us in a short time, as soon as possible. Your presence with me is very indispensable, in view of urgency of questions and the pace of affairs . . . I hope that you will return here as soon as you receive this letter.'

Lawrence set out for Wejh as quickly as he could. The modern-day Crusader would soon be embarking on his greatest adventure. The Arab Revolt was about to explode across southern Syria.

CHAPTER 9

The Gates of Palestine

O N THE VERY day that Captain Lawrence – now attired in billowing Arab robes instead of British khaki – set off on his first combat mission, more than 20,000 British and Anzac soldiers were assaulting the fortified city of Gaza, the historic gateway from Sinai into Palestine. It was here that desert met sown, and the men of what was now called 'Eastern Frontier Force' – Australian Light Horse (ALH), New Zealand Mounted Rifles, British Yeomanry, Scotch, Welsh and East Anglian infantry, and such exotica as the new Imperial Camel Corps and two Light Car Patrols – relished the transition from the sandy wastes of Sinai to the pastures, plough-lands, orchards and market-gardens of Palestine.

They arrived as winter turned to spring, so the wells and cisterns were full, the downs carpeted with grass and flowers, the fields golden with ripening barley. In places, 'English-looking brooks fringed with kingcups' tumbled down little gullies.[1] Desert-starved horses chomped greedily at grass and grain. Men discovered cool, sweet, clean water in the wells, fresh fruit in the markets and soft almonds in the orchards.[2] Many, too, as they passed from wilderness to Promised Land, took note of the ruinous monuments to 4,000 years of military history. Gaza is as old as the book of Genesis in the Bible.[3] Gaza was the place where the blinded Samson brought down the Temple of Dagon on the heads of the Philistines.[4] Gaza was the great fortress-city that had defied the warlords of every age – Egyptian pharaohs, Assyrian kings, Persian emperors; Alexander the Great and the Caesars; Richard the Lionheart and Saladin; and many more. Napoleon, who captured the city in 1799, deemed it 'the outpost of Africa, the door of Asia'.[5]

The Crusaders seemed to have loomed large in the minds of the Christian soldiers of Eastern Force. Lieutenant Joe McPherson, the camel-transport officer, also a devout Catholic, turned down promotion into 'a soft, safe, and honourable job in Cairo' to emulate those who had marched 'to the Wars of the Cross and Crescent in the days of King John'.[6] Lieutenant-Colonel Guy Powles of the New Zealand Mounted Rifles was pleased to report that 'the famous Stone of Baldwin' – a Crusader monument found on an excavation site at Arish – had been re-erected in its original location. He speculated that Khan Yunus, the southernmost village in Palestine, was 'most likely the "Darum" of the Crusaders of King Richard the Lionheart', and that by advancing out of Sinai 'we were fairly launched upon the Tenth Crusade'.[7]

What had brought them to Gaza, these men of the Tenth Crusade? Six months before they emerged from the desert, they had parried the Ottomans' left hook at Romani, bundled the enemy backwards through the north-western oasis zone, and watched them disappear across the 60-mile sand desert between Bir al-Abd and Arish. They had chosen the battleground: chosen to fight on their own side of the waterless waste, close to their own bases of supply, far from those of the enemy. They had done this knowing that logistics were nine-tenths of the art of war in the desert; and this had been confirmed by victory over an enemy whose water bottles had run dry in the summer heat.

The Romani position had proved itself ideal for the long-term defence of Egypt and the canal, for it secured the only route by which large enemy forces might be projected across the desert. The War Cabinet in London was more than satisfied. The 'Westerners', led by General Sir William ('Wully') Robertson, Chief of the Imperial General Staff, were in the ascendant. The battles of Verdun and the Somme were raging on the Western Front. The Brusilov offensive was storming to success on the Eastern. By contrast, the Ottoman fronts were secondary, the Egyptian Expeditionary Force's strategic mission defensive, and nothing substantive had changed since Robertson had written to General Murray in March reiterating his view that 'Egypt must be regarded as my general reserve'.[8]

The War Cabinet's directives provided a general framework; they did not settle the question how best to make use of available resources to maximise security. Murray had already raised the possibility of pushing a force across the desert to Arish – perhaps a relatively small force that could be supplied by sea – this to become a forward outpost threatening the flank and rear of any renewed Ottoman thrust towards the canal. Nothing in Murray's instructions precluded this: he was free to use his forces in whatever way seemed best for the defence of Egypt.[9] Yet there is quite a difference between static and aggressive defence, for the latter is liable to reconfigure the conflict in unexpected ways and lead to 'mission creep'. So it was in Sinai in the autumn of 1916.

* * *

September, October and November were quiet months on the Egyptian front. The armies were widely separated by the water gap, so contact was limited to aerial reconnaissance, mounted patrols and two long-distance raids on small Ottoman garrisons. The British infantry saw nothing of the enemy except the occasional aircraft overhead. Behind a forward screen of mounted patrols, theirs was the dull duty of digging a succession of temporary firebases covering the railhead, now advancing, alongside water-pipe and wire road, at a rate of 15 miles a month.

Conditions were harsh in the barren sector between Abd and Arish. Tents offered too obvious a mark to enemy aircraft, so the men lived in 'bivvies', often nothing more than scrapes in the ground with a propped-up blanket or ground sheet over the top – though they would scavenge where they could for bits of sacking, canvas, Bedouin cloth or palm-branches to gain extra protection from the sun.[10]

Somewhere behind them were the construction teams, a troop of Yeomanry doing advance-guard, followed by the military surveyors laying out the line, then thousands of Egyptian Labour Corps swarming like ants to dig a cutting or build a bank, 'the natives performing their work almost entirely by using little spades and fig-baskets', recalled Yeomanry medical officer Teichman, 'the sand being scooped into the latter and removed as quickly as possible.'[11] Royal Engineers were busy laying telegraph and telephone lines. The Army Service Corps was delivering supplies. The Camel Transport Corps was moving them to the railhead. William Massey, the official London correspondent, watched the camel trains in fascination:

> One line you would meet would be transporting iron water-pipes twice as long as the animal, and as the animals proceeded at their steady 2½ miles an hour gait, the pipes moved up and down like engine beams ... A camel carrying timber is packed up so high that he seems hopelessly overloaded, while a column bearing barbed wire for entanglements looks for all the world as if, by some monstrous freak of nature, the Army had bred gigantic porcupines with long legs for its service.[12]

Massey was equally struck by the way in which entire temporary settlements in the desert would spring up one month and vanish the next. One such staging-post, between Mazar and Arish, was Kilometre 128. In December 1916 there was a line of vast canvas tanks, supported with posts and sandbags, containing thousands of gallons of water, running along half a mile of railway sidings. Beyond were encampments for thousands of men and beasts. 'Camel trains bearing a vast amount of supplies to relieve pressure on the railway, where everything continued to give way to the water trains, could be traced like great veins on the surface of the desert.'[13] A month later, Kilometre 128 was gone.

> Anyone moving along the desert railway today would gather no idea of the vast organisation required to build that undertaking, or of the labour involved in carrying the army and its supplies along that iron road. Sand has blown over the camping-grounds which had accommodated divisions, and not a sign of their presence remains ... The troops were the destroyers as well as the creators of their own vast works ...'[14]

The march across Sinai turned the war into a precise, methodical, industrial operation. 'They built the railway, the pipeline, reservoirs and pumping-stations, [and] fortified positions, and entrenched as they moved forward step-by-step, camp succeeding camp, with wonderful regularity.'[15] The 250km railway across Sinai from Ismailia to Rafa took a whole year to build, for materials were in heavy demand from other theatres and had to be transported across submarine-infested waters.[16] The achievement was phenomenal, representing a massive investment in advanced industrial technique to make possible the projection of military force across the desert. Massey thought the railway 'a band of metal more precious than gold', and the reservoirs of purified Nile water 'a jewel as priceless as all the treasures of Ind'.[17]

* * *

But to what purpose? By the time a leap towards Arish had become possible, much had changed. The Battle of Verdun had ended: the French had held the line, but the effort had cost them 540,000 casualties. The Battle of the Somme had also ended – without a breakthrough, despite 420,000 British and 195,000 French casualties. The Brusilov offensive had undermined German efforts at Verdun and Austro-Hungarian efforts against Italy, but it, too, had finally fizzled out, having cost an estimated 1,400,000 Russian casualties. Rumania, bribed to join the Entente with a promise of territorial gains and encouraged by Brusilov's early successes, had entered the war in August only to find itself overrun by December.[18] The year 1916 – with its great offensives, more costly in blood and treasure than anything ever known – ended as it had begun, in the stalemate of frozen fronts. Nor was that all. The Battle of the Atlantic – the struggle of German U-boats against British shipping – was turning critical. The average monthly loss rose from 131,000 tons in the period April to September to 276,000 tons in November to February; by the winter of 1916/17, the British were losing the submarine war and facing the real possibility of starvation and surrender.[19]

Morale was sinking. The waste of life at the front and growing privation at home had ruptured the jingoism of 1914: millions of soldiers and workers were turning against the war. The dams of the social order were, in fact, set soon to burst. The Russian Revolution would begin in March 1917, the French Army would mutiny in April, and the Italian Army collapse in October. Britain was not immune. There had been strikes on the Clyde and in South Wales during 1915, and a full-scale mutiny would break out against the brutal regime at the 'Bull Ring' military training-camp at Etaples in September 1917.

Britain's rulers sensed the rising discontent. Unless they could win the war soon, they were liable to be forced into a compromise peace by some sort of popular revolt against the carnage, privation and waste. They found themselves engaged in a war of attrition – what the Germans called *Materialschlacht* – and this required 'total war': centralised control and direction of all available industrial and manpower resources for the single purpose of destroying the enemy's capacity and will to resist. What was needed, they told themselves, and their people, was 'a more energetic conduct of the war'; and perhaps – somewhere, somehow, at some point – this would make possible 'the knock-out blow'.

In Britain as elsewhere in the winter of 1916/17, the crisis of the war became a crisis of government. Opposition to the Asquith government centred on the flamboyant and opportunistic David Lloyd George, former chancellor of the exchequer, former minister of munitions, latterly secretary of state for war. Asquith was overturned in a parliamentary coup and Lloyd George became prime minister on 7 December. Lloyd George immediately set up a War Cabinet of five men – himself, the Tory leader Andrew Bonar Law, the Labour leader Arthur Henderson and two leading imperial viceroys, Alfred Milner and George Curzon.[20] This had the effect of formalising the division between 'Easterners' and 'Westerners', the War Cabinet tilting to the former, the Imperial General Staff to the latter.

Usually interpreted as an argument about grand strategy, it was in fact multi-dimensional. The generals had a narrowly professional view of the matter: they wanted to win the war in the only way they believed it could be done – by concentrating on the principal enemy (Germany) on the main front (the Western) – and therefore were opposed to, as they saw it, wasting resources on 'side-shows'. 'Briefly,' Robertson had explained in a cable to Murray in March 1916, 'my policy is . . . Refuse to take offensive action in the Balkans unless the situation changes very much. To keep Egypt reasonably secure. To keep a reserve in Egypt for India as long as it seems likely to be required. To get everyone else to France . . .'[21]

Lloyd George, on the other hand, had long advocated 'knocking out the props' of Imperial Germany. The supposed 'props' were, of course, the Austro-Hungarians, the Bulgarians and the Ottomans. The implication was a defensive stance on the Western Front and offensive action in the Balkans and the Middle East. The metaphor was misconceived: Germany was in fact propping up its allies, not vice versa. But the underlying point was valid: if the Western Front was impenetrable, did it not make sense to apply pressure to other parts of the wide arc of the Central Powers' militarised perimeter? Lloyd George thought so. William Robertson did not. Nor, of course, did Douglas Haig, the British commander-in-chief in France.

The argument about strategy had less significance than either its protagonists at the time or military historians afterwards assumed. The First World War was neither an eighteenth-century 'war of position' nor a nineteenth-century 'war of manoeuvre': it was a twentieth-century 'war of attrition'. It took the form of a gigantic siege of the Central Powers, and its outcome was decided by the greater degradation of the manpower, materiel and morale of the besieged than of the besiegers. But this took time, and there was no short-cut. Most strategic movement was still restricted to the speed of marching men and animals, and, because the technology of firepower had leapfrogged ahead of battlefield mobility and communications, the tactical advantage lay with the defender, and battles tended to be static and protracted. These factors benefited the besieged. Since the Central Powers were operating on internal lines, they were able, as long as their strength endured, to move forces between fronts to block enemy offensives. Where military pressure was applied was therefore a secondary matter.

The politicians, though, were not concerned with military strategy alone. Their closer relationship with civil society made them more sensitive to casualties, shortages, the stalemate on the Western Front and the increasingly sullen public mood. The new prime minister, in particular, wanted a morale-raising victory. And where better to seek one than in the Holy Land? Lloyd George, too, had his Crusader fixation. Freddie Maurice at the War Office wrote to his friend Arthur Lynden-Bell, Murray's number two in Cairo, about the change in government line: 'The prime minister is very anxious, naturally, for some success to enliven the winter gloom which has settled upon England, and he looks to you to get it for him. He talks somewhat vaguely of a campaign in Palestine, and I think he has at the back of his mind the hope of a triumphant entry into Jerusalem.'[22]

Britain's political leaders were also world statesmen – empire-builders acutely aware that the central axis of British global power ran from the homeland, through the Mediterranean, along the Suez Canal, down the African coast, and across the Arabian Sea to India and the East. As well as remaining sensitive to any renewed Ottoman thrust – with its attendant risk of an Islamic surge – the Easterners were increasingly preoccupied with the dangers and opportunities represented by the apparent crumbling of Ottoman power. Not only did they wish to position Britain to fill the probable vacuum; they were in fact plotting with their French and Russian allies for a vast expansion of European colonial power in the Middle East.

Robertson's cables to Murray reflected his reluctance to support the Easterners' strategy: 'your primary mission remains unchanged,' he insisted, 'that is to say, it is the defence of Egypt'. On the other hand, Murray was informed that the prime minister wished him 'to make the maximum possible effort during the winter' – even though no additional troops were immediately available. Murray was keen: 'You may rely on me . . . to push on as rapidly as I can. I shall not stop acting offensively until I see that I am in danger of risking the defence of Egypt.'[23]

A particular concern was that the Ottomans had also been building a new desert railway. Djemal Pasha had hired the services of the celebrated German engineer Heinrich Meissner, who had worked on both the Baghdad and Hijaz Railways. Two hundred miles of iron track were taken from reserve dumps on the Hijaz. Eighty miles of line elsewhere were ripped up to supply iron sleepers. Additional wooden sleepers were cut from Lebanese timber. By October 1915, the first 100 miles of new line to Beersheba were open. From there, construction continued, first to Auja on the frontier, then beyond to Kossaima by the end of 1916.[24] By the time the British line reached Mazar, midway between Abd and Arish, a rival Ottoman line was advancing in the opposite direction, some 60 miles to the south-east, towards the alternative central route across Sinai.

Murray's military appreciation was sound. A leap to Arish would block the coastal route to Suez, place a British force on the flank of the central route, and provide a forward base for reconnaissance and raiding.[25] It would also position the British for an invasion of Palestine – should they wish it. At the very least, the capture of Beersheba would bring the Hijaz Railway within range of British aircraft, imperilling Ottoman communications with Medina, and might even trigger a rising of the Arab population of southern Syria, 'who are known to be very disaffected towards [the] Turks' – though Murray seems to have favoured more than this, arguing that an offensive would prevent the Ottomans sending troops to other fronts, and might even stretch them to breaking-point in southern Palestine.[26]

His hunch was about to be tested. After three months during which most British and Anzac soldiers had seen very little of the enemy, they were to fight a succession of major battles between late December 1916 and mid-April 1917, culminating in two fierce assaults on the fortress-city of Gaza.

* * *

As the sun came up over Magdhaba on 23 December, the bivouac fires of around 1,500 men of the 80th (Anatolian) Regiment blanketed the position in smoke. Harry Chauvel, watching with his brigadiers and staff 4 miles to the north, could not see much. Magdhaba was a small desert settlement about 25 miles inland on the eastern bank of the Wadi Arish, a wide cutting with a gravel base carved across the desert by occasional torrents of winter flood-water, its flanks strewn with stone.

Chauvel's men had crossed the desert from Mazar to Arish two nights before, and, reaching the wadi where it met the sea, had delighted in their escape from the misery of the dunes. 'The hard-going for the horses seemed almost miraculous after the months of sand,' said General Cox, commander of 1st Brigade, Australian Light Horse, 'and, as the shoes of the horses struck fire on the stones in the bed of the wadi, the men laughed with delight. Sinai was behind them.'[27]

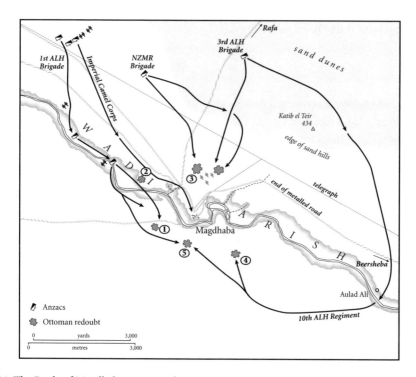

11. The Battle of Magdhaba, 23 December 1916.

They had come expecting to fight the Ottomans at Arish. It was the largest settlement in Sinai, an old caravan-route town of fort, mosque and flat-roofed houses coated in yellow plaster; the men, arriving after months marooned in desolate desert encampments, relished its clean little souk selling dates, figs and vines.[28] But the Ottomans were gone. Though they had built strong entrenchments around the town, they no doubt feared encirclement by horsemen and an assault supported by naval gunfire. Where were they now?

Kress von Kressenstein, the Bavarian officer in overall command in southern Palestine, had in fact urged complete withdrawal from Sinai, considering the Ottoman position untenable. He had been overruled 'on political grounds'.[29] As the British aerial spotters quickly established, the Ottomans had pulled back in two directions, some going east along the coast to Rafa, others inland south-south-east to Magdhaba.

Lieutenant-General Sir Philip Chetwode – newly appointed commander of the Desert Column (as the forward elements of Eastern Force were known) – had splashed ashore on the beach at Arish on the morning of 22 December. The infantry of 52nd Division were already marching in from the west to secure the position, and a camel convoy of fresh supplies was scheduled for arrival that evening. So Chetwode – a keen 'thruster' – ordered Chauvel and the Anzac Mounted Division out on a second night march: they were to hit Magdhaba at dawn the following day.[30]

* * *

The Anzacs were refining a new kind of mobile desert warfare. Romani, Katia, Oghratina and Abd had taught valuable lessons. The British infantry could not keep up with their Ottoman counterparts, especially in shifting sand; so offensive action, if the enemy was to be caught and run down, depended on the cavalry. But the cavalry – or mounted infantry – of the Anzac force lacked firepower: Chauvel's line had been too lightweight to break the Ottoman rearguards during the pursuit after Romani. A partial solution had been found with the establishment of the Imperial Camel Corps Brigade (ICC). This by now comprised 18 companies, each of 175 men, 10 of them Australian, 6 British and 2 New Zealander. The brigade also included the Hong Kong and Singapore Batteries, each formed of six 9-pounder mountain-guns (manned by Indian crews), and a squadron of eight Vickers heavy machine-guns (with British crews). Additional firepower was provided by Lewis light machine-guns, three per company. After a shaky start – when the ICC had failed to attract sufficient volunteers – the unit evolved into an elite special-operations outfit with a strong *esprit de corps*.[31]

The cameliers were not intended to be fought as mounted infantry. Racing into action on camels, let alone attempting a quick getaway in retreat, was considered altogether too hazardous. What the corps offered was exceptional strategic mobility in the desert, for the camel is a superb example of evolutionary adaptation. Food in the form of fat is stored in humps. Water is stored throughout the body tissues. Super-efficient kidneys create high-concentrate waste to conserve liquid. Blood temperature rises to absorb heat and reduce perspiration. The animal has feet that are both spreading for walking on sand and padded for walking on stones. It has a long neck for efficient foraging on desert trees and scrub. The result is an ideal mode of transport for off-road movement in desert and semi-desert environments; indeed, for any kind of movement in Central Asia, the Middle East and North Africa before modern roads. Camels can go for about a week without water, and can then consume up to 30 gallons at a single watering. They can survive much longer without food, and can subsist on stuff of the most forbidding nature: a camel can eat a prickly-pear cactus, for example – flesh, leathery skin, thorns like large needles, the whole lot – as if was ice-cream. And they can be expected to travel up to 25 miles a day carrying a maximum load of about 350lbs.[32] A horse, by contrast, needs to drink between 5 and 10 gallons a day, requires quality fodder or grazing and takes a maximum load of about 250lbs.

Men may love dogs and horses, but never camels. The camel is a large, smelly, supercilious, temperamental, tic-infested beast with a number of revolting habits, especially during the months-long rutting season, when males extrude a pink ball of flesh through their mouths, secrete foul-smelling matter from their neck glands, and use their tails to spray urine over their back legs. Half the camels to be had in Egypt were also afflicted with mange (a mammalian skin disease caused by parasitic mites). Worst of all, camels are unpredictable and the males can be dangerously, even lethally violent, especially in the months-long rutting season.

Such 'magnoon' camels (as Australian cameliers dubbed them) are liable to launch sudden charges on unsuspecting victims – presumably those arbitrarily perceived to be rivals in the rut. The Camel Transport Corps recorded 380 British officers sent to hospital with camel bites in one year, 70 of whom actually lost limbs.[33] 'There was one man-killer ... with a most unsavoury reputation,' wrote 'Trooper Bluegum' (the *nom de plume* of Oliver Hogue, a light-horseman who became a camelier).

He killed a few men and sent several to hospital. Anon he went on trek with an Anzac battalion, and, after a spell of decent behaviour, broke out again and threatened to slaughter a whole section. He was laid out temporarily

with a crack on the skull, but the rider was taking no more chances. Next
day he loitered behind on the trek, blew the camel's brains out, and reported
to the OC [officer commanding] that the camel had died of a broken heart.[34]

What made the awkward relationship between man and camel worthwhile
was the ICC's capacity to project firepower over long distances. The ICC could
put between 1,600 and 1,700 men into its firing-line, almost double that of
an ALH brigade. As Chauvel scanned the enemy position at Magdhaba, he
knew that his command packed a harder punch than at Romani. The Anzac
Mounted Division, an elite of desert-wise combat veterans, retained their key
advantages of speed, surprise and élan; but the Camel Corps now provided a
strong infantry pivot with plenty of firepower on which the mounties could
manoeuvre.

* * *

The column had set out an hour after midnight, riding down the firm ground
of the east bank of the wadi – fast, confident, disciplined. 'Speech and smoking
were forbidden,' reported the Australian official historian. 'The long column of
ghostly horsemen was speedily blanketed in a heavy cloud of fine clayey dust;
the only sound was the pounding of hooves, the clank of stirrup against stirrup,
and the occasional neighing and snorting of the horses. Each hour was ...
divided into 40 minutes' riding, ten minutes' leading, and ten minutes' halt.'[35]
When they saw the flickering specks of the Turks' campfires in the distance,
they drew rein and waited while the staff went forward to reconnoitre.

The wait was long. The Turkish trenches were hard to make out across an
expanse of flat ground, and Chauvel needed air reconnaissance. The first
aircraft arrived around 6.30am, flying low, bombing the Turks, drawing fire to
reveal enemy positions. The first report was not dropped until just before 8am,
however, and only then was Chauvel confident enough to issue orders. He
would remain heavily dependent on the reports of the airmen throughout the
ensuing battle.

The wadi was a straggling gorge about 25 feet deep, extending north-west to
south-east, the sides broken by numerous little side-gullies. The sand desert
encroached close to the wadi on the western side, but there was a plain several
hundred yards wide on the opposite bank, and it was here that the few buildings of the settlement were located; the plain was covered with mounds and
scrub. The Ottomans had constructed a ring of trench redoubts, located so as
to provide mutual fire-support, of which five, two on the western side of the
wadi, three on the eastern, were substantial earthworks.[36]

A concentrated attack on Redoubt No. 2, the most northerly, was to be the epicentre of the battle. Chauvel deployed the Inverness and Somerset Batteries of Royal Horse Artillery (RHA) on a slight rise about 2 miles north of this redoubt, and directed the Imperial Camel Corps to launch a direct attack upon it. Chaytor's New Zealand Mounted Rifles Brigade was to swing wide on the left and then loop southwards to attack Redoubt No. 3. Royston's 3rd Light Horse Brigade was to move alongside the New Zealanders, but to swing wider still. Then came the news – from a pilot who had landed his plane close to divisional HQ around 10am – that some of the Turks were escaping southwards. This report – greatly exaggerated – reshaped the battle, for Chauvel now ordered Royston to send his 10th Light Horse Regiment on a galloping loop southwards to cut off any retreat, and Cox to take the 1st Light Horse Brigade, so far held in reserve, straight down the wadi from the north to get at the Turks as they pulled out.[37]

* * *

Most of the Turks were not going anywhere: they were determinedly defending their trenches. Cox's charge ran into concentrated fire from rifles, machine-guns and artillery, and he promptly ordered his men into the cover of the wadi, where they dismounted and linked up with the cameliers. Henceforward, between 11am and 2pm, progress was barely perceptible as the battle took the form of a cautious long-range firefight. But in the course of these three hours, fire superiority gradually passed from Turkish infantryman to Anzac trooper. The fire of the two RHA batteries on the rise was supplemented by that of the Hong Kong and Singapore mountain-guns, first at 3,000 yards' range, then at 1,000. The effect was to suppress much of the outgoing fire from Redoubt No. 2 as the Turkish infantry cowered.

Meantime, cameliers and light-horsemen were advancing in rushes, one troop firing while another made a dash. Little by little, the circle of skirmishers around the redoubt, once dispersed and distant, became concentrated and close; as it did so, its fire became more lethal.[38] 'They were all under cover in excellently prepared trenches,' reported Bluegum, 'while the Anzacs were attacking in the open. But the latter's marksmanship at long ranges was far superior. The crests of the redoubts were lashed with bullets, so that the Turks feared to raise their heads, and their fire grew erratic. Nearer and nearer drew the attacking force. Hotter and hotter grew the fire.'[39] By 2pm, some men were only 100 yards from the Turkish trenches.

At this point, however, Chauvel issued orders to break off the action. He was tormented by worries about water. His engineers had failed to find any, his horses had not drunk water since leaving Arish, and they were now facing the long ride back before they would get any.

The margin between victory and failure was narrow. The clincher was the exceptional character of Chauvel's brigadiers. They exercised field command close-up with their men and were expected to be independent-minded. The order reached 'Fighting Charlie' Cox of 1st Light Horse just as his men were fixing bayonets to storm Redoubt No. 2. 'Take that damn thing away,' he told the messenger, 'and let me see it for the first time in half an hour.'

A regiment of Light Horse and two companies of Camels then launched a bayonet charge that carried them into the Turkish trenches. The defenders surrendered *en masse*. This was the fulcrum of the battle. The remaining Turkish redoubts fell in rapid succession, some to wild mounted charges that rode straight over the earthworks. At 4.30pm, with darkness descending, the last shot was heard, and Chauvel's men had become a chaotic mass of mingled units spread across the 2 square miles of the enemy position.[40] About them were some 100 Turkish dead, 300 wounded and 1,300 prisoners. Given the character of the battle, their own casualties had been relatively light: 22 killed and 124 wounded.[41] This was testimony to the field-craft and marksmanship of the Anzac troopers. The final victory depended upon a combination of fire superiority and moral dominance. The Turkish infantry – tough peasant-soldiers of a traditional empire – were dogged enough while their trenches were secure, but lacked the nerve to resist an Anzac bayonet charge.

* * *

Two weeks later, the Anzac Mounted Division and the Imperial Camel Corps were again riding through the night, this time headed by Chetwode in person and reinforced by 5th (Yeomanry) Mounted Brigade and No. 7 Light Car Patrol (of six Ford cars, each mounting a machine-gun). The target was Rafa on the Turco-Egyptian border, almost 30 miles north-north-east of Arish – the last town in Sinai. Dawn on 9 January 1917 revealed an enemy position of formidable strength set amid an open landscape of grass, barley and wild flowers. The position was formed of a hilltop redoubt on the northern side and three earthwork complexes to the south, the whole arranged in a diamond pattern just under a mile across, with trenches on rising ground and placed to maximise cross-fire and enfilade. The approaches to the position were almost devoid of cover for a distance of about 2,000 yards. It was defended by about 2,000 men of the 31st (Anatolian) Regiment. Reinforcements lay only 12 miles distant. Chetwode considered its capture by dismounted cavalry virtually impossible.[42]

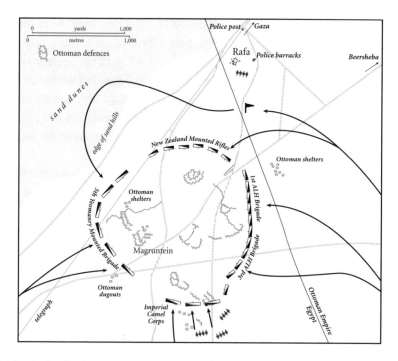

12. The Battle of Rafa, 9 January 1917.

Chauvel was undaunted. He spent the middle hours of the day constructing a complete ring of riflemen around the enemy position: New Zealanders to the north, 1st and 3rd Light Horse to the east, Camels to the south, 5th Yeomanry closing the circle on the west. As at Magdhaba, the battle became a slow-motion firefight, but this time against defenders with clear fields of fire across barren, sloping ground. The Turkish infantry would sometimes climb onto their parapets to shoot at men lying in the open below.[43] As well as trenches, three lines of them in places, there were numerous individual pits 'extremely difficult to locate until you were right on them', some designed to take a machine-gun and perhaps two or three riflemen, others a lone sniper; one brave Turk was found buried up to his armpits behind a small aloe plant.[44] Machine-guns and artillery were pushed well forward to give close-range covering fire; the battle was notable for the way in which British and Indian gunners exposed themselves to deliver direct fire over open sights at the enemy works.[45] Aircraft dropped smoke-balls to indicate enemy positions and – for the first time in the campaign – used wireless communication to direct artillery fire.[46]

By late afternoon, despite heavy casualties, few of the attackers were closer than 1,000 yards and ammunition was running out. Then came the news that two columns of enemy reinforcements, around 2,500 men in all, were moving on the position from the east. History now repeated itself: Chauvel got his superior's permission to break off the action at 4.25pm; the Yeomanry, at a standstill for some time on the western face, were pulled out of the line at once; Chetwode mounted his horse and rode for Arish.[47] But the orders came too late for the New Zealanders, whose plucky brigadier, aware that time was pressing, had decided to fix bayonets and rush Hill 255, the northern redoubt that was the key to the Ottoman position.

Covered by a tremendous fire of rifles, Lewis guns and heavy machine-guns that made the trenches on top of the hill 'smoke like a furnace', the New Zealanders first advanced to within 800 yards, then dressed their line, and next stormed up the slopes in two tempestuous rushes. Despite the fire, the Turks resisted stoutly to the end, some standing in the open to aim. But, unnerved by the charge, their shooting was ragged and, before the end, menaced by the bayonet, their resistance collapsed.[48]

Meanwhile, on the opposite side of the battlefield, around 600 cameliers, two companies of Australians and one of British, had performed a similar feat, charging with the bayonet to overrun the southernmost works and win a lodgement inside the enemy position. Trooper Bluegum was witness:

> the accurate and well-sustained fire of our guns, maxims, and rifles at length achieved a superiority of fire over the garrison, which enabled the attackers to approach, by well-timed advances, nearer and nearer the Turkish trenches. The cordon tightened. An ever-closing circle menaced the defenders. When within striking distance, a glitter of steel flashed all round the circle.[49]

The Turks had been seen fixing their own bayonets; 'accepting the challenge with a great roar,' reports the Australian *Official History*, the cameliers 'rushed at the stronghold. But as they reached the trenches, the Turks raised a number of white flags, and a moment later the panting assailants, who were almost too exhausted after their long charge for further effort, were shaking hands with the enemy all along the line.'[50]

Thereafter, the enemy positions fell one by one and, as darkness descended, the victory was complete. The Turks had lost 200 killed, 170 wounded and 1,400 taken prisoner. The Desert Column had 70 killed and 400 wounded – three times the losses at Magdhaba.[51] The duration and intensity of the firefight was evident in the expenditure of ammunition: the attackers had used 1,637 artillery shells and 410,000 rifle rounds in all (that is, 4.5 shells and 1,100 rounds for each casualty inflicted).[52]

But the military achievement had been extraordinary. A mobile arm of tremendous reach and punch had been successfully deployed to eliminate a series of heavily entrenched positions held by strong garrisons of determined infantry. This arm had been pushed to the uttermost limit. Men were sometimes two nights in the saddle without sleep and would fight a battle in between. Horses sometimes went a day or more without water. Surprise was achieved and enemy positions easily surrounded, but the firing-line was paper thin, and success depended on enterprising officers, the bonds of mateship, a growing *esprit de corps*, and the confidence and élan of tough, self-reliant, outdoor men.

* * *

Gaza sits on a small hill about 2 miles from the sea. At the time of the First World War, it was a major communications centre for its region, sitting astride the north–south coast road, and connected by another main road with Beersheba about 25 miles inland to the south-east. With an abundant water-supply, it was a town of about 40,000 people. Extending around it for up to a mile and a half was a network of tracks, gardens, olive groves and small fields, bounded by prickly-pear cactus hedges. The hedges grew up to 10 feet tall and 15 feet thick, and were more impenetrable than barbed wire; during the fighting, attempts to clear the way by artillery bombardment would make little impression. Beyond the garden zone lay a tangled belt of sand dunes on the seaward side, and a series of ridges and rolling hills on the inland side.

A few miles south of the city ran the Wadi Ghuzze, a formidable natural obstacle, 100 yards broad in places, with rugged banks up to 30 or 40 feet high. After their double defeat at Magdhaba and Rafa, the Ottomans had held the edge of the Ghuzze until early March, but then, anticipating attack, had abruptly withdrawn to the Gaza–Beersheba line. Kress von Kressenstein had gone unheeded in opposing the attempt to hold forward positions in north-eastern Sinai, and the Ottomans had paid a heavy price for this political gesture. His advice now carried greater weight. The defenders of Palestine were too few to hold a long line with an open desert flank against three divisions of infantry and 11,000 horsemen. They would instead make their stand in the complex terrain of Gaza, where the defensive resilience of the Ottoman infantry would play to greatest advantage. Here, for months, these infantry had been digging, lacing with trenches the jumble of hills, crooked lanes and cactus banks around the town, creating a sprawling Western Front-type fortress. Air reconnaissance failed to reveal either the extent of the works – the trenches were too well concealed – or the size of the garrison – 4,000 men, not the 2,000 of British estimates.[53]

The axis of the coming battle was a long, narrow, north–south ridge called Sire, which ended at a prominent hill, Ali Muntar, overlooking and dominating the city on its south-eastern edge. Either side of Sire were other ridges, a short one to the west, Sheluf, along which ran the coast road from Rafa to Gaza, a higher one to the east, Burjabiya, which terminated at another prominent hill, Mansura, about 3 miles south-east of the city, and a fourth, farther east again, Sheikh Abbas. Like the four fingers of a hand pointing north-east from the Wadi Ghuzze, these ridges represented the main approaches to Gaza from the south. Though Sire was the primary axis, it offered too narrow a corridor of advance and was exposed to enfilading fire from the defences around the city.[54] The ideal, therefore, was a broad-front advance through the sand dunes and along the length of the three western ridges, with a flank guard on Sheikh Abbas to protect against counter-attack from the east. This much was inherent in any attempt to storm Gaza from the south – equally apparent to both the British high command and their Turco-German counterparts.

* * *

But was Gaza to be attacked? This was far from certain at the beginning of 1917. Murray received a cable in early January discouraging large-scale operations in Palestine till later in the year, because a major spring offensive was planned on the Western Front. On the other hand, he was informed, the prime minister remained keen to see operations pursued in the Middle East with as much vigour as resources allowed. Lloyd George's view was soon affirmed by a joint Anglo-French strategy conference held in Calais on 26 February, where it was agreed that offensive action should be launched across several theatres.[55] Even Robertson conceded the potential propaganda value of victories in Palestine, writing on 31 January that 'If we do not get a big success in the west this year, we shall have difficulty in retaining popular support [for] the war ... If therefore we are still fighting next winter and could have a good thing based on Egypt, we ought to get good value out of it, and moreover it is the only theatre where we can operate in wintertime and so keep up public interest.'[56]

Murray was confident he had enough men to push forward against Gaza; indeed, his worry became that the Ottomans might slip away before he could bring them to battle.[57] Lieutenant-General Sir Charles Dobell's Eastern Force had been reorganised and now comprised three territorial infantry divisions (52nd, 53rd and 54th), two mounted divisions (Anzac and Imperial), plus the Imperial Camel Corps. Chetwode's Desert Column remained the spearhead, but with the addition of Dallas's 53rd (Welsh) Division. Well handled, this force might have broken through. The artillery and air support was good, the territorials would fight with grit given the chance, and the mounted divisions had evolved into elite shock-troops. The weak link was the British high command.

'The English are taking over everything,' reported Trooper Idriess of the 5th Light Horse, 'and in new organisations they put unknown officers over officers who have proved themselves in the field.'[58] The problem started at the top with Murray. Physically somewhat frail and accustomed to his comforts, he remained most of the time at his headquarters at the Savoy Hotel in Cairo. His rare visits to the front were made in a luxury train equipped with a sleeping carriage for each officer and an ample supply of food, drink and tobacco. This did not endear him to either Anzac troopers or Glaswegian territorials camped out in the desert.[59] Equally bad – and no doubt reflecting both his remoteness from the fighting and a typical prejudice against 'colonials' – he sometimes failed to give due credit to his men. Reading a newspaper report of Romani, Chauvel wrote to his wife: 'I am afraid my men will be very angry when they see it. I cannot understand why the old man cannot do justice to those to whom he owed so much . . .'[60]

Murray's senior appointments were often ill-judged. Dobell had been successful commanding small forces in the Camerouns and the Western Desert, but he would prove incapable of managing a large-scale industrial battle like Gaza.[61] Chetwode was a competent officer, but he was placed in the anomalous position of commanding both the mounted corps and the infantry division scheduled for the main assault – but not the two reserve divisions.[62] The biggest problem, however, was Major-General A.G. Dallas, whose Welsh infantry were to spearhead the attack. Command and control at his headquarters would break down so completely during the battle that his brigadiers would afterwards inform Chetwode that they were collectively unwilling ever to fight under Dallas's leadership again.[63] As well as being the wrong team for the job in hand, moreover, the British commanders at First Gaza were in the wrong places. Murray in his luxury train was too far from the front to control the action. Dobell and Chetwode shared neighbouring HQs, leaving the cavalry commander out of touch with his forward elements and cramped by the presence of his superior. Compounding the difficulties was a shortage of experienced staff officers, resulting, according to the *Official History*, in 'excessive strain, lack of sleep and consequent liability to error'.[64]

Dobell's plan was sound enough in theory. The cavalry was to move through the open country east of Gaza and form a screen to prevent the Ottomans either evacuating the city or reinforcing it. The 54th (East Anglian) Division was to move up behind them and cover the flank of the main infantry assault. This was to be mounted by 53rd Division. The 160th Brigade would advance along the Sire Ridge, 158th along the Burjabiya Ridge, and 159th would form the divisional reserve. The 52nd (Lowland) Division was to act as general reserve in the vicinity of the Wadi Ghuzze.[65]

The problem was that the British punch was underpowered in relation to an enemy who was stronger than he appeared. Murray, egged on by the politicians back home, was, in effect, attempting to replicate Magdhaba and Rafa on a bigger scale. He wanted to project as strong a force as possible to the furthest limit of the supply-chain. The railway and water-pipe had reached only as far as Rafa, 15 miles from the Wadi Ghuzze, the British jumping-off point. It was necessary to improvise 15 trains of animals and vehicles to bring up the water, food and ammunition to sustain a 24-hour operation. Beyond that, everything would depend on the rapid capture of Gaza to gain access to its wells and landing-places.[66]

Lengthening the odds against success was the fact that Kress and his staff had anticipated the British plan, and their own was a carefully measured response. Kress intended to fight a 'cauldron' battle around Gaza, drawing the main force of the British attack down upon it and consuming its strength in the defensive labyrinth his men had created there. The bulk of his force, 12,000 infantry and 1,500 cavalry, was held back in three separate battle-groups, one at Beersheba away to the south-east (one infantry and one cavalry brigade), one at Tell el-Sheria (16th Division), and one in reserve near Huj (3rd Division). The 53rd Division was also on its way, marching down the coast road from Jaffa.[67] Kress lacked either the infantry for linear defence or the cavalry to contest the open ground between Gaza and Beersheba. His plan was for an elastic defence involving a *masse de manoeuvre* pivoting upon a trench-fortress.

* * *

The British marched to battle on the morning of 26 March through nocturnal darkness and then a thick fog that did not clear until gone 7 o'clock. The mounties, well used to night riding, reached all their allotted positions by mid-morning. The Anzacs closed the cordon around the city with the capture of Jebalieh, a mile and a half north of Gaza, at about 10.30. The infantry were another matter. The 53rd Division, delayed in a wearisome 12-mile approach-march in darkness and fog, did not reach its assembly-point until 8.30. But it then did nothing for more than three hours, despite a succession of tetchy messages from Chetwode to Dallas, who was in fact away from his headquarters and uncontactable for two hours. 'When are you going to begin your attack?' asked the last message at 12 o'clock. 'Time is of vital importance. No general staff officer at your headquarters for two hours.'[68] Half the daylight –

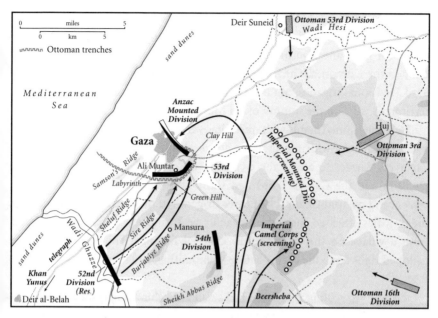

13. The First Battle of Gaza, 26–27 March 1917, showing the situation late on the first day.

half the precious window of time – had been lost before the Welsh infantry got going.

They moved into a storm of fire. Ion Idriess and his mates in the 5th Light Horse watched from a distance.

> Our position was unique, miles of the semi-circle battle was spread like a panorama before us . . . We could see the shells bursting over miles of country, see the attacking battalions . . . we watched the huge bulk of Ali Muntar turning into a roaring volcano, its cactus crest obliterated by the smoke and earth that vividly showed the crimson-black flame of explosions. Toiling across the exposed country at its base, we watched the little toy men of the 53rd Division plodding in waves towards the grim fortress, roaring under its machine-gun fire . . . The poor Welshmen, coming up the open slopes towards the redoubts, were utterly exposed . . . Shrapnel had merged in a writhing cloud over the advancing men. They plodded out of a haze of earth and smoke only to disappear into another barrage. It was pitifully sublime. When within close rifle-range, line after line lay down and fired while other lines ran past them to lie down and fire in turn. And thus they were slowly but so steadily advancing, under terrific fire. Every yard must have seemed death to them. We could see in between the smoke-wreaths that when each line jumped up, it left big gaps.[69]

The attack slowed amid the cactus hedges near the top of the 300-foot hill and spread across two subsidiary mounds, Clay Hill to the south-east, Green Hill to the south-west, and also into a tangle of gardens and trenches near the city dubbed 'the Labyrinth'. The fighting of the late afternoon sucked in all three of 53rd Division's brigades, but by 6 o'clock, as the sun began to set, the Welsh territorials were on the summit of Ali Muntar.[70]

Here they joined hands with Australians and New Zealanders, for Chetwode had, at 1 o'clock, with the infantry attack finally under way, sent orders to Chauvel's Anzacs to attack the city from the north. The Imperial Mounted Division and the Camel Corps had shuffled northwards to fill gaps in the screen, and by 4pm Chauvel had three brigades in motion. Idriess was among them. Rifles crackled through the cactus walls and machine-guns chattered from a village on the right as they charged forward. The 5th Light Horse galloped right up to the cactus before dismounting, and then:

> the pear was spitting at us as the Turks standing behind simply fired through the juicy leaves. The horse-holders grabbed the horses while each man slashed with his bayonet to cut a wall through those cactus hedges. The colonel was firing with his revolver at the juice spots bursting through the leaves . . . Then . . . man after man tore through the cactus to be met by the bayonets of the Turks, six to one. It was just berserk slaughter. A man sprang at the closest Turk and thrust, and sprang aside and thrust again and again. Some men howled as they rushed, others cursed to the shivery feeling of steel on steel. The grunting breaths, the gritting teeth and staring eyes of the lunging Turk, the sobbing scream as a bayonet ripped home. The Turkish battalion simply melted away: it was all over in minutes. Men lay horribly bloody and dead; others writhed on the stained grass, while all through the cactus lanes our men were chasing demented Turks.[71]

The Anzacs were now in the suburbs fighting house-to-house. The battle dissolved into numerous local actions. In one place they charged and captured two Austrian Krupp guns. Turkish infantry then counter-attacked, hurtling down the road in a dense mass, waving rifles with bayonets fixed, shouting 'Allah al-Akbar! Allah al-Akbar! Finish Australia!' An officer levelled a machine-gun over the shoulder of a trooper 'and blazed away, taking the massed Turks in the flank: they fell in writhing masses sprayed by the Hotchkiss bullets, and melted away under the cross-fire of the New Zealanders'.

But only 70 yards away, a Turkish machine-gun was firing from a house. A group of New Zealanders under a corporal swung round one of the captured guns, put a shell in the breach, and fidgeted with the firing mechanism until it suddenly went off, blasting a hole clean through the house and tumbling out twenty-eight Turkish prisoners. A second shell smashed another house, full of riflemen, who emerged coughing from the fumes.[72]

The Tommies had taken Ali Muntar. The Anzacs were fighting in the streets of Gaza. Major von Tiller, the German garrison commander, had accepted defeat and given orders to destroy documents and blow up the wireless station. Kress, directing operations from Tell el-Sheria, assumed Gaza was lost and instructed his relief forces to halt for the night. But as the sun set, the victorious Welshmen and Anzacs received the order to retire. The response was disbelief. Chauvel argued with Chetwode on the phone. Chaytor, the New Zealand commander, demanded the order in writing before he would comply. Ryrie refused to move until he had collected every man of his 2nd Light Horse. Idriess records 'the utter amazement of all troops', the officers shrieking for signallers to confirm the order, the men gazing down the abandoned streets of an all-but captured city.[73]

* * *

Dobell's and Chetwode's HQs were located on the edge of the Wadi Ghuzze: too far from the main action to assess the flow of battle and issue appropriate orders.[74] They had been panicked by evidence that Kress's planned counter-attack was unfolding, with forces from Beersheba, Tell el-Sheria and Huj closing in on the British right flank. In fact, Kress had been as frustrated by delay as the British, and had so far got few of his men into action.[75] But Chetwode and Dobell, unaware that Gaza had effectively fallen, feared that the Anzacs might be cut off without access to water, and ordered them to retire. The unintended effect was to unravel all the gains of the day.

The withdrawal of the cavalry screen would expose the eastern flank of the infantry, so Dallas was ordered to link up the 53rd Division's right with the 54th Division's left. But the no-one had told Dallas that the 54th had moved from its relatively exposed position at Sheikh Abbas to a position farther west, closer to the 53rd, on Burjabiya Ridge. Assuming he was being instructed to form a new line extending all the way to Sheikh Abbas, he abandoned Ali Muntar – the key to Gaza. The mistake was discovered only at 5am the following morning. Orders were immediately issued for its reoccupation, but a strong Turkish counter-attack threw the advanced elements of the Welsh off the summit as they arrived.[76] By mid-morning, two divisions of British infantry were holding a tongue-like salient of hillside projecting northwards, exposed to heavy fire from three sides.[77]

Rafael de Nogales had a panoramic view of the Ottoman counter-attack on the British salient no less impressive than that of Ion Idriess of the Welsh infantry attack over the same ground the day before. The front was:

enveloped in thick smoke, from which burst incessant tongues of flame, and through which tore the smoking arcs of the shells. Upon the plain, and along the summits of the red encircling hills, gashed with deep ravines, the units that suffered the heaviest losses continually fell back, one after another, to fill up their ranks; and deploying anew in battle formation, hastened to reinforce our line of fire, in spite of the deadly work of the enemy's artillery [and] machine-guns . . .

It seemed to Nogales 'as if Richard Coeur-de-Lion and Sultan Saladin them-selves had come to life amid the carnage'.[78]

Private 'Ron' Surry of the Essex Regiment had spent 26 March carrying ammo forward for the 53rd Division, but the following day he and his mates found themselves in the thick of it. Ordered to advance as dawn was breaking, they crossed 2,000–3,000 yards under heavy fire, covering the final distance to the enemy wire in a series of short rushes, and then received the order to charge. 'Men fell like flies, and in the rush I vividly remember getting hung up in the barbed wire. In an agony of fear, I frantically tried to free myself. It seemed hours before I could disentangle my legs, yet it could not have been longer than a couple of minutes. With a bound I leapt into the trench.'

The Turks counter-attacked, and the Essex men charged forward to meet them: 'The Turks stopped, some knelt down and fired, then as we got nearer they turned and fled. We had gained the next line.' A fresh counter-attack was beaten off. Then the order came to work to the right to clear more of the captured trench. 'I . . . had to climb over whole rows of bodies piled two or three feet high. It was simply awful and the stench was simply chronic. We . . . pushed on over the ever-increasing blackened bodies.'

The Turks counter-attacked again, filing down the trench, but Surry's group waited for them in a traverse and bayoneted them as they came through. Established on the slopes of Ali Muntar, the Essex men passed forward sand-bags to create a parapet on the reverse of the trench.[79]

But the main threat was not to the front: Surry's battalion was holding the head of a sausage-shaped salient, and around midday a strong attack on the right flank threatened to get in behind it. Most of the British infantry had gone two nights without sleep and were now in their second day of battle. The Turks, on the other hand, had rested in their positions overnight and been reinforced by reserves. The exhausted Tommies were being attacked by thousands of rela-tively fresh men. Their position was untenable.[80]

The order was 'every man for himself', and the remnants of Surry's company evacuated the trench and became part of a chaotic fighting retreat. He and one of his mates found themselves in an improvised firing-line of Queen's Royal

West Surreys, 'extended on a hill repulsing an attack. We threw ourselves down and helped them to pour lead into the enemy. Our rifles became so hot that it was with difficulty that we fired them.' To his left was a fellow with both legs blown off crying for water.[81]

Surry's battalion had begun the day 1,000 strong; by nightfall the survivors numbered 200. The British Army was back on the Wadi Ghuzze, where the action had begun, having suffered 4,000 casualties in two days' fighting. The Ottomans had suffered far fewer – about 2,500 – and they had won an unequivocal victory over a more numerous, more professional, better equipped enemy. They had done this despite the misfiring of Kress's plan – due, he said, to 'typically Turkish' delays – for a converging counter-attack to crumple the British right on the 26th. In the event, however, this had been sufficient to panic a British high command that was too inexperienced, and too remote from the fighting, to be able to assess accurately the dynamics of the battle.

This could not be admitted, so there was a cover-up. Newspaper placards in London read: 'A Brilliant British Victory. 20,000 Turks Defeated.' The news relayed to the public reflected Murray's military dispatch: 'On 26 and 27 March, we were heavily engaged east of the Ghuzze with a force of about 20,000 of the enemy. We inflicted very heavy losses on him; I estimate his casualties at between 6,000 and 7,000 men, and we have in addition taken 900 prisoners, including general commanding and the whole divisional staff of 53rd Turkish Division.'

Pressed for detail when the facts did not stack up, Murray blamed the fog on the morning of the 26th for the failure to take Gaza. The men of the Desert Column knew otherwise. One senior officer wrote: 'It might be said that the real accidents of the day, which robbed the troops of the fruits of their victory, were not so much the result of the sea fog in the morning as the fog of war among the high command in the evening.' The Ottomans also knew better. A note dropped by an enemy airman over British lines read: 'You beat us at communiqués, but we beat you at Gaza.'[82]

* * *

The Ottomans knew the truth, but the War Cabinet at home did not: it was dependent on Murray's false testimony. 'The early telegrams about the First Battle of Gaza affected the General Staff very much indeed,' recalled Robertson, who, a convinced Westerner, now found it harder to resist Lloyd George's insistence on a strategic pivot to the Middle East.[83] As another high-ranking Easterner, Lord Milner, expressed it in a letter to the prime minister: 'As things are, the Turk is crumbling ... Having got him on the run, should we not keep him on the run?'[84] The War Cabinet thought so.

Murray's victory cables were not viewed in isolation: they had arrived at a moment of danger, frustration and opportunity that, in combination, seemed to strengthen the case for an Eastern strategy. The Russian Revolution had begun on 9 March. A five-day urban insurrection had brought down the tsar and installed a new provisional government. The implications were unclear. Some thought a new democratic Russia would prove a stronger ally. Others feared a military collapse (though few in London or Paris yet appreciated the explosive power of the social forces that had been unleashed). Either way, military support for the Russian war-effort – most obviously in Transcaucasia – became an urgent priority. What seemed to make this more practical was General Maude's capture of Baghdad on 11 March, the culmination of a steady three-month advance down both banks of the Tigris by some 165,000 Anglo-Indian troops. Gains on the Western Front tended, by comparison, to be dismally limited and costly.[85] The Battle of Arras (9–15 April) was destined to replicate the usual pattern: Vimy Ridge was taken on the first day, but thereafter breaches in the line were quickly sealed, the offensive ground down, no breakthrough occurred, and the final toll was 85,000 casualties.[86] The Battle of the Atlantic rose to its supreme crisis at the same time, the tonnage lost being 298,000 in January, 468,000 in February, 500,000 in March and 849,000 in April. This proved to be the wartime peak – the tide of battle was about the turn – but no-one knew this at the time, and the shipping losses of early spring 1917 were unsustainable. 'During this month [April],' recalled Churchill, the former first lord of the Admiralty, 'it was calculated that one in four merchant ships leaving the United Kingdom never returned. The U-boat was rapidly undermining not only the life of the British islands, but the foundations of the Allies' strength; and the danger of their collapse in 1918 began to loom black and imminent.'[87]

The winter blues of 1916/17 had found expression in a 20-page internal 'appreciation' exploring the implications 'in the event of the failure of the Entente Powers to obtain a decision in the main theatres during the coming summer'. The author was probably the director of military intelligence at the War Office. It identified three main British war aims: the maintenance of maritime supremacy; the preservation of the balance of power in Europe; and the security of Egypt, India and the Persian Gulf. This was unexceptional. The conclusion, reconfigured in the light of current circumstances, was not. It was premised on the assumption that Germany would remain undefeated in 1917, and that the pressure for a negotiated compromise peace would then become irresistible. This outcome, the author argued, would be compatible with the first and second war aims, but not with the third; indeed, it would undermine the third, since Germany would be freed up by peace in Europe to pursue its imperial ambitions in the Middle East. 'From Aleppo they [the Germans] could operate against Armenia, towards Mesopotamia, or towards Syria and Egypt . . . In these conditions, the maintenance of adequate garrisons for the defence of Mesopotamia and Egypt would place an intolerable strain upon our resources.' The key, it seemed, was Aleppo, the northern Syrian city that stood at the main junction of the entire Middle Eastern railway and road system. The ultimate military objective had to be Muslimiye Junction, just north of Aleppo, from which railway lines extended west across Anatolia to Constantinople, east along the southern edge of Armenia towards Mesopotamia, and south through the length of Syria and down into Arabia.[88]

The many reasons for a 'Tenth Crusade' – imperial, strategic, political, whimsical – crowded out any sober assessment. Even Robertson seems to have been swayed. He cabled Murray directing him to 'develop his recent success to the fullest possible extent and to adopt a more offensive role in general'. Freddie Maurice, the director of military operations at the War Office, wrote to Lynden-Bell in Cairo explaining why military reservations had to be set aside:

> The political arguments in favour of going on are . . . very strong. In the first place, we require to put the screw on tighter and tighter here in England in order to reduce imports, particularly food, so as to save shipping, and also to get hold of the men who are available in the country . . . the government feels that its hands must be strengthened as much as possible by military successes, and the moral prestige of a success in Palestine would be very great on the public mind.[89]

The objective, Murray learned to his consternation, was not simply Gaza, but Jerusalem.[90] He had been taken at his word. Had he not reported that the Turks had been defeated with heavy loss? So be it, came the response from London: one more push should break them and deliver the Holy City to the Entente. Murray's cover-up had turned into a trap. His reputation could now be salvaged only by the rapid capture of Gaza. But in the three weeks between the first and second battles, the prospects of success had dimmed.

* * *

Kress had been encouraged by the ineptitude of the British infantry attack at First Gaza, but also chastened by the relative failure of his counter-stroke and the narrowness of the victory. His advantage, it was clear, lay not in manoeuvre – especially given the number and quality of the enemy's mounted

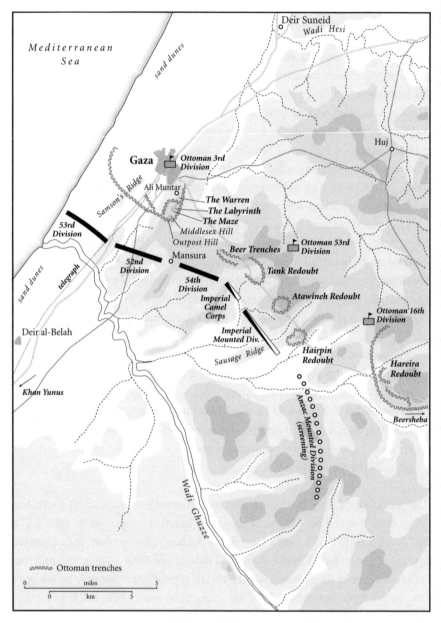

14. The Second Battle of Gaza, 19–20 April 1917, showing the situation at zero hour.

units – but in the doggedness of the Ottoman infantry in digging and defending trenches. The German commander therefore had them construct a 15-mile line of earthworks between the sea and Tell el-Sheria. The curving western extent ran through about 3 miles of sand dunes, and then the trenches ran over

Samson's Ridge, through the cactus thickets south of the town, to a point on the Sire Ridge about a mile and a half south of Ali Muntar. In this vicinity was a series of trench complexes – the Maze, the Labyrinth, the Warren – and of hilltop redoubts – Outpost Hill, Middlesex Hill, Green Hill – which formed the core of the defensive system. East of this was a gap of just under 1,000 yards of open ground, and then the first of a series of separate trench redoubts – Beer Trenches, Tank Redoubt, Atawineh Redoubt, Hairpin Redoubt and Hareira Redoubt. The redoubts were placed on rising ground, the approaches over open slopes laced with barbed wire, and the various works were close enough for mutual support and so arranged as to maximise converging fire. Available to defend this line were 15,000 men, 85 machine-guns, 90 field-guns and 10 aircraft.[91] Murray's opponent had closed down the chances of another mounted *coup de main* based on surprise and speed. If the battle was to be fought sooner rather than later – and the War Cabinet had made itself clear on that – the British generals were going to have to fight something akin to a head-on trench battle in the manner of the Western Front.

The Eastern Frontier Force was not well prepared for such a battle. For sure, units left behind in March were now brought forward, putting 7,000 more men into the line, and doubling the number of guns: the Ottomans would be outnumbered in the coming battle two-to-one.[92] But the plan was to launch a grand assault along some 15,000 yards of front. Three infantry divisions, each with two brigades up and one in reserve, were to advance side by side, the 53rd Welsh through the sand dunes, 52nd Lowland direct on Ali Muntar, and 54th East Anglian towards the open ground beyond.

This would be the main attack. But to pin the Ottomans in their eastern redoubts and prevent them reinforcing Gaza, the line was to be extended by the Camels, Imperial Mounted and Anzac Mounted: lack of manpower meant that Murray was being forced to use his cavalry as infantry. With 170 guns, there were only enough for 1 per 100 yards of front – compared with, for example, 1 per 12 yards of front at the Battle of Arras. Nor were the guns of adequate calibre. No less than 154 of them were the 18-pounder field-guns or 4.5-inch howitzers of the divisional artilleries. Except for the guns of the French cruiser *Requin* and two British monitors off the coast, the only medium guns available – capable of smashing trenches – were twelve 60-pounders and two 6-inch and two 8-inch howitzers.[93] Even these, in the event, underperformed – partly because the Royal Flying Corps had only twenty-one serviceable aircraft available and could not meet the demand for aerial observation.[94] The Ottoman artillery, by contrast, had been registered on the approaches in the weeks before the battle, and was to be wireless-directed by German and Austrian pilots during the fighting.[95]

Nor did the British have enough shells to sustain a long bombardment. Murray was planning an industrial battle without an industrial stockpile. The British supply problem remained acute. By digging in along the Gaza–Beersheba line and shutting the British out of southern Palestine, Kress was denying them access to the region's water, fodder and food reserves (in that order of importance). Though the railway and water-pipe had by now reached Deir al-Belah, just 5 miles short of the Wadi Ghuzze, and though carrying-capacity was being augmented by seaborne transport, the logistical strain was extreme. The supply-line itself was consuming most of what it carried. Of the 600,000 gallons of water a day being pumped from Kantara on the canal, for example, only 137,000 reached the end of the 120-mile pipeline, and from there only 37,000 reached the troops in the front-line, the rest being consumed by the railway, the technical staff, the labourers and the animals along the way.[96] What did reach the terminus then had to be transported the remaining distance to the front by camel-train. The improvement on the situation during the March battle was marginal. Prodded by his superiors into a battle of materiel, Murray was dependent on logistics geared only to a short battle of manoeuvre.

Few senior officers entered the battle with much confidence. Chauvel and Chetwode, the two most experienced generals, were opposed to it and, according to General Mott, the replacement for Dallas at the head of 53rd Division, 'There never appeared to be anything in the conception of the plan beyond brute force, without the adequate artillery to carry it through.'[97]

The men moved into position on 17 April, spent the following day in consolidation and preparation, and then, after a two-hour artillery bombardment, the main attack went in at 7.30 on the morning of the 19th. Some considered the preliminary bombardment worse than pointless. According to General Smith, commanding 52nd Division:

> This bombardment was the most futile thing possible, resulting . . . only in warning the enemy of the point of attack and in gross waste of ammunition. The fire-trenches were the object of the bombardment, and to think that any intelligent enemy will hold his front-line trenches in strength when there is no threat of an infantry attack is ridiculous – considering the distance apart of the opposing forces.[98]

General Sandilands, the artillery commander of 54th Division, spent two hours trying to persuade his superior to call off the planned assault, arguing:

> I have not got the ammunition for it. Even one round per gun per minute, I shall have nothing left to fight a battle with . . . I can't guarantee to drop a

single shell into the single line of trenches over 2,000 yards away ... when the infantry start to move forward, they will be mown down in swathes. It is just murder.

The results were as predicted; but it was Sandilands, of course, who was sacked after the battle.[99]

Nowhere along the line was the artillery capable of providing the weight of fire necessary to its three basic tasks of trench destruction, counter-battery fire and infantry support. Some 3,000 gas shells had been supplied, but these proved sheer waste. The gas was evaporated by the heat and dispersed by the wind so quickly that the Turks appear never to have realised they were under gas attack.[100] The Ottoman trenches and wire remained substantially intact, and the defenders continued to operate their weapons with confidence as the slopes before them filled with lines of slow-moving specks, thousands of them, each a man lumbering beneath a heavy pack, weighed down with weapons, tools and 200 rounds, hunched forward over his rifle against the storm of steel.[101]

Nothing went right. Eight old tanks had been delivered to the Palestine front, and six of these went into action on 19 April. The tank was an ingenious combination of internal-combustion engine, caterpillar tracks, plate armour and firepower (either heavy machine-guns or quick-firing artillery). In time, it would revolutionise the battlefield. For the present, however, solutions to the technical problems raised by the tank's combination of attributes were crude. Pulling 28 tons of weight, the Vickers Mark 1 could manage only 2mph as it clanked its way forward. Breakdowns were common, and ditching an ever-present danger due to the driver's limited visibility and the machine's meagre power-to-weight ratio. The eight men jammed inside, none of whom had room to stand or move around, were battered by severe bumping and jolting, and might be thrown against jagged, sometimes red-hot machinery. The cab was filled with ear-splitting noise from the engine and the guns, and by fumes from oil, petrol and exhaust. Temperatures could reach 50°C. Tank crews suffered headaches, vomiting and sometimes collapse.

Additional problems arose at Gaza. Sand clogged the machinery, especially the tracks, and the heat of the sun added to that of the engines turned the cabs into cookers. Worst of all, the tanks were used singly and spread along the front, making each one a magnet for artillery fire as soon as it appeared. The men inside were concussed, blinded by splinters, torn apart by flying fragments, or burnt to death when their tank 'brewed up'. Only two of the six tanks actually entered an enemy redoubt, and most of the crews – who tended to be technically minded junior officers and engineering-industry workers – became casualties. Infantry bunching in the lee of the tanks – as they invariably did – also suffered heavily from the shell-fire the vehicles attracted.

Could it have been different? Dobell's basic error – for he, under Murray, was responsible for the tactical plan – was to violate the principle of concentration of force. Nowhere along the line was there, as there might have been, an attack in depth supported by massed artillery, airpower and armour.[102] The tanks were, even at this early stage in their development, formidable weapons. Lynden-Bell had watched a demonstration and concluded that 'if we can only get the Turks to stand, I feel we will frighten them out of their lives.'[103]

The attack on Tank Redoubt confirmed the potential. It involved a brigade of East Anglian territorials, two battalions of Australian cameliers and a tank called *The Nutty*. The fire was ferocious and some units had lost 50 per cent of their men by the time they reached the enemy works. But the presence of a tank seemed to fanaticise the attackers and terrify the defenders. The Australians and Tommies fixed bayonets and charged screaming through clouds of smoke,' recalled Trooper Idriess.

> The tank rolled on with her shell-pierced machinery grating and shrieking, fumes sizzling out from the shell-holes in her sides. It was a terrible charge. In the last few yards, the monster grew red-hot and belched dense clouds of smoke, but whatever was left of its crew either stuck to or had fastened the steering-gear so that the great thing clanked on, tearing up rows of barbed wire, until in the very centre of the redoubt it burst into flames. Only thirty Australians reached the redoubt and twenty British infantry. They were madmen. The Turks lost their nerve at the blazing tank groaning upon them, at the glint of steel as maniacs burst from the smoke. They fled, 600 of them, under Germans and Austrians.[104]

But the vanguard who broke into the Ottoman redoubts here and in one or two other places were always too few to hold the ground they had taken. The assault recoiled all along the line. The British Army suffered 6,400 casualties, three-quarters of them in the two infantry divisions, the 52nd and 54th, which had attacked the centre of the enemy position astride Sire Ridge.[105] Ottoman casualties were fewer than a third as many.

Nogales, despite having traversed the horrors of the battlefield that night – looters stripping corpses, the ripped and mashed remains, the moaning of the wounded, the howls of jackals feeding on the carrion – was eventually overcome with a strange sense of the historic grandeur of the common soldier of the East.

I noted near me, standing motionless as a sphinx, one of our sentinels, an Anatolian with aquiline nose, high cheek-bones, flat back of head, contemplating with a gaze at once proud and sombre the dusty horizons of the desert. With his profile, the long nose making almost one line with the slanting forehead, his medium-sized but muscular body garbed in a lead-coloured uniform, his calloused but shapely hands resting on the mouth of his rifle, our sentinel appeared as one of the ancient Hittite sculptures set down living in our own time . . .

It seemed to Nogales that 'Time had rounded the cycle of ten thousand years in an hour.'[106]

* * *

Kress von Kressenstein considered the battle a walkover. None of his positions had ever been in serious peril and his losses were 'trifling'. So confident was he that he contemplated a general advance to drive the British back over the Wadi Ghuzze, but 'shortage of munitions and supplies made a counter-offensive on a large sector out of the question'. He settled for 'the comparative peace of trench warfare'.[107] The mood in the British ranks was despondent: it was being said that Gaza was another Gallipoli.[108]

Murray accepted no blame for the debacle. Dobell was selected as fall guy. Summoned to GHQ in Cairo, he was told of his removal from command and ordered to return home forthwith. Murray's cable explained that he was being recalled owing to 'poor health'. Lynden-Bell elaborated in a letter to Maurice on 23 April: it turned out that Dobell had got 'a very bad touch of the sun' at First Gaza, and that it was 'quite clear to us all that he was absolutely abnormal and quite different to what he used to be'. Dobell was replaced by Chetwode. Lynden-Bell was confident this would be an improvement, partly, it seems, because the new Eastern Force commander was 'sensible enough to wear an enormous thick hat'.[109] Murray also blamed the soldiers. He complained that his best divisions (formed of regulars) had been withdrawn; the implication was that the territorial divisions were second-rate.[110] Not that the battle should be regarded as a defeat. Lynden-Bell reflected the official line in Cairo when he wrote to Maurice: 'In the circumstances, it would obviously have been unwise with our small force to attempt to push home the attack on Ali Muntar. We therefore decided to take things quietly and carry on the job methodically.'[111]

* * *

London was not impressed. In fact, on the very day Lynden-Bell was penning his 'in the circumstances' letter, the War Cabinet agreed unanimously upon the dismissal of Murray. The Savoy Hotel commander had finally been rumbled.

Murray had not been without virtue. He had grasped that static defence on the line of the canal exposed the waterway to attack and was wasteful of manpower and resources. He had pushed for aggressive defence based on forward bases and active patrolling and raiding. He had overseen the massive logistical effort – railway, water-pipe, wire road, camel trains, labour corps – necessary to project military force across the desert. He had cleared Sinai of Ottoman soldiers, and brought 35,000 of his own men to the edge of Palestine. He had laid the firm foundation from which the conquest of the Middle East in the final year of the war would be launched. His replacement in command of the Egyptian Expeditionary Force considered Murray's preparatory work to have been 'the cornerstone' of his own successes.[112]

But Murray was not a field commander; he was merely the efficient manager of an industrial process. The War Cabinet now wanted a conqueror, a Crusader, a military hero.

News of their decision to replace Murray was delayed for six weeks only because they took time finding their man. He took some persuading. His initial reaction was to regard reassignment from the Western Front as demotion. The prime minister reassured him: 'I told him, in the presence of Sir William Robertson, that he was to ask us for such reinforcements and supplies as he found necessary, and we would do our best to provide them. "If you do not ask, it will be your fault. If you do ask and do not get what you need, it will be ours." I said the Cabinet expected "Jerusalem before Christmas".'[113]

On 21 June 1917, Lieutenant-General Sir Edmund Allenby boarded a train at Charing Cross on the first leg of a week-long journey to Alexandria. He assumed command in Cairo at midnight on the 28th. Palestine was to be his supreme opportunity as a general. He was destined to become the architect of two of the most astonishing military victories of the First World War – victories that would make him the conqueror of first Jerusalem, then Damascus.

Captain Lawrence would come to see him as something of a latter-day Richard the Lionheart. But of Allenby's arrival at Cairo GHQ, Lawrence for the present knew nothing. Nor, for that matter, did GHQ, at that precise moment, know anything of Captain Lawrence. For, at the beginning of May, with a party of about fifty Arabs, he had ridden east and disappeared into the desert. And that was the last that anyone had heard.

CHAPTER 10

Aqaba

Captain Lawrence's return from Wadi Ais to Wejh had been eagerly anticipated. He arrived on 14 April to find Feisal much flustered by his month-long absence. The immediate worry was a false rumour that the French were landing 60,000 men in Syria. The suspicion that France had predatory designs on the country seemed confirmed; and to this was now added another – that Britain was colluding in these designs.[1]

Arab doubts centred on Major Pierce Joyce, a broad, tall, career soldier with a penchant for efficiency and order, whose main role was the management of bases, supplies and the British specialist units attached to the revolt. Lawrence came to see in him 'a serene, unchanging, comfortable spirit ... more patient than any recorded archangel'.[2] Joyce, like other British officers, was actively discouraging any Arab move north, in preference for a large-scale operation to sever the railway at Medain Saleh/Al-Ula and thereby force the surrender of the Medina garrison.[3]

That this was British policy was confirmed in a private letter from Clayton to Lawrence awaiting him upon his return. 'The move to Aqaba on the part of Feisal', wrote the Arab Bureau chief, 'is not at present desirable ... It is questionable whether, in the present circumstances, the presence of an Arab force at Aqaba would be desirable, as it would unsettle tribes which are better left quiet until the time is more ripe.'[4] Joyce's efforts to confine Feisal to the Hijaz reflected his instructions from Cairo. They also chimed with Colonel Brémond's yet more insistent agitation to the same effect. Powerful leverage in this regard was provided by Feisal's dependence on the flow of British money, supplies, munitions and weaponry. The sherif began to fear that Syria would slip from the Arab grasp.[5]

This danger was real. Two months before, Feisal and Lawrence had had a private conversation of immeasurable significance for both their personal relationship and the future of the Arab Revolt. It involved the sharing of a secret that was to bind these two men together – Arab desert prince and British archaeologist turned soldier – in a political conspiracy that would last through the war and beyond.

Lawrence had been worried by Brémond's lobbying for an Anglo-French landing at Aqaba, the port at the northern head of the gulf of the same name that gave access to the Red Sea. In Anglo-French hands, possession of the port could be used to keep the Arabs bottled up in the Hijaz. In Arab hands, it might be used as the forward base of a spreading insurgency. A second consideration was the political impact: an Anglo-French seizure of Aqaba would have compromised the Hashemites' standing in Syria, reducing them to little more than the Arabian tribal auxiliaries of an essentially European operation.

Eager both to alert Feisal to French designs and to cement his own relationship with the Arab leader, Lawrence decided to reveal that the McMahon Correspondence – and in particular, the fourth letter of the exchange, the one promising Arab independence across virtually the whole of Arabia, Syria and Iraq – could not be relied upon. What made this so was the Sykes–Picot Agreement: a secret protocol in which three allied imperial powers – Britain, France and Russia – set out a joint plan to carve up the Middle East after the war.[6]

* * *

Cairo had been fully informed about the Sykes–Picot Agreement only in April 1916, by which time it had committed itself to the undertakings contained in the McMahon Correspondence. The contradictions were immediately apparent and the cause of much anxiety. The reaction of Lawrence's friend Hogarth was typical: 'The conclusion of this agreement is of no immediate service to our Arab policy as pursued here, and will only not be a grave disadvantage if, for some time to come, it is kept strictly secret.'[7]

This was to understate the duplicity and moral depravity inherent in the situation. On 4 March 1915, tsarist Russia had resubmitted an old claim to control over the Straits of Constantinople. This had alerted its British and French allies to the need to agree upon a distribution of Ottoman spoils. On 21 November that year, Sir Edward Grey, the British foreign secretary, had suggested joint discussions on the matter. The French had appointed their former Beirut consul, François Georges-Picot, as their representative, the British, Sir Mark Sykes, a wealthy minor aristocrat and Tory MP who, widely travelled in the Ottoman Empire, considered himself something of a Middle East expert. Sykes – arrogant and ambitious, a liar, schemer and charlatan –

seems to have been the kind of man who slipped easily into the role of empire-builder a century ago. The ever-perceptive Lawrence detected his hollowness: Sykes was, he wrote in *Seven Pillars*, 'the imaginative advocate of unconvincing world movements . . . a bundle of prejudices, intuitions, half-sciences. His ideas were of the outside, and he lacked patience to test materials before choosing his style of building. He would take an aspect of the truth, detach it from circumstances, inflate it, twist and model it.'[8] Sykes seems to have been the principal architect of the agreement that came to bear his and Georges-Picot's name. Its aim was little short of the total dismemberment of the Ottoman Empire.

Petrograd was allocated Constantinople and the four eastern provinces of Anatolia, with their mainly Armenian populations. Paris was granted most of the Syria coast, much of southern Anatolia, and parts of the province of Mosul in northern Iraq. A colour-coded map was provided, and these 'French' areas were shaded blue. London was awarded most of Mesopotamia, including Basra and Baghdad, and this was shown red. In addition, two large territories were marked as single blocks, one, allocated to France and labelled 'A', extending across inland Syria and central Iraq, the other, allocated to Britain and labelled 'B', extending across Transjordan and northern Arabia. These were to have 'independent' Arab rulers, but they would be subject to supervision by the respective imperial powers. Finally, Palestine (shown brown on the map) was to be governed by some sort of international administration – though the underlying assumption was that Britain would be dominant here given the likelihood that its army would end the war in control of the place, and that it straddled British imperial communications.[9]

Sykes–Picot anticipated the British government's pivot to the East under Lloyd George. Turkish atrocities had been a common theme of liberal rhetoric in the nineteenth century. The new prime minister picked up the fallen banner. The right-wing novelist John Buchan, installed as 'director of information', was encouraged to launch an anti-Turkish propaganda campaign. The slogan 'The Turk Must Go!' proved popular. So, too, did echoes of the Crusades – tinged, in Lloyd George's case, with the Nonconformist evangelism of the Welsh valleys. Liberal humanitarianism and Christian piety chimed with a more prosaic consideration: that the cost of the war in blood and treasure – the 'sacrifices' of the British people – could be justified only by commensurate territorial gains. For the prime minister, this was, of course, the real issue. As he later explained: 'For the British Empire, the fight with Turkey had a special importance of its own . . . The Turkish Empire lay right across the track by land or water to our great possessions in the East – India, Burma, Malaya, Borneo, Hong Kong, and the Dominions of Australia and New Zealand.' A heady vision for an expanded and remodelled British Empire took hold in the new War Cabinet. With the addition of German colonies in Africa and Ottoman colonies in the Middle East, a vast condominium centred on the Indian Ocean became possible, a continent-spanning arc of imperial territory extending from South Africa, through East Africa, the Middle East, the Indian subcontinent and South-East Asia, all the way to Australasia.[10]

* * *

Lloyd George had a particular interest in one place on this arc: Palestine. He had intervened personally in the Sykes–Picot negotiations to prevent its dismemberment, arguing that it would not be worth winning the Holy Land only to 'hew it in pieces before the Lord'.[11] It is doubtful that the Lord cared, but British statesmen most certainly did, for Palestine sat astride the land-bridge from Africa to Asia that was the empire's main communications chokepoint. This matter had exercised Whitehall minds for almost a century, certainly since the days of Lord Palmerston, who had canvassed with the Ottoman sultan the idea of 'returning' European Jews to the Promised Land, confident in the belief that the grateful settlers would become a pro-British bulwark in an unstable region.[12] This idea was now revived at the highest levels of government, encouraged by an increasingly outspoken pro-Zionist lobby, which included the influential Liberal newspaper, the *Manchester Guardian*. 'The whole future of the British Empire as a sea empire', explained the paper's military correspondent in November 1915, depended upon Palestine becoming a buffer state inhabited by 'an intensely patriotic race'.[13]

Palestine duly became the focus of another scheme involving the indefatigable Mark Sykes. In a curious concatenation of circumstances, the issue, like so many others that eventful April of 1917, had just gone live. As the U-boat war peaked in the Atlantic, British armies crashed to defeat at Arras and Gaza, and Lawrence answered an urgent summons from Feisal to return to Wejh, disturbing news of an anti-Jewish pogrom in Jaffa was brought to Cairo by Sarah Aaronsohn. Sarah was sister to the agronomist brothers Aaron and Alexander, both of whom were committed Zionists now working abroad for the cause. Djemal Pasha had ordered the evacuation of the coastal city, fearing a British landing from the sea to take the Gaza defences in the rear. Though the order was no doubt carried out with the customary incompetence, corruption and brutality of the Ottoman state, there was in fact no 'pogrom'. Nonetheless, Aaron Aaronsohn, the older brother, who was now at the centre of a Zionist network extending from the Middle East to London to New York, concocted a sensational news story that eventually spread widely. 'Grave Reports – Terrible Outrages – Threats of Wholesale Massacre' claimed the *Jewish Chronicle* in

London. 'Cruelties to Jews Deported in Jaffa – Djemal Pasha Blamed' proclaimed the *New York Times*.

Aaronsohn was greatly assisted in disseminating the story by a new friend: Sir Mark Sykes. He, in turn, was encouraged by a small but increasingly influential pro-Zionist lobby in London. Fellow Tory MP William Ormsby-Gore, for example, cabled Sykes to say, 'I think we ought to use pogroms in Palestine as propaganda. Any spicy tales of atrocity would be eagerly welcomed by the propaganda people here, and Aaron Aaronsohn could send some lurid stories to the Jewish papers.'[14]

The 'Jaffa Pogrom' of April 1916 was a contrivance of wartime propaganda. Whose interest did it serve? The Jews of Palestine numbered about 60,000 in a population of 700,000 at the time of the First World War. Many belonged to ancient families, spoke Arabic as their first language and were highly assimilated into local society.[15] Some, like the Aaronsohns, were recent immigrants, often of Eastern European origin, and a large proportion of these lived in new pioneer settlements and were committed Zionists. They enjoyed the support of an international Zionist movement which included wealthy sponsors like the Rothschilds and influential politicians like former British Home Secretary Sir Herbert Samuel. Most politically active European Jews, however, were not Zionists; the majority were relatively poor, many faced persecution, and they were therefore more likely to be on the left than to support what many regarded as, at best, an irrelevance and a pipedream, at worst, a form of predatory nationalism. Such doubts were well-grounded. Zionism – the aspiration to create a Jewish homeland – could succeed only through an alliance with imperialism. Theodor Herzl, the Hungarian-born founder of the Zionist movement, had canvassed Argentina, Uganda and even Madagascar as possible homelands, before soliciting the support of first the Ottoman sultan and then the German Kaiser in an effort to secure access to the biblical 'Promised Land'.

With the outbreak of the First World War, Zionist attentions shifted to Britain. With Herzl dead, Chaim Weizmann, a Russian émigré who became a chemistry lecturer (and explosives expert) at Manchester University, had emerged as a leading figure in the Zionist movement. He had the ear of his MP, Arthur Balfour, the former Tory prime minister and the new foreign secretary in Lloyd George's wartime coalition. Weizmann saw a 'providential coincidence' between British and Zionist interests. 'Palestine will fall within the influence of England,' he explained. 'We could easily move a million Jews into Palestine within the next 50–60 years, and England would have a very effective and strong barrier, and we would have a country ...' He took every opportunity to advance the Zionist case with Britain's leaders, telling the cabinet minister Sir Robert Cecil, for example, that 'a Jewish Palestine would be a safeguard to England, in particular in respect to the Suez Canal'.[16]

From late 1916 onwards, Sykes acted as the Mephistopheles of the growing convergence between Zionism and British imperialism. Following conversations with Aaron Aaronsohn in Cairo, he convened a secret meeting in London on 7 February 1917 attended by Walter Rothschild, Herbert Samuel, Chaim Weizmann and other leading British 'Jewish gentlemen'.[17] Events did the rest. The Russian Revolution had the twin effect of making Zionists previously hostile to the anti-semitic tsarist regime more willing to countenance an alliance with the Entente, and the British more open to the attractions of Zionism as an essentially right-wing movement in a Europe swinging sharply to the left.[18] Equally significant was US entry into the war. This was yet another of the dramatic events of April 1917: Congress declared war on the German Empire on 6 April. Many Americans were Jews; few were Muslims, Turks or Arabs. Here was a powerful new reason to raise the Zionist banner and rally international Jewry behind the Entente. The Jaffa 'pogrom' was perfectly timed in this respect, and Zionist propaganda was henceforward heavily coloured with Crusader-type racism. 'It is high time to abandon our previous forgiving attitude towards Turks,' Aaronsohn cabled one of his American contacts.

> Now that Turks have committed those crimes, Jewish attitude and American public opinion must undergo complete change. Only efficient way to quick release of Jewish populations from Turkish clutches is to attack latter thoroughly in the field and everywhere … We must present a united front, and concentrate Jewish influence on wresting Palestine from Turkish hands.[19]

The British government was finally persuaded towards the end of 1917. An Anglo-Zionist alliance appeared to offer three things: Jewish recruits for the war; a pro-British settler enclave in the Middle East after the war; and an opportunity to freeze the French out of Palestine.[20] Thus the famous 'Balfour Declaration', which took the form of an open letter from the foreign secretary to Lord Walter Rothschild. It stated:

> His Majesty's Government view with favour the establishment in Palestine of a national home for the Jewish people, and will use their best endeavours to facilitate the achievement of this object, it being clearly understood that nothing shall be done which may prejudice the civil and religious rights of existing non-Jewish communities in Palestine, or the rights and political status enjoyed by Jews in any other country.[21]

The document was highly disingenuous. The two aims – the establishment of a Jewish homeland and the safeguarding of the rights of the existing non-Jewish

population – were incompatible. All of Palestine was occupied. Zionist settlement usually involved using Jewish funds raised abroad to buy land from
absentee Arab landlords and then evicting Arab tenant-farmers whose families
might have occupied the land since time immemorial. The British were offering
to facilitate ethnic cleansing.[22] The more far-sighted of them knew this. 'In
Palestine,' Balfour explained after the war:

> we do not propose even to go through the form of consulting the wishes of
> the present inhabitants of the country ... The four Great Powers are
> committed to Zionism. And Zionism, be it right or wrong, good or bad, is
> rooted in age-long tradition, in present needs, in future hopes, of far
> profounder import than the prejudices of the 700,000 Arabs who now
> inhabit that ancient land.[23]

Thus, in furtherance of its ambition for world empire, Britain's rulers had sold
the Middle East twice, first to the Arabs, then to the Entente. But they had sold
Palestine three times, first to the Arabs, then to themselves and finally to the
Zionists. Politicians like Lloyd George claimed that Britain was fighting a war
to defend the freedom of Europe against an autocratic and aggressive Germany.
Many of their actions give the lie to that claim, but few are so blatant as the
Sykes–Picot Agreement and the Balfour Declaration. These undertakings
reveal the war in the Middle East – like the wider war of which it was part – to
have been a struggle between rival alliances of great powers for empire and
profit.[24] It was T.E. Lawrence's tragedy that he experienced this *Realpolitik* of
European imperialism as an inner psychic crisis.

* * *

Aqaba in 1917 was a small settlement of single-storey mud houses on the
edge of a pebble beach fringed with date-palms. It was dominated by a
stone fort, which housed the local Ottoman governor and a small garrison
of soldiers. A post and telegraph office connected the place to the outside
world. In ancient and medieval times, Aqaba had been a town of some standing,
but after the fifteenth century it had fallen into decay.[25] By the time Lawrence
arrived there in early July, whatever residual dignity it may have retained
had been lost: 'Through the whirling dust we perceived that Aqaba was all
a ruin. Repeated naval bombardments had degraded the place to its
original rubbish, and the poor remains of the houses stood about in a
litter ... Aqaba was dirty and contemptible, and the wind howled miserably
across it.'[26]

Yet the town's scant and scruffy appearance belied its significance. Aqaba was one of those otherwise obscure places that the exigencies of war may suddenly place under history's spotlight. It was located on two major route-ways. One of these ran from Cairo to Suez and across the southern track through Sinai. This was a Hajj road used by pilgrims from North Africa whose intention was either to take ship at Aqaba and pass down the Red Sea to Jiddah or to continue overland through western Arabia. The other was a north–south route, for Aqaba lay at the point where the Wadi Araba, part of the Great Rift Valley, became the Gulf of Aqaba, the seaway that skirted the eastern edge of Sinai and emptied into the Red Sea. As well as the Wadi Araba, running due north, Aqaba was also connected with Ma'an and the Hijaz Railway by a route which began as a camel track through the Wadi Itm immediately north of the town.

Though Aqaba had ceased to be an active port, it might become so again. Indeed, for this precise reason, just as Gaza was the British Army's gateway into Palestine, so was Aqaba the Arab Army's gateway into Syria. Such were the geographical constraints that it was difficult to imagine a system of military logistics capable of carrying the insurgency northwards that did not involve possession of the town; only here, it seemed, could the necessary bulk supplies be landed close enough to the prospective fighting-front. For the Arabs, Lawrence wrote, 'Aqaba spelt plenty in food, money, guns, advisors.'[27] As long as the Ottomans held it, moreover, it constituted a wedge driven between the Egyptian Expeditionary Force in front of Gaza and any Arab forces attempting to move north along the Hijaz Railway. The British high command had long been anxious about Aqaba. From there the Ottomans might threaten Murray's flank, send raiding parties into Sinai and project jihadist propaganda down the Red Sea coast. They might even turn it into a German submarine base.[28] According to Lawrence, 'The British staff felt the inconvenience of this uncontained enemy base in all their efforts to prolong their right wing against Beersheba . . .' The aim had to be to get Aqaba 'at once, while it was yet lightly held.'[29]

* * *

The Royal Navy, supported by the French, had bombarded Aqaba on numerous occasions since the beginning of the war, sometimes sending landing parties ashore. The garrison had been about 100 in 1914, and was still only about 300 in the middle of 1917, mainly Ottoman-Arab Gendarmerie.[30] That such a relatively small garrison might easily be overwhelmed was obvious. But then what? As reconnaissance flights had confirmed, the real military problem was not the town garrison. Aqaba was ringed by high mountains to north and east, and the

'Lawrence of Arabia.' The archaeologist and wartime officer T.E. Lawrence is transformed into a matinee idol in Lowell Thomas's 1919 West End show.

2. The Young Turks, the triumvirate of dictators who ruled the Ottoman Empire during the First World War: (top) Ismail Enver Pasha (1881–1922), (bottom left) Mehmed Talaat Pasha (1874–1921) and (bottom right) Ahmed Djemal Pasha (1872–1922).

The German generals: (top) Otto Liman von Sanders (1855–1929), (bottom left) Erich von
ılkenhayn (1861–1922) and (bottom right) Freiherr Kress von Kressenstein (1870–1948).

LEADERS

4. The British and Australian generals: (top left) Archibald Murray (1860–1945), the manager of industrialised logistics; (top right) Edmund Allenby (1861–1936), the thrusting field commander; and (bottom) Henry Chauvel (1865–1945), the dashing light cavalryman.

5. The Cairo spooks: (left) Gilbert Clayton (1875–1929), (below right) David Hogarth (1862–1927) and (bottom) Stewart Newcombe (1878–1956).

6. The Hashemite sherifs: (top) Feisal (1883–1933), (bottom left) Hussein (1854–1931) and (botto right) Abdullah (1882–1951).

7. The Arab commanders: (top left) Auda abu Tayi (1874–1924), the desert warlord; (right) Ali ibn el-Hussein el-Harithi (dates uncertain), the young chieftain; and (left) Jafar al-Askari (1887–1936), the regular officer.

8. The imperial politicians: (left) David Lloyd George (1863–1945), who wanted Jerusalem as a Christmas present; (below right) Henry McMahon (1862–1949), who conjured the wartime alliance with the Arabs; and (bottom left) Mark Sykes (1879–1919), who plotted the post-war land grab with the French and the Zionist

ARMIES

The Ottoman infantryman: soldiers are recruited (top) and prepare to march (bottom) in orthern Palestine.

10. British firepower and Australian mobility.
Artillery (top): a battery of 60-pounder heavy guns at a
British military camp.
Airpower (above): a Bristol Fighter of No. 1 Squadron,
Royal Flying Corps, Palestine.
Cavalry (right): trooper of the Australian Light Horse.

1. The camel. Above, a Bedouin army on the move. Feisal (in white), at the head of his Ageyl bodyguard, leads his army to Wejh. Below, a Bedouin army in camp. The sprawl of tent-groups implies separate tribal contingents.

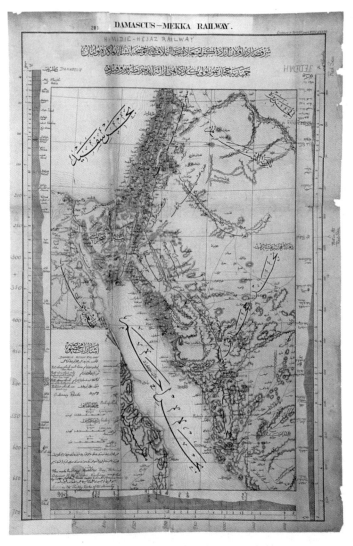

12. The train. Above, the industrialisation of piety: an Ottoman map of the Hijaz Railway from Damascus to Medina. Below, power, piety and prestige: an Ottoman construction battalion poses for a photo.

13. Special ops.
Above, the Imperial Camel Corps advance north after attacking Mudawwara.
Left, an Australian trooper of the Imperial Camel Corps.
Below, the Hijaz Armoured Car Battery at Tooth Hill camp.

OUTPOST HILL   MIDDLESEX HILL   GREEN HILL   ALI EL MUNTAR   FRYER HILL   ANZAC RIDGE
THE WARREN   QUARRY

WEST TOWN   EAST TOWN
Sheikh Hasan   MEDITERRANEAN SEA   Sheikh Redwan   Sand Dunes

14. Gaza: the landscape. Top, a view towards Gaza from British start-lines on Burjabiye Ridge. Gaza itself is left of centre. Middle, a view over Gaza from Ali Muntar Hill, looking west towards the sea. Note the complex terrain of small fields bounded by cactus. Bottom left, Ali Muntar Hill: the dominant feature. And bottom right, cactus hedge: an impenetrable obstacle.

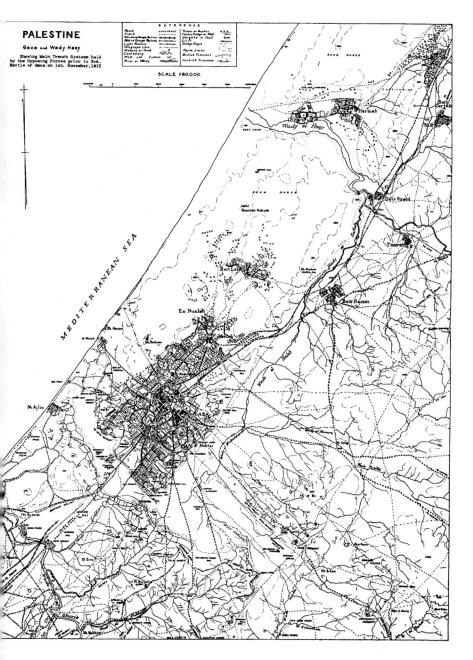

5. Gaza: a First World War trench-fortress. This British military map – based on aerial reconnaissance – shows the lace-like network of gullies, hedges and trenches around Gaza.

16. Gaza: men and machines. (Clockwise from the top) Tommies: British soldiers at rest in a gully near Gaza. *Mehmetchiks*: Ottoman soldiers man a trench near Gaza. Machine-guns: an Ottoman machine-gun unit poses for a photo. Armour: a British Mark 1 tank on top of an Ottoman trench.

17. Aqaba and Mudawwara. Left, the final charge into Aqaba. Below, a montage of aerial reconnaissance photos shows the battle-scape of Mudawwara. The railway is the line on the right. The station is a miniature fortress formed of blockhouses and trenches. The northernmost of three hilltop redoubts is clearly visible towards the top left.

BATTLES

18. Megiddo: the end of empire.
Left, Ottoman prisoners under escort.
Note their ragged appearance.

The Wadi Fara.

The Barada Gorge.

Sherifian irregulars enter Damascus.
Ottoman prisoners are marched away.

. Imperialism, old and new: above, victims of the Armenian Genocide, and below, a colour-coded
ap of the planned Sykes–Picot carve-up.

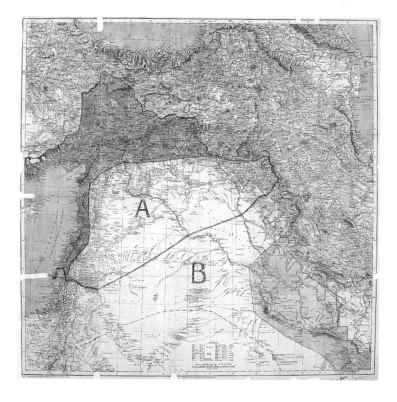

DEMONS

20. Betrayal.
To the right, General Allenby enters Jerusalem as conqueror, and below, Prince Feisal departing his meeting with Allenby after the fall of Damascus.

Below left, Lawrence after the war, and right, Dahoum, whom Lawrence loved, and who perished in the wartime famine and epidemic in northern Syria.

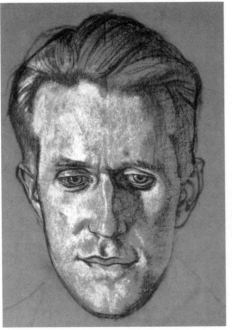

key route inland lay though these mountains along the Wadi Itm, a long, winding, steep-sided gorge where the track narrowed in places to a single camel-width. A British officer who saw this ground a year later passed grim comment on its defensive potential: 'The bottom of the gorge was in some places only a few yards wide. Every now and then we turned a corner where a low-lying spur jutted out across the valley and offered an ideal rear-guard position. At one of these places, one company with two or three machine-guns could have stopped an army corps . . .'[31]

Three major posts, each with a garrison of about 100 men, guarded the route, Guweira on the northern approaches to the wadi, Kithara at a point where the gorge divided and the main path turned sharply to the west and narrowed to a single track, and Khadra by the southern entrance. In addition, at Resafeh, a network of trenches, gun-pits and observation-posts was located beside some wells on a shelf of rock that formed a bend in the gorge; the defenders had clear fields of fire down hundreds of yards of track in either direction.[32]

That the British could land a large enough force to overwhelm the garrison at Aqaba itself was not in doubt. The issue was whether they could fight their way down the Wadi Itm before the Ottomans had time to bring up sufficient reinforcements to lock the position shut. The danger was of yet another Gallipoli or Gaza: a trench-war stalemate expensive in manpower and materiel. It was this strategic problem that had turned Aqaba into a political problem. Had it been possible to take the port and open a route into the interior by a sudden seaborne *coup de main*, the British – no doubt with a token French force in tow – might have stormed into southern Syria and blocked the Arab routes out of the Hijaz. As it was, given their anxiety about an independent Arab advance, British officialdom preferred that the Ottomans should retain Aqaba than that the Arabs should take it. As Clayton spelt out in an internal memorandum: 'the occupation of Aqaba by Arab troops might well result in the Arabs claiming the place hereafter, and it is by no means improbable that after the war Aqaba may be of considerable importance to the future defence scheme of Egypt. It is thus essential that Aqaba should remain in British hands after the war.'[33] Imperial politics had trumped military strategy.

Lawrence had other ideas. He had already decided that Damascus was the prize the Arabs must aspire to if the French were to be thwarted. 'One night we all swore not go Mecca till after we had Damascus,' he scribbled in his note-book. 'Great fun when I insisted on taking the oath too.'[34] The implication was a strategy of 'extension in depth', and this was something to which Feisal himself now seemed openly to subscribe.[35] He rebuffed Brémond's offer of military advice on the grounds that 'scientific military knowledge' was not needed in tribal warfare.[36] Major Joyce also found himself hitting a wall: 'Feisal's whole attention is now turned northwards and he considers the actual taking of Medina the work of Abdullah, Ali and Zeid.' A week later, more of the same: 'He cares little about Medina . . . I have endeavoured to confine Feisal to local ambitions and military operations, but from somewhere he has developed very wide ideas.' Joyce suspected that these 'wide ideas' included Damascus.[37]

Joyce may have known that Feisal's Arab advisors were urging an advance up the coast into Syria. He seems not to have suspected the role of the enigmatic little officer who had become the Arab leader's confidant. Not that Lawrence was promoting an advance up the coast: he knew the difficult ground about Aqaba. What he had in mind, in fact, was an alternative of extraordinary audacity.[38]

* * *

Much hinged upon a recent arrival at Feisal's headquarters at Wejh: Auda abu Tayi. Auda was the foremost fighting chieftain of the Howeitat, the tribe whose territory straddled the desert and semi-desert regions of southernmost Syria – the territory through which any Arab advance north would have to pass. Without Auda's Howeitat, the Hashemites would remain bottled in the Hijaz for evermore.

Auda was about 50 in 1917, his black hair streaked with white, but he was still, reported Lawrence:

> strong and straight, loosely built, spare, and active as a much younger man. His face was magnificent, even to its lines and hollows . . . He had large eloquent eyes, like black velvet in richness. His forehead was low and broad, his nose very high and sharp, powerfully hooked, his mouth rather large, and his beard and moustaches trimmed to a point, in Howeitat style, with the lower jaw shaven underneath.

Lawrence saw in Auda 'a knight-errant'; he was more truly a figure from Homer.

> His hospitality was sweeping . . . His generosity kept him always poor, despite the profits of a hundred raids. He had married twenty-eight times, had been wounded thirteen times, and in the battles he provoked had seen all his tribesmen hurt, and most of his relations slain. He himself had killed seventy-five men, all Arabs, by his own hand in battle . . . Of the number of dead Turks he could give no account: they did not enter his register.

A man of extremes, an Arab Achilles, he could fly into ferocious rages, when men would flee his presence as that of a 'wild beast', yet he loved to shout out stories against himself, invent others at the expense of his guests, and could at times be 'simple as a child, direct, honest, kind-hearted, and warmly loved'. Auda lived life, and imagined life, as a saga: 'His mind was stored with tales of old raids, and epic poems of fights, and he overflowed with them on the nearest listener. If he had no listener, he would very likely sing them to himself in his tremendous voice, deep, resonant, and loud.'

Auda's leadership had raised the Abu Tayi clan to supremacy among the wider Howeitat tribe. He was rated 'the greatest fighting man in northern Arabia', and his followers became 'the first fighters of the desert, with a tradition of desperate courage, and a sense of superiority which never left them while there was life and work to do . . . but which had reduced them from 1,200 men to less than 500 in 30 years'. Lawrence logged the fighting strength of the Abu Tayi in 1917 at 535 camel-men and 25 horsemen.

He met Auda for the first time immediately upon his return to Wejh in April. The Howeitat chieftain drew back Feisal's tent-flap and boomed out a salutation. Feisal rose to meet him. In Lawrence's eyes they made 'a splendid pair, as unlike as possible, but typical of much that was best in Arabia, Feisal the prophet, and Auda the warrior, each looking his part to perfection, and each immediately understanding and liking the other'.[39]

To Lawrence they must have seemed incarnations of the legends of the past. Liddell Hart, who knew Lawrence well after the war, thinks he saw in Auda 'an inverted Crusading baron who seemed to have marched straight out of Lawrence's former medieval dream-world to greet him'.[40] But the dream obscured a harsher truth: there was perhaps more to Lawrence's perception than he would have cared to admit. Feisal was the personification of a form of Arab nationalism distorted by Hashemite ambition and its dependence on British imperialism. Auda was a tribal patriarch, a warrior-chieftain, an outlawed robber-baron, a man rooted in traditions that owed nothing to the ideologies and movements of the modern world; he was a pre-modern who fought for glory, booty and honour. The dependence of 'the prophet' on 'the warrior' therefore had this deeper significance: it confirmed that Arab nationalism, uprooted from the barracks and cities of Syria, had become a withered weed of the desert, sustained only by British gold and Bedouin raiding. This must inform our answer to an old question: whose idea was the Aqaba campaign?[41]

* * *

No definitive answer is ever likely to be given. Discussions were had and decisions made in the secret conclaves of Feisal's command tent at Wejh in the
spring of 1917. No official written record was made. Even had it been, the subtleties of interpersonal influence, often perhaps the fruit of prior conversations,
might easily have gone unnoticed. What we can say is this. Other British officers,
in deference to both conventional military wisdom and the promptings of their
French allies, were unanimous in urging Feisal to remain focused on operations
in the Hijaz. Feisal himself was a somewhat timid politician; ambitious, for sure,
and a charming diplomat and coalition-builder, but neither a great commander
gifted with wide strategic vision, nor a desert warrior with fire in his belly in the
Auda mould; he was, in one British officer's judgement, 'a man who can't stand
the racket'.[42] In any case, the state-building ambition of Feisal and his brothers
– not to mention the Ottoman-Arab officers they recruited to their cause –
inclined them to prioritise building up the strength of their regular army and
waging conventional warfare; they needed their tribesmen, but they were not
guerrilla leaders by choice. The tribal sheikhs who joined them, on the other
hand, were not so much nationalists waging a war of liberation as traditional
desert raiders with followings inflated by foreign guns and gold. Because of this,
as long as the war lasted, Lawrence was ever anxious that the tribesmen would
be diverted from their military objectives to softer, more lucrative targets; and
dispersal laden with loot after a successful operation was a perennial problem.

Lawrence seems to stand outside this tangle of interests. As an officer, he
was not a regular but a wartime maverick, one much given to deep reading and
reflection, and endowed with a first-class brain. As a latter-day romantic, he
idealised the Bedouin as a special people, untainted by modernity, unspoilt by
materialism and corruption, men in the mould of the legendary heroes of
medieval literature. As an Arabist, a man who knew the language, the people
and the region, a man who now counted many Arabs as comrades-in-arms, he
was appalled by the secret diplomacy to which he was privy. Lawrence straddled boxes, fitting into none, and thus was uniquely placed to think outside
them all. He had encouraged the move to Wejh. He had reconfigured the war in
his fevered head at Wadi Ais. And now he was the shy, quiet, shadowy, almost
imperceptible mover and shaker who gently guided other men in the direction
of their inclinations. Towards Aqaba. And then Damascus.

Attempts to deny his influence fall flat. He was, after all, in his capacity as
liaison officer, the plug in the socket connecting Feisal's Arab Northern Army to
its British supply-chain. But he was, of course, much more, for he had forged a
special relationship with 'his' leader, based on a mix of cultural empathy, sound
advice and proven political loyalty. The last must have had exceptional significance. While other British officers were party to a conspiracy to keep the Sykes–

Picot Agreement secret – Clayton, Newcombe and Wilson all reported, with varying degrees of disquiet, that Hussein had no knowledge of its details – Lawrence had divulged what he knew to Feisal.[43] Now, though, he went much further: he planned a daring deep-penetration raid designed to project an Arab commando force through the deserts of northern Arabia into southern Syria, there to raise the local tribes and descend upon Aqaba from the landward side. The effect would be to turn the Wadi Itm from an Ottoman defence-work directed against troops landing at Aqaba into an Arab defence-work against reinforcements from the north. It was, Lawrence later explained, to be 'an extreme example of a turning movement, since it involved a desert journey of 600 miles to capture a trench within gunfire of our ships'.[44]

Of this, Lawrence could tell Cairo nothing: Clayton's letter had been unequivocal, and he could have been in no doubt that, had he revealed his intentions, he would have received a direct order not to proceed. Therefore: 'I decided to go my own way, with or without orders.'[45] All the British knew was that some sort of Arab raid was planned, directed northwards up the railway to Maan; but it barely impinged on the consciousness of fellow officers, for Lawrence was studiously vague, only a handful of men were involved, and Feisal's primary focus appeared to remain Medain Saleh/Al-Ula. 'The venture was a private one,' Lawrence wrote. 'I had no orders to do it, and took nothing British with me. Feisal provided money, camels, stores and explosives.'[46]

* * *

On 9 May 1917, Lawrence set off into the desert in the company of Sherif Nasir, the widely respected expedition commander, Nesib el-Bekri, a cheerful Syrian nationalist keen to spread the message in the north, and Auda abu Tayi, who would rally his tribesmen when they reached the Wadi Sirhan. They were accompanied by about forty-five camel-men, some of them Howeitat followers of Auda, others gaily attired Ageyl mercenaries. The Ageyl had been recruited from the towns of the Hijaz and the Nejd for Ottoman service, but had gone over wholesale to the sherif of Mecca at the beginning of the revolt. Many Sherifian leaders had bodyguards formed of these men. They served as long as they were paid and would go where they were directed – unlike the Bedouin tribesmen, who came and went as they pleased and rarely left their tribal districts – so they provided ballast to Sherifian forces. Lawrence later recruited his own Ageyl bodyguard – looking like 'a bed of tulips' in their multi-coloured garb – and he considered them loyal, reliable and brave. The party set off well equipped with rifles, ammunition, water, supplies, 20,000 gold sovereigns to aid recruitment, and a large quantity of explosives – which, Lawrence soon discovered, was also an aid to recruitment, since 'the noise of dynamite explosions we find everywhere the most effective propagandist measure possible'.[47]

The first leg of the journey, from Wejh north-east to the railway near Diraa, took ten days and was relatively easy, except that Lawrence experienced an outbreak of boils and fever that added physical misery to an increasingly troubled mind. This, though, was nothing to what followed: the crossing of Al-Houl. A flat, desolate, waterless waste devoid of life, it was one of the most pitiless expanses of desert in Arabia. They faced it, moreover, as the summer heat soared towards its maximum and a furnace *khamsin* wind blew across it. Immense and implacable, Al-Houl made men seem tiny, their efforts puny. 'The only sounds,' Lawrence recalled, 'were the hollow echoes, like the shutting down of pavements over vaulted places, of rotten stone slab on stone slab when they tilted under our camels' feet, and the slow but piercing rustle of the sand, as it crept slowly westward, before the hot wind of the open desert ...' As the wind became half-gale:

> our shrivelled lips cracked open, and the skin of our faces chapped, while our eyelids, gone granular, seemed to creep back and lay bare our shrinking eyes. The Arabs drew their headcloths tightly across their noses, and pulled the brow-folds forward, so that they became visors for them, with only a narrow loose-flapping slit of vision. At this stifling price, they kept their flesh unbroken, for they feared the sand particles which would wear open the chaps into a painful wound ...[48]

Soon afterwards, crossing another desolate wilderness, the dried mud-flats of Biseita, from which the sun reflected like a mirror and cut 'flame-yellow' into eyes, the party realised that a man had gone missing. His fully laden camel was still present, but not the rider: he must have dozed off and fallen from his mount. His name was Gasim. His sole companion was handicapped by a foundering camel. The other Bedouin did not count him a fellow tribesman. That left only Lawrence, whose man he was, who might attempt a rescue. Here was a test he resented and at first contemplated shirking, for Gasim had proved a worthless man and Lawrence's temper was 'very unheroic'. But he returned, nonetheless, found Gasim, half-mad in the desert sun, and brought him safely back.

Then the worst was over: the party reached the Wadi Sirhan, the great south-east/north-west routeway that led from northern Arabia to the eastern edge of Syria, where a long series of depressions with wells and grazing marked the traditional desert camping-grounds of the Howeitat. Here was rest and refreshment before the next phase of the campaign. But Lawrence could not relax. The daily round of hospitality and feasting became a torment. The wadi was found to be alive with poisonous snakes. And the comings and goings of tribal diplomacy gnawed at a rising sense of guilt that was in danger of becoming a debilitating mental illness.[49]

* * *

The imperial powers had no designs on Arabia, and the war in the Hijaz had been a clean war to decide whether Ottoman or Hashemite should rule there. Not so the new war about to be launched in southern Syria. Among these Howeitat, Lawrence was now campaigning with men slated for dispossession in the secret protocols of Sykes–Picot. Other officers in the know shared the moral unease, coupled with a sense that two-faced dealing was liable to backfire. Wilson had written in March:

> I feel very strongly that the settlement of Syria etc. should not be arranged behind his [Hussein's] back, so to speak. He is, in my opinion, well deserving of the trust of the British government, and I feel sure we will greatly regret it in the future if we are not quite open and frank with him now over the whole matter.

Joyce concurred in a separate note in April:

> I feel confident that it is essential that the limits of the Arab movement be defined as soon as possible . . . it should be defined to what extent we intend to support their schemes. Otherwise the trust they have hitherto placed in us and all the assistance that has been rendered will be practically nullified.

Newcombe bubbled with indication in May: Sykes's policy, he wrote:

> entails throwing great responsibility on our government to see the . . . Arab cause through to the end. Otherwise we are hoodwinking the sherif and his people, and playing a very false game in which officers attached to the sherif's army are inevitably committed and which I know causes anxiety in several officers' minds, in case we let them down.[50]

But in one officer's mind in particular. On 2 June Lawrence wrote in his notebook: 'Dined with Auda. Lies.' Later, in *Seven Pillars*, he expanded:

> Arabs believed in persons, not in institutions. They saw in me a free agent of the British government, and demanded from me an endorsement of our written promises. So I had to join the conspiracy, and, for what my word was

worth, assured my men of their reward. In our two years' partnership under
fire, they grew accustomed to believing me, and to think my government,
like myself, well-meaning towards them. In this hope they performed some
fine things; but of course, instead of being proud of what we did together, I
was continually and bitterly ashamed.[51]

The Hijaz war had been an adventure that could be lived like a medieval legend.
The Syrian war now beginning was a political betrayal, something a man of
Lawrence's sensibilities could experience only as a psychic crisis. He began to
crack at once. 'Can't stand another day here,' he wrote in his diary on 5 June.
'Will ride north and chuck it.' In his notebook he clarified his motives for the
benefit of his superior: 'Clayton. I've decided to go off alone to Damascus,
hoping to get killed on the way. For all sakes, try and clear this show up before
it goes further. We are calling them to fight for us on a lie, and I can't stand it.'[52]

While recruitment continued at Nebk in the Wadi Sirhan, Lawrence
embarked on a long, dangerous, far-ranging journey into central Syria. The
men around him, caught up in a commotion of movement-building, their
comings and goings accompanied by wild shouts and fusillades, now appeared
as if characters from a Greek tragedy, blind to their fate, hapless and naive on
the way to their doom. Guilt-laden, his mind incapable of rest in the cacophony
of the Howeitat encampment, his confusion compounded by his anomalous
position as a British officer acting in defiance of orders, imperial interest and
conventional military thinking, he slunk away.

Lawrence covered more than 300 miles in just under two weeks. The escape
was a tonic. However confused and self-destructive his mood when setting out,
he turned the journey to good account. It was partly a reconnaissance, a chance
to refresh his knowledge of a landscape he knew, but to see it in a new way,
through the eyes of the guerrilla leader he had become. The journey was a
small-scale diversionary raid. Recruiting a small group of tribesmen, he dyna-
mited a railway bridge 50 miles north of Damascus and stirred up a general
security panic in the Baalbek region – thereby diverting Ottoman attention
from Aqaba. On the way back, he made contact with the Arab underground
and anti-Ottoman tribal leaders, including Nuri al-Shaalan, the great Ruwalla
autocrat of the eastern deserts, whom Lawrence found:

very old; livid, and worn, with a grey sorrow and remorse upon him, and a
bitter smile the only mobility in his face. Upon his coarse eyelashes, the
eyelids sagged down in tired folds, through which, from the overhead sun, a
red light glittered into his eye sockets and made them look like fiery pits in
which the man was slowly burning.

The meeting took place at Azrak, an oasis settlement with a Roman fort of black basalt that once blocked the north-western egress of desert raiders coming down the Wadi Sirhan. The old man rekindled Lawrence's inner anguish by brandishing documents and demanding to know which of Britain's contradictory promises were to be believed. Upon Lawrence's answer might depend the hope of winning the Ruwalla when the rebellion rolled northwards. 'The abyss opened before me suddenly . . . In the Hijaz, the sherifs were every-thing, and ourselves accessory; but in this distant north, the repute of Mecca was low, and that of England very great. Our importance grew; our words were more weighty; indeed, a year later, I was almost the chief crook of our gang.'[53]

Despite the awkward encounter with Nuri al-Shaalan – or perhaps, in part, because of it – Lawrence returned to Nebk in better mind. The journey – the escape – had been a catharsis, enabling him to complete the painful and protracted metamorphosis that had begun three months before when he had first confided to Feisal the secret protocols of the Anglo-French agreement. Since then, a wide gap had opened between him and his fellow countrymen. He had betrayed the secrets of British imperialism. He had rejected British military strategy. He had disobeyed orders not to advance on Aqaba. And now, finally, he resolved to placate the furies of guilt still raging inside his head by seeking all-out victory for his Arab comrades-in-arms: 'I salved myself with the hope that, by leading the Arabs madly in the final victory, I would establish them, with arms in their hands, in a position so assured (if not dominant) that expediency would counsel to the Great Powers a fair settlement of their claims.'[54]

* * *

By the day of Lawrence's return to Nebk, 18 June, all was set: the commando force of 50 had swelled to a small army of 700, mainly Howeitat, but with some Ruwalla, Sherarat and Kawachiba. Leaving 200 of these to guard the tribal tents in the Wadi Sirhan, the rest set out due west for the wells at Bair, two days' hard riding away. The Ottoman engineers had made a botched job of blowing the ancient shafts: one was filled in, two badly damaged and one unaffected. The raiders soon had three wells in use – ample for their force – and they paused at Bair for a week, using the time to reconnoitre the wells at Jefer, the next station, to make contact with the tribes between Maan and Aqaba, and to mount diver-sionary raids to the north, dynamiting the railway at Sultani, Atwi, Minifer and elsewhere – 'demolitions . . . of a pin-prick character, meant only to distract the Turks, and advertise our coming to the Arabs'.[55]

On 28 June, the Arab force set out for Jefer, where they found the Ottoman sabotage had been more thorough, and it was a struggle to dig out one well, though this proved sufficient when it was done. By now, the desert was buzzing with news of the proximity of a Sherifian force, but amid the cross-currents of rumour and report, combined with the distraction of the railway demolitions, the Ottoman high command failed either to locate the enemy or divine his objective.

Meanwhile, a flying column dispatched by Sherif Nasir had combined with local tribesmen to attack a police post at Fuweilah, about 15 miles south-west of Maan on the Aqaba road. The post was taken, but some soldiers escaped back to Maan, the main Ottoman military base in southern Syria, and raised the alarm. As it happened, a battalion of the 178th Regiment had just arrived at the town. It was immediately ordered to proceed to Fuweilah.

The main Sherifian force moved out the following day, 1 July, to attack the line near Ghadir al-Hajj Station. This, again, was a diversionary raid. The force used up all its remaining explosive, blowing up ten bridges and numerous rails, and easily driving back a rash sally by the little station garrison. The Sherifians then rode west, stopping about 5 miles from the line to make fires and bake bread, hoping that the noise of the explosions and telegraphed reports from the station would draw down to Ghadir al-Hajj the Ottoman reserves stationed at Maan.

But the plan unravelled. The men of the flying column brought news that an Ottoman battalion had already marched from Maan to Fuweilah: the road to Aqaba – assumed to be defended by only a string of small posts of around 100 men – had been blocked by a force of more than 500. These, finding Fuweilah itself a place of death overflown by vultures, had taken up position in a village called Abu al-Lissan – a collection of mud houses around a spring at the bottom of a valley overlooked by low hills.

Far sooner than anticipated, the crisis of the campaign had come, for if this force were not defeated and the road to Aqaba opened, the Sherifian vanguard would be left hanging in the air, without the strong forward base necessary to sustain an insurgency in southern Syria. Worse, the tribes already in revolt might be crushed by Ottoman retribution and the whole nascent movement in the region decapitated at birth.

There are moments, moreover – perhaps more often than is realised – when battle is less a matter of strategy than of politics; and particularly so in revolutionary war. The Arab masses of southern Syria were watching. Was this the moment to turn on the hated Turk? Was this the moment for the village to storm the police station? Some hotheads had already moved into action, but they were few. Most remained uncertain, passive, still deciding. Were these Bedouin who had ridden out of the desert mere raiders? Or were they, indeed, as some proclaimed, the vanguard of an Arab revolution that would sweep the

Turks away? The same question in reverse was being asked in all the little Ottoman posts along the road. Was this a tinpot rebellion, to be scotched by a determined stand followed by punitive action? Or was it the beginning of a conflagration?

On hearing the news, therefore, that an Ottoman battalion had blocked the Aqaba road, that it was in fact astride the main pass through the Batra Hills down onto the Guweira Plain, the little Sherifian army had no choice but to accept the challenge of battle – not simply to clear the way, but to win the moral dominance on which successful revolutionary insurrection depends.

* * *

Arriving near dawn, the tribesmen dismounted and scattered unobserved to form a wide ring on the crests above the village. The Ottoman commander had neglected to post lookouts. From the cover of walls and rocks they commenced a firefight at long range, shooting from perhaps 500 yards away, while the Ottoman infantry took cover in the little complex of houses, gardens and gullies at the base of the valley.

So it continued for many hours, the men lying on open ground under the summer sun, their rifles becoming too hot to hold, rocks burning into arms and breasts. Skin peeled away. Throats swelled with thirst and lips cracked open. Heads thudded with heat. 'It was terribly hot,' recalled Lawrence, 'hotter than ever before I had felt it in Arabia ... Some even of the tough tribesmen broke down under the cruelty of the sun, and crawled or had to be thrown under rocks to recover in the shade.' The Ottomans, trapped in the little valley, were hotter still, and they could see nothing to shoot at. Even their little mountain-guns were of no avail, the twenty rounds of shrapnel they fired all flying high and bursting uselessly in the Arab rear.

This was battle at its most tentative. Casualties were few, positions unchanged and the sun was setting. Lawrence and Nasir had crept into a hollow in a desperate effort to assuage their thirst from a trickle of muddy water. Auda appeared, 'striding down powerfully, his eyes bloodshot, and staring, his knotty face working with excitement'. Dropping down to share the shade, he asked, 'Well, how is it with the Howeitat? All talk and no work?'

Tempers had grown short, and Lawrence shot back, 'By God, indeed, they shoot a lot and hit a little.'

Auda flew into a rage, flung down his headcloth, and ran up the hill to his men, yelling at them to rally to him. Lawrence followed, unnerved, fearing he may have precipitated disaster. Struggling to where Auda stood glaring down at the Turks, he was told, 'Get your camel, if you wish to see the old man's work.'

By the time that Lawrence, Nasir and the 400 camel-men had mounted and gathered in a hollow just below one of the crests, the climax of the battle was upon them. They heard 'yells and shots in a sudden torrent from beyond the crest'. And then:

> There were our fifty horsemen coming down the last slope into the main valley like a runaway, at full gallop, shooting from the saddle. As we watched two or three went down, but the rest thundered forward at a marvellous speed, and the Turkish infantry who had been huddled together under the cliff, ready to cut their desperate way out towards Maan in the first dusk, began to sway in and out, and finally broke before the rush.

Auda led the charge and was targeted by a volley. Two bullets smashed his field-glasses, one pierced his revolver-holster, three struck his sheathed sword, and his horse was killed under him; yet he survived the battle without a wound.

The camel-men plunged over the crest to join the charge and head off the fleeing enemy. 'The slope was not too steep for a camel-gallop, but steep enough to make their pace terrific, and their course uncontrollable; indeed, it was very difficult to sit the wildly-plunging animals at all.' The camel charge came down the slope at nearly 30 miles an hour, its momentum unstoppable. The Arabs extended to left and right as the hill widened closer to the base, sweeping round the flanks of the enemy mass. 'The Turks fired a few shots, but mostly only shrieked and turned to run; and the bullets they did send at us were not very harmful, since it took much to bring a charging camel down in a heap.' Lawrence, though, in the first moments of the collision, shooting into the Turks with his pistol, hit his own camel in the back of the head, causing it to drop 'as though it had been pole-axed'. He flew through the air to crash down and wait in dazed anticipation of his own death.

But the battle was soon over. It ended in a swirling mass of frenzied point-blank shooting around the spring in the fading light of dusk. This was massacre more than fighting, for the Turks had been broken by the sudden, wild, careering charge of horse from one direction, camelry from another, and most of the 300 or so known to have perished were shot down now, in the final five minutes.

The bitterness of the tribesmen was great, for Ottoman rule was brutal. Only two days' before, in the fighting at Fuweilah, some mounted police had got in among Howeitat tents and stabbed to death an old man, six women and seven children. Nasir and Lawrence struggled to save lives, and 160 prisoners, including three officers, were taken. Some fugitives may have been killed further afield, going uncounted, while some likely escaped in the darkness. The

Sherifians, by contrast, had only two killed and several wounded: a slight loss for the destruction of an entire battalion.[56]

The insurgents camped for the night and sent out dispatches proclaiming their victory. Some were sent to the chiefs of the coastal Howeitat, encouraging them to place local Ottoman posts under siege until the main Sherifian force arrived. Others went to the commanders of the main Ottoman garrisons on the road south at Guweira, Kithara and Khadra, informing them that they would be spared if they surrendered, and sent as prisoners to Egypt. The policy worked. When the Sherifians reached Guweira, 22 miles south of Abu al-Lissan on 4 July, the local chief had already taken the surrender of the 120-strong garrison manning 'the three little stone houses' that constituted the post. They then travelled down the Wadi Itm until they reached the next major post, Kithara, 18 miles from Guweira. Here the garrison, seventy-strong, was more defiant, for 'they were on a cliff, commanding the valley, a strong place which might be costly to carry by open assault'. But on the night of 4/5 July there was an eclipse, and the Arabs overran the position without loss in the confusion and darkness, 'while the superstitious Turkish soldiers were firing rifles and clanging copper pots to rescue their threatened satellite'. Beyond Kithara, one small Ottoman position after another was found abandoned, the scattered outposts having been withdrawn to the safety of Khadra, 15 miles farther on. Concentrated here, too, was the garrison of Aqaba itself, so that the post was defended by some 300 men, all massed at the mouth of the Wadi Itm to contest egress to the coastal plain. Here the final drama of the campaign was played out.

The Arab force had by now swelled to 1,000, with more arriving all the time, but two attempts to negotiate were met by shots, and a third produced only an offer to surrender in two days if no relief came from Maan. This would not do. Food was running out and the tribesmen could not be compelled to wait. An engagement, on the other hand, was likely to be costly, both for the attackers on the way in, and for the defenders, who would probably be massacred. Negotiations were resumed, and the commander now agreed to surrender at daybreak the following morning (6 July), his honour presumably satisfied by the moderate delay.

This, however, was to take no account of the ever-shifting shape of an Arab battle. For more men arrived during the night, bringing to 2,000 the total of Howeitat tribesmen ranged on the crags about the Ottoman post, many knowing nothing of any agreement. General firing broke out at dawn, and Nasir, Lawrence and the small contingent of Ageyl they had brought from the Hijaz had to march between the lines to stop the action. The surrender then went ahead as planned, the Turks flinging up their arms and crying 'Muslim, Muslim' as soon as the Arabs appeared. The total of prisoners rose to 600.[57]

The miniature army then advanced the final few miles to the sea, breaking into a charge at the end, a dust-wreathed rush of cavalry, camel-riders and local hill-men, eager for loot, racing into history. Near the head was an Ageyl camel-man bearing a great crimson standard, raised aloft on a spiked and tasselled pole, the fabric holed and ripped by battle. Lawrence captured the scene on camera: as if the imaging technology of the twentieth century had recorded a ghost from the twelfth.[58] For an Arab tribal army had emerged once again from the desert, as so often in the past, and was embarked upon a war of conquest to bring down an empire.

CHAPTER II

Bull Loose

I T WAS THE strangest of meetings. Lieutenant-General Sir Edmund Allenby had been less than two weeks in his new post. A big man, heavily built but immaculately attired, he was a highly accomplished professional cavalry officer who had commanded a mounted column in the Boer War, the British Expeditionary Force's Cavalry Division in 1914, and then successively the Cavalry Corps, the V Corps, and the Third Army on the Western Front.

His was a dominating presence, his sharp mind and brusque manner exuding self-confidence, his ferocious temper a terror to the hesitant, the sloppy and the careless. Eruptions of the volcano were often triggered by minor breaches of regulations: he had made himself unpopular as pre-war inspector-general of cavalry with an obsession about the wearing of chin-straps, and latterly, as commander of the Third Army, with an equal (and perhaps more justifiable) obsession about the wearing of steel helmets. He seems to have got worse with advancing years and rank. Archibald Wavell, who served on his staff in Palestine and later wrote his biography, was in no doubt 'that in Allenby increasing authority brought increasing asperity. He who had been a noticeably easy-going young officer and a good-humoured squadron-commander, was a strict colonel, an irascible brigadier, and an explosive general.' His nickname, a reference to both his size and his temper, was 'The Bull'.[1] He could hardly have been more different from the undersized junior officer in front of him. Especially at this moment, for Captain Lawrence, hot-foot from Aqaba after two months in the desert, had returned to Cairo to discover that moths had eaten his uniform. Allenby, in consequence, found himself in the company of 'a little bare-footed skirted person'.[2]

Lawrence had arrived in Cairo at midday on 10 July. His first port of call had been the Arab Bureau for a meeting with his chief, Gilbert Clayton. The British spymaster was astonished to see him. He had had no knowledge of his whereabouts for two months, and only days before had speculated that Lawrence was in the Maan area, where a large iron bridge had been reported blown-up. He was even more astonished when he learned that Aqaba had fallen. Lawrence's arrival had preceded any another news of this momentous event, for he had left for Cairo the day after the Arabs entered the town, crossing Sinai on the southern route, the old pilgrim road, travelling the 160 miles from Aqaba to Suez in 49 hours. Haste was dictated by urgency. Defensive posts had been set up before Lawrence departed, but the little Arab army would disintegrate without food, ammunition and modern weapons for its new recruits. Continuing by train to Cairo, Lawrence had noticed Admiral Wemyss in a group of officers at Ismailia Station. Within hours, a ship loaded with stores was on its way to Aqaba. A couple of days later, after meeting Clayton and dropping his bombshell, he was ushered into the presence of the new commander-in-chief.[3]

Lawrence asked for supplies, arms and 200,000 gold sovereigns. He was unsure of the impression he made.

> Allenby could not make out how much was genuine actor and how much charlatan: the problem was working behind his eyes and I left him to its difficulties. He did not ask many questions, or talk much, but studied the map and listened to my explanation of the nature of eastern Syria and the inhabitants. At the end he put up his chin and said quite directly, 'Well, I will do for you what I can', and that ended it. I was not sure how far I had caught him, but in the future we learned that he always meant exactly what he said, and that what Allenby could do was enough for the very greediest of his subjects.[4]

Allenby – like so many others before and since – never did quite sort out what he thought of Lawrence.[5] Shortly after the latter's death, he described him as 'a character difficult to know' and one who 'had his private reasons for all he did'.[6] But if he suspected Lawrence of charlatanism, he also detected extraordinary qualities – and how could he not, following the fall of Aqaba? So much so, in fact, that he cabled Robertson in London on 16 July with a summary of Lawrence's plans, giving his opinion that 'even the partial success of Captain Lawrence's scheme would seriously disorganise Turkish railway communications south of Aleppo, while its complete success would destroy effectively his only main artery of communication ... and might further be expected to produce extensive local risings throughout the Jordan Valley'.[7] A second cable to similar effect followed on 19 July.[8]

Captain Lawrence's military activities were suddenly being discussed at the highest level of the British military command. This would continue to be the case until the end of the war. No other officer attached to the Arab forces would receive a fraction of this attention. Allenby knew that Lawrence was in a class of his own. 'The fact is,' he would cable Robertson in October, 'only Lawrence can deal with the Arabs effectively.'[9] Writing as a retired field-marshal after the war, Allenby was unstinting in his praise, describing Lawrence as 'the mainspring of the Arab movement'.[10] His ideals, independence of mind and intellectual gifts had made him a brilliant war-leader. 'Lawrence was under my command, but, after acquainting him with my strategical plan, I gave him a free hand. His cooperation was marked by the utmost loyalty, and I never had anything but praise for his work, which, indeed, was invaluable throughout the campaign.'[11]

When he first heard the news of the change of command, Lawrence had worried that 'we would have trouble for six months teaching him [Allenby]', since it had taken that long to persuade Murray and Lynden-Bell of the value of Arab operations. 'The peace army had prepared for war by forming a caste habit,' wrote Lawrence, 'which tried all ideas by King's Regulations and rejected such as transgressed in matter or even in manner . . .'[12]

But Allenby was in a different mould and had decided immediately that the Arabs were to be supplied in full. Lawrence reciprocated with hero-worship. Allenby – who was twice Lawrence's age – became a father-figure. This becomes apparent in a psychoanalytically complex passage in *Seven Pillars of Wisdom* in which Lawrence attempts to define his attitude:

> Allenby came nearest to my longings, but I had to avoid him, and keep out of the sight of the man whom I wanted to worship, not daring to bow down, for fear lest he show feet of clay . . . Yet what an idol the man was . . . From such a height the world looked flat . . . He was not to be judged by our standards, any more than the sharpness of the bow of a liner was to be judged by the sharpness of razors . . . He, like a tank, could smash through groves of guilty disaster.[13]

Allenby, then, was greatness itself, a supreme being, a deity – that is, in psychoanalytical terms, the all-powerful patriarch of the unconscious mind, that mythic figure of the dream-world with the authority to expunge guilt and doubt. Lawrence had attempted to recover his mental balance in May by closer identification with the Arab cause. Did he not thereby betray his own people? Allenby's support was reassurance that he did not: that the avenging father was not angry. Yet he dared not 'bow down' lest the idol show 'feet of clay'. For was Allenby not still a military incarnation of Sykes–Picot? Was the whole Arab war not a mere artefact of British gold and guns? 'All he required of us,' Lawrence wrote ten years later:

was a turnover of native opinion from the Turk to the British; and I took advantage of that need of his, to make him the stepfather of the Arab National Movement – a movement which he did not understand and for whose success his instinct had little sympathy. He is a very large, downright, and splendid person, and the being publicly yoked with a counter-jumping opportunist like me must often gall him deeply.[14]

It was an extraordinary, though semi-detached, military partnership; surely one of the strangest in history. Two very different wars were now inextricably linked, each dominated, from a British perspective, by two very different men. Wavell knew and admired both. In his view, 'Lawrence had great courage, versatility, and quickness of mind, but Allenby was unquestionably the stronger and greater character of the two outstanding figures in this campaign.'[15] Lawrence would have agreed: Allenby was 'the graven image all of us worshipped'.[16]

But the comparison is facile: it misses a deeper truth. The partnership between the two men was dependent on the difference, each playing a role that the other could not, each doing so in such a way as to achieve what some – usually without understanding what they mean – like to call 'greatness'. For 'greatness', or 'genius', or whatever term one uses, is a social relationship defined by an historical moment. Political and military leaders are personifications of the social forces at whose head they stand, and only to the degree that their attitudes and aptitudes correspond to the needs of the moment, are they elevated towards 'greatness' or 'genius', becoming the highest expression and embodiment of mass social praxis.

Lawrence was an exceptional man, but also an awkward and troubled one, his psyche inaccessible beneath its neurosis-armour. He might, in other circumstances, have lived out his time in the relative obscurity of an Oxbridge college. As it was, the peculiarities of his personality, the historical conjuncture of the Arab Revolt, and the sequence of accidents that brought him to Feisal's camp in October 1916, these combined to create 'Lawrence of Arabia'.

Allenby, too, in his very different way, was 'the man of the moment'. His family were traditional English gentry with a house on the East Anglian coast and a small estate in the Norfolk countryside. He had been a sound rather than distinguished pupil at Haileybury and had twice failed the Indian Civil Service entrance exams. Though his family had no tradition of military service, he then applied to Sandhurst and was successful, embarking on a career as a soldier, with no especially strong sense of vocation. He was never what used to be called 'a keen soldier': it was simply his job. And later, on campaign, he would often express his dislike of war, and of soldiering in general. He would fill letters home with descriptions of the flowers and birds of the countryside. English rural pursuits remained his passions – riding, hunting, fishing – though he enjoyed travel, was an enthusiastic reader, and absorbed information like a sponge.

A famous eye surgeon invited to dine with Allenby in Cairo found himself on the receiving end:

> He put me next to him and began pumping me on my subject. Did I know anything about diseases of the eye in previous campaigns in Egypt and Palestine? Had I written anything about it or published it? ... Whether it was a fly expert from the British Museum, a railway engineer, an expert on town-planning, or a naturalist who could tell him something about the flora and fauna of the country, he had them all up and sucked their brains of anything they could tell him.

Allenby went away with some of the doctor's books on archaeology and history, and when he returned them, requested more.[17] 'His mind had breadth and poise rather than any great depth,' wrote Wavell. 'He had not a creative and imaginative brain, like Marlborough: his military genius was colder and stiffer, like that of Wellington, the very embodiment of character and common sense.'[18]

Allenby, then, was neither a hidebound member of the military caste nor a brilliant innovator: he was a solid but thoughtful professional, rooted in conventional soldiering, but willing to improvise. This mental agility was underpinned by his own unstinting diligence, and by the way in which his dominant and dynamic personality energised all with whom he came in contact.

Crucially, Allenby was a delegator. The story went round that, immediately after his arrival in Cairo, he had been presented with a large pile of papers by a major-general of the staff. They concerned such matters as dress, discipline and the administration of martial law. The new commander-in-chief studied the first two or three, then pitched the entire pile into the far corner of the room, issuing a firm order that his time was never again to be wasted on matters that should be dealt with by a junior officer. A few days' later, he was off on his first visit to the front.[19] His predecessor had failed to delegate and become immersed in paperwork and trivia. He had also failed to empower the men under him by giving them responsibility, supporting their work, and making them feel valued. Murray's army, headed by a bureaucrat, had become listless; Allenby, instinctively a field commander, set out to create a 'band of brothers'.[20]

'Not only was he a born leader of men, with a most determined and resolute character,' wrote one of his Tank Corps officers in France, 'but he possessed an extremely imaginative and far-seeing mind, and was not afraid to depart from stereotyped methods of warfare.'[21] This had been evident through much of

Allenby's career, not least in his conduct of the Battle of Arras on the Western Front in April 1917. Instead of the prolonged artillery preparation that had become standard (and served warning on the enemy of what to expect), he opted for a short, intense bombardment. The men of Third Army then rushed the enemy trenches, taking the Germans by surprise, surging forward three and a half miles in places, the greatest single-day advance by the British Army on the Western Front since 1914. Because the offensive had then degenerated into the usual bloody attrition, Allenby emerged from the battle with tarnished reputation: Arras, in the end, seemed to confirm the assessment of him as a strange mix of calm scientific soldier and stubborn, hot-tempered 'Bull'. Yet in fighting a battle of attrition, he was merely conforming to Haig's way of war. Palestine was to be his supreme opportunity, for here, with his own independent command, Allenby's distinctive combination of personal dominance, cavalryman's flair and a thinking general's openness to new ideas would allow him to triumph.[22]

The change of command was a tonic. The Egyptian Expeditionary Force (EEF), demoralised by its double failure in front of Gaza and the tedium of trench-war stalemate, was now languishing in the fast-rising heat and sickness of the summer. The new commander's first mission was to restore discipline, morale and a sense of purpose. The Australian *Official History* – never excessive in its praise of British generals – described 'the Allenby effect' in a famous passage:

He went through the hot, dusty camps of his army like a strong, fresh, reviving wind. He would dash up in his car to a Light Horse regiment, shake hands with a few officers, inspect hurriedly, but with a sure eye to good and bad points, the horses of, perhaps, a single squadron, and be gone in a few minutes, leaving a great trail of dust behind him. His tall and massive, but restlessly active figure, his keen eyes and prominent hooked nose, his terse and forcible speech, and his imperious bearing, radiated an impression of tremendous resolution, quick decision and steely discipline. Troops who caught only one fleeting glimpse of him felt that here at last was a man with the natural qualities of a great and driving commander who, given a great task and supplied, as Allenby was, with a great scheme for its accomplishment, would relentlessly force it through to its conclusion. At last, they had a commander who would live among them and lead them. Within a week of his arrival, Allenby had stamped his personality on the mind of every trooper of the horse and every infantryman of the line.[23]

Officers came to dread his sudden descents. Warnings would be broadcast whenever the chief was on the move: 'BL' for 'Bull loose', or BBL for 'Bloody

Bull loose'. Sometimes he would emerge on horseback, his huge form obvious in the approaching dust-cloud, or he would be chauffeured at top-speed in a Rolls-Royce staff car; though on one early visit, he turned up in a Ford truck driven by an Australian 'clad only in a sleeveless vest and very attenuated shorts'.[24]

Even before his first tour of inspection at the front – a week after reaching Cairo – he had begun a clear-out of GHQ. 'You know,' he explained to a medical officer, 'General Headquarters' roots in Cairo and Ismailia are like alfalfa grass. They are getting too deep into the ground and want pulling up. Moreover, staff officers are like partridges: they are the better for being shot over.'[25] Some 'brass' were purged and sent home, others relocated to Allenby's new, sweltering, fly-blown GHQ at Khan Yunus in Palestine. Geoffrey Inchbald, a junior officer with the Imperial Camel Corps, bore witness to the transformation: 'I have never seen such an array of brass gathered together as I found in the bars and dining-rooms [of Cairo's top hotels] on the first occasion, nor so few as on my second visit.[26]

This played well among the other ranks. Caste privilege and incompetent officers are demoralising. The mood lifts in an army when soldiers sense they are well looked after and effectively led. The new commander was the talk of the trenches. 'Rumour had it that many a muddler had been sent back to London,' reported Sergeant Hatton of the Middlesex Imperial Yeomanry.

> This new general rode about among the troops with only an orderly, instead of a retinue of 30, and spoke to the men themselves, asking after their comfort, if rations were good, and when they last had leave … There's nothing a soldier dislikes so much as being unnecessarily messed about … But under Allenby nothing was done without a purpose. At his advent, our rations and water almost immediately became more regular …[27]

Trooper Ion Idriess also gave grudging approval to the new regime: 'General Allenby has put the whole Anzac Division on B Class. Says they are frightfully overworked. The division is to have a month's spell. Miracles never cease in this land.' He and his mates found themselves transported to Marakeh beach: 'No doubt this is a real spell. No idiotic stirrup polishing or such like tommy-rot. Plenty of bathing, sleep, and fresh water. Just enough training to keep us fit.'[28]

Private John Beer of the newly arrived 60th (London) Division was also impressed by what he called 'the Palestine Riviera', where 'it was quite a treat to go to bed in pyjamas in a bell tent near the sea … a tent nowadays being quite a high form of living, especially after living out in the open, in the desert, with shortage of water …'[29]

Equally important was the growing sense of purpose, of 'getting ready', that pervaded all ranks.[30] As well as infecting the EEF with his own dynamism and ramping up the level of military activity, Allenby took his men into his confidence and instilled a sense of shared purpose. 'Everyone is in a great state of delight at getting a move on at last,' reported Noel Drury, an officer of the Royal Dublin Fusiliers, 'and, specially, as we know beforehand the general outline of the scheme. Why does no other commander realise that the men are capable of taking an intelligent interest in things ...? Thank goodness, Allenby has some common sense and understands his Tommy Atkins.'[31]

Allenby belonged to a rare species: a First World War general who bonded with his men. Despite his shyness, aloofness and volcanic temper – despite the barriers of social class and military caste that separated officers from other ranks in the armies of the age – Allenby won the approval and confidence of the men of the Egyptian Expeditionary Force. This would not be the least factor in the triumphs to come.

* * *

The Ottoman Army also acquired a new commander in the summer of 1917. He was none other than Imperial Germany's former commander-in-chief on the Western Front. General Erich von Falkenhayn had succeeded to the supreme command in September 1914, following his predecessor's defeat at the Battle of the Marne. A traditional career soldier from an impoverished aristocratic background, Falkenhayn's dispatches from China during the Boxer Rebellion (1900) had attracted the attention of the Kaiser and secured him royal favour. Tall, slim and smart, with close-cropped hair, military moustache and steely stare, he was the picture of a Prussian officer. But his stern aloofness – as so often among the officer caste of the age – masked neurotic doubt and indecision. His failed masterwork had been Verdun, a monstrous battle of attrition designed to 'bleed to death' the French nation. It lasted ten months, consumed two-thirds of a million casualties, and left both sides numbed by the horror and futility of the fighting.

Yet Falkenhayn's ruthlessness was not matched by tenacity of purpose. Moltke had sensed this, writing to the Kaiser in January 1915 that his successor, 'despite an apparently strong will ... does not possess the inner forces of spirit and soul to draft and carry through operations of great scope ...' This was military historian Liddell Hart's assessment, too: 'Falkenhayn was history's latest example of the folly of half measures; the ablest and most scientific general – "penny wise, pound foolish" – who ever ruined his country by a refusal to take calculated risks.'

Verdun was the result: a battle that involved no risk, merely stubborn, head-on, unrelenting carnage.[32] The butt of increasing criticism, Falkenhayn had resigned his post in August 1916. He subsequently accepted command of the Ninth Army in Rumania, which had just declared war on the side of the Entente. In a whirlwind six-week campaign, Rumania was overrun and knocked out of the war.[33] His military reputation somewhat restored, Falkenhayn was soon dispatched on the mission that brought him to the Middle East in the summer of 1917. Baghdad had fallen to Maude's Anglo-Indian Army on 11 March 1917, and the German field-marshal arrived at Constantinople in early May charged with its recovery. In late July, when Allenby was *en route* to Cairo, Falkenhayn arrived in Aleppo to assume command of the new *Yilderim* army group being formed to undertake the task.[34]

* * *

Yilderim was Turkish for 'Thunderbolt'. It had been the epithet of Sultan Bayezid I in honour of his victory over the Crusaders at Nicopolis in 1396. It implied, of course, a powerful, fast-moving strike-force. *Yilderim*'s order of battle would eventually include two full armies, the existing Eighth Army commanded by General Freiherr Kress von Kressenstein in southern Palestine, and a new Seventh Army under General Fevzi Pasha, which included divisions withdrawn from service in Europe, where the collapse of Rumania in December and the overthrow of the tsar in March had eased the pressure on the Ottoman Empire's Austro-Hungarian and Bulgarian allies and released two Ottoman corps for redeployment.

Yilderim was to be stiffened with a spine of 6,500 hand-picked German specialist troops. This 'Asia Corps' – or 'Pasha II' as the Ottomans knew it – absorbed existing German units in theatre ('Pasha I'), and would later receive further reinforcements from Germany, eventually numbering seven infantry battalions, each supplied with six heavy machine-guns and eighteen light machine-guns, and further supported by attached units of additional machine-guns (a company of six), trench mortars (a section of four), mountain-guns (an assault platoon of two) and a troop of cavalry. The Asia Corps was also provided with separate batteries of howitzers, field-guns, mountain-guns and anti-aircraft guns, as well as wireless, telephone, hospital and sanitation units, a transport column of 400 lorries and an air component of four squadrons of eight aircraft apiece. With the firepower of a division and the transport column of a corps, Pasha II represented a major escalation of Germany's war-effort in the Middle East.[35]

Falkenhayn, fresh from conquest in the Balkans, came to Aleppo with a grandiose vision of conquest. He was supported by Enver Pasha, the Ottoman war minister, a man also given to Napoleonic schemes. Enver had announced the formation of *Yilderim* and the plan to retake Baghdad during a visit to the Syrian front in June. The Ottoman Empire had lost its nominal authority over Tripoli in October 1911, over Cairo in November 1914, over Mecca in June 1916, and over Baghdad in March 1917. Its claim to Arab-Islamic leadership was in peril. It was for this reason that it remained determined to cling to Medina, and a similar imperative underlay the proposed pivot to Mesopotamia.

Falkenhayn had at first concurred, but the British build-up on the Gaza front during the summer persuaded him otherwise. At a council of war in August he clashed with Enver, arguing that the defence of Palestine was the priority. But his alternative proposal was equally unrealistic: he envisaged a dramatic assault on Allenby's desert flank to roll up the British line and send the Egyptian Expeditionary Force back across Sinai. *Yilderim* – 'Army Group F' as the Germans called it – would then be railed back to Aleppo and projected into Mesopotamia for the descent on Baghdad.

Djemal Pasha was opposed to both schemes. He had his own reasons: Syria was his bailiwick, and increasingly he ruled there as a semi-independent potentate, a political and military strongman with his own territorial base. He therefore opposed any strategy that threatened to weaken the Ottoman line in southern Palestine. As it happened, this was the right call. Jerusalem, Damascus and Aleppo were threatened by Allenby's army, not Maude's. The fall of Baghdad had brought the campaign in Mesopotamia to a temporary impasse. The Anglo-Indian army had reached the limit of its existing communications, and distance and the ferocious summer heat precluded any early resumption of the offensive. The challenges confronting any Ottoman drive in the opposite direction were forbidding: had *Yilderim* been sent to Mesopotamia, it would have found itself at the end of a 500-mile-long supply-line confronting an entrenched army that by the end of 1917 had swelled to 400,000 men.[36] Allenby's army, on the other hand, was 50 miles from Jerusalem, 200 from Damascus, 350 from Aleppo and, should he break through at Gaza, he would be running with the grain of the Levantine communications system. He was, however, far too strong to be dislodged from his toehold along the Wadi Ghuzze. That meant that the only coherent Ottoman strategy was that favoured by Djemal: concentration for a defensive battle on the Gaza line.[37]

The Turco-German high command thus found itself deeply divided. Mustapha Kemal, the hero of Gallipoli, resigned his command of the Seventh Army in protest at Falkenhayn's interference (the more compliant Fevzi Pasha was his replacement). The pique of the emerging Turkish nationalist leader is easy to understand. The *Yilderim* headquarters staff consisted of sixty-five Germans and only nine Turks, most of the latter relatively junior liaison officers. Djemal Pasha also threatened to resign, indignant about his partial eclipse. The compromise that kept him in post was a muddle: Falkenhayn would rule south of Jerusalem and west of the Dead Sea, Djemal in Syria and the Hijaz – a divided command.[38]

There was tension, too, between the established German officers of the Military Mission – who knew the limitations of the Ottoman infrastructure – and the new men of Asia Corps. Kress considered Falkenhayn's offensive ambitions hopelessly optimistic 'at a time when the Anatolian railway could not ensure effective maintenance even of the weak Turkish forces in Palestine, Mesopotamia, and the Hijaz'. He continued:

> Indeed, by this date, the Turkish Army . . . was neither trained nor equipped in a manner suited to modern warfare, and was utterly unfit for any serious offensive operations. Those who knew its true state were amazed that it had succeeded in maintaining itself without serious disaster for close on three years of intensive fighting.[39]

Liman von Sanders was equally sceptical. Falkenhayn had disdained to consult him. Liman responded with ironic comment born of years of frustration in the Ottoman service.

> The German officers of course acted on the experience they had gathered in the theatres of the German fronts, and assumed that here, as in Germany, all orders issued would be carried out. In Turkey one can make the most beautiful plans and prepare the execution by drawings and perfect orders, and something entirely different will be done, or perhaps nothing at all.[40]

Even with local cooperation, much was simply impossible. The ambitiously conceived *Yilderim* army assembling at Aleppo still comprised only three divisions at the end of the summer. Such were the heavy transport requirements of the Asia Corps that it would still be stuck at Haidar Pasha Station on the eastern shore of the Bosphorus as the Third Battle of Gaza was fought. The further projection of force beyond Aleppo – whether to Mesopotamia or Palestine – was dependent on rail and road communications close to collapse. The flow of rations, basic kit and medical supplies to existing units was so erratic that Kress's Eighth Army was losing 3,000 to 4,000 men a month to sickness, and had on average 25 per cent of its strength hospitalised at any one time. 'This lack of men prevented the frequent reliefs of divisions so necessary for rest and training of troops; the inefficiency of the railway service on the lines of communication resulted in a constant shortage of supplies . . .'[41]

Desertion had become an epidemic. About 300,000 men had absconded by the end of 1917, and the back areas teemed with bands of deserters living as outlaws. Every division had lost thousands, many in transit, many from the front, so that divisions were no larger than regiments. 'The Turkish soldier, particularly the Anatolian, is excellent fighting material,' explained Liman. 'Well looked after, sufficiently nourished, properly trained, and calmly led, these men will accomplish the highest aims.' Instead, however:

> For about two years now a great part of the troops have not been granted sufficient time for training, They have been torn apart, before the small and large units have been properly cemented together . . . When sent to the rail-road station, the men for the most part did not know each other or their superiors. They only knew they were being sent to some bad place. Hence they ran away whenever they could, and risked being shot while running. They jumped from the cars in motion, from the marching column in covered terrain, or from the bivouac, or from their billets.[42]

Politicians and generals might concoct ambitious plans for sweeping conquest. But the Ottoman Empire, after three years of modern industrialised warfare, was grinding down. It was as much as field commanders like Kress could do to hold the line. Such were the pressures on the infrastructure that it was mid-September before the transport of Seventh Army from Aleppo to the front could begin, and Fevzi Pasha's HQ did not reach Hebron until 27 October. Long before the new German commander could marshal the forces to attempt a desert *Blitzkrieg*, Allenby was ready with his own sledgehammer blow. When it fell, Falkenhayn himself was still in Aleppo.[43] For his German officers, the name *Yilderim* had come to seem grimly ironic.

* * *

For six months, from late April to late October 1917, the war in Palestine was not far different from that on the Western Front. Men on both sides faced the discomfort and tedium – 'almost a prison life', according to one fed-up Tommy – of trench-war stalemate.[44] The main difference was the climate, especially as the temperature soared to summer-time peaks in excess of 40°C, made worse by scorching *khamsin* winds.[45] 'I shall never forget a scene I saw on 25 April 1917,' wrote Sergeant Minshall of 74th (Yeomanry) Division. 'We were working at full pressure trenching and wiring in the burning sun. The hot winds parched men's lips and throats until some were overcome with the heat and had to be carried to our position. To see big strong men crying like little children for water, "precious water", was terrible.'[46]

Albert 'Ron' Surry, a signaller in the 54th (East Anglian) Division, recalled the misery of simply manning the trenches: 'It was terrifically hot, and the water in the bottles soon reached a temperature near boiling point. The sun beat mercilessly down, and we became reduced almost to a state of exhaustion, so that it was with difficulty that we were able to breathe.' He was sent out on a patrol, despite suffering from dysentery, and collapsed when he returned: 'I lay on the bottom of the trench beaten, without cover from the broiling sun, as at that time we were not issued with khaki bivouac sheets, and we were not allowed to spread a blanket across the top of the trench as it made a too conspicuous object for aerial observations.'[47]

Compounding the misery was the dust of Palestine – in contrast to the sand of Sinai. 'Sand one can put up with quite easily,' thought Lieutenant Case, a Royal Engineers officer with the 60th (London) Division, 'for although unpleasant in one's food and in one's clothes, it is always clean and easy to shake away, but dust is absolutely filthy. It covers everything, and gets everywhere. It will require all the willpower I possess to live in this filthy, vile dust-fog for long, and not develop a temper like a demon.'[48]

Unable to wash without a long trek to the sea, men became infested with vermin. Woollen underclothes and a flannel 'spine pad' inside tunics designed to protect against heatstroke spawned colonies of lice. 'I am smothered with lice,' wrote Private Blunt of the Civil Service Rifles, 60th Division. 'Every morning and whenever there is a spare minute, everyone takes off their shirts and opens their trousers to hunt out lice ...'.

Fleas infested the bodies of men and beasts. 'I am sitting in my dug-out now and it's just 2 o'clock in the morning,' Stanley Goodland, Somerset Light Infantry, 75th Division, explained to his wife. 'We've been heavily shelled all night and have had no rest. I can't sleep now, for we have an epidemic of fleas and mice in these trenches. Last night, when I woke up to do duty, I was a mass of bites and I think nowhere on my body could you have put a five-shilling bit without touching a spot. Tonight it's just as bad.'

The flies were also a torment. 'Flies by the million pestering one whenever one stays still, flies in your drink, flies in your food, flies in your tent, flies wherever they can be most inconvenient and annoying' (Lieutenant Case). The heat and the flies made daytime sleep impossible, adding to the crushing tedium of trench life.

Then there were the scorpions. They would creep unseen into blankets, and it was wise to shake them out before sleep; but unwelcome visitors might arrive during the night. 'The moment you touched him with a stick,' observed Anthony Bluett of the Camel Corps, describing an encounter with a scorpion, 'he elevated his poisonous battering-ram, which was as long as himself, and struck and struck again in an ecstasy of rage, until he actually poisoned himself and died from his own blows.[49]

The water was too little and often infected. The diet was usually dull, monotonous, and unhealthy: mainly bully beef, 'Maconochie' stew (a tinned mixture of scraps of meat and overcooked chunks of carrot and turnip floating in gravy), and army biscuits of tooth-shattering hardness. The meat-and-veg stew had a regrettable effect on men's insides. 'One of the features of the night marches was the frightful stink,' noted Doug Calcutt, a Cockney private in 60th Division. 'The Maconochie stew ration gave the troops flatulence of a particularly offensive nature. So we marched along in air released by hundreds of men breaking wind.'[50]

The worst of it was that the rotten diet – especially the lack of fresh fruit and vegetables – contributed to an epidemic of septic sores. Bites and scratches routinely became infected as plagues of flies attacked the smallest wound. The Worcestershire Yeomanry medical officer Captain Teichman reported that 'the slightest scratch from the barbed-wire caused septic sores, which were often followed by serious inflammation'; in May the sickness rate in his brigade amounted to 10 per cent hospital admissions daily due to septic sores; 'everyone was thoroughly stale and listless.'[51] Other men were struck down by 'sandfly fever', which 'left those attacked limp and exhausted for days', yet others by malaria, including 3,000 of the newly arrived 10th Division, who had contracted the disease in the Balkans.[52]

Allenby declared war on the flies, issuing wire swatters and ordering all men not directly involved with the enemy to spend 15 minutes killing flies at sunset when they settled.[53] The success or otherwise of the commander-in-chief's campaign against the flies is not recorded.

* * *

But as summer passed into autumn, a new mood pervaded the Egyptian Expeditionary Force. It was partly 'the Allenby effect'. When he arrived, the army, in Wavell's words, 'were discouraged and cynical: they had lost faith in the higher command and themselves . . . The force was in the doldrums, becalmed and dispirited, held between failure and success.'[54] The transformation was absolute: 'Allenby introduced into the army a new and incalculably improved moral tone,' reported the Australian *Official History*. But this was not just down to the personality of the commander-in-chief: the soldiers knew that he had the backing of London, that the army was doubling in size, and that massive new infrastructure was being put in place.

What had hitherto been a rather casual military adventure with no definite goal was suddenly converted into a stern, clear-cut campaign with nothing short of the complete destruction of the Turkish force in Palestine and the capture of Jerusalem as its immediate objective. All ranks were conscious that at last they had emerged from the wilderness, and that the Promised Land was shining before them.[55]

The vibes from London had grown stronger through the summer. General Nivelle, the new head of the French Army, had launched an offensive in Champagne on the Western Front proclaiming, 'We have a formula . . . victory is certain.' He did not. The French lost 120,000 men in five days. A month later, Nivelle was sacked. By that time, his army was paralysed by a wave of mutinies. The *poilus* (French rank-and-file soldiers) had had enough. The revolt started in late April, grew in May and peaked in June. Desertion became an epidemic, entire units refused to go back into the line, and demonstrations were held in which soldiers sang revolutionary songs. Around 40,000 men were directly involved, and 68 divisions were affected. During one two-week period, the front-line was virtually denuded of French troops.[56]

The situation on the Eastern Front was even more disastrous. The so-called 'Kerensky offensive' in July fell apart before it got going. Unstable and unpopular, Russia's provisional government had offered a revolutionary people further carnage and impoverishment. Many of the conscript *muzhiks* had simply refused to leave their trenches. The offensive had been a 'complete failure', reported General Brusilov, because 'the officers, from the company commander to the commander-in-chief, have no power'.[57] Soon tens of thousands would be arresting officers, fraternising with the enemy, and debating the Bolshevik programme of 'peace, bread, and land'; others would simply head for home, shooting officers who tried to stop them.[58]

All hope of ending the war in 1917 had evaporated. Popular support for it was turning into mass opposition. The shift to the left across war-ravaged Europe was becoming a landslide. Telegrams from London squawked the need for good news from the Holy Land: 'During the coming autumn and winter,' read an August cable to Allenby, 'it is necessary to strike the Turks as hard as possible, since a good success achieved against them will tend to strengthen the morale and staying-power of this country during a season when important successes in Europe may not be feasible . . .'

A corollary of the Entente's sagging fortunes was the availability of Ottoman troops for service in the Middle East and the possibility that *Yilderim* would prevent Maude securing the Mesopotamian oil-fields.

The Turks may shortly be free to concentrate the greater part of their forces against you and Maude in view of the Russian situation ... In order to take advantage of the Arab situation and to relieve the pressure upon Maude by forcing the enemy to divert troops to Palestine, it is important that you should press the Turks opposed to you to the fullest extent of your variable resources as early as possible in September.[59]

* * *

The government was eager to supply the men and materiel to make this possible. With Allenby's request for seven infantry divisions, three mounted divisions, full complements of divisional and corps artillery, and five squadrons of aircraft, London complied except for a slight shortfall in guns. The EEF commander was able to reorganise his army into three full corps. The Desert Mounted Corps, commanded by Chauvel, comprised the Anzac, Australian and Yeomanry Mounted Divisions, each of three brigades, plus the Imperial Camel Corps Brigade. XX Corps, under Chetwode, comprised the 10th (Irish), 53rd (Welsh), 60th (London) and 74th (Yeomanry) Division (the Irish and the Londoners having been transferred from Salonika, the Yeomanry having been dismounted and reorganised as infantry). XXI Corps, under Bulfin, comprised the 52nd (Lowland), 54th (East Anglian) and 75th (Wessex) Division (the latter formed of territorial battalions previously stationed in India).

Most divisions had a full equipment of 36 field-guns (18-pounders) and 12 howitzers (either 3.7-inch or 4.5-inch). The corps artillery totalled 2 medium field-guns (6-inch), 28 heavy field-guns (60-pounders), 50 medium howitzers (6-inch), and 8 heavy howitzers (8-inch). The Desert Mounted Corps was equipped with a further 46 guns, mainly Royal Horse Artillery 18-pounders. This was sufficient. The army had the gun-power to neutralise enemy batteries, smash his trenches, cut the wire, and provide covering fire as infantry and cavalry went in. The grand total of the EEF's new order of battle was 75,000 rifles, 17,000 sabres and 475 guns – roughly twice Murray's strength at the Second Battle of Gaza, and roughly twice that of Kress von Kressenstein currently.[60]

A commensurate infrastructure was necessary to sustain such a host on the edge of the desert. The further industrialisation of Sinai was essential. Kantara on the canal became a port with quays where ocean-going steamers could be berthed and unloaded. Beyond the port were huge railway sidings, sheds and workshops, miles of metalled road, acres of store-dumps, and a town-sized settlement of huts and tents.[61] The Sinai Railway was doubled. It was also extended from Rafa to the Wadi Ghuzze in two directions, along the coast north-eastwards through Khan Yunus to Belah, and eastwards inland to Shellal. Beyond the main railheads, little Decauville spur-lines were laid to bring supplies closer to different parts of the front. Some of these were within sight and range of enemy guns. Tommy drivers gave their miniature locomotives names like 'Iron Duke', 'Lion' and 'Jerusalem Cuckoo'. One line would later carry 850 tons of artillery ammunition to the gun batteries in a single day of fighting.[62]

The carrying-capacity of even the doubled line across the desert was insufficient. But Britain was both an industrial and a maritime power, so alongside the train worked the steamer. A fleet of small vessels of 1,000 to 1,500 tons burden plied the route between Port Said and Belah. The ships would anchor about 150 yards offshore, and would then be unloaded into small boats. Egyptian, Maltese and West African labourers worked the boats, though the most proficient proved to be Raratongans from the South Pacific serving with the New Zealanders. Most could carry four 60-pounder shells at a time, and 30 of them could do as much work in a day as 170 British soldiers.[63]

Vast dumps accumulated at the port and the railheads. The management and onward transhipment of supplies from the dumps was another industrial process, involving caterpillar tractors, fleets of lorries and a web of wire roads.[64] But here, because of the limited supply of motor transport, the condition of the roads, and the clogging sand and dust, modernity and tradition intersected. Supplying XX Corps with its water, for example, were 73 lorries, but also 6,000 camels.[65] The armies of the First World War were only semi-industrialised. As well as 96,000 fighting men (and about 100,000 other military personnel and 60,000 native labourers in the rear areas), there were 46,000 horses, 40,000 camels, 15,000 mules and 3,500 donkeys working for the Egyptian Expeditionary Force in late 1917.[66]

The Turks would be driven from Jerusalem when a prophet of God brought the waters of the Nile to Palestine: so ran the Arab prophecy. Transliterated into Arabic, Allenby's name could be read as *Allah en nebi* ('the prophet of God'). And sure enough, the British water-pipe had brought the waters of the Nile to Palestine.[67]

But it could not bring enough. Water was the single biggest problem. It was in short supply on the edge of the desert, it was heavy to carry, and total consumption was in excess of half a million gallons per day. Army engineers were busy all the time laying pipelines, constructing reservoirs and searching for new sources of supply. A branch pipeline was laid from Rafa to Shellal, and spare pipe-sections were stockpiled for future use. A lucky strike at Khan Yunus was yielding 100,000 gallons a day. Wells at Belah provided additional water, though suitable for animals only. Spring-water – slightly saline, but potable – had been tapped at Shellal, and a rock-basin was dammed to create a half-million-gallon capacity reservoir, with facilities for the filling of 2,000 camel water-containers an hour (25,000 gallons). As well as the divisional supply-trains – a mix of tractors, trucks, camels and mules for carrying forward water, food and munitions – GHQ created a reserve train of four 'heavy burden' camel companies (about 7,000 beasts) for use in emergencies. Shortly before the offensive began, further wells were opened up on the desert flank and provided with pumps and canvas troughs – at Esani, 10 miles south-west of Beersheba, and at Khalassa and Asluj, 16 miles south of it.[68]

The improved water supply was adequate – though limited – so long as the enlarged army remained stationery. Once mobile warfare resumed, however, the transport links would snap in a dozen places: the rapid capture of enemy wells would be critical, especially on the inland flank. To prepare men for the ordeal to come, water abstinence became part of an intensive training programme. The ration was limited to half a gallon a day for all purposes over a period of three weeks.[69] Units would be sent on long marches in full pack through waterless desert and limited to a quart of water per man. Marches might culminate in simulated combat, with advances, wire-cutting and charges, while shells whistled overhead.

The training served several purposes: it acclimatised and reconditioned newly arrived units; it counteracted the debilitating effect of trench warfare; it prepared the army for the hard marching and fighting to come; and it rekindled a sense of mission and *esprit de corps*. Trench raids across no-man's-land – as well as serving practical purposes like collecting intelligence and intimidating the enemy – were also designed to foster an offensive spirit.

Most men conceded the value of training and raids, even if they complained at the time; they were far less tolerant of the endless routine of fatigues, drill and 'bull'. Latent class antagonisms were sometimes pricked. 'All grousing and grumbling in fine style', recorded the Londoner Doug Calcutt. '"Fuck the Army!" being the prevailing sentiment.' Bullying NCOs and snobbish officers were especially hated. But the dominant mood seems to have been aggressive and confident. A mix of time in the line, time spent training and time relaxing on the 'Palestine Riviera' kept men fresh, fit and eager. Allenby was forging an instrument of victory.[70]

* * *

The Ottoman defences around Gaza had been sufficient to defeat two British assaults in the spring. In the intervening six months, these defences had been greatly strengthened. The deep belt of trenches and cactus-hedges around the town was now manned by the 3rd and 53rd Divisions of XXII Corps. Along the road running south-east from Gaza to Beersheba lay a series of strong trench-redoubts defended by XX Corps – Beer Trenches and Tank Redoubt (54th Division), Atawineh and Hairpin Redoubts (26th Division), and Hareira and Sheria Redoubts (16th Division). At Hareira, about 15 miles inland, the line was bent back, running about 5 miles eastwards along a deep wadi to Sheria, the hook thus formed constituting a heavily defended but 'refused' left flank. The 7th Division was in reserve north of Gaza.

Beersheba, 15 miles south-east of Hareira, had been organised as a detached fortress. On the eve of battle it was defended not by Kress von Kressenstein's Eighth Army, but by III Corps of Fevzi Pasha's Seventh, part of the new *Yilderim* force: 27th Division was entrenched in the high ground around the town, 3rd Cavalry Division active in the surrounding area, and 24th Division in reserve. The 19th Division was in reserve north of Beersheba and the 12th Depot Regiment was on the Jerusalem–Hebron road.

British intelligence estimated total Ottoman strength at between 40,000 to 45,000 rifles, 1,500 sabres and 300 guns.[71] This appears to have been a gross overestimate. The average strength of the Ottoman divisions was only 3,000 men – the equivalent of a British brigade, the theoretical strength of an Ottoman regiment. The true totals were probably closer to 32,000 rifles, 1,400 sabres and 270 guns. Two-thirds of these were defending the main Gaza–Hareira–Sheria line.[72]

South of Gaza, for a distance of about three miles from the sea to Sheikh Abbas Ridge, the British and Ottoman trenches ran close, typically only a few hundred yards apart. Then the British line bent back to run south-west along the ridge-line until it met the Wadi Ghuzze. The wide region beyond was, of course, the preserve of Desert Mounted Corps, which, with a massive numerical advantage over the opposing Ottoman horse, was securely in control of the open ground. The Ottoman calculation was to discount the desert flank. Kress had the balance of his force on his right, in anticipation of another direct assault on Gaza. He knew, of course, that the enemy's greatest advantage was in the mounted arm – a 10:1 advantage as against less than 2:1 in infantry and artillery. But the desert was waterless, except for the wells at Beersheba, so he assumed that sustained, large-scale operations, especially by cavalry, whose horses would require 5 gallons a day, were not possible. 'Owing to the shortage of water', he wrote on 15 October, 'it is impossible that large mounted forces will operate from the east of Beersheba.'[73] He was wrong.

Lieutenant-General Sir Philip Chetwode had produced a detailed military 'appreciation' of the situation on the Gaza front back in May. Chetwode – commander of Desert Column under Murray and now XX Corps under Allenby – was another Boer War cavalryman with a wise head on his shoulders.

He had been ably assisted by Brigadier-General Guy Dawnay – whom Lawrence, in fact, considered the main architect of the new offensive.

> Beneath his mathematical surface were hidden passionate many-sided convictions, a reasoned scholarship in higher warfare, and a brilliant bitterness of judgement . . . He was the least professional of soldiers, a banker who read Greek history, a strategist unashamed, and a burning poet with strength to deny the littleness of daily things . . . Dawnay was not the man to fight a straight battle. He sought to destroy the enemy's strength with the least fuss, not by hitting it directly, but by studying his moral weaknesses and developing them . . .[74]

The plan, as all good plans tend to be, was simple enough: the real challenge, as ever, was to make its execution feasible. Chetwode proposed feinting against Gaza to fix the Turks and draw in reserves, while massing for an attack on the left of the Ottoman line. 'The enemy has put all his best work, all his wire, into the Gaza front as far as Atawineh. His works in the Hareira area are certainly formidable, but there he has not the depth that he has elsewhere, nor the wire; nor have we elsewhere the observation that we should have in attacking his left flank.'

The pivot of the battle, then, was to be the Hareira–Sheria complex of redoubts guarding the left of the main Ottoman position. But the first objective would be Beersheba, the detached trench-fortress on the far left, the capture of which would allow the British cavalry to water and then swing north-west to outflank Hareira–Sheria while the infantry attacked it from the south and south-east. The plan would permit the British to make effective use of their 'great preponderance of mounted troops'; and to use them in such a way that they might break into the enemy rear, cut the Gaza road, and make possible the total destruction of the Ottoman Eighth Army.[75]

Allenby studied the Chetwode/Dawnay plan and approved it, but then developed it further, knowing well enough that no plan survives first contact with the enemy.[76] The heady vision of a rapid mounted breakthrough had something in common with Falkenhayn's scheme for a desert *Blitzkrieg*: neither paid sufficient attention to the capabilities and intelligence of the enemy. In particular, Allenby had to allow for the proven doggedness of Ottoman infantry defending entrenchments. So a range of options and alternatives was built into the plan. A succession of blows would be landed on different parts of the enemy line. As well as pinning him in his trenches and drawing down his reserves, the aim was to keep him off-balance and confused. The intention would be to smash through on the desert flank; but there would be a readiness to respond to such exigencies and opportunities as might arise elsewhere.[77]

The basic plan was as follows. Bulfin's XXI Corps, with 36,000 men and 218 guns, was to launch a direct attack on Gaza to fix the enemy's attention on his right flank. Chetwode's XX Corps and Chauvel's Desert Mounted Corps, with a total of 47,500 infantry, 11,000 cavalry and 242 guns – the main strike-force – would hit the enemy's left, first attacking Beersheba, then the Hareira–Sheria complex. The 5,000 men of Barrow's Yeomanry Mounted Division would act as a covering force in the centre.

For the plan to work, the Ottomans had to be convinced, both before and in the early stages of the battle, that Gaza was again the main target. The danger was of an untimely strengthening of the enemy's left. An elaborate, multi-faceted deception plan was therefore developed. Camps were laid out on Cyprus, as if preparations were under way for a coastal landing at Alexandretta, deep in the Ottoman rear.[78] Lawrence organised a bridge-blowing raid on the Yarmuk Valley (abortive in the event), to further focus the enemy on the security of Syria.[79] The Royal Navy was active along the coast off Gaza, taking soundings and collecting a fleet of small boats, as if landings in the enemy rear were intended; an impression confirmed by badly enciphered wireless communications on a wavelength the enemy was known to access.[80] Strong cavalry reconnaissances, pushed up close to the Beersheba defences, became fortnightly events, so as to accustom the enemy to a high level of merely 'demonstrative' activity in the sector.[81] The bulk of the army was kept in front of Gaza as long as possible, and the strike-force was moved, secretly and rapidly, to its assembly points only at the last moment, its abandoned camps left standing, lights showing at night.[82] Extensions to the light railway and the digging of new wells in the desert were delayed. So was the accumulation of dumps of rations and munitions, and when it was done, the work was performed at night and the results heavily camouflaged.[83]

Perhaps the most ingenious deception device was that concocted by intelligence officer Richard Meinertzhagen. Having compiled a dummy staff-officer's notebook full of false information about plans and problems, he rode out towards enemy lines on 10 October until he attracted the attention of a mounted patrol and induced it to give chase. When they appeared to draw rein, he stopped, dismounted and fired. Provoked into resuming the chase, the patrol this time blazed away as they galloped forward. 'Now was my chance,' Meinertzhagen wrote in his diary, 'and in my effort to mount I loosened my haversack, field-glasses, water-bottle, dropped my rifle, previously stained with some fresh blood from my horse, and in fact did everything to make them believe I was hit and that my flight was disorderly.'[84]

The haversack – which, to add authenticity, also contained some personal letters – was recovered by the patrol. The contents of the notebook implied, of course, that the main British effort would directed against Gaza. Kress, though he considered the possibility of a ruse, was inclined to take the notebook at face-value – in large part, no doubt, because it confirmed his own assumption.[85]

The Gaza deception campaign was a complete success. Critical to it was that the Egyptian Expeditionary Force had, for the first time, wrested air supremacy from its enemies. Allenby had requested five squadrons of aircraft in July; this request had been very nearly met, and he had four squadrons available for service, over sixty machines, on the eve of battle. The Palestine Brigade of the Royal Flying Corps (RFC), with main aerodromes at Belah and Nuran, was commanded by Brigadier-General Geoffrey Salmond, an artillery officer who had become one of the pioneers of British military aviation as early as 1913. Salmond was an example of the emerging class of intelligent, visionary, enterprising officers who flourished in the new techno-war. He often flew in person, for, as one of his flight-sergeants observed in relation to an operation in January 1917, 'he was not the type to sit at the Savoy Hotel like General Murray and his staff. He was as keen as the pilots ... to see that the work went as planned.'[86]

RFC air-crew were largely a self-selecting military elite – 'cavaliers of the air' – but they had been hamstrung on the Palestine front by second-rate kit until the summer of 1917. Marginal technical superiority – in speed and performance – is often decisive in air war. A new machine, the Bristol Fighter, now gave the RFC the edge. One of the most successful fighter aircraft of the First World War – over 3,000 would be built between summer 1917 and autumn 1918 – it was unquestionably superior to all the varied aircraft flown by German, Austrian and Turkish pilots during the campaign.[87] Though complete control of the airspace was impossible – the aircraft available were too few and too slow – enemy pilots quickly discovered the new-found superiority of their opponents and tended to fly high and avoid contact.[88]

* * *

Allenby had hoped to attack in September, to give his army time to push deep into Palestine before the rains came. But men and guns were still in transit at this time, and he preferred the greater certainty of victory when preparations were complete.[89] October, then. The end of the month, in fact. The offensive was scheduled to begin early on the morning of the 31st.

Bernard Blaser, a scout and mapper with the London Scottish, was making his final preparations the afternoon before. He and his mates would be assaulting the trenches south of Beersheba the following morning. Each man was given two grenades and an extra bandolier of ammo. Some were allocated coloured flare-lights as location signals for aerial spotters, others wire-cutters and circular saws.

Forty-eight hours' rations were issued, consisting of bully beef, biscuit, jam and dried fruit, together with a small bottle of tea and rum. A hot meal was served; the last we were to have from the cooks for many weeks. The camp was cleared up, everything packed, and we made ready to start. We were in position by midnight, and the attack was to be launched at dawn.[90]

Ion Idriess and the Australian Light Horse were also on the move that night, headed east of Beersheba. Horses had been given their fill of fodder and water, each man allocated three days' rations, and they were now riding down a metalled road between the hills amid a rumble of artillery, transport and ambulances. 'We knew it led to Beersheba. All were excited, each in his own quiet way. I had that queer, almost subconscious fear I have when I know that soon I will be under heavy fire, and then we must advance into it.'[91]

The heat of the day was gone, but not the dust and thirst. The London newsman W.T. Massey watched the night-time approach march:

Where the tracks were sandy, some brigades often appeared to be advancing through one of London's own particular fogs. Men's faces became caked with yellow dust, their nostrils hot and burning, and parched throats could not be relieved because of the necessity of conserving the water allowance. A hot day was in prospect on the morrow, and the fear of having to fight on an empty water-bottle prevented many a gallant fellow broaching his supply before daybreak.[92]

Away to the west, the guns were booming and flashing at Gaza. The bombardment that had begun three days before was rising to its crescendo.

Almost 150,000 men – Turkish, Arab, German, Austrian on one side; English, Scottish, Welsh, Irish, Australian, New Zealander on the other – were preparing for battle. Many were overawed by a sense of history. Palestine was one of the world's most contested battlegrounds. Now it was their turn. The Third Battle of Gaza was to be the greatest battle in the Levant since the Ottoman conquest of the Middle East four centuries before.

CHAPTER 12

The Railway War

L AWRENCE HAD ALREADY decided to pull out when the Arab lookout on top of the hill shouted down that a train was standing at Hallat Ammar Station. By the time he had climbed up to look for himself, the train was moving. Racing back down the slope, he yelled to his men to get into position, and there was a wild scramble over sand and rock.

The 80-odd riflemen were posted in a line just below the lip of a low ridge running parallel with the railway and about 150 yards from it. Two sergeant-instructors had set up their weapons at one end of this line, about 300 yards from the intended demolition, and so placed that they would take the train in enfilade. Yells, an Australian, 'long, thin, and sinuous, his suppled body lounging in unmilitary curves', had charge of two Lewis light machine-guns, and Brooke, 'a stocky English yeoman, workmanlike and silent', operated a Stokes mortar; accordingly they were known as 'Lewis' and 'Stokes'. Salem, Feisal's best slave and one of four with the expedition, having pleaded for the honour of operating the exploder, was waiting in some hollows at the bottom of the ridge. Lawrence had spent some hours the previous day planting a 50lb charge of blasting gelatine on top of a bridge and then burying the 200-yard cable. He now placed himself on a little hillock near the bridge from which he could signal to Salem when the moment for detonation came.

One man continued to keep watch from the hilltop: a necessary precaution, for if the train were to halt and the troops it carried disembark behind the hill, the raiders would be taken in the rear. But it kept coming, making as much speed as it could. The Ottomans aboard, already alerted to the presence of a raiding party in the area, opened a random fire into the desert. The racket of steam engine and shooting sounded steadily louder as the train approached the waiting men. Salem 'danced round the exploder on his knees, crying with excitement, and calling urgently on God to make him fruitful'. But Lawrence became anxious. There was a lot of firing from the train. How many men was this? Were there enough Arabs to deal with them? The fight would be at close-quarters, and escape hazardous if things went wrong.

Much had already gone wrong. Lawrence had set out from Aqaba on 7 September intending to attack Mudawwara, an oasis settlement with a substantial water-supply about 100 miles south of Maan. Disruption of the water installations here would have imposed a heavy logistical burden on the Ottomans, forcing them to fill trains with water, both to service the railway and supply their garrisons. But bickering between rival clans of Howeitat at Guweira had prevented him raising the 300 men he needed, and he had returned to Aqaba to seek Feisal's assistance. Setting out again a week later, he had barely a third of the number he wanted: about 100 tribesmen, 4 slaves and 10 freedmen of Feisal's, and the 2 British Army weapon specialists. Nor had the tribal tensions been resolved. The most senior Arab leader present was Zaal abu Tayi, Auda's nephew, but only 25 were his clansmen, and the rest questioned his authority, so Lawrence found himself *de facto* leader of an expedition that was 'not a happy family'. They headed east, nonetheless, through the mountains of Rum, with their towering red-sandstone cliffs and black-basalt screes, then out across the baked mud-flats beyond and through the sand desert, reaching Mudawwara, 50 miles distant, late on the second day (17 September). But the position was too strong to attack: reconnaissance revealed a long line of station buildings transformed into blockhouses, and a garrison estimated at 200 to 300 strong.

After camping for the night, the raiders headed south, towards a range of low hills, seeking a place for an ambush. Having selected a site and laid a charge, they began the long wait for a train. Before one came, however, the Arabs detailed to guard the camels climbed to the top of the ridge and were seen silhouetted against the skyline both from Mudawwara Station, about 9 miles to the north, and Hallat Ammar Station, 4 miles to the south. It was already sunset, too late for the Turks to react to what they had seen. But early next day, a detachment of about forty set out from Hallat Ammar. Some thirty Bedouin were dispatched to distract them. Around noon, matters became critical when a further 100 Turks headed out from Mudawwara. The raiding party was in danger of having its line of retreat cut off. Precipitate withdrawal was delayed only by the last-minute sighting of the train at Hallat Ammar, steam up, about to move.

The ambush site had been well-chosen. The main hill provided a vantage-point for observation and concealed the presence of the raiding party. The railway turned a double dog-leg at this point, running east–west for a short distance, parallel with the 50ft high ledge of rock where the Arab riflemen were

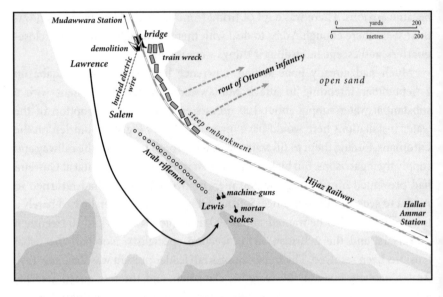

15. The Hallat Ammar Ambush, 19 September 1917.

posted on the morning of 19 September. Just beyond the second dog-leg, as the line resumed its northward progress, it passed over a low, two-arched bridge. This was ideal for a demolition. The locomotive was likely to plunge into the wadi, pulling the carriages behind with it; and even if the locomotive somehow got clear, the carriages would be derailed by the broken arch and their own forward momentum.

But Lawrence's anxiety increased when the train 'rocked with screaming whistles into view around the bend'. Instead of one engine, there were two, and these were followed by ten box-wagons, rifle-muzzles at every door and window, and little sandbag emplacements of Ottoman soldiers on the roofs. He made the snap decision to detonate the charge under the second locomotive, 'so that however little the mine's effect, the uninjured engine should not be able to uncouple and drag the carriages away'.

The two locomotives steamed past the rocky ledge which concealed Lewis guns, Stokes mortar, the over-excited Salem with his exploder and eighty Arab riflemen. When the driver of the second engine was over the bridge, Lawrence raised his hand. 'There followed a terrific roar, and the line vanished from sight behind a spouting column of black dust and smoke 100 feet high and wide. Out of the darkness came shattering crashes and long, loud metallic clangings of ripped steel, with many lumps of iron and plate; while one entire wheel of a locomotive whirled up suddenly black out of the cloud against the sky, and sailed musically over our heads to fall slowly and heavily into the desert behind.

Except for the flight of these, there succeeded a deathly silence, with no cry of men or rifle-shot, as the now-grey mist of the explosion drifted from the line towards us, and over our ridge until it was lost in the hills.'

The bridge was destroyed by the blast. The front engine was derailed and left listing, its cab burst, steam hissing at pressure. The cab and tender of the second engine were torn to strips and cast amid the rubble of the bridge, 'a blanched pile of smoking iron'. The front wagon had plunged into the mini wadi. Filled with typhus victims, 'the smash had killed all but three or four, and had rolled dead and dying into a bleeding heap against the splintered end'. The succeeding wagons were derailed and damaged, some with buckled frames. Parts of cylinders, wheels, pistons and boiler-plating had been hurled up to 300 yards from the centre of the blast. The effects of the explosion had exceeded expectations.

In the momentary lull, as the protagonists – dazed Turks in the broken wagons, awestruck Arabs on the ledge above – came to their senses, Lawrence raced to join the British NCOs. As he did so, the Arabs surged forward to within 20 yards or so of the wrecked train. The little desert battlefield was soon alive with lethal close-range fire, the bullets ripping into the woodwork of the slumped carriages as soldiers tumbled from the doors. Then the machine-guns opened up. Though disadvantaged by their height – resulting in plunging rather than sweeping fire – the Lewis guns were angled along the enemy line, 'and the long rows of Turks on the carriage roofs rolled over, and were swept off the top like bales of cotton before the furious shower of bullets which stormed along the roofs and splashed clouds of yellow chips from the planking'. The Turks who managed to get clear scurried behind the railway embankment, which sloped steeply on the far side, and there improvised a firing line, shooting back through the wheels at the Bedouin opposite.

A protracted firefight might have ensued, but this the Arabs could not afford with columns approaching from north and south: they needed a quick end. 'The enemy in the crescent of the curving line were secure from the machine-guns. But Stokes slipped in his first shell, and after a few seconds there came a crash as it burst beyond the train in the desert. He touched the elevating screw, and his second shot fell just by the trucks in the deep hollow below the bridge where the Turks were taking refuge. It made a shambles of the place. The survivors of the group broke out in a panic across the desert, throwing away their rifles and equipment as they ran. This was the opportunity of the Lewis gunners. The sergeant grimly traversed with drum after drum, till the open sand was littered with bodies.'

* * *

It had taken 10 minutes. The fighting had been sudden, bloody and one-sided. Seventy Turks had been slain, most killed by the Stokes mortar or the Lewis machine-guns, with another thirty wounded and ninety taken prisoner. Only two Arabs had been killed and three wounded.

The moment it ended, the Arabs rushed the train and tore it part. The scene was transformed from one of close-quarters killing to one of frenzied plundering.

> The valley was a weird sight. The Arabs, gone raving mad, were rushing about at top speed bareheaded and half-naked, screaming, shooting into the air, clawing one another nail and fist, while they burst open trucks and staggered back and forward with immense bales, which they ripped by the railside, and tossed through, smashing what they did not want. There were scores of carpets spread about; dozens of mattresses and flowered quilts; blankets in heaps; clothes for men and women in full variety; clocks, cooking-pots, food, ornaments and weapons … Camels had become common property. Each man frantically loaded the nearest with what it could carry and shooed it westward into the void, while he turned to his next fancy.

The withdrawal was chaotic but successful. The Bedouin fled westwards across the desert with their booty as soon as they could, the war band now transformed into 'a stumbling baggage-caravan'. Lawrence and the two NCOs remained behind to bring off the electrical cable and the guns. They were assisted by Zaal and his cousin, who rushed back with some camels in the nick of time. The train-wreck and the dead were then left to the little columns of Turks trudging towards the battlefield from Mudawwara and Hallat Ammar Stations.[1]

* * *

The Hijaz Railway extended for 800 miles between Damascus and Medina. A single-track, narrow-gauge railway, it had been constructed between 1900 and 1908, ostensibly to transport Hajj pilgrims to the Islamic Holy Land. It reduced the journey-time from a month to three days, and made it much safer and cheaper, mainly because it cut out the Bedouin camel-men, wayside traders and raiding parties. Because of this, the construction of the railway had been contested, and parts of it had been militarised before the war, with some station buildings loop-holed for defence. The railway, in any case, served a strategic as well as a religious purpose. A work of piety that strengthened the sultan-caliph's claim to religious leadership over the world's Muslims, a monument to industrial civilisation and the Ottoman Empire's modernising aspirations, it also enhanced the ruling power's capacity to project military force into Arabia.

In a sense, too, the railway was a frontier. To the west lay the more settled regions of Syria and the Hijaz: regions, until the war at least, under effective Ottoman control. To the east lay hundreds of miles of desert: a *barbaricum* populated by nomadic pastoralists and ruled by tribal potentates. The 79 stations along the line, one every 10 miles on average, often located at places of gathering and camping used by nomads, caravans and raiding parties for thousands of years, functioned like little frontier-posts.[2] Most comprised one, two, or at most three modest, single-storey, flat-roofed buildings constructed of stone blocks. The defensive potential of these was easily realised: steel shutters, loopholes knocked through walls, and mud-brick or sandbag parapets on the rooftops converted them into blockhouses; connecting lines of stone breast-work turned two or three such into a miniature desert fort; stretches of trench, cut in zigzags of fire-bay and traverse, provided effective outworks. The iron road had first transformed the landscape by replacing traditional camel-mounted movement with industrialised movement; now the war transformed it again, converting a civil railway into a military life-line, pilgrim stations into desert forts.[3]

But this was not enough. The stations, like beads on a thread laid across the desert, were too few and too low-sited to be secure. Wide, unseen spaces lay beyond them, and many were overshadowed by high ground nearby. So the evolving Ottoman counter-insurgency required new blockhouses and fortlets in the gaps between stations – perhaps two, three or four, such that each little post was within sight of the next – and also hilltop redoubts, usually a ring of trench, breastwork, sandbags and loopholes.[4] The narrow double-stripe of iron rail thus widened into a militarised band a mile or two across, a zone of posts for watching the line, of firebases arranged for mutual support, and of garrisons to defend them and patrol the ground between. Each desert station was manned by 100, 200 or 300 soldiers. Each little post was defended by a section or a platoon. Thousands of men spread out along 800 miles of desert.

It was as much as the creaking Ottoman war-effort could do to guard the line; there was nothing to spare to patrol and contest, let alone occupy and control, the tens of thousands of square miles of desert beyond. And though the railway the Ottoman Army clung to, and depended upon, and were deployed to defend, represented industry, empire and modernity, it was what it was: a one-dimensional line between two fixed points. But the desert was not like this: it was formed of two dimensions and an infinity of points. And the desert was the domain of the camel. The war, at one level, was a contest between the train and the camel – a contest the camel was destined to win.

* * *

For sure, the long age of the camel was coming to an end. The one-humped dromedary seems to have been domesticated in southern Arabia some time after 3000 BC, but its use was limited until a serviceable saddle was developed around 1200 BC. This transformed the camel into an effective beast of burden – 'the ship of the desert' – but even then the impact was limited, and the Arabs, the nomadic camel-men of the desert, remained a marginal people. The South Arabian saddle had limited load-bearing capacity, and the alternative cushion-saddle for riding provided only a precarious perch. The technical problem was the hump. The saddle of a horse goes in the middle of the downward-curving back; in the case of the camel, no such simple solution is possible, for that is precisely where the hump is. It was another thousand years before a saddle was developed that so distributed the weight that the camel became capable of bearing heavy loads.

The ideal position for a camel saddle is, of course, on top of the hump, so that weight is evenly distributed and bears down on the rib-cage rather than on either the neck and shoulders or the pelvis. But the hump itself is soft tissue, so simply placing a cushioned seat atop the hump is efficient neither in spreading weight nor in providing a secure perch. The solution to this problem seems to have emerged towards the end of the first millennium BC. Like many transformative inventions – like the wheel and the plough – the basic idea is very simple. The North Arabian saddle comprises a four-sided wooden frame which fits over the camel's hump and rests on top of its rib-cage. It is heavily cushioned beneath to prevent rubbing and sores, and can then be adapted either to carry loads, with the burden slung in equal proportions on either side, or to take a rider, who sits between raised pommels front and back on a cushioned platform supported by the frame on top of the hump.

The impact of the North Arabian saddle on world history is hard to overestimate. It transformed camel-breeding nomads into merchant princes, and camel-mounted warriors into conquerors and empire-builders. It shifted decisively the military balance between desert and sown; between, that is, the Bedouin of Arabia and the civilisations of Iraq, Syria and Egypt. Indirectly, it was responsible for making Arabic the language and Islam the religion of the Middle East and North Africa.[5] Now, at the end of its long supremacy, the camel was to win one final victory: over the train. For the camel, unlike the train, could move in two dimensions across the desert.[6]

The mobility of a camel-mounted commando was enhanced by its self-sufficiency. Water and grazing were found *en route*, and each man could carry six weeks' food on his saddle, in the form of a 45lb bag of flour for making bread. 'This', explained Lawrence, 'gave us a range of over a thousand miles out and home, and that . . . was more than ever we needed, even in so large a country as Arabia.'[7] Because of this, the Arab guerrillas of 1917 were able to strike pretty much anywhere, anytime; and the effect was to stretch time and space, forcing the Turks to consume resources both in waiting and in dispersal. It was tip and run. That was all it took. 'We used the smallest force in the quickest time at the farthest place. If the action had continued till the enemy had changed his dispositions to resist it, we would have been breaking the spirit of our fundamental rule of denying him targets.'[8]

Lawrence was the child of a maritime nation. He knew Francis Bacon's dictum that 'He who commands the sea is at great liberty, and may take as much or as little of the war as he will.' The camel in the desert was like a ship at sea:

> Camel raiding parties, self-contained as ships, could cruise without danger along any part of the enemy's land-frontier, just out of sight of his posts along the edge of cultivation, and tap or raid into his lines where it seemed fittest or easiest and most profitable, with a sure retreat always behind them into an element which the Turks could not enter.[9]

By thus constituting themselves as 'the silent threat of a vast, unknown desert', the Arabs achieved an almost exponential multiplication of force; or, from another angle, an almost exponential economy of force. Since a camel-mounted raiding party setting out from Aqaba could reach Damascus in about ten days, every station on the Hijaz Railway, all the way to Medina, was under threat of attack. Against an insurgency that was everywhere and nowhere, to defend the railway line at all was to defend the whole of it. Thus might 100 men tie down 1,000, even 10,000.

The only alternative would have been an active counter-insurgency of light mobile columns, fast enough to overhaul the raiders, numerous enough to string a net around them. Thus, slowly, through a long process of attrition, might the guerrillas have been destroyed, or rounded up, or driven away. But the cost in men, beasts, materiel and supplies would have been prodigious.

The British had managed it against the Boers, but it had taken them two years and required a ten to one superiority in numbers. The British divided the open *veldt* into segments by erecting hundreds of miles of wire fencing. They guarded the fences by erecting 10,000 blockhouses, each garrisoned by seven men. Their army eventually numbered a quarter of a million – dwarfing in size the *entire* Boer population, men, women and children – and some 80,000 of these were mounted. Converging columns of mounted troops would attempt to run down the elusive commandos. Giant 'drives' – one soldier every 12 yards, advancing 20 miles a day – would sweep the *veldt*. The cost was £1.5 million a week, and the British lost five men for every Boer killed or captured. This colossal military effort was directed at a force that never exceeded 40,000, and by the end was barely 20,000. What made victory possible was the massive predominance of the British Empire in manpower and resources over the two small Boer Republics.[10] Where were the Ottomans to find the means to wage such a war?

* * *

Only by such preponderance of force can regular soldiers prevail over guerrilla insurgents embedded in the landscape and its lifeways. The former are invaders, outsiders, an alien presence; the latter are rooted in local society, organically part of its families, villages and tribes. This basic dichotomy manifests itself in a dozen practical, potentially deadly, ways. The regular is imposed on the military landscape and is dependent on heavy equipment, modern communications and external supply. His intelligence relies upon on observation posts, patrols and interrogation; and his security entails an array of fortified posts and concentrated firepower. The invaders are therefore highly visible, relatively immobile and poorly informed.

Compare the well-rooted guerrilla. He is mobile and largely self-sufficient or sustained by local supply. Being part of the native population, he is gifted with superb intelligence about his enemies, yet can make himself invisible whenever he chooses, even when in plain sight, since he is indistinguishable from the civilians around him. The regular strives to dominate landscape by visible threat. But wherever he is, he finds that his enemy is not. How did Lawrence put it? 'It seemed a regular soldier might be helpless without a target, owning only what he sat on, and subjugating only what, by order, he could poke his rifle at.'[11] The guerrilla controls the rest – everywhere beyond the range of the regular's rifle. He does this not by occupying fixed points, but by perpetual motion, by multiplying force by velocity, thereby stretching space, so that the guerrilla becomes a virtual presence everywhere the regular is absent. Being a phantom, being everywhere and nowhere, he is the master of all unseen space. No less important, because he is an immanent presence, because he is of the place, he can always wait, lying low whenever he wishes, striking only when opportunity beckons; thus he can stretch time as well as space.

The military asymmetry of Ottoman regular and Sherifian insurgent was mirrored in the anthropological asymmetry of Anatolian (or Syrian) peasant as against Bedouin nomad. For a peasant is rooted to one spot. His whole life is spent in a neighbourhood only a few miles wide, working the same fields, inhabiting the cottage of his birth, burying his parents in a village cemetery used generation after generation. In the mind of the peasant, the land is consecrated with sweat and blood, his and his ancestors', and his instinct is to cling to it with grim determination. It comes naturally, therefore, to the peasant soldier to stand fast, to dig in, to find security in melding himself with the earth.

The nomad is the polar opposite: to stay still is death; only in movement, unceasing movement, is there life, for its substance – water and grazing – is found scattered in patches. And because it is barren, because it is a desolation of sun and sand, the Bedouin has little liking for the desert: his vision of paradise is a land flowing with water and lush-green with living things. The nomad, unlike the peasant, has no love for the earth, and no inclination to linger. So if the Arabian war was a war of regular and guerrilla, it was also a war of peasant and nomad, one that pitted the resilience and tenacity of the peasant-conscript defending a breastwork against the fluidity of the camel-mounted raider.

This was to continue an ancient conflict – one several millennia old – but now reconfigured by modern weaponry. It is expedient upon the guerrilla to strike without warning, to kill quickly and to retreat with haste – before the alerted enemy has to time to concentrate superior force. By stretching time and space, the guerrilla imposes dispersion on his opponent and thereby weakens his separate detachments to the point where they become vulnerable. But the stretching of time and space is strategic, not tactical. On the contrary, time must be compressed when the moment comes to strike. For, the moment the guerrilla reveals himself, his enemy begins to concentrate.

So it was at Hallat Ammar, where Lawrence's commando was threatened by two converging columns north and south, two pincers threatening to cut off its retreat. But the battle was over in 10 minutes, and the raiders escaped. This was typical of the railway war, which comprised numerous, small, fleeting firefights. And in such fights, modern weapons gave the guerrillas the tactical edge. In the past, armed with spears, slings or muskets, it had taken time to kill. But magazine rifles, machine-guns and mortars were long-range, rapid-fire, precision weapons able to kill quickly. The camel allowed the Sherifian irregular to stretch strategic time and space; the Lee-Enfield allowed him to compress tactical time.

As the Arab insurgency swelled around them, the Ottomans became increasingly helpless. Once it got a grip – once it had secured a northern base and been extended into Syria – the Ottoman Empire was doomed. It lacked the numbers, the mobility, and the instincts to wage an effective counter-insurgency war. The initiative lay wholly with its enemies, who were free to strike only when and where they chose, and who would do so only when confident of success and easy escape. The Ottoman infantryman found himself engaged in an unwinnable war with an army of phantoms.

The exceptional economy of force achieved by the guerrillas becomes clear in a comparison of combat strengths. It is estimated that the Arab Northern, Southern, and Eastern Armies comprised a maximum of 5,000 regulars and fluctuating forces of up to 20,000 irregulars. Prince Feisal's Northern Army – the strategic cutting-edge of the Revolt – numbered a maximum of 8,000 regulars and irregulars, but often had as few as 3,000 men actually in the field.[12] The contrast with the size of Allenby's Egyptian Expeditionary Force (EEF) is marked: by the autumn of 1918, its total ration strength in theatre had grown to 340,000, giving a front-line combat strength of 57,000 rifles, 12,000 sabres and 540 guns.[13]

How do these relative strengths compare with the Ottoman distribution of force west and east of the Jordan? British intelligence estimates for the autumn of 1918 were as follows. Facing the British in Palestine were the Eighth Army of 10,000 rifles and 157 guns, and the Seventh Army of 7,000 rifles and 111 guns. Facing the Arabs in Syria and Arabia were the Fourth Army of 6,000 rifles, 2,000 sabres and 74 guns, a further 6,000 rifles and 30 guns deployed on the Hijaz Railway, and a garrison at Medina of 9,000 rifles. In addition, there was a general reserve of 3,000 rifles and 30 guns.[14] This means that, even counting only front-line combat strength – that is, ignoring Allenby's huge logistical 'tail' – the Arabs achieved an extraordinary economy of force relative to the British. For, while 69,000 British faced 17,000 Turks west of the Jordan, 3,000–8,000 Arabs faced 14,000 Turks in Syria, and a further 25,000 Arabs faced 21,000 Turks in Syria and Arabia combined.

Put simply, there were more Turks fighting 25,000 Arabs (at the most) than there were fighting 340,000 British; more precisely, the economy of force of the Arab campaign overall, measured in terms of manpower deployment, was at least 17 times higher than that of the British, while that of Prince Feisal's Northern Army, even assuming a maximum strength of 8,000, was a staggering 35 times higher.

* * *

The Hallat Ammar Ambush was one of many military operations mounted by the Arab Northern Army in the last six months of 1917. Aqaba swelled into a major depot as the Royal Navy transported successive contingents of Feisal's existing forces from Wejh, as new tribal recruits flooded in from southern

Syria, and as an increasing number of former Ottoman Arab officers, many from the prisoner-of-war camps of Egypt, arrived to join the revolt. 'The slide towards the sherif was obvious when Nasir was here,' wrote Lawrence, 'and has become immense, almost impossible, since Feisal arrived [on 23 August]. He is unable even to see all the head sheikhs of the newcomers.'[15] The Navy also organised regular supply-convoys – though barely keeping pace with need – and great dumps of rations and munitions accumulated. Admiral Wemyss's flagship, HMS *Euryalus*, a four-funnelled armoured cruiser, sat at anchor, its two 9-inch and twelve 6-inch guns spreading a protective mantle over the growing tented encampment onshore.

The camp was built around Feisal's tent complex, which included accommodation for himself, his retinue and his guards, as well as reception, dining and sleeping areas for his many guests. A large part of the campsite was occupied by the Hashemite regulars, whose drilling became a feature of camp life. There was also a canteen for British officers, who arrived in growing numbers, and others serving the crews of machine-guns, mortars, mountain-guns, armoured cars and aircraft. Another area was occupied by a community of traders, many from the Hijaz, and on the fringes was a shifting population of tribesmen in temporary encampments.[16]

To some military professionals it looked shambolic. Feisal's army had been placed under Allenby's command – an arrangement negotiated with the Emir Hussein by Lawrence himself on a flying visit to the Hijaz in late July – and British officers were taking a keen interest in its conduct. Replying to one critical intelligence report, Lawrence wrote to Clayton, 'I don't think that any [report] of the Arab situation will be of much use to you unless its author can see for himself the difference between a national rising and a [military] campaign.'

The 'Arab situation' required officers of special stamp. One such was Major Pierce Joyce, now reassigned from Wejh to Aqaba, a man whose love of order was, unusually, coupled with an easy-going, unassuming and ever-patient manner.[17] Technically his superior officer, Joyce gave Lawrence a free hand and provided him with solid backing, becoming, in the words of Liddell Hart, 'a strong shaft for Lawrence's spearhead'.[18]

An advanced post was also established at Guweira, about 35 miles inland, on the far side of the Wadi Itm – an essential precaution, for had the Ottomans reoccupied the wadi, the Anglo-Arab forces would have been bottled up on the coast. Auda based himself at Guweira, holding it with about 600 Howeitat tribesmen for a month and a half following the fall of Aqaba, gaining the time needed for consolidation and build-up. The Ottomans retook Abu al-Lissan and Fuweilah, but were hamstrung in their efforts to advance farther by a water problem.

The Aqaba road drops steeply from Fuweilah to a hot, sandy plain, waterless across the 20 miles to Guweira, making it incumbent to carry large quantities to support any advance towards the town. Auda compounded the enemy's difficulties by mounting diversionary attacks on the railway line, blowing bridges and ripping up rails in at least three places.[19] Lawrence considered these measures more than enough. The 'indirect approach' was Aqaba's best defence: 'by extended threats on the railway,' he argued, 'we can force the Turks to increase their forces there, and I believe the Hijaz line is already working to full capacity to support the troops now between Deraa and Medain Salih. For this reason I do not think they can at once defend it, and attack Aqaba on the necessary scale.'[20]

So it proved. The Ottomans turned Maan into a major base for up to 6,000 troops and 16 guns, constructing strong fortifications on the hilltops covering the approaches to the station and the town. Their strategy was to establish outlying posts beyond Maan on the roads leading from the dry plain of Guweira up into the well-watered Hills of Edom; posts which would also cover Maan and the railway line. The garrison at Abu al-Lissan/Fuweilah, 2,000 strong, was one of these. In mid-August an Ottoman force occupied Delagha, about 10 miles north-west of Abu al-Lissan. This closed the second of the three routes.

But the initiative was passing from the Ottomans to the Arabs as the Aqaba build-up neared completion. A temporary landing-strip had been laid out at Kuntilla (reconnoitred by Lawrence), and bombing missions commenced at the end of August, when four Royal Flying Corps aircraft dropped more than 100 bombs on Maan, Abu al-Lissan and Fuweilah, hitting an engine-shed, barracks and an encampment. Meanwhile, Arab forces infiltrated northwards along the eastern edge of the Wadi Araba, penetrated into the hill-country along the third, unguarded routeway, and established an advanced post at Wadi Musa (near Petra). The Arab line came to resemble a giant crescent anchored on Wadi Musa in the north, Guweira in the south, and bent outwards in the middle around the Ottoman posts at Delagha and Abu al-Lissan/Fuweilah.[21]

In late September, a large raiding party – 200 Bedouin and 30 regulars with 2 machine-guns – attacked the Ottoman timber-cutting operation at Shobek, about 15 miles north of Wadi Musa. The timber was needed to keep the trains running – the war having terminated the supply of South Wales coal – and a branch line had been constructed to carry it down to the main line at Uneiza. The raiders took the village, captured its garrison, and ripped up 300 rails, but failed to overwhelm the Ottoman company guarding the forest.[22] The raid may have triggered the strong Ottoman riposte that followed a month later, however: an attempt to eliminate the Arab forward base at Wadi Musa, where a decisive battle was fought on 21 October.

The man charged with suppressing the Arab Revolt in Syria was Mehmed Djemal Pasha, commander of the Fourth Army, known as Djemal Pasha *Kuchuk* ('the Lesser') to distinguish him from Ahmed Djemal Pasha *Biyuk* ('the Greater'), the Ottoman triumvir and regional viceroy.[23] Djemal *Kuchuk* dispatched three infantry battalions, a Circassian cavalry regiment, a company of mounted infantry and eight guns in an effort to dislodge the Arabs holding Wadi Musa. Converging in three columns, they faced fierce resistance from 350 regulars, 180 tribesmen and 2 mountain-guns ensconced in the hills around Petra.[24] These were commanded by Maulud Mukhlus, a former Ottoman officer, a keen Arab nationalist, Feisal's *aide-de-camp* and, according to Lawrence, 'a fire-eating Mesopotamian cavalryman' who had proved himself a hard-driving martinet.

Maulud's detachment of mule-mounted infantry had become 'excellent soldiers, capable of instant obedience, and of attack in open order, prodigies in the Arab ranks'.[25] This they demonstrated in the savage little battle fought on the red-rose cliffs around the ancient city. It opened with artillery fire on the Arab positions, supported by aerial bombing by a single aircraft coming in at only 300 metres. The Ottomans launched three separate assaults. The Arabs opened their centre and drew the enemy against the cliffs, while manoeuvring around their flanks to catch them in cross-fire. The Ottoman columns were smashed and forced to withdraw after losing 200 killed and wounded. Arab casualties were about 40.

Maulud had held the entry-point into the uplands open, and to maintain this the garrison was soon reinforced to 800. A month later an Ottoman push towards Guweira was equally unsuccessful and, before the year was out, a combination of mounting pressure along the main Aqaba–Maan road and continual attacks on the railway had compelled Djemal to draw in his horns and establish a tight defensive perimeter around Maan.[26]

* * *

Lawrence followed his successful ambush at Hallat Ammar on 19 September with a second raid just over a week later, 150-strong and this time with a plentiful reserve of pack-camels. Finding a suitable location was growing harder as the war intensified and the density of Ottoman posts along the line increased ('we found ourselves beset on all sides by enemy blockhouses'). A mine was eventually planted on a bridge near Shedia – two hours' work – at a point 2,500 yards from the nearest post to the south, 4,000 yards from that to the north. On the first day, no train passed. On the second, a water train went over the mine without detonating it (it was Lawrence's first use of an automatic 'contact' mine). An electric mine was therefore placed over the automatic one – another two hours' work – and the wait resumed.

Finally, at 8am on 6 October, a twelve-wagon train came steaming down the line from Maan. Lawrence signalled, the plunger went down, the engine was consumed in 'noise, dust and blackness'. A few bursts from the Lewis guns, and the Arabs stormed the train 'in a wild torrent'. The mine had taken out one arch of the bridge and destroyed the locomotive beyond repair. About twenty Turks were killed, and others, including four officers, taken prisoner. The couplings broke and the last four wagons drifted away downhill, but the other eight were ransacked, yielding about 70 tons of foodstuffs. In less than an hour, the wagons were emptied, the camels loaded, but there was no time to fire the train: Lawrence and the last two Arabs pulled out with 'about 40 Turks coming up fast and only 400 yards off'. There had been no Arab casualties.[27]

Lawrence's two raids were models of efficiency, but they were only two among many – the great majority involving no British officers at all. In the months of July, August and September 1917, the railway between Maan and Medina was attacked on average once every three days. Some 30 bridges were destroyed and about 10,000 rails torn up.[28] The following month, about two weeks after Lawrence's Shedia ambush and around the time Maulud was fighting the Battle of Wadi Musa, some 2,000 Bedouin were involved in three separate attacks on the 75-mile stretch of the railway south of Hallat Ammar. A train was derailed, about 250 Turks killed or captured, and a hilltop redoubt held by 180 men overwhelmed and held for four days.[29] One estimate has seventeen engines and scores of wagons destroyed in the last four months of 1917.[30]

The capture of Wejh at the beginning of the year had paralysed the Ottoman garrison at Medina by extending its flank and compelling dispersion of force. Now, towards the end of the year, following the capture of Aqaba and its transformation into a major military base, the garrison at Maan had also been thrown onto the defensive by a further stretching of space and the distraction of effort this imposed. This had been achieved partly by the occupation of Wadi Musa on the left, partly by aerial bombing in the centre, but above all by railway raids on the right that had left the Ottoman command with no option but to dribble its precious manpower into a hundred tiny posts. The British *Official History* was correct in its assessment: 'Little enough could have been done to stop the enemy had he come forward with determination, but so harassed was he that he never could muster the nerve for the attempt.'[31]

* * *

Less than a week after his second train-wrecking exploit, Lawrence took a 90-minute flight over the Negev Desert to be delivered to General Allenby's field headquarters at Arish.[32] Questioned closely about strategy, Lawrence explained that the intention was not to break the railway line, but to keep it 'just in working order – but only just – to Medina'. Thus would the Ottomans consume themselves in defending the line and maintaining the garrison at its end. To break the line would turn Maan into a railhead and the war into a siege. For this the Bedouin were ill-suited. Whereas wrecking trains was 'honourable, easy, and profitable', a siege would be a mistake 'till our regular army was trained and equipped and numerous enough to invest Maan'. Quizzed also about Wadi Musa, Lawrence claimed that the place was 'impregnable' and a trap for the blundering enemy – blundering because blind, for the Arabs moved in small, fast, fluid groups, and 'the truth was that the Turks acted in complete fog with regard to us'.[33]

But debriefing was not the main purpose of the summons. Allenby was preparing for his big push against the Gaza–Beersheba line, and the Sherifian guerrillas on his extreme right had an open flank before them. Might they mount an operation against the Ottoman communications far behind the lines? Might they even raise a tribal insurrection deep in the enemy's rear? The ideal target was Deraa, a railway town about 60 miles south of Damascus, the place at which the Palestine line branched off the main Hijaz line. The entire Palestine rail network, with connections to Haifa, Jaffa, Jerusalem, Gaza and Beersheba, would be cut off if Deraa were to be taken. Lawrence himself described the town as 'the navel of the Turkish armies in Syria, the common point of all their fronts'.[34]

But the risk was prodigious. If the EEF failed to break through decisively, any rebellion would be isolated and the result might be 'horrible massacres' and the premature ruin of 'the best asset Feisal held for eventual success'. It was not to be contemplated at this stage in the campaign, especially given the lateness of the season and the likelihood that the winter rains would soon bring any advance to a standstill. Lawrence proposed instead a deep-penetration raid to destroy one of the larger railway bridges over the Yarmuk.[35] Such was the steep gradient of the gorge that no less than fifteen major bridges, many incorporating large ironwork sections, had been required to carry wide curves of track. Blowing just one of these would close down rail communications with the Palestine front until repairs could be effected – no easy matter given the engineering complexities.[36] Lawrence discussed the plan with Clayton following his meeting with Allenby. When the scheme was put to the commander-in-chief, he approved, adding a request that the bridge be blown on 5 November or on one of the three succeeding days.[37]

* * *

The expedition set out on 24 October. It was led by Sherif Ali ibn el-Hussein el-Harithi, described by Lawrence as 'physically splendid . . . impertinent, head-strong, conceited, as reckless in word as in deed . . . the ideal many-sided leader who could turn to effect any mad situation as it arose'. Ali's affiliations were to the tribes about Azrak, the Beni Sakhr and the Serahin, from whom it was hoped he would be able to recruit volunteers. Another of the party was Emir Abd el-Kader, an Algerian nationalist exile who controlled a number of villages settled with his own people on the north bank of the Yarmuk; he, too, was a potential recruiter, or at least a smoother of paths. Later, they would be joined by Mifleh el-Gomaan, a sheikh of the local Beni Sakhr, who would greet the party when it reached Bair with 'a public show in which all the men, horses, and camels in the place turned out and welcomed us . . . with wild cheers and gallopings and curvettings, and much firing of shots, and shouting'. The British were represented by Captain George Lloyd from the Arab Bureau, Lieutenant Wood of the Royal Engineers, and a company of Indian soldiers with two Vickers heavy machine-guns; Lloyd craved adventure, Wood was the explosives man, and the Indians would provide the covering fire. The expedition crossed the railway just south of Shedia and then circled wide through the desert oases of Jefer, Bair and Azrak.

But nothing went right. Recruitment was poor. The preferred target was crawling with enemy soldiers. Abd el-Kader disappeared – an event widely predicted – and Lawrence guessed he had gone over to the Turks and alerted them to the raiders' presence. The Indians could not keep up with the Arabs, reducing the column's speed from 50 to 35 miles a day, yet speed was of the essence, because they were a small party intent on attacking a target deep in enemy territory – more than 400 miles from Aqaba via Azrak – in an area both heavily populated and strongly garrisoned. The actual raid would involve travelling 80 miles in 13 hours if the party was to reach its target and return to safety east of the railway in a single night. To make matters worse, it was wet and muddy.

Lawrence might have called the whole thing off. He did not. But the attack on the bridge at Tell Shehab on 7 November was abortive. As the demolition party crept forward in the darkness, someone dropped a rifle. The clatter alerted the Turkish sentries, who started firing. The Beni Sakhr fired back, but the Serahin, acting as porters and fearing the dynamite they were carrying would explode if they were hit, hurled it into the ravine. With the alarm raised and no means of blowing the bridge, Lawrence ordered evacuation.

The raiders raced eastwards amid a clamour of activity in the Syrian villages they passed. Cold, wet, tired and hungry, they got clear without upset or loss, but were a bitterly disappointed group of men. There was, however, a reserve supply of gelatine – enough to blow a train – and the sixty or so Beni Sakhr and Serahin volunteers wanted to recover some honour from the fiasco. So the Indians, who were suffering most, were sent back to Azrak, and the rest made for the railway line.

It was a madcap scheme. They planted their mine on a small masonry culvert and took position in some curving hills. But only 60 yards of cable was available, so the ends had to be buried until a train came, and then the exploder attached at the last minute. The operator (Lawrence) then had to sit by a bush so small that it was sufficient only to hide the device. Two trains in fact went by before the mine could be triggered – the first because the cable was yet to be laid, the second because the mechanism failed despite repeated efforts, leaving Lawrence 'sitting on a naked bank in full view of a Turkish troop-train, crawling past 50 yards away at walking pace'. Time seemed to stand still. The British officer hoped he would pass as a casual Bedouin shepherd. Ottoman officers gathered at the ends of the carriages to stare and point. Lawrence waved back and grinned nervously. Miraculously, no-one fired.

The raiders then spent their second night camping at the ambush site. Finally, at 10am on 11 November, another train came around the bend, whistling loudly, travelling at top speed down the gradient, 'a splendid two-engined thing of twelve passenger coaches'. Lawrence hit the plunger and the mine went off. But he was far too close. 'The ground spouted blackly into my face, and I was sent spinning, to sit up with shirt torn to my shoulder, and the blood dripping from long ragged scratches on my left arm. Between my knees lay the exploder, crushed under a twisted sheet of sooty iron. In front of me was the scalded and smoking upper half of a man.'

The whole boiler of the first engine had been destroyed. The locomotive had toppled from the broken bridge into the wadi. The second locomotive had also dropped into the void. The first three coaches had telescoped and been smashed to pieces. The rest were badly derailed, the listing boxes zigzagged along the track. One of them was a saloon car decorated with flags: an Ottoman general was on the train. The ground was strewn with dead, for the coaches had been packed, but some 200 soldiers had survived the smash and were now lining the embankment – far too many for a guerrilla commando of 60 riflemen without machine-guns.

As shooting erupted, Lawrence found himself in the middle. With great pain in his right foot and head still dizzy with shock, he stumbled as he ran for cover. Ali rushed forward to help, followed by twenty of his men, but seven of these were killed by Ottoman fire before the group scrambled to safety. Lawrence found that, in addition to cuts, bruises and a broken toe, he had five bullet grazes and his clothes were ripped to pieces. The raiders repulsed an Ottoman probe by about forty men, but then, taking their chance, scurried up the hill to their rear, mounted the nearest camels, and fled east into the desert.

Returning to Azrak in the bitterly cold wind and rain of approaching winter, Lawrence contemplated his first substantive failure: the Yarmuk operation had been abortive, enemy communications between Damascus and Palestine were unimpaired, and the Minifer ambush had ended in defeat, with a third of his men down and the rest routed.

In the event, it did not matter: news shortly reached Azrak that Allenby had broken the line and taken Gaza. The war was going well in Palestine.[38]

* * *

Lawrence had attempted to resolve the contradictions inherent in his position by committing himself wholeheartedly to the Arab cause; that is, by 'going native'. This was confirmed by George Lloyd, the Cambridge-educated aristocrat, Tory MP, wartime captain, and Arab Bureau colleague who had accompanied Lawrence on the first part of the journey to the Yarmuk gorge. The two were friends, and Lawrence had unburdened himself to Lloyd. 'L not working for HMG [His Majesty's Government],' Lloyd scribbled in his notebook after one especially intimate conversation, 'but for Sherif [Hussein].'[39]

Lawrence's Arab allegiance was proving an inadequate salve, however. In part, perhaps, this was because neither Feisal nor his Bedouin followers conformed to Lawrence's heroic ideal. The sherif was an essentially weak personality, easily afflicted with despondency and indecision; 'Feisal does not get any bigger,' wrote Hogarth, 'even T.E.L. admits that . . . [Lawrence] is not well and talks rather hopelessly about the Arab future he once believed in.'[40] As for the tribesmen, they fought not for some ideal of Arab unity and independence, but for pay and plunder. Auda may have been a romantic desert warrior, but he was also an avaricious tribal potentate. British intelligence established that he was in communication with the Ottomans within a month of taking Aqaba – the achievement having raised the price of his services – and Lawrence was needed to renegotiate terms. Auda was assured that money and munitions were coming from Allenby; in the meantime, he might like an advance instalment. 'Auda saw that the immediate moment would not be unprofitable; that Feisal would be highly profitable; and that the Turks would be always with him if other resources failed. So he agreed, in a very good temper, to accept my advance; and with it, to keep the Howeitat well-fed and cheerful.' Reporting to Cairo, Lawrence was economical with the truth, for 'the crowd wanted book-heroes and would not understand how . . . human old Auda was.'[41] But this was a repeating story. A month later, Lawrence found himself unable to raise the men and camels he needed to raid the railway because 'three sub-tribes I was relying on were not yet paid, and Auda abu Tayi was making trouble by his greediness and his attempt to assume authority over all the Howeitat'.[42] The Yarmuk raid was stymied by lack of enthusiasm for a purely military operation that was both dangerous and without prospect of loot; Auda was among those who refused to participate, as was Zaal, success having changed the 'hard-riding gallant of spring into a prudent man, whose new wealth made life precious to him'.[43]

Lawrence was wrestling, too, with the psychic demons of the battlefield. There is no such thing as a 'clean war'. Battle is never romantic, always ugly. The Arab war was fought in a pitiless waste of sand, gravel and rock, where much of the killing was close-up and visceral, the wounded were left to die in the sun, and prisoners, if taken, were herded along until many had perished of thirst, hunger and exhaustion. Soldiers have only a limited capacity to endure the privations, stresses and horrors of war; all have their breaking-point.[44] When this is reached, the mind can implode as the trauma of recent experience connects with older psychic complexes. Post-traumatic stress disorder (PTSD) – as we now call it – can then give rise to a wide range of symptoms, and varying degrees of dysfunction. It can manifest itself in sleeplessness, recurring nightmares and flashbacks; in memory loss and lack of concentration; in shame, loss of self-esteem and emotional numbness; in hyper-vigilance, hyper-arousal and hyper-activity; but also in retreat from the world, panic attacks and attempted suicide.[45] In extreme cases, it can trigger full-blown psychosis, where the mind's ability to distinguish between the demons inside and the reality outside dissolves, in whole or in part, and the personality becomes deeply fractured.

To one acquaintance Lawrence had written a vivid *Boy's Own* account of Hallat Ammar, ending, 'I hope this sounds the fun it is ... It's the most amateurish, Buffalo-Billy sort of performance, and the only people who do it well are the Bedouin.' But this was façade. He wrote another letter around the same time to Oxford friend Edward Leeds very different in tone: 'I hope when the nightmare ends that I will wake up and become alive again. This killing and killing of Turks is horrible ... you charge in at the finish and find them all over the place in bits, and still alive many of them, and know that you have done hundreds in the same way and must do hundreds more if you can.'[46] He felt that his quota of courage was fast being drained. 'I'm not going to last this game much longer,' he told Leeds. 'Nerves going and temper wearing thin ...'[47] Lloyd heard the same on the way to the Yarmuk gorge: 'He opened his heart to me last night and told me that he felt there was so much for him still to do in this world, places to dig, peoples to help, that it seemed horrible to have it all cut off, as he feels it will be, for he feels that, while he may do the job, he has little or no chance of getting away himself.'[48]

Yet he survived the Yarmuk only to plunge wilfully into the reckless danger of Minifer. He had a zest for life, but courted his own destruction. He had become a deranged action-hero possessed by a death-wish. He would soon descend deeper into the darkness. Within days of his return from the Yarmuk – if his own account is to be trusted – he would walk into enemy-occupied Deraa, where he would be arrested, tortured and raped: a psychic trauma to cap them all.

CHAPTER 13

The Third Battle of Gaza

THE PRELUDE WAS the greatest artillery bombardment ever known in the Middle East. The heavy guns of an army corps and the field-guns and howitzers of three divisions – 218 guns in total – opened on Gaza on 27 October.[1] 'Suddenly,' recalled London correspondent W.T. Massey, 'there was a terrific burst of fire on about 4 miles of front. Vivid fan-shaped flashes stabbed the sky, the bright moonlight of the East did not dim the guns' lightning, and their thunderous voices were a challenge the enemy was powerless to refuse.' So the Ottoman guns replied, their fire rising to a fury, then ebbing away as the British guns found them. Sound-ranging sections detected between 16 and 24 guns south of Gaza; after two days of bombardment, only 10 remained; after six days, only 4. Other British guns pulverised the front-line defences or doused bivouac areas and communication centres with gas shells.[2]

The land-based artillery was joined on 29 October by the guns of the British cruiser *Grafton*, the French battleship *Requin*, seven destroyers, five monitors, two river gunboats, and some smaller vessels. The naval gunfire, including that of the huge 14-inch guns of the monitor *Raglan*, ranged over the Ottoman rear areas, targeting the railway, road bridges and ammo dumps. An ammunition train took a direct hit and exploded with the force of an earthquake, spreading a wreckage of torn and twisted metal across several hundred square yards. Two shells took out the centre of the main stone bridge over the Wadi Hesi, the fire directed by a seaplane and coming in over 14,000 yards.[3]

As well as preparing the way for the infantry attacks to come, the bombardment had two other effects: it fixed the enemy's attention on Gaza; and it muffled the sounds of 60,000 men marching or riding upon Beersheba, 25 miles to the south-east.

* * *

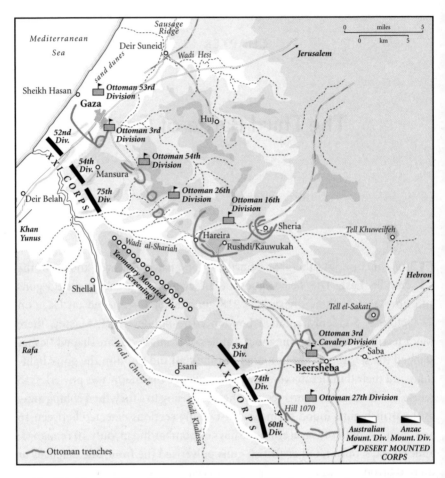

16. The Third Battle of Gaza, 29 October–7 November 1917, showing the situation at zero hour.

Beersheba, like Gaza, was a city of fable. Abraham had dug a well, planted trees and pastured sheep here. It had been the southernmost settlement of the ancient Israelite kingdom. The Romans had stationed a garrison in the town. In 1917, it contained an administrative centre, a post and telegraph office, a mosque, a market of a dozen shops, the homes of about 800 people and, crucially, seven ancient wells supplying abundant good water.[4] It was also a local communications hub, with roads or tracks radiating north-east to Hebron, Bethlehem and Jerusalem, south to Sinai and Aqaba, and north-west across the coastal plain to Gaza. The recent arrival of the railway had further enhanced its importance, turning it into what an Arab Bureau report described as 'a military settlement built on German lines'.[5]

The battle would turn on possession of Beersheba and its wells. Kress von Kressenstein was almost right when he averred that no large mounted force could operate east of Beersheba for lack of water. And the British mounted force was very large: in fact, one of the largest forces of regular cavalry ever assembled in the history of war. Desert Mounted Corps and XX Corps combined, the cavalry and infantry arms respectively of Allenby's massive right-hook, required 400,000 gallons of water, weighing 2,000 tons, per day.[6] By opening new wells at Esani, Khalassa and Asluj, by allocating all of XXI Corps' transport to the strike-force, and by sending men forward with full water-bottles on the night of 30/31 October, the British could make their attack. But that is all they could do. The Egyptian Camel Transport Corps' 35,000 pack-animals could supply only so much water.[7] And each mile the front moved forward, so much the less would it be. Indeed, in the event of a fast-moving offensive of the kind envisaged, with Chauvel's cavalry sweeping forward to take the enemy in flank and rear, it would be none at all: horses go faster than camels. Beersheba itself was the principal local water-source, and it was vital to seize it before the Turks could destroy the wells. Either Abraham's well was captured on the first day, or Allenby's plan would fall to bits on the second.

The town lay on the edge of the Judaean Hills in a hollow surrounded by high ground to the north, east and south, but with a relatively open plain to the west, the most likely direction of attack. It was in the west, therefore, that the defences were especially strong, with more or less continuous trench-lines on commanding ground. These were solidly constructed, many of them cut into rock, with dugouts, some overhead cover, and barbed wire fixed to iron stanchions along the front. Forward of the main line were machine-gun emplacements and concealed sniper positions. In all, Beersheba was defended by about 3,500 infantry, 1,400 cavalry, 60 machine-guns and 28 cannon.[8]

The British plan was to employ the infantry of the 60th (London) and 74th (Yeomanry) Divisions of XX Corps in an assault on the main defences, fixing the Turks in the defence of what they considered their most vulnerable sector. Meantime, Desert Mounted Corps, comprising Anzac Mounted Division, Australian Mounted Division and 7th Mounted Brigade, was to work through the hills and attack from the east, throwing out strong flank-guards against enemy reinforcements approaching from the direction of Hebron; ideally, the cavalry would cut in behind the defenders of Beersheba to block their escape and ensure their destruction. A 'special operations' force of seventy Arab irregulars stiffened with British machine-gunners and commanded by Lieutenant-Colonel Stewart Newcombe was to make a wide detour to the east with the aim of striking the Hebron road. Its mission was to harass enemy reinforcements and attempt to raise the tribes in the Ottoman rear.[9]

* * *

By 3am, the men of XX Corps were in position. They had marched about 8 miles through the night and were now deployed some 2,000 to 2,500 yards from the enemy trenches. The 74th Division was to attack on the left from due west, 60th Division on the right from the south-west. Each division had two brigades forward and one in reserve. The main initial objective was the commanding height of Hill 1070.

Just before 6am the British guns – 16 heavy and 104 medium – burst into action. The Ottoman trenches on the hill were deluged with exploding shells and disappeared in clouds of dust – so dense that it became impossible for the gunners to judge the effects of their fire, forcing a pause in the bombardment while the dust settled. Then, at 8.30am, the Londoners of 181st Brigade stormed Hill 1070 and captured it in 10 minutes with the loss of only 100 men. The guns had shattered the defence: it turned out that every single machine-gun had been destroyed or buried.[10]

Now the artillery moved forward and came into action at wire-cutting range against the main line. For an hour and half, the guns attempted to blast gaps through which the infantry could advance on the Ottoman positions either side of Hill 1070. The effects were limited: when the Londoners and Yeomanry went forward at 12.15, they found most of the wire intact and had to cut their way through.[11] But the dust cloud raised by the barrage hitting the Ottoman trenches allowed the wire-cutting parties to work relatively unimpeded.[12]

Bernard Blaser of 60th Division's London Scottish had found the waiting hard. The sun was hot, but water had to be conserved, for no-one knew when bottles might be replenished. And through the morning hours, with the sounds of battle all around, each man was prey to his fears. 'Suddenly a gun boomed out from directly behind us, then another, being followed in quick succession by the batteries on our right and left. Thank heaven it would not be long now!'[13]

A short distance away, another London Division man, Doug Calcutt of the Queen's Westminster Rifles, was also waiting to go over. But he and his mates found themselves too close to the guns: they were hit by both Ottoman counter-battery fire and the premature burst of a British shell. 'High explosive is bursting between us and the guns. Shrapnel comes over. Bursts above us and rains down on us. Steady stream of wounds. Young Morrison, elbow. Brown, arm. Low, head, and so on and so on.'[14]

At zero, the guns would lift to form a creeping barrage. The London Scottish tensed for action: 'All was ready, bayonets fixed, magazines filled, and the men of the first wave crouched just below the skyline of the ridge waiting for the signal . . . Their faces were a study, and in them could be read a mixture of curiosity, alarm and expectation.' Blaser, whose job was to operate alongside the battalion commander, marking his position with a standard, watched the first and second waves advance:

> The men moved forward and gained the crest. That was the psychological moment. I fully expected to see them shot down like flies, but not a man was hit. As each approached, a keen observer would have faintly distinguished a momentary falter, a mere semblance of hesitation, as though preparing to receive a shock ... In a flash it had passed, the man was on the skyline, and reassured by seeing his comrades descending the hill unhurt before him, he, too, pushed forward and was lost to view.[15]

Private Blunt was in the first wave:

> It was necessary to get over the ridge and off the skyline as quickly as possible. Once over the ridge it was a rush down the valley and a charge up the opposite ridge, where the Turkish trenches were at the top ... Bullets were falling everywhere. Several of our lads were hit ... In the excitement I did not have the 'wind up' one little bit ... Every minute I was expecting a bullet to get me, but my good luck stuck to me ... When we got to the Turkish trenches, we jumped straight in and shot or bayoneted or took prisoner all that was there.[16]

The bombardment had done its work. The machine-guns had again been knocked out.[17] Most of the traumatised defenders had fled, leaving a litter of abandoned kit and the broken bodies of fallen comrades. 'Upon the faces of them all was the stamp of death,' reported Blaser. 'But what was this? A gurgling sound as of laboured breathing emanated from one figure huddled up on the bottom of the trench. He was unconscious and in a deplorable condition, with his right jaw blown away and one foot hanging by a thread ...'[18]

It was much the same elsewhere: enemy resistance was weak, and the British infantry stormed to success with light casualties. By 1.30 they had captured a long stretch of front-line trenches to the south-west of Beersheba, and were setting up an outpost line 2,000 yards beyond this. A third attack was then mounted immediately to the north, along the line of the Wadi Saba, by two brigades, one of 74th Division, the other of 53rd (Welsh) Division. This encountered little more than scattered sniper-fire, and by 7 o'clock in the evening the position was taken. For a total loss of fewer than 1,200 men, XX Corps had occupied 3 miles of entrenchments and captured 500 Turks and 6 field-guns. The infantry had completed its work for the day.[19]

* * *

The success of the assault was a vindication of the British Army's new tactical doctrine for offensive action. This doctrine, fully developed by the winter of 1916/17, was the result of major reappraisals based on Western Front experience, in particular that of the Battle of the Somme in the summer and autumn of 1916.

The central problem, of course, was the 'storm of steel' in no-man's-land. Rifles had maximum ranges of about 2,000 yards, and a rifleman could load two clips into his magazine and then fire 10 aimed rounds in about a minute. Heavy machine-guns, with about twice the range, might take the same time to spray a full belt of 250 rounds across an area 500 yards wide. Field-guns, with ranges in excess of 6,500 yards, could maintain a steady four rounds a minute, or twenty rounds a minute in a crisis. A single shrapnel shell could scatter perhaps 250 high-velocity bullets across 50 yards of 'beaten' ground, while high-explosive shells killed by concussion, blast and the effect of countless flying shards of hot metal.[20] In the half century since the American Civil War, the increased killing-power of weaponry had transformed the battlefield, making it a lethal space for anyone standing in the open. The simple fact was that incoming fire had to be cut to a small fraction of its potential maximum if attacking troops were to have any chance of getting across the open ground between opposing trench-lines.

Gun-power was critical. The old dictum 'artillery conquers, infantry occupies' was writ large in hastily updated military manuals. Gunners now waged a sophisticated techno-battle involving sights and elevator-screws, flash-spotting and sound-ranging, aerial observation, telephone and wireless communication, and mapping and plotting. Massed artillery could now execute 'creeping barrages' – a wall of exploding shells advancing just ahead of assault troops – or 'box barrages' – three walls of exploding shells designed to shut enemy forces out of a designated area. Such was the range, accuracy, rate of fire and destructive power of modern artillery that it could, in sufficient concentration, suppress all defensive fire, allowing infantry to cross no-man's-land and get into the enemy trench system without loss. This was the ideal, rarely realised in full, but henceforward the essential basis of all offensive tactics: the working assumption was that infantry could not get forward without artillery, and the more of it there was, and the better the coordination of guns and infantry, the more likely an attack was to succeed.[21]

Infantry practice had also been transformed. The shift from massed linear formations to a loosely structured battle-scape of open-order lines, fire and movement, and small, semi-independent, all-arms sections was more or less complete by the third winter of the war. The change had begun, in the British Army at least, before 1914, largely in response to Boer War experience of fighting skilled marksmen armed with modern rifles. British doctrine included the use of extended formations, advances in short rushes, and the slow build-up of a firing-line at about 200 yards distance from the enemy.[22] But at the beginning of the war, British officers still thought primarily in terms of lines, rifles and massed musketry – much as Marlborough and Wellington had done. No longer by 1917. The forward elements of an assault might still be deployed in lines, but with 5–6 yards between each man, and perhaps 50 yards between each successive 'wave'. The rear elements, on the other hand, would typically advance in single file, each section or platoon thus forming a 'worm', with the company or battalion of which they were part said to be in 'artillery formation'. Some tacticians wondered whether the forward elements should not also be 'worms'. Others, more radical still, thought in terms of 'blobs': sections or platoons operating as more or less self-contained clusters of men, who would seek their own way forward, adapting to the ground, improvising responses to enemy resistance.

'Blob' tactics represented the most complete expression of the potential inherent in the new all-arms platoon. Each was divided into four sections of between six and ten men. Each section might have a different specialised role as Stokes gunners, Lewis gunners, riflemen, rifle-grenadiers or 'bombers'. Practice varied, functions might be combined, and the trend was towards a more all-purpose infantryman. But the essential principle held: the platoon became an all-arms miniature army, with its own artillery, machine-gun and 'storm-troop' capacity.

The Stokes mortar was a lightweight infantry-support weapon comprising a 3-inch cylinder mounted on base-plate and bipod. Bombs could be projected over several hundred yards, and, once the weapon was ranged in, at such a rapid rate that half a dozen might be in flight simultaneously. Because of the mortar's very high trajectory, operators could remain under cover while dropping bombs into enemy trenches.[23]

The Lewis light machine-gun was equally important. Highly portable, it could be carried by one man, dropped onto its small bipod in a trice, and immediately open fire at a rate of 100 rounds a minute. It was fed by pan-shaped magazines holding 47 rounds, so a full team comprised five men, the firer, the loader, and three more carrying bags of spare ammo.[24]

Grenades – an old weapon of war – had to be reinvented in the First World War in the context of trench warfare. Improvised 'jam-tin bombs' were eventually replaced by mass-produced Mills bombs, the latter a fragmentation grenade whose 'pineapple' casing was designed to shatter into lethal shards of flying metal. The range of hand-grenades was only about 30 yards, however, and a demand for greater range was met first by trench catapults, then rifle-grenades – a bomb mounted on a metal rod that could be fired out of an ordinary rifle ten times as far as a man could throw it.[25]

The new weapons revolutionised small-unit tactics. The specialist sections of a platoon might operate in a flexible 'diamond' formation of four 'blobs', with riflemen and bombers moving through gaps to 'infiltrate' the enemy position, Lewis gunners providing covering fire, and mortar men and rifle-grenadiers using their weapons like tiny howitzers.[26]

Blaser describes the London Scottish going forward in this way at Beersheba on 31 October:

> The front-line companies arranged themselves in sections of bombers, grenadiers, riflemen and Lewis gunners, for each section would advance as a 'blob' 50 yards from the next on either side. The attack formation was in waves of sections or 'blobs', and there were to be two companies in the front-line, one in support, and one in reserve.[27]

Just as the artillery acted to suppress enemy fire for the infantry as a whole, so the 'fire' sections of the platoon acted to suppress it for their own 'shock' sections. The army in action was becoming more integrated and more decentralised at the same time – enabling it to fight what some were calling 'the deep battle'.

Deep in several senses. An offensive battle required weeks, if not months, of reconnaissance, planning and preparation, stockpiling of munitions, registering of guns, massing of divisions, training of men, and much else. It could be expected to last for days, if not weeks, and to involve not only front-line combat, but wide-ranging artillery attacks on enemy batteries, communications, command and control, and his attempts to bring forward reserves and supplies. And because defences were in depth, attacks, too, had to be mounted in depth. General Ivor Maxse, a leading British tactical theorist, considered a stacking up of successive assault waves a precondition of success: 'a single line will fail; two lines will usually fail; three lines will sometimes fail, but four lines will usually succeed'. The two basic reasons for this were the depth of the defences to be penetrated and the limits of endurance of the fighting man: 'Under existing conditions, only one definite offensive blow can be expected from one body of infantry in one operation ... There is a limit to human endurance in battle, and once that limit is reached, the reaction is severe.'[28]

The deep battle and the new platoon tactics had an impact on soldiers' relationship with the landscape. Men were obliged to weave their way through it, hugging the ground, clinging to its little havens, sensing its subtleties. So they became more conscious of its contours, more intimate with the earth as they moved across it, more viscerally aware of the slight, critical, life-and-death nuances of the geographic spaces around them. A paradox: for the First World War was, at the same time, a global war of machines, millions of men, and fronts hundreds of miles long.

* * *

The infantry action west and south-west of Beersheba closed down around seven in the evening on 31 October, having torn open a 3-mile gap in the defences. But the town remained in enemy hands, Chauvel's Australians were still 3 miles east of it, and only an hour of daylight remained. Desert Mounted Corps' horses had not drunk for 24 hours. Chauvel had earlier wired Allenby requesting permission to fall back on alternative water supplies if necessary. Allenby's reply was characteristic: 'The Chief orders you to capture Beersheba today, in order to secure water and take prisoners.'[29]

The head of Desert Mounted Corps had started out at 6pm the previous day. Chauvel's 11,000 horse had then ridden between 25 and 30 miles through the moonlit night. All had reached their initial positions by 8am, two hours after sunrise. But no direct assault on Beersheba was possible, for the Ottomans occupied two commanding eminences north-east of the town. These guarded the Hebron road, down which reinforcements were due to pass, and threatened the flank of any force operating against Beersheba from the east. Both had to be captured.[30]

Ryrie's 2nd Australian Light Horse Brigade was ordered to take Tell el-Sakati, about 5 miles from Beersheba, to block the Hebron road, secure Chauvel's outer flank, and take possession of some nearby water. As the horsemen came into view, they were shelled with shrapnel, and as they got closer, riflemen and machine-guns opened up. Forced to dismount, they found themselves in rough ground with plenty of cover. Working forward, they gradually established fire superiority, and by 1pm Tell el-Sakati had been captured. The brigade spent the rest of the day guarding the position.[31]

Tell el-Saba proved much tougher. Three miles east of Beersheba, it was a major trench-fortress overlooking the open plain which Chauvel's men would have to cross to take the town; it was, in New Zealander Guy Powles' view, 'the keep of the Beersheba position'. The 1,000ft mound, the site of an ancient settlement at the junction of two wadis, was protected by cliffs on the south and steep slopes elsewhere. The top, about 400 yards by 200, was rocky but flat. It was heavily entrenched, with positions for two tiers of riflemen and machine-gunners with good fields of fire. Its capture was the mission of the New Zealand

Mounted Rifles, 1st Australian Light Horse Brigade, and the Somerset and Inverness horse-gun batteries.

The Canterbury and Auckland Regiments galloped in from the east and then dismounted about half a mile from the tell to fight their way forward on foot. The Somerset Battery kept pace, coming into action first at 3,000 yards, then leaping forward to a new position only 1,200 yards from the enemy trenches. The priority was to pinpoint and destroy machine-guns. Fire was directed onto these by signalling officers with flags observing from the front-line. A section of Somerset guns was then repositioned to target other machine-guns on the north face. The Inverness Battery, operating at a range of 2,600 yards, concentrated its fire on a nest of machine-guns in some caves east of the tell. The Australians, meantime, had opened an attack from the south, easing the pressure on the New Zealanders, as some of the defenders were redeployed to deal with them.

By 1.30pm, though the Canterburys were stalled on the right, some of the Aucklanders had got to within 300 yards of the Ottoman trenches and had Hotchkiss machine-guns placed to enfilade them. Even so, it was gone 2 o'clock before the firing-line was strong enough to begin the final assault. Advancing by short rushes, under covering fire from field-guns and machine-guns, groups of Aucklanders headed for the plateau. At 2.40 the first trenches on the eastern flank of the tell were captured: 60 prisoners were taken, as well as 3 machine-guns, 2 of which were now turned on the enemy.[32] 'We watched excitedly,' recalled Trooper Idriess:

> as we saw the New Zealanders, like little men, advancing in short rushes. Then further along, the 1st Light Horse Brigade began advancing in bent-backed rushes. Machine-gun, rifle and artillery fire increased in fury. Then we caught the gleam of bayonets. We strained our eyes as one line of men were almost at a trench. They were into it. Faintly we heard shouts as line after line surged on. Quickly the firing from Tell el-Saba died down. Then we saw it was taken.[33]

The final rush had come at 3 o'clock, the Aucklanders, reinforced by some Wellingtons from the reserve, surging up the last few yards, soon followed by the Canterburys on their right, the Australians on their left. Another seventy Ottomans were captured, along with two more machine-guns, while the remainder streamed west in flight.[34]

But the struggle for Tell el-Saba had cost six precious hours. A heavily entrenched hilltop redoubt with determined defenders and plentiful machine-guns, its capture had really been a job for infantry backed by heavy guns. Two brigades of dismounted infantry with two batteries of horse artillery simply did not have the firepower to manage the job with any alacrity. The only way to avoid a bloodbath and provide a reasonable chance of success had been cautious dribbling forward to build up a firing-line. The price was paid in time. And it was another four hours before Chauvel had his command reorganised and redeployed for the next phase of the operation – just one hour before sundown.

* * *

What was the correct way to use cavalry on battlefields dominated by a storm of steel? Traditionalists still argued for shock action, l'arme blanche (the sabre), and 'cavalry spirit'. Others insisted that all cavalry had to become mounted infantry, using horses for movement, but doing their fighting on foot with the rifle. Allenby – like so many First World War generals, a cavalryman – took a middle position. As inspector-general of cavalry between 1910 and 1914, he had supported the introduction of machine-guns and stressed the importance of firepower, yet argued that modern warfare still offered many opportunities for mounted action.[35] Fate ordained that he should be afforded the supreme opportunity to demonstrate that he was right, for in Palestine he commanded one of history's last great cavalry armies.[36]

The density of men and guns on the Western Front, and battlefields scored with trenches, pitted with shell-holes, laced with wire and churned into mires of mud, confounded plans for mounted action again and again. The massed divisions of cavalry waited four years to exploit a 'breakthrough' that never came: a triumph of hope over experience. But the wide open spaces of the Eastern Front – and later of Russia during the Civil War – saw much cavalry action. Here, the relationship between force and space was more balanced, the opportunity for movement and manoeuvre greater. So, too, in the Middle East. Without continuous trench-lines ranged in depth, on battlefields where gaps could be punched right through the defences, or a masse de manoeuvre projected around an open flank, cavalry might execute a Blitzkrieg as surely as panzers a generation later.

Chauvel had the strategic instincts of a cavalryman, but the tactical caution of the mounted infantryman he truly was. Accounts differ as to what passed between him and his senior officers, and who it was who finally made the decision to launch a mounted charge across 4 miles of open ground against entrenched infantry, machine-guns and artillery. What is beyond doubt is that at about 4.30 in the afternoon Chauvel ordered Major-General Hodgson, the British commander of the Australian Mounted Division, to take Beersheba before dark. What seems equally certain is that, regardless of whether or not he actually said so, Chauvel must have known that, given the distance and the time, the only way this could be done was by a mounted charge – though both Hodgson and Brigadier-General Grant, commander of 4th Australian Light Horse Brigade, later recalled having made that decision themselves.[37]

The brigade deployed on a front of two regiments, 4th Australian Light Horse (ALH) on the right, 12th on the left, with 11th in reserve. Each regiment was formed in three lines, one squadron behind the other, about 300 yards apart. The individual troopers were spaced at intervals of about four or five paces. There were about 800 of them. The outcome of the entire battle had come to depend upon these men: thus had all the giant forces set in motion by the war in the Middle East become momentarily concentrated.

The attack was supported by covering fire from the brigade machine-guns and two batteries of artillery. The 5th Mounted Brigade was ordered to follow the 4th ALH in direct support, and the 7th Mounted to advance south of the town; meantime, the 1st and 3rd ALH Brigades were already moving to the north of it. Grant's brigade was, in fact, the spearhead of a massed assault on Beersheba by virtually two entire cavalry divisions.[38]

Pressure of time had precluded reconnaissance: the Turks were known to be entrenched, but their location and strength were uncertain. As the horsemen appeared on the plain, moving at a trot, the Turkish gunners opened up with shrapnel. But the range was long and the target scattered and fast-moving, so casualties were minimal. At about two miles, the Turkish machine-guns joined in, but by now the British artillery was replying with a destructive fire wherever gun-flashes showed along the line. The distance closed further, and then came the musketry, erratic at first, then rapid and sustained. Men and horses went down, but the speed of the charge accelerated, rising now to a pounding gallop. Nostrils flaring, eyes bulging, manes and tails streaming, the walers came on through swirling red dust and the half-light of early evening, the troopers yelling, waving bayonets, high on adrenalin.

Courage is a social attitude; or perhaps a collective madness. Ion Idriess, participating in another charge that day, discovered that:

> the thrill, the comradeship, the knowledge that soon hell would open out, filled us all ... with the terrible intoxication of war ... I think all men get scared at times like these; but there comes a sort of laughing courage from deep within the heart of each, or from some source he never knew existed; and when he feels like that, he will gallop into the most blinding death with an utterly unexplainable, don't care, shrieking laugh upon his lips.

In fact, though few noticed at the time, the fire weakened as the range closed. Such was the speed and awesomeness of the charge that the Turkish infantry, having set their sights at 800 yards or more, never adjusted them, firing high and wild over the last few hundred yards. The guns, too, missed their mark, balls of flaming shrapnel bursting behind as the Light Horse raced on. 'The last half-mile was a berserk gallop,' reported Idriess, watching through his glasses, 'with the squadrons in magnificent line, a heart-throbbing sight as they plunged up the slope, the horses leaping redoubt trenches ...'

The leading wave jumped over the first and second trenches – 4ft wide and 8ft deep – and headed straight into the town. The second wave leapt from their horses and plunged into a frenzy of stabbing, hacking, clubbing, bombing and point-blank shooting. The third wave careered into the mêlée. Bayonets plunged into the bellies of horses overhead. A barrage of stick grenades exploded and destroyed half a troop. A man pinned beneath his horse exchanged shots with a Turk. The corpse of Sergeant-Major Wilson, firmly seated, galloped on, while Major Featherstonehaugh, when his horse went down, charged forward on foot, emptied his revolver into the nearest Turks, then fell, shot through both legs.

The men of the 4th Light Horse killed thirty or forty Turks before the remnant surrendered, those of the 12th about sixty. As the fighting subsided and the stretcher-bearers gathered the dead and wounded, they discovered the casualties to be amazingly few: thirty-one killed and thirty-six wounded, most of them in the savage few minutes of fighting at the Turkish trenches. Their open order, their speed, the great dust clouds raised by such numbers of galloping horse had protected them from the metal storm. So, too, had the sheer audacity of the charge, for, as Wavell commented, 'it requires extremely well-trained and disciplined units to adjust sights calmly and to produce good fire-effect in the face of galloping horsemen.'

The Ottoman garrison commander had ordered the evacuation of the town before the charge began, but he was taken by surprise at the sudden onset and escaped with only minutes to spare. His German engineers lacked the time to blow all their charges: most of the wells were captured intact. More than 1,000 prisoners were gathered up, 100 or so at the western trenches, the rest across the town, along with 9 field-guns. Though some 1,250 men escaped to fight again, the unexpected speed of the attack had shattered the Ottoman 27th Division as a military formation. As at Magdhaba and Rafa, Kress's defence of an isolated bastion had proved costly in the face of Chauvel's massed cavalry.[39]

The charge of the 4th Australian Light Horse Brigade at Beersheba has become a legend and grown in the telling. The Ottomans were evacuating and the western trenches were not fully manned. Beersheba was not the climax of the battle: the conquest of the town eliminated a flank bastion, solved the immediate water problem, and allowed XX Corps to advance on the main Ottoman position – but that is all. On the other hand, failure to take Beersheba on 31 October would have dislocated Allenby's entire offensive, reducing it to frontal slugging, perhaps bringing it to eventual defeat. And as a tactical demonstration of the still-enduring power of cavalry at the beginning of the twentieth century, it surely stands supreme. As a German staff officer captured in the town reported: 'We did not believe that the charge would be pushed home. That seemed an impossible intention. I have heard a great deal of the fighting quality of Australian soldiers. They are not soldiers at all: they are madmen.'[40]

* * *

The battle's centre of gravity now shifted to the British right. Desert Mounted Corps and XX Corps need time to water, reorganise, reconnoitre and redeploy for the assault on the flank of the main Ottoman position, the Hareira–Sheria complex; they would not be ready before 3 November at the earliest. To keep the enemy guessing and off-balance in the interim, Allenby ordered the planned infantry attack on Gaza to commence on the night of 1/2 November.

At 11pm, the 7th Scottish Rifles stormed Umbrella Hill, a projecting strong-point flanking the south-eastern end of a 5,000-yard long attack front that extended to the sea. The position was taken in half an hour. Then, at 3am, the main attack went in, covered by an intense 10-minute artillery bombardment. Much of the ground was loose, heavy, wearisome sand, piled into great dunes up to 150ft high. Beyond the sand on the right of the attack front, where the ground sloped gently upwards, was a maze of cactus-lined lanes and fields. The Turkish trenches, revetted with timber and sandbags, fronted by wire and in one place a minefield, dominated the approaches and were ranged in depth. But darkness shrouded the leading waves, allowing them to get into the enemy's forward line and commence a subterranean battle inside the trench system. Four brigades were employed, 156th Brigade of the 52nd (Lowland) Division on the right, and 161st, 162nd and 163rd of the 54th (East Anglian) Division in the centre and on the left. They were supported by six tanks. After three-and-a-half hours' fighting, Sheikh Hassan, a height overlooking the town's anchorage north-west of Gaza and, at 3,000 yards from the start-lines, the most distant of the planned objectives, was taken.[41]

XXI Corps had punched clean through the Ottoman defences on the far left of the British line. The Imperial Service Cavalry Brigade – three regiments of lancers, 1,500 horsemen, from the princely states of Jodhpur, Mysore and

Hyderabad – were duly moved forward to attempt a breakout. Before they could do so, the Ottomans counter-attacked. Two regiments of the 7th Division, sent in haste from Kress's reserve, marched to the sound of the guns, drove back the advanced elements of the 4th Northamptonshires, and then launched a full-scale assault, 2,000 strong, aimed at retaking Sheikh Hassan and driving the British back down the coast.

This effort was shattered by two murderous bombardments, the first by XXI Corps' heavy artillery, the second by even more powerful naval guns offshore. The survivors went to ground and set about improvising a new line. The fighting subsided and the front stabilised.[42]

About 1,000 Turks had been killed and some 550 captured. XXI Corps' losses were also heavy – about 350 killed, 2,000 wounded and 350 missing – but the attack had fulfilled Allenby's expectations, keeping his opponent anxiously focused on Gaza and compelled to commit another division to its defence. Even the tenacity with which the Turkish infantry defended their ground conformed to the British plan. Kress had discovered at First Gaza that an elastic defence based on depth and manoeuvre was beyond the capacity of the Ottoman Army. He had been forced to dig in and hold fast. But now the greatest virtue of the Turkish soldier – his tenacity in defence – was to be turned against him.[43]

* * *

Around the time of the Light Horse charge at Beersheba on the evening of 31 October, Stewart Newcombe's special-ops unit was far behind Ottoman lines cutting the telegraph line to Jerusalem. Hearing of Beersheba's capture, he took a gamble and the following morning moved his miniature force of 100 or so camel-mounted Arab irregulars and British machine-gunners onto the Hebron road. His thinking was that such brazen action might trigger a local uprising and, either way, the British cavalry should reach him soon enough. On the first day, Newcombe's force was attacked by about 100 Turks, who were repulsed with loss. By the morning of the 2nd, they had blocked all movement along the road for 40 hours. But their time was up: 100 Germans were coming down the road in lorries from Hebron, and another German officer was leading two companies of Ottoman infantry up the road from the south. With most of his machine-guns knocked out and twenty men down, Newcombe surrendered.

The impact, however, had been out of all proportion. No less than six Ottoman battalions had been sent against Newcombe's force. A German officer later reported on the pandemonium in Hebron:

The place was like a disturbed ants' nest. The staff of army headquarters was standing beside its horses saddled for hasty retreat ... Mounted Turkish gendarmes dashed through the excited populace. The main body of the English was said to be only a few kilometres off. As in all panics of this sort, rumour had grossly exaggerated the facts. A whimsical touch was given to the affair by an old Arab procuress, who in the midst of the universal terror was calmly preparing to meet the enemy with a band of scantily clad dancing-girls wearing transparent veils.[44]

The fall of Beersheba, followed by news of Newcombe's raid, jangled the nerves of the Ottoman high command. Falkenhayn had already dispatched the 19th Division from the *Yilderim* reserve, and ordered Fevzi Pasha, commander of Seventh Army, to counter-attack from the north-east with the aim of retaking the town. Fevzi requested a further three Eighth Army battalions from Sheria to assist, and these Kress duly supplied. The Ottoman forces were vectored on Khuweilfeh, an ancient tell in a complex of low hills with good local water, situated about 12 miles north-east of Beersheba, and therefore on the flank of the planned British sweep on the Hareira–Sheria complex. As well as the newly arrived 19th Division, the force assembled and entrenched at Khuweilfeh comprised the 3rd Cavalry Division, part of the 24th Division and elements of the 27th Division.

The British high command was equally aware of the importance of the position, not only in view of its location, but also because the wells at Beersheba had proved inadequate to meet demand, and a strong *khamsin* wind had added to the thirst of men and beasts, making the capture of additional water supplies a tactical priority. The 7th Mounted Brigade assaulted the Ottoman trenches on 2 November, but was driven back. They were joined by the 53rd Division and the 1st Light Horse Brigade during the night, and the attack was resumed the following day. But the Ottomans had also been reinforced, and again, after a hard day's fighting, remained firmly in control of Tell Khuweilfeh.

So it was to continue for four days more – a disjointed battle in a maze of little hills and gullies. The New Zealand officer Powles considered it 'mountain warfare', and the Australian Trooper Idriess reported the hills as 'all gorges and frowning bastions of rock fissured by tortuous ravines', the slopes covered in a 'stunted green-grey bush', the ground ideal for 'ambuscades'. A long succession of attacks and counter-attacks made little difference. The advantage was with the defender, especially as he controlled the wells, whereas the British were dependent for water, food and ammunition on supplies carried down 12 miles of rough, stony track from Beersheba.

Men and beasts along much of the British line were wilting from lack of water. Major Vivian Gilbert was marching up with the London Division.

> Our heads ached and our eyes became bloodshot and dim in the blinding glare reflected from the sand. After a time our tongues began to swell so that they seemed to fill the insides of our mouths, which had gone dry. It was with difficulty that we could speak. Then our lips commenced to swell; they turned a purplish black and burst; sand blew in the open cuts, and flies persistently settled on the wounds, driving us almost mad.

Some horses had to go two, even three days without water. Khuweilfeh became an obsession because 'it holds water, water, water' (Idriess). The water crisis was so acute that the entire Australian Mounted Division had to return to the rail terminus at Karm to drink.[45]

* * *

Success at Third Gaza was close-run. But if the grand assault on Hareira–Sheria had to be postponed until 6 November, it did not have to be cancelled. The stage was being set for a decisive clash of arms. The long struggle of the Welsh infantry on the bloody slopes of Khuweilfeh had completed that process. The model was Blenheim: attacks on either flank to fix the enemy and draw down his reserves; a thinning of the centre to feed the threatened flanks; then a hammer-blow to smash through the weakened centre and break the enemy army in two.

The Ottoman line had become anchored on two trench-bastions, Gaza to the west, Khuweilfeh to the east. But the effort to defend them, and in the latter case the attempt to concentrate a *masse de manoeuvre* for a counter-stroke, had drained their centre and reserves. On the night of 5/6 November, the main bulk of Desert Mounted Corps and XX Corps was finally moving into position opposite the Hareira–Sheria complex. This comprised a number of distinct trench-systems extending for about 15 miles. The Hareira Redoubt formed the western flank. A southward-projecting salient was created by the Rushdi and Kauwukah systems. A further 5 miles of trenches extended eastwards on the opposite side of the Beersheba railway. Just to the north was the Sheria Redoubt, the main position guarding the eastern flank.

The works had been much embellished over the preceding six months, and were now in considerable depth and heavily wired. They commanded an extensive field of fire over an open rolling plain. But the defenders were reduced to a few thousand, whereas the British strike-force comprised three infantry divisions – from left to right, 10th (Irish), 60th (London) and 74th (Yeomanry). West of the 10th, in the 15-mile-wide gap between XXI and XX Corps, was the Australian Mounted Division and, on the opposite flank, beyond the 74th and covering the British flank and rear, was a large force comprising 53rd Division – still battling in the hills around Khuweilfeh – Yeomanry Mounted Division, the Imperial Camel Brigade and the New Zealand Mounted Rifles.

The attack was opened by 74th Division at 5am, its three brigades, in echelon from the left, advancing westwards with the aim of rolling up the line of trenches east of the railway. The ground was devoid of cover, and the pace of the advance tended to outrun artillery support, which, in any case, was hampered by lack of up-to-date reconnaissance of enemy works. But the infantry swept forward, covered by their own machine-guns and, by 1.30 in the afternoon, had captured all their objectives.

By this time, the artillery had cut the wire in front of the Rushdi and Kauwukah trenches, and the men of 60th and 10th Division were advancing, some in extended lines with fourteen paces between each man, others in 'artillery formation' of platoon-sized 'blobs'. Doug Calcutt, the browned-off private with the Queen's Westminster Rifles, 60th Division, was in the thick of it. One minute he was hugging the ground shielding his head against shrapnel with his water-bottle, the next he was up and over the brow of a hill into an inferno of fire, heading for 'a line of trenches on the top of a ridge and the whole line punctuated with clouds of flying earth. The barrage. Then we commence. We have ears for nothing else but the bullets and machine-guns.' Gunner Powell and his mates, also with 60th Division, were lugging forward a Stokes mortar to provide close support.

> Our own field-guns and machine-guns were firing close above our heads. The noise was unbearable, beyond description; I was literally stunned by the cacophony, unable even to think clearly. In front of us was a long downward slope, and then a rise towards the Turkish trenches, but these were quite blanketed in a fog of smoke and dust. The sand all over this slope was spurting up where bullets were striking it as [if] it were a hailstorm. The ground was soon dotted with prostrate figures. Everywhere men were throwing up their arms and falling, headlong, some to lie still, others to writhe and scream in agony.

In fact, the casualties were not too heavy. The guns laid down a creeping barrage, tearing up the wire and suppressing enemy fire. The 60th lost only 300, and the total for the day, spread across three divisions, was 1,300. Once into the enemy trenches, the fighting was usually a brief flurry of shooting, stabbing and bombing, and then the Turks ran or surrendered. Clearing the trenches could, however, be nerve-wracking. 'They proved to be a maze which we were ordered to scour, proceeding in various directions,' reported Calcutt. 'I had the bayonet held out in front, loaded and finger on trigger. Dodged along, saw somebody. I started, he started, we both smiled. It was Humphreys with bomb with the pin out working in my direction.'

By late afternoon, elements of both the 74th and 60th Divisions were closing on the Sheria Redoubt. The plan was to rush it after nightfall. But the Turks, preparing to pull out, fired a great depot of stores and munitions at Sheria Station, and the flames illuminated the whole area for the enemy machine-gunners, blinding the British infantry: a bayonet charge became too risky.[46]

The Ottomans were attempting a partial retreat to a new line. Kress had commenced a withdrawal from Gaza, now deemed untenable, on 5 November, with the intention of redeploying his Eighth Army along the Wadi Hesi, about 5 miles to the north. Fevzi's Seventh Army, on the other hand, centred on the Khuweilfeh position, was standing firm. The hope was that the whole front might be stabilised on this new alignment.

Late on the 6th, it became known that Gaza was being evacuated, and when 75th Division went forward in the early hours, it found the enemy trenches empty. 'A wonderful sight greeted us,' recalled one Somerset Light Infantry lieutenant. 'We were abreast of Gaza close on our left. The country was interlaced with trenches and dense cactus-hedges; also bushes and trees grew plentifully; all affording excellent cover, especially for machine-guns. But not a shot was fired at us and we advanced unopposed.' By dawn, the British infantry had captured Ali Muntar, the great mound south-east of the town that was the key to its possession.

The Eighth Army was in full retreat, and Gaza, which had defied capture for nine months, was in British hands. But in the centre, the 'Zuheilika Group' – an improvised formation of about 1,000 men – moved into Sheria to reinforce the remnants of the Ottoman 16th Division, and a strong position was taken on the north side of the wadi that ran through the town, with well-placed artillery and machine-guns able to sweep the approaches. The Londoners of 60th Division took heavy casualties when they stormed forward on the morning of the 7th. But they were far too numerous to be stopped. The Turks were driven out of the town and away to the north. It was the same at the Hareira Redoubt. Though the Irish of 10th Division had to cross a flat plain under fire from artillery, machine-guns and rifles that morning, their attack was equally successful. Only at Khuweilfeh did the weary struggle of the Welsh infantry continue through another full day of hard fighting; but even here, finally, the enemy drew off in conformity with the general retirement farther west.[47]

By evening, it was clear that the Egyptian Expeditionary Force had won a great victory. The Turks were in retreat all along the line, and such was their condition, and such the numbers of enemy horse seeking to get among them, that their prospects of forming a durable line any time soon seemed bleak. Allenby's plan was for Chauvel's cavalry army to cut in behind as many as possible and seal off their retreat. He still hoped to trap a large part of Kress's Eighth Army south of the Wadi Hesi, while riding down and routing those who did succeed in getting north. He sensed that the total destruction of the force that had contested control of the desert between Egypt and Palestine for three long years was within his grasp.

But the enemy was not broken yet. The dogged Ottoman infantry, badly supplied and equipped, often hungry, thirsty and ragged, almost always heavily outnumbered, may have endured a week of intensive battle, sustained severe losses, and been driven from its trenches; yet its formations were intact. After almost a year of trench-war stalemate, tens of thousands of men were in motion across southern Palestine on the night of 7/8 November. But the extent of Allenby's victory was still in doubt. Would the defeated Turks escape to fight again? Would the victorious British be able to take Jerusalem before the rains set in?

CHAPTER 14

Jerusalem

MAJOR-GENERAL 'JIMMY' Shea, commander of 60th Division, had gone forward to reconnoitre in a borrowed light car. It was early afternoon on 8 November 1917, the first day of the British pursuit after Third Gaza. It was proving harder than anticipated. The Ottoman rearguards were fighting a succession of positions designed to hold up the British advance while immovable stores were destroyed and the main mass of the retreating army got clear. Shea's Londoners were now stalled by a strong force entrenched on a commanding ridge a mile or two from Huj, the terminus of a small railway branch-line 10 miles inland from the coast. A column of about 2,000 men was in hasty retreat behind them. The Huj position was holding open the gap through which the remnants of Kress's army were still streaming.

The view from the light car was discouraging: Shea saw a wide expanse of open ground with serious firepower deployed on the ridge above. In fact, there were about 300 Turkish infantry, 4 machine-guns, a battery of German mountain-guns, another of Austrian 75mm field-guns, and a third, also Austrian, of 150mm howitzers. An infantry assault was liable to be slow and bloody. Could the cavalry perhaps turn the position? After all, this was a rear-guard with both flanks in the air.

The nearest mounted contingent were some yeomanry of 5th Mounted Brigade. Lieutenant-Colonel Cheape – a master of foxhounds and commander of the Warwickshire Yeomanry – collected one and a half squadrons of his own regiment and another one and a half of Worcesters: 170 men in all. No fire support was available: the brigade machine-guns had been sent to the rear with the pack-animals to water earlier that day, and the horse-guns had been outpaced in the rapid advance. The only thing in Cheape's favour was a low rise in front of the left-centre of the enemy position which concealed the approach

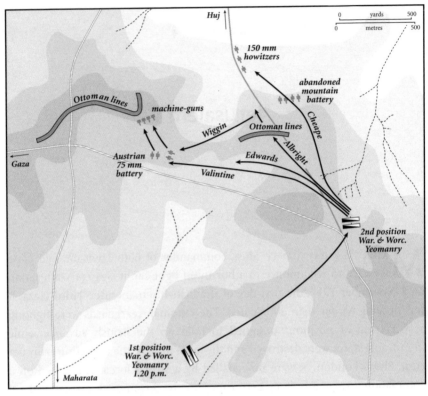

17. The Yeomanry action at Huj, 8 November 1917.

of his force until within about 800 yards, and afforded intermittent cover save for the final 200 to 300 yards.

Everything then happened very fast, as it tends to in mounted action. Advancing in a column of squadrons, Cheape's force unfolded to launch three distinct attacks. The leading squadron of Worcesters was directed against a force of about 200 Turkish infantry positioned between the mountain-guns on the enemy left and the field-guns and machine-guns in the centre. Cutting into the enemy line, this squadron then turned inwards along the ridge. They were supported by the full squadron of Warwicks and the half squadron of Worcesters, who crested the rise behind which they had advanced and charged the guns in the middle of the ridge frontally. Meantime, the remaining half squadron of Warwicks, swung wide to the right, rode around the eastern end of the ridge, and came in on the enemy rear, where they intercepted a small force attempting to get away to the north and cut down the crews of the three howitzers.

All three charges were made with drawn sabres. All three carried home. 'The gunners were nearly all Germans and Austrians, and they fought well,' reported

W.T. Massey. 'They splashed the valley with shrapnel, and during the few moments' lull when the yeomanry were lost to view behind the mound, they set their shell fuses to zero to make them burst at the mouth of the guns and act as case-shot.' Lieutenant Mercer was with the leading squadron of Worcesters: 'Machine-guns and rifles opened up on us the moment we topped the rise behind which we had formed up. I remember thinking that the sound of crackling bullets was like a hailstorm on an iron-roofed building ... A whole heap of men and horses went down 20 or 30 yards from the muzzles of the guns.'

Captain Williams of the Warwicks recalled the collision with the enemy gunners:

> They had served their guns until our advanced line was within 20 yards and then threw themselves under their guns. Few remained standing and, where they did, were instantly sabred. Others running away from the guns, threw themselves on the ground on being overtaken and thus saved themselves, for it was found almost impossible to sabre a man lying down at the pace we were travelling.

Having overrun the guns, the yeomanry swept on up the ridge to take the machine-guns, and, as Massey reports, 'having used the white arm [sabres] against their crews, the guns were turned onto the retreating Turks and decimated their ranks'.

The fighting had been savage. The casualties of the yeomanry were very high: all 3 squadron commanders were killed and 6 other officers wounded; 26 troopers were killed and 40 wounded; and no less than 100 horses were lost. The majority of the casualties were brought down during the charge to contact, though some also fell in the brief flurries of hand-to-hand fighting on the ridge, sabre against saw-bayonet, especially those involving the Austrian and German gunners, many of whom died fighting. In total, 11 guns and 4 machine-guns were captured, and some 70 men taken prisoner.[1]

The yeomanry charge at Huj cleared the way for the advance of 60th Division towards the Wadi Hesi. It also confirmed the lesson of Beersheba: that mounted charges against fixed positions could succeed. Speed could provide protection against firepower as surely as the armour of a tank or the trenches of the infantry. It limited the period of exposure, made range adjustment problematic, and unnerved those against whom it was directed; advantages that could be greatly enhanced by adopting an open-order formation and by the great clouds of dust thrown up by large masses of fast-moving horse in a dry environment. Thus, even without effective covering fire, a small force of charging yeomanry had been sufficient to rout a force two or three times their size and capture three batteries of guns. It was certainly a vindication of Allenby's compromise position on mounted tactics in modern warfare. As he cabled Robertson in London: 'The charge was at once carried out in face of heavy gun, machine-gun, and rifle fire with gallantry and dash worthy of the best traditions of British cavalry.'[2]

* * *

A very different sort of battle was raging a few miles to the north-east: a veritable meat-grinder of a battle. Moving north along the coast, the lead brigade of the 52nd (Lowland) Division had got across the Wadi Hesi near its mouth before dark on the 7 November, thereby turning the right flank of the new line Kress von Kressenstein was attempting to establish. The second brigade crossed during the night, the third early the following day. On the division's right, however, beyond the coastal dunes, was a low, rolling north–south ridge of rock and baked clay, about 3 miles long, covering the road and rail routes out of Gaza on the northern side of the wadi. This was Sausage Ridge, and, since it guarded their flank and escape-route, the Turks had dug deep, sandbag-revetted trenches and posted a strong garrison. The approach was across a 3-mile-wide open plain in full view of the defenders on the ridge.

The 155th Brigade launched an assault in the afternoon, but a threatened counter-attack on its left flank forced it to halt and face north. The 157th Brigade then advanced against the southern portion of the ridge, gaining a footing late in the day, but was then embroiled in a see-saw battle of attack and counter-attack that continued into the night. For several hours, Lowland Scot and Anatolian Turk engaged in a primeval close-quarters struggle with bullet, bomb and bayonet. Officers and NCOs went down, but little groups of men, clinging to patches of the slope, fought on. Finally, guided through the darkness by Turkish flares and the continual explosions of artillery, the 6th Highland Light Infantry led a final assault on the ridge. Approaching from the southern flank, they took the Turks, preoccupied by events to their front, by surprise. Gathering up the remnants of other units on their way, they gained momentum and stormed into the nearest trenches with the bayonet. This settled the matter. The Turks began to run and the Highland Light Infantry swept forward. Soon there were hundreds of Turks streaming away down the gullies and slopes on the eastern side of Sausage Ridge.[3]

The victory had been costly: 700 casualties in the two attacking brigades.[4] And it had taken all day, allowing thousands of Ottoman soldiers to make good their escape.[5] The two arms of a British pincer that might have closed the northern exit from Gaza had been held open by the Ottoman rearguards at Huj and Sausage Ridge just long enough to allow most of the men of Eighth Army to get away. They were not yet safe, but what might have become a trap was now merely a close pursuit. Everything depended on the speed of the cavalry and their ability to get among the ragged columns streaming north and turn retreat into rout.

* * *

Allenby knew what was at stake. He had relearned an old lesson at Arras earlier that year: that an army, physically and mentally exhausted by the effort, easily relapses into lethargy after battle; yet that is precisely when it must push on relentlessly to complete the victory if the full benefit is to be gained. When Guy Dawnay submitted draft orders for the pursuit, Allenby amended the proposed limit of advance with a line farther north and enquired whether it would be impossible to reach this. Dawnay replied, 'Not necessarily impossible, but ...' Allenby cut him off: 'No but. In pursuit you must always stretch possibilities to the limit. Troops having beaten the enemy will want to rest. They must be given objectives, not those you think they will reach, but the furthest they could possibly reach.'[6]

The rout of Kress's Eighth Army was close. Matters reached their nadir on 9 November, the day after Huj and Sausage Ridge. Trooper Idriess and his mates in the 5th Light Horse saw the evidence of near-panic as they pushed forward that day.

> Our horses soon were stepping in and out among the confusion of Turkish baggage, gear and equipment, and occasionally a blood-stained Turk. At dark we rode on a large Arab town ... Hundreds upon hundreds of Turkish wagons in jumbled masses of wreckage and confusion. Some were piled upon the other where bomb and shell had blown them ... But hundreds of wagons were quite unharmed, their horses and bullocks and mules still yoked to the wagons, in a pitiable state ... Countless rifles, stacks of cases of ammunition, wagons loaded to the brim with shiny brass bombs, farriers' gear, saddlery, armourers' gear, wagons loaded with doctors' gear, provisions, confusion indescribable: the baggage of an army in full retreat.[7]

A short while later, 5th Light Horse stumbled upon an abandoned German officers' camp of mud, stone and thatch houses surrounded by prickly-pear hedges on a low hilltop. Strewn about the abandoned wagons were clothes, greatcoats, gas-masks, cartridges, violins, sheet-music and photographs of women. The place stank of beer: the bungs had been pulled from a dozen great casks just before the Aussies galloped up.[8]

Hustling the enemy northwards were both the troopers of Desert Mounted Corps and the airmen of the Royal Flying Corps. Rumours of their coming rippled through the retreating columns. 'On the afternoon of 9 November,' recalled Kress:

> panic broke out at El-Tine, the main ammunition depot and railhead behind the Eighth Army front, among the large number of troops there assembled ... This did more to break the heart of the Eighth Army and diminish its fighting strength than all the hard fighting that had gone before. Several bombing attacks by powerful enemy flying-formations had caused explosions in the big ammunition-dump, and cut all telegraphic and telephonic communication. Suddenly news spread that the enemy's cavalry had broken through ... Although this report was false and fantastic, it caused such agitation that many formations began to retreat without orders and broke into flight.

Troops, transport and technical personnel were scattered. Some officers and men did not stop until they reached Jerusalem, or even Damascus. Units lost contact with their supply columns. Army communications broke down completely. Rumours of the breakthrough reached Jerusalem and spread tremors of alarm across the city.[9]

This, however, proved to be the low point. 'Thanks to the energy and devotion of a number of German and Turkish officers,' noted Kress, 'order was in a measure restored on the following day.'[10] Thanks were also due to the physical impossibility of sustaining the pursuit at the speed and scale necessary to harry the Eighth Army to destruction. The airmen flew sorties to the limits of endurance, but they were too few to be decisive. Only Desert Mounted Corps possessed the necessary combination of speed and shock-power; but it was breaking down from thirst, hunger and exhaustion. The Dorset Yeomanry was forced to cover 60 miles in 54 hours without water for its horses. The Lincolnshire Yeomanry may have held the record: 84 hours without water.[11] Some of the London Division's artillery horses had to be shot when they collapsed from thirst.[12] On 9 November, the second day of the pursuit, only one of the three mounted divisions, Anzac, was actually able to advance on the enemy; both Australian Mounted and the Yeomanry were forced to ride off in search of water. At the front, it was not simply a matter of finding wells. Small village wells often lacked pumps, and the retreating Ottomans had usually destroyed the pumps at larger wells. Many mounted units were reduced to improvising ropes of bridle reins and telephone cable to haul up one canvas bucket at a time: a very time-consuming way of watering thirsty horses. Oil drums and petrol tins became prized additions to unit inventories.[13]

The supply situation was almost as critical. The British were advancing far beyond their railheads, and the separate Ottoman railway system was of different gauge and short of rolling stock, so was of no immediate use. The Royal Navy was able to unload some supplies at points on the coast, but never enough, and even these had still to be transported inland. The gaps between railhead or beach and the advancing front-line were filled by camels and lorries, but the distances were increasing all the time.[14] No less than five infantry divisions were stalled on 10 November by lack of logistics to carry them forward.[15]

The search for water added scores of miles to the distances covered. Units marched in a curious succession of reverses and zigzags. It all added to the growing exhaustion and sickness. 'One whole bloody day spent in getting half a bloody drink,' moaned one Middlesex Yeomanry trooper.[16] 'At every halt the men automatically fell asleep,' recalled Sergeant Hatton of the same unit, 'as we had now had no sleep for five nights. In fact, we rocked in our saddles as we rode, and we were heavily laden with equipment . . .'[17]

Captain Teichman, the Worcestershire Yeomanry medical officer, made this assessment on 11 November:

During the morning a large number of sick men and horses were evacuated. The strain was beginning to tell: we had now been on the move for fourteen days, and the horses had on more than one occasion been forty-eight hours without water and often twenty-four. On many occasions the latter had been equally long without their saddles off. The men were badly in want of sleep, and many had broken out again with septic sores, chiefly on account of their inability to wash or take their clothes off for the past two weeks.[18]

The infantry were equally miserable. When the 60th (London) Division was finally granted some rest on the night of 9/10 November, Private Blunt of the Civil Service Rifles wrote in his diary:

Rations nothing but bully beef, biscuits, and jam. No cigarettes. Not one night's proper rest and continually on the march. We had marched and fought from Beersheba to the sea. Owing to casualties, the battalion is now only just over half strength. Everyone seems just beat and worn-out. I am as weak as a kitten, feeling done up all over. My face is covered with septic sores, and my feet are all blistered . . . I hope I shall never go through such a period again.[19]

* * *

The Eighth Army survived by the narrowest of margins. Its rearguards held the pincers apart just long enough on 8 November to allow its fleeing columns to escape across the Wadi Hesi. The pursuing regiments of horse were too few, too slow and too tired to get in among them and turn retreat into rout on the 9th. Launching its attack from the edge of the desert, advancing from there across the semi-arid zone of southernmost Palestine, the Egyptian Expeditionary Force had been prevented from landing a killer-blow by lack of water. 'Nearly every fight was a fight for water,' according to Chetwode, XX Corps commander, 'and if you did not drive the enemy off the water, you had to go back to where you started from and begin all over again.'[20]

On the third and fourth days of the retreat, the Ottoman Army began to recover. Regimental officers were reassembling their men and restoring order. Staff officers were establishing fresh lines of communication and supply. The high command was working on a new line of defence. The balance of advantage was shifting. The Ottomans were falling back on their bases as the British advanced away from theirs. They were reforming in the defensible hill-country of Judaea. The geography favoured them increasingly. The coastal plain, about 25 miles wide at Gaza, narrows to about 12 miles at Jaffa, the rugged spurs and valleys of the central mountain-massif approaching ever closer to the sea. A ladder of minor rivers, often marshy and muddy, provides a succession of defensible east–west lines across the plain, while control of the hills to the east covers the approaches to Jerusalem and threatens the flank of any army moving north up the coast.[21]

By the 12 November, Falkenhayn had about 20,000 men deployed on a 20-mile-long convex line covering Junction Station, the connection between the Jerusalem branch-line and the rest of the Palestine network. His force was spread too thin – and he wasted some of his strength in an ill-conceived and wholly ineffective counter-attack on the British right – but the position was a good one, with a succession of rocky hills crowned with mud villages girded by cactus-hedges and orchards, from which the Ottoman infantry had clear sweeps over bare, open slopes. These villages were converted into forts and became the framework of the defence.[22]

Allenby, still driving his army to the limit, was determined to punch through this line before it could solidify. Ignoring the threat posed by Falkenhayn's counter-attack – it petered out more through weariness than anything done by the dismounted Australians opposing it – he ordered a general attack along the whole line, employing, from left to right, Anzac Mounted, Yeomanry, 52nd (Lowland), 75th (Wessex) and Australian Mounted.

The battle began at 7am on 13 November. By mid-morning the British had captured a series of outlying positions with little opposition, and there was then

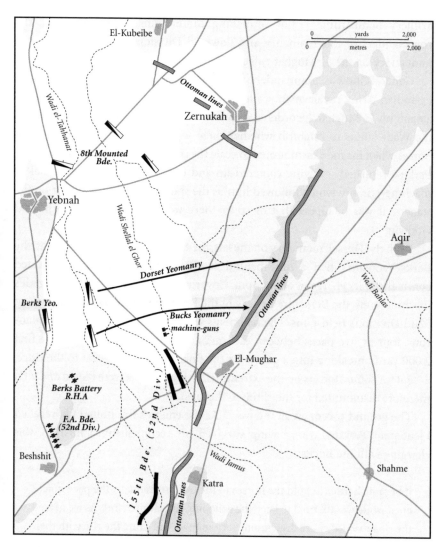

18. The Battle of El-Mughar, 13 November 1917.

a lull as the guns were hauled forward. The second phase was much harder. The crux of the battle became the village of El-Mughar, a strong Ottoman position facing the right-centre of the British line, at the junction, as it happened, of the Yeomanry and Lowland Divisions. The 155th Brigade, having overrun Beshshit village, sent forward two battalions late morning, one against Katra, the other against El-Mughar, twin strongpoints overlooking the Wadi Jamus. The Lowlanders were pinned down by shrapnel and machine-gun fire several hundred yards from their objectives, unable to get out of the wadi, even when reinforced by the reserve battalion. The brigade commander requested an artillery bombardment. But something more dramatic was pending: the commanders of the Yeomanry and Lowland Divisions had decided upon a joint attack on the El-Mughar ridge.[23]

General Godwin, commander of 6th Mounted Brigade, was a much admired ex-Indian Army cavalryman. Called upon to support the Lowlanders' stalled assault on El-Mughar, he ordered a reconnaissance of the approaches through the Wadi Jamus to establish whether there would be cover available for led horses when his men dismounted to scale the opposite ridge. When Lieutenant Perkins returned – having cantered up and down the wadi under a hail of machine-gun fire which followed him 'as the spotlight follows a dancer on the stage' – it was to report that of cover there was none. 'We'll gallop it,' said Godwin.

With the Dorset Yeomanry on the left, the Bucks Yeomanry on the right, the Berks Yeomanry half a mile behind – 800 men in total – 6th Mounted commenced its charge at about 3pm. Covering fire was given by the brigade's machine-guns, the Berkshire Battery of the Royal Horse Artillery, and some of 52nd Division's field-guns. The regiments went forward in columns of squadrons, four or five paces between each man, advancing at a trot over the first 2,000 yards, breaking into a gallop for the final 1,000-yard ascent to the ridge, except for some Dorsets on the extreme left, whose horses were blown and who therefore dismounted for the climb to the crest.

The ground was open all the way.[24] 'As the enemy's fire hotted up,' recalled Lieutenant Perkins, who, having survived his reconnaissance mission, was charging with the Bucks:

> it became harder to hold the horses to the trot, so gradually the pace quickened while we still tried to keep the galloping squadron in line. As we neared the ridge, swords were drawn, and very soon we breasting the rise with their gun-blasts feeling like pillows hitting one's face. Then in seconds they were all around us, some shooting, some scrambling out of slit trenches, and some sensibly falling flat on their faces. It had taken us, I suppose, a bit over five minutes.[25]

The Yeomanry had taken the ridge, but the enemy still held the village of El-Mughar. This was now assaulted by dismounted Berks Yeomanry and two battalions of Lowland infantry. By 5pm the fighting was over, all pockets of resistance overcome, many enemy captured, others escaping down the rocky eastern slope. The yeomanry charge had been decisive. It had cost 6th Mounted Brigade 16 killed, 114 wounded and 265 horses – 16 per cent of its personnel, 33 per cent of its mounts. The losses of 52nd Division's 155th Brigade had been much higher – 482 men in total, 315 among the two battalions of Borderers who stormed El-Mughar, 167 among the two of Royal Scots Fusiliers who took Katra. The Ottomans had suffered far more heavily, however: of the 5,000 defenders of the El-Mughar/Katra position, 400 had been killed in the two villages, many by shell-fire, 200 by the yeomanry on the ridge, and a total of 1,500 had been captured, along with 2 field-guns and 38 machine-guns.[26]

Yet again, a head-on mounted charge had carried against entrenched infantry backed by artillery and machine-guns. Lieutenant Perkins grasped the simple truth: the speed and shock had been too much for the defenders.

A line of horsemen appear out of a wadi two miles away, but too far to shoot at. Soon they are in range, but by then another line of horsemen emerge, and apparently your rifle fire and the machine-guns show no dramatic result. In your growing anxiety, your aim is dodgy to say the least, and again a third lot of horsemen appear. It is all very quick, and even in those days, when most men were used to horses, the galloping onrush is frightening – so, do you stand pat or run?[27]

As hundreds of Turks streamed down the eastern slope of the ridge and made for Aqir, another hilltop settlement a couple of miles to the east, the 22nd Yeomanry Brigade set off in pursuit. But their forward elements were ambushed and pinned down by heavy fire when they reached the village. Refet Bey, the commander of the Ottoman XXII Corps, realising that the yeomanry were set to power straight through the front, had concealed an improvised line of clerks, orderlies and headquarters staff in a small wadi. He could be seen calmly riding to and fro on a white horse on the far bank. The action of this little group of men – about a company's strength – was sufficient to halt the British advance until nightfall and allow the fugitives from the day's fighting to make their escape.[28]

The line had also cracked farther south. The 75th Division had taken Mesmiye and 300 prisoners by late evening, and during the following night pushed forward, supported by some armoured cars, to Junction Station itself. Night marches are nerve-wracking, however, especially when, as in this case, they are punctuated by determined counter-attacks by hundreds of enemy emerging from the darkness screaming *Allah al-Akbar*. The division's forward unit, an Indian Army battalion of Outram's Rifles, was ordered to hold its ground until dawn, the blazing lights of the station in view ahead. Come first light and two Australian armoured cars raced past into the station to find it abandoned. Rumour had it that Kress von Kressenstein himself had left on the last train out. The enemy had not had time to destroy two locomotives, some rolling stock, and abundant stores of food, petrol and ammunition.[29] It had been a hasty departure by a weak and demoralised army with a broken front and at risk of annihilation.

The capture of El-Mughar ridge drove the Seventh Army eastwards into the hills, breaking its link with the Eighth Army on the plain, splitting *Yilderim* in two. The capture of Junction Station severed its railway connection to the outside world, reducing its communications to just two main roads, that to Nablus in the north, that via Jericho eastwards across the Jordan Valley. This was the strategic situation created by the week-long Battle of Gaza and the ten-day pursuit that followed.

The British had advanced 60 miles along the coast and 40 miles into the hills, hustling their enemies backwards all the way. The cost had been high: the British had suffered 6,000 casualties, and, by driving men and beasts to their uttermost, and by extending supply-lines to the point of breakdown, the pursuit had, in Dawnay's words, 'reached the limit of what is possible'. The Egyptian Expeditionary Force was exhausted. Between 29 October and 14 November, in a region critically short of water, the cavalry had averaged 170 miles. In nine days, the 52nd Division had marched 70 miles and fought four major actions. 'I am sure you would be astonished if only I could tell you of the marching and fighting of this period,' wrote Captain Case of the Royal Engineers to his family. 'This would have been magnificent even with a decent climate, good food, water and roads, but considering the wild country, the heat and the shortage of water, I think the achievement must be one of the foremost that the war has produced.'

So it was, and the losses of the enemy had been prodigious, with 10,000 men, 100 machine-guns, and 80 cannon captured, the degraded remnant demoralised and disorganised. But they had survived, and they were now safely across the River Auja in the north, and retreating deep into the Judaean Hills to the east, making a pause inevitable.

But for how long? The danger was that the frazzled enemy be given time to regroup and dig in. Allenby was determined to prevent it. 'So ends the first phase,' concluded Case in his letter home. 'What will the second bring forth?'[30]

* * *

Edmund Allenby was an avid reader. Two books he especially valued at the present time were the Bible and Sir George Adam Smith's *Historical Geography of the Holy Land*.[31] Though the latter was a work of piety written by a Scottish theologian, it was probably the most useful thing available in London when Allenby set out for Palestine. The prime minister – a man of religious conviction himself, albeit of a somewhat morally wayward kind – certainly thought so. Allenby's copy had been his present. 'I was convinced,' Lloyd George later explained, 'that this work was a better guide to a military leader whose task was to reach Jerusalem than any survey found in the pigeon-holes of the War Office.'[32] Maybe so. Even the colour pull-out maps may have been useful, since the main alternative was maps prepared decades before by the archaeologists of the Palestine Exploration Fund.[33] At the very least, perusing the pages of the *Historical Geography* in mid-November 1917 would have given the commander of the Egyptian Expeditionary Force food for thought.

The description of the western approaches to the Holy City was alarming.

> This great barrier [the hill-country of Judaea] . . . is penetrated by a number
> of defiles . . . Few are straight; most of them sharply curve. The sides are
> steep, and often precipitous, frequently with no path between save the rough
> torrent-bed, arranged in rapids of loose shingle, or in level steps of lime-
> stone strata, which at the mouth of the defile are often tilted almost perpen-
> dicularly into easily defended obstacles of passage . . . Everything conspires
> to give the few inhabitants easy means of defence against large armies. It is
> a country of ambushes, entanglements, surprises, where large armies have
> no room to fight, and the defenders can remain hidden; where the essentials
> of war are nimbleness and the sure foot, the power of scramble and of rush.

Sir George continued with a gloomy report on history's many failures to penetrate this 'great barrier'. Only once, it seemed, had a would-be conqueror of Jerusalem approaching from the west been blessed with success.[34] All the rest – Philistines, Assyrians, Greeks, Romans, Crusaders and many more – had failed. Especially poignant – given the talk in the army of this being 'the Last Crusade' – was the fate of Richard the Lionheart, who had come within sight of the Holy City in 1192, but could not bear to look upon it, knowing he was unable to reach it.[35]

Allenby might have blanched. Some senior officers advised against an advance through the mountains, especially at the onset of winter, with lines of communications already at the limit.[36] The War Office cabled caution: Allenby was not to be 'drawn into a position which you can only hold with difficulty'; he was to be aware that 'the situation in Europe is such that it may be necessary to reduce our forces in the East to the bare minimum required for defensive purposes this summer'.[37]

There were other options. Though an offensive on both fronts was precluded by logistical constraints, Allenby might have screened the Seventh Army in the hills while striking against the Eighth on the coast. Victory on the Auja might have allowed him to swing east through Nablus, sever the Seventh Army's communications, and force the surrender of Jerusalem by an indirect approach.[38] But the strategic argument was finely balanced, for the Ottomans were reeling from recent defeats, and the preponderance of British military power – a three-to-one advantage – was potentially overwhelming. And the balance tipped when political arguments were added. Jerusalem was one of the world's greatest prizes; not for any economic or strategic value it had, but because, as a holy city of three religions, it was an ideological icon.

Jerusalem's 70,000 people were a mix of Muslims, Christians and Jews. The Christians were divided into a multitude of sects: Greek Orthodox, Roman Catholic, English Protestant, German Evangelical, Armenian Apostolic, Russian Orthodox, Copts and many others (though the numbers of foreign residents had, of course, been greatly reduced by the war). The streets of the Old City were an archaeological treasure-trove of ancient buildings redolent with mythic and historic significance. Jerusalem was the City of David, the location of Solomon's Temple, the site of Christ's crucifixion, the place where Muhammad met Abraham and Moses.[39] The great powers had squabbled over rival claims to be 'protector' of Jerusalem, or of one or another of its various sects, for the best part of a century. Now the British government had come forward as would-be 'liberator'. The French and Italians had duly appended military detachments to Allenby's army as tokens of shared interest.

Equally acute were Ottoman sensitivities, for the empire's claim to the caliphate had already been eroded by the loss of Cairo, Mecca and Baghdad; the sultan's authority as guardian of Islam and leader of *jihad* would ring hollow indeed if yet another of the holy cities were to be lost to the infidel.[40]

Jerusalem it had to be, then – by the direct approach. If so, it had to be soon. Allenby knew that 'if we had given the Turks time to organise a defence, we should never have stormed the heights'.[41] Accordingly, after a pause of only a day on 17 November, the new offensive began. It was, of course, a gamble, and the terrain, the weather, and the dogged endurance of Ottoman soldiers defending strong positions ensured that the struggle lasted a month and was bitterly fought.

* * *

The city of Jerusalem stands about 2,700 feet above sea-level at the summit of a long north–south plateau. To the east the land drops abruptly into the Rift Valley of the Jordan, but to the west it tips more slowly in a ripple of steep-sided spurs and gorges. The western routes – of which there were few, and all but one mere stone tracks – followed the valleys. The villages, perched high on the

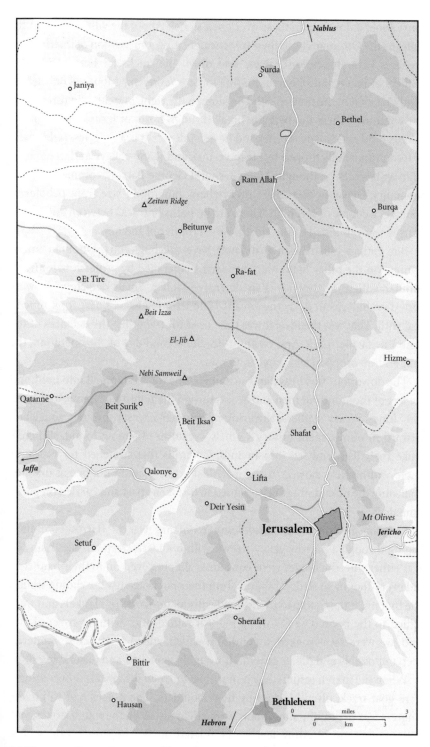

19. The area of operations around Jerusalem, 18 November–9 December 1917.

spurs, looked down upon these over open slopes. About the villages and on the plateaus the Ottomans built their trenches, creating a succession of interlocking firebases with stupendous views. And down the tracks far below came the soldiers of Lieutenant-General Bulfin's force – Yeomanry Mounted on the left, 52nd Division in the centre, 75th Division on the right, marching in three separate columns – their aim being to break through north of Jerusalem to cut the Nablus road and isolate the city and its defenders.[42] 'It is a waterless wilderness of tumultuous hills broken by steep ravines and stony valleys and marked by built-up terraces . . .' thought Major-General George Barrow, commanding the Yeomanry Division. 'Stones are everywhere, ranging in size from pebbles to boulders a couple of feet high. There are no paths or tracks between villages . . .' Barrow was reminded of the North-West Frontier of India.[43]

But Pathan hill-tribesmen did not have machine-guns. Ottoman infantrymen, on the other hand, were modern soldiers led by professional officers familiar with the latest ideas in defensive tactics. Small detachments were posted on hilltops to delay the advance and then fall back. These took time to deal with. That was the idea: it was time used to strengthen the defences of the main line farther back. And on the 19th, the second day of the operation, the temperature dropped and it began to rain.

The downpour was heavy and sustained. The tracks slumped into mud, and the feet of thousands of men and beasts turned them into a deep mash of slime and stones. Weary soldiers, shivering in summer kit, wet through, squelched forward in numb, silent misery. Camels, creatures of sun and sand, slithered, broke their legs, and fell into ravines. Columns that stretched for miles on single-width tracks slowed to a crawl. Most artillery could not be got forward at all, only the mountain-guns, designed to be taken apart and carried on pack-animals.[44]

Sergeant Hatton of the Middlesex Yeomanry was in Barrow's column. Edging through a narrow valley strewn with boulders, steep terraces rising in tiers either side, the horses were 'constantly slipping even on to their haunches and every foot or so striking sparks from their hoofs against the sliding stones'. The first night they camped in the open without top-coats or blankets and were chilled to the bone. The following night it rained, and, 'without cover of any kind, we were soon soaked, a condition which, added to the cold, rendered sleep impossible and life in general thoroughly wretched and miserable'.

When the march resumed next morning, the road disappeared, becoming a mere goat-track, often blocked by huge boulders. The horses had to be led, progress was 'dreadfully slow', boots were 'cut to pieces on the rough stones', and 'with aching and bleeding feet we blundered on'. At the third camp, where numerous groups of men huddled against terrace walls, permission was given to brew up over little fires. It was only a pinch of tea and sugar in boiling water, no milk, but it was a warming comfort. Then, as darkness fell, the skies opened again, and the rain came down in sheets, drenching everything within half an hour; it was, Hatton scribbled in his diary, 'the most wretched night of the war'.[45]

Only now, on 21 November, as the British columns reached the main Ottoman line, did the real fighting begin. In the north, the yeomanry were halted at the Zeitun Ridge, their 1,000 or so dismounted riflemen, with only four mountain-guns in support, unable to make any headway against about 3,000 entrenched Turks and several well-handled batteries. The 52nd Division captured the village of Beit Izza in the centre, but was unable to proceed further against the mesh of hilltop firebases ahead. The narrowness of the valleys restricted the breadth of attack fronts, whereas each Ottoman position was supported by others, so that converging fire tended to be concentrated on comparatively small bodies of men trying to move forward. Of particular importance, at the junction of the 52nd and 75th Divisions, was Nebi Samweil. This great mount was the Mizpah ('watch-tower') of the Old Testament, and in the village mosque on the summit were reputed to lie the remains of the Prophet Samuel. About eight miles north-west of the Holy City, it stands almost 3,000 feet high, with uninterrupted views in all directions, and is considered 'the Key to Jerusalem'.[46] It now became the cauldron of battle.

It was stormed and taken after sunset by Outram's Rifles and the Duke of Cornwall's Light Infantry from 75th Division. They were followed onto the summit by a battalion of Gurkhas and one of Hampshires. The capture seems to have been a fluke: the defenders were not anticipating a night attack and, about to be relieved, were taken by surprise as they prepared to leave. But the British then found themselves holding an exposed salient against fire from neighbouring heights. All attempts over the next three days by successive battalions of 52nd and 75th Division to capture El-Jib, a major eminence a mile or so north of Nebi Samweil, broke down about a mile from the village. Without artillery to suppress incoming fire, the storm of steel proved impenetrable.

Equally hopeless was the ongoing struggle on Nebi Samweil itself. The British lodgement, reinforced by Scots Lowlanders, was deluged with shell-fire and subjected to a relentless succession of counter-attacks.[47] Here, Major Kermack's company of the 7th Royal Scots found themselves. Like Sergeant Hatton's troop of Middlesex Yeomanry a few miles to the north, they had endured days and nights of pelting rain. They were dressed in thin drill tunics and shorts designed for an Egyptian summer. Cold and wet, hollow-eyed and half-starved, they now found themselves crouched under a terrace ledge on the side of Nebi Samweil. They were down to 50 or 60 men, quarter strength, when ordered to attack the main Ottoman position facing them. The mood was one of hopelessness. 'Our time on the ledges had given ample evidence that the Turk artillery was in greatly superior strength and dominated the situation.' Kermack was right: they were immediately pinned down by artillery, machine-gun, and rifle fire, and they spent the rest of a very long day cowering under rock. It was the same everywhere on the division front: 'We were held up along the whole line.'[48]

Hatton, too, bore witness to the power of the Ottoman artillery. A camel-gun sauntered onto the skyline near his troop's position. The enemy guns opened up and the shelling went on for hours. 'Into one group of some eight horses near me a shell fell direct; it must have killed a number outright, but the remainder, panic-stricken, careered backwards and fell, a mass of dead, dying, and maddened life, over a terrace.' Then he saw a shell land in a hollow where a group of badly wounded men had been gathered by the stretcher-bearers. A regimental padre had been going among them.

> I turned away sickened and hid my face in my hands, but summoning courage to look in a moment or two, saw that by some miraculous chance the padre was unhurt, and was sitting up in a dazed fashion gazing round him. Many of the dying were now dead, having been literally blown to pieces. Limbs and parts of limbs with the flesh exposed lay around. Stretchers were smashed to fragments, and the whole sight was a holocaust of slaughter. The padre soon collected himself, and calmly moved about among those still alive, turning them over, gathering the remnants of this his flock about him and continuing his message of peace and absolution.[49]

On the 24 November, Allenby issued orders for the attacks to be discontinued. It was clear his attempt to take Jerusalem 'on the run' had failed. The three British divisions had lost 2,000 men and been defeated at almost every point along the line by an Ottoman force that was probably only about one-third the size. Since the British had captured virtually no ground, there were no estimates of Ottoman casualties, but it seems likely they were far fewer. Breaking through was going to involve fresh troops, plenty of guns, better logistics and a different strategy. That would take time to organise.[50]

* * *

During the pause in the British offensive, the Ottomans launched a series of determined counter-attacks in an effort to retake Nebi Samweil and buy time for a further build-up of *Yilderim* forces in defence of Jerusalem. The attacks were spearheaded by some 3,000 Ottoman 'stormtroopers'. Wearing modified German-style steel helmets, carrying canvas shoulder-bags full of German-design stick grenades, and equipped with new German-made 1917 Mausers, these specialist soldiers were trained in the new infantry assault tactics pioneered on the Western Front. Their German mentors advocated surprise, speed, infiltration and deep penetration. Supporting artillery-fire was to be sudden and concentrated in time and space. Machine-guns were to be moved forward with the assault detachments to suppress enemy fire and disperse counter-attacks. The stormtroopers were taught to operate in small groups, to use their initiative to work their way forward, and then to fight it out at close-quarters with bombs as much as firearms. Bombers were to 'close on the trench at all possible speed, throwing their grenades, lie down while the grenades burst, and then rush the trench without hesitation'. The basic rule was that 'the boldest decision is always the best'.[51]

Two squadrons of 3rd Australian Light Horse holding a ridge at El-Burj towards the southern end of the British line had direct experience of the new tactics when suddenly attacked by the Storm Battalion of *Yilderim's* 19th Division in the early hours of 1 December. The Aussies were driven back by around 500 men charging forward with cries of *Allah al-Akbar* and volleys of stick grenades.

Clinging to the reverse slope of the ridge, they halted a second bombing attack with rifle and machine-gun fire at 20 yards range. They were soon joined by parties of Royal Scots Fusiliers and some Gloucester Yeomanry. The Scots counter-attacked with Mills grenades, taking the Turks in flank, sending one detachment back down the slope in flight. The composite line of Australians, Scotsmen and Gloucesters then held on until dawn, throwing back three separate Turkish attacks between 2am and 6am.

First light revealed the Turks to be trapped, unable to move forward, but with retreat now barred by some Australian machine-guns. Two detachments, one of Light Horse, the other of Royal Scots, then worked around the enemy flanks and induced the entire force to surrender. About 170 were taken prisoner; another 100 or so dead were counted nearby; the assumption was that the rest had fallen elsewhere and that the entire battalion had been annihilated.[52]

Thus were roles reversed during the succession of Ottoman counter-attacks mounted between 27 November and 1 December. Falkenhayn had planned an elaborate series of attacks to fix the British line and break through where he had detected a 5-mile gap on the northern front between the left flank of the Yeomanry Mounted Division in the hills and the right flank of the 54th (East Anglian) Division near the plain. The plan was sound in theory: an attempt to cut across the fragile communications of the divisions fighting in front of

Jerusalem. But the hill-country favoured the defence, attacks were costly, and the Ottoman Army lacked the numbers, logistics and skills – perhaps even, at some root level, the cultural attitudes – to carry out the textbook schemes of its German staff officers. The British high command was alarmed and found itself compelled to feed in units willy-nilly to hold the line. But there was never any real prospect of a breakthrough – against an army of combat veterans three times as numerous and with an enviable record of victory – and the main consequence of the operation was that Falkenhayn suffered further casualties he could ill-afford.[53]

The Seventh Army was reduced to about 15,000 men, the equivalent of a corps, and many were deeply demoralised, the moral decay evident in the numbers deserting. More than 5,000 deserters, including 200 officers, were arrested in Jerusalem during a round-up. Major von Papen, serving with the German Military Mission, wrote to Count Bernstorff, the new German ambassador to the Porte, on 21 November:

> We have had a very bad time. The breakdown of the army, after having to relinquish the good positions in which it had remained for so long, is so complete that I could never have dreamed of such a thing. But for this dissolution we should still be able to make a stand south of Jerusalem even today. But now the Seventh Army bolts from every cavalry patrol.

Papen favoured withdrawal from Jerusalem, but knew that Enver, the hawkish Ottoman war minister, opposed it on political grounds. 'From a military point of view it is a mistake, for this shattered army can only be put together again if entirely removed from contact with the enemy and fitted out with new divisions.' Germanic arrogance infected Papen's view. In truth, the Ottoman soldier remained dogged in adversity.[54] But Papen was right about the hopelessness of the Jerusalem position in the last month of 1917.

* * *

Allenby sensed this, too, and was unrepentant about his run at the mountain barrier:

> Had the attempt not been made at once, or had it been pressed with less determination, the enemy would have had time to reinforce his defences in the passes lower down, and the conquest of the plateau would then have been slow, costly and precarious. As it was, positions had been won from which the final attack could be prepared and delivered with good prospects of success.[55]

Nonetheless, he left nothing to chance. The fought-out XXI Corps was swapped with the relatively rested XX Corps on the coast. The supply crisis was eased with the arrival of 2,000 donkeys from Egypt to serve as pack-animals in the hills. The main axis of attack was shifted south to avoid the most difficult country and make proper use of the one good road – that from Jaffa to Jerusalem – to facilitate maximum artillery deployment. The cavalry component was reduced, since opportunities for mounted action were limited and horsemen lacked the necessary firepower; virtually all the fighting this time was to be done by infantry divisions with full complements of guns.[56]

The plan was far less ambitious than that a fortnight before. Instead of pivoting on the right and swinging north to cut the Nablus road, the army would pivot on the left and advance through the gap between Nebi Samweil and Jerusalem. Thus, instead of trapping the Seventh Army by severing its communications to the north, it would be pushed backwards: instead of destruction, the aim now was merely to defeat the Turks and drive them away. While 10th (Irish) Division guarded the northern flank, 74th (Yeomanry) and 60th (London) were to launch the main attack from the west, and a composite force of 53rd (Welsh) Division, a Yeomanry regiment, a heavy battery and some armoured cars – known as 'Mott's Detachment' – were to advance up the Hebron road to mount a separate attack from the south.

In the event, General Mott displayed excruciating caution, taking five days to move his column 50 miles, despite encountering almost no enemy opposition. By the time he reached the outskirts of Jerusalem, on 8 December, the battle was all but decided. Though rain and mist had slowed progress, and despite 74th Division being stalled around Nebi Samweil, 60th took a number of Ottoman positions with relative ease during the day, and was poised to spring forward to the Nablus road.

The crumbling of resistance was palpable. 'Their positions west of Jerusalem had been hewn out of the hillside with great labour more than a year previously,' wrote Wavell:

and in places provided three tiers of fire. Stubbornly defended, they should have been impregnable, and the Turk at his normal fighting level would certainly have made the assault a perilous enterprise. But the succession of defeats had shaken the morale of the Seventh Army, and its best remaining troops had been expended in the fruitless counter-attacks of the previous ten days.[57]

Though they did not yet know it, as they camped on the night of 8/9 December on the ground they held and tried to snatch some sleep, the weary British, Scots, Welsh, Indian and Gurkha infantry had won the battle for Jerusalem.

* * *

How exactly does one surrender a great historic city? It is not an everyday event and the mayor of Jerusalem was not sure. But the Ottoman garrison had fled in the night, the governor had handed the keys to the mayor before himself departing, and the priority was surely to protect the city by delivering them to the conquering army as soon as possible.

A small party of dignitaries in greatcoats, tunics, fezzes and *kalpaks* duly set out under a white flag. Two random cooks of the 20th London Battalion, however – the first representatives of the British Empire encountered – refused to have anything to do with them. Pressing on, the mayor's party then met two sergeants of the 19th London Battalion – still in summer shorts, boots and puttees encrusted with mud. The sergeants were not sure what to do, so everyone posed for a group photograph. The city fathers next encountered two artillery majors, who promptly disappeared to get advice. The mayor, it seemed, was gradually ascending the British military hierarchy: progress of sorts.

Lieutenant-Colonel Bayley of the Royal Field Artillery now arrived. He clearly considered himself of sufficient rank to make an important decision, so he took possession of the keys, and then stood around chatting for a while. Next on the scene was Brigadier-General Watson, who, with Bayley and an escort of ten gunners, accompanied the mayor's party back into the city. Finally, Major-General Shea, commander of 60th Division, having consulted with Lieutenant-General Chetwode, his corps commander, about the etiquette, headed into the city and formally accepted its surrender.[58]

* * *

Three separate battles had been fought for possession of Jerusalem over the preceding three weeks. The first, the British offensive of 21–24 November, had been a clear-cut Ottoman victory. The second, the Ottoman counter-attacks of 27 November–1 December, had been an equally clear-cut British victory. The third, by comparison, had lasted barely a day and been far less bloody. The 60th Division, which had done most of the fighting on 8 December, suffered only 550 casualties.

The blood-letting, privation and anguish of the first two battles had drained away the Seventh Army's will to combat, and, fearing total collapse and possible annihilation, the Ottoman high command had given the order to withdraw on the night of 8/9 December. Though 1,000 or so men were captured, along with 5 guns and 12 machine-guns, this was but a small fraction of the erstwhile defenders of Jerusalem.[59] Largely due to Mott's failure to push forward quickly and cut in around the relatively undefended eastern flank of the city, most of the retreating Turks had got clean away.[60] Yet again – as at Romani, Gaza, Wadi Hesi and Junction Station – the Ottoman Army had escaped to fight another day.

* * *

On 11 December, General Allenby made his formal entry into Jerusalem. It was a carefully stage-managed event for both a local and an international audience. After a *Blitzkrieg* campaign of 40 days and 18,000 casualties, he had stormed the mountain barrier to become – by one estimate – history's 34th conqueror of Jerusalem.[61] He was, moreover, the first Christian conqueror since the Crusades, for the city had been ruled by the Ottomans for four centuries, and by Muslims of some kind for seven. He had triumphed where Richard the Lionheart – a schoolroom English hero – had failed.

Christian piety; the Bible stories and the Holy Land; the Crusades and the romance of medieval chivalry – these were far more pervasive elements of European culture in *la belle époque* than they would be even twenty-five years later. The diaries, letters and memoirs of Allenby's soldiers were suffused with a sense of the historic and religious significance of the campaign. This sentiment was widely shared at home, not least in the House of Commons, which cheered when news of the capture of Jerusalem was announced, and in the pages of the London *Times*, which, apparently without irony, proclaimed 'the liberation' of the city.[62]

Bernard Braser of the London Scottish was typical: 'To free the Holy Land from a policy of organised murder, a tyranny so awful and despicable as to cause the hearts of the most apathetic to revolt in disgust, was in itself sufficient to urge us to great efforts, to suffer increased hardships without complaint.' He saw in his mind pictures of King Richard swinging a battle-axe, Samson battling the Philistines, and David bringing down Goliath.[63] These themes played to the whole of Europe; but celebration was, of course, restricted to Entente capitals.

The conquerors were anxious, however, to mute the message, in deference to an international audience, many of whom were unlikely to have found Crusader triumphalism inspirational. Twenty years before, the German Kaiser had entered Jerusalem through a specially cut hole in the city wall wearing Prussian uniform and riding a white horse. Unlike the brash *nouveau*-monarchy of Imperial Germany, the British Establishment had centuries of practice at getting the tone right. 'In the event of Jerusalem being occupied,' Robertson had cabled Allenby on 21 November, 'it would be of considerable political importance if you, on officially entering the city, dismount at the city gate and enter on foot. German Emperor rode in and the saying went round "a better man than he walked". Advantage of contrast in conduct will be obvious.'[64]

So Allenby climbed down from his Rolls-Royce staff car at the Jaffa Gate and walked into the city, followed by a small retinue of officers. The scene was framed by four honour guards – fifty British soldiers (a judicious mix of English, Welsh, Scots, and Irish), fifty Anzac (both Australians and New Zealanders), twenty French and twenty Italian. (Indian Muslim soldiers, meantime, were deployed to guard Islamic monuments around the city.) From the steps of the Tower of David, just inside the Jaffa Gate, a conciliatory proclamation was read out in seven languages (English, French, Italian, Russian, Arabic, Hebrew and Greek). Though Jerusalem was under martial law, all three of the great religions of the city would be respected, all holy places protected, all pious practices safeguarded.[65]

Major T.E. Lawrence had arrived just in time for the ceremony. Though rather junior, he had secured an invitation. Decked out in clean uniform and red tabs, he walked in the little procession of senior officers and staff through the Jaffa Gate. Though he considered the ceremony 'impressive in its way', he noted the deliberate low key, the absence of 'show'.[66] He seems to have been deeply affected by the historical drama of the moment: 'for me it was the most memorable event of the war, the one which, for historical reasons, made a stronger appeal than anything on Earth'.

But he was too brooding, too troubled by inner demons, to be altogether swept up. 'By my failure I had fettered the unknowing English, and dishonoured the unknowing Arabs, in a way only to be repaired by our triumphal entry into a liberated Damascus. The ceremony of the Jaffa Gate gave me a new determination.'[67]

CHAPTER 15

The Mountains of Moab

THE 'FAILURE' ON which Lawrence reflected at the Jaffa Gate was not simply the bungling of the Yarmuk raid. This had been compounded by the scale of Allenby's success, by which the Arab cause was diminished in proportion. 'We would have been by now, not in Jerusalem, but in Haifa, or Damascus, or Aleppo, had I not shrunk in October from the danger of a general rising against the Turks.'[1]

Lawrence was now prone to abrupt, manic-depressive oscillations of mood, swinging from elation at his own part in a great historic drama to near-suicidal despondency. The Yarmuk operation had been a dangerous, deep-penetration raid, the getaway a narrow escape. The Minifer ambush had been a hazardous, last-minute improvisation which had placed Lawrence in full view of a crowded Turkish troop-train only 50 yards away.

He had then immediately courted death again by donning disguise and entering enemy-occupied Deraa as a spy. He was seized by a group of Turkish soldiers, though not as a suspected enemy agent, but as a young man able to satisfy the lust of the Ottoman commandant. Resisting the subsequent advances, he was flogged severely and sadistically. Then, broken and bloody, he was sexually abused. It was an experience of violent homosexual rape which seems to have engendered profound feelings of guilt and shame, and to have inflicted permanent psychological damage.[2] Left in an outbuilding, Lawrence had escaped during the night, but he was left too mentally anguished to relax amid the bustle of the new Arab forward base at Azrak, to which he at first returned after his ordeal.

Azrak, about 50 miles east of the railway, was an oasis village in the eastern desert, its collection of stone houses and palm groves clustered near an old, square Roman frontier fort built of black-basalt blocks. The raiding party had taken up residence in the fort after the attack on the Yarmuk. The little mosque was cleaned for use, sentries posted in the upper towers, and rooms made habitable by covering the split-stone rafters of the roofs with brushwood, palm-branches and wads of clay.

For a while, despite solid rain and the howling of wild dogs at night – 'ghostly guardians ... the mythical builders of the fort' – the ruins provided a sort of haven. But as news spread that the followers of the sherif of Mecca were there, the fort became an embassy, hosting a trickle of visitors that soon swelled to a flood. Sometimes it was a column of Bedouin tribesmen, rushing in on camels, shooting into the air. Another time it might be a cavalcade of Druse horsemen from the mountains, a party of warlike peasants from the upland plain, a stiff procession of Syrian town dignitaries, a ragged crowd of Armenian refugees, or a marching company of Arab deserters from the Ottoman Army. 'Always they came, day after day, till the desert to the north of us, which had been trackless when we came, was all starred out with grey roads.'[3]

Lawrence, in his deeply troubled state, found intolerable the slow routines of Arab diplomacy – the polite rituals of guest-friendship with its greetings, coffee-grinding, mutton-feasting and gift-exchange. He again sensed acutely 'the fraudulence of an alien preaching others' liberty', and found the old doubt gnawing deeper as to whether 'the British government could really keep the spirit of its promises'. So, despite rain, sleet, and snow, he left for Aqaba, a gruelling ride in which he drove himself to the limit – and his sole companion well beyond it, to the point of blubbering, self-pitying despair. He arrived, it was said, wraith-like, white and withdrawn.[4]

A few days later, he was flown to Allenby's headquarters in Palestine. The great breakthrough campaign from Gaza to Jerusalem was approaching its triumphal conclusion and Allenby was planning ahead. To secure his eastern flank, which was coming to rest on the Jordan Valley, he was eager for the Arabs to advance up the western side, through the Mountains of Moab. This region, a well-watered upland plateau, was a source of grain and fodder for the Ottoman Army and wood-fuel for the Hijaz Railway, making it an important strategic asset. An Arab advance, moreover, would allow the two allied armies to link up across the intervening valley and squeeze out the Ottoman garrison at Jericho and the Ottoman fleet being used to ferry grain across the Dead Sea.[5]

The scheme, from Lawrence's perspective, had much appeal. Here was a proposal for an Arab advance deep into Syria – an advance to match that of the British in Palestine. Feisal and the Arab high command were eager to move north, and now they could expect more effective British support. After a short rest as Wingate's guest at the British Residency, the young liaison officer – 'looking much fitter and better than when I last saw him' in Hogarth's view – returned to Aqaba with a renewed sense of mission.[6]

* * *

Jafar Pasha al-Askari had disembarked at Aqaba on 18 August 1917. Jafar was one of the growing band of Arab nationalist officers who had defected from the Ottoman service to the Sherifian. Wounded and captured at the Battle of Agagir in the Western Desert in February 1916, he had been 'turned', thanks in part to the solicitous attentions of Gilbert Clayton, David Hogarth and T.E. Lawrence of the Arab Bureau, but mainly to the news of the hangings of Arab leaders in Damascus and Beirut. 'Many members of these [secret] societies had been arrested, savagely humiliated, and subjected to the most inhumane and outrageous torture,' he later wrote. 'I made up my mind there and then to seek revenge, and to make every effort to join the sherif of Mecca at the earliest possible opportunity.'[7]

Two days steaming up the Red Sea on HMS *Hardinge* from Wejh had brought him and 800 Sherifian regulars to the new forward base of Prince Feisal's Arab Northern Army. Another 800 would arrive within five days.[8] Jafar knew the *Hardinge*, a workhorse of Admiral Wemyss's Red Sea task force, for it was the ship that had carried him from Cairo to Wejh the previous January.

Appointed to overall command of Feisal's regulars, Jafar spent six months recruiting and training, before leading his men in their first major operation, an attack on the railway, in early August. Then came the summons to Aqaba: a surprise, for few seem to have been aware of the objective of the small expeditionary force that had set out two months earlier under Sherif Nasir, Auda abu Tayi and Captain Lawrence. But the potential was obvious: 'the appearance of Emir Feisal at Aqaba would put new heart into the tribes and spread the movement northwards, causing the enemy much fear and consternation.'[9]

By the beginning of 1918, Feisal's Regular Army numbered about 2,000 men. Despite grandiloquent military nomenclature – so-called 'divisions' were in fact of battalion strength – it seemed a tiny force when set against Allenby's 95,000. Each of its two divisions comprised an infantry regiment (or brigade) formed of two battalions, each of 400 men, supported by a mounted section, some artillery, signals units, explosives experts and a floating periphery of tribal irregulars. One of the infantry battalions was mule-mounted, and there was, additionally, a small battalion, 150 strong, of Hijazi camel-men.[10]

Many of the infantry wore British combat uniforms with khaki *keffiyehs*. This was straightforward for Iraqi Arabs from prisoner-of-war camps who had served in the Ottoman Army. It was sometimes problematic with recruits from the Hijaz and the Yemen, who were 'unaccustomed to obeying orders and wearing army uniforms'. Trousers were a particular issue, and Jafar was compelled to design 'a new form of dress, consisting of an upper garment resembling an army jacket, complete with epaulettes, pockets, buttons and sleeves, and a lower one like a Scottish kilt, only longer, all of which I arranged to be made from sand-coloured cloth'. Many of the mule-mounted battalion, on the other hand, wore Arab *sirwal* baggy trousers (for comfort) and the grey sweaters of the Egyptian Army.

The standard small-arm was the Short Lee-Enfield rifle, though the mule-men were supplied with old (Japanese) Arisaka rifles.[11] The miniature army's artillery was 'a motley collection of various models and types' – two British 18-pounder field-guns, two Ottoman 77mm field-guns, two Egyptian mountain-guns, and 'two small, elderly mountain-guns under the French officer Captain Pisani, which were so antique we dubbed them "Napoleon's Guns"'.[12]

Military proficiency took time to acquire. In the early autumn, the Aqaba camp became so overcrowded and insanitary that there was an epidemic of cholera.[13] Still, such was the orderly layout of a Sherifian camp near Abu al-Lissan that it was mistaken for an Ottoman one and accidentally bombed by passing British aircraft.[14] And when Lawrence passed by Maulud Muklus's camp in the hills during the bitter winter that followed, he was struck by the stolid endurance of the 500 regulars stationed there for two months without relief.

> They had no tents to live in, only shallow dugouts on the hillside, lined with rough stone. They had no fuel except sparse wet wormwood . . . They had no clothes but khaki drill uniform of the ordinary British summer sort. They slept in their verminous pits on empty or half-empty flour-sacks, six or eight of them together in a knotted bunch, that enough of their worn blankets might be pooled for warmth. Rather more than half of them died or were mutilated by the cold and wet. And yet the others maintained their watch, wholly without available support, exchanging shots daily with the Turkish outposts, and protected only by the weather from crushing counter-attack.[15]

Here was a clue to the disproportionate importance of these 2,000 men of the Sherifian Regular Army. For the tribesmen came and went as the inclination took them. They were like a fluid in motion. Strategically, they would ride, concentrate, strike and disperse. Tactically, they would snipe and shift, dissolving away before superior force in one place to re-coagulate in another, seeking the point of least resistance. Like guerrillas in general, they would not defend fixed positions, for mobility, speed and evasion were the ABC of their military doctrine. This had the effect of stretching the Ottoman occupation, in time and space, towards the limit of its resistance. But it could never actually break it, so long as the capacity for decisive battle against concentrated force was lacking. Provided the Ottomans remained secure in their fortified bases, they could always renew their strength for further effort. And when they sallied forth again, the irregulars were prone to melt away before their greater fire-power. To hold ground, contest ground, turn ground into a killing-field and place of decision required a solid line of disciplined soldiers with modern firearms.

It did not necessarily require great numbers of them. Such was the tying down of men and materiel in static garrisons that the enemy's active columns were necessarily small. A single battalion of Jafar's regulars and a couple of guns were often sufficient: a solid firebase in the centre of the battlefield on which the tribesmen could pivot in manoeuvre. Maulud's battle at Wadi Musa the previous October had been of this kind: a miniature Cannae in which his dismounted mule-men staged a fighting withdrawal in the centre to lure the enemy forward as the tribesmen scampered along the rock-walls either side to envelop the flanks. There would be more like it.

Not that battle – let alone victorious battle – was essential to strategic effect. Often it was enough that the regulars simply existed. Through the autumn, the mere presence of Jafar's 2,000 recruits in training at Aqaba had been sufficient to deter an Ottoman advance from Abu al-Lissan to recapture the town. The tribal contingents might have dissolved before a relatively small punitive column. The existence of the regular battalions meant that a larger column was necessary: this imposed an impossible logistical burden: and thus was Aqaba secured.

As the war spread into Syria and the Sherifian regulars played an increasing role, the British and French commitment also ramped up. The British Military Mission, headed by Lieutenant-Colonel Pierce Joyce, was a composite special operations unit comprising: the Hijaz Armoured Car Battery of three Rolls-Royce armoured cars, mounting machine-guns and serviced by Ford tenders; two 10-pounder guns carried on Talbot lorries; a company of Egyptian Camel Corps; and X Flight (four aircraft) of the Royal Flying Corps. Such was its importance that, by February 1918, the Arab front had a small Cairo-based staff headed by Lieutenant-Colonel Alan Dawnay.[16] To formalise matters further, in March 1918 Lawrence was promoted lieutenant-colonel, making him equal in rank to Joyce. The thinking was that each performed comparable liaison duties, only Lawrence was attached to the tribesmen, Joyce to the regulars. The

British contribution was supplemented by that of a small French Military Mission under Captain Pisani, comprising two mountain-guns and four machine-guns.[17]

Lawrence remained semi-detached, both physically, in that his whereabouts and activities were often a mystery to his nominal superiors, and psychologically, in that his identification with the Arab cause, at least as he understood it, remained unwavering. This was symbolised by his recruitment of a personal bodyguard (though he was, of course, under threat, often moving through tribal areas where allegiances were uncertain, and with a price on his head that was steadily rising, since the Ottoman authorities were kept informed about his activities by their excellent desert intelligence network).

The men he hired were Ageyl, the professional mercenaries of the Hijaz and Nejd villages traditionally employed by Arab leaders as personal retainers. To secure their allegiance and good service, he paid the standard rate for man and camel, but supplied the mount himself, so that each man earned the full value of his pay, and would, when necessary, be prepared to push his animal to the limit, for 'my rides were long, hard, and sudden'. They were commanded by Abdullah al-Nahabi (Abdullah 'the Robber'), a young man who had solicited Lawrence's favour with gifts of two fine saddle-bags, and who came with the recommendation of Ibn Dakhil, the captain of Feisal's bodyguard. Many of the recruits were lawless men, 'fellows whose dash had got them into trouble elsewhere', but the rules of Bedouin service were strict and, once pledged, they were bound to give loyal service. Lawrence says that 90 served in all and nearly 60 died; though he was rarely accompanied on mission by more than 30 at a time. 'Fellows were very proud of being in my bodyguard, which developed a professionalism almost flamboyant. They dressed like a bed of tulips, in every colour but white; for that was my constant wear, and they did not wish to presume ...'[18]

* * *

The capture of Jerusalem had transformed the strategic relationship between the British and Arab forces. As long as the Egyptian Expeditionary Force (EEF) was stalled in front of Gaza, it was separated from the Arab Northern Army at Aqaba by 135 miles of desert. Jerusalem, on the other hand, perched close to the western escarpment of the Jordan Valley, was a mere 20 miles from the Dead Sea, 40 from the King's Highway on the opposite, eastern escarpment. This was the ancient north–south road that ran across the upland plateau of southern Syria.

The plateau, formed of sandy limestone and about 200 miles in length from the Yarmuk Gorge to the Plain of Guweira, is tilted, lower in the north, higher in the south; but because the Rift Valley also tilts, the eastern escarpment is a soaring edifice several thousand feet high along the whole of its length. The plateau, moreover, is broken by a succession of east–west wadis, some of them forming gigantic gorges, especially in the south. In the east, though, the ground is more gentle, the hills sloping down to merge with the desert about 20 miles from the King's Highway; and it was along this interface between desert and sown that the old caravan route used to run; and, by the time of the First World War, the Hijaz Railway. The plateau enjoys a relatively temperate climate with good rainfall, so it is corn-growing land with numerous small towns and villages of Arab farmers. Four sizeable market-towns spaced at intervals along the King's Highway – from south to north, Shobek, Tafila, Kerak and Madaba – were the local centres of Ottoman power – and the key strategic targets in any struggle for control of the region.[19]

Until early 1918, the Arabs could make little headway, for the Ottomans had reoccupied Abu al-Lissan, a barrier to a direct advance on Maan, and a threat to the flank of any push towards Shobek. But the drip-drip of attacks on the railway forced them to draw in their horns and divert men to the defence of the stations. This opened the way for the Arab Northern Army to attempt its most ambitious strategic thrust so far: a three-fold convergence on Tafila from west, south and east.

Sherif Nasir led a force of 300 regulars and 1,500 tribesmen, mainly Beni Sakhr, but with some Howeitat under Auda abu Tayi, with 8 machine-guns and 2 mountain-guns on a wide sweep through the eastern desert to fall upon Jurf al-Darwish Station, 35 miles north of Maan. The Arabs took position during the night and struck at dawn. The railway line was cut north and south of the station to block the arrival of reinforcements. A lone Ottoman gun was silenced by the two Arab mountain-guns. The tribesmen then launched an unscheduled camel-charge, and the Ottomans fled their trenches for the safety of the station build-ings. When a shell penetrated a wall, the tribesmen charged again, and the demoralised defenders surrendered. The Arabs had suffered only 2 casualties, the Ottomans 20, with 200 captured, along with all their guns, mules, equipment and a train-load of delicacies destined for the officers' messes of the besieged garrison at Medina. The only sourness was that the weather broke, delaying the onward advance to Tafila, and ten men froze to death in a single night of bitter cold.[20]

The southern column, meantime, formed of hardy sheepskin-clad villagers from Wadi Musa led by Sherif Abdul Mayin, advanced to Shobek, raised the local tribesmen, put the Ottoman garrison to flight, and then set about destroying the branch-line used to supply wood-fuel to the Hijaz Railway. The third column, mainly Jazi tribesmen (a Howeitat clan) under Sherif Mastur, came by way of the Wadi Araba and the great eastern escarpment.[21]

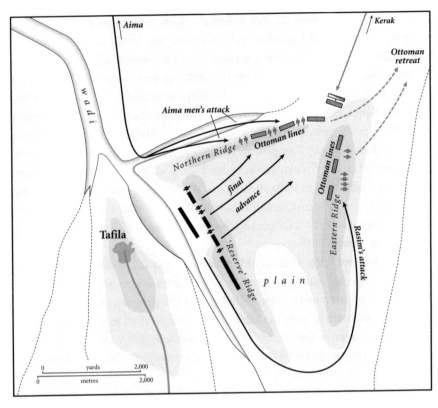

20. The Battle of Tafila, 25 January 1918.

As the Sherifian forces approached Tafila, however, they were fired upon by local townsmen. The paramount sheikh of Tafila, Dhiab al-Auran, was a Sherifian sympathiser, but there was bad blood between town and tribe, and it was at first uncertain how far his writ would run. In the event, a ceasefire was arranged, the population came over to the rebels, and the position of the little Ottoman garrison of 150 men, who retreated inside Government House, became untenable. Their surrender was arranged once Nasir's regulars were on hand to receive it. Among the captives was an Arab officer, Captain Zeki al-Halabi, who had already been in touch with Feisal. He was immediately appointed the Sherifian district officer for Tafila.[22]

The threat to their control of the plateau alarmed the Ottoman high command, and on 23 January Lieutenant-Colonel Hamid Fakhri Bey duly set out from Kerak with a composite brigade of 48th Division troops intent on recapturing Tafila. About 1,000 men in all, it comprised 3 infantry battalions, a cavalry detachment, 2 Austrian mountain-guns and about 30 machine-guns of various calibres. To oppose them were about 600 Arabs, some regulars, but mainly tribesmen, with 4 mountain-guns and about a dozen machine-guns.[23] These had been joined by Sherif Zeid, the Emir of Mecca's youngest son, Jafar, and Lawrence.

A tactical retreat might have been the wisest course. But this would have exposed the people of Tafila to Ottoman retribution – Hamid Fakhri was threatening precisely this as he approached the town – as well as being a major setback to the campaign. Instead, at first, there was unhappy compromise: Zeid – despite his youth, in overall command, and unsure of himself in a crisis – had followed the advice of Jafar and pulled his men back to the high ground west of the town. This caused panic among the inhabitants; though not necessarily, as Lawrence quickly discovered, a decision to flee.

> It was freezing hard, the ground all over ice and snow, and in the dark narrow streets the crying and confusion were terrible. I went out and walked about, listening. The men were in a passion of fear. . . . It was important to know the real public opinion, and soon we saw that they were in horror of the Turks, ready to do all in their physical capacity to support against them a leader with any fighting intention.[24]

The entire battle, in fact, was driven by spontaneous local initiative and on-the-spot decisions by often quite junior officers. There was no prior plan, and no proper direction from the Sherifian leadership. The command vacuum allowed Lawrence to play a major role in improvising a victory amid chaos.[25]

* * *

Outpost fighting had, in fact, broken out on the afternoon of 24 January, and when Zeid was persuaded to send a small force of regulars – a dozen mule-mounted infantry, a couple of machine-guns and a mountain-gun – back across the ravine the following morning, townsmen and tribesmen took courage. Most local men had some sort of firearm, however antiquated, and a thin firing-line slowly formed east of the town on a low ridge that lay across the Ottomans' path. Lawrence dubbed this the 'reserve' ridge, for it looked out over a triangular plain about 2 miles across, enclosed by two further ridges, on the north and the east, between which, at the north-eastern apex of the plain, ran the road to Kerak.

Tribal horsemen and groups of snipers in the rock and scrub skirmished with the Ottoman column as it drew closer during the morning, but then fell back across the plain towards the reserve ridge in the early afternoon. Hamid Fakhri proceeded to deploy his men on the ends of the northern and eastern ridges either side of the road.[26] His advance had first slowed and now came to a halt. This was to prove fatal. The shock and awe of a rapid onset might have broken the Arab will. Instead, the enemy's hesitancy implied weakness, and the defenders' confidence rose. The delay also allowed time for Zeid to transfer all his forces across the ravine, and for hundreds of local men to reach the battlefield.

Through the middle of the afternoon, the battle took the form of a long-range firefight. The Arabs generally had the better of it, for they knew the ground, and Lawrence had earlier paced out the distance across the plain, whereas the Ottomans, despite superior firepower, 'had not the range and fumbled it'. From the Arab point of view, the Ottomans had been halted and fixed in position on the far side of the plain, their line an inverted triangle on the distant ridge-tops, their commander unable to recover the initiative. In this curious little battle on the edge of a remote Arab town – so anomalous in the great war of mass and machine that had engulfed the world – power was flowing from one side of the plain to the other.

'We reminded one another that movement was the law of strategy, and started moving': thus Lawrence in his somewhat flippant account of the battle in *Seven Pillars*. Rasim Bey, a cheerful Syrian artillery officer who, since his defection, had had charge of Feisal's guns, took 80 mounted men and 5 light machine-guns to envelop the Ottoman left. Meantime, a hundred or so armed peasants from Aima, a village a few miles to the north-west, had begun a simultaneous assault on the Ottoman right, supported by 3 light machine-guns sent from the main line. They approached unseen along the ridge to within about 300 yards of the enemy.

Late in the afternoon, while fire from the mountain-gun and a battery of Vickers machine-guns on the reserve ridge plunged onto the Ottoman positions, chipping deadly shards of flint from the bare rock, separate firefights erupted at either end of the line. The Ottoman infantry on the flanks found themselves under fire from three sides, and many of their machine-guns proved useless, unable to depress sufficiently to target men clinging to the slopes beneath. On the right, the enemy's order to change front to deal with the flank threat seems to have been misinterpreted by the Aima men. The Arab machine-gun commander watched amazed as the villagers charged up the hill and the enemy broke and ran: 'as soon as the Turkish soldiers got up to change their direction, the peasants thought they were preparing to flee. They cheered loudly and attacked. The unit fell into disorder, which, strangely, spread to other units. The machine-guns were left lying on the ground, and clamour arose on both sides.'

Everything now happened very fast. As both flanks crumpled, Zeid and Lawrence urged the main line on the reserve ridge forward, and a stream of

Arabs raced across the plain. Mohammad ibn Ghasib, commander of Zeid's household retinue, 'led them on his camel, in shining wind-billowed robes, holding the crimson banner of the Ageyl high over his head'. On the opposite side of the field, Hamid Fakhri mounted his horse and ordered his staff into the line with rifles. But he was hit and fell to the ground mortally wounded. The whole Ottoman line dissolved into a mob of fugitives heading north.

Few survived. The Arabs poured after them on foot, on horse, on camel. Not only the Arabs: 'The Armenians, crouching behind us all day anxiously, now drew their knives and howled to one another in Turkish as they leaped forward.' Others, too, along the way, no doubt nursing bitter grievance of their own, arose to kill, far from the battlefield. So perhaps only 50 or so made it back to safety, and maybe 600 perished, including most of the wounded, who lay out the night after the battle and died in the snow. Around 250 were taken prisoner, and the booty included 2 mountain-guns, 27 machine-guns, and 200 horses and mules. The Arabs had about 100 casualties.[27]

* * *

Three days later, on 28 January, a separate Arab force, seventy horsemen under Sherif Abdullah ibn Hamza – prodded into action by Lawrence, hot-foot from Tafila – attacked the Ottoman naval base at Mezraa on the eastern shore of the Dead Sea. The flotilla stationed there supplied grain from the Kerak region to Ottoman garrisons on the farther shore. The raiders struck at dawn and caught the enemy sleeping. They burnt down the base huts, scuttled 6 sailing dhows and a motor-launch, and took 60 prisoners and 10 tons of grain.[28] The operation – an anomaly: the destruction of a fleet by irregular cavalry – had been a total success. It no doubt contributed to a growing sense of panic on the Ottoman side, evidenced by the abandonment of Kerak and a withdrawal to the railway, leaving the whole of the mountain massif open to an Arab advance.[29]

But the Ottomans had overreacted. The Arab offensive was abruptly stalled by Zeid's timidity, shortage of funds, the onset of severe winter weather, and perhaps – in a curious quirk of social psychology – the experience of victory itself, with its draining of energy and tumble of emotions; victory, Lawrence thought, 'upsets the Arab army'.[30]

With Zeid's little force snow-bound at Tafila, Lawrence headed south to collect the additional £30,000 he calculated was needed to get the revolt rolling northwards again. When he returned on 11 February, after a three-day journey along muddy tracks in rain and snow, it was to discover that Zeid had lapsed into complete passivity. 'Zeid hummed and hawed, and threw away his chance of making profit from it [the victory at Tafila]. He had the country from

Madaba at his feet. These Arabs are the most ghastly material to build into a design.'[31]

Worse was to come. When the weather improved two days later, Lawrence set out on a reconnaissance to the north, returning on 18 February with the news that the prospects were good. But by then the funds had gone. Zeid – young, shy, easily worked upon by avaricious tribal elders – had already dispensed the new tranche of British gold brought to Tafila only a week before. Lawrence was stunned, and soon plunged into depression. The Arab offensive was stone-dead. Tafila itself was likely to be retaken (it was, on 6 March).

Lawrence himself was at fault, having placed trust in untrustworthy men. He felt personally betrayed; and, no doubt, at a deeper level, was gnawed by the insoluble contradiction between the romantic ideal on which his psychic well-being was founded and the corruption of it with which he was obliged to wrestle.

In flight from this reality once again, he left Tafila for Allenby's headquarters, there, physically exhausted and mentally anguished, to appeal for transfer to 'some smaller part elsewhere'. He had 'made a mess of things'; he was 'tired to death of free-will'; he had been wounded five times and 'dreaded further pain'; hunger, cold and dirt had 'poisoned my hurts into a festering mass of sores'. Above all, there was 'the rankling fraudulence ... that pretence to lead the national uprising of another race, the daily posturing in alien dress, preaching in alien speech: with behind it a sense that the "promises" on which the Arabs worked were worth what their armed strength would be when the moment of fulfilment came'; and, with the 'fraudulence', the blood-price charged to his account, 'the causeless and ineffectual deaths of those 20 Arabs and 700 Turks' at Tafila. 'My will had gone, and I feared longer to be alone, lest the winds of circumstance or absolute power or lust blow my empty soul away.'[32]

* * *

The mood at Allenby's headquarters when Lawrence reached it could hardly have been more different. A two-month argument in London between Westerners (mainly generals) and Easterners (mainly politicians) had just concluded with a firm decision to make the defeat of the Ottoman Empire the main strategic priority. Allenby's plan, proposed after the fall of Jerusalem, for a limited advance in Palestine and operations east of the Jordan to cut the Hijaz Railway at Amman had been rejected. The Chief of the Imperial General Staff (CIGS) had been compelled to cable a demand for alternative plans for either 'the conquest of the whole of Palestine', or, better still, an 'advance through Palestine and Syria to the vicinity of Aleppo'. A quaint touch was a supplementary note that 'Palestine is to be considered as embracing the whole country between Dan and Beersheba' – a biblical flourish that bore the imprint of the prime minister, since Dan did not appear on modern maps, and archaeologists could not agree on the location of the site.[33] Allenby replied that it could not be done without more troops; the effect of which was to ratchet up the row in London, for the implication was a diversion of force from other fronts. The dispute reached the Supreme War Council in Versailles, a new body set up in November to coordinate Entente strategy (and also to enable Lloyd George, 'the Welsh wizard', to sideline his own CIGS, the intractable Westerner 'Wully' Robertson).

Robertson's influence was on the wane. Tainted by association with the murderous futility of Passchendaele, his reputation was further compromised when Allenby captured Jerusalem without the massive reinforcement the Cabinet had been told would be necessary. General Sir Henry Wilson – a 'political general' unpopular with many of his colleagues, a trimmer willing to run on the Eastern wind, and, by his own admission, the ugliest man in the army – had been appointed Britain's permanent representative at Versailles. Then, in mid-February, Wilson replaced Robertson at the War Office. He was soon informing ministers that action in the Middle East was the priority, lest 'we run a grave risk of permitting the Germans to establish themselves in a position which will eventually lead to the downfall of our Eastern Empire'.[34]

The Supreme War Council had already agreed to remain on the defensive in France, Italy and the Balkans, in order to 'undertake a decisive offensive against Turkey with a view to the annihilation of the Turkish armies and the collapse of Turkish resistance'. The effects might be far-reaching: perhaps even direct contact between the Entente powers and 'such elements of resistance to German domination as may still exist in Rumania and Southern Russia'.[35] General Jan Smuts, now a member of Britain's Imperial War Cabinet, was dispatched to Palestine in early February to discuss implementation of the plan.

The conclusion was that the available resources were insufficient to sustain simultaneous offensives in both Mesopotamia and Palestine: it had to be one or the other. And that, since the Mesopotamian force was further from Aleppo, had more onerous railway requirements, and would be exposed to a counter-offensive against its right flank in the event of a march across Transcaucasia, it should remain on the defensive: the decision would be sought in Palestine. Accordingly, two infantry divisions and a cavalry brigade were to be transferred from Mesopotamia to the Egyptian Expeditionary Force. These, with the addition of an Indian cavalry division from France, would bring Allenby's strength up to ten infantry divisions, four mounted divisions and a mounted brigade.[36]

* * *

Politics, not military strategy, had shaped this policy. The prospects for the Entente looked grim in the last winter of the war. The Bolsheviks had taken power in Russia and ended the war on the Eastern Front, freeing millions of German, Austro-Hungarian and Ottoman soldiers for service elsewhere. The French Army, paralysed by a wave of mutinies in the spring, had remained on the defensive ever since, its morale too fragile for the generals to risk sending the *poilus* over the top once more. The Italian Army had been routed at the Battle of Caporetto in October, and hundreds of thousands of men had cast aside their rifles and headed for home, many shouting revolutionary slogans or singing the 'Internationale'; only 70 miles back, deep inside Italian territory, were the generals finally able to improvise a new line. Serbia had been overrun in 1915, Rumania in 1916, and the Salonika Front across the southern Balkans had remained locked in hopeless stalemate ever since. And there was Passchendaele, where, during three months of drenching rain in late 1917, 2 million men had fought each other for possession of patches of slime and rubble, where thousands cut down by the storm of steel were sucked into the mud and disappeared forever, and where the survivors fought a primeval struggle with firearms, bombs and clubs inside a maze of shell-smashed trenches reeking of gas, shit and rotting bodies. Haig's most monstrous battle achieved nothing. The opposing lines had moved a few miles, but were as strongly defended as ever. The stalemate was unbroken. The war went on.

It had now lasted more than three years. Some 10 million were dead, perhaps twice that number maimed in body or mind, and hunger and disease stalked the cities of Europe. The popular mood was sullen and seditious. There were mutinies, strikes and demonstrations. Basil Thomson of Scotland Yard reported 'a rather sudden growth of pacifism'. Police agents recorded ominous graffiti in army latrines: 'What the hell are we fighting for? Only the capitalists.' One gloomy police report noted: 'There is scarcely a community or group of people in England now among whom the principles of socialism and extreme democratic control are not beginning to be listened to with ever-increasing eagerness ... There is no gathering of working people in the country which is not disposed to regard capitalism as a proven failure.' *The Times*, alert to the current of anxiety among its readers, ran a series of articles on 'The Ferment of Revolution'. That fourth winter of the war, the British political elite – like its counterparts elsewhere – had reason to fear that it was losing its grip; that the bitterness of the common people was reaching critical mass; that the contagion of revolution might soon spread from Red Petrograd through the whole rotting social fabric of war-ravaged Europe.[37]

Britain's leaders wanted a morale-boosting victory, and where better to seek it than in the Holy Land? But they were also empire-builders, and in this regard, too, the Middle East was a priority. 'If Russia collapsed,' Lloyd George had told the War Cabinet long before it actually did so:

> it would be beyond our power to beat Germany, as the blockade would become to a great extent ineffective, and the whole of the enemy's forces would become available to oppose the Western allies. We could not contemplate with equanimity the prospect of entering a peace conference with the enemy in possession of a large slice of allied territory before we had completed the conquest of Mesopotamia and Syria.[38]

The Germans might be unbeatable on the Western Front. A compromise peace might eventually be necessary. Let Britain, therefore, ensure that she had secured her spoils before coming to the negotiating table.

But if Russia's 'collapse' made 'the conquest of Mesopotamia and Syria' more pressing, it also served to expose it as the naked imperial land-grab that it was. When the armed workers, soldiers and sailors of the Petrograd Soviet – a democratic mass assembly of the city's working population – stormed the Winter Palace and brought down the pro-war provisional government in November 1917, they gained possession of countless files of secret documents filled with evidence of the corruption of the old European order it was their mission to destroy. Among these was the Sykes–Picot Agreement. The Bolsheviks – committed to world peace and the self-determination of peoples – promptly published this, along with many other secret treaties.

The global impact was hardly less than that of the revolution itself. Djemal Pasha wrote immediately to Feisal:

> There is only one standpoint from which your revolt can be justified in the interests of the Arabs, and that is the possibility of establishing an independent Arab government ... But what sort of an independence can you conceive in an Arab government to be established, after Palestine has become an international country, as the Allied [Entente] governments have openly and officially declared, with Syria completely under French domination, and with Iraq and the whole of Mesopotamia forming part and parcel of British possessions?[39]

The political crisis – for such it was for Britain's imperial elite in the Middle East – was compounded by the almost simultaneous publication of the Balfour Declaration, proposing a Jewish 'national home' in Palestine. Already a 'Jewish

Regiment' or 'Jewish Legion' was being formed. It would eventually comprise five battalions of Royal Fusiliers, with recruits drawn from Britain, Canada, the USA and the Zionist settlements in Palestine. They were to fight, in the words of one of their commanding officers, 'not only for the British cause, but also for the restoration of the Jewish people to the Promised Land'.[40] Long before the first of them arrived at the front in June 1918, the British advance from Gaza had given substance to the Balfour Declaration. Zionist settlers gave Allenby's soldiers a warm welcome. Most were of European origin. Many were English speakers. The soldiers reciprocated: many commented upon the friendliness of the people and the prosperity of their farms. In places, where British soldiers were camped near Zionist villages, there were joint celebrations of the fall of Jerusalem.[41]

The foreign capital that had created these islands of colonial settlement was invisible. What was more apparent was the contrast with the Arab villages, where the people were poorer, more guarded, seemingly remote and alien; a social distance lengthened in the racist lens through which the invading soldiery viewed the native people of the region.[42] The gulf was obvious in Jerusalem. The British Army had been welcomed by many among its cosmo-politan, multi-confessional population, but, in the words of the Australian *Official History*:

> mingling with demonstrative Christians and Jews, sullen and calculating, rejoicing as little at the arrival of the British as they had in the occupation of the Turks, were the Arabs who make up so large a part of the population . . . These silent Arabs served to remind the representatives of the government in London that Jerusalem is sacred to others beside Christian and Jew; that the Arab race is the parent of both the Hebrew and the Christian; that in a war for the right of self-determination it had the master-claim to all Palestine; and that the Mosque of Umar in Jerusalem is one of the most sacred of all Muslim shrines. All the trouble which was to follow after the Armistice in the settlement of the Arab claims was foreshadowed as General Shea drove through the streets of Jerusalem.[43]

Gilbert Clayton, the British spy-master, foresaw trouble immediately. He explained his concerns at length in a letter to Mark Sykes. The lack of any state-ment against annexations following the Sykes–Picot revelations was causing 'distrust and uneasiness'. The Balfour Declaration had 'made a profound impression on both Christians and Muslims, who view with little short of dismay the prospect of seeing Palestine and even eventually Syria in the hands of the Jews'. This double whammy of a diplomatic démarche prepared the ground 'for German-inspired ... propaganda' and 'an attractive proposal for independence under nominal Turkish suzerainty'.[44]

Clayton was right to worry. Only a minority felt any sort of allegiance to the Entente. Most were indifferent, but a good many fought on the opposite side, either as members of local Ottoman militias, or in raiding parties sanctioned by Ottoman authority so long as they targeted pro-Sherifian communities. Whichever side they fought on, the Arab combatants usually had no higher motives, no commitment to 'a cause'; they were essentially hired guns licensed to loot and rustle.[45] The British were in a bidding war with the Ottomans for mercenary service. Before the end of 1916, when the war was still confined to the Hijaz, they had already shelled out nearly a million pounds to the Sherifians.[46]

The conduit by which British gold reached Bedouin warriors was, of course, the traditional tribal hierarchy of sherifs and sheikhs. Sykes–Picot and the Balfour Declaration revealed the perfidiousness of the British and thus imperilled this vital relationship between imperial power and local client. Anglo-Arab relations continued problematic for the next six months, despite strenuous British efforts at damage-control.[47] Sherif Hussein, who forwarded Djemal's letter to Feisal on to the British, was naïve enough to accept the ready reassurances which came back. Feisal was not, and he kept open a line of communication to the Turks until at least the summer of 1918. Various factors tended to hold Feisal to his existing allegiance – filial loyalty, the influence of his British advisors, an empowering flow of British gold and supplies, and the logic and momentum of the war itself. But many of Feisal's regular officers were even more sceptical than he. In early April, they presented him with a memorandum questioning the subordination of the Arab Northern Army to the Egyptian Expeditionary Force (Feisal having been placed under Allenby's command the previous August). Shortly afterwards, there was virtual mutiny when an operation against the railway broke down in bad weather and logistical failure; Arab officers voiced bitter recriminations against their British advisors.[48] The immediate crisis was resolved, but the underlying tensions were not, and a succession of military setbacks over the next two months would bring Anglo-Arab relations to their lowest point.

* * *

Allenby had ordered two secondary operations in late December 1917. The aim had been to push the Ottomans back and secure some defensive depth and elbow-room for his own forces; in particular, he wanted Jaffa and Jerusalem, at opposite ends of his line, beyond artillery range.

The first operation, on the night of 20/21 December, was a brilliantly conceived and executed crossing of the River Auja north of Jaffa, which was to be developed as a major forward supply-base, with port and rail terminus. The river, up to 50 feet wide and 12 feet deep, with swampy banks on the south and sandy ridges on the north, afforded the enemy a strong defensive position. Though solid rain had turned the approaches to mud and the stream to a torrent, men of the 52nd (Lowland) Division crossed on rafts and bridges in the darkness, took the Ottomans by surprise, established a secure bridgehead on the north bank, and then, over the following two days, drove the enemy back 5 miles.[49]

A second, larger operation was mounted in the centre and on the right of the line, this was designed to push the Ottomans away from Jerusalem. It happened to coincide with a powerful enemy counter-attack, launched on the night of 26/27 December. While the 53rd (Welsh) and 60th (London) Divisions took the main weight of this attack in front of the city, the 10th (Irish) and 74th (Yeomanry) Divisions advanced through the hills to the west to threaten the enemy flank and bring them to a halt. The whole British line then rolled forward over the following three days (28–30 December), the Ottomans recoiling several miles.[50]

The fighting north of the Holy City was stubborn and sometimes ugly. Lieutenant Chipperfield, in charge of four London Division machine-guns, gave up taking prisoners:

We spend the rest of the day committing atrocities, shooting everything that moves – wounded, stretcher-bearers, Red Crescent parties . . . Constant barrages and attacks. We are mainly firing short bursts at anything we can see. Fool of a Turk coming up to take his place in the line, stands at full height to fire his rifle from the shoulder. Give him five rounds, knock his head off and see it fall before he drops.

Bernard Blaser and his mates, also of the London Division, were equally frenzied:

The sight of the recumbent and bleeding forms of our comrades lying around did not tend to promote feelings of mercy, and the tactics of the Turks had so incensed us that bayonets got to work slick and sure. Turks who had been doing their utmost to mow us down were now on their bended knees; angry oaths were uttered, and cries for mercy arose above the din; but no quarter was given; a few bayonet thrusts, a few shots fired point-blank, and they toppled over dead.[51]

There was then a long pause. The EEF had lost 30 per cent of its fighting strength and almost outrun its communications by the end of 1917. 'I could not deploy more troops, even if I had them,' Allenby cabled Robertson on 3 January, 'until my railway line is doubled.'[52] The rain and mud of winter compounded the supply problem, and effectively precluded further combat operations before the weather turned. 'One's sole interest in life is food,' wrote one 74th Division major in his diary, 'and I feel sure we shall soon be cutting each other's throats for a tin of bully. There have lately been a good many cases of men stealing each other's iron rations in the regiment.' Allenby had to pull entire divisions out of the line because 'I can't feed them with certainty, and even now, a fortnight's heavy rain would bring me near starvation.'[53] The priority was to build the railways and roads needed to sustain a new offensive when the time came; and meantime hold fast and wait for spring.

* * *

By mid-February, when Lawrence arrived at headquarters from Tafila, the plan was for a big push. Allenby wanted first to secure the Jordan Valley and attack the Hijaz Railway as a way of strengthening the Arab Revolt. Then, as the weather improved and his new rail communications caught up with his army, he wanted to break through on the left flank and drive up the coast through Haifa, Tyre, Sidon and Beirut. Meantime, a subsidiary column would push eastwards, south of Lake Tiberias, down the Yarmuk Valley, and onto the direct road to Damascus, working in tandem with the Arabs. Such was the heady vision. The first stage was to pinch out the Ottoman garrison at Jericho, the ancient settlement about 15 miles north-east of Jerusalem that lay amid a tangled mass of stony ridges, sheer cliffs, and deep gorges a short distance from the River Jordan. The Londoners of 60th Division stumbled forward to fix the enemy in his trenches, while the Anzacs flanked the position on the night of 20/21 February to render it untenable; the Turks, however, as usual, evacuated in good time, retreating across the Jordan, except for a bridgehead on the west bank at Ghoraniyeh.[54]

The second stage of the operation involved a general advance between the Nablus road in the west and the Jordan in the east as far as the Wadi Auja.[55] Four days of fighting (9–12 March) succeeded in winning virtually all objectives – despite the rugged terrain, the difficulty moving artillery and the numerous enemy machine-guns hidden in caves – and this placed Allenby's army abreast of the tracks on the far side of the river that led up the eastern escarpment towards Amman.[56]

Ten days later, General Shea led a large battle-group – 'Shea's Force' – across the Jordan to raid Amman and attempt to block the Hijaz Railway by

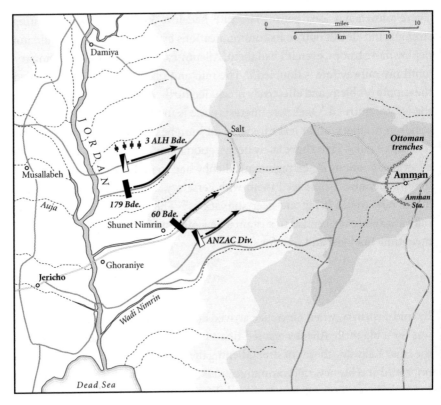

21. The Amman raid, 21 March–2 April 1918.

destroying a major tunnel and viaduct. The intention was partly to draw the Turks north – away from Tafila and Maan – and make it easier for Feisal's forces to move forward. It was also to fix the enemy's attention on events east of the Jordan, in particular to make him anxious for the security of the vital railway junction at Deraa.[57]

Shea's own 60th Division was to advance down the rough metalled road that ran across the valley from Jerusalem through Jericho, over the Ghoraniyeh Bridge, to Shunet Nimrin at the base of the eastern escarpment, up the defile from there to Salt near the summit, then across the plateau to Amman. One Anzac mounted brigade was to advance on the left using a track to the north of the road; the rest of the Anzac Mounted Division, along with the Imperial Camel Brigade, was to advance on the right, using more southerly tracks leading directly to Amman.

Much of the valley below and the plateau above is relatively easy going. The escarpment itself, however, is a 4,000-foot tower of crags and gorges. And, as luck would have it, Shea's columns had no sooner set out than they faced a pitiless downpour destined to last for two days that first slowed the river crossing, then the ascent.[58] The river doubled its size, overflowed its banks, and ran in spate at 12 miles per hour. Men attempting to cross at fords or swim over to secure ropes 'were swept away like corks'.[59] The mountain tracks proved impassable to wheels and fell apart in the downpour, the long files of pack-animals, laden with supplies and munitions, slithering to a standstill.

'First to go were the mess donkeys,' recalled one London Scottish officer, 'which one after the other subsided on the track and resolutely refused to try any more. Some of the mules caught the infection and also stopped.'[60] Camels found the going harder still. 'Many of them did the splits with their legs splaying out in either direction,' reported an Imperial Camel Corps officer, 'others slipped and went over the side of the ravine, and even if they were not fatally injured by the fall, there was no chance of getting them back again, so that we had to climb down, remove their loads, and shoot them where they lay.'[61] It took Shea's Force five days to cover the 25 miles to get within striking distance of Amman; even then, men and beasts were so exhausted they were compelled to spend a further day, 26 March, resting.[62] By then, the Turks were ready for them.

The delay had been fatal. Skander Bey, commander of the Ottoman 48th Division, had been ordered to Salt earlier that month. But his men had been spread along the Hijaz Railway on garrison duty, and many were destined not reach him until the fighting was over. When Shea's columns marched on the Jordan, Skander's defensive screen guarding 25 miles of river line amounted to 'a force of 80 to 100 infantry, a few cavalry and some machine-gun detachments'. His animal transport was inadequate, especially for moving machine-guns, he was short of field telephones and the Arabs had cut the existing telegraph-lines, so that communication between corps and division involved an eight-hour ride each way by a mounted orderly.

His stop-gap position at Shunet Nimrin was quickly turned because, with barely 600 men to hand, his flanks were in the air. Falling back to Salt, there was strength only for a defence of the town itself, so the British were soon lapping round both sides, while the Arabs in the town were sniping at the Ottoman rear.

A little later, an enemy cavalry regiment entered the town by the north-west. The Arabs, taking courage, attacked our sanitary company ... and began to murder our sick and wounded. The penetration of the enemy into the town made our own position untenable ... the whole danger of the enveloping movement was apparent. The weak forces were no longer able to hold their position, especially in view of the disaffection of the Arabs. But as we were entirely surrounded, retirement during the day was impossible. Till dark, a determined resistance was our only hope.[63]

The defenders of Salt fell back on Amman on the night of 25/26 March. They found the position there well fortified and strongly garrisoned. Djemal Pasha (the Lesser), commander of Fourth Army, had arrived to take command in person. Good telephone and telegraph communications were open. The supply of guns and munitions was plentiful. The troops were being fed on freshly baked bread. The inhabitants – mainly Circassian refugees from tsarist Russia – were friendly and had helped dig the trenches.[64] More men were arriving all the time.

The delays to the British advance – mainly due to the weather, partly to the resistance of Skander's detachments – had given General Otto Liman von Sanders just the time he needed. There had been radical changes in the enemy high command. Djemal Pasha (the Greater), the viceroy of Syria, had been recalled to Constantinople. Kress von Kressenstein had been superseded by Djevad Pasha at the head of the Ottoman Eighth Army. And Falkenhayn had gone – compromised in the eyes of his German superiors by the fall of Jerusalem, and in those of his Ottoman allies by his arrogance and German-dominated staff.

Liman, head of the German Military Mission since 1913, the victorious defender of Gallipoli in 1915, was at once an efficient Prussian aristocratic officer and a man sufficiently in tune with the realities of the Ottoman Empire not to attempt the impossible. In Wavell's view, he had 'less brilliance in manoeuvre than Falkenhayn, but was a staunch fighter on the defensive, and had better knowledge of the Turks and their methods', adding that 'he worked through a Turkish rather than a German staff'.[65] Allenby concurred: 'He appears to have a better understanding of the Turks, and to be less unpopular than ... Falkenhayn. Him, they hated.'[66]

Falkenhayn's 'brilliance in manoeuvre' had, of course, done him no good in Palestine. Brilliance does not exist in the abstract; generalship involves adaptation to concrete circumstances. Falkenhayn had concocted schemes on maps that could not be carried out by the men on the ground: thus he failed.[67] Liman, because he did not do this, was – as Allenby sensed – a more formidable enemy.

Though taken by surprise, once informed of the enemy thrust towards Amman, Liman ordered the Fourth Army, headquartered at Damascus, to have every available man converge on the town from north and south, and the Seventh Army, at Nablus, meantime to dispatch a force eastwards across the Jordan to threaten the British rear. The Amman garrison of fewer than 2,000 men was swelled to perhaps 5,000, including many Germans, supplied with around 70 machine-guns and 10 field-guns. Four days of attacks by the Anzacs, the Camels and the London Division's 181st Brigade made little impression. Only three mountain batteries were available, the weather was atrocious, the terrain rugged, and the Turks fought with their usual tenacity in defence of fixed positions, the Germans with their customary professionalism.[68]

Skander Bey witnessed the effects of Ottoman fire: 'Wave after wave advanced and reached within 500 yards of our position, where they were checked by the stubborn resistance of the troops in position . . .'[69] A.S. Benbow of the Camel Corps found himself advancing through a hail of fire when he stumbled and was hurled to the ground by a haversack heavy with 200 rounds of ammo. He made no attempt to get up. Bullets were hissing through the air and cracking on the stones all around. So he scraped with bare hands in the soft ground, but, for fear of attracting enemy fire, 'could only dig a hole large enough to put my head in'. He then folded his arms in front of his miniature dugout as extra protection and attempted to lie still. 'This was by no means an easy task as bullets were slashing up the ground and glancing off stones all round me, and their sickening thud and splash made me wince in a most uncomfortable manner.'[70]

The British attacked two days running, paused on the third, then resumed the offensive on the fourth. Though they made some gains, and though Ottoman battalions were reduced in places to a mere fifty men – 'the hospitals in Amman were filled to overflowing with wounded' – the enemy line held.[71]

In the rear, meantime, Salt was under attack by a separate Ottoman force, and the Jordan had risen 9 feet and swept away several bridges; so the supply situation was critical and the line of retreat imperilled. Allenby gave the order to withdraw and, by the evening of 2 April, except for troops detailed to hold a bridgehead at Ghoraniyeh, the whole force was back across the Jordan. There had been 1,350 casualties. Although about 1,000 prisoners had been taken, neither tunnel nor viaduct had been blown, a large quantity of supplies had been lost, and the Turks had won an indisputable victory. The Arabs, moreover, had been treated to a stark demonstration of the limits of British power.[72]

* * *

The Amman raid had been planned as part of a combined operation with the Arab Northern Army – the first of its kind. Instead of advancing on the axis Shobek, Tafila, Kerak and Madaba, the Arab focus shifted eastwards to the railway, and the plan was now to sever the line at Amman, Maan and Mudawwara. Despite the British defeat in the north, the Arabs went ahead and mounted a full-scale attack on Maan a week later.

Lawrence, Feisal and Jafar had all favoured operations to cut the line north of Maan, taking advantage of the distraction provided by the British threat to Amman, but the plan was modified at the insistence of Sherifian officers eager

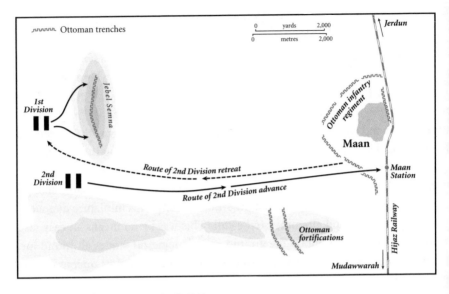

22. The Battle of Maan, 13–17 April 1918.

to employ the new regular army in a conventional battle. The motives appear to have been a mix of professional pride, nationalist ambition and suspicion of British advice. The result was a compromise.[73] Three columns were formed. The southern column, commanded by Nuri al-Said, first stormed Ghadir al-Hajj Station south of Maan, destroying 1,000 rails, on 11 April, and looped back to join the central column under Maulud Mukhlus for a direct assault on Jebel Semna, a dominating mound south-west of Maan, on the 13th. This assault, by 1st Division's two battalions of regular infantry, supported by Captain Pisani's guns, the British armoured cars and Auda's Howeitat cavalry, succeeded, bringing the Arabs within striking distance of the main defences around Maan Station.[74]

Meantime, the northern column under Jafar al-Askari – 2nd Division's two battalions of regulars, an 18-pounder gun and about 500 tribesmen – had attacked Jerdun, north of Maan, on the 12th. The infantry had advanced from the east under supporting fire from the 18-pounder, but had then stalled about 400 yards from the station. Jafar had found his 200 Howeitat cavalry milling about aimlessly and bellowed at them to support their comrades.

This exhortation had the desired effect: as one man they fell upon the station from the rear and quickly got the better of the defenders. The Turkish garrison commander was mortally wounded and made a gesture of surrender to me, whereupon his soldiers threw down their arms and left their trenches to give themselves up. There were about 200 of them. We seized the station, and the tribesmen looted all the weapons, ammunition, military supplies and stores they could lay their hands on.

After burning the station, Jafar's men moved south, tearing up 3,000 rails as they went, eventually joining 1st Division at Jebel Semna.[75]

The reunited Sherifian Regular Army now prepared for an assault on the most important Ottoman military base in southern Syria. Maan was a major communications hub. Routeways radiated from it like the spokes of a wheel: north to Amman, Deraa and Damascus; north-east to the desert oases of Jefer, Bair and the Wadi Sirhan; south-east to Mudawwara and the Hijaz; south-west to Aqaba and the Red Sea; and north-west to Wadi Musa, Shobek and the King's Highway. Because it was blessed with a plentiful water-supply, due to nearby limestone springs, a substantial medieval town had developed at Maan, with a strong Bedouin and commercial character, and this later became the seat of an Ottoman district governor. When the Hijaz Railway reached it in 1904, the town comprised about 500 flat-roofed mud houses a mile or so north of the station, and another 200 or so half a mile farther north again. A large station complex was established, and Maan came to be regarded as 'the Gateway to Arabia'.[76]

Control of Maan provided the Ottoman Army with a strong base for the accommodation of soldiers, materiel and supplies that could be moved rapidly in any of several directions. The town and the station were low-lying, but they were ringed by a series of rounded hills. Instead of continuous lines, therefore, the garrison had created a series of separate upslope strong-points, with linear trenches just below the upper contours of hills and ridges, and ring-trench redoubts on the summits. Attackers approaching across the open plains below were liable to be caught in cross-fire from two or more of these elevated firebases.

Jebel Semna was an outwork of this system. Its capture on 13 April had taken three hours and been achieved with light casualties (though these had included Maulud, the veteran Arab general, who had been shot from his horse and carried from the field with a painfully shattered thigh-bone). The inner works were more formidable. The western approach to Maan Station from the direction of Jebel Semna was a wide, flat plain overlooked by fortified ridges, all of them entrenched and wired. The ridge immediately west of the station – known as 'the Hill of the Birds' – was especially strong, with a 725m trench facing west, another of 500m south-west. Behind lay the station itself, a complex of masonry buildings functioning as blockhouses, and hereabouts lay the main encampment of the Ottoman garrison, up to 4,000 regulars of the Fourth Army's II Corps.

Elated by a string of successes – Ghadir al-Hajj, Jerdun, Semna – Feisal's Arab officers were now determined to attack this modern trench-fortress. The easiest approach – offering plenty of cover – would have been from the direction of town, which lay north-west of the station. But the inhabitants were divided into pro-Ottoman and pro-Sherifian factions of uncertain proportion, and it was deemed inadvisable to turn the place into a battlefield and risk the townsmen rallying to the Turk. This meant a direct assault across the open western approach.[77]

Jafar mounted several smaller operations to tighten the investment around the station and win better positions for his artillery. Then, on 16 April, under close covering fire, Nuri al-Said led the 2nd Division across the plain, around the southern edge of the Hill of the Birds, and towards the station complex, occupying positions 500 yards, in places only 200 yards, from the Ottoman lines. The following evening, the cavalry, regulars and tribesmen, rushed the station itself and captured the engine-shed. But the French guns ceased fire when Captain Pisani's ammunition gave out – he had warned in vain of the risk before the attack – and the Bedouin failed to mount a planned attack from the eastern flank. Nuri's infantry were unable to storm the trenches south and west of the station. The men in the engine-shed were left isolated under intense fire.

Though the siege of Maan Station lasted two days and nights, in the end the attackers were forced to retreat. The Arabs lost half their officers and a quarter of their rank-and-file, many in the final withdrawal across the plain under fire from massed riflemen and machine-guns on the ridge. Lawrence watched the sad spectacle of defeat unfold: the plain was 'littered with crumpled khaki figures, and the eyes of the wounded men, gone all rich with pain, stared accusingly at us as they were carried past. The human control had gone from their broken bodies, and their torn flesh took free play with its own nerves, and shook them helplessly.' Jafar pulled his men back to Jebel Semna.[78] The struggle for Maan became a stalemate. It would continue for five months.

Lawrence later praised the fighting qualities displayed by the Sherifian regulars: 'we had never expected such excellent spirit and work from our infantry, who fought steadily and cheerfully, under machine-gun fire, making clever use of ground ... The general conduct showed us that, given fair technical equipment, the Arabs were good enough for anything, with no need of British stiffening, however weighty the affair.' But he lamented the waste. The task was too much for 'such slender resources', and the attack had been pressed 'in the face of the truth'. He congratulated himself on having prevented delivery of bayonets, for 'had we had them, Nuri would once more have charged home, and all of us would have been spent'.[79]

Lawrence was perhaps too critical. The Battle of Maan was the largest single engagement of the Arab war, involving up to 4,000 Ottomans and 3,000 Arabs in a fiercely contested 5-day struggle. The Sherifian regulars had fought exceptionally well in the face of severe losses. The Ottomans were sufficiently spooked to send 3,000 reinforcements to boost the garrison. The railway below Maan was wrecked beyond repair, the town's communications with Mudawwara and the garrisons to the south permanently broken. The line to the north, upon which Maan was dependent for supplies, was under regular attack. The combined effect was to leave the Ottomans east of the Jordan more tied to static garrison duty than ever before, having to surrender initiative and mobility in order to defend key strong-points and keep open their line of communication. Despite tactical defeat, therefore, the Arab campaign of April 1918 can be considered a strategic success.[80]

* * *

It was the unnecessary carnage that preyed on Lawrence's mind and contributed to another of his periodic mood-swings. War is an experience of extremes. Moments of euphoria alternate with moments of depravity and horror. *Seven Pillars* is a dark book that makes little mention of the former. But others, who fought with him, bore testimony to Lawrence's standing among the Arabs. An Australian pilot serving with X Flight at Aqaba, one Stan Nunan, wrote home in December 1917 of 'a wonderful Englishman', 'a real live superman', one who had captured the town with 'a ragtime army of Arabs'.

> One day he will be in his red tabs as a staff major and the next in Bedouin dress – bare feet, flowing robes, and headdress ... Goes out with a few of his dusky cutthroats and a few camels loaded with guncotton and blows up trains and the line to Mecca. The Arabs stop him in the street to kiss his robes. The record of his exploits would fill a book. He is the most unassuming fellow you ever met.[81]

Army mechanic S.C. Rolls, serving with the Hijaz Armoured Car Company, was also witness to the Lawrence effect. He had never heard of Lawrence when appointed his driver in the final phase of the war. He was therefore astonished by the reception accorded the small, shy, self-effacing British lieutenant-colonel upon arrival at Feisal's camp at Guweira. 'As we drove towards the rock, the whole army seemed to come out of its tents, and Arab horsemen, riding bare-back, galloped round and round us furiously, with flying cloaks and brandished rifles, crying out of their throats, "Ya Aurans! Ya Aurans!", as though the name of my companion was a battle-cry.'[82]

A few months later, Rolls watched another Lawrentian advent, this time by air, landing at an Arab encampment at Jefer in the eastern desert. Again, the surge towards the leader, the brandishing of weapons, the shouting of the name.

> We rushed forward, the Arabs rushed forward, everybody seemed to hasten to greet the man who, without any official announcement from first to last, was recognised by all as the moving spirit of the whole campaign ... The Arabs ... touch his knee with reverent hands, kiss his shoulder, his head ... Instead of swinging him up on our shoulders, we watch while Feisal advances through the lane cleared in the mob by his black slaves to meet him. There is a smile on the ivory bearded face. They clasp hands, and quickly the Arabian prince embraces our Lawrence, once, twice ...[83]

But always, behind the pageantry of war, behind its challenges and excitements, lurked twin demons, Doubt and Guilt, gnawing like vultures at the innards of an all-too-sensitive mind. Lawrence had been depressed before witnessing the torn and twisted bodies carried off the battlefield at Maan. Both of his Arab servants, Ali and Uthman (named Daud and Farraj in *Seven Pillars*) – teenagers who had perhaps reminded him of Dahoum – were dead. Ali/Daud had died of cold during the winter at Azraq. The life had then gone out of his bereaved friend, a boon companion since early childhood, one who had previously been so mischievous and high-spirited, but was now 'dark and hard, leaden-eyed and old ... grey and silent, very much alone'.

Then, in early April, during a minor skirmish with a Turkish patrol near the railway, Uthman/Farraj had been shot and fallen from his camel. When his fellows reached him, they found him terribly wounded and in great pain. Then a fresh alarm: a party of fifty Turks and a motor trolley approaching down the line. Uthman/Farraj was bundled into a blanket, but 'he screamed so pitifully that we had not the heart to hurt him more'. The bullet had smashed right through and damaged the spine. The Arabs thought he had only hours to live, and to Lawrence he seemed 'sunken in that loneliness which came to hurt men who believed death near'.

But they could not leave him, for the Turks had been known to 'burn alive our hapless wounded'; the understanding was that those wounded who could not be moved should be finished off by their friends. So it fell to Lawrence to kill Uthman/Farraj.

> I knelt down beside him, holding my pistol near the ground by his head, so that he should not see my purpose; but he must have guessed it, for he

opened his eyes and clutched me with his harsh, scaly hand ... I waited for a moment and he said, 'Daud will be angry with you', the old smile coming back strangely to his grey face. I replied, 'Salute him from me', and he gave the formal answer, 'God give you peace', and shut his eyes to make my work easier.[84]

* * *

The British had failed at Amman, then the Arabs at Maan. The Ottoman Empire's peasant infantry was as tenacious as ever in defence of trenches, its grip on its Syrian strong-points still secure. Yet Allenby was determined to try again before the summer heat, especially when a deputation of Beni Sakhr arrived at his headquarters and offered assistance in a fresh attempt on Salt. Their fighting men were presently camped at Themed near Madaba, they said, and if the British moved soon they would have 20,000 tribal allies fighting with them on the escarpment.

It was a castle in the air. As Lawrence – who arrived at headquarters in the middle of the subsequent operation – wryly observed, the deputation was that of a single clan, it could 'in no circumstances raise more than 400 men', and 'at the moment there was not a single tent on Themed'.[85]

Though the objective was more modest than that of a month before – the aim was to seize Salt and consolidate it as a forward base on the far side of the Jordan – the difficulties were no less, for the Ottoman defences had thickened. Skander Bey's 48th Division had moved down to Shunet Nimrin, the position astride the Salt road at the base of the escarpment. They sensed a fresh attack pending and, though the ground was too hard for entrenchment, had worked night and day building stone sangars, terraced into the slopes and ranged in depth.[86]

The plan was for the 60th Division, backed by the New Zealand Mounted Rifles, to assault the position at Shunet Nimrin. At the same time, the Australian and Anzac Divisions were to advance up the eastern side of the valley, block the bridges and fords against Ottoman reinforcements from the west, and then send the bulk of their men up the tracks from the valley to the escarpment and take the town. The Ottoman VIII Corps would then be caught between the Londoners on the plain and the Australians behind them on the heights. The operation, commanded by Chauvel, began early on 30 April.[87]

All went well at first. The Londoners rushed the outer defensive line at Shunet Nimrin under the cover of a heavy artillery bombardment – Skander Bey reckoned twenty batteries were in action – but were then stalled by the stronger second line. This need not have mattered, for theirs was essentially a

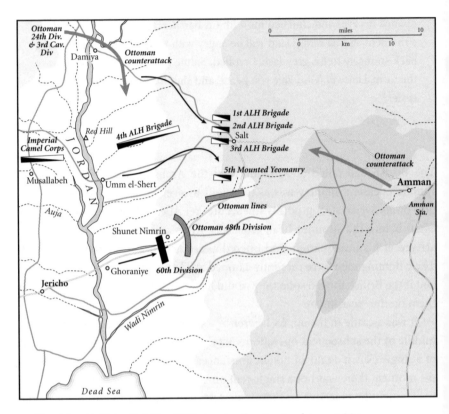

23. The Salt raid, 30 April–4 May 1918, showing the situation late on 1 May.

fixing operation, and the intensity of the subsequent fighting ensured that the defenders could do little about events elsewhere. The struggle was to continue through the night, often hand-to-hand, and as early as the second morning many Ottoman regiments had lost half their men and all their best officers. By the fourth and final day, rations would be exhausted and ammunition running out.[88]

Meantime, the 4th Australian Light Horse Brigade had advanced to cover the bridge at Damiya. This done, the 3rd Australian Light Horse headed up the Damiya track, and the 5th Mounted Yeomanry up the more southerly Umm el-Shert track. Later in the day, two more Light Horse brigades followed them. The 3rd Brigade captured Salt before the end of the day, and the following morning the three Light Horse brigades were deployed in a defensive ring around the town, while the Yeomanry had begun pushing down the main road towards the rear of the defenders of Shunet Nimrin.[89]

Then disaster struck. On hearing of the British operation, Liman von Saunders had immediately ordered the Ottoman 24th Division – two infantry regiments, a storm battalion and a pioneer company, under the capable command of Colonel Böhme – to cross the Jordan and attack the enemy rear. They were to do this in conjunction with Colonel Essad Bey's 3rd Cavalry Division and Caucasus Cavalry Brigade, along with two companies of infantry, a machine-gun detachment and a pioneer unit of the German Asia Corps.

Böhme got his men across the Jordan on the night of 30 April/1 May. Dawn found them concealed among the low mud-hills on the eastern bank of the river. Brigadier-General William Grant's 4th Light Horse was deployed facing west towards the Damiya Bridge. Though Grant feared an attack, he had no inkling of the imminence of the storm when, at about 7am on 1 May, it broke across the valley in a sudden eruption of rifle and machine-gun fire.[90] Soon afterwards, 'wave after wave of infantry in open order, and very boldly led, debouched from the mud-hills and struck straight across the plain'.[91] At the same time, more infantry appeared on Grant's right, and enemy cavalry could be seen circling wide to envelop his flank. It was soon clear, too, that his left was also threatened, with the enemy – who appear to have outnumbered his 800 dismounted riflemen at least three to one – pushing south towards Red Hill in an effort to cut off his retreat.[92] 'The attack was a complete surprise for the enemy,' recalled Liman. 'Before the Turkish horsemen and running skirmish lines could meet them, the British cavalry [sic] avoided the attack and galloped away to the south in disorder.'[93]

By 10am, Grant's line was being crumpled up, his guns in danger of capture. He was deployed in the lower foothills of the escarpment, a succession of rough ridges and gullies running east–west towards the river, an intricate obstacle course for wheels. B Battery, the Honourable Artillery Company (HAC), lost one of its four field-guns, stuck in a wadi, as it attempted to extricate itself. Worse followed an hour later. By then the light-horsemen had been driven back too far, and A Battery HAC and the Notts Battery, Royal Horse Artillery, had no room to retreat when they came under machine-gun fire at 700 yards' range. The limber teams were shot down and the batteries immobilised. The guns were served as long as possible, and then, as the enemy closed to 200 yards, all eight were abandoned. The Turks also overran a stranded armoured car and around fifty wagons, ambulances and water-carts.[94]

The situation remained critical for several hours. As the line was rolled up from the right, the 4th, 12th and 11th Light Horse Regiments tumbling southwards across steep rock-strewn gullies under covering fire from Hotchkiss light machine-guns, the enemy pressed forward also on the left, overrunning Red Hill, narrowing the avenue of escape to the south. It became a race between Turkish infantry on the plain moving to close the exit and Australian troopers struggling to lead their horses across deeply corrugated foothills. 'I shall never forget the horror of that ride, slipping, sliding, crawling from ledge to ledge. A slip and a horse would topple over and fall for perhaps 100 feet. At times, we had to force them to drop from ledge to ledge like goats. Here and there, one would miss a ledge, and that would be the end of that particular horse.'[95]

Only in the mid-afternoon was some sort of firing-line stabilised across the valley with the arrival of the Middlesex Yeomanry and the Auckland Mounted Rifles on the left. Any further retreat would have carried the Turks across the line of the Umm el-Shert ford and track, cutting off the retreat of the entire cavalry force at Salt; even as it was, the position was perilously shallow, and with the forces available there was little chance of getting forward again.

Chauvel's divisions now occupied an elongated salient. On the southern face, the Londoners were unable to break into the fortress of Shunet Nimrin frontally, and the Yeomanry in the hills above were equally unable to get down the road to take it in the rear. At the eastern tip of the salient, the Australian cordon around Salt was under growing enemy pressure, was running out of ammunition and was in danger of being cut off. And on the northern front, a thin line of dismounted riflemen, liable to be rushed at any moment, were all that was preventing the Ottoman 24th Division getting into the British rear. Hard fighting on 2 and 3 May were sufficient to hold the ground, but no more, so Allenby finally gave the order to break off the action.

* * *

Sergeant Hatton's troop of Middlesex Yeomanry were among the last to pull out. On outpost duty, he had been dismissive when two scouts reported at dusk on 4 May 'thousands of the enemy about 100 yards to our front massing under cover of a ridge'. At 8 o'clock that night, gunfire erupted in the darkness 'like hell's furies let loose'. Hatton's unit had not been told of the general retirement, and they now discovered that they were alone, 'left out as the last covering force'. Spooked by 'huge black masses' seen in front of them, the order to retire was followed by a rush for the horses and a madcap ride across heavily broken ground in pitch darkness.

The scene at the Ghoraniyeh bridgehead, when Hatton's scattered sections finally reached it, bordered on pandemonium.

It was not a 'disorderly rout'; it was like a man who, while pretending not to hurry, was walking just as fast as ever could without breaking into a run. As the pathways converged to the bridge, the 'traffic jam' became more intense ... One moment we were riding beside stragglers from the Camel Corps, then a group of British and Indian soldiers all mixed up together;

ambulance wagons, guns and limbers, camel cacholets, tall Indian Sikhs, short Indian Gurkhas, London lads, Australian bushmen, all 'going the same way home'.[96]

The plight of the wounded was especially grim. Some light-horsemen were taken down the escarpment on horseback, riding in front of one of their mates, 'under excruciating agonies, sticking it out'. Others endured the misery of the camel cacholets: each beast carried two men in chairs or stretchers, one either side, but the jerky motion inflicted 'hellish torture upon the wounded'. The most distressing sight seen by Trooper Henry Bostock that day was 'a man shot through the head, his brains protruding from the outward bullet-hole. He was groaning pitifully, and it seemed possible he would not reach the valley alive.' Many could not be moved at all, of course, and they were simply abandoned to 'Turkish chivalry'.[97]

Earlier, while the fighting still raged at Shunet Nimrin, the Londoners had been evacuating their dead in the night. Bernard Blaser of the London Scottish saw the bodies laid out ready and two wagons arrive to collect them.

Each lifeless body was lifted into the wagons; ten, twenty, thirty, and more, the very best of fellows; men with whom we had lived, with whom we had laughed, men with whom we had discussed the past and planned the future, now all covered with blood and dust, tattered and disfigured – dead. It was a horrible sight . . . Not a sound broke the grim silence save the dull thud as each limp form found its place at the bottom of the wagon. When all were in, the wagons rumbled away with their ghastly loads.

The following evening they buried them in a little battlefield cemetery by the Jordan, the battalion, now down to just 200 men, forming a hollow square around the open graves, heads bared and bowed over reversed rifles as the padre read the service.[98]

The British were lucky to have made good their escape, and to have suffered only 1,600 casualties.[99] Exhaustion and lack of reserves had limited the scale of the Ottoman victory. Liman, in fact, had been reluctant to close the pocket: 'I was certain that our weak and exhausted troops were unequal to the desperate battle which was bound to ensue when the British saw their line of retreat threatened.' The German commander wanted the invaders to be left an escape-route. And once he had them in flight, he knew a counter-stroke was beyond his available strength.[100] Senior Turkish officers concurred. Skander Bey, fighting at Shunet Nimrin, saw, on the afternoon of 4 May, 'long columns . . . coming from Salt, moving rapidly and in the open, towards the Jordan on our right flank. There was no doubt that the enemy had evacuated for a second time. But the VIII Corps had no troops and no strength with which to make a counter-attack.'[101]

* * *

On the face of it, three defeats in a month. And as the crushing summer heat set in, another front reduced to weary stalemate. Underfed, disease-ridden, in uniforms ragged and patched, the heavily outnumbered *Mehmetchiks* still maintained an unbroken line, and Amman, Maan and Salt still stood as bastions of Ottoman power on the imperial frontier.

Nor was this the sum of Anglo-Arab woe. Events far away had drained the reserves of manpower that might yet have achieved a breakthrough. Suddenly, along the Western Front, a storm of violence had been unleashed that seemed to confirm every 'Westerner' general's deprecation of sideshows. The 'Ludendorff offensive' began on 21 March 1918. Two days later, the British Cabinet learned that the Germans, attacking on a broad front astride the Somme, had advanced 12 miles and captured 600 guns: that they had, in fact, broken the line. In two weeks, they penetrated 40 miles and inflicted a quarter of a million casualties. Then, on 9 April, they struck again, this time in Flanders. Within two days, the Channel ports were in danger, and Haig, the British commander-in-chief, issued a desperate order of the day: 'There must be no retirement. With our backs to the wall and believing in the justice of our cause, each one must fight on to the end.' Three further major German thrusts followed in May, June and July. Each was weaker than the last, until the German Army's offensive power was exhausted and the attacks finally petered out.[102]

But that was in the future. On 27 March, at the height of the crisis, London cabled Allenby to inform him that he was henceforward to remain on the defensive in Palestine, so that as many men as possible could be dispatched to the Western Front. During April and May, a total of twenty-four infantry battalions, nine yeomanry regiments, and five and a half batteries of heavy artillery were dispatched.[103] These were combat-veterans. The whole of 52nd (Lowland) Division went, having served in Gallipoli, Sinai and Palestine. Likewise the 74th (Yeomanry) Division, another crack outfit. 'It was a "hard-boiled unit" that landed at Marseilles in the summer of 1918,' recalled artillery officer Douglas Thorburn.

> We were all burnt to a mahogany colour by the desert sun. We were practised in gunnery of all possible varieties. Gunners and drivers were skilled workmen and knew their jobs and were proud of their skill . . . I do

not think I exaggerate when I say that as a fighting machine we were ten times the value of the inexperienced organisation that had left the Western Front two-and-a-half years before.[104]

These soldiers were gradually replaced by regiments of Indian troops. Most of the new arrivals had no war experience. Most were trained more for parade-ground smartness than in the field-craft of a modern industrialised battlefield. The Indians would require time to make ready.[105] There would be no major offensive until the autumn, at the earliest.

At a deeper level, however, the stage for the great climax of the war in the Middle East had been constructed. The scenery was yet to be installed, and the players were still learning their roles. But the essential framework of the battle to come was already in place. And, in the strange way of history's process, the tactical defeats at Amman, Maan and Salt formed part of that structure. For the strategic effect had been to convince the Ottoman high command that their greatest danger lay in the east; and, accordingly, they made permanent adjust-ment in their distribution of force, henceforward leaving a third of their men on the far side of the Jordan. This notion – that the British offensive, when it came, would be a great thrust across the Syrian plateau – was carefully nurtured in the months ahead and sank deep roots in the minds of the enemy. Wavell, who knew Allenby well, considered it part of a grand deception planned from the start.

When Chauvel, chastened by defeat at Salt, expressed regret at his failure, Allenby's retort was emphatic: 'Failure be damned! It's been a great success.'[106] So it had been. For the fierce fighting in the Mountains of Moab in the spring of 1918 had drawn the Turk's attention. Whereas the British general's plan was to land his killer-blow not there, but 50 miles to the west, beside the sea, in the Plain of Sharon.

CHAPTER 16

Special Operations

Tʜᴇ sᴘʀɪɴɢ ᴏғғᴇɴsɪᴠᴇ – of the British against Amman and Salt, of the Arabs against Maan – had ended in failure. The heady hopes raised by the capture of Jerusalem in December had been shattered by the continuing resilience of the Ottoman infantryman in defence of entrenchments. He had again interposed a military impasse.

The news from afar was equally alarming. The Germans had broken through on the Western Front. General Ludendorff's gamble – to hazard his remaining reserves of military power on an all-out offensive to break the line before the Americans arrived in force – was looking like it might succeed. If it did – if Haig's army was sundered from its French allies and driven back to the Channel ports – the Germans would dictate the peace. Their Ottoman appendage would then be restored to power across the Middle East. So the shock of Sykes–Picot and the Balfour Declaration was now compounded by British military failure in both Syria and France. The Arabs appeared to have backed a loser. Might it not be better to cut a deal with the Turks?

June was a critical month. On the 4th, Feisal had a private meeting with Zionist leader Chaim Weizmann in Aqaba. It lasted only 45 minutes. Weizmann was disingenuous about long-term Zionist intentions. Feisal was guarded and non-committal. The encounter cannot have been reassuring, since Weizmann was now operating under the protective mantle of the Balfour Declaration – the very fact of the meeting having been facilitated was testimony to that – and the aims of the Zionist movement were no great secret. Lawrence, who met the Zionist leader shortly afterwards, reported that Weizmann 'hopes for a completely Jewish Palestine in fifty years, and a Jewish Palestine under a British façade for the moment'.

Around this time, a letter arrived from Djemal the Lesser, the commander of the Ottoman Fourth Army, offering, according to Lawrence, 'independence to Arabia and autonomy to Syria, and half the riches of Turkey to Feisal, if the Arab Army would rejoin the Turks against the British'. Feisal replied on 10 June setting out his terms for a separate peace, proposing, among other things, 'that Syria's future relationships with Turkey should be modelled on the relationship between Prussia, Austria and Hungary'. There seems to have been little doubt in Lawrence's mind that – as he put it in a private conversation with Liddell Hart after the war – Feisal was 'selling us'.

Then came a dramatic diplomatic *volte-face*. The British Foreign Office appeared, on 16 June, to endorse the 'Declaration of the Seven', a memorandum drawn up by a group of Syrian oppositionists in Cairo a couple of months before. Though still tainted by some possible ambiguity – it was yet another artefact of the mercurial Mark Sykes – it seemed on the face of it to provide straightforward support for Arab independence without any of the hedging and qualification of the McMahon Correspondence. It was, accordingly, received with acclaim in Feisal's camp. Echoing in spirit US President Woodrow Wilson's very public commitment to national autonomy and the self-determination of peoples – and, for that matter, though rather belatedly and altogether less convincingly, that of the British prime minister – it seemed to indicate that the world had moved on from the shameless secret diplomacy of 1916.[1]

One important factor in sustaining Feisal's allegiance was, perhaps, his special relationship with Lawrence, who had become both confidant and fellow conspirator. Much that the British officer knew he seems not to have divulged to his superiors. As he later wrote: 'We feared that the British might be shaken at Feisal's apparent mistrust of them in entertaining separate negotiations, after their own model. Yet, in fairness to the fighting Arabs, we could not close all avenues of accommodation with Turkey.'[2] Feisal and Lawrence were heading for Damascus in the same chariot, both knowing that the more ground they covered, the greater the prospects for Arab independence in the post-war settlement – regardless of letters, declarations, treaties and other pieces of paper.

But even the special relationship was now under strain. The failure of the combined Anglo-Arab offensive in April made Damascus suddenly seem far distant, even unreachable. And while the standing of Allenby, the regular army general, was little affected by the setback, it was quite otherwise with Feisal, the prophet-prince, the leader of a national insurgency.

Lawrence, with his instinctive feel for the subtleties of the historical process, sensed the danger in stasis. He knew that the revolt could not come to rest. It was motion, or it was nothing. If it did not advance, the energy to sustain it would quickly drain way.

We on the Arab front had been exciting Eastern Syria, since 1916, for a revolt near Damascus, and our material was now ready and afoot. To hold it still in that excited readiness during another year risked our over-passing the crisis ineffectually ... His [Feisal's] fellows were living on their nerves (rebellion is harder than war), and their nerves were wearing thin.[3]

The tide of revolt had rippled northward for almost two years, the mass of local tribesmen entering the fray as the rebel vanguard reached them, then falling away again as it passed onward. It seemed a natural rhythm, in harmony with the ways of the desert. Plunder was honourable, but such was the sparseness of tribal life that what was little to others was much in an Arabian camp. The war – especially the railway raids – was all too profitable. Poor men soon became rich; then, sated to the modest limit of Bedouin avarice, they found themselves with much to lose, and, like comfortable men everywhere, became averse to risk.

Even of Auda's men was this true. 'The Howeitat remain absolutely loyal to Feisal, but are getting very weary of fighting, and have, besides, profited so materially in Sherifian service as to value their lives dearly. They still show splendid dash and courage when in action, but it is becoming ever more diffi-cult to persuade them into the firing-line.' Auda himself, Lawrence reported, was using Turkish prisoners-of-war to build himself a fortified palace of mud-brick – roofed with plundered telegraph poles – at Jefer.[4] The martial energy of the veterans was being dissipated by a glut of booty. New recruits were needed to sustain the momentum. Only fresh triumphs would attract them.

To, as it were, re-boot the insurgency, Lawrence came up with a bold scheme for an Arab-only run at Deraa and Damascus. The April operations had cut a 65-mile gap in the railway line between Maan and Mudawwara which it was impossible for the Ottomans to repair ('eight stations and all the rails and bridges have been smashed to atoms by us'). This isolated the garrisons farther south, forcing them to shift for themselves, eliminating them as a factor in the wider war. The 15,000 or so men in the Hijaz could easily be contained and neutralised by local tribesmen. Lawrence therefore proposed reassigning Ali's and Abdullah's regulars to Feisal's Northern Army, which, supplemented with additional local recruitment, might create a concentrated force of about 10,000 men.

He first proposed dividing this force into two, 8,000 to besiege Maan, 2,000 to form a mobile strike-force to act against Deraa and beyond. He later modi-fied this to a three-fold scheme, reducing the size of the proposed Maan force in order to create a third detachment to operate in the Mountains of Moab. 'My plan for containing Maan, holding the Moab plateau, and simultaneously raising the Hauran was actually to capture Damascus, and so destroy the Turkish Palestine army between my hammer and Allenby's anvil.' In essence, the Maan and Moab forces were to fix the enemy in his positions, while the mobile strike-force – Lawrence's *masse de manoeuvre* – was to break into the rear, disrupt his communications, and perhaps, by raising a tribal revolt in the Jebel Druse, create a new forward base for an attempt on Damascus itself. Critical to the scheme was 'a regal gift' from Allenby.

The decision was taken in May to turn most of the Imperial Camel Corps – useful in the Sinai Desert, less so in Palestine – into conventional cavalry. This released 2,000 camels for service elsewhere. The British Quartermaster-General wanted them for transport. Lawrence trumped him, telling Allenby it would enable him 'to put a thousand men into Deraa any day you please'. Joyce thought Lawrence 'like a boy released from school' when he returned to Feisal's camp at Abu al-Lissan with the news on 22 May. He had good reason to be pleased: 'It was an immense, a regal gift: the gift of unlimited mobility. The Arabs could now win their war when and where they liked.'[5]

In the event, the plan for an Arab-only operation – ambitious, but well conceived – was never put to the test. The Sherif Hussein refused to release the Sherifian regulars in the Hijaz for service in the north. Indeed, he became obstructive in his refusal, inventing excuses to prevent Feisal visiting him, and pretending the line was faulty when Lawrence tried speaking on the phone. He continued obdurate in response to a personal letter in which Lawrence set out the compelling strategic reasons for the transfer. The problem was political. A rift had opened between Mecca and the Arab Northern Army. Hussein was a traditional desert potentate whose power-base was the Hijaz and the local Bedouin tribes. Feisal had evolved into an ambitious Arab politician who now stood at the head of a Syrian nationalist insurgency. Hussein's centre of gravity remained Mecca; Feisal's was fast shifting towards Damascus. The old man seems to have become jealous of his son's success and suspicious of his growing independence.

Nor was Feisal the only perceived threat to Hussein's aspiration to become the ruler of a unitary Arab state after the war. There was also Ibn Saud, the lord of the fanatic Wahhabi of central Arabia, who had thrown off his nominal allegiance to the Ottoman sultan, yet was showing no inclination to transfer it to the newly self-styled 'king of the Arabs'. As Colonel Wilson, the British representative at Jiddah, reported of Hussein: 'He is preoccupied with the Saud question, and the tone of their recent letters is very acrid . . . the real ground of their disagreement is that the king regards Ibn Saud as his chief opponent to his personal ascendancy and to his scheme of unification in Arabia.'

Hussein's anxiety about Arabia was laced with doubt about the British position. The Indian government – running the war in the Gulf – maintained close diplomatic ties with Ibn Saud. The British government was focused on Syria and cared little for the Hijaz. How would it play out if it came to a shooting war with Ibn Saud for control of Arabia? Feisal's British-backed Syrian campaign began to seem far away; Hussein needed soldiers at home.[6]

It did not matter. Lawrence's plan for an Arab-only advance into northern Syria had been superseded. A month after securing the 2,000 camels, Lawrence was again at Allenby's headquarters, where he learned that the grand offensive postponed in the spring was back on, now scheduled for September: the British and the Arabs would be advancing in tandem after all.[7] The Indian troops sent to replace the British divisions withdrawn for service in France had arrived promptly and trained hard: they were ready for action sooner than anticipated.

The news, from an Arab point of view, was a mixed blessing. They would henceforward be a junior partner in the struggle for Syria, and might find themselves competing for the laurels of victory when it came. The risk was that, instead of Feisal's men entering Damascus as the vanguard of a national liberation struggle, they might end up as little more than the auxiliaries of a predatory imperial power.[8] On the other hand, the Sherifian cause was at a low ebb in the summer of 1918; there were fears for its very survival. Dawnay worried that the Ottomans, with an estimated 6,000 men available, might attempt an offensive thrust at Feisal's 2,000, now based at Wuheida, a sprawling tribal encampment a few miles south-west of Maan. 'Should they do so,' he wrote to Joyce on 15 July, 'the result might well be disastrous. Meanwhile, our greatest security lies in the fact that the Turks, at present, have no conception of Feisal's actual strength (or weakness) . . .' It was vital to persuade the enemy that Feisal's forces were growing and that a new offensive was imminent – otherwise 'the old Turk might well take heart to have a whack which would not improbably send us spinning.'[9]

It would be two months before Allenby was ready to launch his great offensive: time enough for the Turks to learn of Feisal's weakness and mount an operation to roll back – if not snuff out altogether – the Syrian insurgency; an eventuality which would have released thousands of Ottoman troops for service on the Palestine front. Dawnay's proposal was to use the two remaining companies of Imperial Camel Corps (the rest having been disbanded), some 300 men, to organise a show of force east of the Jordan. Lawrence, previously reluctant to see British troops *en masse* in the Arab theatre, was enthusiastic. Accordingly, Dawnay requested their deployment, and this was granted, subject to the stipulations that, because they were needed for the coming offensive, they were to avoid heavy casualties, and were to be returned by late August.

This provided sufficient time for a long trek to strike at opposite ends of the Ottoman line. The plan was for the cameliers to march across Sinai to Aqaba, from there to Mudawwara, and then to participate in a night attack to capture the position. They would then disappear into the eastern desert *en route* for Azrak, camping there before striking out to attack the railway somewhere in the north, with the bridge and tunnel near Amman, which the British raid in the spring had failed to destroy, as possible targets. Dawnay felt this Camel Corps raid would do the trick: 'if they appear just at Mudawwara and then in the area north of Maan, we add considerably to our chance of fooling the Turk until after other events make it unnecessary to do so any longer'.[10]

* * *

The Arab war had become multi-dimensional. As well as pinprick guerrilla attacks on the railway line, it also involved deep-penetration raids by small commando forces to attack key strategic assets, and conventional campaigns for control of territory in which regular soldiers, albeit supported by irregulars, sometimes fought pitched battles. None of this diminished the importance of the railway war. There was no let-up in the intensity of attacks, not even when the entire 65-mile stretch between Maan and Mudawwara was permanently destroyed; the focus simply shifted to other parts of the line. Indeed, if anything, the failure of the spring offensive gave added significance to the railway. Attacks on the line north of Maan prevented the garrison from taking the offensive by keeping it fully occupied defending its communications. They also provided opportunities for looting to encourage tribal recruitment.

Attacks also become more professional, evolving from something akin to a traditional Bedouin *ghazzu* into the precursor of modern special ops, sometimes with sophisticated coordination of armour, artillery and airpower. Lawrence later told Liddell Hart that 'the war showed me that a combination of armoured cars and aircraft could rule the desert'.[11]

Like many enthusiasts for techno-fixes, he overstated the case. All weapon systems have strengths and weaknesses. Armoured cars could not negotiate rocky slopes. Aircraft were grounded in bad weather. Many of the new machines of war were at an early stage of development, suffering from severe technical limitations and frequent mechanical breakdown. Their novelty and unreliability made them risky investments, so production runs were limited and the tendency was to supply too few to make any advantage decisive. Balanced on the cusp of modernity, the First World War remained a war of marching men, and of horses, mules, and camels, as well as of machines. In truth, the railway war was not ended by armoured cars and aircraft alone, but by these in clever combination with mobile artillery and camel-mounted riflemen.

* * *

Mudawwara, like Maan, was an Ottoman fortress of the railway war that had for long proved impregnable. An oasis settlement on the ancient caravan route through western Arabia, its importance was enhanced by the advent of the Hajj pilgrimage in the seventh century. It acquired a large stone fort in the eighteenth century and, of course, a railway station in the early twentieth. The first attempt on what Lawrence called 'the great water-station' was made as early as September 1917, but the guerrillas decided against an assault after reconnaissance revealed the place to comprise a long line of solidly constructed stone buildings defended by about 200 men. The guerrillas' technological advantage was slight – an electric detonator, a Stokes mortar and two Lewis guns – and they counted only 116 riflemen: insufficient for an assault, since 'our first tactical principle was safety-play'. So they headed south in search of alternative opportunity, and three days later mounted the highly successful attack on a train near Hallat Ammar Station. The intention then had been to return soon, with artillery and more men, and attack under cover of night, 'but actually one accident after another saved Mudawwara, month by month, so that it was not till August 1918 that it at last met the fate so long overdue . . .'[12]

In the meantime, there were three further abortive attempts. In late December, a very different sort of operation was organised – a fully motorised reconnaissance by a small British composite unit of three Rolls-Royce armoured cars, three Rolls-Royce tenders, and two Talbot lorries mounting 10-pounder mountain-guns. The cars were officered by Captain Dowsett and Lieutenant Gilman, the guns by Captain Brodie, and the force as a whole by Colonel Pierce Joyce, head of the British contingent at Aqaba. Lawrence tagged along as 'spectator'. Before the main operation, two tenders were loaded with petrol and rations at Guweira and then taken across the desert to the railway to test the viability of the route: they found easy going for vehicles, especially on the mud flats beyond Wadi Rum, where the speedometers sometimes touched 65mph. The entire force of eight motors then set off early on 31 December, reaching the vicinity of Mudawwara at sundown. Deciding the country was too open and the enemy blockhouses too numerous, they drove north up the line looking for somewhere to mount an attack.

Returning to the overnight campsite at Tooth Hill used by the scouting party on 27/28 December, they launched an attack from there on the defences of Tell Shahm Station. Joyce and Lawrence watched the first phase of the battle through binoculars from a hilltop 'like the best regular generals'. An Ottoman outpost on a low rise ('Siddons' Ridge') – a single trench with a miniature bunker at either end – was shelled by Brodie's mountain-guns and then machine-gunned by Dowsett's armoured cars. The vehicles prowled around the enemy position, spraying the trench when targets appeared, but were unable to mount the slope. The return Ottoman fire was ragged and ineffective: 'Armoured car work seemed fighting de luxe,' thought Lawrence, 'for our troops, being steel-covered, could come to no hurt.' But this was a stand-off: though the cars were immune to rifle-fire, they were powerless to compel the surrender of the post without infantry to storm it.[13]

Lawrence, the romantic medievalist, loved machines, speed and firepower. Such different preoccupations were not unusual at the time. Many Europeans subscribed to a primitive jingoism that amounted to little more than the worship of totems – the flag, the crown, the nation, the empire – even as they engaged in a very modern kind of mass killing. Interwar fascism would elevate the contradiction to a yet higher level, combining 'blood and soil' mysticism with an enthusiastic embrace of techno-charged modernity. Thus were the myths of the tenth century harnessed to the military technology of the twentieth. It would take thirty years of war, poverty and genocide between 1914 and 1945 to shatter this ideological nexus and reveal nationalism and industrialised militarism to be the twin monsters of a world gone mad. As yet, though, an armoured car in the desert – a mechanised Crusader knight – could be experienced as 'fighting de luxe'.

Not that the Rolls-Royce armoured car was particularly luxurious. Essentially a steel-plated version of a conventional 'Silver Ghost' motor-car, the chassis had a strengthened back-axle designed to support a steel cylinder, 5 feet in diameter, with a revolving turret. The turret mounted a Vickers-Maxim machine-gun. The armour plates, which also covered bonnet and radiator, were three-eighths of an inch thick and bullet-proof. There was an open wooden platform at the back where ammunition was stored in boxes. The high speed Lawrence experienced was achieved by an engine of 40/50hp and a four-speed gearbox. Double wheels allowed the cars to continue even with a puncture until a scheduled stop. The interior, which contained two mattresses, two rifles, a rubber water-bottle and a first-aid kit, was exceptionally cramped.

Though the nominal crew was three – a driver and two gunners – there was not really room, and usually only two men were carried. When driving, they would sit side-by-side on the floor, backs supported by slings, legs outstretched in front, bums resting on little piles of mats, peering through slits in the armour. When in action, the gunner had to stand up; but only the shortest of men could be fully upright and not be forced to stoop over the Vickers. The driver, meantime, still sitting, endeavoured to feed the cartridge-belt into the gun while still managing the steering-wheel. Unsurprisingly, armoured car men tended to be short; 'tall men, who had to half double themselves up,' reported S.C. Rolls of the Hijaz Armoured Car Company, 'took up very much more room and were always cramped and uncomfortable, and on this account were generally considered the least desirable to work with.' The summer heat in the desert was so great 'that men inside the cars were in danger of being cooked like rabbits in a saucepan'.[14]

Quite apart from the obvious problem of mechanical breakdown, especially with rough usage on campaign, much else could go wrong. Ground at all rough or broken was impassable and, with restricted driver vision, cars were liable to ditch, bog in sand, or jolt and break an axle. The immunity to small-arms fire was relative, not absolute, and the vulnerability to artillery fire high, with the chilling danger of 'brewing up', with men trapped inside the metalwork of a burning vehicle. The effectiveness of the car's own armament was somewhat impeded by the limited vision of both gunner and driver. It was the age-old problem of armour: to protect was to restrict.

Brodie's guns had been equally incapable of delivering a decision in the curious little skirmish at Siddons' Ridge. They lacked the weight of shot to have serious effect on men in trenches, being mere 10-pounder mountain-guns. These were updated versions of the 'screw guns' developed in the late nineteenth century for use in colonial warfare, where, according to one observer, they 'proved most successful in dislodging unruly natives'. Used particularly on the North-West Frontier of India, they were immortalised by Kipling ('It's worse if you fights or you runs: you can go where you please, you can skid up the trees, but you don't get away from the guns!'). Their chief characteristics were that they were relatively light and were designed to be broken down and transported in parts on mules or camels. The gun barrel, for example, comprised two parts, a breech and a chase, and these screwed together: thus 'screw gun'. They could be unloaded and assembled relatively quickly – the manual allowed 180 seconds – and then, except for their low calibre, they operated very much like standard field-guns, being quick-firing rifled breech-loaders with a maximum range of about 6,000 yards. Sam Brodie's Royal Field Artillery 'motor section' represented an adaptation, in that two assembled guns were carried on the flat beds of open trucks. These could be fired from their mounts – making Brodie's Talbots some of the first mobile gun-platforms – but they were usually offloaded and fired from the ground.[15]

The 10-pounders made little impression on Siddons' Ridge, however, and the gunners soon attracted small-arms fire: the main disadvantage of light artillery operating in close support was, of course, its vulnerability. So the raiding party headed off to attack Tell Shahm Station, clearly visible in the distance. Brodie set up his guns and shelled the station compound – transformed into a miniature desert fort – at a range of about 2,000 yards. The compound offered a much better target than a mere earthwork, and the Ottoman defenders trickled away to their main hilltop redoubt a few hundred yards to the north. The armoured cars rolled up to the station and machine-gunned the doors and windows. That was all: without infantry, nothing further could be done. The raid had been 'more jest than operation'. Neither Joyce nor Lawrence had employed armoured cars before: 'Our anxiety and forethought had been all to reach the railway through the manifold difficulties of the plains and hills. When we did reach, we were entirely unready for action, with not a thought of tactics or method . . .'[16]

If the raid on 1 January had been little more than a training exercise, that on 22 January was a full-scale attack. It again involved the British mobile column, this time with the addition of five Talbot tenders, but also Captain Pisani's two guns, some Arab guns, a contingent of Sherifian regulars, and over a thousand irregulars from different tribes.[17] Not least, this time there was an air component. The British Military Mission had acquired its own mini air force – X Flight of the Royal Flying Corps/Royal Air Force – soon after the capture of Aqaba.[18] The new service attracted modern-minded young officers who tended to be imaginative and enterprising. The airmen had established an advanced landing-ground at Disi, about 30 miles east of Guweira, and were now able to offer strong air-support to an Anglo-Arab attack on Mudawwara.[19]

X Flight's four aircraft were obsolescent. The BE2e was a rather slow two-seater designed mainly as a reconnaissance plane and light bomber. It was dangerously vulnerable to the new classes of German fighter in action over Palestine. Where unchallenged in the air, however, its impact on the battle-space could be transformative. As well as providing a flow of first-rate reconnaissance reports, including sketch-maps and, increasingly, air-photos, they could function as mobile artillery in active support of ground operations, each aircraft carrying one 100lb bomb or an equivalent weight of smaller bombs.[20]

On the morning of 22 January, X Flight opened the attack on Mudawwara by dropping three 100lb bombs and four 20lb bombs, destroying an ammunition dump and a water tank. One of Brodie's mountain-guns shelled a strongly defended hilltop redoubt about 1,000 yards west of the station ('Central Redoubt'), while the other was manhandled across 400 yards of soft sand in an effort to bring the station itself under fire.

But that was the summit of achievement. The second gun had to be withdrawn because of the intensity of fire from the station. And, though Sherif Feisal himself was in overall command, supported by Nuri al-Said, his chief-of-staff, the Arabs failed to mount an attack. The reasons are obscure, but whether due to squabbles between rival sheikhs or a revival of ancient feuds, the Beni Atiyeh men melted away and brought the planned assault to nought. Lack of water and food then forced a retreat before a new plan could be made for the following day.[21] Feisal wrote bitterly to his brother:

> As for us, we failed in our raid on Mudawwara. And there is no explanation for our retreat except the will of Allah. We reached Mudawwara with large numbers ... and we found in front of us about 200. There was a slight skirmish involving artillery and planes. The detachment did not attack on the first day. No-one knows the reason except Allah: laziness, hesitation and spinelessness.[22]

* * *

So again Mudawwara was reprieved, and again three months were to pass before another attempt was made. This was coordinated with the large-scale Arab operation against Maan in mid-April, for which it was, in effect, a diversionary attack. Lawrence, having just borne witness to the carnage of the main battle, caught up with the British, Egyptian and Bedouin mobile column at Tooth Hill on the night of 18/19 April. Joyce was ill, so it was commanded by Alan Dawnay.

Lawrence was amused by the incongruous regularity of Dawnay's desert camp:

> It was a wonderful show, for the cars were parked geometrically here, and the armoured cars place there, and sentries and pickets were out in all the proper places, with machine-guns trained and ready. Everything was ready, even the Arabs, put in a tactical place behind a hill, where they were in support but out of sight and hearing of the line ... the only thing lacking was an enemy ...

The battle plan was also a precisely timed choreograph: 'He unfolded a paper, and read me his operational orders, orthodox-sounding things with zero timings and a sequence of following movements. Each unit had its appointed duty.'[23]

The column again included the three armoured cars with their Rolls-Royce tenders, and the two mountain-guns in their Talbot lorries. But these were now joined by a detachment of Ford light cars mounting Hotchkiss machine-guns, and a demolitions unit headed by Captain Hornby, with explosives carried in spare tenders and lorries. Alongside the British specialists were a 100-strong company of Egyptian Camel Corps under Captain Peake, and a detachment of Imran tribesmen under Sherif Hazaa. Because of language difficulties and possible tension between the Egyptians and the Bedouin, Lawrence tactfully offered his services as Dawnay's 'interpreter'. Dawnay gave him a warm welcome.

The attack began at dawn on 19 April. The cars surprised the sleepy Ottoman soldiers in their trenches at 'Plain Post' (the terms are those of Dawnay's plan), and they stumbled out with their hands up: 'It was like plucking a ripe peach.'[24] Hornby then raced forward in two Rolls-Royce tenders and blew up 'Bridge A' with 120 slabs of gun-cotton; 'the roar nearly lifted Dawnay and myself out of our third tender ... and I showed Hornby the cheaper way of the drainage holes as mine-chambers'.[25]

Covered by fire from the 10-pounders and the cars' machine-guns, Peake's Egyptians and Hazaa's Arabs then prepared to storm 'Rock Post' – a steep, rocky knoll surmounted by a stone ring-work and a blockhouse.[26] Before they could do so, however, the nine remaining defenders, 'frightened by the splashing and splattering of the four machine-guns', surrendered: 'So that was peach the second.'[27]

There was then a pause in the actual fighting as Dawnay, Hornby and Lawrence raced up and down the line in Rolls-Royces laden with two tons of gun-cotton and carried out a series of demolitions:

> bridges and rails roared up about us on all sides, whenever fancy took us, or there was a target. The officers and crews of the cars covered us, and sometimes covered themselves, under the turrets or wings of their cars, when stones or iron fragments came sailing musically through the smoky air ... It was fighting de luxe, and demolitions de luxe, and we enjoyed ourselves.[28]

After lunch, 'South Post' was captured – to the very minute scheduled in Dawnay's plan, but not as the manual prescribed. The Egyptians, as good regular infantry, expected to advance on it in a succession of alternate rushes. The Bedouin were 'too wound up', however, thought it 'a steeplechase', and 'did a camel-charge up the mound and over into the breastworks and trenches'. The Turks again surrendered.[29]

Lawrence continues the story:

> Then came the central act of the day, the assault upon the station. Peake drew down towards it from the north, moving his men with repeated efforts, hardly, for they were not fierce, or thirsty for honour. Brodie opened on it

with his usual mathematical nicety, while the aeroplanes appeared overhead to the minute, circled round in their cold-blooded way, and dropped whistling bombs into its trenches. The armoured cars went forward snuffing smoke, and a file of Turks waving white things rose slowly out of the ramp ending their main trench, and moved in a dejected group towards them.[30]

The Turks – 31 were taken prisoner – ceased to matter: the victory won, there was a frenzied rush on the booty. The cars beat the camels, and Lawrence's trophy was the station bell, 'a fine piece of dignified Damascus brass-work'. A minute later, the Bedouin arrived, 'and there was the maddest looting in their history. Two hundred rifles, 80,000 rounds of ammunition, many bombs, much food, and clothes, were in the station, and everybody smashed and profited'. A camel set off a trip-mine and caused a minor panic. An Egyptian officer put a guard on a storehouse because his men were short of food. The situation turned ugly. Shooting began, and Lawrence later confided that 'we were all within a hair's breadth of getting scragged'. A tense mediation followed. And then a compromise: the Egyptians would take what they needed, then the tribesmen have all that remained.[31]

By the end, most of Hazaa's men were sated and made off to their homes, leaving only a handful the following morning. But the Turks at Ramleh, the next station to the south, had heard the news from Tell Shahm and fled, leaving the station shut up and abandoned, so this too was captured early on the 20th; the remainder of that day was spent in demolitions. But the loot at Ramleh dispersed the remaining tribesmen, so it was a much depleted force that reached Mudawwara, the strongest post by far, on the third day. The one hope was that the garrison would be spooked into surrender or flight as their comrades had been, but when cars and camels were spotted at a distance east of the station, two little Austrian mountain-howitzers opened up at 7,000 yards range. Outgunned and without cover on the approaches, the raiders could not risk an attack; so they veered away to the south, blew up a bridge, and then, returning north again, 'went on destroying line and bridges, meaning to make our break a permanent one, a demolition too serious for Fakhri [the Ottoman commander at Medina] ever to restore'.[32]

Though Mudawwara had survived again, it did so now as an isolated outpost, cut off from Maan, for the break in the line, 65 miles long, was beyond repair as the creaking Ottoman military approached its terminal crisis. The main purpose of the mission had therefore been accomplished: all the garrisons to the south were now isolated, unable to get north to reinforce the defence of Palestine and Syria, unable to receive reinforcement or resupply. The strategic aim had not changed: previously, when the Ottomans were determined to hold on, the intention had been to overstretch them with pinprick attacks that left the line just serviceable; now, when they needed to concentrate their forces for a life-and-death struggle in the north, the intention was to make their dispersal permanent by blocking their avenue of retreat.[33]

* * *

Lawrence was a pioneer not only of modern guerrilla warfare, but also of special operations and combined-arms tactics. He and other officers, both British and Arab, were creating mobile columns of elite specialist troops and using them to carry out deep-penetration raids behind enemy lines. These columns mounted attacks on key installations in which airpower, armour, artillery and assault troops worked in carefully coordinated and synchronised combination.

The First World War was a global war of machines and mass. Because of this, wherever the ratio of machine-power to front-line was high, the result was trench-war stalemate. Much of the fighting in Palestine was of this kind. But where the ratio was lower, where firepower was subsumed by space, another kind of war developed; one where the industrialisation of war, instead of creating an impasse, made possible the projection of highly mobile and precisely targeted force. The railway war, which had begun as traditional Bedouin raiding writ large, later became a matter of aircraft, artillery and armoured cars. Or, more accurately, it became a matter of both: a war of the camel and of the machine.

The Ottomans had no riposte. Crippled by the sclerotic infrastructure of a medieval empire, they lacked not only the machines but even the camels necessary to an active counter-insurgency. Unable to strike at the depots and encampments of their enemy – perhaps, indeed, lacking the imagination and enterprise to wish to – all they could do, this army of peasant-conscript infantry led by often corrupt and semi-literate officers, was to dig in and wait for him to come to them. So it was that, by a slow process of attrition, ever more of the Hijaz Railway had become untenable, ever more of it broken beyond repair, and the remaining garrisons ever more beleaguered in their isolated station-fortresses.

Mudawwara was one of these. Four Anglo-Arab expeditions over the preceding year had failed to capture it. The station comprised a long line of stone buildings converted into blockhouses and surrounded by trenches. The approaches were open except on the west, but here the Ottomans had created three hilltop redoubts, each a loop-holed ring-work of piled stone, on the heights that dominated the station. Though the position was a strong one, it had survived thus far more by luck than by design.

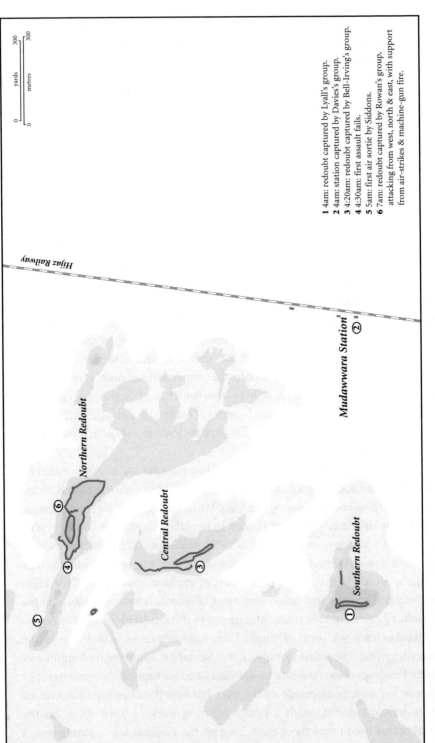

Hijaz Railway

Mudawwara Station ②

Northern Redoubt

Central Redoubt

Southern Redoubt

① ④ ⑤ ⑥ ③

yards 0 300
metres 0 300

1 4am: redoubt captured by Lyall's group.
2 4am: station captured by Davies's group.
3 4:20am: redoubt captured by Bell-Irving's group.
4 4:30am: first assault fails.
5 5am: first air sortie by Siddons.
6 7am: redoubt captured by Rowan's group, attacking from west, north & east, with support from air-strikes & machine-gun fire.

24. The Battle of Mudawwara, 8 August 1918.

In the summer of 1918, therefore, Mudawwara was the obvious target for Alan Dawnay's scheme to breathe fresh life into the flagging Arab insurgency with a demonstrative display of British military power. Accordingly, a new expedition to attack the oasis was formed in July, this time headed by Major Robert Buxton, commander of the (much reduced, but still formidable) Imperial Camel Corps (ICC), comprising 16 officers, 300 other ranks, 400 camels, 6 Lewis guns, and a field ambulance with 4 medical officers. Orders were 'to seize Mudawwara with the primary object of destroying the enemy's valuable water-supply'.

The ICC duly arrived at Aqaba at the end of the month after a 160-mile trek across Sinai. Two days later, the column, reinforced by 22 Egyptian Camel Corps, and, carrying 260 rounds of small-arms ammunition per man, 2,000 rounds per Lewis gun and 7,500lbs of gun-cotton, headed down the Wadi Itm. They camped overnight at Wadi Rum, then rendezvoused at Disi the following day with Brodie's 30 men and a demolitions expert. Because of previous difficulties controlling Arab tribesmen and coordinating their efforts with those of British regulars, the decision was not to include Bedouin. On the afternoon of 6 August, the advanced elements approached to within a few hundred yards of the Ottoman redoubts without being detected. The British then established camp 3 miles to the west, and there made detailed plans for an attack based on their own reconnaissance and earlier air-photos.

* * *

By 4am on the morning of 8 August, Buxton was getting anxious. The action had been scheduled to commence at 3.45, but there was still silence. Then a Mills bomb exploded in the Southern Redoubt, quickly followed by others. Captain Lyall's assault group – three officers and fifty other ranks – had taken off their boots, crept up the slope, and crouched down behind the stone sangar at the top. They had not been detected. Most of the occupants were asleep. Then, all of a sudden, they hurled a volley of grenades and stormed over the top with the bayonet. It was over in an instant, though Lieutenant Jones was killed.

At almost exactly the same time, Lieutenant Davies and his group of thirty men hit the station. They, too, had not been noticed before reaching the buildings. They paused for a few moments, then put grenades through the windows, and immediately charged in with the bayonet. The Ottoman trumpeter was shot just as he put his instrument to his lips to sound the alarm; Davies took the trumpet as a regimental trophy. A green Verey light announced the capture of the station, closely followed by a red one from the Southern Redoubt. Twenty minutes later, as the darkness lifted, a third column – three officers and ninety-five other ranks under Captain Bell-Irving – captured the Central Redoubt. Lieutenant Radloff's assault commando were over the sangars and among the guns and tents before the defenders knew what was happening.

Three other columns were also at large in the glimmering light. Two had gone north and south to sever the telegraph line and blow up the rails either side of Mudawwara Station, cutting it off from the outside world. Another small column took position in front of the strongly held Northern Redoubt; the plan was for this to be attacked in the rear by other columns when they came up. But the Turks here were making a serious fight of it (they had an artillery piece), and at 4.30am a runner reached Brodie to request artillery fire, both high-explosive and shrapnel, on the Northern Redoubt. Half an hour later, Captain Siddons, flew over in a single-seater BE12a, and began signalling in morse using a klaxon. The content was intemperate. He had flown in to provide air-support, but he had no information from the officers on the ground. Where was he to attack?

Buxton's officers seem to have been unwilling to act without orders – a weakness in special ops, especially on this occasion, since the commander was at the station and out of contact due to signals failure. So Corporal Fox raced across 300 yards of flat ground under machine-gun fire to re-establish communications. A prearranged signal 'HLN' – meaning 'Bomb Northern Redoubt' – was then laid out on the ground. Siddons duly dropped ten 20lb bombs on the position and fired 80 machine-gun rounds into it. Just under an hour later, X Flight's three other aircraft appeared – two more BE12s and a BE2e – and these attacked the redoubt with another 25 bombs and almost 500 rounds. The ICC Lewis guns were brought to bear, and Lieutenant Rowan's assault group closed on the position from west, north and east. At 7 o'clock, the defenders streamed out waving anything white they found to hand.

Save for the shooting up and capture of a small Turkish patrol approaching from the south, and the deliberate demolition of the station infrastructure and 2,000 yards of rails, the little battle was over. It had lasted three hours and cost only four killed and ten wounded (who were treated in an improvised hospital set up in the eighteenth century Ottoman fort, along with the rather more numerous Ottoman casualties). It had been a minor masterpiece of modern special ops. The attackers had used darkness and stealth to close with the enemy. They had attacked and captured three positions by the 'shock and awe' effect of a sudden storm of close-quarters violence. And they had crushed the main centre of resistance by calling down artillery fire and air-strikes. By this means, they had killed 21 Turks, captured 150 others, along with two guns and three machine-guns, and taken possession of a fortified station and 3 strong hilltop redoubts that had defied a succession of earlier raids.[34]

When he heard the news, Lawrence was suitably impressed. 'This fine performance settled the isolated fate of the Turkish corps at Medina beyond question, whatever might be our fortune away by Deraa, and whatever reverses our little containing army in front of Maan might suffer before or after . . .'[35]

The original plan had been for the ICC to trek north after hitting Mudawwara and strike a second blow 250 miles away. This proved abortive: the column was sighted by German reconnaissance aircraft; the route to the railway was occupied by a Bedouin tribe of uncertain sympathy; and the district to be attacked was thick with enemy patrols. The risks were too great, the mission was called off, and Buxton headed away, 'very sadly'.[36]

In the wider scheme of things, it did not matter. The raid had secured Mudawwara, denied the enemy the initiative, and kept alive his anxiety about the security of the Mountains of Moab. The Arab fighters had been rallied during the low point in the final summer of the war. A month later, Allenby's sledgehammer blow would fall at the opposite end of the line.

CHAPTER 17

Armageddon

THE HEAT OF the desert is a dry heat. That of the Jordan Valley is heavy and humid. Because it lies 1,200 feet below sea-level, the air pressure is greater, the atmosphere denser. In the summer, when the temperature can occasionally hit 50°C in the shade, human existence is reduced to hopeless torment during the hours of daylight. Sergeant 'Appy' Hatton and the Middlesex Yeomanry were camped near Ghoraniyeh Bridge about 50 yards from the river in the summer of 1918. They were among several thousand horsemen, mainly Anzac, interned in the valley through the four hottest months of the year. 'The heaviness of the atmosphere and the dampness of the heat', recalled Hatton, 'made the climate that of a typical hot-swamp region, and men who had been on constant service for four years had not the strength to withstand the conditions, so that the sick parade every morning was a sorry sight.' Between 9am and 4pm, the heat was unbearable, and men would lie naked and prostrate under their mosquito nets, heads throbbing, bodies dripping, all energy and willpower gone. When they stirred themselves to eat, they found the army staple of tinned meat – monotonous and nutritionally deficient at the best of times – melted into a sticky coagulate of oil and fibre that was virtually inedible.

The British high command contributed a dose of stupidity to the heat crisis. Allenby, in his ascent of the military hierarchy, had accumulated a thickening crust of arrogance. He objected to 'shorts' as unsoldierly for mounted men and a risk to health. A message was heliographed from the relatively cool mountains into the furnace below to the effect that any officer whose men were found wearing shorts would be severely dealt with. 'The result of the prohibition,' reported the Australian *Official History* was that 'for some time men were condemned to ride and work in their heavy riding-breeches and leggings, and were constantly saturated with perspiration, though without a change of clothing.' Strong representations eventually produced a compromise: the men could wear khaki-drill trousers.

Contact with the enemy was virtually zero. The Turks might as well have been on the moon. The real enemies were the heat, the vermin and the sickness. Millions of mosquitoes bred in the swamps along the river. Men on patrol wore muslin veils around their pith-helmets and muslin gauntlets on their hands as protection. Men at night heard them buzzing relentlessly against their mosquito nets. The ground was alive with small adders, tarantula spiders, six-inch centipedes and huge black scorpions. A man's arm could swell to twice its size in less than ten minutes after a scorpion sting.

Veterans attested the flies of the Jordan Valley a greater plague than those of Gallipoli and Sinai. 'It made any attempt at meal-taking a quarter of an hour of sheer exasperation. One had to keep waving your left hand over bread and jam the whole time, and then they would settle in dozens on the other end as you placed one end in your mouth.' Some men found the tiny sandflies even worse. Lieutenant Goodsall of the Royal Field Artillery was one of them:

Sand-flies are the worst insect pests I have ever encountered ... They are almost too small to see, and they find their way into everything, clothes, bedding and through mosquito-netting. Wherever they bite, they set up the most violent irritation, and as they attack in hundreds all over the body, life becomes a mild form of hell. To scratch one's self is useless.

Men fell sick in their hundreds – from sandfly fever, malaria, septic sores and 'Jordan boils'. Virtually everyone was periodically afflicted with stomach disorders. The Middlesex Yeomanry did a month in the line, a month resting in the hills, then another month in the line. 'Our second sojourn was worse than the first: it was hotter, if anything, and we suffered the same wearying discomfort from flies and dust, the same depletion of strength from fever, boils, and malaria, until the regiment almost ceased to exist except as a skeleton. This last month in the valley remains a nightmare to all who endured it.'[1]

When, finally, the horsemen filed away, they did so secretly, at night, and they left behind an eerie shadow of themselves: the camps vacated were left standing, 15,000 dummy horses of canvas and straw filled the deserted horse-lines, and mules drew sleighs across the ground to raise clouds of dust and simulate activity. That was not all. New campsites were laid out and tents pitched. Battalions of infantry marched purposefully from Jerusalem into the valley – only to return by lorries in the night, to repeat the performance the following day. Additional bridges were thrown across the Jordan. Wireless messages continued to be transmitted from a corps headquarters which had in fact moved away. The principal Jerusalem hotel was cleared and new telephone lines laid for the transfer of an army staff that never arrived. Billets were labelled in anticipation of a troop concentration that existed only in imagination. A race meeting was advertised, but none was actually planned. Agents were dispatched to bargain for supplies of fodder in the Amman region, but these would never be collected.[2]

This was at the eastern end of the line: a false impression of strength, of build-up, of an imminent offensive blow when the worst of the heat had passed. The opposite performance was played out at the western end: a false impression of nothing – when in fact there was the greatest possible concentration of men, horses and guns. Three complete divisions were moved from the Jordan Valley and the Judaean Hills to the Plain of Sharon; but they were moved at night and then hidden in olive and orange groves north of Jaffa, or were moved into empty tents erected long before in existing camps.[3]

Otto Liman von Saunders, the canny defensive fighter who had defeated every British effort on Gallipoli, may have been more in tune than his predecessor, Erich von Falkenhayn, with the military aptitudes of the Ottoman soldier. But the relationship between mass and space in Palestine in 1918 was very different from that on the Gallipoli peninsula in 1915. Falkenhayn had favoured large reserves, kept well back from the front-line, and a strategy of defence in depth through manoeuvre and counter-attack. Liman understood that the Ottoman Army lacked both the mobility and the verve to deliver this; that a successful defence had to depend primarily on the traditional tenacity of the Anatolian peasant-conscript in a trench. So he moved most of his men back into the line.

The Eighth Army, now commanded by Djevad Pasha, held the Plain of Sharon sector near the coast. The Seventh Army, now under Mustapha Kemal Pasha, who shared with Liman the laurels of Gallipoli, was in the Judaean Hills. And the Fourth Army, still led by Mehmet Djemal Pasha 'the Lesser', lay beyond the Jordan, some of its regiments massed in conventional trench-lines in anticipation of a new British thrust at Salt and Amman, others holding fortified outposts along the railway against the tribal insurgency. But 'army' was, in every case, a misnomer. British intelligence estimated the Ottoman strength opposing Allenby in September 1918 at 2,000 sabres, 23,000 rifles and 340 guns.[4] Each 'army' was, therefore, the equivalent of an under-strength division, with correspondingly small corps, divisions, regiments and battalions.

The manpower crisis had been immediately apparent when Liman – who estimated his strength even lower than the British – first arrived at the front in March. 'The Turkish battalions, which I saw at the front, numbered 120 to 150 rifles. According to a written report, the Eighth Army had 3,902 rifles available for the defence of the left sector with a front of 28 kilometres. And thus it was everywhere.'[5] Allenby was not the only one practising deception; Liman did the same, in an effort to convey an impression of strength. Wireless messages announcing the arrival of reinforcements were sent in ciphers the British were known to have broken. Long columns were then set marching to deceive enemy aviators and convince enemy intelligence of the truth of the messages.[6] The manpower crisis grew worse through the summer. In June, Liman cabled Enver, the war minister, that 'the strongest Turkish regiments [brigades] average 350–400 rifles, in addition to machine-guns, and many Turkish regiments are weaker'.[7]

It was not simply a lack of recruits, though the burden of four years of attrition on the empire's reserve of 12 million Anatolian Turks was now acute, especially given crumbling support for the war among Syrians and Iraqis – an indirect, unmeasurable, but surely not inconsiderable effect of the Arab Revolt.[8] Equally problematic was the deployment of such forces as were available. In March, Liman had urged the abandonment of the Hijaz and withdrawal to a line abreast the Dead Sea. The Arab Revolt had made the defence of the railway 'an almost impossible military task'; the British advance had made it 'unnatural and impracticable to continue indefinitely the defence as far as Medina'. But it was not to be: 'The railroad had been built with money contributed by the entire Islamic world, and the troops along the railroad as far as Medina were the only support of the Turks in this large Arabian section. They were the only connecting link of the [Ottoman] Empire with the holy cities of Islam . . .'[9]

More questionable still was a new pivot to Caucasia. The pan-Turkish fantasies of the Committee of Union and Progress (CUP) leadership had been revived by the collapse of tsarist Russia, the ancient enemy, an event which seemed to have created a power-vacuum across a large swathe of Central Asia.[10] Six divisions, some of them 9,000 strong – troops desperately needed in Palestine – were diverted to the Caucasus front. Some of Liman's own men were poached: he lost many good officers when Enver offered promotion and double pay to those who volunteered for service in the Caucasus.[11] Liman was despairing. Total Ottoman Army combat strength had fallen precipitously from a peak of 800,000 in 1915 to an estimated 400,000 in March 1917 and a mere 200,000 by March 1918.[12] The German general considered the Ottoman Empire incapable of major operations on more than one front, the proposed Caucasus campaign a hopeless adventure. 'It is my firm conviction that the operations in East Caucasus, with their indefinite objectives, will and must fail,' he cabled Berlin on 1 August. 'All such Turkish projects since the beginning of the war have failed, but I have never been listened to, and shall not be listened to in this case, until it is too late.'[13]

The Caucasus adventure also imposed additional strain on a rudimentary logistical infrastructure now close to collapse. The transport system simply could not supply the quantities of munitions, food and other necessities required. Much of what was moved was siphoned away by corrupt officials before it reached the front. Local supplies became unobtainable because the peasants feared their produce would be plundered without payment by undisciplined requisition squads. At the front, pack-animals died in their hundreds from hunger and thirst. The soldiers, in consequence, were 'undernourished, very poorly clothed and wretchedly shod'. According to Liman:

> the Turkish soldiers had no summer clothes, but wore their cloth uniforms, which might better be called rags. They suffered the more as fully three-fourths of them had not had any underclothing for a long time, and wore their clothes next to the body. That . . . the British or Indian dead left before the Turkish front were promptly robbed and found naked is not to be looked upon as intentional cruelty. It appeared to the Turkish soldiers the only means of procuring clothing, linen, or boots. All orders against the spoliation of the dead were in vain.

Malaria and dysentery were at epidemic levels, front-line medical services minimal, and the hospitals in the rear overcrowded and undersupplied.

British propaganda exploited the degraded condition of the Turkish rank-and-file, making air-drops of 'the most beautifully illustrated pamphlets showing the physical comforts the Turkish soldier enjoyed in British captivity'. Some crossed the lines, or took the first opportunity to surrender, but these were few compared with the torrent of men who deserted and disappeared into the Ottoman rear areas. By the end, the deserters probably outnumbered those still serving with the colours. Many, organised in outlaw gangs, survived by pillaging military stores, adding to the supply crisis at the front.[14]

The Ottoman line, which extended from the coast across central Palestine, the Jordan Valley and southern Syria to Amman, was 70 miles long. If British intelligence estimates were right, there were fewer than 400 men per mile available in September 1918. These were far too few. But the terminal crisis of the Ottoman Empire was not a merely quantitative matter. The collapsing economy, the hollowed-out social order, the breakdown of discipline and cohesion, the pervading sense of decay and death, these now found expression in the degradation of the Ottoman soldier. Liman became convinced that his army was incapable of anything other than static defence: 'The utmost that could be expected, from the present condition of the deteriorated regiments, was that they might hold their ground against attack.' He abandoned all plans for offensive action.

Some of his German colleagues feared worse: that their soldiers would not fight at all. 'The Turks were tired of the war and unwilling to fight,' wrote Lieutenant Heiden, 'as evidenced by the mass desertions of Turkish soldiers.'

> These deserters took with them not only their rifles and hand-grenades, but also machine-guns. The headquarters of the Eighth Army took energetic steps by guarding the country in the rear, but trucks with armed infantry had to be sent after these deserters, with whom sometimes regular actions took place ... I was told several times that unless peace was made ... the soldiers would go over to the enemy or desert, and that they would fight no longer.

Lieutenant Ricks agreed. He, too, had seen the despair in the face of Little Mehmet, now hollow-cheeked, his uniform rags and patches, his feet shod in animal skins tied with string. Ricks knew 'that the Turks did not intend to stand at the great British attack that was expected'.[15]

The Empire of the Ottomans, once so awesome and splendid, had been worn down to a flimsy façade. Its reserves of human resistance had been consumed by four years of industrialised attrition and guerrilla insurgency. It retained only a semblance of power. The whole edifice was set to collapse at the first impact of Allenby's sledgehammer.

* * *

On 17 September, two days before the British offensive was due to open, an Indian sergeant deserted and disclosed to the Ottomans that a heavy attack was planned in the coastal sector. But on the same day came reports that Arab guerrillas had blown up sections of the railway north and south of Deraa, 70 miles away, at the opposite end of the line. Liman's attention remained fixed on the east. The Indian sergeant may have been a plant. If not, he may have been aware only of a diversionary attack. Regardless, any attempt to redeploy now, seemingly at the eleventh hour, especially given the lack of transport and the communications bottlenecks in the rear, would have been to court disaster. In any case, for months past all the signs had been that Allenby's plan was to attack in the east, not the west, to strike again across the Jordan and into the Mountains of Moab. Had not a large Anglo-Arab force massed at Azrak, opposite Amman, in the second week in September? Were not the British buying up local barley to create fodder-dumps for large bodies of horse? Was not an attempt being made to cut out the key railway junction at Deraa?[16]

Liman was, in fact, being mesmerised by a succession of strokes too rapid and varied to be analysed rationally. Lawrence, now an accomplished military conjuror, had concocted a plan with built-in flexibility, to be modified as circumstances required. There were two main potential targets, Amman and Deraa. The significance of Amman was that it was the obvious primary objective of any British offensive across the Jordan: the easiest place to aim for in order to cut the railway and effect a junction with Feisal's Arabs. To worry at Amman was to feed the Ottoman illusion that Allenby was coming this way. Deraa, on the other hand, was a major railway town, where the Hijaz connected with the Haifa Railway and the rest of the Palestine network. To take Deraa was to sever the rail communications of all three Ottoman armies to the south – the Eighth and Seventh in Palestine, the Fourth in Syria – and to block the latter's escape-route north to Damascus. Such was its importance, moreover, that any threat to it was likely to draw down Ottoman reserves. On the eve of the great offensive, the potential strategic value of a strike against Deraa was very high. But it lay far beyond the reach of Allenby's cavalry; only the Arabs could cut the Ottoman jugular.[17]

The Arab force massed at Azrak – commanded by Sherif Nasir – numbered about a thousand men. The regular component comprised: 450 Arab camel-men, 4 Arab Vickers (heavy machine-guns), 20 Arab Hotchkiss (light machine-guns), a French battery of 4 Schneider 65mm guns, 2 British aircraft, 3 British armoured cars with tenders, an Egyptian Camel Corps demolition company, and a section of camel-mounted Gurkha Rifles. Nasir and Lawrence also had their respective Ageyl bodyguard contingents. Around this core gravitated a fluctuating mass of tribesmen – Auda's Howeitat, Nuri al-Shaalan's Ruwalla (who had finally come out openly for the sherif of Mecca), contingents of Serahin and Druses, and peasants from the villages of the Hauran, the volcanic plateau of central Syria. When the column marched on 14 September, the core thousand had been swelled by 300 Ruwalla horsemen, and Nuri al-Shaalan had some 2,000 Ruwalla camel-men camped in the Wadi Sirhan awaiting an order to move.[18]

The modified plan was to cut the three arms of the 'T' centred on Deraa – that is, the railway lines to south, north and west – thereby isolating the town and cutting the communications of each of the three Ottoman armies to the south in two places. The first operation was against the railway between Deraa and Amman. This would encourage the Ottomans in their belief that Amman was under threat, and prevent Fourth Army reinforcements moving up the line to Deraa, the main target.

But a raiding party formed of Peake's Egyptian demolition team and the camel-Gurkhas was misdirected by its guides to a section of the line occupied by the families and flocks of tribesmen fighting with the rebels on the understanding there would be no action in this area. The Serahin refused to let the party proceed, for fear of Ottoman reprisals, and the mission had to be aborted. There was no time to reschedule – Peake's men were needed for the attack north of Deraa – so Lawrence decided to attempt the job on his own.

A camel reconnaissance revealed a section where there were 'two good bridges', and the line seemed very much at ease, insufficiently guarded'. He returned on 16 September with two armoured cars, one to engage a nearby blockhouse, the other to escort his tender down to the larger of the two bridges, a four-arched structure, so that he could blow it with 150lbs of gun-cotton. As the demolition group approached the bridge, the little blockhouse garrison of about eight men became active, climbing out of their trenches and advancing towards the demolition party. The armoured cars came into action, two Turks were shot down, the rest began to flee, then changed their minds and came forward to surrender. This allowed Lawrence half an hour of quiet in which to arrange a technically perfect demolition:

> we stood on the pier-buttresses, which were conveniently flat-headed, to clear the drainage-holes in the arch-spandrils. In these, six small charges were inserted zig-zag, and with their explosion all the arches were scientifi-cally shattered, the demolition being a fine example of that finest sort, which left the skeleton of the bridge intact indeed, but tottering, so that the enemy had a first labour to destroy the wreck, before they could begin to rebuild.

But the prisoners overloaded the cars as they set off on the return-journey, and just 300 yards from the railway there was a sudden crash, a loud cracking of wood and rending of metal, and one side of Lawrence's tender tipped down and came to a violent halt, the weight of the body resting on one of the back wheels. A spring bracket had 'a sheer break which nothing but a workshop could mend'. The Turks approaching from neighbouring posts were perhaps ten minutes away. The mission had been risky without infantry support, and now the price to be paid might be a Rolls-Royce and a heap of valuable kit.

'A Rolls in the desert was above rubies, and we had never lost one yet, though we had been driving in them for 18 months, without one inch of made road, across country of the vilest, at speed, day or night, doing perhaps 20,000 miles, carrying a ton of goods and four or five men up. This was our first structural accident in our team of nine.' Lawrence's driver improvised a temporary repair.

> Rolls ... our strongest and most resourceful man, the ready mechanic, whose skill and advice largely kept our cars in running order, was nearly in tears over the mishap. The knot of us, officers and men, English, Arabs and Turks, crowded round him and watched his face anxiously. As he realised

that he, a private, commanded in this emergency, even the stubble on his jaw seemed to harden in sullen determination.[19]

The following morning, 17 September, the main column overwhelmed the Ottoman post at Tell Arar, 5 miles north of Deraa, and then spent the rest of the day carrying out a series of extensive demolitions designed to close the line for a sustained period. 'So 10 miles of the Damascus line was freely ours . . . It was the only railway to Palestine and Hijaz, and I could hardly believe our fortune; hardly believe that our word to Allenby was fulfilled so simply and so soon.'[20]

Meantime, that same afternoon, a column of Nuri's camel-mounted regulars, with artillery support, attacked Mezerib Station, on the western arm of railway, the line from Deraa to Haifa. Lawrence, having witnessed the attack on Tell Arar in the morning, was present again to see Pisani's guns smash the buildings and trucks in the station, and Nuri walk forward at the head of 100 of his infantry to receive the surrender of the 40 soldiers still alive. Peake's demolition men were still at work on the Damascus line, but the raiders did their best to make a permanent break, clearing the station, burning rolling stock, breaking points, planting 'tulip' mines along the track and ripping down the telegraph.

> This station was most rich; and the hundreds of Haurani peasants hurled themselves into it in frenzy, plundering. Men, women and children came running, and fought like dogs over every object. Even the doors and windows, the door-frames and window-frames, and the steps of the stairs were carried off. One hopeful blew in the safe, and found postage-stamps inside. Others smashed open the long-range of wagons in the sidings, to find in them all manner of goods for the Turkish army in Palestine. Tons were carried off. Yet more was strewn in wreckage on the ground.[21]

The disintegration of the *ancien régime*, its powerlessness increasingly evident, was turning into a carnival of looting.

An attempt on 18 September to destroy the bridge over the Yarmuk at Tell el-Shebab – the target of the abortive mission a year before – was checked by the arrival of a trainload of German and Turkish soldiers. This was news good enough: confirmation that the Deraa operation was drawing Liman's reserves east of the Jordan. By the following morning, its mission fully accomplished, Nuri's column was back at its new forward base at Umtaiye, about 20 miles south-east of Deraa.[22] In the distance could be heard the rumble of the guns, the majority massed on the coast, where there was one for every 50 yards of British front, the heaviest concentration of firepower in the history of Palestine.[23] The Battle of Megiddo had begun.

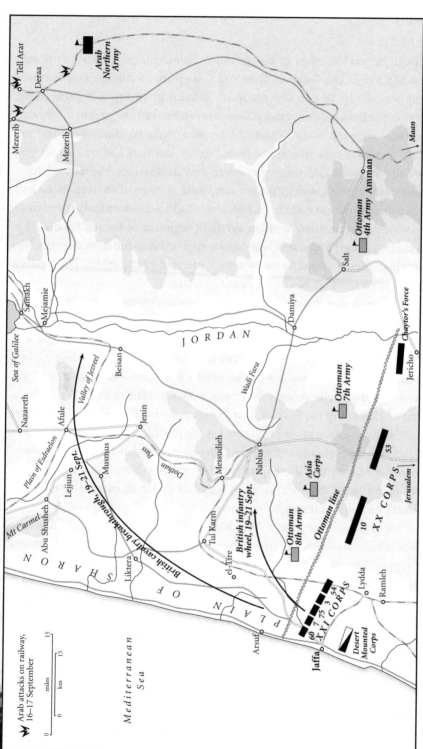

25. The Battle of Megiddo, 19–25 September 1918, showing the situation at zero hour and the direction of the main British attack.

* * *

Though he had lost many of his veteran British territorial infantry – the men who had fought the Gallipoli, Sinai and Gaza battles – Allenby's replacement army was similar in size and not much inferior in quality to it predecessor. Many of the Indian infantry battalions were combat-raw and new to the theatre, and there were too many British officers who spoke no Hindustani, and too many Indian officers who spoke little English. But they had trained up well over the summer, and two experienced Indian divisions had arrived from Mesopotamia. The cavalry, furthermore, were stronger than ever. None had been withdrawn from Palestine, whereas two Indian divisions had arrived from the Western Front, along with an excellent regiment of French Spahis. This meant that Desert Mounted Corps now comprised four full divisions, 4th, 5th, Australian Mounted and Anzac Mounted: a total of 12,000 sabres. The artillery was also stronger than before: 540 guns in total.[24]

The British therefore enjoyed a two-to-one advantage in overall numbers, and a six-to-one advantage in cavalry. But this is to understate the imbalance. The Fourth Army was wholly preoccupied with defending the Hijaz Railway against the Arabs, so that Liman had only 17,000 rifles in the line against Allenby's 57,000. The success of the British deception plan had created yet further imbalance, for Allenby had massed 35,000 infantry and 383 guns on a front of 15 miles in the Plain of Sharon, where Liman had only 8,000 infantry and 130 guns: a four-to-one advantage at the planned *Schwerpunkt*, the point of decision, the place where breakthrough was intended. Behind these infantry, moreover, Allenby had three-quarters of his cavalry. None were in the front-line: all remained mounted to act as a mobile *masse de manoeuvre* once the infantry had broken through.[25]

This great military mass – 'the sharp end' of the Egyptian Expeditionary Force (EEF) – was sustained by a semi-mechanised and industrial-scale system of supply. The total ration strength in theatre, including all troops and the 80,000 Egyptian labourers of the Camel Transport Corps, was 340,000.[26] But if all labour working anywhere on the line of communications, including Sinai and Egypt, be included, the total rose to almost 470,000. Also in military service were 75,000 horses, 39,000 mules, 35,000 camels and 11,000 donkeys. Mechanical transport eventually numbered 290 tractors, 190 caterpillar-trucks, 1,700 lorries, 2,100 cars and vans, and 1,600 motorcycles.

Second Lieutenant James Robertson, who had volunteered in Glasgow in November 1915 and since risen from the ranks, was part of this huge 'logistical tail'. On 7 September he left Jerusalem with a convoy of 14 tractors and 28 cater-pillars to a depot in the Jordan Valley a few miles north of Jericho. For a month, the job was to haul supplies from the depot to the Ghoraniyeh bridgehead, often working through the night, sometimes for days on end, exhausted by lack of sleep, drenched in sweat as the heat of the machines was added to that of the valley.[27] 'Sweat saves blood' goes the military adage. So it was in September 1918. Behind the front-line was the equivalent of an industrial city of half a million workers. Much of the technology – like the Holts caterpillars – was cutting-edge. The movement of supplies, which peaked in August 1918, rose to a daily average of 2,317 tonnes.[28] The stockpiles included almost 1,000 shells for every gun.[29]

Such was the imbalance, Wavell was convinced that 'the battle was practically won before a shot was fired'.[30] Another officer thought the British offensive that of 'a tiger against a tomcat'.[31] Liman's assessment was scarcely more optimistic. He contemplated wholesale retreat to a line abreast the Sea of Galilee and along the Yarmuk Gorge, the historic defence-line of central Syria. Only his army's chronic lack of mobility prevented it.

> On account of the limited marching capacity of the Turkish soldiers and of the very low mobility of all draft animals, I considered that the holding of our positions to the last gave us more favourable prospects than a long retreat with Turkish troops with impaired morale. The lack of sufficient troops to establish rearward positions of support was fraught with danger for the retreat; it was also the cause of the collapse of the front.[32]

But even Liman, as he later admitted, underestimated the moral decay of the Ottoman Army. He had not peered deeply enough into the dark heart of Little Mehmet. Armies are held together on the battlefield by some strange compound of discipline, solidarity, pride and hope. The compound can dissolve in an instant amid the chaos and terror of battle. Panic can then disintegrate an army of tens of thousands into human atoms in a matter of minutes. Then it ceases to be an army and becomes an inchoate mass of frightened, desperate, fleeing humanity.

That time had now come for the Ottoman Army in Palestine. It had taken four years of carnage, privation and fear, until finally, *Mehmetchik* – hungry, ragged, sensing his enemy's overwhelming superiority, believing his cause defeated, reduced now to the bare hope of personal survival – would fight no more. 'In my reckonings,' Liman confessed, 'I made the mistake that, while considering possible a step-by-step retreat of units, I had not calculated upon the collapse of whole divisions. During the entire campaign, I had observed such failure in Turkish troops under my command but once ... [and] never in defence.'[33]

* * *

The guns on the coast opened fire at 4.30am on 19 September. For 15 minutes the Ottoman trenches were subject to sudden and intense fire from every available gun. They disappeared in the smoke and dust of more than a thousand explosions a minute. Signal rockets soared skywards from the murk: the defenders summoning help. But there was no time, for this was no preliminary bombardment: it was zero hour itself. The infantry were already moving, five divisions of Lieutenant-General Sir Edward Bulfin's XXI Corps; from left to right, the 60th, 7th, 75th, 3rd and 54th. Only the last, the East Anglians, were wholly British; the other four divisions were formed of composite brigades of one British and three Indian battalions. Many of these men were facing the inferno of modern battle for the first time. It did not matter. They entered the enemy's front-line trenches under cover of the artillery bombardment, which was planned as a creeping barrage, advancing at a speed of 100 yards a minute.

The defences were organised in two main lines. The first ran along a low sandy ridge and had a depth of about 3,000 yards. The trenches were well-constructed, but the barbed wire was limited, and the decision had been against using the guns to cut it; instead, the forward assault units were supplied with wire-cutters and a mixture of planks, corrugated-iron sheets, and stuffed sandbags. A second line lay two to three miles behind the first, but the trenches here were neither continuous nor protected by wire.

As the line of erupting shells advanced deeper into the Ottoman trench-system, the infantry found themselves advancing against almost non-existent resistance. A volley of grenades, a bayonet charge and the defenders, stunned and confused, usually surrendered *en masse*. Soon, as the advance penetrated deeper, hundreds could be seen fleeing across the open ground to the north. A measure of the enemy's broken will was that mere handfuls of men found themselves making mass captures. Forty men of the 125th (Napier's) Rifles took 200 prisoners and 6 machine-guns. A British captain and six men of the same regiment captured a battery of three 105mm howitzers. Another battery, of 150mm howitzers, was captured by a wounded Indian NCO of the 92nd Punjabis and four wounded men of the 1st Guides Infantry.

The 60th Division, on the coast, advanced 7,000 yards in about two and a half hours, and by 7am was clean through both Ottoman lines. The 3rd, 75th and 7th Divisions also carried the front system at the first rush. Only on Bulfin's right was there significant resistance, but even here the 54th Division, supported by a French contingent it had under orders, Détachment Français de Palestine et Syrie, secured all its primary objectives, despite facing the only Turkish counterattack of the day, and clashing with elements of the elite German Asia Corps.

The 54th Division was the hinge of a gigantic gate opening at the coast and swinging north-east. By 5pm, barely 12 hours after the start of the attack, the

60th Division had advanced more than 16 miles to the railway junction at Tul Karm, which it captured before dark, taking prisoner the garrison of 500 men. The advance of the three divisions on the right conformed to that of the 60th, so that the infantry of XXI Corps were executing a vast wheel designed to herd the Eighth Army away from the coast and cut off the Seventh Army still in the hills. By the end of the first day, Bulfin's infantry attack had shattered two entire Ottoman divisions, taken 7,000 prisoners, and captured 100 guns. Meantime, the 10th and 53rd Divisions of Lieutenant-General Sir Philip Chetwode's XX Corps, ranged along the 30 miles of front that ran though the Judaean Hills and down to the Jordan, had launched a diversionary attack to engage the Seventh Army frontally and keep the enemy guessing about the direction of the main British effort.[34]

General Liman von Sanders at his Nazareth headquarters had only a hazy idea of what was happening. Arab saboteurs (or someone) had cut many of the telegraph and telephone lines. At 7am all communications with Tul Karm ceased. Around the same time, Eighth Army headquarters stopped responding to wireless messages (it had been overrun and its commander had become a fugitive behind enemy lines). It was gone 9 o'clock before Colonel von Oppen, commander of the Asia Corps, holding the hinge position between the Eighth Army on the coast and the Seventh Army in the hills, got through to Liman on the phone to inform him that the whole of the right flank had collapsed. The German commander-in-chief was stunned. Nothing had prepared him for this.

'Up to this day,' he wrote ten years later:

no exhaustive account has appeared of the complete and sudden collapse of the 7th Division in the western part of the coastal sector, and of the adjoining two regiments of the 20th Division. Though the force was very small for such a large sector, it had stood up well in prior battles. After two hours of drum-fire, they had completely disappeared on 19 September, before a hostile infantry attack had been launched. Nor did I ever during the retreat see officers or small parts of this division.

There was worse, Oppen explained: strong forces of enemy cavalry were advancing northwards along the coast – deep into the Ottoman rear.[35]

* * *

Lieutenant-General Sir Henry Chauvel's Desert Mounted Corps had been waiting for the gate to open: three divisions, 5th Cavalry on the left, 4th Cavalry on the right, Australian Mounted behind. They included British Yeomanry,

Indian Lancers and Australian Light Horse.[36] All 9,000 of them, whether cavalry proper or mounted infantry, had had impressed upon them the need for aggressive shock-tactics. Dismounted action was to be a last resort. The enemy was to be charged on sight.[37] The weapons were to be the lance, the sabre and the bayonet.[38] The plan was for mounted breakout followed by relentless mounted pursuit to hound the defeated enemy to destruction.

Within two hours of the opening barrage, the 5th Division was moving forward along the seashore, covered by the cliffs that bordered the beach, and by 8.30am they were in the open country beyond the abandoned Ottoman fortifications. The 4th Division, further inland, got off to a slower start, but by 10am they, too, were through.[39] The Middlesex Yeomanry were with them, and Sergeant Hatton bore witness to the ease of the preceding infantry battle.

> Shortly before 9 o'clock, with the other regiments of our brigade, the 29th Lancers and Jacob's Horse … we rode off through gaps in the wire and quickly passed over the Turkish trenches. The signs of battle were fewer than would be supposed. Here and there the loose huddled body of a dead Turk, or one badly wounded calling for 'moyah' [water], a few forsaken machine-guns, an occasional field-piece, several dead donkeys and pack-ponies; but nowhere were the heaps of slain that had formed such grim testimony to the attacking troops at the smash-up of the Beersheba-Gaza line.[40]

Writing later in the *Cavalry Journal*, Lieutenant-Colonel Rex Osborn tried to imagine the view from the air as Chauvel's cavalry army cantered forward:

> From 10.00 hours onwards, a hostile aeroplane observer, if one had been available, flying over the Plain of Sharon would have seen a remarkable sight – 94 squadrons, disposed in great breadth and in great depth, hurrying forward relentlessly on a decisive mission – a mission of which all cavalry soldiers have dreamed, but in which few have been privileged to partake.[41]

The cavalry's orders were simple: they were to avoid formed enemy bodies if they could, push forward as rapidly as possible, break into the Plain of Esdraelon, and block the roads and railways behind the Ottoman front by seizing the town of Afule. It was an exceptionally bold plan, aiming for the deepest and fastest possible penetration, so as to bring about the complete destruction of the Eighth and Seventh Armies.[42] Critical to the operation were the passes through the Carmel Range which led from the Plain of Sharon to that of Esdraelon. Near the northern exits, commanding the roads between Palestine and Syria, lay the ancient site of Megiddo. Hereabouts were many of history's greatest battles fought. Among the victories won near Megiddo was that of Pharaoh Thutmose III over the King of Kadesh in the fifteenth century BC, that of Saladin over the Crusader Kingdom of Jerusalem in 1187, and that of the Mamluks over the Mongols in 1260. Even Bonaparte had fought a battle here, in 1799, during his siege of nearby Acre. And Megiddo was the biblical Armageddon, which, according to the *Book of Revelation*, was to be the site of the final battle between good and evil at the end of time.[43]

The plan now was for the 5th Division to wheel wide on the left and enter the northern plain via Abu Shushe, while the 4th Division wheeled more tightly and used the Musmus Pass, debouching at Lejjun (Megiddo itself). By 2.30am on the morning of 20 September – less than 24 hours after zero – the two lead brigades of 5th Division were through the northern pass and into the plain beyond. The 13th Brigade made straight for Nazareth, which was about 7 miles north of Afule in the hills of Galilee on the far side of the plain. When shooting started around the town, Liman was still in his pyjamas as he clambered into a car to make a rapid exit. The vanguard, the Gloucestershire Yeomanry, charged into the town, and confused fighting erupted in the streets, where Liman, now dressed, returned to organise the defence. Though the Gloucesters briefly overran the Ottoman GHQ, 13th Brigade, encumbered with 1,250 prisoners, and without adequate support, was forced to pull back to the plain.[44]

Even before this shock, Liman had begun to grasp the full scale of the disaster unfolding. He had given orders to Major Frey to block the Musmus Pass with a scratch force of gendarmerie and part of a depot regiment – six companies with twelve machine-guns in all.[45] They were too late. Though part of the lead brigade had lost its way and missed the entrance to the pass – causing a delay of two hours – the advanced elements of 4th Cavalry reached the northern exit before dawn on the morning of the second day. They had covered about 40 miles in less than 24 hours, the last of it slipping and slithering in single file down a rocky goat track. Comprising two armoured cars and 2nd Lancers, they overwhelmed a party of 100 Turks sitting around campfires with arms piled, and entered the town. By 5.30am, 2nd Lancers had watered, fed and breakfasted, and were again on the move, led by the 30-year-old Captain Davison, in command because his superior regimental officers were indisposed.

Ten minutes later, the lancers collided with Major Frey's column, hurrying up to block the pass, and the centre squadron immediately came under fire. Davison ordered this squadron and the armoured cars to engage the enemy frontally, and sent his reserve squadron round to the right, along a slight depression, to execute a flank attack. The officer commanding the third squadron, seeing the manoeuvre, made an independent decision to cooperate. The enemy were ranged in two lines, one behind the other, and these were attacked simultaneously by the two squadrons.

A charge of lancers was terrifying. The weapon was held under the arm, balanced by being gripped well forward, and the razor-sharp point was driven at the enemy with the force of a galloping horse. It had long reach, was easily directed, and inflicted ghastly wounds, often fatal. The action was over in five minutes. Though three enemy machine-guns were manned until the moment of impact, the Turks were so shaken by the spectacle that they fired high, and only one lancer was wounded and twelve horses killed. Once among the enemy, the Indians speared 46 Turks, and virtually all the rest, numbering 470, quickly surrendered. As the regiments of 4th Cavalry streamed out of the pass into the plain, they passed 'these poor Johnnies squatting disconsolately on the ground'. For many of the British and Indian troopers, they were the first enemy they had seen.[46]

The 4th Division entered Afule in the centre of the plain at about 8am, shortly after 5th Division. Much rolling stock, three aircraft, and an abundance of medical and other stores were captured. Leaving the 5th in occupation of the town, it then headed off down the Valley of Jezreel towards Beisan, around 15 miles to the south-east. 'Way on our right,' recalled Sergeant Hatton, 'we could just see the white stone houses of Nazareth, set among olive trees upon the slope of a hill-side, and throughout the day, wherever one looked to left or right, miles upon miles of moving cavalry met the eye.'

On the way, riding forward to reconnoitre, Hatton's commanding officer, Lieutenant-Colonel Lawson, was surprised and captured by a Turkish detachment retreating northwards. According to the divisional commander, Lawson:

> explained the situation to the Turkish officers and showed them on his map how hopelessly they were placed, with British troops on all sides of them. This strange conference, held in indifferent French, ended in the position of captured and captors being reversed; and the officer led back to his regiment 800 armed Turkish officers and men as prisoners-of-war.

The moral collapse of Ottoman resistance appeared absolute.

Beisan was another nodal point on the Palestine communications network. Situated where the Valley of Jezreel entered the Valley of the Jordan, it lay on a dog-leg of the Deraa–Haifa railway, astride a new motor-road from Nablus. It was captured at 4.30 in the afternoon, the garrison offering little resistance. All the northern escape-routes for the men of the Eighth and Seventh Armies had been blocked. As Hatton explained, the two Turkish armies west of the Jordan were now surrounded, and as the infantry were still pounding away at them on the original line, and the troops down in the Jordan Valley, the Chaytor Force, were also engaging the Fourth Army, we realised that before long they would be driven back on us.' The 4th Cavalry Division had advanced 70 miles in 36 hours. It had lost only 26 horses. The effect was that, by the evening of the second day of the battle, two Ottoman armies were doomed.[47]

* * *

They were already disintegrating. The third arm of the cavalry breakthrough, that of Australian Mounted, had followed 4th Division through the Musmus Pass and then turned sharply south-east towards Jenin, a major town on the road and railway between Nablus and Afule. As 10th Australian Light Horse approached the town from the north-west on the evening of the 20th, it encountered a large body of Turks with some Germans waiting in a grove in expectation of attack from the south. A single squadron peeled off and charged, and the entire mass, 1,900 men, immediately surrendered – at odds of 50 to 1.

The 10th Light Horse, supported by the 9th, then entered Jenin as darkness fell: a few hundred horsemen in the midst of about 3,000 enemy soldiers. Only some German machine-gunners showed much fight. Most of the Turks simply surrendered. Then pandemonium broke across the town, as men, women and children fell upon the immense stores of food, clothing and equipment in the stores; fires broke out as dumps were set alight.

The 10th Light Horse meantime moved to block the southern approaches to the town. A machine-gun section commanded by one Lieutenant Patterson lost its way and found itself on the road ahead of the main body. A large column of enemy was marching up from the south. The Australians opened fire. The Turks began to deploy. Patterson rode forward and demanded their surrender, claiming to stand at the head of a large force. The request was translated by a German nurse who happened to be with the column and spoke good English. The bluff was believed, and 2,800 men surrendered to Patterson's 23.[48]

On the evening of the same day, the third of the battle, the eastern escape-route via the Jordan Valley was also blocked. This was the work of airpower. Nablus had fallen around noon, the infantry of 10th Division advancing from the south, as the troopers of 5th Australian Light Horse Brigade, temporarily detached from division, entered from the west. The fall of Nablus terminated all organised resistance by the Eighth and Seventh Armies. The greater part of the former had already been taken prisoner. A long column of survivors retreating down the road to the north was intercepted when it reached Jenin. Another column started north-east from Nablus along the motor-road constructed by the Turks through the Wadi Fara to Beisan. The first part of the journey passed through a precipitous gorge where the road was cut into the hill-side. Here, at dawn on 21 September, RAF reconnaissance plans spotted the main mass of Mustapha Kemal's Seventh Army strung out in a 5-mile-long column of men, animals, carts, lorries and guns. For four hours that morning, the column was the target of sustained air-attack, with nearly ninety sorties flown, the aircraft sometimes bombing and strafing only a few yards overhead. The Wadi Fara was transformed into a valley of death.

'The enemy's line was stretched along a narrow and steeply winding road that threaded the mountainside, overhanging a deep chasm,' explained the RAF war diary. 'It was difficult, if not impossible, for troops caught here to scatter or take effective cover. Every two minutes two machines arrived over the column, and every half an hour an additional formation of six machines bombed and machine-gunned it . . .'

The head of the column was struck first, blocking the road, bringing everything to a halt. In what followed, nine tons of bombs were dropped and 56,000 machine-gun rounds fired into the inert, helpless mass of flesh below. Desperate men tried to escape by climbing out of the wadi or descending into the gorge. Others prostrated themselves on the ground or waved frantically in an effort to surrender. 'As a result of the bombing, the road was completely blocked,' the war diary continued. 'Motor transport was blown across the road. Wagons, horses, oxen, guns and limbers were an inextricable mess of ruin. In all, 87 guns, 54 motor-wagons, 4 motor-cars, and 932 wagons were destroyed or captured.'

Not a single aircraft was lost: the Wadi Fara was a one-sided massacre. The pilots could see what they were doing, and many were traumatised, some reduced to tears, asking not to be sent up again. Brigadier Biffy Borton, who commanded the wing of seven squadrons responsible for Wadi Fara, wrote to his father afterwards: 'General Salmond [the RAF commander in Palestine], who came up to stay with me, went out to the scene next day, and was absolutely appalled at the havoc which could be produced by aircraft. We are commonly alluded to as butchers.'[49]

The demoralised and disorganised survivors scattered into the hills. Most were rounded up in the next few days. Very few made it across the Jordan. The Ottoman Seventh Army, like the Eighth, had ceased to exist.[50]

That same day, General Allenby, returning to GHQ after a drive down to Lejjun, found time to write to his wife. 'I think that the Turkish army is practically destroyed,' he told her.

We have taken well over 20,000 prisoners and some 120 or more guns. I think we shall get all guns and many more prisoners. My losses are very slight ... I went and passed through thousands of prisoners today, many of them Germans. Most of them are dog tired. I should not be surprised if we get 30,000 eventually; there must be hundreds scattered among the mountains, still, who will surrender if we push the infantry in. All my troops have marched and fought grandly; some of the infantry have done 20 miles, across mountains, today.[51]

Two days later, he wrote again with further details.

Prisoners still roll in; and the roads and defiles of the mountains are encumbered with guns, wagons, motor-lorries and all sorts of stores. It will take weeks to collect them ... I've been going round hospitals today. All the sick and wounded are very cheerful and content. I've told them they've done the biggest thing in the war – having totally destroyed two armies in 36 hours![52]

* * *

Only the Fourth Army remained. This had taken little part in the fighting so far and was substantially intact. The completeness of Allenby's victory in Palestine had, however, rendered its position untenable. Its centre of gravity was still at Maan, but the Arabs had cut its supply-line near Deraa, and Allenby was now intent on the capture of the town, as a preliminary to a combined Anglo-Arab advance on Damascus. Already, British and Australian cavalry were in the Jordan Valley well to the north of Maan. Chaytor's Force – Anzac Mounted Division, a brigade of Indian infantry, two Zionist battalions, two West Indian regiments, seven batteries of artillery – had been operating on Allenby's outer flank, charged with preventing any movement west of Ottoman reinforcements, guarding XX Corps' right as it went forward in the Judaean Hills, securing the Damiya bridge over the Jordan, then advancing on Salt and Amman. Major-General Chaytor, the New Zealander now in command of the original Anzac division, accomplished his mission with such success that his men were in Salt by the evening of the 23rd, and had captured Amman after a fierce little battle around the Citadel on the 25th.[53]

On the day Amman was captured, another fierce little battle took place more than 50 miles to the north, at Samakh, 'a mean little mud village' by the Jordan, on the southern edge of the Sea of Galilee. Samakh had momentarily assumed decisive importance. It was the anchor of an interim defensive line that Liman was struggling to construct in an effort to keep open an escape-route from Palestine eastwards down the Yarmuk Gorge. It had to be held if anything was to be salvaged from the wreckage of the Seventh and Eighth

Armies; and in order to block the British pursuit and give the still-intact Fourth Army on the far side of the Jordan more time to get north. Liman, accordingly, had ordered an emergency rearguard action at Samakh, telling the post commandant, Captain von Keyserling, to hold at all costs.

Pursuit to the uttermost was a core maxim for Allenby – a specific application of the generic maxim that 'sweat saves blood'. The chief had met Chauvel at Megiddo on the 22nd. The casualties had been minimal. Two armies had been destroyed. The only constraints on forward movement were geographical and logistical. The British and Anzac high command was in jubilant mood. The danger was that the ease and apparent completeness of the victory would cause officers and men to relax. So when Chauvel told Allenby that he had taken 15,000 prisoners, Allenby replied, 'No bloody good to me! I want 30,000 before you've done.'

Nothing was to be given time to coalesce and consolidate. Any solid enemy body was likely to gain substance as the flotsam and jetsam of defeat re-coagulated around it. No such body was to be allowed to stand. Chauvel gave Brigadier-General Grant's 4th Light Horse Brigade – the men who had charged at Beersheba the year before – the task of eliminating the Samakh rearguard. They set out at 2.30am on 25 September. The ground was flat as a pancake, so the night approach served them well. But as the 11th Light Horse Regiment appeared out of the darkness, machine-guns and rifles opened fire. 'The bullets whistled low over our heads, like the rustle of an immense flight of swallows,' recalled Ernest Hammond, 'and in the distance we saw pin-points of light dancing along the muzzles of the guns like flickers of lightning.'

'What orders, colonel?' shouted a squadron leader in the gloom. Grant was under-strength and had been promised reinforcements, but he was not inclined to wait and lose the advantage of darkness and surprise. So Lieutenant-Colonel Parsons was ordered to mount an immediate attack. 'Form line and charge the guns!' While C Squadron took position on a low hill east of the town overlooking the road and railway, A and B Squadrons formed two lines of half-squadrons and charged, yelling loudly, waving swords, covered by the fire of the regiment's machine-guns. Cavalry pits brought down some horses, bullets many more, and both squadrons veered away from the fire and diverged, Major Loynes on the left heading into the town itself, Major Costello looping wide on the right.

Soon the Anzac troopers were dismounted and engaged in a close-quarters gun battle in the streets. The defenders were well-hidden and outnumbered the Australians two-to-one. Germans fired concealed machine-guns and lobbed grenades from upper-floor windows. The battle was static for about an hour, until Grant ordered up the Hotchkiss machine-guns and a reserve squadron from 12th Regiment. Then the Australians began to move forward again. Buildings were contested, room by room, floor by floor, with bombs and bayonets in some of most bitter hand-to-hand fighting of the campaign. As the defenders gave way, some tried to escape across the lake in a motor-boat, but it was caught by Hotchkiss fire and exploded, while other fugitives were mown down along the railway. When the savage little battle ended, the Light Horse had 14 dead, 29 wounded, and about half their animals killed. They counted 98 enemy dead, and 23 officers and 341 rank-and-file were taken prisoner, of whom about 150 were German.[54]

Samakh completed the conquest of Palestine. Acre and Haifa, on the coast, had been captured by a separate mounted column on 23 September, so the way was clear to create two massive pincers moving around either side of the Sea of Galilee, with Damascus as the final objective of both. Barrow's 4th Division was to move east via Irbid to capture Deraa, intercept the anticipated retreat of the Ottoman Fourth Army, and then take the road north to Damascus: a total distance of 140 miles. Meantime, Hodgson's Australian Mounted, followed by Macandrew's 5th, was to take the western road around the lake, cross the Jordan at Jisr Benat Yakub ('the Bridge of the Daughters of Jacob'), and head for Damascus via Kuneitra and Sasa: a distance of 90 miles. Both columns were to travel light and fast, living off local supplies of water, fodder and food: they were to achieve the destruction of the Ottoman forces in Syria by breaking free of the long and ponderous EEF supply-system.[55]

* * *

The Arabs, too, were on the move. A council of war at Umtaiye on 24 September had agreed Lawrence's proposal that Feisal's army should relocate to a new position at Sheikh Saad village. About 15 miles north-west of Deraa, it would place the Arabs on the flank of both the east–west route down the Yarmuk Gorge and the north–south route to Damascus. Its occupation would mean pressing hard on Deraa and the Ottoman lines of retreat, and positioning the Arabs both to cooperate with the British and to make a run for Damascus when the time came.

The move was complete by dawn on the 27th. Soon afterwards the news came that the Ottomans were evacuating Deraa. A little later a plane dropped a message with further intelligence: two columns of Turks were approaching, one from Mezerib in the west, 2,000 strong, the other from Deraa to the south, 6,000 strong.[56] 'The nearer 2,000 seemed more our size,' reported Lawrence. 'We would meet them with 500 men and scatter them. Therefore we called half our mounted infantry, with most of the Hotchkiss automatics, and two of Pisani's

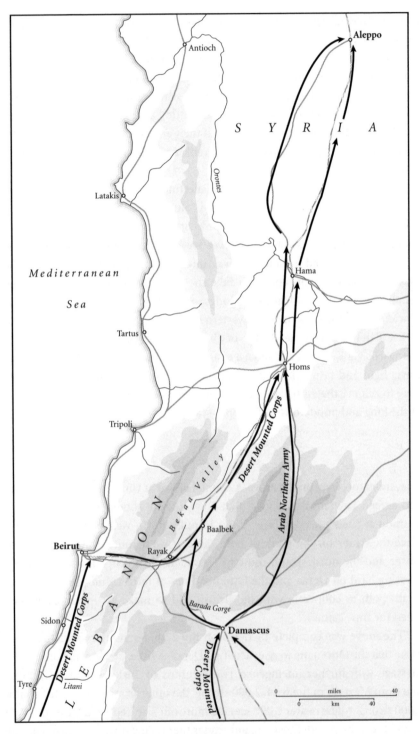

26. The race from Damascus to Aleppo, October 1918.

guns, to go down south against them.' There was another consideration: the Arab village of Tafas lay directly in the path of the retreating column, and the Sheikh of Tafas, Talal el-Hareidhin, had been fighting with the Sherifian forces for the past year. Talal feared for his village.[57]

The Sheikh of Tafas was famous in the region of Deraa.

Talal was an outlaw, with a price upon his head, but so great in his district that he rode about when and where he pleased, and lodged with whom he would. He had fallen out with the Turks over the military service of one of his villagers two years before, and in the first year and the second had killed, according to one report, some twenty-three Turks with his own hand.

He dressed in dashing Haurani fashion. 'His sheepskin coat was of the finest Angora obtainable, covered in green broadcloth, ornamented with silk patches, and designs in brown braid. His other clothes were silk, and his high boots, his silver saddle, his sword, his dagger and his rifle matched his reputation.'[58]

Talal urged haste. Half way to the village, the Sherifian column passed a group of mounted Arabs herding some prisoners towards Sheikh Saad. The victims had been stripped and were being beaten forward. It was a time of vengeance: these were Turks of the police battalion from Deraa, 'beneath whose iniquities the Arabs of the neighbourhood had run with tears and blood innumerable times'. There was disquieting news: the retreating Turkish column, mostly mounted lancers, had already reached Tafas. And a little further, when the village came in view, the news was found to be true.

The village lay there stilly before us, under the slow wreaths of white smoke, as we rode to it guardedly. Some grey heaps seemed to hide in the long grass, embracing the ground in that close way which corpses had. These we knew were dead Arab men and women. But from one a little figure tottered off, as though to escape from us. It was a child, three or four years old, whose dirty smock was stained red all over one shoulder and side. When near we saw that it was blood from a large half-fibrous wound, perhaps a lance thrust, just where neck and body joined.

The child became frightened, then dropped in a heap, gushing blood, and died. Among other bodies were four dead babies.

On the outskirts were some low mud walls, of sheepfolds, and on one lay something red and white. I looked close and saw the body of a woman folded across it, bottom upwards, nailed there by a saw bayonet whose haft stuck hideously into the air from between her naked legs. She had been pregnant, and about her lay others, perhaps twenty in all, variously killed, but set out in accord with obscene taste.

A terrible madness of war had descended on this little upland village basking in clear air and warm sunshine. The lancers were a military elite, stalwarts of a doomed empire, men embittered by defeat and the treachery of an enemy within. A swollen rage had burst inside the village and destroyed its people in a sudden frenzy of rape, murder and desecration. The madness now infected the witnesses. As it did so, it drew upon deep layers of bitterness, accumulating over four centuries among the common people, a piling up of collective memories of bullying, conscription, extortion and the rule of the gendarme.

Talal withdrew inside himself and sat alone on his horse. Time passed. Then he drew his *keffiyeh* about his face, drove his stirrups into his horse's flanks, and galloped headlong towards the tail of the Turkish column, to perish in a hail of rifle and machine-gun bullets.

Auda, looking 'very cold and grim', took command. 'God give him mercy,' he said. 'We will take his price.' Then he led the Haurani peasants forward in a battle of vengeance and annihilation.[59] The order was given: 'No prisoners!' The Arab attack split the enemy column in three. The smallest section, formed mainly of German and Austrian machine-gunners grouped around three motor-cars, fought magnificently, repelling a succession of attacks, but was eventually overwhelmed. The fight against the other two was a running battle over many miles, gaining momentum as the peasants flowing on either side of the fleeing Turks mounted themselves on abandoned donkeys, mules and horses, and re-armed with discarded rifles, revolvers and bayonets.

'There lay upon us a madness, born of the horror of Tafas or of its story; so that we killed and killed, even blowing in the heads of the fallen and of the animals, as though their death and running blood could slake the agony of our brains.' It continued until nightfall, by which time 'the rich plain behind us was scattered over with the dead bodies of men and animals'. Only 200 or so of the central section of the broken column survived, many of them Germans, taken prisoner by a group of Arabs lately arrived who had not known of Tafas.

But their respite was short. A fallen Arab with a shattered thigh was found to have been tortured, 'bayonets having been hammered through his shoulder and other leg into the ground, pinning him out like a collected insect'. So an end was made of the prisoners. 'We ranged our Hotchkiss on them, and pointed to him silently. They said nothing in the moment before we opened fire. And at the last, their heap ceased moving ... and we mounted again and rode slowly home ... in the gloom which felt so chill now that the sun had gone down.'[60]

* * *

Deraa had fallen on the same day and was immediately plunged into a chaos of killing and looting. Lawrence raced to the scene by camel, passing 'through a country of murder and night terror', outpacing his companions to enter Deraa alone at dawn on 28 September. General Barrow's 4th Cavalry Division was approaching from the west. Lawrence was eager to see an Arab administration established before it arrived. He was also fearful of accidental clashes between British and Sherifian forces if the former were unaware that Deraa was already in Arab hands.

Making contact with Barrow was not straightforward: it meant crossing a war zone and then establishing his identity. His being mistaken for an enemy, a native and then a spy by the first British soldiers he encountered seems to have appealed to Lawrence's impish sense of humour. When he eventually found his way to Barrow, he continued mischievous, telling the somewhat perplexed general that a Sherifian administration already existed, sentries had been posted and that his men would be welcomed as guests of the Arabs. Barrow, lacking instructions otherwise, conformed. Upon entering the town and catching sight of a pennon outside the new headquarters of the Sherif Nasir – the former Ottoman commandant's office – Barrow saluted. A political milestone had been passed: a British column, effecting junction with an Arab column, had conceded the legitimacy of an interim Sherifian administration.

Barrow was, nonetheless, appalled by the mayhem; in particular by the looting of a hospital train trapped in the town when the line to the north was cut.

> In the cab of the engine was the dead driver and a mortally wounded fireman. The Arab soldiers were going through the train, tearing off the clothing of the groaning and stricken Turks, regardless of gaping wounds and broken limbs, and cutting their victims' throats . . . it was a sight that no average civilised human being could bear unmoved.

Much of the town was in flames, hardly a building remained undamaged, and dead animals lay everywhere. Despite Lawrence's objections, Barrow insisted on restoring order at the station.[61]

* * *

Fifty miles to the south, General Chaytor's Anzac Mounted Division, in possession of Amman for three days, received news that a large Ottoman column had been sighted to the south: the Maan Detachment of Ottoman II Corps. A message was dropped over the column informing its commander that all water supplies on the road ahead had been secured, and that his force would be bombed on the morrow if he did not surrender. Contact was made by 5th Light Horse with the Ottoman vanguard the following day, 29 September, and shortly afterwards a trolley came down the line with a message from Colonel Ali Bey requesting a meeting. Before this could be arranged, another message arrived offering surrender.

On the hills east and west of the Ottoman column were thousands of armed men mounted on horses and camels: tribesmen of the Beni Sakhr. Their watchful presence was the essential background to the negotiation now in progress. 'After their withdrawal from Maan,' reported the Australian *Official History*:

> the Turks had marched north to Ziza, with the picturesque tribesmen, burning to strike and plunder, but fearful of risk, prowling like jackals around them. Riding their mean-looking but spirited Arab ponies, they galloped in wide circles about the fugitive force, uttering wild shouts, firing their rifles into the air, and threatening each hapless straggler with pillage and murder.

Ali Bey wished to surrender to the Australians to save his men from the Arabs. But he refused to do so until assured that sufficient protective force was on hand: one regiment of Light Horse was not enough. Warned of the tense three-way confrontation and the alarming danger of a massacre, Chaytor ordered Brigadier-General Ryrie – the 55-year-old hard-fighting, heavyweight bushman who commanded 2nd Brigade – to Ziza with as many of his men as he could muster. When he arrived, the situation had grown still more alarming. 'The 5th Regiment were concentrated, waiting reinforcements, while the Turks in their trenches were standing to arms holding off the Arabs with shell and machine-gun fire,' reported the commander of the 7th, who had arrived with Ryrie. 'The vulture appearance of the Arabs, who were willing that we should do the fighting and they the looting, will not readily be forgotten.'

Ryrie took an extraordinary decision. Having advised Ali Bey of his intentions, he led his men through the ring of Arabs, entered the enemy lines, and ordered his men to fight side-by-side with the Turkish infantry in defence of their trenches. He had with him two Arab sheikhs, and these he now used as hostages, telling them that if the Ottoman camp was attacked during the night, they would both be shot.

> The sheikhs sent out messengers to inform their followers of this threat, and the Turks and Australians proceeded, after years of bitter fighting, to bivouac

together. They gathered about the same fires, exchanging their food, making chapattis together, and by many signs expressing reciprocal respect and admiration. The Australians, although outnumbered eight to one, had no concern for their safety, and the confidence with which they moved about the armed lines was a tribute to the honour of the Turks.

Thus, again, the Australian *Official History*.

The New Zealand Brigade arrived at 8am the following morning. Most of the Turks then laid down their arms, though Ryrie allowed a few hundred to keep their rifles as supplementary escorts, and the whole column headed north to Amman. The prisoners numbered 5,000.

The elimination of the Maan column was the culmination of a spectacular nine days' campaigning by Chaytor's Force, which had bagged 10,000 prisoners, 57 guns, 132 machine-guns, 11 railway engines and 106 trucks. Casualties had been minimal: a mere 139 killed, wounded and missing.[62]

* * *

By mid-afternoon on 30 September, Lawrence, being driven in *Blue Mist*, his Rolls-Royce tender, was at Kiswe, just 10 miles short of Damascus. He heard firing to the right, near the Hijaz Railway. Then he saw it: a Turkish column of about 2,000 ragged men stumbling forward in the dust, some halting now and then to spray bullets or shrapnel at their pursuers, before resuming their weary trek. All about them were the horsemen and camel-men of Sherif Nasir, Nuri el-Shaalan and Auda abu Tayi. This was the Deraa column, which three days before had been 6,000, now reduced by steady attrition to only a third as many. Thus had the Parthians defeated the Romans, the Arabs the Byzantines, the Saracens the Crusaders: by employing an 'Eastern way of war', based on light cavalry and shooting; a war of mobility and missiles; of distance, evasion and harassment: a war of the wasp.

It was nearly the end. Nuri al-Shaalan's Ruwalla, hanging on both flanks, were herding the remnants of the column towards Jebel Mania. There, lying in wait, were Auda's Howeitat, and their local friends, the Wuld Ali. Lawrence motored across to suggest cooperation with the British, coming up an hour or so behind, and then drove down to secure the assistance of the Middlesex Yeomanry and a battery of horse guns.

The extra pressure broke the column into a stream of men who, abandoning guns and transport, headed for a col between the twin peaks of Jebel Mania, seemingly towards emptiness and safety. 'However, in that empty land was Auda waiting for them, and in that night of his last battle against the Turks, the deadly old man killed and killed, plundered and plundered, captured and captured, till dawn came and showed him his work finished.' Tired by then of killing, the 600 survivors he took prisoner. It was the culmination of two weeks during which Feisal's Arab Northern Army had killed about 5,000 Turks, taken about 8,000 prisoners, and captured 30 guns and 150 machine-guns.[63]

* * *

Two other columns of Djemal *Kuchuk*'s fugitive Fourth Army were also on the move that day, one streaming north-east from Damascus towards Homs, the other north-west down the Barada Gorge towards Baalbek and Beirut. General Chauvel's Australian Mounted Division was ordered forward in an effort to block both routes. When the 5th Australian Light Horse Brigade reached the southern lip of the gorge, they found themselves looking down precipitous cliffs upon a crowded mass of troops, transport and trains a few hundred feet below. River, road and railway ran down this gorge, and the great majority of the men fleeing Damascus seem to have chosen it, for the Homs road was almost waterless. But the gorge was only about 100 yards wide, and the column therefore stretched for miles.

First on the scene, at about 4.30 in the afternoon, were the 2nd New Zealand Machine-Gun Squadron (with six Hotchkiss) and the French Régiment Mixte Marche de Cavalerie. Two miles to the west, the 9th Australian Light Horse also reached the lip of the gorge. Meantime, the eastern end, near Damascus, was blocked by the 14th Australian Light Horse.

Rarely have riflemen and machine-gunners been offered such a target: densely packed, soon virtually static and within relatively close range. One official report ran as follows:

German machine-gunners, operating from the tops of motor-lorries and trains, defied the challenge to surrender, and all along the gorge the unequal issue was joined. The result was sheer slaughter. The light-horsemen, firing with fearful accuracy, shot the column to a standstill and then to silence. For miles the bed of the gorge was a shambles of Turks and Germans, camels and horses and mules.

Another official report stated:

The wretched Turks, seeing that to go forward meant complete destruction, turned back, only to fall into the hands of the 14th ALH . . . The enemy, or at least the Germans in his ranks, attempted resistance, but his situation was hopeless. Some struggled through, others turned back, while the Australians fired and fired till the road was littered with bodies of men and animals and the wreckage of transport wagons.

Four hundred bodies were later counted. Four thousand were taken prisoner. It took several days to burn the vehicles and reopen the road.[64]

* * *

By the end of the fighting on 30 September, the last sizeable fractions of the Ottoman Fourth Army had been destroyed on Jebel Mania and in the Barada Gorge. Though an estimated 17,000 Ottoman fugitives were escaping north-wards, only about 4,000 of these were considered effective rifles: these were all that remained of the whole of the Ottoman armies in Palestine and Syria, which, on 19 September, appear to have had a ration strength of more than 100,000. Most of the destruction had been wrought by the Desert Mounted Corps, which had taken a total of 47,000 prisoners, including a final haul of 12,000 when they entered Damascus on 1 October.[65]

Feisal's Arab Northern Army also had its bag: 5,000 enemy killed, 8,000 taken prisoner, 30 guns and 150 machine-guns captured.[66] This, though, meas-ures only part of the Arab contribution to victory. Allenby's army at Megiddo had faced only about 17,000 Turks in Palestine, whereas Feisal had faced 14,000 in Syria, the other Arab armies a further 12,000 in the Hijaz. These figures must be set against those for the British and Arab armies respectively. Allenby's combat strength was 69,000 foot and horse, but his massive 'logistical tail' brought his manpower total up to a third of a million (counting ration strength) or half a million (counting all war-related labour in theatre). Arab strength, on the other hand, comprised about 5,000 regulars and a fluctuating force of about 20,000 tribesmen, whose logistics amounted to little more than Alan Dawnay's British Military Mission. These figures reveal the draining effect of the long 'war of the flea' between June 1916 and August 1918 that preceded the short 'war of the wasp' in September 1918. In crude terms, the Arab Revolt had more than halved the Ottoman force available to defend Palestine against Allenby.[67]

Admittedly, the Arab regulars were too few to storm strong Ottoman posts, and the Arab tribesmen were guerrillas only; this being so, the Sherifians could not have brought about the sudden and total collapse of September 1918 by their own unaided efforts. On the other hand, it seems highly unlikely that Allenby could have broken through so decisively west of the Jordan but for the enemy's preoccupation with a (failing) counter-insurgency war in Arabia and Syria. The war in the heart of the Middle East was a hybrid of two very different but highly complementary parts, a large, conventional, highly mechanised army operating in tandem with a desert-based tribal insurgency.

This, moreover, is to take account only of the more measurable impacts of the Arab Revolt. Considered as an idea percolating through the pores of the Ottoman Middle East, Feisal's insurgency was like an acid eating away the social and military fabric from the inside. Disaffection and desertion among Ottoman Arab soldiers had reached such a pitch that Turkish officers no longer trusted them. Liman, contemplating a withdrawal to a new line abreast the Sea of Galilee, 'gave up the idea, because we would have had to relinquish the Hijaz Railway ... and we no longer could have stopped the progress of the Arab insurrection in the rear of our army'.[68] The effect, therefore, was to reduce the number of reliable guards available as the zone of insecurity to be guarded widened: a classic scissors crisis. The final eruption of activity east of the Jordan in September – the breaking of communications, the destruction of the railway, the raiding of depots, the cutting-up of retreating columns – was merely the culmination of a process that had already hollowed out Ottoman Arabism from within.

* * *

On the night of 30 September, it seemed that Damascus might be burning. Explosions were lighting up the sky. Shells were bursting like fireworks in the upper darkness. Lawrence felt 'sick at heart to think of the great town laid in ashes as the price of the freedom we were bringing her'.

It was a false alarm. The Germans, among the last to leave, were setting fire to the dumps and ammunition stores.

> When dawn came, we drove to the head of the ridge, which stood over the oasis of the city, almost afraid to look out north for the ruins we would see; but instead of ruins were silent gardens, blurred green with the early mist, in whose circuit nestled the glowing city, beautiful as ever, like a pearl in the morning sun. The uproar of the night had shrunk to a thin column of black smoke . . .[69]

Damascus had never been a fortress. Situated on the great trade-routes of the Middle East, it had always been a city of merchants and bazaars, of artisans and guilds; and, given its abundance of fresh water and relatively cool upland-plateau location, a city of gardens and orchards. Syrians, Greeks, Romans, Arabs and Ottomans had ruled here, and the city's population – 300,000 before the war – was of diverse origin and religion. But it was the Arab-Islamic heritage that was predominant. Damascus had been the first capital of their global empire when the Arabs, welded into a politico-military power by the new religion of Islam, burst out of the desert in the mid-seventh century AD. It was one of the six great cities of Arab Islam, and, until 30 September 1918, the only one still held by the Ottoman Empire. But unlike so many great cities, which have been fortresses as well as political, cultural and economic centres, the fate of Damascus had usually been decided by battles outside the city.[70]

So it was now. Battles on the Plain of Sharon and in the Judaean Hills, battles in the Plain of Esdraelon and at Amman, massacres in the Wadi Fara, at Tafas, on Mania and in the Barada Gorge, these were the struggles that had ended four centuries of Ottoman rule over Damascus. The Turks had gone. Mile upon mile of fugitives were streaming away to the north; no longer armies, or even parts of armies; merely broken fragments, clusters of men held together more by instinctive solidarity than any military discipline or purpose, seeking only to escape from war and death.

Politics knows no vacuum. But who would now rule in 'liberated' Damascus? Allenby had at first discouraged Feisal from making a run for Damascus: Arab pressure around Deraa was critical to his operations in Palestine. But when the scale of his victory became apparent, and the great city became an immediately achievable objective, the position changed. The British Foreign Office had approved a Sherifian interim administration, and Allenby had issued new instructions to Feisal on 25 September:

> There is no objection to Your Highness entering Damascus as soon as you consider that you can do so with safety. I am sending troops to Damascus, and I hope that they will arrive there in four or five days from today. I trust Your Highness's forces will be able to cooperate, but you should not relax your pressure in the Deraa district, as it is of vital importance to cut off the Turkish forces which are retreating north from Maan, Amman, and Salt.[71]

He sent complementary orders to his own commanders, advising them that the Arabs should, if possible, be allowed to enter the city first, and that any administration set up by Feisal should be respected. Lawrence approved, and saw the wisdom:

> He hoped we would go in first, partly because he was generous, and knew how much more than a mere trophy of victory Damascus would be for the Arabs; and partly for prudential reasons. Feisal's movement it was which made the country friendly to the Allies as they advanced, which enabled convoys to go up and down without escort, towns to be administered without garrison. And Allenby valued and used the Arabs not for their fighting, but for their preaching ... It was our burden to make each new yard of country ours in sentiment before we took it.[72]

Lawrence drove into Damascus at 9am on 1 October. The streets were 'nearly impassable with the crowds, who yelled themselves hoarse, danced, cut themselves with swords and daggers, and fired volleys into the air. Nasir, Nuri Shaalan, Auda abu Tayi and myself were cheered by name, covered with flowers, kissed indefinitely, and splashed with attar of roses from the house-tops'.[73]

But the political situation was contested. The Damascene political class was divided into two factions. One was headed by the brothers Abd el-Kader and Muhammad Said, two emirs whose main base of support was the 15,000-strong Algerian exile community, from whom they had recruited a powerful armed retinue. The Algerians were temporisers. Abd el-Kader had briefly associated himself with the Arab Revolt – visiting Hussein in Mecca and Feisal at Aqaba – but then, back in Damascus, had returned to his Ottoman allegiance.

On 29 September, Muhammad Said was proclaimed the head of a provisional municipal administration by a hastily assembled meeting of notables. The Algerians raised the Sherifian flag – the very one, Abd el-Kader claimed, that had been given to him by Hussein in Mecca – and announced their recognition of the sherif of Mecca as 'king of the Arabs'. The departing Ottoman general Djemal *Kuchuk* added his support to the new administration.

Feisal's followers in the city at first accepted this *fait accompli*. During the day, a large demonstration had attacked the main Ottoman prison and released the 4,000 inmates. Shukri al-Ayoubi was one of those freed. He and Ali al-Rikabi were the leaders of the other major faction in the city. Both were long-term supporters of the Arab Revolt. But Shukri, perhaps somewhat disoriented at his sudden release, accepted the new Algerian regime, and Ali was away from the city visiting General Barrow's headquarters.

The situation was transformed the following morning with the arrival of the principal Sherifian military leaders – Nasir, Auda, Nuri and Lawrence – and that of their army. 'On the morrow of 1 October 1918,' wrote Subhi al-Umari, the Syrian officer who had command of Feisal's machine-guns:

we [regular] units of the Arab Army marched towards Damascus and entered it from the Gate of God ... The populace were gathered all the way ... in their thousands, on rooftops, men, women, and children. All were greeting us with clapping, songs and anthems, ululations, flowers, rosewater sprayed on us ... I cannot describe the feeling that possessed me on that hour. My tears were flowing, and my heart nearly stopped from excitement ... The type of joy we were experiencing amidst the thousands of the people was a different type of joy, greater than all the joys that a human being may normally experience in a lifetime. I do not believe that I can describe it, neither could anyone else who has not experienced and tasted it.

The Sherifian leaders headed for the Town Hall as soon as they entered the city. The Algerians' claim to power was based on little more than the number of their armed followers. Though many harboured (well justified) suspicions about Hashemite ambition and British duplicity, the Algerians appear to have been mere opportunists, their attempted coup an exercise in the self-advancement of a clientelist retinue. Had they been genuine Arab nationalists advancing a programme of reform, matters might have played out differently. As it was, the Algerians were too few to prevail, and suspicion of their leaders too strong for their usurpation to be tolerated in the absence of the military power to underwrite it. Though there was a fierce altercation in the Council Chamber – Auda himself knocked back Abd el-Kader when he came at Lawrence with a dagger – the two brothers were driven from the Town Hall. An attempt at armed rebellion that night – the Algerians joined by some Druses – amounted to little more than rioting and looting, and was easily crushed by the Sherifian Army. Muhammad Said surrendered and was exiled. Abd el-Kader went on the run, and was hunted down and killed a few weeks later.[74]

Shukri al-Ayoubi established a new municipal authority, though he soon resigned the leading position in favour of Ali al-Rikabi. Work was immediately begun to re-establish order and essential services. Lawrence – misfit, maverick, archaeologist, intelligence officer, guerrilla leader – now assumed a new role, that of urban administrator, attending to police, water-supply, electricity, sanitation, fire prevention, food-supply, telegraph and currency.[75] Much was already in hand when, two days later, on 3 October, Feisal made his triumphal entry into Damascus. Allenby also arrived, and the two men met for the first time, by prearrangement, at the Victoria Hotel. Lawrence thought, 'They were a strange contrast: Feisal, large-eyed, colourless and worn, like a fine dagger; Allenby, gigantic and red and merry, fit representative of the power which had thrown a girdle of humour and strong dealing around the world.'[76]

But he wrote little about what transpired. The disappointment was bitter. The late struggle between the Algerian and Sherifian factions shrank to the status of an historical footnote. The gun-toting Arab tribesmen outside, the cheering Damascene crowds, Feisal's regular officers, the writers and teachers of the nationalist underground, the *fellahin* of the upcountry villages, the Arabic-speaking peoples of the Middle East in general: the hopes of all were already being scoured out by the *Realpolitik* of an imperial carve-up. Feisal was told that France was to be the 'protecting power' in Syria; that Lebanon would be under direct French rule; that the Arab administration in Damascus would be subject to 'French guidance'; that Feisal was to have a French liaison officer.

General Chauvel, who was present, observed the reaction.

Feisal objected very strongly. He said that he knew nothing of France in the matter; that he was prepared to have British assistance; that he understood from the advisor whom Allenby sent him that the Arabs were to have the whole of Syria, including the Lebanon, but excluding Palestine; that a country without a port was no good to him; and that he declined to have a French liaison officer or to recognise French guidance in any way.

The chief turned to Lawrence and said: 'But did you not tell him that the French were to have the protectorate over Syria?' Lawrence said: 'No, sir, I know nothing about it.' The chief then said: 'But you knew definitely that he, Feisal, was to have nothing to do with Lebanon?' Lawrence said: 'No, sir, I did not.'[77]

* * *

The day before, Lawrence had visited the military hospital. A thousand dead, dying, and prostrate, mainly dysentery cases, lay untended there. As he passed from the blazing sunlight of the courtyard to the inside, he was met first by the sickening stench of thirty corpses, some fresh, some putrid and yellow-black, some swollen to twice or thrice their size, a few burst open and liquid with decay. Rats scurried about and gnawed the bodies. The ground was discoloured by streams of dried blood and shit.

Further in, the corpses were in bed, in lines, 'each man rigid on his stinking pallet, from which the liquid muck had dripped and stiffened on the floor'. Beyond were some still alive: as Lawrence recalled:

> [he] suddenly heard a sighing breath, and turned abruptly to meet the open eyes of these outstretched men fixed on me like beads, while *Aman, Aman* ('pity, pity, pardon') rustled from their twisted lips. There was a brown wavering as they tried to lift their hands, and a thin fluttering like withered leaves, as they vainly fell back again upon the beds ...
>
> Outside the walls we could hear Damascus and its hundreds of thousands merry-making, drunken on liberty after five subject-centuries, too happy to see misery or to relieve it. And within these walls lay these hundreds, enduring, in our neglect, not Death the strong spirit, with quiet hands and wings, but slow physical corruption, a piecemeal rotting of the envelope of flesh about the hopeless spirit of longing to escape.

Lawrence arranged for doctors to attend, and pressed some Turkish prisoners into service as a burial detail. The following day, he was still there at the hospital, possessed with a mission to reform and make good. The bodies were gone. Filth was burnt. Patients were cleaned up, given fresh shirts, placed back on reversed mattresses. Enough water was secured, and some food. The place began to smell of disinfectant.

But things were not yet up to army standards, and the bizarre denouement was an altercation between Lawrence and a visiting British medical officer, who was scandalised by the conditions, and viewed the man who admitted to being sort of in charge – dressed in 'skirts and sandals' – with disgust. The officer erupted in anger. Lawrence:

> cackled out like a duck, with the wild laughter which often took me at moments of strain . . . He had not entered the charnel-house of yesterday, or smelt it, or seen us burying those bodies of ultimate degradation, whose memory had woken me up again and again, sweating and trembling in my bed this early morning. So he misunderstood, and glared at me, muttering about a bloody brute. I laughed out again, and angered him so much that he smacked me over the face and stalked off, leaving me more ashamed than angry, for in my heart I felt that he was right, and that anyone who had, like me, pushed through to success a rebellion of the weak against their masters, must come out of it so stained that nothing in the world would make him clean again.[78]

* * *

The psychic demons were in the ascendant now. Death and Decay held dominion. The modern Crusade had been a will-o'-the-wisp; instead there was greed and betrayal. The fantasy had dissolved.

The beloved was among the dead. The Bedouin Apollo – the beautiful boy for whom the knight-errant had performed heroic deeds – had perished; not nobly, not famously, but in obscurity, unrecorded, among the anonymous of one of history's great convulsions, most probably in the squalor of the famine and typhus epidemic that killed a third of the people of northern Syria in 1916. 'The strongest motive throughout had been a personal one . . . present to me, I think, every hour of these two years,' Lawrence wrote at the end of *Seven Pillars*. He had waged war for love of Dahoum: 'I liked a particular Arab very much, and I thought that freedom for the race would be an acceptable present.' But he learned before the end that Dahoum – the incarnation of an ideal, an essence of Arabism, symbol of a mythic desert people who were clean and austere and 'pure' – was dead. And thus was the unravelling of the delicate construct of his mind complete.

Much later, commenting on a romantic travelogue, *Adventures in Arabia* by William Seabrook, he wrote:

It just shows you how time and experience take the zest out of adventure. If I'd written the tale of my first travels in Syria, hunting Crusader castles, I might have done this sort of thing. Indeed, I probably did it, cautiously, in letters home. Later I went to the very bottom of Arab life – and came back with the news that the seven pillars were fallen down.

Dahoum became a metaphor of aspiration and failure. 'I loved you, so I drew these tides of men into my hands, and wrote my will across the sky in stars to gain you Freedom,' Lawrence wrote in the dedication to *Seven Pillars*. But Death took Dahoum, and the worms consumed his body, before the gift could be delivered. Just as well, for the gift had spoiled. 'Men prayed me that I set our work, the inviolate house, as a memory of you. But for fit monument, I shattered it, unfinished. And now the little things creep out to patch themselves hovels in the marred shadow of your gift.'[79]

After Feisal had departed from his meeting with Allenby on 3 October, Lawrence stayed behind to tell the chief that he was due for leave and wished to be sent home. Allenby demurred, but Lawrence insisted, and finally the general agreed.

At 7pm on 4 October, Lawrence was driven from Damascus in *Blue Mist*, his Rolls-Royce tender, at the start of a long journey back to England.[80] He carried in his head psychic wounds that would eventually bring him to the brink of suicide.

He had decided to leave two days beforehand. He had listened to the muezzin sounding the call to prayer across the city on the night of 1 October. He had followed the so-familiar words, repeated five times a day: 'God alone is great. I testify there are no gods but God. And Muhammad is the Prophet of God. Come to prayer. Come to security. God alone is great. There are no gods but God.' Then he heard the muezzin lower his voice and add: 'And He is very good to us this day, O people of Damascus.' And hearing it, Lawrence was reminded of his loneliness and fraudulence: 'since only for me of the tens of thousands in the city was that phrase meaningless'.

I had been born free, and a stranger to those whom I had led for the two years, and tonight it seemed that I had given them all my gift, this false liberty drawn down to them by spells and wickedness, and nothing was left me but to go away. The dead army of my hopes, now turned to fact, confronted me, and my will, the worn instrument which had so long frayed our path, broke suddenly in my hand and fell useless.[81]

Epilogue

T HREE WEEKS AFTER Lawrence's departure, the Anglo-Arab forces approached the ancient city of Aleppo in northern Syria. Since the opening of the Battle of Megiddo on 19 September, they had destroyed three Ottoman armies. Of some 100,000 men, fewer than 20,000 had escaped to the north, and the majority of these were fugitives.

The Egyptian Expeditionary Force, straining to catch them, was at the furthest limit of its logistics. Damascus was 150 miles from its main bases, Aleppo an additional 200 miles beyond. Exhaustion and sickness were, in any case, taking their toll after five weeks of continuous operations. The spearhead now compromised the attenuated 5th Mounted Division of Major-General MacAndrew, down to around 1,500 sabres, supported by Sherif Nasir's 1,500 Arab irregulars, two batteries of horse-guns, three armoured-car batteries, three light-car patrols and an RAF squadron.

On 23 October, MacAndrew's cavalry discovered a line of entrenched Turks about three miles south of Aleppo. They did not seem inclined to budge. A request that the city be surrendered was rebuffed. On the 25th, however, the blocking position was outflanked by Nasir's Bedouin, who entered the city from the east, stirred the local population into action and engaged the garrison in street-fighting. The position was rendered untenable, and the Turks withdrew from both Aleppo and the trenches to the south later that night.

The main body – formed of the two improvised divisions that had been defending the trenches – pulled back to a position near the village of Haritan about eight miles north-west of the city, where they blocked the Alexandretta road and threatened the road and rail line north from Aleppo to the vital junction at Muslimiya, close to the border with Anatolia.

The Jodhpur and Mysore Lancers launched a series of charges. The first cleared the Turks off a rocky knoll at the front of their position, but the main line was too strong. There were only about 3,000 Turks, but they were holding their ground, and each effort of the lancers was beaten back by rifle, machine-gun and artillery fire.

It was the last significant engagement of the war. On 31 October, the Entente and the Ottoman Empire, their respective representatives meeting on a British warship anchored in Mudros harbour on the island of Lemnos, agreed an armistice.

The Ottomans had now lost dominion over their Middle Eastern empire. The war had ended at the boundary between Arabic-speaking Syria and Turkish-speaking Anatolia. But here, on the border of their homeland, in the final few days, some Turks had rallied and formed a line. The man who led them was Mustapha Kemal Pasha.

A 37-year-old brigadier, Kemal was now appointed supreme commander on the southern front. In the last days of 1918, the war over, Kemal's men, though ragged, hungry and few, manned a line of posts between Alexandretta on the coast and Mosul in northern Iraq.[1] In the fires of military disaster, the poor alloy of Ottomanism was hardening into the iron of Turkish nationalism.

* * *

Another brand of nationalism was being forged in Cairo. Despite colonial occupation, wartime privation and the brutal treatment of labour conscripts, the Egyptian people had remained largely indifferent to the Ottoman call to *jihad*. But now the war was over, and a new world was in the making. President Wilson had proclaimed 'the self-determination of peoples'. The Bolsheviks were supporting national liberation movements. Even the British seemed to have endorsed Arab claims to independence. Perhaps, after all, it *had* been a war for freedom.

Saad Zaghlul Pasha, the leader of Wafd, the main Arab nationalist party in Cairo, duly proposed that he head a delegation to the Versailles Peace Conference to put forward Egypt's claim to independence. It seemed only fair. Egyptians had been forced to play their part. Roughly a third of men aged between 17 and 35 had been conscripted into the labour battalions. Buildings, animals and crops had been requisitioned. Poverty and hunger, in consequence, stalked the land. Egypt had paid a heavy price for Britain's war.

Zaghlul caught the mood. A campaign of committees and petitions soon swelled into a broad national movement. So Zaghlul was arrested and deported to Malta. And that was the trigger: Egypt exploded into revolution.

Student demonstrations on 9 March 1919 turned into a full-scale student strike the following day. This produced the first violent clashes with security forces. As news spread, the revolt became general across Egypt's cities. Soon the country was engulfed by violence, with attacks on trams, railway lines, police posts and military installations. Within a week, the British had lost control of Upper Egypt.

Workers joined the revolt, with strikes of dockers, transport workers, factory operatives, postmen and printers. So did ordinary villagers: large parts of the countryside became no-go areas for the British. Allenby, charged with restoring order, was in no doubt that the whole country was nationalist in sentiment, while professing to detect a sinister external influence: 'The movement has been really well organised, and the whole nation is against us, including the *fellahin* of Upper and Lower Egypt. I have little doubt that there is strong alien support below it all, and there are evident signs of Bolshevism.' He feared the native security forces would be affected: 'The Egyptian Army and Police have behaved well, up to now, but we can't expect them to stand firm against the fervour of a nationalist outburst.' He was concerned, too, about his Indian soldiers: 'if the Egyptian revolution takes a religious hue, my Muslims will be sorely tried'.

Troops looking forward to rapid demobilisation from the Egyptian Expeditionary Force were disappointed. Tens of thousands were rushed to Egypt. A murderous repression rolled back the nationalist movement in late March and April. More than 1,000 Egyptians were killed, over 1,500 imprisoned and 57 executed. Nonetheless, major concessions were necessary to quell the unrest – Zaghlul was released and allowed to proceed to Paris – and the movement would fizz for several years yet, with fresh outbreaks of protest and further police terror to crush them.

Many of the British and Australian soldiers redeployed to Egypt were reluctant, sullen, even mutinous. They wanted to go home, of course, but they were also infected by the radical mood. Some 3,000 British soldiers awaiting demobilisation at Kantara were ordered to break the railway strike. They refused. 'Some trade union microbe has got into them ...' Allenby complained. 'I can't shoot them all for mutiny ... one reason given by the men was that to work on the railway would be "strike-breaking".'[2]

Despite its great victory over the Ottomans only months before, Britain's imperial elite, caught between a popular anti-colonial revolt and a restive army of working-class conscripts, seemed closer to losing Egypt and Suez in the spring of 1919 than at any time during the war itself.

* * *

A new London show opened in August 1919 to enthusiastic reviews. *The Daily Telegraph* was particularly gushing. The show had, it seemed, introduced audiences to a hitherto little-known war hero, one who 'went to Arabia and, practically unaided, raised for the first time almost since history began a great homogeneous Arab army'. Despite this, the *Telegraph* explained, the hero in question 'would probably soon have been forgotten', had it not been for the efforts of 'Mr Lowell Thomas and his moving pictures'; thanks to these, 'Thomas Lawrence is definitely marked as one of the elect'.

Lowell Thomas, an experienced journalist and lecturer, had been dispatched with cameraman Harry Chase by the US government in 1917 to collect material to encourage American support for the war. Disappointed by the grim realities of trench warfare on the Western Front, Thomas had headed east in search of a more romantic war. There he met Lawrence, first briefly in Jerusalem, then over several days in Aqaba. Lawrence, seeing a chance to publicise the Arab cause, was cooperative. But Thomas, the veteran newshound, seems to have known at once that his angle would be the young British archaeologist himself, who had become, as he later put it, 'the Uncrowned King of Arabia'.

Thomas's travelogue – a mix of moving images, coloured stills and breathless commentary – was a blockbuster success. So much so that it had to be moved from the Royal Opera House to the Albert Hall, then to the Philharmonic Hall, and finally to the Queen's Hall, eventually being seen by more than a million people in London alone (rising to 4 million as Thomas toured the provinces and then the British Empire).

Lawrence, Thomas told his audiences, 'is a young man whose name will go down in history beside those of Sir Francis Drake, Sir Walter Raleigh, Lord Clive, Charles Gordon, and all the other famous heroes of Great Britain's glorious past'. Such was his allure that he was reduced to moving about London in disguise to shake off female admirers, reporters, publishers and hero-worshippers. If so, little wonder: Thomas was proclaiming night after night that 'Lawrence had accomplished more toward unifying the peoples of Arabia than all of the sultans and emirs since the days of the great caliphs 600 years ago.'

The legend of 'Lawrence of Arabia' was thus a confection of Lowell Thomas. And this first of many reconstructions of Thomas Edward Lawrence as hero and celebrity was richly ironic. For what was Lowell Thomas's blockbuster show, 'With Allenby in Palestine and Lawrence in Arabia', if not a modern-day version of a *roman d'aventure*? Lawrence had become – as, perhaps, in his teenage dreams, he had hoped to become – an Arthurian hero.

But the dream had long since faded in the bitter light of intrigue and betrayal, bleached out by the secret diplomacy of the war and the backroom deals of the peace.

When Thomas's show opened in London, Lawrence was back from Versailles, where he had served on Feisal's staff. He knew that the British were making way for the French in Syria, that Feisal's fragile regime in Damascus was in mortal peril. The knowledge had plunged him into depression. Living at Oxford and dividing his time between his family home in Polstead Road and All Souls, where he had been awarded a fellowship, he would, reported his mother, 'sometimes sit the entire morning between breakfast and lunch in the same position, without moving, and with the same expression on his face'.[3]

* * *

The Syrians made their final stand at the Pass of Maysalun, about 12 miles west of Damascus, on 24 July 1920. They were very few, perhaps 1,000 regulars and some 2,000 volunteers who had rushed from the city to join them. Feisal had already capitulated to French demands, but he had faced furious demonstrations, and his advice to offer no resistance to the advance of General Gourand's army from the coast had been ignored. But the superiority of the enemy, 12,000 strong, supported by artillery, tanks and bombers, was overwhelming.

It might have been otherwise. Though the Syrian nationalist underground had been crushed by Ottoman repression in 1915 and 1916, the cause had since swelled into a flood tide, fed by the confidence engendered by the Sherifian victory over the Ottomans, anger at the machinations of the Versailles powers, and expectations aroused by the global revolutionary surge originating in Russia. What doomed the Syrians was the conservative timidity of their Hashemite leaders. The Syrians might have geared up for a people's war against imperialism. They might even have unleashed a land war of the Syrian *fellahin*. At that very moment, on the far side of the Black Sea and the Caucasus, a newly forged 'Red Army' of workers and peasants was engaged in a life-and-death struggle against counter-revolutionary 'Whites' backed by eight separate armies of foreign invaders – a struggle from which the Reds would eventually emerge victorious. But the Arab Kingdom of Syria was a regime of sheikhs and landlords who feared their own people more than the French, and Feisal's capitulations and pusillanimity had destroyed any chance of mass resistance.

In the circumstances, the Battle of Maysalun was hard-fought. Despite a tank charge against the centre and cavalry attacks on both flanks, the Syrian line held for several hours. When it broke, around mid-morning, the fugitives were bombed from the air.

The French entered Damascus the following day. Gourand, arriving in the captured city on the 26 July, headed straight for the tomb of Saladin, the Islamic leader who had defeated the Crusaders seven centuries before. 'Saladin,' he announced, 'we're back.'[4]

* * *

Another battle had been fought on the very same day as Maysalun. A column of 800 British soldiers had been sent to relieve a small post on the Euphrates under siege from local tribesmen. The heat was crushing, water ran out and the column was forced to halt and make camp, the men in a state of collapse. The British force was then attacked by about a thousand Iraqi Arabs.

An attempt to retreat turned into disaster: as darkness fell, the numbers of the attackers grew, the column fell apart, and the soldiers were picked off in the scrub. Over 300 were killed or taken prisoner. The defeat imperilled the security of Baghdad, and the British high command contemplated wholesale withdrawal from the Euphrates Valley.

As their own cause spiralled into terminal crisis, the Syrian nationalists had urged their Iraqi compatriots to open a second front: 'Get up! Demand your rights! Demand your complete independence!'

The Iraqis had needed little urging. The Government of India administration had replaced Iraqis with foreigners in the civil service. It had refused Iraqi nationalists the opportunity to travel to Versailles to put their case before the world. Its control over the country had been reaffirmed by a League of Nations decision in April 1920. This last had provoked a storm of protest. The repression that followed proved to be petrol on the fire. During June the British lost control of large parts of the country, and by late July there were an estimated 130,000 rebels in action, 60,000 of them equipped with firearms. The security forces found themselves waging a full-scale counter-insurgency war. 'The difficulty in coping with Arabs,' explained one British officer, 'is the extraordinary manner in which they seem to appear from nowhere, and their mobility.'

Lawrence might have smiled. His comments on what he had seen of Anglo-Indian operations in Iraq in 1916 had been scathing. Now, writing in *The Sunday Times* on 22 August 1920, his judgement was no less unequivocal:

The people of England have been led in Mesopotamia into a trap from which it will be hard to escape with dignity and honour. They have been tricked into it by a steady withholding of information. The Baghdad communiqués are belated, insincere, incomplete. Things have been far worse than we have been told, our administration more bloody and inefficient than the public knows. It is a disgrace to our imperial record, and may soon be too inflamed for any ordinary cure. We today are not far from a disaster.

In the event, reinforcements were rushed in and the reconquest of the country commenced. Blockhouses were built to guard the railways. Punitive columns seized livestock and burned villages. The RAF dropped 100 tons of bombs. Poison gas was used and found to have 'excellent moral effect'. More than 10,000 Iraqis were killed.

A year later, in August 1921, the British installed a puppet ruler in a rigged election: Feisal. They had already made a similar arrangement with Abdullah, Feisal's older brother, offering him Transjordan in return for his giving up plans to attack the French in Syria. Thus did the British Empire endeavour to stabilise its, and its French allies', Middle Eastern conquests: by establishing Hashemite client regimes.

The Iraqi aerial bombing experiment had been instructive. It had been found to be much more efficient in 'pacifying' native villages than dispatching a punitive column. One officer in particular took note. According to Wing Commander Arthur Harris, the Arabs and Kurds 'now know what real bombing means in casualties and damage. Within 45 minutes, a full-size village can be practically wiped out and a third of its inhabitants killed or injured.'[5] 'Bomber' Harris had found his life's mission.

Churchill concurred: he, too, was becoming a firm advocate of air-power as a low-cost form of imperial policing. In fact, in government conclave in London, he was proposing dropping aerial gas-bombs. By chance, the very same idea was the subject of a bitter parody in the pages of The Times.

It is odd that we do not use poison gas on these occasions. Bombing the houses is a patchy way of getting the women and children, and our infantry always incur losses in shooting down the Arab men. By gas attacks, the whole population of offending districts could be wiped out neatly; and as a method of government, it would be no more immoral than the present system.

The author of the piece was Lawrence.[6]

* * *

September 1922: four years since Megiddo, seven since Gallipoli, and the film of history seemed to be rerunning. A British army, dug in behind barbed wire, confronted a Turkish army at Chanak on the Asian shore of the Dardanelles. A British fleet was anchored in the Straits to support them. More men, guns and aircraft were on their way. London had ordered the British commander on the spot to deliver an ultimatum. The Prime Minister, David Lloyd George, was determined 'not to run away before Mustapha Kemal'.

The fate of the Ottoman Empire had been decided in a new round of 'peace' negotiations following the Versailles settlement that had concluded with the

Treaty of Sèvres in August 1920. Representatives of the Ottoman sultan-caliph in Constantinople had been among the signatories.

The Young Turk triumvirs were long gone, each to his fate. Talaat was gunned down by an Armenian holocaust survivor in Berlin, where he had taken refuge, on 15 March 1921. Djemal, too, was tracked down by an Armenian hit-squad, in the Georgian city of Tbilisi, and killed on 25 July 1922. Enver, the self-styled 'little Napoleon' of the Committee of Union and Progress, and its leading protagonist of pan-Turkish imperialism, died true to the faith, in August 1922, in command of a Muslim militia fighting the Reds on one of the many obscure Central Asian battlefields of the Russian Civil War.

The sultan-caliph remained – now a puppet of the Versailles powers, held captive in his capital by a British, French and Italian occupation garrison, a gormless spectator at the rape of his country. For Turkey was to be dismembered and large parts of it distributed to France, Italy, Greece and Armenia. The Turks were to retain only northern and central Anatolia, the western shore of the Sea of Marmara, and a small enclave around Constantinople, the last two areas to be demilitarised.

Foreign armies of occupation were already on hand to enforce the new arrangements. The Italians had landed at Adalia in April 1919, the Greeks at Smyrna in May 1919, and a combined Allied force was in Constantinople. The Treaty of Sèvres was the starting-gun for a full-scale offensive by the Greeks. The effect was to plunge Turkey into two years of ferocious violence, marked by wholesale ethnic-cleansing and massacre.

Clausewitz had remarked that 'it is impossible to achieve the conquest of a great state'. So it proved in the Turkish heartland of Anatolia. The peasants rallied to Mustapha Kemal's Turkish Nationalists. The villages rose in a people's war against foreign aggressors intent on murder, rape and dispossession. And when the Greek army disintegrated in the face of Kemal's final offensive in August 1922, the Greeks – both soldiers and civilians – were, quite literally, driven into the sea by vengeful hordes of Turks. Smyrna became a city of fire and massacre. Almost half a million Ottoman Greeks fled across the Aegean.

But Kemal had no wish to follow up with a war against the British at Chanak. Nor, it turned out, had Lieutenant-General Sir Charles Harington, Britain's man on the spot, any wish to start one. He disobeyed orders, failed to deliver London's ultimatum, and opened negotiations with the Nationalists. Within a month, the Graeco-Turkish War was over, and the British were preparing to pull out.

Harington was right. The Greeks were defeated. The French and Italians had backed away from confrontation. British public opinion was against war.

The Cabinet was lukewarm. Kemal's Nationalists were in secure control of Anatolia, enjoyed mass support and were getting munitions from the Bolsheviks. Lloyd George found himself suddenly isolated in advocating a new war of imperial annexation in the Near East. On 19 October, the Tories, meeting in the Carlton Club withdrew their support from the Coalition government. The Tories won the subsequent election.

'We cannot alone act as the policeman of the world,' the Tory leader Andrew Bonar Law had written in a letter to *The Times*. It was a frank admission of the limits of imperial power.[7] Lloyd George had failed to recognise such limits, and because of this, because his warmongering and empire-building went beyond them, his premiership was terminated by the phoenix-like resurgence of an old enemy – the Anatolian peasant-soldier.

* * *

Two years later, in September 1924, war came again to the Hijaz. For six years, ever since the end of the Great War, the Emir Hussein had displayed an almost childlike disbelief in the endless perfidy of his former wartime ally. When, in the summer of 1921, four months after the close of the Cairo Conference, he was asked to endorse the resulting imperial *fait accompli* – one that violated every tenet of the McMahon Correspondence – he was incredulous. To compound matters, he was at the same time expected to sign both the Treaty of Versailles and a declaration recognising French authority over Syria. This, he learned, was to be the basis of an Anglo-Hashemite treaty providing for financial subsidies and British guarantees against Saudi aggression. The emissary who conveyed the offer – considered by Colonial Secretary Winston Churchill the best man for the job – was T.E. Lawrence.

Hussein proved obdurate. 'His ambitions are as large as his conceit,' Lawrence cabled his superiors, 'and he showed unpleasant jealousy of his sons ... Reason is entirely wasted on him, since he believes himself all-wise and all-competent, and is flattered by his entourage in every idiotic thing he does ... His titles have turned his head and made him complacently absurd.' Lawrence became increasingly frustrated and depressed. 'This is the beastliest trip I ever had', he wrote to his artist friend Eric Kennington.

Lawrence the Orientalist, now playing the role of imperial diplomat, saw in Hussein only a cantankerous old man. Suspicion of his sons Abdullah and Feisal – both now client rulers under British hegemony – was mere 'jealousy'. Opposition to Anglo-French partition of the Middle East defied 'reason'. Hussein's aspiration to rule the independent and united Arab state the British had promised made him 'idiotic' and 'absurd'.

There was no deal. So the British left 'the king of the Hijaz' to his fate. In the absence of Abdullah and Feisal, the defence of the kingdom became the responsibility of the insipid Ali. The Saudi *ikhwan*, the warrior-brothers of the Wahhabi cult, 3,000-strong, invaded the Hijaz and closed around Taif. On the night of 4 September, Ali abandoned the town, stealing away under the cover of darkness, leaving the inhabitants to the mercy of their enemies. The *ikhwan* entered the town and put it to the sack. Homes were destroyed and the market looted. The town leaders were dragged from the mosque where they had taken refuge and cut to pieces. More than 300 were killed in a few hours. Bodies were thrown down wells.

Hussein appealed to the British for support. None was offered. It was soon clear to all that the Hashemites were isolated and defenceless. The terror at Taif had communicated a clear message across the Hijaz. Ibn Saud now consolidated his advantage by guaranteeing freedom of access to the Islamic holy cities. The leading merchants of Jiddah, meeting on 3 October, called on Hussein to abdicate in favour of his son Ali. This tipped the balance against the regime and, on 16 October, the leader of the Arab Revolt – the emir of Mecca, the self-styled 'king of the Hijaz', the aspiring 'king of the Arabs' – sailed from his homeland into exile forever. On board the steamer on which he departed, along with his personal possessions, was £800,000 in gold sovereigns, some of it profits of the Hajj, the rest what was left of Britain's wartime subsidies.

On the day that Hussein sailed, four warriors of the *ikhwan* entered Mecca – now an abandoned ghost-town of shuttered shops and empty streets – and read out the proclamations of the new Saudi ruler.[8]

* * *

Wars do not usually have the outcomes intended or foreseen, either by the winners or the losers. Violence has its own dynamic and logic: swept into war's churning vortex of killing, destruction, displacement and hatred, humanity is prone to lose control of the forces of destruction it has unleashed, and of the destiny it is attempting to shape.[9]

In the Great War in the Middle East, everything changed and nothing changed. The Ottoman Empire collapsed, but the social order of the Middle East remained. The Turkish pashas were overthrown, but the sheikhs and landlords were not. The old police posts were captured, but new ones were built, and in the end the only difference was the uniforms. The Turks fled, but the British and the French replaced them. Hussein of Mecca sailed away, but Ibn Saud of Riyadh took over.

The Arab Revolt had been a mirage in the desert. Uprooted from the towns and villages of Syria and transplanted to the encampments of the Bedouin, Arab nationalism acquired an exotic form devoid of real substance. The Hashemites were ambitious reactionaries. Their followers were tribal raiders. Their power was a flow of foreign gold, guns and grain. They reached Damascus, the highest summit of Arab aspiration, not as the leaders of a revolutionary army – not as 'the Reds' of the Middle East with a call to the peasants of Syria and Iraq to seize the land – but as the hired guns of the British Empire.

The Arab Revolt was a false hope, and history turned back on itself. Instead, in a richly ironic twist, it was Turkey that produced a real national movement – one that defeated its own reactionaries and collaborators, ejected a Greek army of conquest and a British army of occupation, and established a strong, modernising, reforming republic.

The Arabs, by contrast, remained under foreign colonial rule. And the new geopolitical order imposed on the Middle East between 1916 and 1921 has remained substantially unchanged in the century since. In consequence, the region has been, and remains today, riven by sectarianism, violence, intractable conflict and untold human suffering.

ENDNOTES

Chapter 1: Holy War?

1. Wilson 1989/1990, 133–6.
2. Wilson 1989/1990, 136.
3. Wilson 1989/1990, 138–9; Moorhead 2003, *passim*.
4. Rogan 2015, 100.
5. MacMunn and Falls 1928, 28.
6. Baedeker 1912, 186–212; Wavell 1936, 4.
7. MacMunn and Falls 1928, 39.
8. Wavell 1928/1936, 27.
9. MacMunn and Falls 1928, 22–5; Wavell 1928/1936, 26–7.
10. Mason 1974/1976, 408–9.
11. Mason 1974/1976, 408.
12. Ulrichsen 2014, 48–9.
13. Spear 1965/1978, 170–8.
14. Waraich 2007.
15. *New York Times* 1916, 9–10.
16. *New York Times* 1916, 6–9.
17. *New York Times* 1916, 7.
18. Faulkner 2013a, 152.
19. Stephenson 1969/1971c, 747–8; Barnett 1970, 292; Mason 1974/1976, 344.
20. Mason 1974/1976, 348–9.
21. Mason 1974/1976, *passim*.
22. Mason 1974/1976, 414.
23. Hobsbawm 1987/1994, 69; James 1994/1995, 219.
24. James 1994/1995, 204.
25. Stephenson 1969/1971b, 435–6.
26. Stephenson 1969/1971c, 746.
27. Ulrichsen 2014, 20–1.
28. Stephenson 1969/1971c, 746–7.
29. Stephenson 1969/1971c, 745–8; Mason 1974/1976, 398–9.
30. Stephenson 1969/1971c, 748–9.
31. Hardman.
32. Hardman; MacMunn and Falls 1928, 11, 13.
33. Hardman.
34. Wilson 1989/1990, 152.
35. Garnett 1938, 190–2; Wilson 1989/1990, 167–9; McGuirk 2007, 10–13.
36. Lapping 1985/1989, 280.
37. Lapping 1985/1989, 280–2; Newsinger 2006, 85–6.
38. Mansfield 1991/1992, 89; Newsinger 2006, 87.
39. Newsinger 2006, 87–8.
40. Newsinger 2006, 88–9.

41. Mansfield 1991/1992, 91–5; Newsinger 2006, 89–94.
42. Mansfield 1991/1992, 97–108; Strachan 2001/2003, 731.
43. Lapping 1985/1989, 287; Mansfield 1991/1992, 108.
44. Faulkner 2011a.
45. Faulkner 2012, 44.
46. Faulkner 2012.
47. *Times History*, III, 299.
48. Newsinger 2006, 98–9.
49. *Times History*, III, 287–8.
50. *Times History*, III, 284.
51. Nicolle 1989, 39–40, 47.
52. Nicolle 1989, 11–13.
53. Nicolle 1989, 41.
54. *Times History*, III, 304–6.
55. Rogan 2015, 68–9.
56. *Times History*, III, 314–15.
57. *Times History*, III, 317.
58. MacMunn and Falls 1928, 17–18.
59. Wavell 1928/1936, 26.
60. Strachan 2001/2003, 734.
61. Morgenthau 1918/2000, 114–16.
62. Morgenthau 1918/2000, 116.
63. Emin 1930, 79; estimates for the ethnic population breakdown of the Ottoman Empire at the time of the First World War are, for a variety of reasons, imprecise. The figures given here are approximations only.
64. Morgenthau 1918/2000, 107.
65. The origin of this frequently cited phrase seems obscure; suffice it to say that it is believed to have emanated from within the German high command in reference to their Austro-Hungarian allies during the First World War.
66. Strachan 2003, 97.
67. Trotsky 1914.
68. Finkel 2005/2006, 8–11.
69. Mansel 1995/2006, 33, 42.
70. Palmer 1992, 37; Petersen 2012.
71. Finkel 2005/2006, 492; Palmer 1992, 150.
72. Nicholson 2005.
73. Stephenson 1969/1971a, 398.
74. Palmer 1992, 189.
75. Stephenson 1969/1971a, 398; Palmer 1992, 192.
76. Strachan 2003, 98.
77. Strachan 2001/2003, 696; Rogan 2015, 47.
78. Strachan 2001/2003, 695–6, 707–8.
79. Lewis and Strachan 2004.
80. Djemal Pasha 1922, 153–4.
81. Weber 1970, 99; Nogales 1926, plate facing 113.
82. *Times History*, IV, 350.
83. Wavell 1928/1936, 29–30.
84. Erickson 2001, 70.
85. Gullet 1923/1941, 116–17.
86. Wavell 1928/1936, 28.
87. Kress von Kressenstein 1922, 'The first expedition against the Suez Canal'.
88. MacMunn and Falls 1928, 28–9.
89. *Times History*, IV, 346–7.
90. Erickson 2001, 70; *Times History*, IV, 349; Vader 1969/1971, 708; Bullock 1988, 20.
91. Aaronsohn 1916, VI; MacMunn and Falls 1928, 40–1; Rogan 2015, 119–22.
92. MacMunn and Falls 1928, 25.
93. MacMunn and Falls 1928, 30, 43–4.
94. MacMunn and Falls 1928, 41.
95. MacMunn and Falls 1928, 41–2.
96. Wavell 1928/1936, 31.
97. Kress von Kressenstein 1922, 'The first expedition against the Suez Canal'.
98. Wavell 1928/1936, 40–1.
99. Garnett 1938, 195–6.

Chapter 2: Young Turks

1. Trumpener 1968, 50–1.
2. Trumpener 1968, 66–7, 272–3.
3. For the approximate value of a 1914 Turkish pound (T£), see 'Notes on the text' on p. XX; Trumpener 1968, 271–2.
4. Trumpener 1968, 282–3; *Purnell* 8, 3546; Haythornthwaite 1992, 380. These estimates are based on approximate 1914 exchange rates for US dollars, German marks and Turkish pounds.
5. Trumpener 1968, 271–83, esp. 283.
6. Luxemburg 1915, chapter 4.
7. Carr 1969/1991, 167.
8. Strachan 2001/2003, 663.
9. Emin 1930, 39.
10. Trumpener 1968, 7–11; Ulrichsen 2014, 25.
11. Nicholson 2005, 8–9.
12. Luxemburg 1915, chapter 4.
13. Luxemburg 1915, chapter 4.
14. Atwood 2013, 14.
15. Atwood 2013, 1.
16. Massie 1992, 782–5.
17. Sampson 1975, 52–7.
18. Wilson 1989/1990, 80, 108, 110.
19. Garnett 1938, 170–5.
20. Garnett 1938, 170–1, 172.
21. Wilson 1989/1990, 104, 110.
22. Wilson 1989/1990, 145.
23. Wilson 1989/1990, 146–7.
24. Atwood 2013, 36.
25. Palmer 1992, 170–1.
26. Finkel 2005/2006, 513.
27. Spilsbury 2013a, 2013b, 2014; Rogan 2015, 17.
28. Emin 1930, 55.
29. Liman von Sanders 1927, 1–3; Erickson 2001, 11.
30. Nogales 1926, 29; Trumpener 1968, *passim*; Weber 1970, *passim*.
31. Morgenthau 1918/2000, 31–2.
32. Ulrichsen 2014, 18.
33. Weber 1970, 80–1.
34. Mansel 1995/2006, 367.
35. Palmer 1992, 217; Mansel 1995/2006, 367; Finkel 2005/2006, 523.
36. Mango 1999/2004, 30–2.
37. Balakian 2003/2004, 110.
38. Trumpener 1968, 9.
39. Finkel 2005/2006, 469.
40. Taylor 1977/1979, 42.
41. Finkel 2005/2006, 447–87 *passim*.
42. Finkel 2005/2006, 447–525 *passim*.
43. Mazower 2004/2005, 274–5; Rogan 2015, 4–5.
44. Faulkner 2013a, 181.
45. Finkel 2005/2006, 514–18.
46. Mazower 2004/2005, 274.
47. Faulkner 2013a, 181–2.
48. Morgenthau 1918/2000, 21.
49. Strachan 2001/2003, 671–2; Anderson 2013/2014, 77–8.
50. Trumpener 1968, 16–17.
51. Morgenthau 1918/2000, 17.
52. Trumpener 1968, 19–20; Weber 1970, 60.
53. Palmer 1992, 221–3.
54. Massie 1992, 467–90 *passim*.
55. Palmer 1992, 223.
56. Churchill 1923–31/1938, 437.
57. Ferguson 1998, 85.
58. Rogan 2015, 4.
59. Rogan 2015, 28, 31, 40, 46.

60. Palmer 1992, 224.
61. Strachan 2001/2003, 644–51.
62. Palmer 1992, 224–5.
63. Morgenthau 1918/2000, 52–3.
64. Djemal 1922, 113.
65. Emin 1930, 63–4.
66. Emin 1930, 70.
67. Emin 1930, 58–9.
68. Churchill 1923–31/1938, 449–50; Strachan 2001/2003, 677–80.

Chapter 3: Little Mehmet

1. Bean 1946/1947, 101–2; Wykes 1969/1971; Carlyon 2001/2003, 165–213 *passim*.
2. Kemal 1969/1971.
3. Bean 1946/1947, 102; Carlyon 2001/2003, 182.
4. Kemal 1969/1971.
5. Strachan 2001/2003, 680.
6. Anderson 2013/2014, 104.
7. Carlyon 2001/2003, 116.
8. Nicolle 2010, 5.
9. Lawrence 1922/2004, 12–23.
10. Lawrence 1922/2004, 683.
11. Wavell 1928/1936, 19,
12. Fasıh 2003, 132, 237 plate.
13. Fasih 2003, 110–12.
14. Barnett 1979/2003, 76.
15. Mango 1999/2004, 108.
16. Fasih 2003, 181.
17. Anderson 2013/2014, 89.
18. Djemal 1922, 205; Murphy 1921/undated, 179–80; Nicolle 2010, 36.
19. Nicolle 2010, 13.
20. Nicolle 2010, 34–7.
21. Rhodes James 1965/1984, 48.
22. Djemal Pasha 1922, 153.
23. Marshall 1947/2000 is the seminal study dealing with this phenomenon.
24. See Steel and Hart 1994/2002, 205–6, for a vivid first-hand description of combat rage.
25. Fasih 2003, 78–9.
26. Mango 1999/2004, 176 and *passim*.
27. Erickson 2001, 9–11, 19.
28. Liman 1927/undated, 8.
29. Erickson 2001, 53–4.
30. Fasih 2003, 182; effendi, bey and pasha were honorific terms in the Ottoman Empire. Officers up to captain were effendis, majors and colonels were beys, and generals were pashas.
31. Nicolle 2010, 19.
32. Nogales 1926, 166.
33. Erickson 2001, 6–7.
34. Liman von Sanders 1927/undated, 74.
35. Marshall 1947/2000, *passim*.
36. Nicolle 2010, 52.
37. Erickson 2001, 15; Porter 2014, 30.
38. Nicolle 2010, 57; Haythornthwaite 1992, *passim*.
39. Erickson 2001, 16–17; Nicolle 2010, 32.
40. Morgenthau 1918/2000, 176–7.
41. Emin 1930, 78, 89–90; Erickson 2001, 16.
42. Strachan 2001/2003, 691.
43. Nogales 1926, 165; Wavell 1928/1936, 10–12; Strachan 2001/2003, 690–1.
44. Emin 1930, 87; Shqiarat et al. 2011, 110.
45. Liman 1927/undated, 107.
46. Emin 1930, 88–9.
47. Djemal 1922, 142–3.
48. *Handbook* 1916, 139n; Nicolle 2010, 22–4.
49. Fasih 2003, *passim*; Nicolle 2010, 42.

50. Nicolle 2010, 24.
51. Fasih 2003, 230 plate 31; Nicolle 2010, 23–4.
52. Fasih 2003, *passim*.
53. Fasih 2003, 154, 167, and *passim*.
54. Nicolle 2010, 52.
55. *Handbook* 1916, 52; Fasih 2003, *passim*; Saunders forthcoming.
56. Liman 1927/undated, 9.
57. Fasih 2003, 167.
58. Liman 1927/undated, 259–60 and *passim*.
59. *Handbook* 1916, 53; Nicolle 1994, 26, 44; Nicolle 2010, 29–30.
60. Nicolle 2010, 32–3.
61. *Handbook* 1916, 10–11, 107; Nicolle 2010, 29, 32–3.
62. Bean 1946, 128; Nicolle 2010, 46, 50–1.
63. Nicolle 2010, 46, 50–1; WEA 2162 at www.iwm.org.uk/collection/item/object/30001748.
64. Erickson 2001, 8; Nicolle 2010, 33, 54–5.
65. Fasih 2003, 122, 157, 190, *passim*.
66. *Handbook* 1916, 66–9; Erickson 2001, 7–8.
67. *Handbook* 1916, 107.
68. Fasih 2003, 169.
69. *Handbook* 1916, 107; Nicolle 2010, 33.
70. Emin 1930, 253; Nicolle 2010, 48–9, 57.
71. Nicolle 2010, 53.
72. Finkel 2005/2006, 529; Erickson 2001, 30–3, 76–7.
73. Erickson 2001, 7.
74. Liman 1927/undated, 24.
75. Nicolle 2010, 15.
76. Erickson 2001, 8–9; Nicolle 2010, 11–14.
77. Nogales 1926, 43.
78. Liman von Sanders 1927/undated, 38–9.
79. Hinterhoff 1969/1971, 500–2; Erickson 2001, 52–8
80. Hinterhoff 1969/1971, 502; Erickson 2001, 58–60.
81. Ulrichsen 2014, 53, 65.
82. Nogales 1926, 130–1.
83. Morgenthau 1918/2000, 208–9.
84. Balakian 2003/2004, 253.
85. Balakian 2003/2004, 257.
86. Balakian 2003/2004, 258.
87. Nogales 1926, 171.
88. Nogales 1926, 172.
89. Morgenthau 1918/2000, 214; Sagall 2013, 159.
90. Wilson 1989/1990, 202.
91. Ulrichsen 2014, 59–62; Rogan 2015, 164–71.
92. Balakian 2003/2004, 346; Fisk 2005, 390.
93. Morgenthau 1918/2000, 224–5.
94. Morgenthau 1918/2000, 225.
95. Morgenthau 1918/2000, 229–31.
96. Morgenthau 1918/2000, 233.
97. Morgenthau 1918/2000, 242–55, esp. 248.
98. Morgenthau 1918/2000, 20, 249.
99. Morgenthau 1918/2000, 223.
100. Morgenthau 1918/2000, 227.
101. Emin 1930, 189–97; Mansel 1995/2006, 360; Balakian 2003/2004, 163–6.
102 Strachan 2001/2003, 705; Balakian 2003/2004, 181–2.
103. Balakian 2003/2004, 164, 179.
104. Balakian 2003/2004, 187.
105. Balakian 2003/2004, 189–90.
106. Balakian 2003/2004, 175–275 *passim*; Fisk 2005, 388–436 *passim*, esp. 398.
107. Balakian 2003/2004, 182–5.
108. Sagall 2013, 158–82 *passim*.
109. Lawrence 1922/2004, 34.
110. Nogales 1926, 123–4.
111. Morgenthau 1918/2000, 197, 204–5; Balakian 2003/2004, 200–1.
112. Balakian 2003/2004, 253–4.

Chapter 4: For Sultan and Caliph

1. Taylor 1963, 68–70; Terraine 1965/1967, 114–15.
2. Taylor 1963, 31; Barnett 1979/2003, 55.
3. Terraine 1965/1967, 115–19.
4. Terraine 1965/1967, 108–9.
5. Taylor 1963, 75–7; Barnett 1979/2003, 185–6; Palmer 1965, 70.
6. Haythornthwaite 1992, 155–6.
7. Trumpener 1998/2000, 84; Erickson 2001, 62–5.
8. Trumpener 1998/2000, 84–5; Erickson 2001, 120–37.
9. Kannengiesser 1927, 269–70.
10. Rogan 2015, 189, 214–17.
11. Crutwell 1934/1982, 339–41; Barnett 1979/2003, 190–1.
12. Wilson, pers. comm.
13. Rogan 2015, 230–1.
14. Crutwell 1934/1982, 341–5.
15. Crutwell 1934/1982, 341–5; Barnett 1979/2003, 191.
16. Crutwell 1934/1982, 345–6; Barnett 1979/2003, 191–2.
17. Crutwell 1934/1982, 346–7; Clark 1969/1971 passim.
18. Garnett 1938, 202.
19. Wilson 1989/1990, 256.
20. Barnett 1979/2003, 192–3.
21. Clark 1969/1971, 1344–7.
22. Wilson 1989/1990, 274.
23. Rogan 2015, 259–60.
24. Wilson 1989/1990, 255–6.
25. Wilson 1989/1990, 268–9; Carver 2003/2004, 152.
26. Rogan 2015, 260–2.
27. Wilson 1989/1990, 256–67 passim.
28. Nogales 1926, 104–7.
29. Wilson 1989/1990, 270–3.
30. Wilson 1989/1990, 274–5; Anderson 2013/2014, 176–8.
31. Nogales 1926, 122–5; Cruttwell 1934/1982, 348–9; Wilson 1989/1990, 273; Anderson 2013/2014, 178.
32. Rogan 2015, 273–4.
33. Wilson 1989/1990, 269.
34. Cruttwell 1934/1982, 606–7.
35. Barnett 1979/2003, 193–4.
36. Terraine 1965/1967, 198; Barnett 1979/2003, 194.
37. Cruttwell 1934/1982, 609–10; Dupuy and Dupuy 1970, 987–8.
38. Cruttwell 1934/1982, 609–10.
39. Wilson 1989/1990, 263, 278.
40. Nicolle 1989, 36–7.
41. Nicolle 1989, 36–7.
42. Times History, X, 236.
43. Rogan 2015, 236–7.
44. Nicolle 1989, 37–8.
45. Wilson 1989/1990, 639.
46. Wilson 1989/1990, 219–20.
47. Wilson 1989/1990, 232–3.
48. Jafar al-Askari 2003, 15–56 passim.
49. Wavell 1928/1936, 35; Nicolle 1989, 5–6.
50. Times History, IX, 285; Nicolle 1989, 6; Clark 2012/2013, 247–8.
51. Times History, IX, 294.
52. Jafar al-Askari 2003, 65.
53. MacMunn and Falls 1928, 106.
54. Jafar al-Askari 2003, 65.
55. Jafar al-Askari 2003, 69–74.
56. Jafar al-Askari 2003, 74–6.
57. Wavell 1928/1936, 36; Nicolle 1989, 12.
58. Wavell 1928/1936, 37; Nicolle 1989, 6–7.
59. Jafar al-Askari 2003, 76.
60. Jafar al-Askari 2003, 78–80.

61. MacMunn and Falls 1928, 125–9; Wavell 1928/1936, 37–8; Jafar al-Askari 2003, 87–92.
62. Wavell 1928/1936, 38.
63. *Times History*, IX, 318–20; Nicolle 1989, 12–13.
64. An estimated 35,000 British, 15,000 French and 60,000 Italian; Nicolle 1989, 8.
65. Nicolle 1989, 8.
66. McGuirk 2007, v.
67. Wilson 1989/1990, 213.
68. McGuirk 2007, 153–6.
69. Wilson 1989/1990, 193–4, 231–2; Howell 2006/2007, 171–2.
70. Wilson 1989/1990, 169.
71. Wilson 1989/1990, 170–2.
72. Wilson 1989/1990, 169–70.
73. Wilson 1989/1990, 178.
74. Wilson 1989/1990, 178.
75. Magraw 1983, 237–9; Hobsbawm 1987/1994, 71.
76. Wilson 1989/1990, 651.
77. Wilson 1989/1990, 222–4.
78. Wavell 1928/1936, 39–40.
79. Wilson 1989/1990, 224–5.
80. Wilson 1989/1990, 164–6, 195.

Chapter 5: Sinai Bridgehead

1. Lynden-Bell: Lynden-Bell to Maurice, 8/2/16.
2. MacMunn and Falls 1928, 85–6.
3. Djemal Pasha 1922, 166–7.
4. Djemal Pasha 1922, 168; Kress von Kressenstein 1922, 'Preparations for a second offensive against the canal'.
5. MacMunn and Falls 1928, 60–4, 71–2.
6. Kress von Kressenstein 1922, 'Preparations for a second offensive against the canal'; Wavell 1928/1936, 46–7.
7. MacMunn and Falls 1928, 157–8.
8. Wavell 1928/1936, 18–19.
9. Kress von Kressenstein 1922, 'Preparations for a second offensive against the canal'.
10. Lynden-Bell: Maurice to Lynden-Bell, 30/3/16.
11. Lynden-Bell: Lynden-Bell to Maurice, 22/5/16.
12. Lynden-Bell: Lynden-Bell to Maurice, 10/6/16.
13. MacMunn and Falls 1928, 23–5.
14. Gullett 1923/1941, 26; Wavell 1928/1936, 32, 40; though there seem to be different versions of the actual words spoken, and some doubt as to whether they originated with Kitchener.
15. Lynden-Bell: Lynden-Bell to Maurice, 16/1/16.
16. Lynden-Bell: Lynden-Bell to Caldwell, 21/12/15; Lynden-Bell to Maurice, 14/2/16.
17. MacMunn and Falls 1928, 96–7; Lynden-Bell: Lynden-Bell to Maurice, 15/3/16.
18. Wavell 1928/1936, 40.
19. Gullett 1923/1941, 41.
20. Keogh 1954, 32–3.
21. Gullet 1923/1941, 40–1.
22. Wavell 1928/1936, 41–2; Keogh 1954, 34.
23. Bullock 1988, 30.
24. *Times History*, X, 381; Wavell 1928/1936, 43.
25. Gullett 1923/1941, 81, 92; Keogh 1954, 42.
26. Hatton undated, 24.
27. Gullett 1923/1941, 82; MacMunn and Falls 1928, 162; Keogh 1954, 30.
28. Gullett 1923/1941, 119.
29. Gullett 1923/1941, 83.
30. Gullett 1923/1941, 82; Keogh 1954, 41–2.
31. Gullett 1923/1941, 83–4; MacMunn and Falls 1928, 163; Keogh 1954, 40.
32. Gullett 1923/1941, 84–5.
33. Thompson 1923, 256–7.
34. Gullett 1923/1941, 84–7; MacMunn and Falls 1928, 163–6.
35. Gullett 1923/1941, 87–8; MacMunn and Falls 1928, 166–8.
36. Gullett 1923/1941, 49.

37. *Times History*, X, 380.
38. Gullett 1923/1941, 89–90; Hill 1978, 48–9.
39. Bean 1946/1947, 154–6; Baly 2003/2004, 6–8.
40. Gullett 1923/1941, 54–60.
41. Gullett 1923/1941, 29–31.
42. Fleming 2012, 3–5.
43. Faulkner 2007, 83.
44. James 1994/1995, 172.
45. Hill 1978, 11–12.
46. Carlyon 2002/2003, 137.
47. Gullett 1923/1941, 36–7.
48. Bean 1946/1947, 5; James 1994/1995, 311.
49. Bean 1921/1941, 130n.
50. Carlyon 2001/2003, 136–7; Herscovitch and Stanton 2008, 53.
51. Carlyon 2001/2003, 135–6.
52. Lynden-Bell: Extracts, 9–10; Lynden-Bell to Maurice, 24/1/16; Lynden-Bell to Maurice, 14/2/16; Hatton undated, 91–2.
53. James 1994/1995, 313; Baly 2003/2004, 35–6.
54. Gullett 1923/1941, 54.
55. Gullett 1923/1941, 57–8; Fleming 2012, 7.
56. Hill 1978, 67.
57. Gullett 1923/1941, 39, 69; Hill 1978, 48; Dearberg 2012, 54.
58. Gullett 1923/1941, 31–2.
59. Fleming 2012, 25, 43–4.
60. Gullett 1923/1941, 63–4.
61. Hill 1978, 1–46 *passim.*
62. Hill 1978, 38–9.
63. Hill 1978, 48.
64. Hill 1978, 35–7, 49.
65. Hill 1978, 13.
66. Gullett 1923/1941, 69, 71–3; Hill 1978, 69–70.
67. Kermack; Loudon, 47–8; Hatton undated, 139–40; Gullett 1923/1941, 107.
68. Lynden-Bell: Lynden-Bell to Maurice, 22/5/16.
69. University of Florida.
70. University of Florida.
71. Gullett 1923/1941, 108–9.
72. Hatton undated, 50.
73. Keogh 1954, 46.
74. Teichman 1921/undated, 48.
75. Surry.
76. Surry.
77. Hinde, 37.
78. Hatton undated, 94.
79. Baly 2003/2004, 15.
80. Loudon, 53–4.
81. Lynden-Bell: Lynden-Bell to Maurice, 7/3/16.
82. Hatton undated, 139.
83. Loudon, 53–4.
84. Teichman 1921/undated, 111.
85. Hatton undated, 52.
86. Lynden-Bell: Lynden-Bell to Maurice, 16/1/16; also 8/2/16.
87. Thompson 1923, 251.
88. Massey 1918, 26.
89. Lynden-Bell: Lynden-Bell to Maurice, 4/9/16.
90. Lynden-Bell: Lynden-Bell to Maurice, 21/12/16.
91. Gullett 1923/1941, 195.
92. Gullett 1923/1941, 337–8.
93. Bullock 1988, 29.
94. Bullock 1988, 29.
95. Wavell 1928/1936, 60–1; Massey 1918, 30.
96. Teichman 1921/undated, 87–8; Thompson 1923, 268; Keogh 1954, 36.
97. Powles 1922, 18–19; Bruce 2002/2003, 32.

98. Wavell 1928/1936, 61–2; Bruce 2002/2003, 35; NHS.
99. Wavell 1928/1936, 62.
100. Massey 1918, 33–4.
101. Bullock 1988, 29.
102. Wavell 1928/1936, 63; Bullock 1988, 23.
103. Badcock 1925, 23, 30.
104. Wavell 1928/1936, 63.
105. McPherson, 1096–7.
106. McPherson, 1080–3.
107. Woodward 2006/2007, 61–2.
108. Blaser undated, 15–17.
109. Hughes 2004, 100–1.
110. Loudon, 37.
111. *Times History*, III, 304–6.
112. Lynden-Bell: Lynden-Bell to Maurice, 16/1/16.
113. Lynden-Bell *passim*.
114. Badcock 1925, 45–7, 81, 100, 152.
115. McPherson, 1073.
116. Hinde, 24.

Chapter 6: The Battle of Romani

1. Thompson 1923, 269; Gullett 1923/1941, 126; Hill 1978, 74–5; Teichman 1921/undated, 57.
2. Lynden-Bell: Lynden-Bell to Maurice, 17/8/16; Teichman 1921/undated, 68.
3. Teichman 1921/undated, 68; Kress von Kressenstein 1922, 'Preparations for a second offensive against the Canal'.
4. Lynden-Bell: Lynden-Bell to Maurice, 17/8/16; Teichman 1921/undated, 63 and *passim*.
5. Teichman 1921/undated, 71.
6. Thompson 1923, 264.
7. Garnett 1938, 196–7.
8. Powles 1922, 26; Keogh 1954, 34.
9. Thompson 1923, 271–3, map 4; Wavell 1928/1936, 46.
10. Loudon, 46–7.
11. Thompson 1923, 273–8.
12. Gullett 1923/1941, 116–17.
13. Hill 1978, 72–5.
14. Gullett 1923/1941, 141; Wavell 1928/1936, 50n.
15. MacMunn and Falls, 1928, 180n.
16. Powles 1922, map facing 32; Gullett 1923/1941, 141; Wavell 1928/1936, 47.
17. Gullett 1923/1941, 135.
18. Keogh 1954, 41.
19. Gullett 1923/1941, 143–5.
20. Gullett 1923/1941, 145–7.
21. Gullett 1923/1941, 147–8.
22. Kermack.
23. *Times History*, X, 393.
24. *Times History*, X, 393.
25. Gullett 1923/1941, 149–50.
26. Gullett 1923/1941, 151–3; Keogh 1954, 52–3.
27. Gullett 1923/1941, 150–2; MacMunn and Falls 1928, 186–7.
28. McPherson, 1099–101; Keogh 1954, 47; Gullett 1923/1941, 156.
29. Gullett 1923/1941, 152–3.
30. Gullett 1923/1941, 152–4; Keogh 1954, 57.
31. Gullet 1923/1941, 157.
32. Gullett 1923/1941, 156.
33. Powles 1922, 32; Gullett 1923/1941, 156–7.
34. Woodward 2006/2007, 67.
35. McPherson, 1102–3.
36. Powles 1922, 32–3; Gullett 1923/1941, 158, 160; MacMunn and Falls 1928, 189.
37. Teichman 1921/undated, 70–1.
38. Teichman 1921/undated, 72.
39. Wavell 1928/1936, 49.

40. MacMunn and Falls 1928, 191.
41. Woodward 2006/2007, 68–9.
42. Gullett 1923/1941, 170.
43. Gullett 1923/1941, 169–71, Map 7.
44. Baly 2003/2004, 30.
45. Gullett 1923/1941, 170–1.
46. Gullett 1923/1941, 172–3; Baly 2003/2004, 31–2.
47. Gullett 1923/1941, 175.
48. Teichman 1921/undated, 77–8.
49. Hill 1978, 83.
50. Gullett 1923/1941, 175–6.
51. Lynden-Bell: Lynden-Bell to Maurice, 17/8/16, 23/8/16.
52. Gullett 1923/1941, 174–6.
53. Gullett 1923/1941, 176–7; MacMunn and Falls 1928, 195.
54. Gullett 1923/1941, 177–84 *passim*; Baly 2003/2004, 33–4.
55. Gullett 1923/1941, 173, 184; MacMunn and Falls 1928, 199.
56. Gullet 1923/1941, 189–90; Wavell 1928/1936, 50–1.
57. Djemal 1922, 171–2.

Chapter 7: The Arab Revolt

1. Bell 1907/1985, 256–61.
2. Doughty 1931/1956, 253 4, 305.
3. Doughty 1931/1956, 259–60.
4. Doughty 1931/1985, 72.
5. Doughty 1931/1956, 11.
6. Garnett 1931/1956, v–vi; Wilson 1989/1990, 53–4, 86–7, 98.
7. Abdullah 1950, 71.
8. Doughty 1931/1985, 140–84 *passim*.
9. Doughty 1931/1985, 184; Bullock 1988, 34; Nicolle 1989, 20–1. My estimate of the increase in the size of Ibn Rashid's army is based on Doughty's estimate of 500 in the 1870s and Nicolle's claim of 'over a thousand well-armed tribesmen' by 1917.
10. Liddell Hart 1934/1935, 148–9.
11. Nicolle 1989, 21–2.
12. Doughty 1931/1956, 260; Lacey 1981/1982, 56–8.
13. Nicolle 1989, 22–3.
14. Lacey 1981/1982, 102–6.
15. Nicolle 1989, 22.
16. Antonius 1946/1965, 123; MacMunn and Falls 1928, 221–4; Nicolle 1989, 23–35.
17. Antonius 1946/1965, 123–4; Nicolle 1989, 35; Allawi 2014, 25–7.
18. Antonius 1946/1965, 122; Abdullah 1950, 73n.
19. Antonius 1946/1965, 161–2.
20. Fromkin 1989/2000, 106–10.
21. Abdullah 1950, 14, 63–4, 153.
22. Fromkin 1989/2000, 111–12; Allawi 2014, 4–7.
23. Barr 2006, 14.
24. Abdullah 1950, 61–2.
25. Barr 2006, 205, 243.
26. Abdullah 1950, 34–6, 38–9; Allawi 2014, 10–19.
27. Allawi 2014, 23.
28. Abdullah 1950, 45.
29. Lacey 1981/1982, 57–8.
30. Antonius 1946/1965, 21–2.
31. Abdullah 1950, 72–3 and 72n.
32. Barr 2006, 13.
33. Abdullah 1950, 66–7.
34. Fromkin 1989/2000, 111.
35. Bell 1907/1985, 36, 136.
36. Saunders forthcoming.
37. Barr 2006, 13–14.
38. Abdullah 1950, 61–2.
39. Antonius 1946/1965, 124–5; Nicholson 2005, 44–5; Allawi 2014, 44–5.

40. Abdullah 1950, 69–70.
41. Abdullah 1950, 82–3.
42. Abdullah 1950, 109.
43. Abdullah 1950, 119–21; Allawi 2014, 45.
44. Abdullah 1950, 128–9.
45. Antonius 1946/1965, 140.
46. Antonius 1946/1965, 144–6.
47. Antonius 1946/1965, 142–3.
48. Antonius 1946/1965, 147–8.
49. Allawi 2014, 48–9.
50. Allawi 2014, 49.
51. Antonius 1946/1965, 131–2.
52. Antonius 1946/1965, 131–2; Allawi 2014, 46.
53. Allawi 2014, 51ff.
54. Mousa 1966, 29.
55. Abdullah 1950, 109–10.
56. Antonius 1946/1965, 127–9.
57. Fromkin 1989/2000, 79–87.
58. Fromkin 1989/2000, 88–91.
59. Wilson 1989/1990, 167.
60. Buchan 1916/1999, 11–12; Barr 2006, 16–18.
61. Abdullah 1950, 132–3.
62. Antonius 1946/1965, 130–4, 142–4.
63. Antonius 1946/1965, 160.
64. Antonius 1946/1965, 164–5, 414–15; Rogan 2015, 280–1.
65. Antonius 1946/1965, 165–7, 415–16.
66. Antonius 1946/1965, 167–8, 416–18.
67. Fromkin 1989/2000, 176–9; Rogan 2015, 282–3.
68. Wilson 1989/1990, 205–11.
69. Antonius 1946/1965, 168–71, 419–20.
70. Only the most tendentious reading of the fourth letter in the McMahon Correspondence can suggest otherwise. David Fromkin's claim that 'Britain did not bind herself to support Hussein's claims anywhere at all' (1989/2000, 183) is refuted by the evidence of numerous contemporary documents that make it clear that leading British protagonists knew perfectly well that the undertakings within the McMahon Correspondence were hopelessly at odds with both general British intentions for the post-war Middle East and the specific provisions of the Sykes–Picot Agreement. Fromkin's pro-Zionist sympathy may have blinded him to the blatancy of the betrayal.
71. Antonius 1946/1965, 171–5, 182–3, 421–7.
72. Antonius 1946/1965, 188; Allawi 2014, 62–6; Rogan 2015, 288–95.
73. Barr 2006, 22–3.
74. Antonius 1946/1965, 184.
75. Rogan 2015, 296–7.
76. Antonius 1946/1965, 208–9.
77. Abdullah 1950, 136–7.
78. Allawi 2014, 66–7.
79. Allawi 2014, 68.
80. Abdullah 1950, 138.
81. El-Edroos 1980, 71; Murphy 2008, 33.
82. El-Edroos 1980, 70–1; Barr 2006, 5–6; Murphy 2008, 26.
83. Antonius 1946/1965, 196n.
84. Liddell Hart 1934/1935, 81; El-Edroos 1980, 71–2; Bullock 1988, 38.
85. Antonius 1946/1965, 197–8; Abdullah 1950, 143.
86. Bruce 2002/2003, 54.
87. Wilson 1989/1990, 287–8.
88. Liddell Hart 1934/1935, 81.
89. Liddell Hart 1934/1935, 85; Wilson 1989/1990, 289.
90. Antonius 1946/1965, 198–9; El-Edroos 1980, 71–2.
91. Armstrong 2012, *passim*; Haleem 2012, *passim*.
92. Haleem 2012, 76–9.
93. Kennedy 2012, *passim*.
94. Irwin 2012, 170–84.
95. Barr 2006, 28.

96. Liddell Hart 1934/1935, 85; Antonius 1946/1965, 199; El-Edroos 1980, 72.
97. El-Edroos 1980, 72.
98. Wilson 1989/1990, 162; Lawrence 1922/2004, 59.
99. Antonius 1946/1965, 199; El-Edroos 1980, 72–3.
100. Lawrence 1922/2004, 156.
101. Liddell Hart 1934/1935, 86; Murphy 2008, 34.
102. Abdullah 1950, 148; Barr 2006, 28.
103. Wilson 1989/1990, 385–7.
104. Abdullah 1950, 147–9.
105. Liddell Hart 1934/1935, 86; El-Edroos 1980, 74.
106. Lawrence 1922/2004, 77–9; El-Edroos 1980, 71.
107. El-Edroos 1980, 65–6.
108. El-Edroos 1980, 68, 71, 73–4.
109. Liddell Hart 1934/1935, 88.
110. Antonius 1946/1965, 118–21; Abdullah 1950, 156n; Allawi 2014, 33–4.
111. Antonius 1946/1965, 112–15; Allawi 2014, 33.
112. Baedeker 1912, lviii–lxiv.
113. Bell 1907/1985, *passim*.
114. Bell 1907/1985, 211–13, 313–19; Aaronsohn 1916, ch. IX.
115. Bell 1907/1985, 37, 209, 291, 295, 309.
116. Bell 1907/1985, 171.
117. Bell 1907/1985, 217.
118. Bell 1907/1985, 262.
119. Bell 1907/1985, 317.
120. Bell 1907/1985, 132, 318; Aaronsohn 1916, chapters IV, V.
121. A peasant revolution in Syria and/or Iraq might well have triggered one in Egypt. This would have reconfigured the entire subsequent history of the Middle East.
122. Antonius 1946/1965, 152–3.
123. Antonius 1946/1965, 157–8.
124. Abdullah 1950, 132.
125. Djemal Pasha 1922, 165.
126. Aaronsohn 1916, VI; Nogales 1926, 164–7.
127. Aaronsohn 1916, II; Djemal Pasha 1922, 167; Nogales 1926, 176–7.
128. Wilson 1989/1990, 111.
129. Aaronsohn 1916, II.
130. Aaronsohn 1916, V; Nogales 1926, 166.
131. Aaronsohn 1916, II, IV; Nogales 1926, 176–7.
132. Aaronsohn 1916, VII–VIII; Nogales 1926, *passim*.
133. Nogales 1926, 176–7, and *passim*.
134. Nogales 1926, 188–9.
135. Aaronsohn 1916, IX.
136. Antonius 1946/1965, 152.
137. Aaronsohn 1916, VI.
138. Aaronsohn 1916, VI.
139. Djemal Pasha 1922, 167.
140. Djemal Pasha 1922, 205–6.
141. Allawi 2014, 57.
142. Fromkin 1989/2000, 102; Barr 2006, 16; Allawi 2014, 52.
143. Karsh and Karsh 1997, 282–3; Uyar 2007.
144. Allawi 2014, 58.
145. Allawi 2014, 58.
146. Antonius 1946/1965, 188–91; Allawi 2014, 58–9, 65–6.
147. Allawi 2014, 59.
148. Mousa 1966, 16.
149. Abdullah 1950, 154–5; Mousa 1966, 23–4; El-Edroos 1980, 91–2; Allawi 2014, 75–6.
150. Wilson 1989/1990, 247–8, 301–7; Lawrence 1922/2004, 47–8.

Chapter 8: A Crusader, an Unknown Desert and a New Way of War

1. Lawrence 1922/2004, 6; Lawrence 1926/1935/1946, 23–4; Mack 1976, 276–7.
2. Wilson 1989/1990, 21–55 *passim*.
3. Jeremy Wilson and Jan Woolf, pers. comm.

4. Mack 1976, 3–55 *passim*. I am indebted to psychiatrist John Mack's outstanding biography of Lawrence, but I think he, like so many 'post-Freudians', tends to understate the psychic depth of neurotic complexes. In particular, I think the taproot of Lawrence's hero complex – which is so central to his historical role – needs more forthright exposition. I have therefore relied heavily on Mack, but have attempted to develop some of his insights further, and have been greatly assisted in this by reading a wide range of psychoanalytical authors, including Donald Winnicott (1964), and by my discussions with Jan Woolf.
5. Wilson 1989/1990, 28–148 *passim*.
6. Mack 1976, 38.
7. Mack 1976, 41–7. The other two books were a copy of Aristophanes and *The Oxford Book of English Verse*; Jeremy Wilson, pers. comm.
8. Mack 1976, 37.
9. Liddell Hart 1934/1935, 16.
10. Wilson 1989/1990, 52, 990.
11. Brooke 1946/1970, 19; Garnett 1938, 184.
12. Garnett 1938, 185–6; Wilson 1989/1990, 151–2.
13. Wilson 1989/1990, 152, 154, 166.
14. I am using 'Orientalism' in the sense defined by Edward Said (1978/2003) in his classic study.
15. Wilson 1989/1990, 95.
16. Lawrence 1922/2004, 361–2.
17. Wilson 1989/1990, 100.
18. Mack 1976, 96–8; Wilson 1989/1990, 543–5.
19. Mack 1976, 43–4.
20. Lawrence 1922/2004, 'To S.A.'. I am grateful to Jan Woolf for sharing insights into the likely character and significance of the Lawrence/Dahoum relationship.
21. Wilson 1989/1990, 85.
22. Wilson 1989/1990, 248–50.
23. Lawrence 2005a.
24. Doughty 1931/1956, 126, 282.
25. Doughty 1931/1956, 41.
26. Doughty 1931/1956, 37.
27. Doughty 1931/1956, 48–72 *passim*.
28. Lawrence 2005b, 65; Lawrence 2005c, 72.
29. Lawrence 2005d, 73–4.
30. Caudwell 1971, *passim*; Jan Woolf, pers. comm.
31. Wilson 1989/1990, 354.
32. Wilson 1989/1990, 190, 226–7.
33. Mack 1976, 140.
34. Mack 1976, 142; Wilson 1989/1990, 300–1; Jeremy Wilson, pers. comm.
35. Wilson 1989/1990, 301–2.
36. Mack 1976, 132.
37. Mack 1976, 142.
38. Lawrence 1922/2004, 37.
39. Wilson 1989/1990, 302.
40. Wilson 1989/1990, 307–9; Anderson 2013/2014, 199–201.
41. Anderson 2013/2014, 196–9.
42. Wilson 1989/1990, 307–9.
43. Lawrence 1922/2004, 75–6.
44. Lawrence 2005d; Lawrence 1922/2004, 60.
45. Lawrence 1922/2004, 75.
46. Lawrence 2005d.
47. Liddell Hart 1934/1935, 127.
48. Allawi 2014, 77–8.
49. Wilson 1989/1990, 385; Lawrence 2005a, 143.
50. Murphy 2008, 46.
51. Lawrence 1922/2004, 76.
52. Anderson 2013/2014, 203–10.
53. Wilson 1989/1990, 317–21.
54. Anderson 2013/2014, 225–6.
55. Anderson 2013/2014, 213–14, 221–2.
56. Wilson 1989/1990, 317–32.
57. Wilson 1989/1990, 325–6.

58. Anderson 2013/2014, 224–5.
59. Wilson 1989/1990, 325.
60. Lawrence 2005e.
61. Wilson 1989/1990, 328–33.
62. Lawrence 1922/2004, 91.
63. Lawrence 1922/2004, 106–18.
64. Lawrence 1922/2004, 118–19.
65. Anderson 2013/2014, 245–6.
66. Anderson 2013/2014, 237–8.
67. Lawrence 1922/2004, 119–21; Anderson 2013/2014, 211, 244.
68. Lawrence 1922/2004, 123–5.
69. Lawrence 1922/2004, 125–6.
70. Mousa 1966, 20–2.
71. Abdullah 1950, 163–5.
72. Murphy 2008, 38.
73. Fromkin 1989/2000, 222.
74. Fromkin 1989/2000, 223.
75. Wilson 1989/1990, 375.
76. Wilson 1989/1990, 355–6.
77. Wilson 1989/1990, 356.
78. Lawrence 2005e; Anderson 2013/2014, 238.
79. Hanson 1989 *passim*; Keegan 1993/1994, 155–217 *passim*.
80. Lawrence 1922/2004, 161, 197; Liddell Hart 1934/1935, 139.
81. Wilson 1989/1990, 346–7.
82. Wilson 1989/1990, 347.
83. Liddell Hart 1934/1935, 133; Wilson 1989/1990, 347–9; Allawi 2014, 85.
84. Lawrence 1922/2004, 132–3.
85. Liddell Hart 1934/1935, 138, 148; Lawrence 2005f; Anderson 2013/2014, 276; Allawi 2014, 85.
86. Lawrence 1922/2004, 135–62 *passim*; Liddell Hart 1934/1935, 138; Wilson 1989/1990, 352; Anderson 2013/2014, 257.
87. Lawrence 1922/2004, 161.
88. Mousa 1966, 59–60.
89. Wilson 1989/1990, 351–2, 355–8; Anderson 2013/2014, 250–1, 258.
90. Wilson 1989/1990, 381–3; Anderson 2013/2014, 276–7.
91. Anderson 2013/2014, 273–4.
92. Wilson 1989/1990, 385–6.
93. Lawrence 1922/2004, 220–1; Liddell Hart 1934/1935, 179–80; Mousa 1966, 57; Lawrence 2005f; 114–15; Anderson 2013/2014, 280–3.
94. Lawrence 1922/2004, 222; Lawrence 2005f, 117–20; Lawrence 2005g, 131.
95. Lawrence 2005g, 131.
96. Lawrence 1922/2004, 191–200.
97. Clausewitz 1832–5/1943, 22–3.
98. Saxe 1757/1944, 121.
99. Sun Tzu 2002/2005, 12.
100. Clausewitz 1832–5/1943, 68–83 *passim*.
101. Lawrence 1922/2004, 195–7.
102. These principles are embedded in three separate, but very similar, military treatises written by Lawrence after the war. These are: 'The evolution of a revolt' (1920; republished in Brown 2005); chapter 35 of *Seven Pillars of Wisdom* (1922 edition; chapter 33 of the 1926/1935 edition); and 'Science of guerrilla warfare' (1929; republished in Brown 2005). We discuss these treatises in relation to Lawrence's role in the war, his standing as a military thinker and his relationship with the theory of guerrilla warfare more generally in Faulkner and Saunders (2010). Also of relevance here is Faulkner and Saunders (2009).

Chapter 9: The Gates of Palestine

1. Teichman 1921/undated, 117–19; Powles 1922, 82–3.
2. Loudon, 62; Bostock 1982, 58–61.
3. *Genesis*, 10.19.
4. *Judges*, 16.
5. Smith 1894/undated, 184–9; Baedeker 1912, 119–20.
6. McPherson, 1143.

7. Powles 1922, 46, 85.
8. Wavell 1928/1936, 57–8; Grainger 2006, 9–10.
9. Grainger 2006, 8–9.
10. Massey 1918, 82–3, 146 facing pic.; Teichman 1921/undated, 81, 96; Powles 1922, 57, 81, 90 pic.
11. Teichman 1921/undated, 92–3.
12. Massey 1918, 83–4.
13. Massey 1918, 89–91.
14. Massey 1918, 81–2.
15. Massey 1918, 80–1.
16. Gullett 1923/1941, 194–5.
17. Massey 1918, 85.
18. Wavell 1928/1936, 58.
19. Churchill 1923–31/1938, 1201.
20. Taylor 1963, 157–9.
21. Bruce 2002/2003, 35–6.
22. Woodward 2006/2007, 77.
23. MacMunn and Falls 1928, 258–61.
24. MacMunn and Falls 1928, 85–6.
25. Keogh 1954, 71–2.
26. Gullett 1923/1941, 203–4; MacMunn and Falls 1928, 259.
27. Gullett 1923/1941, 208–9.
28. Powles 1922, 59–61.
29. Kress von Kressenstein, 505–6.
30. Gullett 1923/1941, 214.
31. Gullett 1923/1941, 210–13.
32. Bulliet 1975, 30–5; Badcock 1925, 81, 100.
33. Bullock 1988, 23.
34. Hogue 1918/2008, 15–18.
35. Gullett 1923/1941, 215–16.
36. The official histories do not agree in their counting and mapping of the redoubts. Five were numbered by the attackers, but the respective plans show five, seven and eight separate earth-works; Powles 1922, 48 facing plan; Gullett 1923/1941, 216–17, Map 9; MacMunn and Falls 1928, Sketch 12.
37. Gullett 1923/1941, 218–19.
38. Gullett 1923/1941, 220–1.
39. Hogue 1918/2008, 54.
40. Gullett 1923/1941, 221–6.
41. Gullett 1923/1941, 227.
42. Gullett 1923/1941, 233–4; Bullock 1988, 41.
43. Baly 2003/2004, 57.
44. Massey 1918, 108; Teichman 1921/undated, 102.
45. Massey 1918, 109, 111–12.
46. Teichman 1921/undated, 104; Baly 2003/2004, 60.
47. Gullett 1923/1941, 239–40.
48. Powles 1922, 75–6; Gullett 1923/1941, 240.
49. Hogue 1918/2008, 66–7.
50. Gullett 1923/1941, 240–1.
51. Gullett 1923/1941, 242.
52. Bullock 1988, 41.
53. Wavell 1928/1936, 67–8, 73; Grainger 2006, 18–22.
54. Wavell 1928/1936, 73–4; Grainger 2006, 21.
55. Bruce 2002/2003, 91.
56. Bruce 2002/2003, 89.
57. Bruce 2002/2003, 90–1.
58. Idriess 1932/1973, 184.
59. Grainger 2006, 10–11; Woodward 2006/2007, 80–1.
60. Hill 1978, 86.
61. Grainger 2006, 19.
62. Wavell 1928/1936, 69–70.
63. Woodward 2006/2007, 85–8.
64. Bruce 2002/2003, 93–4.
65. Wavell 1928/1936, 71–2.

66. Wavell 1928/1936, 71.
67. Kress von Kressenstein 1922, 506–7.
68. Baly 2003/2004, 68–70; Grainger 2006, 26–8.
69. Idriess 1932/1973, 191–2.
70. Wavell 1928/1936, 77; Grainger 2006, 28–9.
71. Idriess 1932/1973, 193–4.
72. Idriess 1932/1973, 195–6.
73. Idriess 1932/1973, 197; Hill 1978, 104–5.
74. Woodward 2006/2007, 85.
75. Kress von Kressenstein 1922, 506–7.
76. Wavell 1928/1936, 78–9.
77. Grainger 2006, 33–5.
78. Nogales 1926, 331–2.
79. Surry.
80. Grainger 2006, 33–4.
81. Surry.
82. Woodward 2006/2007, 91–3.
83. Woodward 2006/2007, 95.
84. Woodward 2006/2007, 93.
85. Dupuy and Dupuy 1970, 963–4, 974.
86. Dupuy and Dupuy 1970, 969.
87. Churchill 1923–31/1938, 1201–3.
88. MacMunn and Falls 1928, 174 facing sketch 9; Woodward 2006/2007, 94–5.
89. Lynden-Bell: Maurice to Lynden-Bell, 5/4/17.
90. Grainger 2006, 37; Woodward 2006/2007, 95–6.
91. Gullett 1923/1941, 324–5 facing map 13; Wavell 1928/1936, 85–6; Keogh 1954, 113; Grainger 2006, 40–1.
92. Grainger 2006, 40.
93. Wavell 1928/1936, 84, 86.
94. Grainger 2006, 40.
95. Guns were 'registered' on predetermined targets – such as known enemy trenches or landmarks on an anticipated avenue of attack – when ranges and bearings were established in advance so that appropriate settings could be made when firing; Grainger 2006, 44–5, 52.
96. Keogh 1954, 125; Grainger 2006, 42–3.
97. Keogh 1954, 115; Woodward 2006/2007, 98.
98. Woodward 2006/2007, 100.
99. Woodward 2006/2007, 102–3.
100. Woodward 2006/2007, 103.
101. Woodward 2006/2007, 101.
102. Keogh 1954, 120.
103. Woodward 2006/2007, 99.
104. Idriess 1932/1973, 213.
105. MacMunn and Falls 1928, 348; Keogh 1954, 118.
106. Nogales 1926, 350.
107. Kress von Kressenstein, 507–8; Keogh 1954, 118.
108. Baly 2003/2004, 90.
109. Lynden-Bell: Lynden-Bell to Maurice, 23/4/17; Woodward 2006/2007, 104.
110. Woodward 2006/2007, 104–5.
111. Lynden-Bell: Lynden-Bell to Maurice, 23/4/17.
112. Wavell 1928/1936, 92; Keogh 1954, 127–8; Bruce 2002/2003, 110.
113. Bruce 2002/2003, 110.

Chapter 10: Aqaba

1. Wilson 1989/1990, 395.
2. Lawrence 1922/2004, 349.
3. Wilson 1989/1990, 389–91, 395–6.
4. Anderson 2013/2014, 290.
5. Wilson 1989/1990, 391–2; Allawi 2014, 90.
6. Wilson 1989/1990, 359–62.
7. Wilson 1989/1990, 279–84.
8. Anderson 2013/2014, 153.

9. Allawi 2014, 99–100.
10. Fromkin 1989/2000, 263–83 *passim*.
11. Fromkin 1989/2000, 268.
12. Fromkin 1989/2000, 268–9.
13. Fromkin 1989/2000, 270–1.
14. Anderson 2013/2014, 298–305.
15. Allawi 2014, 104.
16. Marshall 1989, 30–4.
17. Anderson 2013/2014, 294.
18. Marshall 1989, 34–5.
19. Anderson 2013/2014, 304–5.
20. Grainger 2006, 178.
21. Allawi 2014, 103.
22. Marshall 1989, 35–40.
23. Lacey 1981/1982, 136.
24. Faulkner 2013b.
25. Baedeker 1912, 213.
26. Lawrence 1922/2004, 338.
27. Wilson 1989/1990, 399.
28. Wavell 1928/1936, 56.
29. Wilson 1989/1990, 398.
30. Wilson 1989/1990, 400; John Scott, pers. comm.
31. Scott 2014, 123; John Scott, pers. comm.
32. Scott 2014, 91–165 *passim*.
33. Wilson 1989/1990, 397.
34. Barr 2006, 102–3.
35. Liddell Hart 1934/1935, 192.
36. Barr 2006, 104.
37. Barr 2006, 114.
38. Jeremy Wilson, pers. comm.
39. Lawrence 1922/2004, 229–31; Bruce 2002/2003, 71; Lawrence 2005h.
40. Liddell Hart, 1934/1935, 183.
41. For contrasting extremes on this question, compare, for example, Liddell Hart 1934/1935, 181–3 ('with Auda, he [Lawrence] concerted a plan') and Mousa 1966, 66–7 ('the whole expedition was planned with no reference to Lawrence').
42. Anderson 2013/2014, 288.
43. Allawi 2014, 101–3.
44. Wilson 1989/1990, 399.
45. Wilson 1989/1990, 397–8.
46. Wilson 1989/1990, 401. Jeremy Wilson suspects that Colonel Wilson knew of the plan, but, realising the importance of secrecy, did not divulge it (pers. comm.).
47. Lawrence 1922/2004, 240–2; Bullock 1988, 53–4; Nicolle 1989, 16, 44–5; Wilson 1989/1990, 406, 412.
48. Lawrence 1922/2004, 263–4.
49. Lawrence 1922/2004, 275–90 *passim*.
50. Wilson 1989/1990, 404–5.
51. Lawrence 1922/2004, 7–8.
52. Wilson 1989/1990, 410.
53. Wilson 1989/1990, 412–13.
54. Wilson 1989/1990, 414.
55. Lawrence 2005i, 137–8.
56. Lawrence 1922/2004, 315–29 *passim*; Lawrence 2005i, 138–9.
57. Lawrence 1922/2004, 332–6; Lawrence 2005i, 139–40.
58. Bullock 1988, 52–3, 59.

Chapter 11: Bull Loose

1. Wavell 1940, 113–14 and *passim*.
2. Lawrence 1922/2004, 347–8.
3. Wilson 1989/1990, 417–19.
4. Lawrence 1922–2004, 348–9.
5. Wavell 1940, 193n.

6. Allenby 1937, in Lawrence 1937, 145–6.
7. Hughes 2004, 36–7.
8. Hughes 2004, 37–9.
9. Hughes 2004, 67.
10. Mack 1976, 177.
11. Lawrence 1937, 145.
12. Lawrence 1922/2004, 346–7.
13. Lawrence 1922/2004, 682–3.
14. Mack 1976, 154.
15. Gardner 1965, 201.
16. Lawrence 1922/2004, 427.
17. Wavell 1940, 193–5.
18. Wavell 1940, 17.
19. Wavell 1940, 188.
20. Keogh 1954, 137.
21. Wavell 1940, 179–80.
22. Wavell 1940, 174–5, 180–3.
23. Gullett 1923/1941, 357.
24. Wavell 1940, 197–8; Woodward 2006/2007, 112–13.
25. Woodward 2006/2007, 112.
26. Woodward 2006/2007, 112.
27. Hatton undated, 145–6.
28. Idriess 1932/1973, 239.
29. Woodward 2006/2007, 129–30.
30. Loudon, 67.
31. Bruce 2002/2003, 113.
32. Horne 1962/1964, 38–45 and *passim*.
33. Liddell Hart 1930/1973, 345–50.
34. Bullock 1988, 70.
35. Wavell 1928/1936, 99; Falls 1930, 675; Bullock 1988, 69–70; Perrett 1999, 29; Erickson 2001, 169.
36. Keogh 1954, 129; Terraine 1965/1967, 198.
37. Djemal Pasha 1922, 182–93.
38. Djemal Pasha 1922, 192–3; Wavell 1928/1936, 99, 109–10.
39. Kress von Kressenstein 1922.
40. Liman 1927/undated, 175–6.
41. Kress von Kressenstein 1922.
42. Liman 1927/undated, 190–2.
43. Wavell 1928/1936, 110n, 113–14.
44. Woodward 2006/2007, 129.
45. Wavell 1928/1936, 104.
46. Woodward 2006/2007, 116.
47. Surry.
48. Woodward 2006/2007, 120.
49. Woodward 2006/2007, 117–19.
50. Woodward 2006/2007, 121.
51. Teichman 1921/undated, 148, 153.
52. Wavell 1928/1936, 104, 112n.
53. Keogh 1954, 124–5; Woodward 2006/2007, 119.
54. Bruce 2002/2003, 112.
55. Gullett 1923/1941, 358.
56. Faulkner 2013a, 202–3.
57. Trotsky 1932–3/1967a, 124–7; Dupuy and Dupuy 1970, 972.
58. Trotsky 1932–3/1967b, 70–2.
59. Hughes 2004, 52.
60. Wavell 1928/1936, 101–2, 112–13; Falls 1930, 14–16.
61. Massey 1920, 34; Wavell 1928/1936, 104.
62. Massey 1920, 34–6.
63. Massey 1920, 36–7.
64. Massey 1920, 45–7.
65. Massey 1920, 45.
66. Massey 1920, 38; Falls 1930, 14.
67. Hatton undated, 183.

68. Falls 1930, 22–3; Keogh 1954, 124, 136–7; Bullock 1988, 62, 67–8.
69. Massey 1920, 31.
70. Hatton undated, 105, 155; Woodward 2006/2007, 123–9.
71. Wavell 1928/1936, 114–15; Keogh 1954, 108–9, 140, 151.
72. Falls 1930, 42n.
73. Grainger 2006, 110.
74. Lawrence 1922/2004, 427–8.
75. Keogh 1954, 130–3; Grainger 2006, 90–4.
76. A guiding principle of Prussian general Helmuth von Moltke 'the Elder' (1800–91).
77. Grainger 2006, 103–5.
78. Keogh 1954, 137.
79. Wilson 1989/1990, 452–7.
80. Wavell 1928/1936, 107; Grainger 2006, 105, 107.
81. Wavell 1928/1936, 106–7.
82. Wavell 1928/1936, 106, 112.
83. Wavell 1928/1936, 106; Keogh 1954, 136–7.
84. Woodward 2006/2007, 132–3.
85. Grainger 2006, 106–7.
86. Seward 2009, 49–50; Hynes 2010, 11.
87. Angelucci and Matricardi 1977, 190–1 and *passim*.
88. Wavell 1928/1936, 107–8.
89. Hughes 2004, 58.
90. Blaser undated, 66.
91. Idriess 1932/1973, 246.
92. Massey 1920, 56.

Chapter 12: The Railway War

1. This account of the Battle of Hallat Ammar is based on Lawrence 1922/2004, 378–417, Lawrence 1926/1935/1946, 352–85, Lawrence 2005j, and the evidence of archaeological fieldwork carried out in October 2013.
2. Winterburn 2012, 173–4.
3. GARP Archive and Saunders forthcoming.
4. GARP Archive and Saunders forthcoming.
5. Bulliett 1975, *passim*, esp. 87–110.
6. Winterburn 2012, 184–5.
7. Liddell Hart 1934/1935, 219.
8. Liddell Hart 1934/1935, 218.
9. Liddell Hart 1934/1935, 218.
10. Faulkner 2011b.
11. Lawrence 1922/2004, 196.
12. El-Edroos 1980, 177–84.
13. Wavell 1928/1936, 194–5.
14. Wavell 1928/1936, 194–5; Falls 1930, 624.
15. Wilson 1989/1990, 437.
16. Wilson 1989/1990, 437; Allawi 2014, 107.
17. Anderson 2013/2014, 351–2.
18. Liddell Hart 1934/1935, 215.
19. Mousa 1966, 86–7.
20. Wilson 1989/1990, 439.
21. Liddell Hart 1934/1935, 226–8; Mousa 1966, 95–6, 121; El-Edroos 1980, 115–18; Wilson 1989/1990, 437–8.
22. Mousa 1966, 122; Shqiarat et al. 2011.
23. MacMunn and Falls 1928, 237; Wavell 1928/1936, 194.
24. Mousa 1966, 124; El-Edroos 1980, 118.
25. Lawrence 1922/2004, 128.
26. Lawrence 1922/2004, 425; Mousa 1966, 124–5; El-Edroos 1980, 118.
27. Lawrence 1922/2004, 417–23;
28. Mousa 1966, 122.
29. Mousa 1966, 122–3.
30. Liddell Hart 1934/1935, 235.
31. Liddell Hart 1934/1935, 227.

32. Anderson 2013/2014, 372–3.
33. Lawrence 1922/2004, 423–5.
34. Liddell Hart 1934/1935, 240.
35. Liddell Hart 1934/1935, 239–40; Wilson 1989/1990, 449–51.
36. Nicholson 2005, 53.
37. Wilson 1989/1990, 451.
38. Lawrence 1922/2004, 449–86; Liddell Hart 1934/1935, 241–4, 248–56; Wilson 1989/1990, 452–7; Lawrence 2005k, 154–6.
39. Anderson 2013/2014, 385.
40. Wilson 1989/1990, 447–9.
41. Liddell Hart 1934/1935, 223–5.
42. Lawrence 2005j, 148.
43. Liddell Hart 1934/1935, 243; Lawrence 2005k, 154.
44. Moran 1945, *passim*.
45. Sherman 2010, 30–1, 178, 183, 231.
46. Wilson 1989/1990, 446–7.
47. Anderson 2013/2014, 380.
48. Anderson 2013/2014, 381.

Chapter 13: The Third Battle of Gaza

1. Grainger 2006, 109.
2. Massey 1920, 74.
3. Massey 1920, 79–80.
4. Baedeker 1912, 170.
5. Bullock 1988, 73–4.
6. Wavell 1928/1936, 102.
7. Badcock 1925, 152.
8. Massy 1920, 59; Falls 1930, 34–5; Woodward 2006/2007, 140.
9. Wavell 1928/1936, 117; Grainger 2006, 105, 113–14.
10. Massey 1920, 57–9.
11. Wavell 1928/1936, 118.
12. Massey 1920, 59.
13. Blaser undated, 72–3.
14. Woodward 2006/2007, 139.
15. Blaser undated, 73–4.
16. Bruce 2002/2003, 129–30.
17. Grainger 2006, 114–15.
18. Blaser undated, 75–6.
19. Wavell 1928/1936, 118–19.
20. Griffith 1994/1996, 38–9; Adkin 2013, 171–261 *passim*.
21. Griffith 1994/1996, 40–4, 66–7, 77; Adkin 2013, 242–3, 250–7.
22. Griffith 1994/1996, 49.
23. Haythornthwaite 1992, 93; Griffith 1994/1996, 115; Adkin 2013, 241–2.
24. Griffith 1994/1996, 115; Adkin 2013, 189.
25. Adkin 2013, 174–7.
26. Griffith 1994/1996, 93–8; Bull 2002, 48–51.
27. Blaser undated, 72.
28. Griffith 1994/1996, 49, 85.
29. Gullett 1923/1941, 394.
30. Wavell 1928/1936, 119–20.
31. Gullett 1923/1941, 388–9; Wavell 1928/1936, 120–1; Grainger 2006, 116.
32. Massey 1920, 62; Powles 1922, 137–8; Gullett 1923/1941, 389–91; Wavell 1928/1936, 121.
33. Idriess 1932/1973, 251.
34. Gullett 1923/1941, 391; Falls 1930, 57.
35. Wavell 1940, 117.
36. Wavell 1940, 127.
37. Woodward 2006/2007, 142–3.
38. Wavell 1928/1936, 122–3.
39. Gullett 1923/1941, 394–404; Wavell 1928/1936, 122–6; Idriess 1932/1973, 248–52; Baly 2003/2004, 109–16; Grainger 2006, 118–23.
40. Gullett 1923/1941, 404.

41. Wavell 1928/1936, 126–9.
42. Grainger 2006, 127–31.
43. Wavell 1928/1936, 129.
44. Wavell 1928/1936, 131; Falls 1930, 82–3; Liddell Hart 1934/1935, 245–7.
45. Powles 1922, 140; Wavell 1928/1936, 131–3; Idriess 1932/1973, 254–5; Keogh 1954, 157–8; Woodward 2006/2007, 146.
46. Wavell 1928/1936, 133–6; Woodward 2006/2007, 146–52.
47. Wavell 1928/1936, 133–7; Bruce 2002/2003, 142; Woodward 2006/2007, 147–53.

Chapter 14: Jerusalem

1. Massey 1920, 91–3; Teichman 1921/undated, 183–5; Wavell 1928/1936, 148; Bullock 1988, 78–9; Bruce 2002/2003, 145; Grainger 2006, 156–7.
2. Hughes 2004, 83.
3. Thompson 1923, 372–90, esp. 388 and pic facing 384; Wavell 1928/1936, 144, 148–9; Grainger 2006, 155.
4. Wavell 1928/1936, 149.
5. Thompson 1923, 384.
6. Woodward 2006/2007, 159.
7. Idriess 1932/1973, 272–3.
8. Idriess 1932/1973, 276.
9. Keogh 1954, 168.
10. Keogh 1954, 168.
11. Bruce 2002/2003, 144.
12. Blaser undated, 89.
13. Keogh 1954, 169; Bostock 1982, 98; Baly 2003/2004, 132.
14. Massey 1920, 97–8.
15. Bruce 2002/2003, 147–8.
16. Woodward 2006/2007, 179.
17. Woodward 2006/2007, 178–9.
18. Woodward 2006/2007, 180.
19. Woodward 2006/2007, 180–1.
20. Woodward 2006/2007, 178.
21. Keogh 1954, 165–6.
22. Keogh 1954, 170–1.
23. Wavell 1928/1936, 151–4; Keogh 1954, 170–2.
24. Wavell 1928/1936, 154–5; Falls 1930, 168–9; Woodward 2006/2007, 186.
25. Woodward 2006/2007, 187.
26. Thompson 1923, 423–5; Wavell 1928/1936, 154–5.
27. Woodward 2006/2007, 188.
28. Falls 1930, 170–1; Keogh 1954, 175.
29. Grainger 2006, 170–2.
30. Wavell 1928/1936, 156; Keogh 1954, 175–6; Bruce 2002/2003, 152; Woodward 2006/2007, 188–9.
31. Wavell 1940, 222–3.
32. Gardner 1965, 114.
33. Grainger 2006, 185.
34. Smith 1894/undated, 286–9.
35. Wavell 1928/1936, 161 and note; Grainger 2006, 201.
36. Gardner 1965, 154.
37. Hughes 2004, 84.
38. Keogh 1954, 176–7; Grainger 2006, 179–80.
39. Baedeker 1912, 20–4.
40. Grainger 2006, 176–7.
41. Bruce 2002/2003, 154.
42. Grainger 2006, 183–5.
43. Woodward 2006/2007, 195.
44. Wavell 1928/1936, 159; Keogh 1954, 180; Grainger 2006, 185.
45. Hatton undated, 183–8.
46. Massey 1920, 142–3; Grainger 2006, 184–5.
47. Wavell 1928/1936, 161; Grainger 2006, 191–3.
48. Kermack.
49. Hatton undated, 189–90.

50. Grainger 2006, 193.
51. Thompson 1923, 461, 472; Falls 1930, 235; Nicolle 1994, 28, 45; Bull 2002, 43–8; Nicolle 2010, 54–5.
52. Gullett 1923/1941, 506–8; Thompson 1923, 470–2; Falls 1930, 234–5.
53. Grainger 2006, 194–9.
54. Gullett 1923/1941, 495–6.
55. Bruce 2002/2003, 158.
56. Wavell 1928/1936, 164–5; Keogh 1954, 182.
57. Wavell 1928/1936, 165–6; Grainger 2006, 204–10.
58. Grainger 2006, 210–11.
59. Massey 1920, 193–4.
60. Grainger 2006, 210–12.
61. Woodward 2006/2007, 202–3.
62. Grainger 2006, 217; *Times History*, XV, 177–80.
63. Blaser undated, 97–8.
64. Hughes 2004, 92–3.
65. *Times History*, XV, 175–7; Grainger 2006, 212–15.
66. Wilson 1989/1990, 463.
67. Lawrence 1922/2004, 508.

Chapter 15: The Mountains of Moab

1. Lawrence 1922/2004, 508.
2. Lawrence 1922/2004, 494–502; Wilson 1989/1990, 459–61; Jeremy Wilson, pers. comm. The Deraa incident has been the subject of intense scrutiny and fierce controversy. Some commentators have denied it happened in any form, others have argued that the account we have is substantially distorted. Jeremy Wilson, the best informed and most measured of Lawrence's many biographers, is convinced of the essential truth of the narrative in *Seven Pillars of Wisdom*. His view is based in part on evidence that the homosexual rape of military prisoners is widespread. There is nothing in Lawrence's account that should occasion surprise, except the candour of the victim in reporting it. It is perhaps worth adding that, if the Deraa incident turned out to be fiction, in whole or in part, we would then be dealing with a highly publicised and elaborate sado-masochistic homosexual fantasy: something at least as significant for Lawrence's biography, and no less demanding in terms of analysis.
3. Lawrence 1922/2004, 487–94.
4. Lawrence 1922/2004, 502–8; Liddell Hart 1934/1935, 257–8.
5. Liddell Hart 1934/1935, 259; Mousa 1966, 126.
6. Wilson 1989/1990, 465–6.
7. Jafar al-Askari 2003, 90–112 *passim*.
8. Jafar al-Askari 2003, 126 and note.
9. Jafar al-Askari 2003, 113–25 *passim*.
10. El-Edroos 1980, 117; Jafar al-Askari 2003, 129–30.
11. Nicolle 1989, 29, 45; Jafar al-Askari 2003, 132.
12. Jafar al-Askari 2003, 136.
13. Jafar al-Askari 2003, 132.
14. Jafar al-Askari 2003, 131.
15. Lawrence 1922/2004, 558.
16. Not to be confused with Brigadier-General Guy Dawnay, the head of Allenby's staff.
17. Liddell Hart 1934/1935, 291n; El-Edroos 1980, 117; Wilson 1989/1990, 477–8, 491–2; John Winterburn, pers. comm.
18. Lawrence 1922/2004, 520–8.
19. Liddell Hart 1934/1935, 263.
20. Lawrence 1922/2004, 531–3; Mousa 1966, 126–7.
21. Lawrence 1922/2004, 534; Mousa 1966, 127.
22. Mousa 1966, 127–9.
23. Mousa 1966, 134–5; Murphy 2008, 64; Lawrence 2005l.
24. Lawrence 1922/2004, 538; Liddell Hart 1934/1935, 269–71; Mousa 1966, 133.
25. Among the many accounts of the battle, that of Mousa 1966 at 132–44, which draws on Arab testimony, provides perhaps the most useful evidence in support of this interpretation. This is somewhat ironic, since Mousa's consistent intention is to deprecate and downplay Lawrence's role. Yet the hard evidence he presents here seems quite compatible with Lawrence's testimony, and this implies (a) a chaotic, uncontrolled battle, (b) a failure of Sherifian leadership, and (c) an opportunity for a man like Lawrence to exercise a degree of centralised control, albeit dependent on getting his advice accepted in the heat of battle.

26. Mousa 1966, 136; Murphy 2008, 62–3.
27. Lawrence 1922/2004, 542–6; Liddell Hart 1934/1935, 274–6; Mousa 1966, 136–8; Murphy 2008, 62–3.
28. Lawrence 1922/2004, 547; Wilson 1989/1990, 477.
29. Liddell Hart 1934/1935, 276.
30. Wilson 1989/1990, 476–7.
31. Wilson 1989/1990, 480.
32. Wilson 1989/1990, 482–3.
33. Hughes 2004, 109–33, esp. 114.
34. Woodward 2006/2007, 215–20.
35. Woodward 2006/2007, 219.
36. Keogh 1954, 200–2.
37. Hochschild 2011, 295–316 *passim*.
38. Woodward 2006/2007, 215.
39. Wilson 1989/1990, 468–9.
40. Patterson 1922/undated, *passim*, esp. i, 23, 68.
41. Powles 1922, 154–5; Hatton undated, 202–4.
42. Surry; Idriess 1932/1973, 272.
43. Gullett 1923/1941, 517.
44. Wilson 1989/1990, 468–9.
45. Rogan 2015, 339–42.
46. Rogan 2015, 309.
47. Rogan 2015, 357–60.
48. Allawi 2014, 108–18, 120–1.
49. Wavell 1928/1936, 169–70.
50. Wavell 1928/1936, 170–2; Bruce 2002/2003, 169.
51. Woodward 2006/2007, 211–12.
52. Woodward 2006/2007, 213.
53. Woodward 2006/2007, 217.
54. Wavell 1928/1936, 177–8.
55. Not to be confused with the River Auja, north of Jaffa, which drains into the Mediterranean rather than the Jordan.
56. Wavell 1928/1936, 178–9.
57. Bruce 2002/2003, 191–2.
58. Wavell 1928/1936, 180–1; Keogh 1954, 208–10.
59. Woodward 2006/2007, 221.
60. Woodward 2006/2007, 223.
61. Inchbald 2005, 169.
62. Wavell 1928/1936, 181; Keogh 1954, 210–12.
63. Skander Bey 1924a.
64. Skander Bey 1924b.
65. Wavell 1940, 244.
66. Bruce 2002/2003, 190.
67. Keogh 1954, 205–6.
68. Falls 1930, 348–9n; Keogh 1954, 212.
69. Skander Bey 1924b.
70. Woodward 2006/2007, 224.
71. Skander Bey 1924b.
72. Skander Bey 1924b; Wavell 1928/1936, 182.
73. Liddell Hart 1934/1935, 290–1.
74. Mousa 1966, 162; El-Edroos 1980, 135–6; Allawi 2014, 121–2.
75. El-Edroos 1980, 135–6; Jafar al-Askari 2003, 138–40.
76. Nicholson 2005, 37; Faulkner and Saunders 2009, 440–1.
77. Lawrence 1922/2004, 600–1; Faulkner and Saunders 2009, 441–3; Saunders forthcoming.
78. Lawrence 1922/2004, 604; Mousa 1966, 162–3; Jafar al-Askari 2003, 142–5; Murphy 2008, 66–7.
79. Lawrence 1922/2004, 604.
80. El-Edroos 1980, 137.
81. Nunan. I am very grateful to John Winterburn for drawing this reference to my attention.
82. Rolls 1937/ 2005, 138.
83. Rolls 1937/2005, 210–11.
84. Lawrence 1922/2004, 596–8; Wilson 1989/1990, 492–3, 495–6.
85. Lawrence 1922/2004, 611.

86. Skander Bey 1924b.
87. Wavell 1928/1936, 184–5.
88. Skander Bey 1924b.
89. Wavell 1928/1936, 185–6.
90. Falls 1930, 375–6, 392–3.
91. Gullett 1923/1941, 615–17.
92. Falls 1930, 375–6.
93. Liman von Sanders 1927/undated, 226.
94. Falls 1930, 376–7.
95. Baly 2003/2004, 210–11.
96. Hatton undated, 241–4.
97. Bostock 1982, 152–3; Black 2008, 10, 109–10.
98. Blaser undated, 240–2.
99. Wavell 1928/1936, 188.
100. Liman von Sanders 1927/undated, 230–1.
101. Skander Bey 1924b.
102. Dupuy and Dupuy 1970, 978–80; Barnett 1979/2003, 168–74.
103. Wavell 1928/1936, 183.
104. Woodward 2006/2007, 230.
105. Wavell 1928/1936, 183.
106. Wavell 1940, 249, 254–5.

Chapter 16: Special Operations

1. Wilson 1989/1990, 511–12, 518–20; Allawi 2014, 108–18.
2. Wilson 1989/1990, 470.
3. Wilson 1989/1990, 502.
4. Wilson 1989/1990, 514–15.
5. Liddell Hart 1934/1935, 303–4, 307–8; Wilson 1989/1990, 503–8, 510–11.
6. Wilson 1989/1990, 521–3.
7. Liddell Hart 1934/1935, 308.
8. Wilson 1989/1990, 516–18.
9. Wilson 1989/1990, 526.
10. Wilson 1989/1990, 526–7.
11. Wilson 1989/1990, 509.
12. Lawrence 1922/2004, 401; Winterburn forthcoming.
13. Lawrence 1922/2004, 515–18; Saunders forthcoming; the low rise was named 'Siddons' Ridge' by the Great Arab Revolt Project.
14. Rolls 1937/undated, 18–20.
15. Stejskal forthcoming.
16. Lawrence 1922/2004, 518–19.
17. Allawi 2014, 119–20.
18. The Royal Flying Corps (part of the Army) and the Royal Naval Air Service (part of the Royal Navy) were merged to form the Royal Air Force, an independent air arm, in April 1918.
19. Winterburn forthcoming.
20. Angelucci and Matricardi 1977, 169, 213.
21. Winterburn forthcoming.
22. Allawi 2014, 120.
23. Lawrence 1922/2004, 605–6.
24. Lawrence 1922/2004, 606; Winterburn forthcoming; 'Plain Post' is probably the same as 'the low rise' Lawrence referred to in relation to the 1 January raid, or what the Great Arab Revolt Project dubbed 'Siddons' Ridge'.
25. Lawrence 1922/2004, 607.
26. Lawrence 1922/2004, 607; Winterburn forthcoming; probably what Lawrence calls 'a blockhouse on a knoll' in relation to the 1 January raid, or what the Great Arab Revolt Project dubbed 'Tell Shahm Fort'.
27. Lawrence 1922/2004; Winterburn forthcoming.
28. Lawrence 1922/2004, 607.
29. Lawrence 1922/2004, 607.
30. Lawrence 1922/2004, 607–8.
31. Lawrence 1922/2004, 608; Wilson 1989/1990, 498.
32. Lawrence 1922/2004, 608–10; Winterburn forthcoming.

33. Wilson 1989/1990, 498–9.
34. Lawrence 1922/2004, 662–3; Inchbald 2005, 199–202; Hynes 2010, 97; Winterburn forthcoming. The detailed reconstructions of the successive operations against Mudawwara in this chapter would have been impossible without the exhaustive researches of my colleague John Winterburn, the Great Arab Revolt Project's landscape archaeologist.
35. Lawrence 1922/2004, 663.
36. Wilson 1989/1990, 538.

Chapter 17: Armageddon

1. Gullett 1923/1941, 638–50 *passim*; Woodward 2006/2007, 245; Hatton undated, 244–50, 256.
2. Wavell 1928/1936, 201; Falls 1964, 55–6.
3. Wavell 1928/1936, 200–1.
4. Wavell 1928/1936, 195; Falls 1964, 38; this estimate excluded 6,000 in the region of Maan (facing the Arabs) and 3,000 in reserve.
5. Liman von Sanders 1927/undated, 204.
6. Liman von Sanders 1927/undated, 208.
7. Liman von Sanders 1927/undated, 241.
8. Liman von Sanders 1927/undated, 218.
9. Liman von Sanders 1927/undated, 207.
10. Rogan 2015, 370–3.
11. Liman von Sanders 1927/undated, 254.
12. Ulrichsen 2014, 69–70.
13. Liman von Sanders 1927/undated, 255–7.
14. Liman von Sanders 1927/undated, 234–6, 243, 256–60, 264–6, 269; Falls 1964, 41–3.
15. Liman von Sanders 1927/undated, 253–4, 265.
16. Falls 1964, 63.
17. Liddell Hart 1934/1935, 330–3; Wilson 1989/1990, 545–6.
18. Lawrence 1922/2004, 710–15; Wilson 1989/1990, 542.
19. Lawrence 1922/2004, 715–21; Rolls 1937/2005, 230–5, back cover.
20. Lawrence 1922/2004, 721–8.
21. Lawrence 1922/2004, 728–32.
22. Wilson 1989/1990, 547.
23. Wavell 1928/1936, 205–6.
24. Falls 1964, 30–1.
25. Wavell 1928/1936, 203.
26. Wavell 1928/1936, 195.
27. Robertson.
28. Badcock 1925, 271, 331.
29. Falls 1964, 52.
30. Wavell 1928/1936, 203.
31. Falls 1964, 49.
32. Liman von Sanders 1927/undated, 273–4.
33. Liman von Sanders 1927/undated, 274.
34. Wavell 1928/1936, 203–8; Falls 1964, 65–75; Perrett 1999, 23–9, 37–43.
35. Liman von Sanders 1927/undated, 275–7.
36. Wavell 1928/1936, 208; Perrett 1999, 23.
37. Hatton undated, 259.
38. Australian Mounted had been issued with swords in the summer of 1918, while Anzac Mounted had elected to remain mounted infantry, with only rifle and bayonet.
39. Wavell 1928/1936, 208.
40. Hatton undated, 258–9.
41. Woodward 2006/2007, 261.
42. Wavell 1928/1936, 208.
43. Falls 1964, 94; Woodward 2006/2007, 255.
44. Wavell 1928/1936, 209; Perrett 1999, 45–6.
45. Liman von Sanders 1927/undated, 278–9.
46. Falls 1930, 518–20; Falls 1964, 90–3; Hatton undated, 259–60.
47. Wavell 1928/1936; Woodward 2006/2007, 262; Hatton undated, 260.
48. Falls 1964, 101–2; Hatton undated 260.
49. Woodward 2006/2007, 263–4; Seward 2009, 201–3.
50. Wavell 1928/1936, 213.

51. Hughes 2004, 181–2.
52. Hughes 2004, 183–4.
53. Wavell 1928/1936, 220–1; Falls 1964, 110–15.
54. Gullett 1923/1941, 730–4; Falls 1964, 108; Baly 2003/2004, 268–70.
55. Wavell 1928/1936, 224.
56. Liddell Hart 1934/1935, 349–54; Wilson 1989/1990, 556.
57. Lawrence 1922/2004, 774.
58. Lawrence 1922/2004, 493.
59. Lawrence 1922/2004, 774–7.
60. Wilson 1989/1990, 557.
61. Liddell Hart 1934/1935, 357–9; Rolls 1937/2005, 246; Falls 1964, 129–30; Wilson 1989/1990, 559–60.
62. Gullett 1923/1941, 724–7; Falls 1964, 113–19.
63. Lawrence 1922/2004, 786–8; Liddell Hart 1934/1935, 364–5.
64. Gullett 1923/1941, 752–4; Falls 1930, 573; Perrett 1999, 77–9.
65. Wavell 1928/1936, 230; Falls 1930, 593.
66. Wilson 1989/1990, 560.
67. Wavell 1928/1936, 194–5; Falls 1930, 408–9; El-Edroos 1980, 178–9.
68. Liman von Sanders 1927/undated, 218, 273.
69. Lawrence 1922/2004, 792–3.
70. Baedeker 1912, 298–305; Falls 1964, 143–4.
71. Wilson 1989/1990, 555–6.
72. Wilson 1989/1990, 560–1.
73. Wilson 1989/1990, 561.
74. Allawi 2014, 138–44.
75. Liddell Hart 1934/1935, 369–71.
76. Allawi 2014, 146.
77. Wilson 1989/1990, 565–7; Allawi 2014, 146–7.
78. Lawrence 1922/2004, 804–9.
79. Wilson 1989/1990, 543–5.
80. Wilson 1989/1990, 568.
81. Wilson 1989/1990, 564.

Epilogue

1. Wavell 1928/1936, 230–3; Falls 1930, 609–618; Mango 1999/2004, 181–2.
2. Lapping 1985/1989, 289–92; Hughes 2004, 229–45; Newsinger 2006, 107–9.
3. Wilson 1989/1990, 489–90, 493–4, 621–6.
4. Barr 2011/2012, 101–3; Allawi 2014, 285–94.
5. Newsinger 2006, 116–19; Barr 2011/2012, 110–13.
6. Brown 2005, 239–40, 243.
7. Walder 1969/1971a; Walder 1969/1971b; Finkel 2005/2006, 539–47; Rogan 2015, 389–90.
8. Lacey 1981/1982, 181–90; Wilson 1989/1990, 656–61.
9. Kolko 1994, *passim*.

TIMELINE

Date	Wider world	Ottoman Empire and Middle East	Egypt/Palestine	Syria	Arabia
1876–1909		Reign of Abdulhamid II.			
1882			British annexation of Egypt.		
1884		German Military Mission arrives in Constantinople.			
1892–1908					Hussein and family held hostage in Constantinople.
1898		German Kaiser visits Constantinople, Damascus and Jerusalem.	Battle of Omdurman: reconquest of Sudan.		
1900–8				Construction of Hijaz Railway.	
1903		Germans granted Berlin-to-Baghdad Railway concession.			
1908		Young Turk Revolution. Oil discovered in Persia.			
1911		Arab nationalist group Al-Fatat founded.			Hussein appointed emir of Mecca.

1911–12	Italo-Turkish War in Libya.	
1911–14		British Museum excavations at Carchemish.
1912–13	Balkan Wars.	
1913		
23 Jan.	Military coup establishes CUP dictatorship in Constantinople.	
Autumn	Arab nationalist group Al-Ahd founded.	
14 Dec.	Liman von Sanders arrives in Constantinople.	
1914		
Jan.		*Wilderness of Zin* survey in eastern Sinai.
Apr.		Secret negotiations between Abdullah and Kitchener in Cairo.
28 July	Churchill seizes Ottoman dreadnoughts *Reshadieh* and *Sultan Osman I*	
4 Aug.	Britain declares war on Germany.	

Ottoman-Sherifian war against Idrisi.

Date	Wider world	Ottoman Empire and Middle East	Egypt/Palestine	Syria	Arabia
10 Aug.		*Goeben* and *Breslau* enter Dardanelles.			
6–11 Sept.	Battle of the Marne.				
16 Oct.		First German gold shipment arrives in Constantinople.			
29 Oct.		Crimean ports bombarded.			
2 Nov.			Britain declares martial law in Egypt.		
5 Nov.	Britain declares war on Ottoman Empire.				
14 Nov.		Grand Mufti declares *jihad* in Constantinople.			
22 Nov.		Britain occupies Basra in Mesopotamia.			
15 Dec.			Lawrence arrives as intelligence officer in Cairo.		
18 Dec.			Britain declares protectorate over Egypt.		
28 Dec.–3 Jan.		Battle of Sarikamish in Caucasus: Ottoman defeat.			
1915					British supply arms and money to Hussein of Mecca.
3 Feb.			First Ottoman attack on Suez Canal defeated.		

Date	Event	
19 Feb.	Dardanelles/Gallipoli campaign begins.	
18 Mar.	Naval battle in Dardanelles Straits: Ottoman victory.	
24 Apr.		Armenian Genocide begins.
25 Apr.	Gallipoli landings.	
May	Battle of Gorlice-Tarnow: Russian collapse on Eastern Front.	Damascus Protocol drawn up.
July		McMahon Correspondence between Cairo and Mecca begins.
21 Aug.		11 Arab nationalists executed in Beirut.
Sept.–Oct.	Artois, Champagne and Loos offensives defeated on Western Front.	
Oct.–Nov.	Serbia overrun.	
6 Nov.	Ctesiphon captured.	
22 Nov.	Senussi campaign begins.	
1916		
8 Jan.	Gallipoli evacuation completed.	
Jan.–July	Murray leads gradual advance across Sinai.	

Date	Wider world	Ottoman Empire and Middle East	Egypt/Palestine	Syria	Arabia
Feb.	British and French negotiate Sykes–Picot Agreement.				
16 Feb.		Capture of Erzerum in Caucasus by Russians.			
21 Feb.	Verdun offensive begins.				
26 Feb.			Battle of Agagia: Senussi defeat.		
Mar.			Maxwell recalled. Murray appointed commander of Egyptian Expeditionary Force.		
18 Apr.		Capture of Trebizond by Russians.			
23 Apr.			Battle of Katia: British defeat.		
29 Apr.		Townshend surrenders at Kut.			
May	Allied powers ratify Sykes–Picot Agreement.		Ali Dinar defeated in Darfur.	Ottoman Army prepares to leave Damascus for Hijaz.	Ottomans attempt to block imports of military supplies into Hijaz.
6 May				21 Arab nationalists executed in Beirut and Damascus.	
4 June	Brusilov offensive begins on Eastern Front.				
10 June					Hussein launches Arab Revolt in Mecca. Sherifian attacks on Mecca and Taif begin.

Date			
16 June			Sherifians capture Jiddah.
27 June			Sherifians capture Rabegh and Yenbo.
30 June			British Military Mission arrives in Jiddah.
1 July	Somme offensive begins.		
9 July			Last of Ottoman garrison surrenders at Mecca.
4 Aug.		Battle of Romani: British victory over Second Canal Expedition.	
5 Aug.		Second Battle of Katia: Anzacs checked.	
8 Aug.		Battle of Bir al-Abd: Anzacs checked.	
1 Sept.		French Military Mission arrives in Alexandria.	Hussein declares himself 'king of the Arabs.'
22 Sept.			Last of Ottoman garrison surrenders at Taif.
Oct.–Nov.		Reoccupation of western oases in Egypt.	Ottoman counter-offensive in Hijaz. Lawrence and Storrs visit Hijaz.
Nov.			Joyce reinforces Rabegh garrison.
Dec.			Battle of Nakhl Mubarak. Defence of Yenbo. Lawrence returns to Hijaz as advisor to Feisal (becomes permanent in Jan.).

Date	Wider world	Ottoman Empire and Middle East	Egypt/Palestine	Syria	Arabia
23 Dec.			Battle of Magdhaba: Anzac victory.		
1917					
Jan.–April	Crisis of Battle of Atlantic.				
9 Jan.			Battle of Rafa: Anzac victory. Ottomans driven out of Sinai.		
18 Jan.					Threat to Rabegh and Yenbo dissolves as Ottomans retreat to Medina.
23 Jan.					Wejh captured by Sherifians with RN support.
Feb.					Garland and Raho attack Hijaz Railway.
4 Feb.			Occupation of Siwah oasis: end of Senussi campaign.		
7 Feb.	Secret high-level Zionist meeting in London.				
Mar.	Russian Revolution begins.				
8 Mar.					Lawrence visits Abdullah at Wadi Ais.
11 Mar.		Capture of Baghdad.			

Date	Event	Event
26–27 Mar.	First Battle of Gaza: Ottoman victory.	Lawrence attacks Aba al-Naam.
Apr.–June	French Army mutinies on Western Front.	
6 Apr.	USA enters war.	
9–15 Apr.	Battle of Arras on Western Front.	
17–19 Apr.	Second Battle of Gaza: Ottoman victory.	
4 May	'Jaffa pogrom' propaganda story breaks.	
9 May		Aqaba mission departs from Wejh.
Late June		Diversionary raid and attacks on line at Minifer and Atwi.
End June–beginning July		March from Bair to capture Aqaba.
28 June	Allenby replaces Murray in command of EEF.	
2 July	Battle of Abu al-Lissan: Sherifian victory.	
6 July	Sherifians capture Aqaba.	
6–16 July		Joyce, Newcombe and Sherifians attack Hijaz Railway in Al-Ula and Sahl al-Matran areas.
Early July	Lawrence crosses Sinai to Cairo to report.	

Date	Wider world	Ottoman Empire and Middle East	Egypt/Palestine	Syria	Arabia
Late July–Aug.				Aqaba developed as forward base.	
24–30 Aug.					Raho and Sherifians attack Hijaz Railway in Mudurij area.
Sept.				Falkenhayn arrives to assume command of *Yilderim*.	
19 Sept.				Hallat Ammar ambush ('First Mudawwara Raid').	
6 Oct.				Shedia ambush.	
12 Oct.				Joyce and Sherifian regulars capture Shobek Castle.	
21 Oct.				Ottomans repelled by Sherifian regulars at Wadi Musa.	
24 Oct.	Italian collapse at Caporetto.				
31 Oct.			Third Battle of Gaza begins. Light Horse charge at Beersheba.		
Early Nov. 1917				Deep-penetration Yarmuk raid fails. Train wrecked at Minifer/Km 172.	
2 Nov.	Balfour Declaration.		Third Battle of Gaza ends:		
7 Nov	Bolshevik Revolution in				

Date				
8 Nov.		Yeomanry charge at Huj. Assault on Sausage Ridge.		
13 Nov.		Battle of Junction Station. Yeomanry charge at El-Mughar.		
Mid Nov. 1917			Lawrence at Azraq. 'Deraa incident'.	
21–4 Nov.		Battle of Nebi Samwel: Ottoman victory.		
22 Nov.	Bolsheviks publish secret treaties.			Ottoman attempts to win over Hussein.
27 Nov.–1 Dec.		Ottoman counter-attacks in Palestine fail.		Joyce tries to explain away Sykes–Picot to Hussein.
Dec.		Lawrence travels to Cairo to report and rest.		
5 Dec.	Armistice on Eastern Front.			
8 Dec.		Second British attack on Jersualem succeeds.		
11 Dec.		Allenby enters Jerusalem.		
31 Dec.–1 Jan.			Attack on Tell Shahm ('Second Mudawwara Raid').	
1918				
Dec.–Feb.			Winter campaign in Dead Sea area.	

Date	Wider world	Ottoman Empire and Middle East	Egypt/Palestine	Syria	Arabia
3 Jan.				Sherifians capture Abu al-Lissan, raid towards Maan, and attack Jurf.	
22 Jan.				Attack on Mudawwara beaten off ('Third Mudawwara Raid').	
25 Jan.				Battle of Tafila: Sherifian victory.	
28 Jan.				Destruction of Ottoman Dead Sea flotilla.	
Feb.				Lawrence goes from Tafila to Guweira and back.	
21 Feb.			Capture of Jericho.		
Mar.			Lawrence in Cairo for conference and rest. Dawnay replaces Joyce as head of British Military Mission.	Lawrence returns to Syria to execute major operation in support of EEF.	
9–12 Mar.			Advance to Wadi Auja line.		
21 Mar.	Ludendorff offensive begins.				
21 Mar.–2 Apr.			First Jordan Raid/Battle of Amman: British defeat.		
Apr.		Ottoman advance in Caucasus.		Lawrence travels widely to rally support for planned offensive.	
12 Apr.				Nuri captures Ghadir al-Hajj.	

13 Apr.	Maulud occupies Jebel Semna.
17 Apr.	Sherifian attack on Maan beaten off, but line cut and siege begins.
19–20 Apr.	Attacks on Tell Shahm and Ramleh: permanent break in railway ('Fourth Mudawwara Raid').
30 Apr.–4 May	Second Jordan Raid/Battle of Salt: British defeat.
May	Sherifian raids destroy 25 railway bridges.
May–July	Lawrence travels widely between Allenby's HQ, Feisal's camp and Sherifian field commands.
4 June	Feisal and Weizmann in inconclusive discussions at Wuheida (Joyce interprets).
July	Lawrence rests in Cairo.
8 Aug.	Buxton's Imperial Camel Corps captures Mudawwara ('Fifth Mudawwara Raid').
16 Sept.–1 Oct.	Arab Northern Army launches major attacks around Deraa and cuts Ottoman rail links.
19 Sept.	Megiddo Offensive begins Ottoman line in Palestine collapses.

Date	Wider world	Ottoman Empire and Middle East	Egypt/Palestine	Syria	Arabia
20 Sept.			Battle of Musmus Pass: Desert Mounted Corps break through.		
21 Sept.			Fall of Nablus. Massacre in the Wadi Fara.		
23 Sept.			Battle of Samakh: Desert Mounted Corps victory. Capture of Acre and Haifa.	Turks abandon Maan.	
27 Sept.				Tafas massacre by Nuri's men.	
28 Sept.	Bulgaria seeks armistice.			Barrow's 4th Cavalry Division and Sherifian advance party enter Deraa.	
29 Sept.	Breaking of Hindenburg Line.				
30 Sept.				Anzacs and Sherifians capture Ottoman II Corps retreating from Maan. Massacre in Barada Gorge. Massacre on Jebel Mania.	
1 Oct.				Australians and leading Sherifian elements enter Damascus.	
3 Oct.				Meeting of Allenby and Feisal in Damascus.	
4 Oct.				Lawrence leaves Damascus for home.	

8 Oct.	Capture of Beirut.
26 Oct.	Anglo-Arabs capture Aleppo. Battle of Haritan: Ottoman victory. Sherifians enter Medina.
31 Oct.	Mudros Armistice.
11 Nov.	Armistice on Western Front.
1919	
Jan.–June	Versailles Peace Conference.
13 Jan.	
Mar.–Apr.	Anti-colonial uprising in Egypt.
Aug.	Lowell Thomas show opens in London.
1920	
June–Aug.	Anti-colonial uprising in Iraq.
July	Battle of Maysalun. French overrun Syria. Feisal forced into exile.

Date	Wider world	Ottoman Empire and Middle East	Egypt/Palestine	Syria	Arabia
1921					
12–30 Mar.		Cairo Conference: Feisal to become King of Iraq and Abdullah Emir of Transjordan.			
15 Mar.		Talaat assassinated in Berlin.			
1922					
25 July		Djemal assassinated in Georgia.			
Aug.		Greek invasion defeated by Turkish Nationalists. Ethnic cleansing in Smyrna and western Anatolia. Enver killed in Central Asia.			
Sept.		Chanak Crisis: Britain backs down.			
1924					
Sept.–Oct.					Hijaz overrun by Saudis. Hussein forced into exile.

BIBLIOGRAPHY

I have not separated primary and secondary sources, since, though the distinction is usually clear, it is not always so. Is Wavell, who served on Allenby's staff, a primary or secondary source when he publishes an account of the Palestine campaign in 1928 and a biography of his former commander in 1940?

I have, where appropriate, referenced with both the original date of publication and that of the edition used, e.g. 1920/1968.

Arab authors are listed under their first name, in accordance with Arabic practice.

* * *

Aaronsohn, A. (1916) *With the Turks in Palestine*, Boston, Houghton Mifflin.
Abdullah (1950) *Memoirs of King Abdullah of Transjordan*, ed. P. Graves, London, Jonathan Cape.
Adkin, M. (2013) *The Western Front Companion*, London, Aurum Press.
Allawi, A.A. (2014) *Faisal I of Iraq*, London, Yale University Press.
Anderson, S. (2013/2014) *Lawrence in Arabia: war, deceit, imperial folly, and the making of the Middle East*, London, Atlantic Books.
Angelucci, E. and Matricardi, P. (1977) *World Aircraft: origins to World War I*, Maidenhead, Sampson Low.
Antonius, G. (1946/1965) *The Arab Awakening*, New York, Capricorn Books.
Armstrong, K. (2012) 'Pilgrimage: why do they do it?', in V. Porter (ed.), *Hajj: journey to the heart of Islam*, London, British Museum Press, 18–25.
Atwood, V.H. (2013) 'The Baghdad Railway', unpublished University of Texas MA dissertation.
Badcock, G.E. (1925) *A History of the Transport Services of the Egyptian Expeditionary Force, 1916–1917–1918*, London, Hugh Rees.
Baedeker, K. (1912) *Palestine and Syria: handbook for travellers*, London, T. Fisher Unwin.
Balakian, P. (2003/2004) *The Burning Tigris: the Armenian Genocide*, London, Heinemann.
Baly, L. (2003/2004) *Horseman, Pass By: the Australian Light Horse in World War I*, Staplehurst, Spellmount.
Barnett, C. (1970) *Britain and Her Army, 1509–1970: a military, political and social survey*, London, Allen Lane.
Barnett, C. (1979/2003) *The Great War*, London, BBC.
Barr, J. (2006) *Setting the Desert on Fire: T.E. Lawrence and Britain's secret war in Arabia, 1916–1918*, London, Bloomsbury.
Barr, J. (2011/2012) *A Line in the Sand: Britain, France and the struggle that shaped the Middle East*, London, Simon & Schuster.
Bean, C.E.W. (1921/1941) *Official History of Australia in the War of 1914–1918, vol. I: the story of ANZAC from the outbreak of war to the end of the first phase of the Gallipoli campaign, May 4th, 1915*, Australian War Memorial digitised online records, www.awm.gov.au
Bean, C.E.W. (1946/1947) *Anzac to Amiens*, Canberra, Australian War Memorial.

Bell, G. (1907/1985) *The Desert and the Sown*, London, Virago Press.

Black, D. (2008) *Red Dust: a classic account of Australian Light Horsemen in Palestine during the First World War*, no place of publication, Leonaur.

Blaser, B. (undated) *Kilts Across the Jordan: being experiences and impressions with the 2nd Battalion 'London Scottish' in Palestine*, Uckfield, Naval & Military Press.

Bostock, H.P. (1982) *The Great Ride*, Perth, Artlook Books.

Brooke, R. (1946/1970) *The Poetical Works of Rupert Brooke*, London, Faber & Faber.

Brown, M (ed.) (2005) *T.E. Lawrence in War and Peace: an anthology of the military writings of Lawrence of Arabia*, London, Greenhill.

Bruce, A. (2002/2003) *The Last Crusade: the Palestine campaign in the First World War*, London, John Murray.

Buchan, J. (1916/1999) *Greenmantle*, Oxford, Oxford University Press.

Bull, S. (2002) *World War I Trench Warfare (2), 1916–18*, Oxford, Osprey.

Bulliet, R.W. (1975) *The Camel and the Wheel*, Cambridge, MA, Harvard University Press.

Bullock, D. (1988) *Allenby's War: the Palestine-Arabian campaigns, 1916–1918*, London, Blandford.

Carlyon, L.A. (2001/2003) *Gallipoli*, London, Bantam.

Carr, W. (1969/1991) *A History of Germany, 1815–1990*, London, Edward Arnold.

Carver, R.M. (2003/2004) *The Turkish Front, 1914–1918: the campaigns at Gallipoli, in Mesopotamia and in Palestine*, London, Pan.

Caudwell, C. (1971) 'T.E. Lawrence: a study in heroism', in *Studies and Further Studies in a Dying Culture*, New York, Monthly Review Press.

Churchill, W.S. (1923–31/1938) *The World Crisis, 1911–1918*, vols. 1–4, London, Odhams Press.

Clark, C. (2012/2013) *The Sleepwalkers: how Europe went to war in 1914*, London, Penguin.

Clark, D. (1969/1971) 'Townshend: surrender, capture, and disgrace', in *Purnell's History of the First World War*, vol. 3, 1340–7.

Clausewitz, C von, (1832–5/1943) *On War*, trans. O.J. Matthijs Jolles, New York, Random House.

Crutwell, C.R.M.F. (1934/1982) *A History of the Great War, 1914–1918*, St Albans, Granada.

Dearberg, N. (2012) 'Aussies on horseback', *Military History Monthly*, 36, 52–7.

Djemal Pasha, A. (1922) *Memories of a Turkish Statesman*, London, Hutchinson.

Doughty, C. (1931/1956) *Passages from Arabia Deserta*, selected by E. Garnett, Harmondsworth, Penguin.

Dupuy, R.E. and Dupuy, T.N. (1970) *The Encyclopedia of Military History, from 3500 BC to the present*, London, Macdonald and Jane's.

El-Edroos, S.A. (1980) *The Hashemite Arab Army, 1908–1979: an appreciation and analysis of military operations*, Amman, The Publishing Committee.

Emin, A. (1930) *Turkey in the World War*, New Haven, Yale University Press.

Erickson, E.J. (2001) *Ordered to Die: a history of the Ottoman Army in the First World War*, Westport, CT, Greenwood.

Falls, C. (1930) *Military Operations, Egypt and Palestine: from June 1917 to the end of the war*, undated reprint: London, Imperial War Museum.

Falls, C. (1964) *Armageddon, 1918*, London, Weidenfeld & Nicolson.

Fasih, M. (2003) *Gallipoli 1915, Bloody Ridge (Lone Pine): diary of Lieutenant Mehmed Fasih, 5th Imperial Ottoman Army*, trans. H.B. Danişman, Istanbul, Denizler Kitabevi.

Faulkner, N. (2007) 'Gordon Childe and Marxist archaeology', *International Socialism*, 116, 81–106.

Faulkner, N. (2011a) 'Dervish dawn, Sudan 1881–1885: the first modern jihad', *Military Times*, 8, 38–45.

Faulkner, N. (2011b) 'Boers, blockhouses, and barbed wire', *Military Times*, 14, 16–23.

Faulkner, N. (2012) 'Omdurman, 2 September 1898', *Military History Monthly*, 25, 38–48.

Faulkner, N. (2013a) *A Marxist History of the World*, London, Pluto.

Faulkner, N. (2013b) *No Glory: the real history of the First World War*, London, Stop the War Coalition.

Faulkner, N. and Saunders, N.J. (2009) 'War without frontiers: the archaeology of the Arab Revolt, 1916–18', in A.C.S. Peacock (ed.), *The Frontiers of the Ottoman World*, Oxford, Oxford University Press for the British Academy, 431–51.

Faulkner, N. and Saunders, N.J. (2010) 'Trains, trenches, and tents: the archaeology of Lawrence of Arabia's war', *Journal of the T.E. Lawrence Society*, 19, 1, 7–21.

Ferguson, N. (1998) *The Pity of War*, London, Penguin.

Finkel, C. (2005/2006) *Osman's Dream: the story of the Ottoman Empire, 1300–1923*, London, John Murray.

Fisk, R. (2005) *The Great War for Civilisation: the conquest of the Middle East*, London, Fourth Estate.

Fleming, R. (2012) *The Australian Army in World War I*, Oxford, Osprey.

Fromkin, D. (1989/2000) *A Peace to End All Peace: the fall of the Ottoman Empire and the creation of the modern Middle East*, London, Phoenix Press.

Gardner, B. (1965) *Allenby*, London, Cassell.

Garnett, E. (1931/1956) 'Introduction', in C.M. Doughty, *Passages from Arabia Deserta*, selected by E. Garnett, Harmondsworth, Penguin.

Garnett, D. (1938) *The Letters of T.E. Lawrence*, London, Jonathan Cape.

Grainger, J.D. (2006) *The Battle for Palestine, 1917*, Woodbridge, The Boydell Press.

Griffith, P. (1994/1996) *Battle Tactics of the Western Front: the British Army's art of attack, 1916–18*, London, Yale University Press.

Gullett, H.S. (1923/1941) *Official History of Australia in the War of 1914–1918, vol. VII: The Australian Imperial Force in Sinai and Palestine, 1914–1918*, Sydney, Angus & Robertson.

Haleem, A. (2012) 'The importance of Hajj: spirit and rituals', in V. Porter (ed.), *Hajj: journey to the heart of Islam*, London, British Museum Press, 26–67.

Handbook of the Turkish Army, 8th Provisional Edition, February 1916, Intelligence Section, Cairo, London, Imperial War Museum.

Hanson, V.D. (1989) *The Western Way of War: infantry battle in Classical Greece*, London, Hodder & Stoughton.

Hardman, F. The Papers of Colonel Fred Hardman, Documents 7233, Imperial War Museum.

Hatton, S.F. (undated) *The Yarn of a Yeoman*, London, Hutchinson.

Haythornthwaite, P.J. (1992) *The World War One Sourcebook*, London, Book Club Associates.

Herscovitch, A. and Stanton, D. (2008) 'History of social security in Australia', *Family Matters*, 80, 51–60 (Australian Institute of Family Studies, www.aifs.gov.au).

Hill, A.J. (1978) *Chauvel of the Light Horse*, Melbourne, Melbourne University Press.

Hinde, E.B. The Private Papers of Major E.B. Hinde, Documents 11178, Imperial War Museum.

Hinterhoff, E. (1969/1971) 'The Campaign in Armenia', in *Purnell's History of the First World War*, vol. 2, 499 503.

Hobsbawm, E. (1987/1994) *The Age of Empire, 1875–1914*, London, Abacus.

Hochschild, A. (2011) *To End All Wars: how the First World War divided Britain*, London, Macmillan.

Hogue, O. (1918/2008) *The Cameliers: a classic account of the Australians of the Imperial Camel Corps during the First World War in the Middle East*, no place of publication, Leonaur.

Horne, A. (1962/1964) *The Price of Glory: Verdun, 1916*, Harmondsworth, Penguin.

Howell, G. (2006/2007) *Daughter of the Desert: the remarkable life of Gertrude Bell*, London, Pan.

Hughes, M. (ed.) (2004) *Allenby in Palestine: the Middle East correspondence of Field-Marshal Viscount Allenby, June 1917–October 1919*, Stroud, Sutton Publishing/Army Records Society.

Hynes, J.P. (2010) *Lawrence of Arabia's Secret Air Force*, Barnsley, Pen & Sword.

Idriess, I. (1932/1973) *The Desert Column*, Penrith, Discovery Press.

Inchbald, G. (2005) *With the Imperial Camel Corps in the Great War: the story of a serving officer with the British 2nd Battalion against the Senussi and during the Palestine campaign*, no place of publication, Leontaur.

Irwin, R. (2012) 'Journey to Mecca: a history (Part 2)', in V. Porter (ed.), *Hajj: journey to the heart of Islam*, London, British Museum Press, 136–219.

Jafar al-Askari (2003) *A Soldier's Story: from Ottoman rule to independent Iraq: the memoirs of Jafar Pasha al-Askari*, trans. Mustafa Tariq al-Askari, London, Arabian Publishing.

James, L. (1994/1995) *The Rise and Fall of the British Empire*, London, Abacus.

Kannengiesser, H. (1927) *The Campaign in Gallipoli*, trans. C.J.P. Ball, London, Hutchinson.

Karsh, E. and Karsh, I. (1997) 'Myth in the desert, or not the Great Arab Revolt', *Middle Eastern Studies*, 33, 2, 267–312.

Keegan, J. (1993/1994) *A History of Warfare*, London, Pimlico.

Kemal, M. (1969/1971) 'Gallipoli: a Turkish view', in *Purnell's History of the First World War*, vol. 2, 774–7.

Kennedy, H. (2012) 'Journey to Mecca: a history', in V. Porter (ed.), *Hajj: journey to the heart of Islam*, London, British Museum Press, 68–135.

Keogh, E.G. (1954) *Suez to Aleppo*, Melbourne, Wilke/Directorate of Military Training.

Kermack, W.R. The Private Papers of Major W.R. Kermack, Documents 11099, Imperial War Museum.

Kolko, G. (1994) *Century of War: politics, conflicts and society since 1914*, New York, New Press.

Kress von Kressenstein, F. (1922) 'The campaign in Palestine from the enemy's side', *Journal of the Royal United Service Institute*, 67, 503–13.

Lacey, R. (1981/1982) *The Kingdom*, London, Fontana.

Lapping, B. (1985/1989) *End of Empire*, London, Paladin.

Lawrence A.W. (ed.) (1937) 'Field-Marshal Viscount Allenby', in *T.E. Lawrence by His Friends*, London, Jonathan Cape, 145–6.

Lawrence, T.E. (1922/2004) *Seven Pillars of Wisdom: the complete 1922 'Oxford' text*, Fordingbridge, J. and N. Wilson.

Lawrence, T.E. (1926/1935/1946) *Seven Pillars of Wisdom: a triumph*, London, Jonathan Cape.

Lawrence, T.E. (2005a) 'Twenty-seven articles', in M. Brown (ed.), *T.E. Lawrence in War and Peace: an anthology of the military writings of Lawrence of Arabia*, London, Greenhill Books, 142–7.

Lawrence, T.E. (2005b) 'Extracts from a diary of a journey, 18 November 1916', in M. Brown (ed.), *T.E. Lawrence in War and Peace: an anthology of the military writings of Lawrence of Arabia*, London, Greenhill Books, 62–8.

Lawrence, T.E. (2005c) 'Extracts from a report on Feisal's operations, 18 November 1916', in M. Brown (ed.), *T.E. Lawrence in War and Peace: an anthology of the military writings of Lawrence of Arabia*, London, Greenhill Books, 68–73.

Lawrence, T.E. (2005d) 'Personal notes on the Sherifial family, 26 November 1916', in M. Brown (ed.), *T.E. Lawrence in War and Peace: an anthology of the military writings of Lawrence of Arabia*, London, Greenhill Books, 79–80.

Lawrence, T.E. (2005e) 'Military notes, 26 November 1916', in M. Brown (ed.), *T.E. Lawrence in War and Peace: an anthology of the military writings of Lawrence of Arabia*, London, Greenhill Books, 76–9.

Lawrence, T.E. (2005f) 'Raids on the railway, 13 May 1917, in M. Brown (ed.), *T.E. Lawrence in War and Peace: an anthology of the military writings of Lawrence of Arabia*, London, Greenhill Books, 111–21.

Lawrence, T.E. (2005g) 'In Sherif Abdullah's camp, 23 May 1917', in M. Brown (ed.), *T.E Lawrence in War and Peace: an anthology of the military writings of Lawrence of Arabia*, London, Greenhill Books, 130–2.

Lawrence, T.E. (2005h) 'The Howeitat and their chiefs, 24 July 1917', in M. Brown (ed.), *T.E. Lawrence in War and Peace: an anthology of the military writings of Lawrence of Arabia*, London, Greenhill Books, 132–4.

Lawrence, T.E. (2005i) 'The occupation of Aqaba, 12 August 1917', in M. Brown (ed.), *T.E. Lawrence in War and Peace: an anthology of the military writings of Lawrence of Arabia*, London, Greenhill Books, 137–40.

Lawrence, T.E. (2005j) 'The raid at Haret Ammar, 8 October 1917', in M. Brown (ed.), *T.E. Lawrence in War and Peace: an anthology of the military writings of Lawrence of Arabia*, London, Greenhill Books, 147–50.

Lawrence, T.E. (2005k) 'A raid, 16 December 1917', in M. Brown (ed.), *T.E. Lawrence in War and Peace: an anthology of the military writings of Lawrence of Arabia*, London, Greenhill Books, 154–6.

Lawrence, T.E. (2005l) 'First reports from Tafila, 11 February 1918', in M. Brown (ed.), *T.E. Lawrence in War and Peace: an anthology of the military writings of Lawrence of Arabia*, London, Greenhill Books, 158.

Lewis J. and Strachan, H. (2004) *The First World War, Episode 4, Jihad*, London, Channel Four.

Liddell Hart, B. (1930/1973) *History of the First World War*, London, Book Club Associates.

Liddell Hart, B. (1934/1935) *'T.E. Lawrence': in Arabia and after*, London, Jonathan Cape.

Liman von Sanders, O. (1927/undated) *Five Years in Turkey*, Uckfield, Naval & Military Press.

Loudon, R. The Private Papers of R Loudon, Documents 1387, Imperial War Museum.

Luxemburg, R. (1915) *The Junius Pamphlet: the crisis of German Social Democracy*, at www.marxists.org

Lynden-Bell, Sir A. The Papers of Major-General Sir Arthur Lynden-Bell, Documents 7826, Imperial War Museum.

Mack, J.E. (1976) *A Prince of Our Disorder: the life of T.E. Lawrence*, Boston, Little, Brown.

MacMunn, G. and Falls, C. (1928) *Military Operations, Egypt and Palestine: from the outbreak of war with Germany to June 1917*, undated reprint: London, Imperial War Museum.

Magraw, R. (1983) *France, 1815–1914: the bourgeois century*, Oxford, Fontana.

Mango, A. (1999/2004) *Atatürk*, London, John Murray.

Mansel, P. (1995/2006) *Constantinople: city of the world's desire, 1453–1924*, London, John Murray.

Mansfield, P. (1991/1992) *A History of the Middle East*, London, Penguin.

Marshall, P. (1989) *Intifada: Zionism, imperialism, and Palestinian resistance*, London, Bookmarks.

Marshall, S.L.A. (1947/2000) *Men Against Fire: the problem of battle command*, Norman, University of Oklahoma Press.

Mason, P. (1974/1976) *A Matter of Honour: an account of the Indian Army, its officers, and men*, Harmondsworth, Penguin.

Massey, W.T. (1918) *The Desert Campaigns*, London, Constable.

Massey, W.T. (1920) *How Jerusalem Was Won*, New York, Charles Scribner's Sons.

Massie, R.K. (1992) *Dreadnought: Britain, Germany, and the coming of the Great War*, London, Jonathan Cape.

Mazower, M. (2004/2005) *Salonika: city of ghosts – Christians, Muslims, and Jews, 1430–1950*, London, Harper.

McGuirk, R. (2007) *The Sanusi's Little War: the amazing story of a forgotten conflict in the Western Desert, 1915–1917*, London, Arabian Publishing.

McPherson, J.W. The Private Papers of Lieutenant J.W. McPherson, Documents 4789, Imperial War Museum.

Moorhead, S. (2003) 'The genesis, conduct and publication of the Wilderness of Zin survey', in C. Leonard Woolley and T.E. Lawrence, 1915/2003, *The Wilderness of Zin*, London, Palestine Exploration Fund/Stacey International, xvii–xliv.

Moran, Lord (1945) *The Anatomy of Courage*, London, Constable.

Morgenthau, H. (1918/2000) *Ambassador Morgenthau's Story*, Ann Arbor, MI, Gomidas Institute.

Mousa, S. (1966) *T.E. Lawrence: an Arab view*, London, Oxford University Press.

Murphy, C.C.R. (1921/undated) *Soldiers of the Prophet*, Uckfield, Naval & Military Press.

Murphy, D. (2008) *The Arab Revolt, 1916–18: Lawrence sets Arabia ablaze*, Oxford, Osprey.

New York Times (1916) 'Loyal India: an interview with Lord Hardinge of Penshurst by the London Correspondent of the New York Times', London, Joseph Causton & Sons.

Newsinger, J. (2006) *The Blood Never Dries: a people's history of the British Empire*, London, Bookmarks.

NHS 'Schistosomiasis (bilharzia)', at www.nhs.uk

Nicolle, D. (1989) *Lawrence and the Arab Revolts*, London, Osprey.

Nicolle, D. (1994) *The Ottoman Army, 1914–18*, Oxford, Osprey.

Nicolle, D. (2010) *Ottoman Infantryman, 1914–18*, Oxford, Osprey.

Nicholson, J. (2005) *The Hejaz Railway*, London, Stacey International.

Nogales, R de (1926) *Four Years Beneath the Crescent*, London, Charles Scribner's Sons.

Nunan, S. The Personal Papers of Stan Nunan, AWM 3DRL6511(A), Australian War Memorial.

Palmer, A. (1965) *The Gardeners of Salonika: the Macedonian campaign, 1915–1918*, London, André Deutsch.

Palmer, A. (1992) *The Decline and Fall of the Ottoman Empire*, London, John Murray.

Patterson, J.H. (1922/undated) *With the Judaeans in the Palestine Campaign*, Uckfield, Naval & Military Press.

Perrett, B (1999) *Megiddo 1918*, Oxford, Osprey.

Petersen, A. (2012) *The Medieval and Ottoman Hajj Route in Jordan: an archaeological and historical study*, Oxford, Oxbow.

Porter, D. (2014) 'The Russian Empire in 1914', *Military History Monthly*, 43, 30–1.

Powles, G. (1922) *The New Zealanders in Sinai and Palestine*, Auckland, Whitcombe and Tombs.

Purnell's History of the First World War, 1969/1971, vols. 1–8.

Rhodes James, R. (1965/1984) *Gallipoli*, London, Pan.

Robertson, J. The Private Papers of J. Robertson, Documents 15013, Imperial War Museum.

Rogan, E. (2015) *The Fall of the Ottomans: the Great War in the Middle East, 1914–1920*, London, Allen Lane.

Rolls S.C. (1937/2005) *Steel Chariots in the Desert: the First World War experiences of Rolls-Royce armoured-car driver with the Duke of Westminster in Libya and in Arabia with T.E. Lawrence*, no place of publication, Leonaur.

Sagall, S. (2013) *Final Solutions: human nature, capitalism and genocide*, London, Pluto Press.

Said, E. (1978/2003) *Orientalism*, London, Penguin.

Sampson, A. (1975) *The Seven Sisters: the great oil companies and the world they made*, London, Hodder & Stoughton.

Saunders, N.J. (forthcoming) *Desert Insurgency: archaeology, T.E. Lawrence and the Great Arab Revolt*, Oxford, Oxford University Press.

Saxe, M. de (1757/1944) *Reveries on the Art of War*, trans. and ed. T.R. Phillips, Harrisburg, Military Service Publishing Company.

Scott, J. (2014) *Conflict Archaeology in Southern Jordan: Wadi Yutm and the Great Arab Revolt, 1916–1918*, unpublished PhD dissertation, University of Bristol.

Seward, D. (2009) *Wings Over the Desert: in action with an RFC pilot in Palestine, 1916–18*, Yeovil, Haynes Publishing.

Sherman, N. (2010) *The Untold War: inside the hearts, minds and souls of our soldiers*, New York, W.W. Norton.

Shqiarat, M., Al-Salameen, Z., Faulkner, N. and Saunders, N.J. (2011) 'Fire and water: tradition and modernity in the archaeology of steam locomotion in a desert war', *Levant*, 43, 1, 98–113.

Skander Bey (1924a) 'The Battles of Salt, Amman and Jordan from the Turkish sources', Part 1, *Journal of the Royal United Services Institution*, 69(474), 334–43.

Skander Bey (1924b) 'The Battles of Salt, Amman and Jordan from the Turkish sources', Part 2, *Journal of the Royal United Services Institution*, 69(475), 488–98.

Smith, G.A. (1894/undated) *The Historical Geography of the Holy Land*, 20th edn., London, Hodder & Stoughton.

Spear, P. (1965/1978) *A History of India*, vol. 2, Harmondsworth, Penguin.

Spilsbury, J. (2013a) 'Tripoli Trappola, Part 1: the battle for Tripoli', *Military History Monthly*, 36, 42–8.

Spilsbury, J. (2013b) 'Tripoli Trappola, Part 2: Italy's hollow conquest', *Military History Monthly*, 37, 32–8.

Spilsbury, J. (2014) 'Thieves united: the First Balkan War, 8 October 1912–30 May 1913', *Military History Monthly*, 42, 38–44.

Steel, N. and Hart, P. (1994/2002) *Defeat at Gallipoli*, London, Pan.

Stejskal, J. (forthcoming) 'The breech-loading 10-pdr mountain-gun'.

Stephenson, J. (1969/1971a) 'Turkey enters the war', in *Purnell's History of the First World War*, vol. 1, 397–401.

Stephenson, J. (1969/1971b) 'Britain, India, and the Middle East', in *Purnell's History of the First World War*, vol. 1, 435–9.

Stephenson, J. (1969/1971c) 'The Indian Army: reform and expansion', in *Purnell's History of the First World War*, vol. 2, 744–51.

Strachan, H. (2001/2003) *The First World War, vol. I: To Arms*, Oxford, Oxford University Press.

Strachan, H. (2003) *The First World War: a new illustrated history*, London, Simon & Schuster.

Sun Tzu (2002/2005) *The Art of War*, trans. J. Minford, London, Penguin.

Surry, A.R. The Private Papers of A.R. Surry, Documents 6096, Imperial War Museum.

Taylor, A.J.P. (1963) *The First World War: an illustrated history*, London, Hamish Hamilton.

Taylor, A.J.P. (1977/1979) *How Wars Begin*, London, Book Club Associates.

Teichman, O. (1921/undated) *Diary of a Yeomanry MO: Egypt, Gallipoli, Palestine and Italy*, Uckfield, Naval & Military Press.

Terraine, J. (1965/1967) *The Great War, 1914–18*, London, Arrow.

Thompson, R.R. (1923) *The Fifty-second (Lowland) Division, 1914–1918*, Glasgow, Maclehose, Jackson.

The Times History of the War, 1914–1919, 21 vols, London, *The Times*.

Trotsky, L. (1914) 'Two armies', *Kievan Thought*, 334 (4 December). Unpublished translation by Pete Glatter from Russian original.

Trotsky, L. (1932–3/1967a) *The History of the Russian Revolution, vol. 2*, London, Sphere Books.

Trotsky, L. (1932–3/1967b) *The History of the Russian Revolution, vol. 3*, London, Sphere Books.

Trumpener, U. (1968) *Germany and the Ottoman Empire, 1914–1918*, Princeton, Princeton University Press.

Trumpener, U. (1998/2000) 'Turkey's war', in H. Strachan (ed.), *The Oxford Illustrated History of the First World War*, Oxford, Oxford University Press.

University of Florida, 'Featured creatures: common name: housefly', at www.entnemdept.ufl.edu

Ulrichsen, K.C. (2014) *The First World War in the Middle East*, London, Hurst & Co.

Uyar, M. (2007) 'Ottoman Arab Officers between nationalism and loyalty', draft text of paper presented to Conference 'Palestine and the First World War – New Perspectives' at Tel Hai Academic College, Upper Galilee, 3–6 September 2007.

Vader, J. (1969/1971) 'Defence of the Suez Canal', in *Purnell's History of the First World War*, vol. 2, 705–11.

Walder, D. (1969/1971a) 'The Chanak crisis', in *Purnell's History of the First World War*, vol. 8, 3477–82.

Walder, D. (1969/1971b) 'The Graeco-Turkish War', in *Purnell's History of the First World War*, vol. 8, 3483–9.

Waraich, M.S. (2007) 'Lord Hardinge bomb case (1912–1915)', at 'Indian Rebels', www.rebelsindia.com.

Wavell, A.P. (1928/1936) *The Palestine Campaigns*, London, Constable.

Wavell, A.P. (1940) *Allenby: a study in greatness*, London, George Harrap.

Weber, F. (1970) *Eagles on the Crescent: Germany, Austria and the diplomacy of the Turkish alliance, 1914–1918*, Ithaca, NY, Cornell University Press.

Wilson, J. (1989/1990) *Lawrence of Arabia: the authorised biography of T.E. Lawrence*, London, Minerva.

Winterburn, J.B. (2012) 'Hadrian and the Hejaz Railway', in N.J. Saunders (ed.) *Beyond the Dead Horizon: studies in modern conflict archaeology*. Oxford, Oxbow Books, 172–87.

Winnicott, D.W. (1964) *The Child, the Family, and the Outside World*, Harmondsworth, Penguin.

Woodward, D.R. (2006/2007) *Forgotten Soldiers of the First World War*, Stroud, Tempus.

Wykes, A. (1969/1971) 'First landings at Gallipoli', in *Purnell's History of the First World War*, vol. 2, 761–73.

INDEX

An index should be useful. There is little value in an undifferentiated list of every passing reference. I have therefore included mainly substantive references, though I have tended to include all references to particular military units. I have also grouped secondary subjects under general headings, so, for example, Ottoman military 'corruption, requisitioning and forced labour' will be found under 'Ottoman Army'. Secondary subjects are listed under general headings in order of their first appearance in the text rather than in alphabetical order.

***